PIONEERING CULTURE:

Mechanics' Institutes and Schools of Arts in Australia

edited by

Philip C Candy
Queensland University of Technology

and

John Laurent
Griffith University

Adelaide
Auslib Press
1994

This publication is available from

Auslib Press
PO Box 622 Blackwood SA 5051
Tel (08)278 4363 Fax (08)278 4000

Price $48.00 plus $8.00 p&h

National Library of Australia cataloguing-in-publication data

Pioneering culture: mechanics' institutes and schools of arts in
  Australia
  Bibliography.
  Includes index.
  ISBN 1 875145 25 7.

1. Mechanics' institutes - History. 2. Adult education -
Australia - History. 3. Technical education - Australia -
History. 4. Australia - Intellectual life. I. Candy, P.C.
(Philip C.). II. Laurent, John, 1947-   .

374.280994

CONTENTS

ACKNOWLEDGMENTS

In preparing this book, we have drawn on the expertise and assistance of colleagues all over Australia and indeed abroad. We are indebted to a range of people - librarians, booksellers, archivists, local historians, curators, researchers, photographers and even office bearers in some institutes that still exist - to all of whom we extend our heartfelt thanks.

Although it is impossible to thank individually everyone who has contributed to this book, we would especially like to acknowledge the following:

Mary Akers, Interpretive Services Manager of Sovereign Hill Historical Park, Ballarat, Vic; Craig Allen of the Bathurst City Library, NSW; Robert Bell, Honorary Secretary of the Ballaarat Mechanics' Institute, Vic; Ann Boyle of the Geraldton Public Library, WA; Lex Brasher of the Queensland Department of Education History Unit; N E Broadsmith, Secretary of the Molong Historical Society, NSW; S Bruce, Honorary Secretary, Taree Literary Institute, NSW; Neville Curnick, Managing Secretary of the Geraldton Cultural Trust, WA; Ellen Elzey, Librarian, Sydney Mechanics' School of Arts, NSW; Pam Firth, former owner of the Healesville Mechanics' Institute building, Vic; Marguerite Garland, Curator of the Colonial Inn Museum, Mudgee, NSW; Una Garland, Senior Librarian at the Muswellbrook Municipal Library, NSW; Anne Grant of the Portland Genealogy Group, Vic; Paul Hager of the Faculty of Education, University of Technology, Sydney; Roger Harris of the University of South Australia; Barbara Heaton of the Newcastle City Council, NSW; Judith Hollingsworth of the State Library of Tasmania at Launceston; Norman Houghton, Geelong Historical Records Centre, Vic; Brian Howes of Barossa Vintage Books, Nuriootpa, SA; Jenny Humphreys, Research Officer, Goulburn Historical Society. NSW; Alan Ives, Archivist at Charles Sturt University, NSW; Marie Johnstone of the Warrnambool Public Library, Vic; Howard Land, Secretary, Sydney Mechanics' School of Arts; Garry Le Duff of the University of South Australia; June Lewis, Leeton Shire Librarian, NSW; Pat Longworth, Treasurer of the Laurieton School of Arts, NSW;

Marie Maguire of Leeton, NSW; Erica Maxwell, of the City of Williamstown Library, Vic; Sue McClarron, State Library of Tasmania at Launceston; Ian and Ilonka McGill of Serendipity Books, Nedlands, WA; Robert McKay of Charnwood, ACT; Keith Moore of the Wellcome Institute for the History of Medicine in London; Norm Neill, Historian with the New South Wales Department of TAFE; Miranda Nicholson, Secretary of the Kincumber School of Arts Committee, NSW; Cassandra Perry of Deakin University Library, Geelong, Vic; Robert Riddel, Architect of Brisbane; Douglas Sellick of the Albany Public Library, WA; Sally Shaw of the East Gippsland Community College of TAFE, Sale, Vic; Ken Smith, University of Sydney Archivist; Larraine Stevens of the Local History Collection, Fremantle City Library, WA; Bob Sumner of the University of South Australia; Noel Tanner, Honorary Secretary of the Swan Guildford Historical Society, WA; Ralph Terbut, New South Wales Department of Water Resources; John Thompson of the University of South Australia; Bill Tighe of the Bathurst District Historical Society, NSW; Geraldine Triffitt, of Mawson, ACT; Bruce Turner, Secretary, Prahran Mechanics' Institute, Vic; Peter Tyrell, Secretary, Nudgee School of Arts, Qld; Lex Weaver, President of the Parkes Historical Society, NSW; Marjorie Weston of the *Kiama Independent*, NSW; Robyne White, Goulburn Historical Society; Lola Wilson, Research Officer with the Kiama and District Historical Society, NSW; and Leila Winchcombe, Secretary, Melbourne Athenaeum.

Others whose assistance has been greatly appreciated include: Staff of the New South Wales, South Australian and Queensland State Archives; the Mitchell Library and the State Library of New South Wales; the John Oxley Library, Queensland; the library of the New South Wales Department of Agriculture and Fisheries; the libraries of the Universities of Sydney, New South Wales and New England, and of the Queensland

University of Technology; the National Library of Australia; the Coober Pedy Community Library; and the libraries of the Sydney, North Sydney and Granville Technical Colleges.

John is also grateful to Margaret Campbell, Ian Lowe and David Burch for helpful discussions, and to the good people at the Antique Bookshop, Cremorne, the Cornstalk Bookshop, Glebe and Optimism Antiques, Tamworth for supplying him with some of the old books he needed to consult, and also to the friendly staff of Mary White College, University of New England, for providing him with such a pleasant working environment while he was writing his chapter on the New South Wales School of Arts.

We would both like to express our grateful thanks to Lynne Bryan, Robyn Daniel, Carrie McNaught, Angela Miller, and Emma Wilcox who battled with a variety of handwritings and manuscripts in all sorts of conditions to produce a consistent format for each chapter. We are of course delighted that Judy and Alan Bundy have agreed to publish this book, and hope that their trust in us, and faith in the importance of this subject will not prove to have been misplaced.

Finally, we would like to thank our contributors for their encouragement, support and above all for their patience. This project has taken several years to come to fruition, and we are grateful to all of them both for entrusting us with their research, and for bearing with us while we edited their work for publication. Whilst acknowledging our indebtedness to all these people, we accept responsibility for the design and execution of the overall book, and hope that it will be of use to others seeking to understand better the significance and impact of the institutes in Australia's cultural history.

P C Candy and J A Laurent
Brisbane
November 1993

'THE LIGHT OF HEAVEN ITSELF': THE CONTRIBUTION OF THE INSTITUTES TO AUSTRALIA'S CULTURAL HISTORY

Philip Candy

It is our privilege to live in times when the much vexed question will scarcely any longer be entertained, whether the great body of the people ought to be instructed. Knowledge, no longer confined to wealth or rank, no longer the depository of the cloistered sage, is all pervading as the light of heaven itself, and may be sought and enjoyed by every willing mind.[1]

W. Smillie, 1842.

INTRODUCTION

On 24 October 1889, an event of momentous significance to Australia took place at Tenterfield in northern New South Wales, not far from the Queensland border. There, at a banquet attended by about 80 people, the Premier of New South Wales - Sir Henry Parkes - delivered a speech which fired the imaginations of many people and which eventually led to Australian Federation on 1 January 1901.[2]

Aside from the dramatic significance of the speech itself, the feature of this presentation that is particularly intriguing is that it took place not in a town hall, or a park, or a railway station or a theatre, but in a School of Arts, a community-based facility very similar in aim and operation to the Birmingham Mechanics' Institute where Sir Henry Parkes had himself obtained so much of his own education and shaped his political and social philosophy.

Of course very few of the thousands of institutes that existed throughout Australia can claim such a special place in the nation's history,[3] but collectively the institute movement made a unique and distinctive contribution to Australia's colonial, and early post-Federation social, cultural, educational, intellectual and architectural landscape.

Probably the most enduring, and certainly the most obvious legacy of the institutes is the buildings they left behind. Anyone who has travelled outside the major cities (and indeed even in the suburbs of larger cities) can hardly fail to have noticed these buildings - often unexpectedly large and substantial - which marked the spread of the institute movement. Referred to in different places as schools of arts, athenaeums, mechanics' institutes, lyceums, literary and scientific institutes, or even simply as institutes, these buildings once blanketed much of Australia. Not all were substantial of course, many were quite modest, and many - both humble and ornate - have since been demolished or converted beyond recognition. But enough of them remain to prompt questions such as: what was the purpose of these institutes, who set them up and why, how long did they last, and perhaps most basically, who used them and for what?

Broadly speaking, the institutes were the forerunners of today's community centres, adult education classes, technical colleges and local libraries, all rolled into one. Set up as local initiatives, though often with support in the form of Government subsidies, the institutes were intended for the benefit of the working-classes - in particular for 'mechanics' (tradesmen or artisans). Though some were formed and led by the workers themselves, most relied on support, encouragement and leadership from among the middle-classes, and in many cases this led to tensions between the aspirations of those for whom they were intended, and those who actually benefited from having the resource in the local community.

Ironically, despite their evident importance to our forebears, and their significance to Australia's cultural history for over one hundred and fifty years, no one knows for certain even how many such institutes there were. Research for this book, however, reveals that there were probably in excess of 2000 nationwide; indeed they were about as ubiquitous as country pubs, local churches, and one-teacher schools. And like pubs, churches and schools, each one bore the unique imprint of the people who established them and patronised them; no two institutes followed identical paths or developed in precisely the same way. But this is not to imply that there are no common factors in their histories. Events such as gold rushes, booms and depressions, wars, federation, the advent of universal primary education, the spread of transport and communications, and continuing population growth provide the backdrop against which institutes in widely separated parts of Australia came into being, served their local communities and, for the most part, faded into oblivion.

In fact, the mechanics' institutes in Australia were themselves part of a much larger movement which spread across the English-speaking world (and indeed even further afield). Accordingly, it is worth briefly exploring their antecedents, in order to understand the interplay of local concerns and broader social and ideological trends that underlay their establishment and diffusion.

THE BIG PICTURE

Conventionally, the history of Australian mechanics' institutes is traced to the precedent provided by the establishment of the Glasgow or the London Mechanics' Institutes in 1823 or alternatively to the foundation of the Edinburgh School of Arts in 1821. While these are no doubt significant milestones in the history of the movement, they are merely particular outcrops in a much broader history, or rather series of histories, because the mechanics' institute movement owes its origins to several different patterns of development.

As Inkster points out, "if the institutes are defined as an extension of radical middle-class culture, then their origins may be found in the 'literary and philosophical societies' of the 1780s and 1790s and the expansion of a radical science culture during the early years of the nineteenth century."[4] If, on the other hand, the mechanics' institutes are seen as part of the radical mobilisation of the working class, then their origins can be traced to the major social and political changes in Britain in the 1820s and 1830s. Yet another precursor might be the adult Sunday Schools, notably Methodist and Quaker, which trace their existence back to the late 1790s or even earlier.[5] It is apparent therefore that the institute 'movement' had several quite different impulses, as well as several quite different ancestors and, as we will show in this book, that there was never unanimity of purpose among the institutes (or even within them) as they evolved and developed in Australia.

It is also worth pointing out that not only were there multiple streams *within* Britain which gave rise to the formation and spread of mechanics' institutes and similar kindred organisations, but Australia was far from the only other place to be affected by what Whitelock has typified as this 'cultural epidemic.' In the late 1790s, for instance, very similar sorts of self-help and mutual improvement institutions sprang up in the United States, and throughout the 1820s and 1830s, libraries, scientific institutions, athenaeums and lyceums spread throughout the New England States, and eventually became widespread throughout the whole country.[6] Not unexpectedly, Canada followed suit, with the first institute being founded in St John's, Newfoundland in 1827[7] and in rapid succession in Montreal (1828), York (1830), and both Toronto, Ontario and Halifax, Nova Scotia in 1831.[8] In New Zealand, three institutes were established in 1841, but there is an unresolved debate about whether the credit for being the first should go to Auckland,[9] Nelson,[10] or Port Nicholson (now Wellington).[11] They also sprang up in the West Indies, South Africa, India, across the Pacific - indeed anywhere that was coloured red on the map of the British Empire. As Whitelock observes,

> There was no centralised policy behind the diaspora of mechanics' institutes throughout the Empire and the English-speaking world. They proliferated because of local initiative driven by common enthusiasms and loyalties. They exemplified the full-blown Victorian self-help principle, although occasionally, as in Australia, some official aid was needed. It could be argued that, as repositories of English culture, educational ideas, books, and journals - and humbug - the institutes contributed more to the sense of imperial community than all the rhetoric in the press and the stately tours by proconsuls. In their heyday in the 1850s, the traveller would have found Hudson's "people's seminaries," easily identifiable with British mechanics' institutes, from the British Pacific islands to India, from Ontario to Otago.[12]

THE INSTITUTES COME TO AUSTRALIA

It is against this background that the movement, fuelled by a mixture of ideals and supported by an assorted coalition of people with quite varied motives, spread to Australia and then throughout the various colonies. The first such organisation was the Van Diemen's Land Mechanics' Institution, established in Hobart in 1827. The next was the Sydney Mechanics' School of Arts, in 1833. This was followed by the original Newcastle Mechanics' Institute in 1835, the Port Phillip Mechanics' Institute and one at Maitland, both in 1839. An abortive attempt to establish an institute in Western Australia took place in 1842, but it was not until 1851 that the Swan River Mechanics' Institute was finally inaugurated; and in the Moreton Bay district, the North Brisbane School of Arts was established in 1849. South Australia's institutes, on the other hand - as was the case in so many other things - had a different history from those of the other colonies. The South Australian Literary and Scientific Association was actually formed in London in 1834, and met for two years until it was subsequently transplanted across the globe in 1836, when the colony was officially settled.

Between these marker events, and across the great expanse of the continent, the institutes spread. Gradually and tentatively at first, and then with greater intensity and vigour as the century progressed, institutes sprang up until, like a carpet of wildflowers, they stretched off to the remotest and most distant corners. Like wildflowers, some flourished, and seemed

3

to be perpetually in bloom. Others withered within a season; some perished for ever, whereas some dropped their seeds and new institutes grew to replace them next time the circumstances were appropriate.

What were the appropriate circumstances? There is no one answer to this question, because some institutes thrived in situations in which others simply failed to take root at all. Some depended on the driving influence of a single person; others seem to have received widespread support from the outset. Some needed the financial backing and patronage of the local élite; others were very much grass-roots organisations whose vitality came from their strong connections with the working-class. Some drew heavily on the intellectual input and evangelical zeal of local - commonly nonconformist - ministers of religion; others had a strictly secular agenda and assiduously weeded out lectures, discussions and library acquisitions with any hint of religious overtones. Some fared best among workers - miners, labourers, railwaymen, shearers, cane cutters and the like; while others developed a more refined, literary and artistic clientele. As Whitelock puts it, "while mechanics' institutes the world over had much in common they were naturally influenced by their local environment and gradually diverged to some extent from the Edinburgh or London models."[13]

LEADING LIGHTS

Wherever the institute movement took hold, it had one or two champions who supported the cause and commonly assisted in the dissemination of its ideals. In Britain, Lord Henry Brougham and Dr George Birkbeck[14] are usually mentioned in this connection; in the United States, Timothy Claxton[15] and Josiah Holbrook.[16] In New Zealand, Jonas Woodward[17] was an important early supporter; and in Canada, Joseph Howe[18] and Rev Dr A Egerton Ryerson.[19] Who fulfilled this role in Australia? Although virtually every institute had its individual stalwarts, who rendered long and distinguished service, several men stand out as having been particularly notable advocates and supporters of the institute movement as a whole.

The first such person is Rev. Dr John Dunmore Lang. Lang first arrived in Sydney in 1823, and died there in 1878. In the intervening fifty-five years, he interested himself in an enormous range of topics related to the progress, development and public life of the colony of NSW. He started schools and colleges, brought boat loads of immigrants mainly from Scotland, gave countless lectures and sermons, travelled widely, served in Parliament, and produced an astonishing array of books, articles, pamphlets and other publications. Apart from lecturing at the School of Arts in Sydney, Lang's major contribution to the movement was to recruit hundreds of Scottish tradesmen as immigrants to the colony. These men shared his belief in the value of education, and formed a substantial nucleus of the foundation membership of the Sydney Mechanics' School of Arts (in 1833) and of the North Brisbane School of Arts (in 1849). Their protestant ethic, like Lang's, was very influential in shaping the agenda of the respective institutes.

The second is Rev. Henry Carmichael, who was employed by Lang as a teacher for his projected Australian College in Sydney. Carmichael travelled to Australia aboard the *Stirling Castle* with a group of Scottish emigrants, and while on the ship he conducted classes for them. Shortly after his arrival in Sydney, with the support of Governor Richard Bourke, he founded the Sydney Mechanics' School of Arts in 1833. Not only did he deliver the

4

inaugural address, which was subsequently published in three lengthy instalments,[20] but he also served as the institution's Vice-President for the first five years. As noted in the *Australian Dictionary of Biography*, "Carmichael's principal achievement lay in the dissemination of advanced educational ideas, which he expounded in three long discourses at mechanics' institutes (1833, 1844 and 1857)."[21] Carmichael can justly claim to be one of the earliest pioneers, not just of the institute movement, but of Australian adult education generally.[22]

The third of these outstanding individuals was Rev. Dr John Woolley, foundation principal and Professor of Classics at the University of Sydney. Woolley was a great believer in the value of a liberal education, a point of view which brought him into conflict with those practical people who argued for a more applied curriculum at the University. However his "creed of 'social sympathy' through a liberal education extended beyond the university ... he believed that academics should take their learning to the wider community... [He] helped to revive the Sydney Mechanics' School of Arts in 1853 (Vice-President 1855; President 1866) and lectured widely for it. [Although] he remained critical of disorder in the School of Arts, he believed it was the most effective instrument for cultural dissemination."[23] Woolley spelt out his ideas about the value of the institute movement in a series of lectures delivered at the Sydney Mechanics' School of Arts and elsewhere, many of which were published either as separate pamphlets, or in a collected set.[24]

The fourth key figure in the Australian institute movement was yet another Rev Dr - John Lillie - a Presbyterian like Lang, but with a calmer and less irascible temperament. Born in Scotland, Lillie arrived in Hobart in 1837 where he lived until 1856, when he returned briefly to Britain before re-emigrating to New Zealand. For sixteen of his nineteen years in Australia - from 1838 to 1854 - he was President of the Hobart Town Mechanics' Institute, where he presented a number of lectures on a variety of subjects. More "a nineteenth century liberal than a traditional Calvinist,"[25] Lillie managed to span secular, scientific and spiritual concerns. His annual presidential addresses, many of which were published in pamphlet form, represented, as Nadel puts it, "the high-water mark of learning publicly disseminated" in Van Diemens Land.[26]

The fifth great advocate of the institutes, and indeed of adult education generally, was one of Australia's earliest leading politicians and statesmen - Sir Henry Parkes. Almost the quintessential Victorian ideal of the self-taught and self-made man, Parkes was born the youngest of seven children and left school early to help support the family by working as a road labourer and in a brickpit. As a youth in the early 1830s he joined the recently-founded Birmingham Mechanics' Institute, and so began a lifetime attachment to learning and to the value of reading. Parkes participated in the diverse range of lectures provided by the Institute, and reflecting back on that period in his life, "liked to think that the educational legacies of his Birmingham days were a love of literature learned through sensitive reading and an appreciation of man's [sic] social and political nature learned at the feet of the town's great orators."[27] Throughout his long career, as both a journalist and as a politician, Parkes was a strong advocate of educational opportunities. For many years he was the editor of *The Empire,* which, "in its concerns about community enlightenment...went well beyond the elementary school system.... It argued vigorously for good public libraries, for institutions of adult education and societies to promote science and the arts. Sydney had its Mechanics' School of Arts...and a Society for Encouragement of Arts, Science, Commerce and

Agriculture, established in 1850. But Parkes thought they all lacked vitality, and pressed for the establishment of a new scientific society and of People's Colleges, adding that because of the philistinism of the colony's wealthier classes, government would need to take the initiative."[28]

The sixth major contributor to the institutes was Frederick Meleng. Unlike the others, Meleng did not have a high public profile, but nevertheless worked tirelessly to promote the institutes in South Australia, and indeed throughout the nation.[29] As the Secretary of the Port Adelaide Institute - one of the largest and most active in the colony - Meleng began to agitate for the establishment of an independent lobby group to represent the interests of the institutes, and so was born the Institutes' Association of South Australia in 1899. Meleng took up the foundational role of General Secretary and also acted as business manager for the *South Australian Institutes' Journal* which, for many years, was a major source of information about the progress of institutes and a forum for discussing issues of common concern. Prior to his untimely and widely-lamented death in 1930, Meleng travelled extensively throughout South Australia and indeed further afield, helping local committees, negotiating and representing individual institutes and the movement as a whole, bulk buying books for the libraries, and generally promoting the educational, cultural and social work of the institutes.

Of course these six people are but a few of the many who contributed to the life and work of the institutes - as patrons, lecturers, committee members, librarians, and simply as active members - over their century and a half of history. It would not be difficult to double their number, by adding people such as: Sir Redmond Barry, a leading figure in early Melbourne who was a founder of the Melbourne Mechanics' Institute, as well as of the University of Melbourne and the Melbourne Public Library (now the State Library of Victoria); Thomas Burgoyne, who repeatedly advocated for the institutes in the Parliament of South Australia and was the first President of the Institutes' Association of South Australia; Joseph Chester, the radical carpenter and cabinetmaker, who contributed so much to the early life of the Swan River and Guildford Mechanics' Institutes; William A Duncan, a leading Roman Catholic intellectual, author, publisher and friend of Sir Henry Parkes, and who was foundation President of the North Brisbane School of Arts; Rev Joseph Johnston, a congregational minister who, "concerned with the intellectual as well as the spiritual needs of the [West Australian] colonists..., often lectured to the Fremantle Mechanics' Institute and when it showed signs of becoming a 'gentlemen's club'... was instrumental in founding the Fremantle Workingmen's Association"[30]; and James Ross, "a Doctor of Laws from Aberdeen University, whom contemporaries styled the 'Birkbeck of Tasmania',"[31] who kept the Van Diemen's Land Institute alive during its perilous early years by making his reading rooms available as a venue for its lectures and library.

Disappointingly, but hardly surprisingly, women do not feature among the early mainstays of the institute movement. As several of the authors show in their chapters, women came to play a much larger role in the institutes only in the twentieth century; in its formative years, the institute movement represented the essence of Victorian patriarchal society. Even in enlightened South Australia, the famous writer and feminist Catherine Helen Spence had to ask her brother to borrow books for her in the 1840s, and when invited to lecture at the South Australian Institute in 1866, she wrote; "I will be very much obliged to Mr Howard Clark if he will deliver it for me, for I am scarcely strong enough for that."[32]   In 1871,

6

however, she did deliver a lecture to the Institute herself, thus becoming the first woman to address a public meeting in the colony.[33] Another, and even more prominent woman contributor to the institute movement was Louisa Lawson - poet, author, publisher and advocate of women's rights - who in 1891 talked her way into the hallowed sanctuary of the Junior Debating Club at the Sydney Mechanics' School of Arts, and was promptly accorded membership by the startled chairman. As a result of this, a rift developed between the Junior and Senior Debating Clubs, but by 1892 the latter's opposition to women crumbled; "on 23 June 1892, Louisa [was] offered membership of the Senior Club. Later, she [was to] represent the clubs on the School of Arts Committee, but she eventually resigned in protest against the nit-picking, circumlocutory discussions that ensured that no significant action ever resulted from any meeting."[34]

FUNCTIONS OF THE INSTITUTES

While the character of the institutes varied markedly across Australia, most of them began life with stern Victorian injunctions about 'useful knowledge,' 'mental and moral improvement,' and 'rational recreation.' Across the nation, and throughout the years, the Rules of various institutes remained remarkably alike, as the following extracts attest:

> The object of the Institution shall be, the diffusion of scientific and other useful knowledge as extensively as possible throughout the Colony of New South Wales.
>
> *Laws and Regulations of the Newcastle Mechanics' Institute,*
> *Library and Museum 1835*

> The objects proposed are, the instruction of the members in the principles of the arts; the diffusion of scientific, literary, and other useful knowledge; and the rational amusement of the members, and cultivation of their tastes.
>
> *Rules of the Launceston*
> *Mechanics' Institute, 1844*

> The objects of the said Institution namely the intellectual improvement of its members and the cultivation of literature science and art shall be promoted by the maintenance of a library and reading-room the delivery of lectures the encouragement of social intellectual and physical recreation and by such other means as the committee of management may from time to time deem advisable.
>
> *Sydney Mechanics' School of Arts*
> *Incorporation Act 1886*

> The objects of the institute shall be the promotion of useful knowledge and rational mental recreation amongst its members, by the following means, as far as may be practicable, viz: The establishment of a library and reading room, lectures,

conversaziones, classes, &c.

*Model Rules for Institutes
in South Australia, 1896*

The purposes for which the Institution known as the Lambton Mechanics' and Miners' Institute is established are the mental and moral improvement and rational recreation of its members, by the maintenance of a Library and Reading Room, by Lectures and Readings, by the formation of classes, and by any other means that may appear desirable to the Committee.

*Rules and Regulations of the
Lambton Mechanics' and Miners' Institute, 1902*

The purposes for which the School of Arts is established are the mental and moral improvement and rational recreation of its members by the maintenance of a Library, Reading-room and Recreation-room, by lectures and readings, by the formation of Classes, and by any other means that may appear desirable to the Committee of Management.

*Rules and Regulations of the Taree
School of Arts 1906*

While the interpretation of these various rules varied both from place to place and over time, most institutes provided some broadly similar combination of facilities and programs, based on libraries and reading rooms, lectures and classes, and "by any other means that may appear desirable to the Committee."

Libraries and reading rooms

Of all the functions performed by the institutes, probably the most universal, the most obvious, and certainly the most extensively documented was the provision of library services. At a time when reading was surprisingly widespread, and other diversions were less common than they are today, there was a thirst for knowledge about what was happening outside one's immediate vicinity, and consequently the provision of books, journals and newspapers was a vital component of the institutes' role.

Even before they had a building, most institutes had a small library, and when a building was erected, the library and reading room were universally regarded as central to its purpose. At the start, the institutes depended primarily on membership subscriptions and donations for their libraries; for these reasons, the libraries were generally small and had quite variegated collections, depending on the interests of the members, the kind of gifts received, what was available from either local or overseas booksellers and, most importantly, on the tastes and interests of the librarian or the library committee.

One way of augmenting the local institute library was through exchanging books - on either a temporary or a permanent basis - with other institutes in the vicinity; this eventually gave way to quite elaborate 'book box' schemes in several states, whereby a central authority took responsibility for buying, and then circulating, a varied stock of reading material to institutes throughout the colony. The other main way in which collections were enhanced was through subsidies provided by the colonial government, though many institutes diverted their book subsidies to other purposes, such as erecting a building.

Where they exist, the catalogues - and even more rarely the borrowers' books - of the institutes' libraries provide quite fascinating insights into the reading habits of both rural and urban Australians. Much can also be inferred from the committee minutes, which contain records of debates about what constituted 'appropriate' reading for the membership. Broadly speaking, committee members could be classified into the 'improvers,' who argued that the institutes existed to provide educational opportunities and improve the moral tone of the community, and the 'entertainers,' who saw the institutes essentially as community facilities providing a wholesome alternative to public houses, billiard parlours and dance halls. The minutes of debates and deliberations by committees across the continent reveal the fascinating dynamics of argument as each group struggled for supremacy.

Whenever governments became involved in providing direct book subsidies, they commonly sought to influence the purchasing policies of the committees, usually away from 'light' literature towards texts on science, history, travel, biography, philosophy and the like. With very rare exceptions, the institute libraries ended up being taken over by municipal councils as responsibility for providing library services was seen as a government matter, and consequently it is still quite possible to find remnants of the institute collections in municipal libraries throughout the nation.

Lectures

Throughout the nineteenth century, the public lecture served as a major vehicle for enlightenment and for entertainment.[35] Perhaps our ancestors a century or more ago were more disciplined than we are, perhaps there were less diversions such as television or cinemas, undoubtedly there was a genuine thirst for knowledge, and almost certainly the tolerance for sitting on hard chairs for long periods had been refined through listening to lengthy sermons! Whatever the case, lectures on a bewildering range of subjects were staple fare in most institutes, even in the remotest locations. At first, these lecture series relied almost entirely on the talent locally available, which in smaller and more remote locations was generally limited to a small pool of educated people: the local doctor, school teacher, ministers of religion and landed farmers. Once each of these local worthies had given a lecture or two on his favourite subject, not surprisingly the lecture series often collapsed, only to be revived whenever a new potential lecturer moved into the district. In larger towns and cities, of course, the pool of potential lecturers was much larger, and the institutes frequently offered an astonishingly diverse range of lectures over the 'season.'

The lectures were reported, often at great length, in the local press. In addition, "by public demand" or "at the insistence of the committee," many were published in their entirety as pamphlets, and have accordingly been preserved for posterity. They make fascinating reading, reflecting as they do the dominant interests and modes of discourse of the middle-class intelligentsia. However it is scarcely surprising that attendances at some lectures were disappointingly low, given the esoteric nature of the subjects, the frequently dry mode of delivery, the "educational and social gulf between lecturers and working-class students,"[36] and the likely state of exhaustion of many members after a day's hard labour in the field, mine or workshop. Little wonder that the nature of the lectures has often been cited as evidence of the middle-class takeover of the institutes although, as John Laurent shows in his chapter, quite complex scientific lectures and those offered by radical orators, managed to draw large and enthusiastic audiences.

As the century progressed, local presenters were supplemented by visiting lecturers. Some accepted the invitation of the local committee; some were sponsored, as in South Australia, by a consortium of institutes; some were paid for by the colonial government (especially in fields such as agriculture or mining); some represented educational organisations (such as University Extension or the Workers' Education Association); and some were enterprising individuals who worked as itinerant lecturers.[37]

These last were nearly always gifted speakers who picked subjects of great contemporary interest. They would arm themselves with maps, charts, and diagrams, with scientific apparatus or with lantern slides (or possibly a combination of all these) and attract huge audiences. Many of them made a handsome living from their craft, as well as bringing that unique combination of scholarship and showmanship to people starved for stimulation and news of the outside world.

Classes

Many of the inadequacies and drawbacks of the lecture scheme have already been alluded to, but one in particular weighed heavily against their educational value: their disjointed nature. For week after week, people would stand in front of the members and expatiate on their chosen subjects, but there was rarely any cumulative development of ideas, or logical connection from one week to the next. To fill this gap, many institutes began class groups.

Some of these were based on the principle of mutual instruction, where members of the class took it in turns to read up on some aspect of the subject and present it to the rest of the group. Related to this was the ever-popular discussion class, where a topic or subject would be selected, and all class members were expected to undertake some reading between meetings so that they could contribute. Often these discussion classes extended over a series of weeks and considered quite controversial subjects such as whether the Australian colonies should form a Federation; whether women were intellectually inferior to men; or whether convicts were a boon or a curse to the society. In her book *Westralian Voices*, Aveling reproduces extracts from three such debates held at the Swan River Mechanics' Institute in Perth between 1853 and 1855; they offer a fascinating insight into the thinking of the participants, as well as the important preoccupations of the times in general.[38]

Other classes were more conventional, in the sense of having a set syllabus, being taught by an instructor, and extending over a period of weeks, sometimes culminating in a test or examination. Three broad categories of classes may be distinguished: basic education for those with limited schooling; general adult education (usually for those with considerable education already); and technical and scientific education.

The extent to which the institutes provided education in the basics - reading, writing and arithmetic - seems to have been largely a function of the times, and of the specific location. As a general rule, those institutes established earlier tended to place more emphasis on basic literacy and numeracy than those formed later in the nineteenth, or early in the twentieth century. Similarly, those in predominantly working-class areas - such as mining, agricultural or industrial communities - placed more stress on these basics than those in more cosmopolitan and better educated environments. In her PhD thesis on literacy in colonial New South Wales, Penglase devotes several pages to the basic educational work of the institutes. She comments that there are relatively few records of such classes,[39] which could be an indication that they were not regarded as a significant, or prestigious, part of the institutes' work.

Turning to the general liberal educational work of the institutes, time and time again in the histories of individual organisations one comes across lists of classes in subjects such as French, Latin, history, geography or philosophy. Such pursuits are likely to have been of limited interest to working-class institute members. Even more distinctly middle-class in their focus and appeal were courses in literature, fine art, drawing and music. While some commentators regarded such topics as edifying and civilising influences, others argued that this was evidence that the institutes were failing to meet the needs and interests of those for whom they were intended (mechanics and artisans), catering instead to decidedly middle-class tastes. There is certainly evidence to suggest that, after an initial blush of enthusiasm, attendance at such classes usually fell off sharply to the point where they ceased to be viable. This in turn was often accompanied by an overall decline in membership of the institute, as working-class members discovered the limitations and shortcomings of the institute's educational program.

Based on the rhetoric which commonly accompanied the formation or revival of particular institutes, and the development of the movement as a whole, it would be reasonable to expect classes on science and technology - the principles underlying the tradesmen's work - to feature prominently in the educational profile of the institutes' movement. However, by and large, although many institutes made desultory forays into subjects like physics, chemistry, engineering (mechanics), hydraulics, geometry, technical drawing and other scientific topics (including phrenology!), it is remarkable how significantly this aspect of their mandate was neglected. As early as 1869, for instance, a Technological Commission was set up by the Victorian Government to inquire into the nature and extent of technical education. It surveyed eighty-seven mechanics' institutes by questionnaire, with fifty-one of them responding. The following extract from the report gives an idea of the relatively undeveloped state of this aspect of the institutes' work at this time:

> To this question--3. Are there in connection with it any classes for practical instruction in any branch of art or trade, or the natural sciences bearing on arts or trade, and by what class of persons are they attended? Out of the fifty-one replies received to date (27th November), only *two* have a class -- Williamstown and Portarlington. That at Williamstown is a ladies' class, for drawing; the other, at Portarlington, seems to embrace most of the objects of such institutions. If to this number we add the Trades' Hall in Melbourne, we have *three* in all doing something of the duty of Mechanics' Institutes; and that is not much for an outlay of £44,486 9s. 9d.![40]

Even more remarkable is how inadequate were the teaching resources to support this work:

> 5. Have you any regular series of models of objects, or good diagrams, for the purpose of aiding the teachers? -- This question was answered by the whole fifty-one with a simple *No*.
> 7. Have you in the Library a sufficiency of elementary or more advanced class-books, suitable for persons who may wish to improve themselves in the principles which underlie their trade or calling? -- Ten replied in the affirmative without any qualification; nine say they have *"a few;"* and the remaining thirty-two declare they have *not*.
> 8. Have you any maps of Australia or of this colony? -- Answered by thirty-six in the affirmative and by fifteen in the negative.[41]

These responses revealed a surprising lack of proper courses in what, at that time, might have been considered to be the bread-and-butter of an institute devoted to mechanics, prompting Bleasdale to comment; "It would appear these places miscalled Mechanics' Institutes are mostly used for reading rooms and occasional lectures, etc."[42]

Nevertheless, as the years passed, many institutes formalised their technical offerings and even sponsored Technical Colleges which, in due course, were taken over by the Technical Education Branch of the relevant Ministry of Education,[43] an interesting though by no means uncommon example of how local community initiative and self-help gradually gave way to Government provision of a needed service.

Museums and art galleries

In many respects, mechanics' institutes and museums formed part of a larger nineteenth century preoccupation with the progress of science, and the dissemination of scientific ideas.[44] As Horton writes, in describing the museum of the Port Adelaide Institute; "The underlying idea of a library and a museum is precisely the same. Both are instruments of intellectual culture, and where combined in an effective degree there is scarcely any limit to the instruction placed ready at hand to those who will accept the opportunities offered."[45]

While not every institute established a museum or art gallery, many did so either as a public resource or as an adjunct to their instructional program.[46] Where museums and art galleries were established, collections varied enormously, depending on the locality, the generosity of the members, and especially on the enthusiasm and expertise of the curator who, in most cases, was also the Secretary and Librarian of the Institute. In mining areas, of course, mineral specimens and geological collections were common; elsewhere, items such as tools and equipment, stuffed birds and animals, ethnological artefacts, sea-shells and fossils, or weapons and militaria formed the basis of the display. As the years went by, many collections were supplemented by gifts of books, papers, household items and other memorabilia from around the world donated by members and other residents in the district. At the Sandhurst Mechanics' Institute in Victoria, for instance, "visitors could marvel at a Lioness, an Indian Tapir, a White Sacred Brahmah Sebu and an Indian Rock Snake, all donated by Dr MacGillivray,"[47] and at the Van Diemen's Land Mechanics' Institute, "among the more notable donations was a native tiger, 5 feet 8 inches long, which the Bridges family of New Norfolk offered on the condition that the institute would have it stuffed."[48] At the Port Adelaide Institute in South Australia, "the museum contained such artefacts as sling stones from New Caledonia, a mat from the New Hebrides, tapa skirts from Fiji, Maori gourds, war clubs from the Solomon Islands, a New Guinea drum, models of Fijian canoes, and New Hebridean weapons,"[49] and elsewhere, equally assorted items were on display. In some places, institutes added extra rooms, or even entire wings, to accommodate the museum holdings and provide for their display. However, lacking either formal policies to guide collection-building or professional curatorial care, many of these collections degenerated into dusty and moth-eaten jumbles, reminiscent of an unsorted garage sale, and were eventually thrown out or broken up.[50] Art Galleries, likewise, suffered a similar chequered fate, though more frequently works of art found their way into municipal galleries, where they have received proper cataloguing, and are conserved for the enjoyment and edification of subsequent generations.

Rational recreation

Virtually every institute included in its objectives a statement about the provision of 'rational recreation' or, as it was sometimes called, 'rational amusement.' What this meant was innocuous, wholesome and, whenever possible, intellectually improving forms of entertainment. A number of institutes formed debating clubs, and many also permitted the playing of chess, draughts and backgammon.

Clearly, however, this was slippery territory and, as with libraries that pandered to the taste for 'light literature,' so it was only a short step from 'Penny readings' to spelling bees and then to general knowledge quizzes. Likewise, 'conversaziones,' originally consisting of recitations and readings interspersed with brief musical items and discussions, gradually gave way to musical evenings, and thence to travelling troupes of singers, dancers and acrobats.

Not unexpectedly, many committees split over the appropriateness of such activities being conducted in the institutes; the 'progressives' versus 'improvers' debate had its counterpart here too. However what probably polarised committees more than anything else was the introduction of billiards. By the end of the nineteenth century, many institutes had amended their objectives to include 'games of skill,' and under this guise, combined with the economic imperative of bringing members back and increasing subscriptions, institutes throughout the country built or devoted special rooms to billiards and employed markers to set-up the games and keep score. Before long, exhibition matches were being played as fundraisers, and in New South Wales at least, the Literary Institutes Association organised tournaments from 1909 onwards among teams from the various schools of arts. Several articles on the subject appear in the *South Australian Institutes' Journal*, and it is instructive that the cover of the first (and only) edition of the *West Australian Librarians' and Institutes' Journal* in 1904 bore a huge, illustrated advertisement for Alcock's, a major supplier of billiard tables and accoutrements.

While this trend was probably inevitable, and certainly strengthened the social side of institute life, for many it represented the end of any serious attention to the lofty educational ideals that had characterised their foundation.

Resource for the local community

In addition to the other activities and services already alluded to, throughout Australia another vital function performed by the institutes - especially in rural areas - was the provision of a place to meet. With regard to pioneering communities, which lacked the civic amenities that today are taken for granted, it is hard to overemphasise the vital importance of a neutral venue for people of different social classes and occupations, and indeed of different religious persuasions, to meet together on an equal footing. Woolley, one of the most ardent and literate supporters of the institutes, in a speech to the Wollongong School of Arts in 1861, even went so far as to claim:

> I am so firmly convinced that the habit of meeting is itself a priceless good, that it would be worthwhile to come [to the Institute] if only to shake hands and go home again.[51]

In addition to this sort of symbolic significance, the institutes served very practical ends as well. In many parts of Australia, the institute hall doubled as a church - or even more than one - before churches were erected, and often also as a school. In the early days of local government, Councils commonly met - sometimes for years - in the institute meeting room, and the hall served as a town hall and civic centre.

Local organisations likewise utilised the institute for meetings where they lacked premises of their own, and in the majority of communities, the institute hall was the venue for any public gathering of any consequence. As with book grants, colonial and state governments provided direct financial aid for the erection of halls; in fact there was a particular frenzy of building and rebuilding activity after the First World War, when many institutes took advantage of government grants, and re-designated their buildings as Memorial Halls.

As well, the institutes provided a focal point for an enormous range of local activities and initiatives. In the histories of those few institutes that have been fully documented, one can find the institutes used for bazaars and concerts, for dances and weddings, for cinemas and emergency shelter. Older residents invariably speak fondly, and local historians write, of the institute as the hub of community life, a place where, as previously mentioned, people met to play cards or chess or billiards, to cook and to sew, to send people away to war and to welcome them home again, and even to keep themselves warm in the depression. While these activities may seem trivial to educational purists, they are vital to the ebb and flow of life in a community, and they also go a long way towards explaining the emotional attachments that many Australians feel towards their local school of arts or mechanics' institute; a feeling that persists to the present day in places.

COMPETITION AND COLLABORATION

Although it is true that every institute started life as a local entity, shaped by the unique combination of local politics, economics, history and demography, there is plenty of evidence that developments in one part of Australia soon affected the aspirations and infrastructure of institutes in other parts. This occurred through the alternating influences of competition and collaboration.

Many of the rivalries between (and within) colonies were reflected in claims made about local institutes, and it is not uncommon to find, especially in the annual reports and prospectuses of particular institutes, claims to be the largest, most modern, best equipped, costliest, or most imposing building in the town/region/colony or continent. Individual towns frequently singled out competitors for particular comparison. Thus Geelong saw itself as deserving a better institute than Newcastle, Ballaarat than Bendigo, Melbourne than Sydney, Fremantle than Perth, and Launceston than Hobart. Civic pride was a powerful motivator in the development of individual institutes.

To counterbalance this, it was not uncommon for institutes to offer and receive help, especially in their formative years. As early as 1840, the Rev T H Osborne, who had recently arrived in Melbourne from Tasmania, stated in his inaugural address to the Melbourne Mechanics' Institution that he was confident that the members of the Van Diemen's Land Institute in Hobart would actively support their development. In many other parts of Australia, the same offer was made and taken up; committee members travelled around offering advice, libraries loaned or gave books to new institutes to help them get started, and sets of rules were passed from institute to institute, to be used as models in setting up a new organisation. This cooperation was most formalised in South Australia, where the South Australian Institute, formed in 1856, and its successor the South Australian Institutes' Association formed in 1899, together provided more than 130 years' continuous support, guidance and leadership to institutes in that state.[52] An abortive attempt was made in 1904 to set-up a similar Western Australian Librarians' and Institutes' Association[53]; and a decade later the short-lived Literary Institutes' Association of New South Wales was inaugurated, with assistance and encouragement from the Institutes' Association of South Australia.[54] Finally in 1927, the Queensland School of Arts Association was formed[55] but, as Carole Inkster points out in her chapter, it was too late to arrest the slide in the status of the Queensland institutes. By that stage, many of the functions they had formerly performed had passed or were passing to other hands; the Associations slowed down, but could not entirely stop, the inevitable decline of the institutes.

SOME COMMON THEMES

Aside from their objectives, referred to earlier, another similarity of many institutes was the composition of the committee. Although it is not universally true, many of the committees were, or soon came to be, dominated by the middle-classes - shopkeepers, lawyers, ministers, teachers, farmers, bankers and civil servants. As the chapters in this book show, this was a common experience, and one which inevitably influenced the institutes' ethos, activities and general membership.

Another feature that many of the longer-surviving institutes had in common was their gradual mutation into centres of amusement and entertainment. The minutes of many institutes are replete with records of the heated arguments between the traditionalists, who wanted to maintain the 'tone' and intention of the original founders, and the progressives who saw that the institute would be overtaken as a centre of social and cultural life if it failed to adapt. A common experience, especially in rural areas that lacked other community facilities, was the watering down of the library, followed or accompanied by recitals and plays in place of erudite lectures, with discussion classes giving way to debating, then chess, and finally billiards. Again, this was not an invariant experience, but common enough across the institutes.

Finally, the common fate of many institutes was to have their activities taken over, one-by-one, by other agencies. Library services would be provided by the Council, new community centres would draw off the public meetings, and theatres would replace their role as auditoriums and cinemas. The local TAFE Colleges would offer the adult education classes that were once their lifeblood, and a series of technological innovations - the gramophone, then radio, then television, then the video recorder - would change the dynamics of family life and of community needs, until finally all that would be left are abandoned and shabby halls such as those described by Warburton:

> Schools of Arts, Mechanics' Institutes, Literary Institutes - what pictures do these words conjure up? Usually we think of old fashioned buildings in city streets, broken-down halls in country towns or a little shack of unpainted wood and rusty iron perched in the middle of nowhere, with a large sagging sign, barely decipherable: "Join our Circulating Library Now - The Cheapest in Town." Floods sometimes wash though them, rats nest in corners, snakes slither along the floor and birds fly through the broken windows. Occasionally one does see a useable Town Hall, run by an elected committee of library-borrowers, but on the whole one would not be straining credibility in thinking of these places as dumps for the local bottle-oh.[56]

While many of these buildings have been bought up and converted into everything from art galleries to banks to antique stores, others have suffered the ultimate ignominy of demolition and nothing remains to mark their passing except perhaps a photograph in a local library.

To others, however, fate has been kinder, and across Australia there is an awakening of sorts to the cultural and architectural value of the old institutes. While some have been modernised and refurbished, others have been lovingly restored, painted in heritage colours to resemble their appearance sixty, eighty or even a hundred years ago. In either case, there is something fitting about mechanics' institutes, schools of arts and memorial halls being embraced by another generation of Australians to become once again a vital part of their local community.

OVERVIEW OF THE BOOK

In view of the number of institutes which at one time or another existed in Australia, and the enormous variations among them, it would be impossible to attempt anything resembling a comprehensive history of the whole movement. Conversely, although there have been a number of histories written of the institute movement in particular states, and even of individual institutions, there has never before been an overview of the movement's development and impact nationally. Consequently, the purpose of this book is to strike a balance between the particular and the general; to consider major trends and patterns, but to illustrate these selectively with representative case studies.

In selecting or commissioning these chapters, it was recognised that the institutes are multifaceted; standing at the headwaters of both adult and technical education, of the provision of public libraries and of community resources. In addition, many of them are remarkable architecturally, or if not, their very ordinariness stands for a category of undistinguished but common vernacular design. Consequently, the chapters selectively illustrate a number of themes simultaneously: they trace the movement from its earliest days to its eventual decline; each State is represented; so too are a range of the institute's forms, both architecturally and organisationally.

There are two chapters where nineteenth-century advocates speak in their own words about the perceived advantages of the institutes. Apart from those two contemporary accounts, the chapters in this book were written by men and women across Australia over a period of almost forty years, from 1955 to 1993. Except for this chapter and the final one, virtually none of them was produced specifically for this book; many of them were originally written as part of theses or dissertations, and have never been published before.

In any collection of papers - especially one which, like this, was written by a range of authors over a long time span - there is a danger that the contributions will lack coherence. We have tried to guard against this in three ways: firstly by selecting chapters that illustrate different aspects of the work of the institutes; secondly through arranging them in a way that provides conceptual continuity; and thirdly by judicious editing mainly for consistency of spelling, references and style, but also to reduce redundancies and repetition.

This first chapter has argued that the development of the Australian institutes can be seen in the context of a much broader, international movement, and also that the development of individual institutions within the Australian colonies was influenced by similar trends elsewhere in the country. While arguing that each institute had a unique mandate and an individual 'personality,' it has also been shown that there were many commonalities between institutes in widely separated parts of the country.

Chapter two, by Elizabeth Webby, takes the theme of historical antecedents further. On a state-by-state basis, she shows that even the earliest institutes always had some sort of precursor - library, reading room or literary society - and that a prevailing concern with self-improvement and social amelioration gave rise to the institutes when they first emerged.

Jill Eastwood's chapter takes the Melbourne Mechanics' Institute as a case study of this general principle, and traces the factors that were operating from its earliest appearance in 1839 until 1870, when the Institute relinquished its working-class focus entirely and embraced the name and the style of an Athenaeum. She also briefly describes the early diffusion of the institutes throughout Victoria, and draws attention to the relationship between dissenting ministers of religion and the spread of the institutes - a recurring theme throughout the rest of the book.

Thomas Osborne's lecture on the advantages of mechanics' institutes has been included for several reasons. For a start, as he was a unitarian minister, it illustrates in a very immediate and forceful way the connections between non-conformity and the institute movement. Secondly, as the inaugural lecture presented at the Melbourne Mechanics' Institute in 1840, it illustrates the sort of concerns that animated the early founders of the institute movement; thirdly it has never been published before in one place; and fourthly it illustrates the subtle and often very personal connections between the institutes (Osborne had come from Hobart, where he had befriended Dr James Ross of the Van Diemen's Land Mechanics' Institute and, within a few years, was to move on to Portland where he took a leading role in establishing the Portland Scientific and General Literary Society[57]).

In chapter five, Brian Hubber traces the effect of the colonial book grant scheme on the development of early Victorian library services through the institutes, and the attempt to rein in the Melbourne Institute in favour of others elsewhere in the Colony. In his chapter, Marc Askew neatly illustrates the fate of one such non-metropolitan institute - that at Geelong - tracing dominant patterns of membership and leadership, the intricacies of local politics, patterns of association and institutional involvement, and their interaction with broader issues in the Colony at the time, such as the discovery of gold. This chapter also shows how both leaders and members brought to bear their experiences gained in mechanics' institutes in Britain.

The chapter by Peter Rose, Wendy Birman and Michael White provides a fascinating overview of the institute movement in Western Australia. Many of the themes already raised - the provision of library services, collaboration between institutes, the middle-class takeover especially of the metropolitan organisations, the impact of the discovery of gold, and the special quality of rural institutes - are seen to have their counterpart here, on the other side of the continent.

Michael Whiting's chapter also has a state-wide purview. It starts with the Sydney Mechanics' School of Arts, but traces the diffusion of the institutes across the colony of New South Wales. He pays particular attention to the educational philosophies of two of the movement's early advocates - Dr John Woolley and Sir Henry Parkes - placing particular emphasis on the liberal adult education role of the institutes. On the surface, John Laurent's chapter would seem to take a rather different point of view, through its focus on the role of the institutes in the early provision of technical and practical education. What he is able to show, however, through analysis of library holdings and lecture series, is that there was a widespread and lively interest in various aspects of science and technology, and that "the dichotomy one frequently finds between 'technical' and 'general' education was not a conspicuous feature in the educational work of New South Wales mechanics' institutes and schools of arts."

In her chapter, also based on the New South Wales experience, and on three case studies in particular, Jean Riley takes a different tack. She shows how - through their lectures and classes, their library holdings and the structures themselves - the institutes contributed to the visual and fine arts, and not just to the 'mechanical' or 'useful arts.' Finally in this sequence, Tessa Raath's chapter provides a valuable summary and overview of the growth and development of the movement throughout New South Wales, before undertaking a survey of the fate of institute buildings in the south-east of the State. Using written sources and local knowledge, she reports a field study which records the present condition and use of a number of former institute buildings - some demolished, some converted to commercial purposes, some taken over for community and civic purposes, and some still operating very much as they always have with local management committees - a pattern that is probably representative of many other parts of Australia.

Steve Kellermeier, by focussing on the architecture of institute buildings in Queensland, follows on from Tessa Raath's concern with the structures themselves. He develops an elegantly simple typology of building types, and then illustrates each of them with representative examples from Queensland. Although the details vary across Australia, depending largely on the climate and the availability of local building materials, this approach to categorising and comparing institute buildings again has its counterpart wherever they were formed.

Continuing with a focus on Queensland, Carole Inkster sketches the main factors that influenced the growth and later the decline of the schools of arts over a period of more than 130 years. Of particular interest is the tension between the drive for respectability brought to the movement by Lang's immigrants on the *Fortitude* (and indeed by a disproportionate number of Scots in Queensland with their strong protestant ethic) and the more radical, working-class influence of labourers in the sugar mills, cattle stations and remote communities.

Wayne Murdoch takes the history of just one Queensland institute - the Rockhampton School of Arts - and shows how the drive for self-improvement flourished in what was then a very remote corner of the British empire. His meticulously documented study shows another side of the institutes - their role as early museums and not simply as libraries - and emphasises the vital importance of the early curators in establishing and maintaining viable collections before the advent of state sponsored museums.

In his chapter on Tasmania, Stefan Petrow deals with the history of not one, but two separate institutes. By comparing and contrasting the progress of the Hobart Town Mechanics' Institute with that of its northern counterpart, the Launceston Mechanics' Institute, he illustrates not only the historic competition between those two cities, but a number of other points about the different impulses that led to the creation and development of institutes generally. This chapter is noteworthy for dealing so comprehensively with the rise and fall of the Hobart Town institution - the earliest in Australia.

While on the subject of Tasmania, we have chosen to include a previously unpublished lecture by the former President of the Hobart Town Institute - Rev Dr John Lillie. The manuscript of this lecture is in the collection of the Wellcome Institute for the History of Medicine in London, and we acknowledge with thanks the permission of the trustees to reproduce the text in this book. This lecture was given in 1854, just after the dissolution of the short-lived Hobart Town Mechanics' School of Arts, a breakaway from the Hobart Town Mechanics' Institute, and it is interesting to note Lillie's comments about the failure of the competitor.

Michael Talbot takes up the opposite theme to competition, namely collaboration, in recounting the unique history of coordination between the South Australian institutes. He shows how first the South Australian Institute, and later the South Australian Institutes' Association, provided leadership and solidarity to that colony's institute movement. Largely because of this extended central influence, the history of South Australian institutes has been more carefully preserved, recorded and analysed than any other state, and Michael Talbot's recent exhaustive and scholarly study of the whole movement[58] provides a model for others in other parts of Australia to emulate.

In her chapter, Amanda Bettesworth not only rounds out the history of the South Australian institutes, but identifies themes that would have their counterpart virtually everywhere in Australia: how the First World War robbed the institutes of their membership base; how there was a flurry of patriotic enthusiasm following the war that resulted in the building or rebuilding of many institutes as memorials; and how changing technology, lifestyles, values and finally the depression progressively eroded many of the institutes' traditional roles and sapped them of their former strength and vitality.

Finally, John Laurent draws together many of the threads from earlier chapters in the book and also attempts to provide an appraisal of the achievements and significance of the movement to Australia's social and even political history. Although commentators have been denouncing the institutes as failures since soon after they began, this chapter argues that they fulfilled a unique role in Australia, and that we would have been much poorer as a society had it not been for the emergence and development of mechanics' institutes, schools of arts, athenaeums, literary institutes and kindred organisations throughout the country.

CONCLUSION

Although I have referred to 'the institute movement' throughout this chapter, the fact is - as I hinted at the beginning - that there were really several different and overlapping 'institute movements' in Australia. The differences between them, however, are not so much a matter of the name that was chosen, but of other, more subtle considerations such as where they were formed (country or city), whether their management was representative of the working-classes or not, and the extent to which they were based on liberal, middle-class values or the principle of genuine emancipation of the working-classes (respectability or radicalism). It is not hard to imagine that different institutes had different 'personalities,' when one considers the range of motives and circumstances that led to their formation. In discussing the spread of the lyceums in the United States, for instance, Cawelti says;

> Behind any broad popular movement of this sort, there is usually a considerable diversity of motives and interests. This was certainly the case with self-culture. In part, the broad interest in popular educational institutions reflected the demand for a common-school education which Americans [and Australians] were soon to undertake as a public responsibility. But other interests temporarily found a common ground in the self-culture movement: there were workers and farmers seeking to increase their skills or to become more successful economically; there were philanthropists who felt a moral duty to extend some of the cultural benefits they enjoyed to the less fortunate; there were businessmen seeking a better trained and more docile labour force, and determined aristocrats who hoped that education would teach the rising classes to respect the leadership of their social superiors. Finally, there were those who dreamed of a society in which all men [sic] would have the opportunity to develop their spiritual and creative potential.[59]

Related to this theme of diversity, is a second: that of difference. As I said at the beginning of the chapter, "there was never unanimity of purpose among the institutes (or even within them) as they evolved and developed in Australia." Hard as it may seem to believe now, looking back at the faded photographs of solemn, middle-aged committee members and the tranquil exteriors of abandoned buildings, the institutes were once the site of animated - even passionate - ideological battles.[60] Not only did books for and against Darwinism sit shoulder to shoulder on the library shelves, and not only did lecture theatres and halls reverberate as speakers argued about female suffrage, transportation, federation or free trade, but the committee rooms themselves witnessed the cut and thrust of heated discussion. As

I have argued elsewhere, such a varied range of motives as those described by Cawelti called forth an equally varied spectrum of opposition to self-education:

> For every clergyman who wanted people to be able to read the scriptures for themselves, there was another who feared that his authority as God's spokesman would be undermined by the ability of members of the congregation to read; for every politician who believed that a better informed, better read, more thoughtful populace would lead to a fuller exercise of democratic rights, there were others who feared the erosion of their power for the same reason; for each radical spokesman who argued that education was "not a charity, but a right,"[61] there was a conservative who wanted to keep the lower orders in their place; for each advocate of literacy as opening the gates of paradise and allowing people to "converse with Herodotus and Livy, Demosthenes and Cicero, Homer and Virgil [and] with Paul and Moses ...," there were yet others who warned against the evil influence of "light literature and works of fiction [that] not only enfeeble the mind but pervert the taste and corrupt the imagination."[62] And against those who saw self-education as the key to a better and more enlightened society, where work and leisure were intertwined,[63] were set patrician traditionalists who rejected the self-educated and self-made man in favour of the traditional idea of a cultivated class that represented, in Cooper's words,[64] "the natural repository of the manners, tastes, tone, and to a certain extent, of the principles of a country."[65]

It is evident that the institutes were far from passive purveyors of a single homogeneous world view, and it is as well to recognise their role in responding to, as well as shaping, Australia's varied political, social, intellectual and cultural inheritance.

This leads me to the third and final point, which is the distinctively Australian character of many institutes. As early as 1851, the Rev Dr J W Hudson, founder of the Scottish and Northern Unions of Literary and Mechanics' Institutes, and author of the pioneering *History of Adult Education*, wrote as follows of the spread of such organisations worldwide:

> It cannot fail to interest every friend of civilisation to observe the extraordinary development of these people's seminaries in the remote regions of the earth. The humble temple of knowledge rears its head adjacent to the abode of the New Zealander and the Sandwich Islander... In the golden, yet uncongenial regions of California, the Mechanics' Institute is located amidst iron houses and coarse tents. In the home of the African, at the Cape, and at Port Natal, near the haunts of the Kaffir, the Literary Association has found a resting-place. Under India's burning sun, the Mechanics' Institute finds friends and members. In Van Diemen's Land, the Athenaeum has its well-built local habitation; and in Australia, the Mechanics' Institute receives ample funds from the government, and possesses a well-filled roll of members.[66]

While it is true that local institutes in Australia must be seen as part of this broader movement, and that the existence of institutes here formed part of a shared consciousness that transcended national boundaries, it is also true that Australia - especially its remote rural parts - put its own unique stamp on the nature and purpose of the institutes.

In all the thousands of words that have been written about the institutes, few are as powerful or as poignant as those contained in a letter written in 1899 to the Queensland Department of Public Instruction, by a group of shearers and labourers working at the Peak Downs Station in western Queensland. In making a case that the government should provide a grant for the recently formed Peak Downs Station School of Arts, they offered the following arguments:

> Firstly - Up to a quite recent period the various woolsheds in the colony were haunted by gangs of professional gamblers, who, at the conclusion of the annual shearing, frequently took away with them, to the cities on the coast, to be expended in vice and debauchery, the greater part of many of the workers' earnings. Since the establishment of woolshed Schools of Arts, in itself a new and recent departure, this evil has rapidly abated; and many men who formerly laboured chiefly for the benefit of the spieler and the publican; are now the possessors of bank accounts, and are contemplating becoming tenants of the crown by selecting small areas of land; mainly for gardening, farming and homestead purposes. It may thus be claimed for the woolshed Schools of Arts, that they are already exercising a direct and an increasingly beneficial effect upon the development of the resources of the colony, and upon the important matter of land settlement. Also, it is worthy of note that the class of settlers brought forward in this manner are of a most desirable type; mostly natives, robust, young, and well acquainted with the conditions of pastoral and agricultural settlement in the colony.

> Secondly - At whatever station these Schools of Arts have been established, a marked and gratifying change is making itself manifest in many aspects of woolshed life; the improvement in manners and the tone of social intercourse being rapid and continuous.

> Thirdly - That no class of workers are more worthy of consideration at the hands of the state, than are the pastoral workers of the colony, who are engaged in the development of its staple industry; whose toil is frequently heavy and severe, the labor being often carried on under conditions of extraordinary discomfort, caused by floods, drought, and other detrimental conditions: and the normal condition of whose lives is one of almost unmitigated hardship.

> Fourthly - That as the woolshed Schools of Arts are essentially similar in character to the similarly named Institutions in the cities and townships; their objects and their methods of working being identical: we, your petitioners, claim that we should receive equivalent consideration at the hands of the Government, and that the usual endowment of ten shillings in the pound should be granted to the Peak Downs School of Arts, in order that its already proved usefulness may thereby be increased.

> Fifthly - That the sum of £9/-/- has been subscribed this year at Peak Downs in furtherance of the objects mentioned. The total number of books in the Library of the Institution is one hundred and ten, and the necessary books for its proper working: - as Minute Book, Cash Book, Ledger, Register, etc., have been provided and kept.[67]

Whatever criticisms can be levelled at the institutes, there must still be much of merit to commend them when a group of workers in a remote and isolated part of the Australian outback were able to claim so much for the educational, cultural, social and even economic impact of this particularly Australian variant of Hudson's "people's seminaries." As Whitelock so aptly observes:

> Altogether, the relics of the institutes - crumbling buildings, the yellowing photographs of bewhiskered committee members and the neglected minute books in museums and archives, the memories that older people have of debates and extension lectures - all these should be viewed with more sympathy and certainly with more gratitude by modern adult educators. The movement started...with such Benthamite benevolence, such Whiggish optimism that human nature could be purified by useful knowledge,... had several achievements to its credit. To dismiss the accompanying rhetoric as naive and inappropriate to a pastoral colony emerging from its former status as a prison farm is to make a modern value judgement that woefully misinterprets the spirit of the times. Above all, in the context of this study, the institutes made the concept of adult learning familiar and acceptable to many members of a frontier society.[68]

In the pages that follow, an attempt is made to rescue the institutes from their undeserved oblivion, to draw attention to the richness of their history, and to celebrate the enormous but largely unheralded contribution which, individually and collectively, they have made to our cultural heritage.

NOTES AND REFERENCES

1. Smillie, W. (1842). Mental Culture. Introductory discourse to the South Australian Literary and Scientific Association and Mechanics' Institute, Queen's Theatre Adelaide, 26 July 1842. *South Australian Magazine,* 1, p.430.

2. Spencer, M. (Comp.).(1970). *Sir Henry Parkes Memorial School of Arts, Tenterfield.* Sydney: The National Trust of Australia (New South Wales).

3. Interestingly, almost forty years earlier, on 16 April 1850, J D Lang had given a lecture in the Sydney Mechanics' School of Arts, in which he had advocated that "for mutual protection and defence, and for general advancement, the five Australian Colonies of New South Wales, Van Diemen's Land, South Australia, Port Phillip and Cooksland, or the Moreton Bay Country [should unite to form] one Great Australian Nation" (Lang. J.D. (1850). *The coming event or, The United Provinces of Australia.* Sydney: D L Welch, printer, p.28).

4. Inkster, I. (1985). Introduction: The context of steam intellect in Britain (to 1851). In Inkster, I. (Ed.), *The steam intellect societies: Essays on culture, education and industry, 1820-1914.* Nottingham: Department of Adult Education, University of Nottingham, p.4.

5. Rowntree, J.W., & Binns, H.B. (1903). *A history of the adult school movement.* London: Headley Brothers [reprinted, with an introduction and notes by C. Charlton (1985).

Nottingham: Department of Adult Education, University of Nottingham].

6.Bode, C. (1968). *The American Lyceum: Town meeting of the mind*. Carbondale, IL: Southern Illinois University Press.

7.Grimson, S. (1965). Mechanics' institutes. *Encyclopedia Canadiana, Vol 6*, p.416.

8.Keane, P. (1975). A study in early problems and policies in adult education: The Halifax Mechanics' Institute. *Histoire Sociale/Social History, 8* (16), note 35, p.261.

9.Colgan, W. (1980). *The Governor's Gift: The Auckland Public Library, 1880-1980*. Auckland: Richards Publishing and Auckland City Council.
Dakin, J.C. (1979). Adult education in early Auckland. *Continuing Education in New Zealand, 11*(2), 48-67.

10.Brereton, C.B. (1948). *History of the Nelson Institute*. Wellington, NZ: A.H. & A.W. Reed.
Hall, D.O.W. (1970). *New Zealand adult education*. London: Michael Joseph.

11.Dakin, J.C. (1978). The origins and beginnings of continuing education in Wellington. *Continuing Education in New Zealand, 10*(1), pp.77-97.
Stevens, J. (1968). 'Brother Fred' and the two cultures: New Zealand's first librarian. *New Zealand Libraries, 31*(5), pp.175-198.

12.Whitelock, D. (1974). *The great tradition: A history of adult education in Australia*. St. Lucia: University of Queensland Press, p.87.

13.*ibid*.

14.Kelly, T. (1957). *George Birkbeck: Pioneer of adult education*. Liverpool: Liverpool University Press.

15.Grattan, C.H. (1959). *American ideas about adult education, 1710-1951*. New York: Bureau of Publications, Teachers College, Columbia University, 20-25.

16.Moreland, W.D., & Goldenstein, E.H. (1985). *Pioneers in adult education*. Chicago: Nelson-Hall, pp. 35-52.

17.Department of Internal Affairs (1991). Jonas Woodward, 1810? - 1881. *The dictionary of New Zealand biography, Vol. 1 - 1769-1869*. Wellington: Allen & Unwin and Department of Internal Affairs, p.609.
Thompson, A.B. (1945). *Adult education in New Zealand: A critical and historical survey*. Wellington: New Zealand Council for Educational Research.

18.Keane, P. (1973). Joseph Howe and adult education. *Acadiensis, 3*(1), 35-49.

19.Wilson, J.D. (1973). Adult education in Upper Canada before 1850. *Journal of Education of the Faculty of Education University of British Columbia, 19*, 43-53.

THE

HISTORY

OF

ADULT EDUCATION,

IN WHICH IS COMPRISED

A FULL AND COMPLETE HISTORY

OF THE

MECHANICS' AND LITERARY INSTITUTIONS,

ATHENÆUM

PHILOSOPHICAL, MENTAL AND CHRISTIAN IMPROVEMENT
SOCIETIES, LITERARY UNIONS, SCHOOLS OF DESIGN, ETC.,
OF GREAT BRITIAN, IRELAND, AMERICA, ETC. ETC.

BY J. W. HUDSON, Ph. D.,

SECRETARY OF THE MANCHESTER ATHENÆUM, FOUNDER OF THE
SCOTTISH AND NORTHERN UNIONS OF LITERARY AND
MECHANICS' INSTITUTIONS, &c.

———

LONDON:
LONGMAN, BROWN, GREEN & LONGMANS, PATERNOSTER ROW,
1851.

Title page from Huason's *History of Adult Education*, 1851

Parkes People's Institute, NSW

Tenterfield School of Arts, NSW, 1992

Laurieton School of Arts, NSW, 1992

Abermain School of Arts, NSW, 1992

W A Duncan, 1811-1885

20.Carmichael, H. (1833). Introductory discourse delivered at the opening of the Sydney Mechanics' School of Arts. *New South Wales Magazine, 1*(2), 65-81; *1*(3), 152-161; *1*(4), 212-217.

21.Nadel, G. (1966). Henry Carmichael. *Australian Dictionary of Biography, Vol 1, 1788-1850*. Melbourne: Melbourne University Press, p.211.

22.Turney, C. (1969). Henry Carmichael - His advanced educational thought and practice. In Turney, C. (Ed.), *Pioneers of Australian Education: A study of the development of education in NSW in the nineteenth century*. Sydney: Sydney University Press.

23.Kable, K.J. (1976). John Woolley. *Australian Dictionary of Biography, Vol 6, 1851-1890*. Melbourne: Melbourne University Press, p.436.

24.Woolley, J. (1862). *Lectures delivered in Australia*. Cambridge: Macmillan.

25.Roe, M. (1967). John Lillie. *Australian Dictionary of Biography, Vol 2, 1788-1850*. Melbourne: Melbourne University Press, p.119.

26.Nadel, G. (1957). *Australia's colonial culture: Ideas, men and institutions in mid-nineteenth century eastern Australia*. Cambridge, Mass: Harvard University Press, p.131.

27.Martin, A.W. (1980). *Henry Parkes: A biography*. Melbourne: Melbourne University Press, p.12.

28.Martin, *op.cit.*, p.90.

29.Sowden, Sir W. (1930). Frederick Edward Meleng - gentleman: A memoir. *South Australian Institutes Journal, 18*(12), 31 August 1930, pp.5-9.

30.Medcalf, M. (1972). Joseph Johnston. *Australian Dictionary of Biography, Vol 4 1851-1890*. Melbourne: Melbourne University Press, p.486.

31.Nadel, Australia's colonial culture, *op.cit.*, p.131.

32.Bridge, C. (1986). *A trunk full of books: History of the State Library of South Australia and its forerunners*. Adelaide: Wakefield Press in association with the State Library of South Australia, p.47.

33.*ibid.*

34.Matthews, B.E. (1987). *Louisa*. Melbourne: McPhee Gribble, with the assistance of the Literature Board of the Australia Council, p.249.

35.Inkster, I. (1980). The public lecture as an instrument of science education for adults: The case of Great Britain, c1750-1850. *Paedagogica Historica, 20*(1), 80-107.

36.Keane, P. (1984). Questions from the past of appropriate methodology for adult learners. *Convergence, 17*(2), p.58.

37. Walker, R. (1981). Lecturers and lecturing in late nineteenth century Australia. In Davison, G., & McLeary, A. (Eds.), *Australia 1888: A bicentennial history bulletin for the study of Australian history centred on the year 1888. Bulletin No. 8.*, pp 78-87.

38. Aveling, M (Ed.). (1979). *Westralian voices: Documents in Western Australian social history.* Nedlands, University of Western Australian Press.

39. Penglase, B.M. (1986). Literacy in colonial New South Wales, 1788-1881. *Unpublished PhD Thesis.* University of Newcastle, p.189.

40. Bleasdale, J.I. (1870). *Practical education: A brief review of its present condition on the Continent of Europe and in Great Britain, etc.* Melbourne: Technological Commission of Victoria, p.23.

41. *ibid.*

42. *ibid.*

43. see, for example, Clarke, E. (1992). *Technical and further education in Queensland: A history, 1860 - 1990.* Brisbane: Department of Education, Queensland Bureau of Employment, Vocational and Further Education and Training, pp 3-18.
Information Services Division, NSW Department of Technical and Further Education (1983). *Spanners, easels and microchips: A history of technical and further education in New South Wales, 1883 - 1983.* Sydney: NSW Council of Technical and Further Education, pp 11-20.
Docherty, J. (1973). Local initiative: The technological schools of art, 1869-1890. In Blake, L.J. (Ed.), *Vision and realisation: A centenary history of state education in Victoria, Vol. 1.* Melbourne: Education Department of Victoria, pp.607-623.

44. Kociumbas, J. (1993). Science as cultural ideology: Museums and mechanics' institutes in early New South Wales and Van Diemen's Land. *Labour History, 64,* 17-33.

45. Horton, H.B. (1902). The museum and art gallery. In F.E. Meleng, *Fifty years of the Port Adelaide Institute, Incorporated, with Supplementary Catalogue.* Adelaide: Vardon & Pritchard, printers, p.55.

46. see also Kohlstedt, S.G (1983). Australian museums of natural history: Public priorities and scientific initiatives in the 19th century. *Historical Records of Australian Science, 5*(4), 1-29.

47. Wallace, R. (1986). *Built on solid foundations: An architectural history of the Sandhurst Mechanics' Institute and School of Mines, McCrae Street, Bendigo.* Bendigo: Bendigo College of TAFE, p.27.

48. Petrow, S. (1993). The life and death of the Hobart Town Mechanics' Institute, 1827-1871. *Tasmanian Historical Research Association Papers and Proceedings, 40*(1), p.15.

49. Page, M. (1981). *Port Adelaide and its Institute, 1851-1979.* Adelaide: Rigby, p.98.

50. see Wayne Murdoch's chapter in this book.

51. Woolley, J. (1865). Schools of arts and colonial nationality. *A lecture delivered at the inauguration of the Wollongong School of Arts, May 28 1861.* Sydney, Reading and Wellbank, printers, p.23.

52. Talbot, M.R. (1992). *A chance to read: A history of the institutes movement in South Australia.* Adelaide: Library Board of South Australia.

53. anon. (1904). An Institutes Association formed. *West Australian Librarians' and Institutes' Journal, 1,* 22-25.

54. anon. (1915). Various views: The Literary Institutes' Association of New South Wales. *South Australian Institutes Journal, 13*(6), p.609.
Literary Institutes' Association of New South Wales (1915). *Program of First Annual Meeting of the Association, 8 March 1915.* Glebe: T.C. Brown & Son, printers, p.2.

55. Kellermeier, S.H. (1980). The School of Arts Association. In Kellermeier, S.H., Schools of Arts - Queensland. *Unpublished Dip.Arch. Thesis.* Brisbane: Queensland Institute of Technology, pp. 87-98.

56. Warburton, J.W. (1963). Schools of arts. *Australian Quarterly, 35*(4), 72-80.

57. Learmonth, N.F. (1968). Portland Mechanics' Institute. *Mimeo.* Portland: Historical Society, p.1.

58. Talbot, *op. cit.*

59. Cawelti, J.G. (1965). *Apostles of the self-made man.* Chicago: University of Chicago Press, pp.83-84.

60. see, for example, Fryar, R. (n.d.). An account...of the growth and development of public institutions at Ballarat, 1856-59. *Unpublished paper.* Ballarat: Ballarat University College.
Keating, C.R. (1980). The Toowoomba Mechanics' School of Arts, 1867-1877. *Unpublished Research Project.* Toowoomba: School of Journalism, Darling Downs Institute of Advanced Education.
Raszewski, C. (1988). The Armidale School of Arts, or Mechanics' Institute, 1859-1871. *Armidale and District Historical Society Journal, 31,* 35-52.
Smith, B.J. (1961). Early Western Australian literature: A guide to colonial and goldfields life. *Unpublished MA Thesis.* Perth: History Department, University of Western Australia, chap. 2.

61. Lovett, W. (1920). *Life and struggles of William Lovett in pursuit of bread, knowledge and freedom.* New York: Knopf, p.142.

62. Ryerson A.E. (1849). A lecture on the social advancement of Canada. *Journal of Education for Upper Canada, 2*(12), p.182.

63. Channing, W.E. (1883). Self-culture: An introductory to the Franklin Lectures, delivered at Boston, September 1838. In Channing, W.E., *The Works of William E Channing DD*

(Rev.ed). Boston: American Unitarian Association, p.32.

Keane, P. (1977). The work/leisure ethic in adult education. *Dalhousie Review, 57*(1), 28-46.

Maurice, F.D. (1855). *Learning and working: Six lectures delivered in Willis's Rooms, London, in June and July 1854.* Cambridge: Macmillan.

64. Cooper, J.F. (1956). *The American democrat.* New York: Knopf, p.89.

65. Candy, P.C. (1991). *Self-direction for lifelong learning: A comprehensive guide to theory and practice.* San Francisco: Jossey-Bass, p.29.

66. Hudson, J.W. (1851). *The history of adult education, in which is comprised a full and complete history of the mechanics' and literary institutes, athenaeums, philosophical, mental and Christian improvement societies, literary unions, schools of design, etc., of Great Britain, Ireland, America, etc., etc.* London: Longmans, pp.xiii-xiv.

67. G.R. Kirkup (Hon. Secretary, Peak Downs School of Arts) to Under Secretary, Queensland Department of Public Instruction, 28 March 1899.

68. Whitelock, *op. cit.*, p.132.

DISPELLING 'THE STAGNANT WATERS OF IGNORANCE': THE EARLY INSTITUTES IN CONTEXT

Elizabeth Webby

INTRODUCTION

In his short-lived newspaper, *The Currency Lad*, the young Australian Horatio Wills wrote on that quintessential nineteenth century theme, the perfectibility of people, mainly through self-education:

> Mankind begin to feel that they are born for some nobler purpose than mere animal existence, and that they are possessed of minds capable of expansion to an almost illimitable extent. The scenery of the moral and intellectual world is, in consequence, undergoing a mighty change. Fertility succeeds to barrenness; and the stagnant waters of ignorance, which formerly sent forth the pestilential vapours of crime and misery, have now given place to those fountains of knowledge, which issue their almost boundless streams to fertilise, enrich, and bless the world.[1]

The growth of the mechanics' institute movement in Australia during the nineteenth century was an important, but far from the only, sign of the new thirst for knowledge. While the institutes were distinguished by being, at least nominally, open to all classes, a host of other, usually more exclusive, societies sprang up in the period from 1820-1850, mostly to die out after a few years.

It is the purpose of this chapter to place the growth and development of the institutes, especially in the first half of last century, into the broader context of organisations and activities designed to foster self-improvement. By doing this, it is hoped not only that the 'movement' will be seen in its true perspective, but that the individual institutions will be seen for what they were: one opportunity among many - especially in cities and larger towns - for people to pursue their individual self-development.

NEW SOUTH WALES

Before 1820, there is little evidence of groups of people meeting together in Australia for other than ceremonial, religious or convivial purposes. On 15 February 1820, the young lawyer George Allen wrote to his brother in England, asking him to send some necessary law books and, if possible, some other, more general, ones since

> . . . this place is not like London for amusements, here we have neither society nor places of amusement, there is not [sic] library here to spend a few hours in; my only employment after the business of the day is to retire to my own room (for I am the only one of the family now left in Sydney) and read my books of which I am sorry to say I have but a slender stock.[2]

A desire to augment such slender stocks by clubbing together to share books with others lies behind many of the societies established in early Australia. In 1821 a group of Sydney gentlemen, including Barron Field, James Bowman, H G Douglas, Frederick Goulburn, John Oxley and Edward Wollstonecraft, founded the Philosophical Society of Australia. One of the Society's regulations was that "Every member shall furnish the Secretary with an alphabetical catalogue of his library, to be digested into one catalogue for the reference of all the members."[3] By 24 July 1822, Field had completed this joint catalogue but very few of the Society's other aims were achieved. These had included

> collecting information with respect to the natural state, capabilities, production, and resources of Australia and the adjacent regions, and publishing from time to time, such information as may be likely to benefit the world at large.[4]

To this end, members were each supposed "to produce a monthly paper, upon some subject connected with the objects of the Society, under penalty of Ten Pounds."[5] But by June 1822, when only three members had given papers, this resolution was suspended, leaving it to "the interest and zeal which (it is hoped) each Member has in the objects of the Society, to lay before them a paper at such time as he may think proper, without any penalty for default."[6] By the end of the year, the Society had ceased to operate.[7]

Unlike both the Philosophical Society, and the mechanics' institutes, most other early groups and societies confined themselves either to the purchase of books and/or newspapers or to the holding of lectures and debates. A Sydney Reading Room had been established even before the Philosophical Society, since its members were informed in the *Sydney Gazette* of 26 August of the arrival of "the first Series of Newspapers & Pamphlets." Further advertisements for the Reading Room appeared in the *Gazette* on 5 and 19 July 1822 and there may have been some links with a "Reading Society" first mentioned on 13 May 1824. It, however, was soon to disband, with its books sold by auction on 1 July 1824. Writing on the establishment of Robert Campbell's Australian Circulating Library in 1825, the previous failures were recalled:

> We have much pleasure in proclaiming the laudable efforts of Mr Campbell, in singly attempting an undertaking, which has thitherto baffled the combined efforts of many respectable individuals. Our Reading Rooms have long since tumbled into forgetfulness, and can scarce be brought to one's remembrance, only when the subscribers recollect that such Institutions were promoted and subscribed to most liberally, but which (like the Sydney and Van Diemen's Land Packet Company) subsided as hastily as they were formed - all owing to the absence of a certain uniformity of sentiment that is required in our community to benefit the public weal. In business we should like to observe men meet upon a par - in the private circle let them be as select as prudence may demand.[8]

But these and other attempts by individuals were equally unsuccessful and, eventually, on 3 February 1826, ten gentlemen met at the Sydney Hotel to found the Australian Subscription Library & Reading Room, eventually to grow into the present State Library of New South Wales. Initially, however, it was a very exclusive enterprise. While the annual subscription of two pounds was no dearer than that for Robert Campbell's Circulating Library, would-be members had also to find an entrance fee of five pounds and be elected by three-fourths of the members present at a balloting. In 1826, also, the gentlemen of Bathurst attempted to establish a Bathurst Literary Society, with similar aims to the Australian Subscription Library and an even more exclusive membership.[9] An attempt to cater for the other classes was made in 1829 with the foundation of the Useful Book Society:

> It will be gratifying to those who have brought with them from England a portion of the characteristic spirit of its inhabitants in the present age, the love of science, and zeal for its universal diffusion, to be informed of the actual formation and hitherto successful progress of a society for the dissemination of useful knowledge among all classes of society in this growing Colony ...

> The object of the present Society is sufficiently apparent in its title. It is simply that of establishing a Library of Useful Knowledge, the contents of which shall be accessible to the whole community, *without the distinction of rank or denomination, whether civil or religious*. For imparting instruction merely spiritual, whether contained in the scriptures or in books founded on those sacred writings, separate societies already abound. For the higher branches of elegant literature, the Subscription Library is more than sufficient to meet the demands of upper classes. But for the middle and lower orders, for such as are either excluded from the associations of the more wealthy, or, being unable to avail themselves of their expensive institutions, have nevertheless a desire for innocent recreation and intellectual improvement, for all in fact, who from taste, necessity, or occupation, prefer that kind of knowledge which may be emphatically designated as '*useful*,' some appropriate establishment to render that knowledge cheap, and access to its various fountains easy, is still a desideratum . . .

> With the view of compassing these objects, it is intended that the subscriptions shall be moderate, the Society unfettered with the appendages of more dignified associations, and every part of its proceedings conducted with an exclusive regard to simplicity and usefulness.

> It is not intended that religious books should be excluded, nor even a proportion of such amusing and popular works as are calculated to afford recreation rather than instruction; a consistency with its professed design, however, will oblige the Society to devote the chief part of its funds to the purchase of elementary scientific works, of those treatises on practical subjects which are most likely to be of service to the farmer, the mechanic, and the tradesman in their respective daily occupations, and of the several cheap periodical publications, such as the *Mechanics' Magazines, Farmer's Magazine, Cottage Monthly Visitor*, etc. which are expressly intended for the instruction of the middle and lower orders.[10]

Once again, however, nothing seems to have come of this venture and it was left to the establishment of the Sydney Mechanics' School of Arts in 1833 to provide a library accessible to all classes.

During the 1830s mechanics' institutes and other literary societies spread through the country regions of New South Wales. Mechanics' institutes were founded at Newcastle in 1835[11] and at Maitland in 1839. Maitland in this year could also boast two book societies, "one in West Maitland, the other in East Maitland, both of which under judicious management are likely to prove flourishing associations."[12] In 1837 a 'Periodical Book Club' was established at Bathurst[13] and in 1839 a Subscription Library and Reading Room at Yass.[14] By 1836 a Book Society was also in operation in Parramatta[15] though it apparently was very exclusive in its membership; a situation about which a 'Parramatta Subscriber' complained bitterly in a letter to the *Commercial Journal*:

> There is a Reading Room now in Parramatta already, but it is of that exclusive nature that it effectually debars the entrance to its precincts, of any one less than gentlemen!! The terms of admission to this Institution renders it exclusive, (being £5 per annum) the very few and very select Persons comprising it, render it exclusive. The very secret manner in which it is conducted makes it exclusive, and above all, one of its members a very great man, (at least in his own estimation), but occupying a very small compass - in space and denominations declared it was exclusive at the formation of the Institution, and said that the few respectable and highly gifted individuals to whose brilliant talents, this precious piece of consummate human wisdom would owe its origin, were determined that, nothing impure, should enter their hallowed sanctuary:- The Emporium of the wit, wisdom, and learning of the far famed town - Parramatta.[16]

Presumably weighed down by criticisms such as these, the reading room faltered, to be replaced in 1841 by the Parramatta Mechanics' Library and Reading Room which, despite its early promise, did not see out the decade.[17] In response to similar complaints throughout the 1830s with respect to the exclusiveness of the Sydney-based Australian Subscription Library, on 19 December 1840, the *Australasian Chronicle*'s leader proposed the formation of a new Public Library, since the Mechanics' Institute Library contained too few works of value and the Australian Subscription Library was open to too few persons. This had perhaps been prompted by a letter from 'A Denizen of the Counting-House,' printed in the *Sydney Morning Herald* on 7 December, deploring that young clerks and other white-collar workers, who would never have got into the Australian Subscription Library, and may have felt the School of Arts beneath them, had "no place where after the duties of the day they may find proper and sufficient relaxation and amusement conjoined with useful instruction." He thought the establishment by them of "a *Subscription Library and Reading Rooms* . . . would be the means of preserving many a young man from much trouble and folly." Whether or not as a result of this letter, the following year saw the foundation of the Commercial Reading Rooms and Library, whose *Rules and Regulations* were printed by Kemp and Fairfax in 1842. At a guinea per annum, its subscription was much lower than the Australian Subscription Library, and, though there was provision for balloting for membership, in practice anyone with the necessary money seems to have been accepted. In a letter to the editor of the *Australian*, 'Senex' remarked.

> Look at the Commercial Library in George Street, men of all ranks meet there, and not only is there no such thing as exclusion in admission to this Institution, but subscribers are invited to join. The fact is established by this Institution, that men may meet without becoming acquaintances or considering themselves bound to salute

each other: and I have there seen men personally obnoxious to each other, quietly enjoy their mental amusement at the same table.[18]

Despite its liberal admission policy, the Commercial Library never seems to have really prospered, and had ceased to exist by 1846. As its full title shows, the emphasis was on the reading rooms, and in the early years it supplied mainly newspapers and magazines. Its subscription was still fairly high, especially as no provision was made, as with the School of Arts and circulating libraries, for quarterly or monthly payments, whilst better collections of books could be found in the latter libraries. Comments in the *Australian* of 19 September 1842 suggest that initially few persons joined the Commercial Library: "We are happy to say that the Society is now in full operation, and from the excellence of the arrangements, we do not doubt that ere long its list of subscribers, as well as its sphere of usefulness, will be very considerably extended." But, within less than two months, it was reported that the Library had lost half its members since July, and hence was financially "exceedingly embarrassed":

> Really, this is one of the most distressing instances of the bad times, when young men are compelled to resign such useful and reasonable recreations, as are afforded them by the library and reading room of this institution.[19]

No doubt as a consequence of this, a slight reduction in the annual subscription, and the dropping of the ten shillings entrance fee, were advertised in the *Australian* of 26 December 1843.

In a series on colonial libraries published in the *Colonial Literary Journal* between 4 and 18 July 1844, the Commercial Library's main defects were seen as the unnecessarily late arrival of British newspapers and the "beggarly account" of books in the library, "(if it be not considered an anomaly to call it a library)." The latter was "a great draw back to its usefulness and its prosperity; and it is, therefore, with unfeigned pleasure we hear of the intended augmentation." To finance this augmentation, the committee decided to run a course of lectures, along the lines of the School of Arts lectures.[20] A letter from 'Yorick,' ostensibly on these lectures, was printed in the *Australian* of 14 May 1844. Most of its space was, however, devoted to the Commercial Library itself, and suggestions for its improvement. After claiming the Library was most useful for just that sort of young clerk referred to in the earlier *Sydney Morning Herald* letter, who could "spend his leisure hours in reading their fascinating pages, instead of wasting both his time, his health, and his means at taverns, billiard rooms, or houses of ill fame," 'Yorick' hoped more people would join and also donate books to build up the scanty collection. The most interesting part of his letter concerns the need to include novels: "The public taste, I much fear, is still so vitiated, that novels *must* be introduced into a library, to make it succeed." 'Yorick's' argument was similar to that used in the previous decade to justify the inclusion of light reading in the School of Arts' Library - novels are necessary to attract members - with the same pious hope that once the taste for reading has been established, "The mind must then be occupied; and when its lighter food is all exhausted, it will be glad to turn to more substantial and wholesome fare." Such theories obviously reckoned without the growing number of novel writers and the growing status of the novel as a literary form. Although the lectures given in aid of the Commercial Library seem to have been fairly successful, it was apparently still unable to purchase sufficient books to satisfy readers' cravings. By 18 July 1846, at the latest, it had ceased to exist, for the *Australian*, chronicle of most of its fortunes, carried an advertisement for Hebblewhite's auction of its books a few days later.

As in Sydney, attempts were made to found book societies, mechanics' institutes and circulating libraries in country districts of New South Wales throughout the 1840s, with similar difficulties in maintaining them in the face of the financial depression and readers' apparent lack of interest in anything but fiction. No mechanics' institute seems to have been operating at Windsor during this period, although there were some circulating libraries. On 25 July 1844, the *Hawkesbury Courier* announced the opening of an apparently short-lived Reading Room, and on 15 January 1846, of a circulating library at the *Courier* Office, to "principally comprise well chosen Novels, Romances, etc." The *Courier* folded only a month after this list appeared and so, presumably, did George Eager's Windsor Library. The next year, a Mr George Walker proposed to open his Windsor Reading Room and Library, "where the advantages of a constant supply of the leading magazines and newspapers of Great Britain, with an excellent collection of standard works, will be secured to subscribers." The Sydney *Age* for 10 April 1847, which printed the announcement, was "happy to hear that Mr Walker has already received promise of very liberal support in his enterprise".

The Parramatta Library, established in 1844, provides another example of the predominant association of circulating libraries with newspaper men in Australian country centres during the 'forties. Edmund Mason, publisher of the *Parramatta Chronicle*, announced on 27 July that he had

> . . . instructed his Sydney Agent to attend the various Book Sales, for the purpose of purchasing Novels, Romances, Travels, Biographies, etc. to be appropriated in establishing a First Class Library in this town.

> The first portion . . . consisting of above one hundred of the most popular Novels and Romances of the day, have been received, to which an addition will be made weekly.

Initially, charges were twopence per volume for one day, and a penny for each subsequent day, with provision for monthly, quarterly and annual subscriptions at a later date. Earlier attempts to establish a library at Parramatta had been unsuccessful, as the *Herald* recalled on 7 April 1841, in its account of the newly-formed Parramatta Mechanics' Library and Reading Room. This had been opened with "about five hundred volumes of useful and entertaining works," and the *Herald* enthused,

> . . . we have no doubt it will be highly beneficial to the Township, as, for years past, this town has been destitute of any thing that could afford rational amusement to any number of the inhabitants; especially the working classes, who, in consequence of this, were rapidly falling into the pernicious habit of spending their evenings in the public houses; but now not a few of them prefer the reading room.

Whether this reformation failed to be maintained, or the infant Society suffered from the seemingly inevitable squabbles amongst its "respectable office bearers," a brief report in the *Herald* for 3 December 1842 announced the dissolution of the "Parramatta Book Society."

The "Parramatta Clerical Book Society," presumably a Church of England body, was, however, still "in good condition."

The fate of various libraries and societies established in Maitland during these years was generally no more fortunate. On 29 May 1840, James Cox, Treasurer and Secretary of the Maitland Book Society, advertised in the *Sydney Morning Herald* a forthcoming meeting "for the sale of the Books of last year, the circulation of one hundred and seventy works just received from England, and payment of subscriptions for the current year." Evidently, the Maitland Book Society had been organised on the common plan of a continuous turn-over of its library. One does not know if it was still in existence by 11 December 1841, when the new *Hunter River Gazette* proposed the formation of a Mechanics' Institute at Maitland. This institution was duly formed, but soon ran into difficulties - on 5 February 1842 its committee announcing the bookseller William Lipscomb had claimed its library for non-payment of debt, "and, if his demands are not satisfied before the 1st March, the books will be delivered into his possession on that day." The *Gazette* thought it "a pity . . . that the members cannot so arrange matters as to enable them to settle the claim . . . without parting with the library, and so make another attempt to carry out the aims of the institution." It would seem that such an attempt was made, though it only staved off the inevitable for, on 7 January 1843, Lipscomb humorously advertised in the *Maitland Mercury* that, "having been appointed Executor to the estate of the late unfortunate Maitland Mechanics' Institute, now deceased and insolvent," he offered its library for sale at reduced prices. Perhaps the Maitland Institute would have done better if it had followed its Sydney counterpart in stocking plenty of fiction; only a few of about one hundred and twenty volumes on this list were novels.

Its death was not, however, the end of the mechanics' institute movement in the Hunter Valley. The Newcastle Mechanics' Institute, founded in 1835, evidently continued to thrive, though not often mentioned in the press. On 23 September 1846, the *Mercury* announced a lecture there on poetry by Dr John Stewart, postponed to 30 September. In addition, the Patrick's Plains Institute seems to have begun in 1845, an account of its first Annual Report being given in the *Mercury* for 9 May 1846. Although having only fifty-eight members, it had sponsored twelve lectures during the year, and owned a library of "216 volumes, on the subjects of arts and sciences, history, biography, travels, philosophy, agriculture, natural history, mechanics, novels, poetry and polite literature, which have been extensively read." Despite these achievements, the committee thought it "improper to disguise the fact, that they have not met with co-operation from that class for which the Society was principally established." But this seems to have been the common complaint of mechanics' institutes, whether English or Australian, idealists ultimately finding most mechanics preferred public houses to reading rooms. On 15 April 1848, the *Mercury* advertised the sale by auction of "100 volumes of outread BOOKS, and other property belonging to the Singleton Mechanics' Institute," which is perhaps to be identified with the Patrick's Plains body. An earlier attempt to found a more high-class "Hunter River Society, For the Promotion of Literature, Science, and The Interests of Agriculture," with obligatory library, does not seem to have gone beyond its announcement in the *Colonial Observer* for 24 September 1842.

Developments in Tasmania during the first half of the century were similar to those in New South Wales, though perhaps because of the closer patterns of settlement, provincial book societies appear to have been more numerous and more successful. The printer Andrew Bent had attempted to open a Public Library and Reading Room in Hobart at the beginning of 1823,[21] but the first successful library was opened by the Wesleyans in 1826. In a publication printed by Bent in 1826, their reasons for commencing the Library are clearly set out: "But so remotely are we situated from the land of books, and so few are possessed of competent libraries, that except within a confined circle, a taste for general reading cannot be gratified by the intelligent, nor cultivated by the young."[22] Later, the sources and nature of the work available are explained:

> One part of the books which now constitute the Library has been purchased; another part is comprised of those volumes which have been gratuitously presented by friends of the infant Institution; and a third part comprises certain books which have been sent from England from time to time, by the Wesleyan Missionary Committee, for the use of the mission at this place....
> The Books comprising the Library are to be of general utility; but while on the one hand, History, Philosophy, and General Science are duly regarded; on the other, Publications that are either frivolous in their composition, or pernicious in their tendency, will be entirely excluded, and Books on Morality and Religion form the prominent feature of the Institution.[23]

The Subscription was ten shillings annually in cash or books, with five pounds making one a life member. In addition, there was to be a number of books "on the plainest and most important subjects of doctrinal and practical Religion; which shall be furnished *gratuitously* to any who may be disposed to apply for them."[24] On 10 October 1827, the *Sydney Gazette* reported, "The Wesleyan Library established about two years since in Hobart Town, by the Rev Mr Carvosso, we are happy to state, is in a flourishing condition, on account of its powerful patronage" - presumably a reference to Governor Arthur.

By 1828 a Hobart Town Book Society had been established, its *Catalogue of Books* being printed in that year by James Ross, who was also its librarian. Although as exclusive as the Australian Subscription Library with respect to membership, it was much less so in its choice of books, including most of the popular novels of the period. As in Sydney, dissatisfaction with the exclusive nature of this Society led to proposals to set up others. In 1829, at a meeting to found a Book Society, it was resolved:

> To limit the subscription to a moderate sum annually. To sell by auction *among the Society annually*, all the Books purchased in the preceding year, so as to increase the funds of the society, and to prevent the expense of forming a library....To have neither Ballot nor Black ball for admission....That every member should have the option of ordering books, equal in cost, to the amount of his subscription....[25]

At a further meeting it was decided, as the *Tasmanian* recorded on 24 April, "That the Society be open to all Housekeepers subject to a code of Regulations to be framed at a General Meeting of those disposed to join in its Establishment.... That the Annual

Subscription be One guinea, with one guinea additional entrance." This move was applauded in the *Australian* on 28 April: "A Club, called a Book Club, is about to be established in Hobart Town, on a moderate and rational scale, the leading principles being to run into no unnecessary expense, and to EXCLUDE *exclusion*." But, in spite of this applause from the sister colony, neither the General Meeting nor the Society is heard of again. The original Book Society continued to prosper:

> At the Annual General Meeting of the Hobart Town Book Society held on Saturday 29 August the affairs of the Society were found to be in a very flourishing state, several new members were enrolled. It was also proposed, we learn, to carry the original intention of the society into effect, of erecting a reading room, and to give it more the character of a really literary institution, by inviting the contributions of learned and scientific men, more especially in recording the researches into the natural productions of this island.[26]

It was presumably to this proposal that the *Tasmanian* of 2 October referred: "We understand that Lieutenant Governor Arthur has been pleased to bestow a piece of land upon the book club, for the purpose of erecting a *Library House*, which will be erected by subscription, upon a very liberal plan."

At Launceston, John Pascoe Fawkner had attempted to found a library as early as 9 February 1825, when he announced, with some of the usual grandiloquence, in the *Tasmanian and Port Dalrymple Advertiser:*

LAUNCESTON READING ROOMS

> As learning expands the mind, produces discoveries which benefit mankind in general, softens the otherwise barbarous manners of men, and conciliates the affections, I beg leave to propose to the Inhabitants of the County of Cornwall the following Plan:- That a READING ROOM, on truly liberal principles, be established by Subscription; and that the Books be purchased by the same Means, either here, at Hobart Town, Sydney, or England. - But, in order that this Plan may ultimately succeed, it will be necessary to divest ourselves of all narrow-minded prejudices, as I firmly hope that those who deplore the prejudices of others will shun their steps. The benefits to be derived from an establishment of this kind would be manifold. In the first place we should have the Gazettes, from England, up to the sailing of each vessel; together with the New Publications of all descriptions worth reading, without being obliged to wait for the extracts in the Hobart Town Gazette. Each Subscriber would have the benefit of reading the whole Collection (a great acquisition) and it would soon form a library, the boast of the Country, and perhaps the envy of our more populous neighbouring towns. Let us set an example that will be glorious to us, at the same time that it is beneficial. In order to obviate one difficulty, I will provide a Room for the use of the Society for Twelve Months, free of expense, this Town being so barren of Public Amusements. - No establishment could be instituted that would tend more to polish the mind, to bind parties to each other by similarity of pursuits, promote disquisitions, and cause a general diffusion of real knowledge, besides placing us in a way of improving by the earliest News from our (Mother, or) Native Country. - The cost to each Subscriber would be, at most, not more than £5;

and what is that, I ask, to any Inhabitant of Launceston, or its Environs? A mere trifle; a labouring man may earn it in a fortnight.

No man of real sense would object to concur with me in the general usefulness of this Proposal, and at such a small expense. Should any person wish to join in endeavouring to accomplish this Plan, I will submit a sketch of the Rules, but to be subject to the Members when assembled.

But either prejudices against emancipists were not so easily put down, or money so easily put up, as Fawkner had hoped, since his proposal seems to have come to nothing. Another attempt of this sort was made in 1826, when, "a meeting [was] held in the School House, at Launceston, on Saturday the 22nd of July, 1826, to consider of the means of establishing an Institution for the Education of Youth, and the advancement of Science and Literature."[27] The establishment of a "valuable and extensive Library and Reading Room for Adults" was also proposed. This library also seems to have gone no further, so that, before and after the brief life of Fawkner's Circulating Library, the Launceston public had to rely on hotels for their reading matter.

James Ross's *Hobart Town Almanac* for 1831 gave a lengthy account of the progress of Hobart's three libraries:

The literary taste of the people also shows itself in a very respectable Book Society, consisting of 60 or 70 members. The annual subscription is two guineas, and the money is regularly forwarded to a bookseller in London who sends in return all the most approved and popular works of the day, reviews, magazines and newspapers. As a sort of appendage to it, there has recently been added a reading room on a small scale, held for the present in the large room above Mr. Deane's library and stationers' store in Elizabeth-street. It is however in contemplation among the public officers, merchants and other influential men in the town to institute a public reading room on a permanent and respectable footing, which may be a general rendezvous for gentlemen from the interior and strangers from abroad, when they visit town. A plan of this building for the purpose has already been made, and with the example of the excellent library at the Cape of Good Hope, of the chamber of commerce at Sydney, and other institutions of the kind, we think it is probable when we compile our little work for another year, that we shall have to commemorate its full establishment as an honour to the town.

Besides this, there is a very valuable little library of useful and instructive books, belonging to members of the Wesleyan persuasion, as also Mrs. Deane's circulating library; and though a great part of the latter consists of novels and other works of a light amusing description, yet in conjunction with the others, its establishment in Hobart-town has done very much good. A reading people can never be a very vicious people; for the very employing of the mind in the quiet rational exercise of perusing a book has, to say the least, a negative good effect, in preventing a sacrifice of time or money in the pursuit of pleasures of a less innocent or more expensive kind.[28]

This is an interesting defence of novel-reading at a time when many people still regarded it as one of the less innocent pleasures.[29] Unfortunately for Ross's argument, however, the Hobart Town Book Society was soon to suffer a series of upheavals, chronicled in all their acrimonious detail in the press, that proved lovers of literature not always quiet and rational.

In 1834, at a general meeting of the society, it was reported "that the general feeling was not only to continue the society as a literary institution, but prospectively to extend it towards the formation of a public library of standard works ancient and modern, and of books of reference."[30] However, it was not until 1836 that the Hobart Town Book Society was finally reconstituted as a public library. On 8 April, the *Courier* enthused "We are happy to see by the advertisement of the meeting of the Book Society to be held on Thursday next, that this remaining glimmer of literature is still alive amongst us, and gaining strength and members," and a week later reported,

> At a numerous meeting of the Hobart Town Book Society held at the Library, Macquarie-street, this day, ... it was resolved unanimously -
>
> That the *Hobart Town Book Society* do henceforth take the name of the HOBART PUBLIC LIBRARY, and that any person residing in Hobart Town, or within five miles thereof, may (on the written proposition of two members of the committee) without ballot be entitled to its privileges, on paying the usual entrance fee and subscription in advance.[31]

Commenting on this decision the following month, the *Courier* said

> The eyes of both the public and the government have all along been directed to the proceedings of this Society, from which in justice to itself something distinctive in the cause of literature should long ago have emanated.
>
> Such as it is, however, it has had one good effect, though of an unmeritorious kind, it has given rise to numerous reading associations throughout the interior. At Bothwell, Richmond, Campbell-town and Norfolk-Plains, incipient libraries already exist. But the great drawback to the ultimate success of all these is the expense of a room to contain the books, etc. Now, as it is the bounden duty of the government to promote a taste for reading and a supply of useful knowledge, we would suggest the propriety of going to the comparatively small expense of annexing an apartment to the public offices, vestries, or other public buildings at each station, for a public library.[32]

After Ross's sale of the *Courier* in 1836, it ceased to devote so much space to the affairs of the Book Society and little further information has been found on the progress of this newly established Public Library. The *Tasmanian* of 27 October 1837 did, however, report a proposal that a section of the Library should "be exclusively devoted to works on science, manufactures, and the arts - more especially to such of these, as are most desirable to see progressing mongst us."

After the failure of the Book Society's reading room, Ross attempted to found a separate institution of this kind. The *Prospectus of a Reading, Literary and News Room, about to be Opened in Hobart Town*, printed in 1832, held out many inducements to subscribers:

The situation which has been chosen for it is one of the most convenient and central in the whole town, being at an equal distance from both wharfs, almost contiguous to the several public offices in Macquarie-street, and readily accessible at a minute's walk from the principal merchant's counting houses, stores and warehouses. The room which is sufficiently capacious, will be neatly fitted up with every requisite, such as globes, maps, writing materials, et cetera. A cheerful fire will be kept up when the season or any of the sudden changes in temperature to which we are liable in this climate, may render that or any other means of personal comfort desirable by the subscribers.[33]

As no conditions of membership are laid down, it would seem that the Reading Room was to be open to all who could afford three guineas a year, or one guinea if they lived further than five miles from Hobart. The tone of the advertisement suggests, however, that Ross anticipated that his members would come mainly from the upper classes. A large selection of British newspapers and magazines, Tasmanian, Sydney, South African, Indian, Singapore and Chinese papers, were to be provided, as well as "some of the most popular novels, &c., a library of the most standard and classical works in English literature, Encyclopaedias, &c.". And since, as Stefan Petrow shows in his chapter, the Hobart Town Mechanics' Institution was at this stage virtually non-existent, Ross also proposed to "commence . . . a regular series of evening lectures on scientific subjects, most suited to the character and probable wants of the youth of this colony." In setting out the need for such instruction, he presented one of the first criticisms of the anti-intellectualism of Australian society:

While the progress of intelligence is marching with rapid strides in Europe and America, in these remote corners, to all useful and elevating purposes it may be said to be stationary. In those countries men of learning or genius, however humble in other respects are as much honoured and consulted, to say the least, as individuals of the largest property, which is still too apt to monopolise respect to the prejudice of what are really higher and nobler, though not perhaps as human nature is constituted more necessary endowments.... Our present excellent and liberal minded monarch alive to the true interests of mankind and awake to the finer feelings of the man, has been known to receive with the most cordial welcome and even to entertain at his table men who though otherwise destitute of worldly wealth had distinguished themselves by their attachment to learning and their fellow men in their generous and disinterested pursuit of useful knowledge. We will not say that there is not a disposition to act similarly in Hobart town, but we must in candour tell our townsmen that the old mammon is still too much an engrossing subject amongst us, and that the professor or rather the possessor of it is still as in the dark ages, too much an idol. Truth and sound reason should be our guide and not the type or custom which others may hold out for our servile imitation.[34]

Despite these worthy sentiments, nothing more was heard of the Reading Room for over a year. Then, on 27 December 1833, the *Courier* advised subscribers to that Institution, "the arrangements will be finally completed by the first of January next." Although in the meantime the subscription had been reduced to two guineas annually for townspeople, the Reading Room does not seem to have prospered, since no further reports of it have come to light.

Having no James Ross to champion them, the affairs of the other libraries and book societies operating in Tasmania during the eighteen-thirties were more briefly chronicled. The Wesleyan Library continued advertising, though apparently without much patronage for its more serious works:

WESLEYAN LIBRARY

The Public will please take notice, the above Library is open to all persons on moderate terms; the Library, which contains nearly 1000 volumes, consists of works on Philosophy, History, Geography, Theology, Astronomy, etc.
Terms - 10s. per annum, full members 20s. per annum.
Catalogues and particulars may be obtained on application to Rev. J. Orton, *Mission House*, or to J Dunn jnr Librarian, *Commercial Bank*.[35]

Ross followed this up with some comments in the next week's *Courier*:

The little glimmerings that we yet have in our *Book Society*, our incipient *Reading Rooms*, at the *Club* and elsewhere, and though last not least, the *Wesleyan Library*, afford a gratifying indication of the general disposition of the people to literary improvement. In mentioning the Wesleyan Library, which is scarcely noticed equal to its merits, we take the opportunity to recommend it especially to public favour, as affording a selection of the best and most useful works, both for circulation and reference at present in the colony, attainable at a low rate. It is in all respects an institution, from the character of the books it comprises, highly deserving of general support.

The 'Club' mentioned in the above passage would seem to have been the Union Club, described as having been established in 1834, with membership limited to two hundred "respectable gentlemen" who had access to their own library.[36] In "A Few Words on the formation of a standard public library, and other literary and scientific institutions in the colony," James Ross, midway through another variation on his common theme, wrote:

The Union Club, lately formed has every prospect of a long and vigorous life, for its materials are joined together by the most effective of all cements of English society - good eating and drinking - and they are less liable to be shaken because the wavering topic of politics, and the undermining vice of gambling, are wholly banished from its circles. Comfort and social intercourse are the pith of its existence.[37]

Presumably much less exclusive were the provincial book societies mentioned in another of Ross's articles. No further information has been found on the one at Campbell-town, but the Norfolk Plains Book Society, with "upwards of 400 Volumes," is listed among the Public Libraries in the 1830 *Hobart Town Almanac* (p.260). On 11 August 1834, the *Launceston Advertiser* printed a request by the Secretary of this Society for members to return their books without delay since "Another supply of books has been received, but nothing can be done to forward their circulation until the state of the Society's affairs is ascertained." In addition, the *Courier* for 24 July 1835 announced a general meeting of another society, the New Norfolk Reading Association. Slightly earlier, on 3 April 1835, the same paper had reported the formation of book societies at both Richmond and Bothwell. The *Colonial Times* for 21 April announced that the Committee of the former Society was "prepared to receive offers from persons who may have works on General Knowledge for sale." Judging by the frequency of newspaper mentions, the Bothwell Literary Society seems to have been the most successful of any of these institutions:

> On Tuesday the 6th September instant, the *First* Anniversary Meeting of the *Literary Society*, Bothwell, (the only existing Institution of this kind in the Island) took place. ... This Society was instituted by a few individuals, lovers of science, who subscribed liberally for the purchase of works of philosophy and general literature - there is already attached to the Institution a very respectable library, both of circulation and reference, in which is to be found a variety of popular periodicals of the day, as well as several British newspapers and a considerable sum has recently been transmitted to London for the purchase of some of the most valuable modern publications - the members are also *increasing*.[38]

Later, the same paper announced:

> *Bothwell Literary Society* - Remote from the distraction of party politics and strife, this little institution we are happy to say is flourishing - considerable additions have been made to the library, and amongst the presentations is a most liberal one, of above *one hundred and fifty volumes of standard works*, by Captain Wood, just landed from the *Dunmore*.[39]

By the time of its second anniversary, as the *Courier* for 22 September 1837 noted, there were over three hundred and fifty volumes in the Bothwell Library and, by 8 November 1837, nearly five hundred volumes. The *Courier* of that date enthused over this demonstration "that to increase the taste for reading it is only necessary to keep up the requisite supply of new, and useful, and interesting publications." A few weeks later it announced the formation of a similar society at Pontville. Amongst the resolutions of the Pontville Literary Society one finds:

> 2dly. That each subscriber name books for procurement to the extent of his subscription; such work or works having been in the Library one year, be at the annual general meeting sold by auction, and at his risk, put up at half price. These and other funds in the hands of the Committee be expended by them in the purchase of books, or otherwise, to the advantage of the Society....

> 9thly. That the amount of each gentleman's annual subscription be one pound, and the ladies' ten shillings.[40]

This appears to have been the first such society to make provision for women members.

Tasmanian libraries and literary institutions continued during the 1840s to be bedevilled by exclusiveness, lack of interest and money, and arguments over the place of fiction. One bright spot, however, was the continuing success of provincial book societies, which hardly managed to get established on the mainland at this period. For most of the 'forties, Hobart readers had to rely on either the Mechanics' Institute Library or one or other of the fluctuating circulating libraries, since the Hobart Town Public Library, formerly the Book Society, appears to have died out in 1840. Certainly by the middle of the decade there was agitation for the formation of a true public library:

> It has been remarked more than once of late in our hearing, what a want there exists in Hobart Town of a Public Library of standard authors, ancient and modern. With many members of the legal profession, a little army of divines, a fearful number of medical men, and very many gentlemen in public offices, or in the enjoyment of independent circumstances, there is no library for the general use of the members of the professions in particular, or for all the classes which have been named. We do think that this is owing to the object never having been properly contemplated or its attainment sought; and that, were a judicious proposal of something of the kind submitted it would obtain very prompt and general support.[41]

But this suggestion was not adopted till 1849, prompted by Governor Denison's inclusion of £200 for the purchase of books for a Public Library in the estimates of government expenditure for that year. Details of the founding of the Library were included in the Preface to its first *Catalogue*, issued in 1849. At the initial meeting, held on 29 May 1849,

> ... fifty-four gentlemen and one lady gave in their names as Members of the Library; and a circular letter requesting the support of the Settlers and Inhabitants of the Colony having been sent to 637 heads of Families, the result was, that, up to the opening of the Library on the 1st August 1849...fourteen persons became Life Members, and one hundred and ten became Annual Subscribers.[42]

As this implies, the Tasmanian Public Library was nearly as exclusive in practice as the Australian Subscription Library. Its progress between the May meeting and the August opening was well-chronicled in the local press, though coloured by their various political viewpoints. On 20 June, the *Hobart Town Courier* wrote: "The subscription to this library, which is to contain works of reference for all classes, is lower than that collected by our Sydney neighbours, where a public library has been founded some time, which now contains 13,700 volumes." Whilst, at ten pounds for Life Membership and two for Annual, the Tasmanian Public Library was somewhat cheaper than the Australian Subscription Library, these charges were obviously still beyond the means of many in the community. And at a later meeting, reported in the *Courier* on 30 June, it was made clear that all classes were not to be admitted, Bishop Nixon's motion for admission by ballot on the Sydney model being carried over Governor Denison's for open membership. This decision earned for the new Library the enmity of the radical *Hobarton Guardian*, which wrote of this "Aristocratic Library":

> We hear that a most expensive house has been taken for the residence of the secretary, one room of which is to be devoted to subscribers for six hours per day, Sundays excepted. We also understand that the room is to be carpeted! etc. etc. We hope the public will protest against one penny of their money being expended for the comfort and extravagance of this library, as they can now see what was the drift of Bishop Nixon in advocating an annual subscription of two pounds.[43]

Returning to the attack four days later with a leader on "The Miscalled 'Public!! Library',", the *Guardian* castigated Nixon for advocating the exclusion of mechanics and other non-gentlemen, even though Denison, in making the original grant of public money, had aimed to found a truly public library. It gave further vent to its anger on 28 July: "This *private* institution will be thrown open at noon on Wednesday next, and will continue so until six in the evening daily, Sundays excepted, for the convenience of officials and accommodation of the *élite* of Hobart Town!"

In Launceston, the Library Society, established in 1845, appears to have been the most liberal of the larger public libraries founded in Australia before 1850, despite the retention of balloting for membership. Provision was made for an unlimited number of members, including ladies, at the low rate of one pound entrance fee and one pound annual subscription, with new books selected by a ballot of members at quarterly meetings. The object of the Society was given as "the establishment of a permanent collection of useful books, in every department of literature." Thus, like the later Hobart Town Public Library, it aimed to exclude novels and seems to have maintained this resolution throughout the 'forties. Nothing further is heard of this Society until 3 April 1847, when a report of one of its annual meetings appeared in the *Examiner*. Although established for nearly two years, it still had only thirty to forty members, possibly because of the exclusion of fiction. All works were, however, accessible to the general public for reference purposes. Later in 1847, the *Examiner* printed a longer account of the Society's Annual General Meeting, including voting on new books. These were mainly scientific, historical and travel works, though Coleridge's *Literary Remains* was also chosen. As retiring president, William Henty, of the famous Victorian pioneering family, presented the customary address "on some of the chief events of the literary and scientific world since the previous meeting," embracing the aims of the Society, literary developments in England and literary institutions in the Southern Hemisphere. He gave a clear expression of the current arguments both for literary societies and against novel reading:

> Looking to the comparatively humble and contracted sphere of our labours, it might be viewed simply as the union of a few to supply their literary wants by a contribution of their means to a common stock; but regarding it as I cannot but do, with the prospect of its securing to us a permanent library of standard authors, and other sources of mental improvement, as one of our best and most available means of cultivating the intellectual taste, and gratifying it when awakened; as a valuable educational institution, using that word in its highest sense as the means of educing and exercising the full powers of the human intellect, and gathering into it the enlarged and refined stores of science, and of an ever increasing and improving literature, I look to it as occupying a high place amongst our local societies. If we regard it even as a mere source of rational occupation, supplying to both young and old the mental gratification derived from books, which in the words of Dr. Channing are worth more, regarded merely as a gratification, than all the luxuries on earth, it claims no ordinary share of our care and attention.

> The great principle which we cherish in the constitution of our society in its permanency. This it is which distinguishes it from the usual features of a book club. Our objects embrace not new books merely or works of passing interest, but authors of merit, whether old or new - standard works of reference and of science. These

44

are our aims, though in the early formation of the society many works of miscellaneous, though I trust not of light reading, may be expected to enter....

To be a lover of reading, was at one time synonymous with being a lover of knowledge; but it is not so now: hardly a lounger over periodicals and serials, but reads in quantity as much as the student, reversing the old maxim, as though he reads many things, he does not read much. The case with the present generation is to instil therefore, not a desire for reading, but a thirst for knowledge and self improvement, to form a sound judgment of books; and direct the mind carefully to study and cherish such as are good and useful, and lead on in the road to the great temple of knowledge, and to discard and avoid those light productions which will assuredly impair the intellectual powers, and detract from the usefulness of him who indulges in them. Towards such ends I feel assured this institution is well calculated to assist.[44]

Subsequent reports in the *Examiner* for 24 June 1848 and 6 June 1849, on new works ordered for the Library Society, show a determination to keep to these high principles. Despite the lack of frivolity in the works selected, the Launceston Library Society was unable to attract any government support. On 10 October 1849, the *Hobart Town Courier*, reporting the Society's Annual General Meeting of a few weeks earlier, announced that a request for such aid "had received a cavalier reply" from the Lieutenant-Governor.

Although no Tasmanian newspapers were published outside Hobart and Launceston during this decade, some information on libraries in other centres can occasionally be found in the major papers. The Bothwell Literary Society continued to flourish in the 'forties, and the *Hobart Town Courier* enthused that this Society had

> ... risen without ostentation, and apparently without effort, by the force and effect of union alone, and the desire to cultivate Science for its own sake, to be by far the best conducted and most apparently useful institution in the island. Some short time since we published an account of their late proceedings, which have been characterised with the desire to promote information, and extend it by precept as well as example amongst the lower orders of the population, and teach them the value of knowledge, by the price which their betters set upon it.[45]

An attempt to found another country library, presumably also to benefit the "lower orders" as well as their betters, was applauded by the *Cornwall Chronicle* in 1847:

> In conjunction with the early closing of shops, at Campbell Town we are glad to find that a library is about to be established, on the premises of the Government Schoolmaster, for which purpose Walter Davidson, Esq., and other influential gentlemen have intimated their intention to subscribe on a liberal scale. A supply of books from Hobart Town is expected shortly, and many of the inhabitants are prepared to subscribe their guinea a year for the privilege of access to a good collection of standard works. We wish the project success.[46]

Unfortunately like so many others, this project does not seem to have enjoyed much success, since nearly three years later, one finds

45

CIRCULATING LIBRARY. In accordance with the expressed wish of many residents in the districts of Campbell Town and Ross, a public library will be opened on the 1st January, at the Macquarie and Ross stores. The library will be supplied during the ensuing year with such books as may be obtained here, but for 1851 arrangements have been made for quarterly shipments direct from London.[47]

VICTORIA

Melbourne, as a sign of the remarkable cultural development which characterised its early years, had, by the eighteen-forties, a Mechanics' Institute, a number of church and other semi-public libraries and a circulating library, though, as an editorial in the *Port Phillip Gazette* regretted, no "public" library along the lines of those in Sydney, Hobart and Launceston:

> It is a fact, at once both singular and lamentable, that although in Britain every town and hamlet, and even every parish, boasts its circulating library, yet in Melbourne, the capital of *Australia Felix*, there is not any establishment of the kind. So far as we are aware, there is no source from which the literary man may obtain books, unless he happen to find works to suit his taste at a bookseller's shop, and then he has to purchase them. There cannot be a doubt, if a public library were formed, and if it were conducted properly, that it would add materially to the enjoyment of the inhabitants of both Town and District.
>
> The idea is not a novel one; it has often occurred to us, and has frequently been brought under our notice by intelligent friends and correspondents. We are induced to refer to the matter at the present moment, because we observe a very fine collection of books in the auction rooms of Messrs. Brodie and Cruikshank, which is to be sold in a few days. The question is, can there be anything done towards forming a Subscription Library at the present moment? "Money is scarce," but the books are likely to sell cheaper on that account. We calculate that two hundred volumes from the collection might be purchased for 3s. a volume, which would only be £30, and that number of really good works would form a select library.[48]

But, as correspondents to both rival papers were quick to point out, there was already in Melbourne a public library of four hundred volumes attached to the Mechanics' Institute. On 18 April, the *Patriot* published a letter from 'G' claiming:

> ... A new and separate Public Library would require an expenditure for suitable premises and Manager or Librarian, which would materially trench upon the funds otherwise applicable for books. Now, as the Mechanics' Institute (now happily purified and re-organised) offers both these indispensables ready formed, together with the services of competent managers, and the nucleus of a Library and Reading Room, would it not be far better to save the cost of rent and Librarian by coalescing with that Institution. - It is to all intents and purposes a Library and Scientific Institution - a library of *general* literature is part of its plan, including periodicals and "light reading" - and I much doubt if Melbourne can afford TWO Public Libraries at present. One pretext for establishing a new Library is the desire to procure novels; - there is no exclusion whatever to such works in the Mechanics' Institute, and were

there funds, it is not to be doubted that a selection of such works would be regularly procured, as well as works of mere science. As, however, it is stated that some of those whose duty it is to direct, refine, and elevate the public taste in literature, as well as in morals, are supporters of the proposed Library, I cannot suppose that there is any wish to direct the reading public of Melbourne, *exclusively*, to the novel writers; and, if there be no such wish, why raise a new Institution, which must certainly injure the old one, by diverting funds from which would be much better employed in enlarging (in every branch of Literature) the Library of the Mechanics' Institution?[49]

Earlier, the *Gazette* of 6 April, in response to a similar letter in the *Port Phillip Herald*, had termed the Mechanics' Institute Library "not suitable for the wants of all classes," which perhaps meant those who considered it too unexclusive. A week later, it reported that sufficient subscribers had come forward to found a Public Library, but not in time to purchase Brodie and Cruikshank's books.

Perhaps these subscribers included many of the gentlemen whose activities were later described as follows:

> ... within the last month, a number of gentlemen have formed themselves into a committee for the purpose of establishing a select and "exclusive" reading club. The members are to be limited to forty in number, and the terms are one guinea entrance fee, and an annual subscription of £2.[50]

Among the supporters of this venture were such Melbourne notables as Charles La Trobe, Redmond Barry, Roger Therry and Dr Howitt, besides "several solicitors, and some of our principal merchants." They were to operate on the usual book club method of auctioning volumes after one year to purchase a fresh lot for the next year. Aside from his connection with this, perhaps unsuccessful, reading club, Sir Redmond Barry stands out, as no one person does in any other colony, as predominantly responsible for the growth of literary culture in early Melbourne. He had been the founder of the Melbourne Mechanics' Institute, and was later to play a major role in the establishment of both the State Library of Victoria and Melbourne University. In addition, as Henry Gyles Turner recorded in his inaugural address to the Australian Literature Society, Barry had earlier turned his own books into a miniature public library. After discussing John Pascoe Fawkner's Melbourne Circulating Library, Turner relates of Barry:

> In the very modest house which in 1842 he occupied in Bourke Street...he set aside one apartment free of access at all times to the working men of the town, and furnished it with the nucleus of a library of good standard works, and current magazines rather more up to date than the solid reading which Fawkner had imported from Van Diemen's Land.[51]

Turner goes on to give a perhaps somewhat rosy picture of Victorian culture in the eighteen-forties, though one in part borne out by the rapid growth in number and quality of newspapers, the large book auctions, and the number and extent of public libraries which sprang up all in the space of ten years:

I have often been told by early colonists that the period from about 1845 to the eruption of the gold miners, was socially and intellectually a most agreeable era. The attractions of a new country, in the foundation of which there was no convict taint, and where the climatic conditions, and the prospects of fortune were so promising, stimulated a very high-class immigration. It was a bright feature of those times that large numbers of young men, scions of good families, flocked out in unusual proportions, and infused into the somewhat primitive surroundings the charm of high culture and refined manners.[52]

Some of these young men no doubt patronised the Melbourne Mechanics' Institute which, like others of its kind, seems generally to have done more for the middle classes than the workers: "In 1849 a Committee on Public Libraries was told that only one member in twenty was a mechanic or artisan, and even these represented the 'upper strata' of the working class."[53]

In contrast to the scarcity of information about Melbourne's circulating libraries, one finds abundant detail on the apparently flourishing concern operated by James Harrison at Geelong. Harrison not only ran a library and book-store but, like so many of his provincial bookselling contemporaries, a newspaper, and fortunately was not chary of space for his own wares. At fifteen shillings a quarter, with two shillings' reduction for advance payments, Harrison's library was almost as expensive as Fawkner's, but he does seem to have made a serious attempt to supply the best light and solid, ancient and modern literature. An advertisement in his *Geelong Advertiser* for 26 June 1841 listed amongst additions to the previous stock of five hundred and fifty volumes, not only the *Waverley Novels*, Miss Porter's *Hungarian Brothers*, Marryat's *Peter Simple*, Cooper's *Prairie* and *Spy* and Mrs Trollope's *Vicar of Wrexhill*, but also *Pride and Prejudice*, Shakespeare's *Plays* and translations of classical authors like Pindar, Anacreon, Virgil and Xenophon. Harrison's "puff" for a further list of additions, several months later, seems in this case to have been truer than usual:

> The recent additions comprise a varied assortment of the most popular works of living authors; although principally comprised of works of fiction, the library will be found to contain a sufficient number of Historical, Biographical, and Scientific works, to render it attractive to the more studious reader, and to blend the "useful" with the "entertaining" in due proportion.[54]

In subsequent years, Harrison continued to provide Geelong readers with the latest and best fiction. In July 1845 he advertised "THREE HUNDRED VOLUMES New and Standard, in addition to the 1500 already comprising the Library."[55] The holdings were not limited to novels, however, and Harrison's library also contained Lang's *Transportation and Colonisation*, the *Port Phillip Magazine*, the *South Australian Magazine*, and the *Tasmanian Journal of Natural Science*. All in all, Harrison's collection would seem to have been equal to that of any other circulating library operating in Australia at the time; regrettably, he was forced to dispose of it shortly after this last advertisement:

BARGAINS OF BOOKS

The undersigned, having determined upon giving up his Circulating Library, in consequence of not having sufficient time to attend to it, will commence selling off the whole of his valuable collection, consisting of eighteen hundred volumes of books in all departments of literature.

The books will remain for sale by private contract at the prices given in the following list, for a few weeks, and the remainder of the stock will then be cleared off by private auction.[56]

The "portion of the Books" listed ranged in price from 1/3d per volume for "odd Volumes of Sir Walter Scott's works," and such obscure novels as the anonymous *Perplexities of Love* (1787), to 4/- per volume for popular works like *Tristram Shandy*, Marryat's *Newton Foster* and Cooper's *Lionel Lincoln*. Nevertheless, all the works were remarkably cheap for that time, especially in Victoria, where book prices generally seem to have been high.

The anonymous proprietor of the new Geelong Circulating Library appears to have been one of those who benefited from the cheapness of Harrison's books. He quickly stepped into the breach, announcing his new library on 1 October, with terms half the price of Harrison's, though for a much smaller and poorer quality collection. A catalogue printed in the *Advertiser* for 29 April 1846 lists only about four hundred volumes, almost all novels, many drawn form Harrison's 1/3d per volume class. Amongst such generally low-quality fiction, however, were a few better works by Cooper, John Galt, Defoe, Gerald Griffin, Thackeray, Scott, Jane Austen, Bulwer Lytton, Godwin, Marryat and Sterne, most of which seem also to have originally been in Harrison's Library. There is no record of this library having survived beyond 1846.

Undoubtedly, the reading public of Geelong was the poorer for Harrison's decision to give up his library in favour of his printing and bookselling activities, and the loss of his excellent collection may have been one of the motivating forces for the subsequent formation of a Mechanics' Institute at Geelong. According to Cary, the prime movers of the Mechanics' Institute were two Scots, Andrew Love and James Harrison. The latter provided a direct link with the first mechanics' institute ever established; that of Glasgow:

James Harrison, while yet a printer's apprentice in that city, became a member of the Glasgow Institute. Convinced of its utility, he quickly sought to establish one in the land of his adoption. March 1841 saw him advocating that cause; he offered to cooperate with anyone who thought the place ripe for such an experiment, [and], as a pledge of sincerity, he promised if it were formed, to do its printing for nothing for the first twelve months.[57]

An earlier attempt to found a Geelong Literary Institution in December 1844 had apparently quickly come to nought. Ironically, the announcement of the commencement of this institution, in the *Advertiser* for 13 January, states that Harrison had been appointed its Secretary and Librarian at a salary of £35; it is possible these new duties, with a probable conflict of interests, may have been partly responsible for the sale of his own library.

The literary institution started with a great flourish: a committee of local worthies was elected, and an inaugural lecture was delivered by the Rev. A Love in October 1845, on 'The advantages to be derived from the study of history.' However, as Cary mentions in his history of the Geelong Mechanics' Institute, "the institution although it imported books,

English papers, and periodicals, did not flourish: it died unnoticed."[58] As in so many other cases, however, it evidently functioned long enough to acquire some sort of a library, since, on 11 September 1847, the *Corio Chronicle* urged that the Geelong Mechanics' Institution amalgamate with "the Literary Association of Geelong (defunct) to obtain use of its library." Three days earlier, the *Chronicle* had been scathing about the poor condition of the Mechanics' Institute:

> Corio has had we hear, for some time, an Institute, in name, similar to the Melbourne School of Arts, but with the exception of half-a-dozen files of colonial papers, and about fifty volumes of dilapidated books, it has nothing to show for its claim, to be ranked amongst the literary institutions of the colony. This will never do, if the Geelongites hope to acquire a scientific character, at all commensurate with their mercantile advancement. The managing committee have a reading room in Yarra-street, and there are funds we are informed for the purchase of a library. If, now they can arrange to have a few lectures delivered in connection with the institute, and adopt some animated plans, of beating up for donation and subscribers, we do not despair, of seeing it soon, in a position to claim from the Government, an annual grant in money, similar to that voted for Melbourne.[59]

The suggestion of amalgamation to improve this library evidently bore fruit, if slowly, since on 22 October 1847, Harrison called in his paper for a Committee meeting of the Literary Institution, "to take into consideration an application for the loan of the books now in the hands of the Secretary." Whether or not the application was approved, when a catalogue of the Mechanics' Institute Library appeared in the *Advertiser* on 13 May 1848, it contained many more than fifty volumes, dilapidated or otherwise. Some were certainly recent purchases, since only a matter of days earlier, the *Chronicle* had announced:

> *Mechanics' Institute* - The frequenters of the Reading Room and subscribers at large to this useful Society, will learn with considerable satisfaction that a fresh lot of books have been added to its Library, chiefly consisting of novels and other such light literature as its shelves were previously much deficient in.[60]

This deficiency of novels, formerly supplied so abundantly by Harrison, may have been one of the main reasons for the apparent lack of interest in the Library. George Arden, better known as a journalist, at this time Secretary of the Mechanics' Institute, prefaced the Library catalogue with:

> As it does not yet seem to be generally known that the Mechanics' Institute possesses a Library which is of course *free* to subscribers the subjoined list of the works now lodged upon its shelves and ready for circulation, distinguishing them according to the usual mode of classification, is published for general information.

Amongst just over three hundred volumes of books, magazines and newspapers listed, were sixty-four volumes of 'Novels, Tales, Etc.,' the largest category, including, of course, *The Waverley Novels*, and equally popular works by James, Lever, Dumas, Cooper, Maria Edgeworth, Hook, Carleton and Le Sage. There were also ten volumes of plays, by Shakespeare, Aeschylus and others, twenty-three of standard poetry by Byron, Pope, Burns,

Southey, Milton, Dryden, Kirke White, Ossian and Scott, with equally standard works like Boswell's *Life of Johnson, Johnson's Works, The Spectator* and *The Tatler* listed under various other headings. Altogether, nearly half the library's holdings were literary works of one sort or another.

Attempts were also made during the 1840s to found a Mechanics' Institute at the other chief Victorian country centre of Portland. On 14 January 1843, the *Portland Guardian* announced the recent formation of a Portland Scientific and General Literary Society, to "embrace the principles of both a Mechanics' Institute and a Debating Society." Interestingly, the Secretary of the newly-formed Society was Rev. Thomas Hamilton Osborne, whose inaugural address to the Melbourne Mechanics' Institute - of which he had earlier been Secretary - is reproduced in this book.

Some weeks later, on 4 February, the *Portland Guardian* reported the Society's intention to send £60 to England to purchase books, whilst, by 8 March, the rival *Portland Mercury* was claiming that, with seventy members and £50 in hand, the Society was a certain success. Despite this hopeful start, and its grandiose title, on 18 December 1848 the Society was declared by the *Guardian* to be "a dead letter and perfectly useless to the inhabitants." In the interval, it seems to have achieved little, and only rated one mention in the press, on 28 June 1845, when the *Port Phillip Gazetteer* stated that La Trobe had sent a donation of five guineas, probably in lieu of a requested government grant. Undaunted, the Portlandians determined to try again, forming a new Reading Society, or Mechanics' Institute, in May 1849. At first, the *Guardian's* outlook was gloomy; in a long editorial, it claimed that, just as the previous Literary Society had been hampered by having elaborate rules but no rulers to carry them out, so this Institute had gone to the opposite extreme by electing office-bearers before it had been properly constituted. 'Temper democratic' seems to be putting in an early appearance here:

> Besides, the idea of a society which could hardly muster two dozen members, to be guilty of the conceit of electing officers with the bombastic titles of 'President,' 'Vice-Presidents,' and all the foppery of a mimic aristocracy! There is too much aping greatness and magnificence to be useful and valuable about such appointments ...in a small community where all are pretty much alike, each struggling, in his own way, for a decent subsistence for himself and his family, and where all these distinctions between each other are so faint, as with difficulty to be discernible, appointments of these kinds are wretchedly out of character. What with Teetotal Presidents, and Presidents for a Benevolent Society, and now, again, Presidents for a Reading Society, almost every man in the place will, in a short time require to prepare himself for a Presidential chair of some kind or other...[61]

Nevertheless, by 23 July, the *Guardian* was prepared to admit that:

> The Mechanics' Institute is through the kind exercises of Messrs. Clay and Claridge becoming a most valuable auxiliary to the improvement and amusement of the town. These gentlemen through their disinterested efforts have made a useful library available to a large class of readers.

An advertisement in the same issue claimed there were already 250 volumes of "Standard Works" in the Library, available for a half-guinea entrance fee and one guinea annual subscription. Some idea of the content of the Library can be gained from the appended list of missing books, which included the tenth volume of Bell's *Shakespeare*, Raley's *Natural Philosophy* and Burke's *On the Sublime and the Beautiful*. Obviously, there could not have been very many works of fiction among the "standards."

In a somewhat sad footnote to these ambitious beginnings, Learmonth chronicles the gradually declining fortunes of the Portland Mechanics' Institute through to its last Annual General Meeting on 27 July 1880, at which the Secretary, Mr F F Levitt, agreed to wind up all the affairs of the Institute by 31 December that year. "And so exit - Portland Mechanics' Institute."[62]

SOUTH AUSTRALIA

In South Australia, a Literary and Scientific Association had been formed even before the settlers had left England, in keeping with the highly-organised system of colonisation adopted there. Like so many of the other plans, however, this had proved unsuccessful, and the Mechanics' Institute subsequently established in 1838 had also become a virtual dead-letter by the eighteen-forties. In a letter, 'Literary Institution,' printed in the *South Australian Odd-Fellows' Magazine* for October 1843, 'W.A.H.' complained that it held no classes, and only one lecture per quarter, instead of every fortnight. In addition, "no books are allowed to be lent out, or taken from the room, *even by the members themselves*." He concluded: "Co-operation and support have been wanting on the part of the inhabitants, to place this Association upon a sure and firm footing." Subsequent criticisms of the inefficiency of the Adelaide Mechanics' Institute were made in letters from 'An Artizan,' published in the *Adelaide Observer* on 17 August 1844 and 1 February 1845. In the first, he voiced the usual complaint that the Institution was not being run by or for mechanics, and, in the second, proclaimed "The only library of reference accessible to Mechanics is *nailed up*, coffined, 'quietly inured,' and thrust into a back warehouse among unsaleable goods." After this, it is not surprising to read in the same paper for 21 August 1847 of an attempt to found another Adelaide Mechanics' Institution, with mention of the two previous failures. By 1 July 1848, as the *South Australian Gazette* reported, this Institution had more than four hundred members, with a library of over two thousand works.

1848 also saw a successful move to merge this new Mechanics' Institution with the South Australian Subscription Library. In her *Diary of A Visit to South Australia in December, 1840 to January, 1841*, now in the National Library, Lady Franklin mentioned on 30 December current efforts to form a Book Society. It was not until 26 October 1844, however, that the *Adelaide Observer* printed the prospectus of the South Australian Subscription Library. Like the Launceston Library Society, it aimed to provide the foundation of a public library, and so did not plan for yearly disposal of books, or consider them the personal property of members. This more liberal attitude was also reflected in the fairly moderate annual subscription of two guineas, and in the allowing of admission without ballot up to 12 November 1844. Further interesting information on the Library is found in a letter from 'O' in answer to criticisms made in the *South Australian Register*:

With regard to the spirit of 'cliquism' of which the Editor of the *Register* expresses so great a horror, the circumstances which could alone have afforded ground for such a charge will, when fairly examined, be the best proof of its falsity. A number of gentlemen having met together for the purpose of forming a Book Club found that there were too many to carry out conveniently the object for which they were assembled - many expedients were proposed, and in the course of the discussion the possibility of establishing a Public Library was suggested. The idea was received with general approbation, and thus the Society, which was before strictly private, assumed a public character, and the foundation of an Institution was laid, which, if the views of its originators are fairly carried out (and I see no reason to doubt that they will be so), is likely to become one of the most important and most useful that a Colony or any other community can possess. . . . As to there not being fifty reading men in Adelaide, the fact of upwards of 100 subscribers having already paid their two guineas towards a library not yet in operation requires no comment.

It is certainly much to be regretted that so great a delay should have taken place in the arrangements for opening the reading-room and circulating the books, and I think we have a right to expect from the labours of the Committee results proportionate to the time they have expended in maturing them.[63]

In earlier comments on the Subscription Library, the *South Australian Register* had drawn a sorry picture of attempts at cultural improvement in Adelaide:

It has been the bane of Adelaide that things begun with spirit have often failed for want of persevering and continued care in the details of management. It would be painful and tedious to enumerate our many miscarriages - our castles in the air. Colleges of which a brick was never laid, - school-houses half finished, and nearly torn again to pieces - clubs again and again revived, but again to sink in poverty and debt - discount societies insolvent - ruining half the town, and finishing (like the Persian who was to swallow his seven brothers), by half ruining themselves - agricultural societies - but we pause - let us rather look forward and that, we may hope for better things, study to avoid the rocks on which we split before. . . .

It will be an error to choose for either office any gentleman, only because he is a gentlemanly nice fellow, and a well read man. . . . Let the Librarian in particular be well acquainted with the *outsides* of books, let him see that they are regularly returned, kept cleanly and in order, and it will matter little to the subscribers what he knows of the *inside*.[64]

Early the next year, too, the *Register* described a recent meeting to determine whether to open the Library's reading room immediately and buy books locally, or follow the usual practice of sending to London for them. James Stephens, a local bookseller, was naturally in favour of the first proposal, saying:

As regards books here, many of the best kind were, to his knowledge, constantly offered, and usually much below English prices. He was sure many purchases might be made here with advantage. A late afflicting dispensation would, most probably, occasion Mr. Shipster's Library to be thrown into the market. It was the best and most valuable ever brought into the colony. Many donations had been received. The books given by Mr. George Morphett were alone more than any member would be likely to read in twelve months....[65]

Nothing further was heard of the progress of this Library for some three years, when the *Observer* reported on a committee meeting to discuss the proposed merger with the Mechanics' Institute. This was agreed to on the terms:

> That there should be a complete amalgamation of the two Societies, under some new title to be agreed upon; that the Mechanics' Institute should contribute, in books and money, an equivalent value to that of the present collection of books of the Subscription Library; and that from the period of junction, one half of the entire subscription to the united institutions should be applied to the purchase of books to increase the library.[66]

In view of the apparent slow progress of the Library, and the disastrous history of Adelaide mechanics' institutes, this merger of resources was obviously extremely wise, though it inevitably must have made the Mechanics' Institute even less the province of the working man than previously. But, as has been seen with the other colonies, difficulties in arranging classes and lectures, and attracting working class support, in practice resulted in all Institutes being little more than subscription libraries under another name.

Besides this public library, there seems to have been a private reading society, the Adelaide Book Club, functioning in 1848, at least, when, on 4 November, Samson and Wicksteed advertised in the *South Australian Gazette* a number of volumes for auction by order of the Club's Secretary. They were mainly recent works such as Leigh's *The Emigrant* (1847), Mrs Gore's *The Popular Member* and Macaulay's *Lays of Ancient Rome* and *Essays*. Whether this auction represented the close of a short-lived venture, or one of the periodic sales held by these kinds of Book Societies, is, in the absence of other evidence, impossible to determine. The South Australian Odd Fellows also apparently ran a library in connection with the Adelaide Lodge, as announced in their *Magazine* for August 1845. The Lodge was said to have 200 volumes and 60 subscribers, whilst "All brothers of whatever lodge may become members on payment of 2s. entrance, and 1d. per week subscription. The books are allowed to circulate" (p.118). Unfortunately, nothing is known about its contents; whatever they were, they were available remarkably cheaply.

Only a little information is available about literary and cultural activities outside Adelaide in the eighteen-forties, as there were no provincial newspapers in South Australia in this decade. As early as 14 January 1843, however, the *Adelaide Examiner* announced that settlers at Balhannah had subscribed to form a public library there "on the most liberal principles." They asked for donations of books and money, since:

> It is the first District Public Library yet constituted in the colony, and being available to a large number of shepherds and agriculturalists dispersed through the Mount Barker country, cannot fail of disseminating much instruction, affording at the same time the means of rational recreation to many whose spare time is now, to use the mildest term, idly thrown away.

Once again, morality and utility are found as the chief handmaidens of culture. On 16 October 1847, the *Adelaide Observer* printed a brief report of the quarterly meeting of the Hindmarsh and Bowden Mechanics' Institute. At that time, it had 40 members, with a library of 250 volumes, plus a further 150 on loan from members, "especially Mr John Ridley," better known for his development of wheat-harvesting machinery.

QUEENSLAND

In 1849, despite this Colony's unpromising beginning as a penal colony, a mechanics' institute was established at Brisbane, largely through the efforts of W A Duncan, formerly a Sydney newspaper man, now sub-collector of customs there. On 22 September, the *Moreton Bay Courier* announced a preliminary meeting to form a "Lyceum For Literary and Scientific Discussion, Lectures, Etc.," and by 6 October was able to report that the Society had sixty members, with Duncan as its President. On 29 November, Duncan was to give the opening lecture on "The Connexion Between Literature and Commerce."

A more practical connection between literature and commerce had earlier been made by Mrs Ann Dowse, wife of the leading Brisbane book auctioneer, who, on 10 June 1848, advertised in the *Courier* the opening of a Circulating Library "at her Cigar and Stationery Establishment." Her collection was composed entirely of volumes of the *Novel Newspaper*, which she also offered for sale. Although the title of Mrs Dowse's establishment suggests a readier appreciation of tobacco than books in Brisbane, no doubt there was plenty of interest in the romantic and sensational works of W.G. Simms, Eugene Sue, Fenimore Cooper, Mrs Radcliffe, Monk Lewis and Victor Hugo, and some may even have borrowed Samuel Richardson's *Pamela*, William Dodd's *Beauties of Shakespeare* or Hannah More's *Coelebs in Search of a Wife*. The *Courier*, at least, was enthusiastic, though it hoped that "some standard works on the various sciences" would be included in future selections.

In at least one other centre in Queensland, moves were also afoot in the first half of last century to promote literary and educational pursuits. On 31 July 1850, a public meeting formed the Ipswich Literary Institution, principally to provide a newspaper reading room and library, following a resolution:

> that the present state and position of this rapidly increasing town make it desirable to establish a public institution for the supply of news and the diffusion of knowledge generally.[67]

Six days later, another meeting established a School of Arts which merged with the embryonic Literary Institution, mainly for the purpose of obtaining the Colonial Government subsidy which was then being made available to schools of arts. In July 1854, the name of the literary institution was formally changed to the Ipswich Subscription Library and Reading Room[68], and four years later, on 11 August 1858, the School of Arts changed its name to the Ipswich Mechanics' School of Arts, and applied for a grant of land for the purpose of erecting a permanent building; a building which subsequently became the Ipswich City Town Hall.[69]

WESTERN AUSTRALIA

An extremely good example of the manifold contrasts between the planned settlement of South Australia and the haphazard colonisation of its western neighbour can be seen in the differences in cultural development of the two states. Although founded nearly ten years earlier than Adelaide, Perth was very far behind when it came to the availability of literature. There were no regular booksellers there in the 'forties, and the only libraries seemingly in operation were two book societies founded in the 'thirties. In various announcements in the *Perth Gazette*, one finds some scraps of information on their activities. On 25 July 1840, the secretary of the Western Australian Book Society advised members, "A new selection of Books having been recently received from England,...the old books now in circulation, will be sold by Auction, and other business transacted...27 inst." By 10 December 1842, the Society was still in operation, though apparently not well-supported:

> At a meeting...held 8 December, it was resolved... That all members who pay their subscriptions due for the year 1840 before the 22nd instant, will be allowed the privilege of reading the books now to be sent for a balance of £22/19/4 being in favour of the Society.

The rival Swan River Reading Society seems to have had a slightly firmer basis. On 29 August 1840, its secretary announced a forthcoming meeting on 10 September: "members requested to pay subscriptions for the ensuing year, new members to apply before the meeting. The members who wish any particular works written for, are requested to give a list of the same at the time of the meeting." On 1 April 1843, the Secretary advertised a "meeting to be held on 8 April to arrange to procure a further supply of books from England," and it was presumably these books that were to be distributed at another meeting on 14 June 1844. As can be seen, both Societies were organised on the principle of a continuous turn-over of books, so neither could be termed a public library in any real sense. In 1842, an attempt was also made to found a Mechanics' Institute at Perth, the *Gazette* for 12 February advertising a meeting three days later, to which "All persons interested are earnestly invited to attend, to hear the report of the Committee." The Institute got as far as holding another meeting on 15 March, "to receive the Report of the Committee appointed at the last meeting, and to elect members." However, it "does not seem to have received very much encouragement from the gentry" or for that matter from the artisans for whom it was intended. The Institute "failed within a few months,"[70] and Perth had to wait until 1851 for a functioning mechanics' institute.[71]

CONCLUSION

From the foregoing survey of libraries and other literary institutions throughout Australia in the first half of the nineteenth century, it is evident that, contrary to popular opinion, mechanics' institutes and schools of arts did not emerge or flourish in an intellectual vacuum. Since the 1820s at least there had been an active - if somewhat uncoordinated - movement for the establishment of circulating and subscription libraries, reading clubs, and various scientific, philosophical and literary societies. Supported and promoted by an alliance of educators, clergymen, booksellers, newspaper proprietors and others, these institutions dedicated to self-education sprang up throughout the colonies, and provided the background against which, and a context within which, the mechanics' institutes developed.

Indeed it is apparent that in many cases the institutes shared with their earlier precursors not

Australian Subscription Library, founded 1826
(reproduced by permission of the State Library of New South Wales)

Dr James Ross, 1786-1883
(portrait by T L Lempriere, 1838. Reproduced by permission of the State Library of New South Wales)

only their philosophical origins, but also the same patrons, committees, premises, lecturers, books and even members. Accordingly, there is considerable continuity between the institutes and their predecessors; a continuity not only in their roles and membership, but in the newspaper accounts of their fluctuating fortunes. Throughout Australia, it was commonly the newspaper proprietors who, as official arbiters of tastes and morals, and as apologists for either radical or conservative points-of-view, sought, both through their own publications and through their support for the cultural work of the local institutes, to dispel "the stagnant waters of ignorance."

NOTES AND REFERENCES

1. Literary institutions. *The Currency Lad*, 27 October 1832

2. George Allen to Joseph Allen, original in the Allen Papers, Mitchell Library

3. Minute Book of the Philosophical Society of Australia, reproduced in *Journal of the Royal Society of New South Wales*, 55(1921), Appendix, p.lxviii.

4.*ibid*, p.lxviii.

5.*ibid*, p.lxviii).

6.*ibid*, xcix.

7.For a brief history of the Society, see Finney, C.M. (1984). *To sail beyond the sunset: Natural history in Australia, 1699-1829*. Adelaide: Rigby, pp. 169-170.

8.Howe's *Weekly Commercial Express*, 23 May 1825.

9. *Sydney Gazette*, 5 April 1826.

10.*Sydney Gazette*, 6 October 1829.

11.See Newcastle Mechanics' Institute Library and Museum (1835). *The laws and regulations of the Newcastle Mechanics' Institute, Library and Museum, founded 2 June 1835*. Sydney: Stephens and Stokes, printers.

12. *Colonist*, 12 October 1839.

13. *Monitor*, 24 March 1837.

14. *Australian*, 1 August 1839.

15. *Colonist*, 13 October 1836.

16.*Commercial Journal*, 16 May 1838.

17.Jervis, J. (1961). *The cradle city of Australia: A history of Parramatta, 1788-1961*. Parramatta: Council of the City of Parramatta, p.124.

18. *Australian,* 4 April 1844.

19.*Dispatch*, 4 November 1842.

20. See the advertisement in the *Australian,* 23 April 1844.

21. *Hobart Town Gazette,* 15 February 1823.

22.Bent, A. (1826). *Observations on the establishment of the Wesleyan Library at Hobart Town, Van Diemen's Land.* Hobart: Andrew Bent, printer, p.3.

23.*ibid*, pp.6-8.

24.*ibid*, p.8.

25.*Tasmanian*, 3 April 1829.

26.*Courier*, 5 September 1829.

27.*Colonial Times*, 4 August 1826.

28.Ross, J. (1831). *Hobart Town almanac.* Hobart: James Ross, printer, pp.99-100.

29. See Nadel, G.H. (1957). The decline in standards. In Nadel, G.H. *Australia's colonial culture: Ideas, men and institutions in mid-nineteenth century Eastern Australia.* Cambridge, Mass., Harvard University Press, pp.88-94.

30.*Courier,* 18 April 1834.

31.*Courier,* 15 April 1836.

32.*Courier,* 6 May 1836.

33.*Courier,* 19 October 1832.

34.*ibid.*

35.*Courier,* 16 September 1836.

36.Elliston, W.G. (1837). *Elliston's Hobart Town almanac and Van Diemen's Land annual.* Hobart: William Gore Elliston, p.42.

37.*Courier,* 21 November 1834.

38.*Courier,* 16 September 1836

39.*Courier,* 18 November 1836.

40.*Courier,* 22 November 1837.

41.*Observer,* 24 June 1845.

42. Tasmanian Public Library (1849). *A catalogue of the Tasmanian Public Library and reading room: systematically arranged; with the rules, regulations, and by-laws, and list of members*. Hobart: Public Library, pp.v-vi.

43. *Hobarton Guardian*, 7 July 1849.

44. *Examiner*, 25 September 1847.

45. *Hobart Town Courier*, 3 January 1840.

46. *Cornwall Chronicle*, 6 February 1847.

47. *Launceston Examiner*, 19 December 1849.

48. *Port Phillip Gazette*, 3 April 1844.

49. *Port Phillip Patriot*, 18 April 1844.

50. *Standard and Port Phillip Gazetteer*, 11 January 1845.

51. Turner, H.G. (1903). *The aims and objects of a literature society*. Melbourne: Echo, p.13.

52. *ibid.*, p.14.

53. Cannon, M.M. (1991). *Old Melbourne Town. Before the gold rush*. Main Ridge, Victoria: Loch Haven Books, p.320.

54. *Geelong Advertiser*, 21 February 1842.

55. *Geelong Advertiser*, 2 July 1845.

56. *Geelong Advertiser*, 10 September 1845.

57. Cary, J.J. (1991). The Geelong Mechanics' Institute. *Investigator, 26* (4), p.152

58. Cary, *op. cit.*, p.151.

59. *Corio Chronicle*, 8 September 1847.

60. *Corio Chronicle*, 4 May 1848.

61. *Portland Guardian*, 11 May 1849.

62. Learmonth, N.F. (1968). Portland Mechanics' Institute. *Unpublished typescript*. Portland: Portland Historical Society, p.2.

63. *Adelaide Observer*, 15 February 1845.

64. *South Australian Register*, 24 December 1844.

65. *South Australian Register,* 7 January 1845.

66. *Adelaide Observer,* 19 February 1848.

67. Slaughter, L.E. (1960). *Ipswich Municipal Centenary.* Brisbane: The Author on behalf of the Ipswich City Council, p.53.

68. *ibid.,* p.54

69. Buchanan, B. (1992). *Council Civic Group and Post Office, Ipswich: Conservation Plan.* Ipswich: Bruce Buchanan Architects Pty Ltd, pp.15-16

70. Stannage, C.T. (1979). *The people of Perth: A social history of Western Australia's capital city.* Perth: Perth City Council, p.76.

71. Nadel, *op. cit.,* p.125. See also chapter seven in this book.

CHAPTER THREE

THE MELBOURNE MECHANICS' INSTITUTE: ITS FIRST THIRTY YEARS

Jill Eastwood

INTRODUCTION

"How can we be cheerful when we are surrounded by a reading public, that is growing too wise for its betters?" It was in 1818 that Mr Flosky - a character in Peacock's satirical novel *Nightmare Abbey* - asked this despairing question.[1] And it was true that a reading public of greater proportions than ever before was developing in England: Through the Sunday schools and dame schools, through Mutual Improvement Societies and individual teachers, the working-classes were gaining a sketchy knowledge of reading and writing.[2] Webb estimates that two-thirds to three-quarters of them were to some extent literate by 1820.[3] Flosky was in a minority when he bemoaned this development, although some people, such as Lord Eldon, expressed a similar view.[4] Reading was becoming a mark of social prestige in an industrial age which demanded new skills and responsibilities and which aroused a greater political and class consciousness in the ordinary people.

Many influential members of English society actively encouraged the desire for education. They felt that "education of the poor was the best security for the morals, and subordination and the peace of countries."[5] Terrified by the excesses of the French Revolution and the widespread discontent of the years after 1815, the ruling classes attempted to ensure that the new education helped to preserve the *status quo*. Henry Brougham, Charles Knight, Harriet Martineau, and Samuel Smiles all assisted in the publication of literature which possessed the *right* ideas, ideas conducive to the maintenance of the existing social order and to the subordination and respect due to social superiors.[6] Because they were concerned to inculcate these "right ideas," the leaders of the education movement did not wish to stimulate free inquiry but rather, as James Mill advocated, "the implanting in the mind through custom or pain and pleasure, an invariable sequence and association of ideas."[7]

It was with these motives and ideas that Brougham and his friends enthusiastically supported the establishment of the first English mechanics' institute at London in 1823. Journeymen and masters, politicians and philanthropists all attended a mass meeting held on 11 November that year to discuss the matter.[8] Joseph Robertson and Thomas Hodgskin, editors of the *Mechanics' Magazine* suggested the establishment of a mechanics' institute, and Dr George Birkbeck, (Lord) Henry Brougham, Lord Denman, J C Hobhouse and S Lushington all gave active support.[9] Publicity, particularly in the *Edinburgh Review*,[10] stimulated the establishment of institutes in other parts of the country and, by 1825, they were widespread and continued to increase.[11] The London Institute went ahead rapidly, creating tremendous enthusiasm on all sides; a spacious lecture hall was opened, a lending library of two thousand volumes was established, and a reading room, newspaper room and chemical laboratory were all set in place. In 1823 Francis Place had seen eight hundred mechanics attending a lecture on chemistry,[12] and over thirteen thousand were enrolled in classes throughout England overall.[13]

The main object of the institutes was to provide scientific instruction for artisans, and to give them the theoretical basis on which their practical work was based. The following statement by Dr Birkbeck as early as 1800 shows his main purpose in supporting the institutes:

> I have become convinced that much pleasure would be communicated to the mechanic in the exercise of his art, and that the mental vacancy which follows a cessation from bodily toil would often be agreeably occupied by a few systematic philosophical ideas, upon which, at his leisure, he might meditate. It must be acknowledged too, that greater satisfaction in the execution of machinery must be experienced when the uses to which it may be applied and the principles on which it operates, are well understood, than where the manual part alone is known, the artisan remaining entirely ignorant of everything besides.[14]

It was for these reasons that Birkbeck's first course of lectures to his Glasgow artisans was on 'The Mechanical Affections of Solid and Fluid Bodies' and was "solely for persons engaged in the Mechanical Arts."[15] Similar ideas are seen in the *Prospectus* of the Manchester Mechanics' Institute:

> This Society has been formed for the purpose of enabling mechanics and artisans, of whatever trade they may be, to become acquainted with such branches of science as are of practical application in the exercise of that trade, that they may possess a more thorough knowledge of their business, acquire a greater degree of skill in the practice of it, and be qualified to make improvements and even new inventions in the arts which they respectively profess.... [T]here is no art which does not depend more or less on scientific principles and to search out what these are, and to point out their practical application, will form the chief objects of this Institution.[16]

There was an essentially utilitarian purpose behind the establishment of the institutes. Behind Brougham's cry of "Knowledge is Power" was an attempt to prevent inquiring minds from turning to those dreadful scoundrels Tom Paine and William Cobbett.[17] It was hoped that the studies made available to them would lead to a greater interest in their daily work and to a more flexible adaptation to new methods. Itinerant lecturers and teachers went about the country to help the artisan "get on in life," and in 1851 J W Hudson wrote:

> The brightest minds in literature and science direct their talents to its development (i.e., education); preparing the ignorant by addresses, by lectures and by writings, to receive and understand the great and interesting truths which the Creator unfolds before them.[18]

Through lectures, classes and libraries these "great and interesting truths" were unfolded in the mechanics' institutes; but not, alas, to the mechanics and artisans for whom they were intended. As early as 1825 Hogg, in the *Mechanics' Magazine*, found that in only four of the thirty-two principal institutes of Lancashire and Cheshire did the working classes attend in considerable numbers, and these four were in "mere hamlets." Similarly, in the Midland Counties, only three out of twenty-one had considerable working class support.[19] A survey of the average membership of the Manchester Institute during the years 1835-41 shows that the greatest number were "clerks, warehousemen, shopkeepers and assistants" and the next biggest group comprised "Merchants, Manufacturers, Artists, Architects, Engravers, Professional Men, [and] Schoolmasters."[20] In evidence given before a Committee appointed by the Society of Arts to inquire into the subject of Industrial Instruction, there are innumerable statements by officials of the Institutes as to the low working class membership and attendance.[21] The Yorkshire Union of Mechanics' Institutes, in its Report of 1841, stated that it is "universally acknowledged that the members...are, nineteen-twentieths of them, not of the class of mechanics, but are connected with the higher branches of the handicrafts, or are clerks in offices, and in many cases young men connected with the liberal professions."[22]

Despite the hard work and enthusiasm put into them, the institutes failed in their purpose, and it is not hard to explain why. The basic problem was "absence of an early and sound intellectual and moral training for the mass of our operatives...they have neither the taste nor the right appreciation."[23] People could read and write a little but found it difficult to understand the language used in lectures which, in any case, were often uncoordinated and poorly taught.[24] There was no opportunity for questions and discussion after the lectures, and many of them slept during the lectures anyway. The Book of Ecclesiasticus summed up the problem in the following words: "The wisdom of a learned man cometh by opportunity of leisure ... therefore how shall he get wisdom who holdeth the plough?"[25] The low attendance at scientific lectures meant a decrease in the number of such lectures given;[26] the excitement of the Reform Bill in the 1830s meant less interest in the mechanics' institutes because there was no opportunity for political discussion there. This in turn led to a drive for membership through the provision of amusing entertainments, exhibitions of art and sculpture, lectures on drama, elocution and music. The majority of people who joined the institutes were not artisans nor serious students; they were not interested in scientific lectures but flocked to talks about Animal Magnetism. Naturally the institutes provided entertainment for the majority who financed them rather than instruction for a small and difficult minority.[27] It was the same with the evening classes: there was no systematic course of instruction, teachers were often inefficient and did not realise the needs and aptitudes of their students.[28] This was not true of Manchester in 1830, where the classes were crowded with earnest pupils and where there were qualified teachers enthusiastic about their work.[29] Few other institutes, however, had this success. The provision of books and newspapers was perhaps their most valuable activity; but few of the artisans could read ponderous academic tomes with pleasure or profit,[30] and light literature was in greater demand. At least opportunities for reading did exist, and people did have access to newspapers.

"Nothing can persuade us that all systems of education are false which do not teach a man his political duties and rights," wrote the editors of the *Mechanics' Magazine*.[31] Yet politics and polemical religion were rigorously excluded from most mechanics' institutes; these were subjects very important to the artisan, and accordingly he went elsewhere, to workingmen's societies and socialist clubs, which would provide them.[32] The workingman did not want an "invariable sequence and association of ideas" implanted in his mind; he wanted to spend his limited free time in pursuits that were interesting and important to him; he insisted on free inquiry. The patronising air of the promoters of these institutes and their utilitarian objects gave the institutes an atmosphere which discouraged mechanics from attending. In its 1841 *Report on the State of Literary, Scientific and Mechanics' Institutions in England,* the Society for the Diffusion of Useful Knowledge points out that the attendance at Socialist institutions were greater than that at mechanics' institutes - although membership was smaller - "and this is believed to arise principally from the fact that the rival institute offers to the workman those things, the exclusion of which from Mechanics' Institutes (especially the right of free inquiry) renders them, if not distasteful, at least uninteresting to him."[33]

These were faults which F D Maurice made a special effort to avoid in his Workingman's College; he insisted continually on the comradeship and co-operation of teachers and pupils.[34] Nevertheless, one must recognise that the idea of mechanics having any right to, or ability for, education was a new and revolutionary one. During the nineteenth century everyone came to be regarded as a human being with a right to the culture and traditions of his or her country equal to the privileged few whose prerogative they had been for so long. It is to Hill and Brougham and their generation that the credit for inspiring such a viewpoint must go. The mechanics' institutes were the first step in the movement for workingmen's education. The great movement of the 'twenties did not succeed, but its development and the causes of its failure provided a valuable warning for the educational leaders of the 'fifties. They help to explain, too, the nature and course of the institute movement in Australia.

THE MELBOURNE MECHANICS' INSTITUTE

The most extraordinary thing about the Melbourne Institute is its establishment in 1839. The settlement had been founded in 1834, recognised two years later,[35] and in 1839 the actual town area was very small indeed - within the narrow boundaries of William, Lonsdale, Swanston and Flinders Streets.[36] The first land sales were held in 1837[37] and, by December 1838, there were only eighteen hundred people in Melbourne, with about seven thousand in the surrounding districts.[38] And yet, in these few years, Melbourne had acquired doctors and lawyers, merchants and hotel-keepers, newspapermen and clergymen, even dressmakers, milliners and tailors.[39] A "grand cricket match" was held in April 1839,[40] a race-meeting during the previous year, and the first hunt with hounds took place in August 1839. Melbourne may have been "a bustling, stirring sort of place from the very pip,"[41] but one can only be amazed at the number of amusements and institutions which were begun in these first three years of a pioneering colony. "Melancholy Accidents" were still frequently reported in the Domestic Intelligence columns of the newspapers, comprising mostly the deaths of unwary wanderers in the great flooded potholes of Collins and Elizabeth Streets;[42] but civilisation was coming fast.

It was on 14 February 1839, that the Union Benefit Society was established, a Friendly Society of the English type formed in Australia by the Melbourne mechanics because "we can perceive nothing to cheer us in the prospect of sickness and adversity, except from our united efforts to save from our weekly earnings, such an amount as may form a fund to relieve those who may be unable to provide for themselves and their families the common necessaries of life."[43] Members of this Society - the builders, stonemasons, blacksmiths, bricklayers, carpenters, painters, plumbers and boat builders of Melbourne[44] - formed a "large and respectable proportion of the community"[45] in 1839. At a general meeting, held at the 'Builders Arms' in September 1839 the formation of a Mechanics' Institute was enthusiastically discussed, but apparently nothing was done.[46] It was not until 4 October that the Master Builders called a public meeting for 5 November at Boots School to establish an institute in the town.[47] A very interested and representative gathering was present; it decided to apply for a subsidy and a land grant from the Governor and many members were enthusiastically enrolled.[48] The following meeting elected the Committee and the Mechanics' Institute was successfully launched.[49]

There is no doubt that most sections of the small Melbourne community were enthusiastically in favour of a Melbourne Mechanics' Institute. Subscriptions of quite large sums were given,[50] and the two public meetings held were crowded. People had been used to the work of the institutes in England, and as with the Cricket Club and the Hunt, wished to see them in Australia also.[51] Since Melbourne was not an industrial society in any sense at all, the English emphasis on teaching mechanics the theoretical principles underlying the functions of their machinery was not really applicable in Australia. In fact, there was a curious mixture of ideas among the supporters of the Institute. The Master Builders themselves wished "the promotion of science in this rising colony; particularly among the young as well as the operative classes."[52] George Arden and Thomas Strode, the *Port Phillip Gazette* editors who were also active members of the Institute, were anxious that the library and lectures would "spread an eager and praiseworthy desire for self-improvement throughout the community."[53] Melbourne was a "sin-prolific"[54] town, and accordingly there was a great deal of emphasis placed on raising the moral tone of the operative classes and on stimulating them to mental activities which would replace drinking and crime.[55] It was apparently not realised that the mechanics who supported the Institute at first, and those few who remained members of it, were not the reprobates with low moral standards, but "a powerful, wealthy and independent body."[56] The members of the Union Benefit Society were all "respectable tradesmen and mechanics" from the upper orders of the working classes, and it was these people who originated and to a certain extent supported the Institute. The Master Builders and the Committee were those who placed most emphasis upon the duty of the Institute to impart popular knowledge, but even they were not primarily concerned with knowledge for mechanics in particular. There is a very interesting address from the Committee, emphasising the value of "experimental philosophy":

> But it is the fortune and happiness of the present age, that the study of nature it appears is preferred to speculations, however sublime, as to what she might be - or from our ideas of harmony and beauty, she ought to be....In an age of such practical diligence and rigorous induction....We are indeed occasionally seduced to wander from that broad and secure path which experimental philosophy is slowly hewing out; but if our conjectures do not cling to us too firmly, on their superficial foundations they will not impede the highway of science.[57]

The writer mentions also natural science, geology, chemistry, physiology and history, but he pays only lip-service to these subjects; his real enthusiasm is in experimental philosophy (or that which today we might loosely describe as physics), not for the benefits it might give to mechanics, but for its own sake. Indeed mechanics are not mentioned in the address. The study of these subjects "are not the absolute necessities of life, but they are those occupations which give to man his surpassing dignity." This is fine prose, but little attention is given to the benefits mechanics will receive from the Institute. Similarly an irate correspondent to the *Herald* is not concerned with the mechanics of Melbourne: "It was founded, Sir, to afford instruction and to encourage the arts and sciences, thus by its means colonial talent was to be fostered and the mists of colonial ignorance dispelled."[58]

The first clause of the Code of Laws of the Institution states that the object of the Institute was: "The diffusion of Scientific and Other Useful Knowledge among its members, and the community generally."[59]

It was only in 1849 that the Committee seems to have felt strongly that the Institute had been primarily established "for the benefit of respectable tradesmen and mechanics";[60] a Mr Harker (MLA Collingwood) held this view some eight years later.[61] Professor W Hearn of Melbourne University and Dr J D Owens (MLA Loddon) viewed it primarily as an establishment for adult education of all classes.[62] Among all these different views and attitudes, there is apparently no single clear idea about the object of the institutes and the sort of function they should perform; the only general agreement seems to be that they were educational institutions.

Membership of the Melbourne Institute fluctuated a great deal in both numbers and character. At no stage could it have been called a working-class organisation, but it did not at once become merely a lending library for people who preferred the "better type" of novel. At the first public meeting to form the Institute, George Arden had attacked the "secret conference," with which apparently John Pascoe Fawkner had some connection, that had drawn up a list of office-bearers for election at the meeting. Only eight of these suggested officials were mechanics, and of the remaining sixteen, "eight could not have been worse chosen." Through the efforts of George Arden and Thomas Strode a meeting consisting entirely of mechanics drew up a list which was adopted by the following meeting. Although these officials "were considered most eligible to carry out the view of the mechanics themselves,"[63] they were indisputably people with power and position in the community:[64] people like Dr Farquhar McCrae, who was Vice President and once had John Pascoe Fawkner thrown out of a meeting on the Road Tax,[65] Redmond Barry, J M Chisholm, Thomas Strode (editor and printer), Alexander Thomson (a surgeon and later settler near Geelong), the Reverend James Clow and his colleague T H Osborne, Captain Smyth, and leading merchant P W Welsh.

These were the people who became officials of the Committee and they were followed by people of a similar type, D G Macarthur and William Westgarth, Edward Curr and Captain Coles. There were other Committee members, some of them probably mechanics, but they were not the leading members and officials; they seldom bothered to attend Committee meetings.[66] It seems to have been generally felt that the people with privileges - those who were endowed with material wealth and those who had had an opportunity to acquire an education - had a responsibility to the less fortunate members of the community.[67] In Australia, as in England, there seems to have been a realisation that the 'lower orders' had a right to education. The people I have mentioned - the lawyers, the doctors, the writers and booksellers, the judges and the politicians - were untiring in their efforts to make the institutes a success.[68] They went to Committee meetings, they lent money, they gave lectures, offered their professional services, solicited members, donated books - all with the most tremendous enthusiasm. Unfortunately they have left few records of the ultimate object behind this enthusiasm, although Reverend T Osborne's inaugural lecture in 1840 on 'The Advantages of Mechanics' Institutes' has survived and was reprinted almost in its entirety in several instalments in the *Port Phillip Gazette* (see chapter four in the present volume - Eds.). Overall, it was the same sort of enthusiasm that produced the English institute movement in the twenties, a fervour for the dissemination of useful knowledge and a recognition of the right of the people to it.

In Melbourne, as in Britain, the mechanics did not regard the Institute as their own organisation. There is a suggestion that membership was at first confined to mechanics;[69] if this were so the restriction was soon lifted. References in the *Annual Reports* indicated an anxiety about this type of member;[70] in 1849 there was apparently an influx of "respectable tradesman and mechanics, being the class of persons for whose benefit societies of this nature are principally intended,"[71] but still they took little part in the running of the Institute. In 1856 classes in English, mathematics and chemistry were established, later Latin, physics and French were introduced: the overwhelming majority of pupils were clerks and shopmen. And by 1865 the Committee was forced to acknowledge that it was "fully aware that the Institute has for many years past ceased to be in the truest sense of the term a "Mechanics' Institute."[72] In 1854 the public recognised this when a proposal to set up a true Workingmen's Society was made and the Institute was described as a "slow-going, middle-class sort of concern."[73] It is sad that the effort and enthusiasm of so many people should have failed in attracting mechanics to the Institute; it is perhaps inevitable that patronage of this type should fail.

A close examination of its activities may help to explain why it did not become an institute for mechanics, and help to define its actual place in Melbourne's social life.

Lectures were an important function of the Institute from the very beginning, although the fluid nature of colonial settlement made it difficult to secure permanent lecturers. Inevitably the lectures were unsystematic and sporadic, the topics decided by the particular fields of those who were willing and able to lecture. Any systematic course of lectures on a certain subject or in any particular field was impossible, and apparently never attempted. During the first year of the Institute's existence, the Reverend Osborne lectured on 'The Advantages of Mechanics' Institutes,' Redmond Barry gave a dissertation on 'Agriculture,' and the Reverend James Forbes a lecture on 'Colonisation.'[74] One of the few detailed records of a lecture is Arden's extremely interesting discussion of 'The Mechanical Agency of the Press in the Dissemination of Useful Knowledge,' which was printed in full by Fawkner. It is an interesting and informative lecture, in which Arden traces the development of writing, emphasises the importance of cheap and numerous Bibles to organised religion, and details the facilities afforded to commerce by the publication of newspapers. He said nothing of what are perhaps the most important effects of printing - the provision of cheap literature, the expansion of a reading public, the development of a political consciousness - aspects of printing which probably would be of most interest to mechanics. Although it was a good lecture, it was a very long one; the language used was academic, even perhaps esoteric,[75] and on the whole would not have appealed to the artisan class. Similarly with Dr Wilmot's lecture on 'Temperance and Temperance Societies':[76] the argument was complex and the language very involved. These lectures of the early years - such as Dr Wilmot's on 'The Present State of Science'[77] and the Most Reverend Patrick Geoghegan's on 'The Existence of a Deity Proved by Nature and Reason'[78] - are on subjects considered of great importance at this period, in contrast with the more entertaining topics of later years - 'Animal Magnetism' in 1850,[79] 'Wit and Humour' and 'Ninevah' in 1854,[80] 'The Stellar Heavens and Mahomedism,' 'On Exhibitions and Gatherings Together for the Good of All,' 'Physiology and Digestion,' and 'Dreams, Somnambulism and Insanity' in 1855.[81] However there was not, I think, any very significant development in the lecture topics; they were too much dependent upon the lecturers available.[82] During the 'forties, lectures were infrequent, partly because of the difficulty in getting lecturers and partly because of the depressed state of the colony. In 1849 a more or less regular annual winter season of lectures was begun; the number and attendances fluctuated from year to year, but on the whole they were well received.[83] 1856 was a particularly good year, with twenty-three lectures being given, most of them attended "by a numerous and respectable audience." The "depressed state of affairs" in 1859 "forced many young men to go to the country in search of work"[84] which meant a bad year for lectures, but the annual winter season was re-established in 1860. There were no courses of lectures held after 1862.

Since we do not know the standard of these lectures, either in presentation or material, it is difficult to judge their value. As far as education for mechanics was concerned, however, they can have been of little use. Smatterings of limited knowledge on various subjects never benefited anybody. They may perhaps have stimulated further inquiry into a subject, but that is about all. As Maurice said of lectures in English institutes, they "did rather graze the surface of men's minds than penetrate into them."[85] Even such lectures as Dr Macadam's on 'Chemistry' or G W Rusden's on 'Representative Institutions' can be of no real value unless questions and discussion follow.[86] This was not permitted. Books containing polemical divinity and other objectionable matter were excluded from the library;[87] religion and politics were not allowed as lecture subjects,[88] and on 21 April 1856, the Committee censured the Debating Class for discussing political and religious topics.[89] This was the fatal mistake of the English institutes. The Australian mechanic may have had a less vital and personal interest in politics at that time, however by 1855 (the year after the Eureka Stockade) he was intimately concerned with them. At any time, it seems to me, the mechanic would be more interested in going to a controversial political lecture than to one on 'The Principles of Beauty in Nature and Art,' and if he did not have that alternative, he would go to the pub. For other classes in the community, perhaps one can say that the lectures provided a pleasant evening's entertainment; not a frivolous evening, but one well spent in gaining culture and the social prestige which accompanies the public knowledge that one is gaining culture. Most of the lectures were apparently well-attended,[90] and must have been an important part of Melbourne's limited social life. They did at least spread a glaze of culture over the raw clay of a utilitarian colonial society.

An abortive attempt to establish evening classes was made in 1848-9,[91] but a really successful series was begun at the instigation of Professor William Hearn, Professor of Economics at the recently established Melbourne University, in 1856.[92] The course ran from July to November, on two evenings a week, at two guineas for a course in one subject. The Reverend W Baxter, Reverend T P Feuner, and Dr John Macadam from Scotch College took classes in English, mathematics and chemistry. Examinations were held at the end of the course and prizes awarded. Although attendance decreased near the time of the General Election, interest was keen and one hundred and eighteen pupils were enrolled. Twenty-nine of them joined all three classes, 23 took two subjects, and 59 joined only one class.[93] Sixty-six pupils enrolled to study etymology and syntax and the history of language and logic in the English class, but the average attendance was only 44. Similarly, in mathematics, the average attendance at classes in arithmetic, algebra and Euclid was only 40, although there were 89 nominal pupils. Fifty-four students were enrolled in the chemistry class, where elementary principles of nomenclature and notation, the chemistry of non-metallic elements and the chemistry of metals were taught to an average class of 42 members. On the whole, it was felt that the classes had been a great success: "we may believe that the demand for instruction in the higher branches of education...is neither forced nor inconsiderable."[94] Applications and attendance fell in the following years, although additional classes were established in Latin, French and experimental physics.[95] The Latin class had the greatest number of applicants (22), but only fourteen commenced and of these only eight attended regularly. The Reverend Baxter considered that this decline was due partly to the laborious nature of the study and the small immediate advance even for the most industrious, and partly because of "the dislike which adults generally have to elementary studies and always to the appearance of being slow or backward."[96] Fourteen people began the English course but in a few months this dwindled to eight regular pupils. In mathematics, ten attended regularly. There were eight in the chemistry class, eighteen doing physics, and thirteen regularly came to French lessons. The biggest and most successful class was in vocal music, which had seventy regular attenders.[97] During the next few years attendance gradually declined (the commercial depression was regarded as a factor in this),[98] and chemistry and physics were discontinued. In 1859 Hebrew and phonographic shorthand classes were introduced. The young men who attended these classes were forced to find work in the country and lack of accommodation was a problem - so it was decided to build a new hall and classrooms at the rear of the present building.[99] During 1860 "the public mind was engaged with important movements which in many cases engaged the leisure time of many of the young men."[100] The vocal music and shorthand classes were continued, but poor attendance led to the cessation of mathematics and language classes. By 1861 it was acknowledged that the classes "in various branches of knowledge, which under the guidance of teachers of acknowledged eminence at one period promised to become a most valuable feature of the Institute, have gradually dwindled away."[101] The year 1862 saw a renewed interest in the large attendance at music, elocution and shorthand, but unfortunately English, mathematics and chemistry classes were never recommenced.

The classes were a valuable feature of the Institute although in these as in other activities the mechanics played but little part. An examination of the occupations of those attending shows that it was mainly middle-class people who attended the classes. For these people, a regular course in these subjects with final examinations to stimulate study must have been of great benefit. It had been hoped, in 1858, that since the University now issued degrees on examination results only, people who could not attend day-time lectures would, through these classes, have an opportunity of gaining a University degree.[102] How many, if any, did so, is impossible to discover. In the absence of any evidence at all, one must presume that the factors which deterred mechanics from attending these classes were the same as those operating in England: the absence of a basic elementary education, on which higher studies could be based, and the absence of any practical incentive to make a mechanic want to spend two or three evenings a week after a hard day's work learning chemistry, French or Latin. It is interesting to note that these classes followed a similar course to those in England: middle-class interests such as music, elocution and dramatics succeeded where English, mathematics and physics had failed. Nevertheless, one can only be amazed that any attempt was made at adult education at all (and in connection - albeit tenuous - with a University!) in a primitive colonial society which had been established for so short a time. It is perhaps significant that their success came after the gold rushes had brought an influx of population and wealth into the colony when earlier attempts had failed completely.

The provision of a lending library and a reading room was the most valuable function of the

Institute, and in time it became its sole function. At first the library was composed of a variety of volumes which had been donated by friends of the Institute or picked up in the colony at sales of personal possessions.[103] Formerly, Fawkner's personal library at his hotel had provided the main reading room of the town; once the Institute had arranged for the purchase of books in England,[104] the library grew quickly and became a valuable asset to the members. By 1845 there were 650 volumes in the library, mainly "works of a standard character in Literature and Science,"[105] such as Robertson's *Historical Works*, Humes *England*, Gibbon's *Decline and Fall of the Roman Empire*, Adam Smith's *Wealth of Nations* and that ubiquitous accoutrement of institute libraries, *The Encyclopaedia Brittanica*. A few popular novels were added also, by authors such as Walter Scott and Fennimore Cooper. In September 1844 a reading room was established by special subscription,[106] and various newspapers, pamphlets and periodicals from Great Britain, Ireland and the colonies were provided. A total of 341 volumes were added to the library during the next year[107] and by 1848 there were over three thousand;[108] but there was a great proportional increase in the romance section, with only two volumes in the 'Politics and Political Economy' section. The Irish element in the Institute was well catered for with three newspapers from Dublin, one from Ulster and two copies of the *Life and Speeches of O'Connell* in the Library.[109] The reading room in particular was extremely popular, so much so that extra accommodation was needed.[110] In 1850 it was admitted that the library, now containing over four thousand volumes, was "a somewhat heterogeneous collection" because of the variety of the donations, and the Committee was building up "a large and rapidly increasing collection of valuable and standard works,"[111] allotting £150 per annum for the purpose. Members were apparently more concerned about light reading than the "more useful and substantial class of works," and the Committee was forced, in 1854, to secure new works by "the most celebrated and select modern fiction authors."[112] "The belief," held by the Committee, "that the character of public institutions is estimated, in some degree by the class of works in their libraries," meant that only a limited portion of the available funds was spent upon fiction; and important new works on engineering, mechanics, and the various branches of natural philosophy[113] still formed the major part of the new books purchased. By 1854, over ten thousand books were in circulation,[114] and this figure increased steadily, from thirteen thousand in 1857 to over twenty thousand in 1860.[115] Many members spent their evenings in the library and reading room,[116] which seemed "to be the departments most constantly made use of."[117] New circulating libraries were formed in the early 'sixties[118] and although membership and circulation both fell somewhat,[119] the level of 1864 was retained for many years.[120] There was also a noticeable decrease in the borrowing of light fiction in proportion to the "increased study of the more important works of literature and science."[121] It seems that the circulating libraries had drawn off those members who were primarily interested in light reading matter; the residue which remained was composed of people mainly interested in gaining information, knowledge and wisdom from books.

Access to books was an important matter in a community where few people had their own libraries. There might be little time or inclination for reading in a pioneering society where practical and material achievements were of prime importance, but those who did yearn for some of the cultural facilities of the country they had left, found them in the Mechanics' Institute. It must be remembered, however, that at any time only a fraction of Melbourne's population were members of the Institute. The reading room was perhaps more important to the community as a whole. Here the papers from the colonies and Great Britain were available, here the latest pamphlets and periodicals could be read. A special reading room subscription enabled non-members of the Institute to read these journals and, although there are no figures available, there are indications that the reading room subscribers greatly outnumbered the actual Institute members.

FINANCE AND GOVERNMENT POLICY

The Institute was almost always in financial difficulties; at first because a feud with Sir George Gipps prevented the Committee from obtaining a subsidy, and later, when Port Phillip gained self-government, because the subsidies it had received were discontinued since the country institutes were regarded as more important.

When the Institute was formed, it was decided to apply for a grant of land and a subsidy.[122] Governor LaTrobe, Patron of the Institute, was very encouraging when a deputation went to see him.[123] It was Gipps who had to give the final answer though. He refused to grant land, but promised £300 when and if building was commenced and a certificate of "probable usefulness" obtained.[124] The Committee was unanimous in its decision to refuse the offer.[125] A later incident indicated the strong antagonism towards Gipps. The Secretary wrote to the *Patriot*, denying the rumour that the Institute had again asked for a grant:

> Sir George's hostility to the Society and of the Committee's refusal of his paltry, trebly qualified promise, as discreditable to himself as it was intended to be insulting to Melbourne....No! No! Sir George! No half measures, no sacrifice of independence by the Committee of the Melbourne Mechanics' Institute. You were once asked and you once refused. That was enough![126]

Gipps was particularly annoyed when he heard that the Institute, together with the churches, had bought land at the minimum price because nobody bid against them, and later sold the land for a good price at public auction.[127] He regarded it as a plan to defraud the Government - "The Mechanics' Institute might be considered by that proceeding to have forfeited all their claims to further assistance, but he could not help regarding the proceeding as wholly fraudulent and little better in reality than the land fraud."[128] So while Sydney received £2,000[129] and Hobart £150[130] each year, the Melbourne Institute received nothing. Despite this setback, building was commenced in 1842 on a site in Collins Street, where the present Athenaeum building stands. The Committee had £1,000 in hand, from subscriptions, donations and the proceeds of their land sale,[131] but maintenance expenses were heavy[132] and they were forced to raise the extra money by mortgage.[133]

The Committee took possession of their "handsome but expensive edifice"[134] in January 1843;[135] the *Gazette* described it as "chaste, and in every respect, worthy."[136] Some income was received by letting the hall and small rooms to various groups and societies, but 1843 was a bad year,[137] with a marked decrease in the number of subscribers.[138] The commercial depression had hit the colony with great force and the attitude of John Stephen, the Secretary and later Town Councillor, aroused much opposition among the public. They disliked an official of the Institute to be also a political partisan.[139] Lectures had ceased, there were no classes, the library was small and the museum non-existent.[140] People had no wish to be associated with such an institute, especially since it was burdened with a £1,250[141] mortgage. Government assistance was essential to keep the institute alive, but by January 1844 there was still no reply from Gipps to the Committee's appeal.[142] Stephen resigned at last,[143] and economies were instituted.[144] But still Westgarth, as Treasurer, was forced to appeal directly to Gipps for aid.[145] The Governor's attitude was rather strange: Westgarth reported that no assistance would be given "both from circumstances relating to the Institute itself, and from the present impoverished state of the Treasury; and (he) further objected on principle to any assistance form governments to such institutions."[146] In reply to a Mr Robinson, the Governor stated that while Port Phillip was part of New South Wales its revenue was only a portion of General Revenue and public concerns here could not be specially helped. Finally, it did not seem that "any large proportion of the Public took an interest in the cause of the Institute."[147] Westgarth noticed that Gipps made constant references to some recent variance between himself and the colonists and this breach may have affected the Governor's decision.[148] A later letter from Gipps veiled with explanations his peremptory refusal to take over the mortgage.[149] Membership increased slightly during the year,[150] the reading room was opened,[151] and a further petition to the Legislative Council[152] brought the promise of an annual grant of £150.[153]

The Institute developed steadily during succeeding years. LaTrobe once again became Patron,[154] Sir George Gipps continued to refuse petitions[155] and Governor Fitzroy was welcomed with an effusive memorial.[156] LaTrobe received very favourably a deputation asking for £10,000 for repairs and building and stated that his views "were not similar" to those of Sir George. He suggested that the present building was inadequate and should be sold. He would then given the Institute a land grant for a new building, or £5,000 for repairs.[157]

It seemed as though a new period of government encouragement and assistance was before the Institute. It did not occur. Lack of money prevented building of the theatre,[158] although the front offices were built and let for £520 per annum.[159] LaTrobe left the colony, and Hotham, his successor, felt it was not proper for a government to give £5,000 to the Institute, even if the state of the revenue had permitted it.[160] And in 1855 the annual grant of £150 was not paid because, Hothan told the Committee, "the Legislative Council have refused to vote sufficient funds."[161] In November the Committee asked once more for their £5,000 and their annual grant, the one was placed on the Estimates for 1856, and the other made available immediately.[162] It was discovered that on 15 August 1853, before he left, LaTrobe had granted the Institute land, sections 10 and 11, between Lonsdale and LaTrobe Streets.[163] The Committee refused to exchange this land for a site behind the Customs House,[164] and apparently later sold it. There is no record of what happened to this land. The Haines government pursued the policy that grants in aid to mechanics' institutes should come from local authorities, since it was not the duty of the government to support such institutes.[165] The Melbourne Institute was once more left to rely upon its own resources.

The numerous mechanics' institutes which sprang up in the country districts during the years after 1855 received no direct government assistance at all after 1857.[166] Treasurer Charles Ebden refused applications from Richmond, Collingwood and Sandhurst,[167] and informed the House that the municipalities had power to erect institutes and that it was no business of the government.[168] The attitude of the succeeding administrations was given by Harker: "There was not, in this colony, the same field of utility for such establishments as there was at home, and besides, it would be better to allow the working men to cultivate a feeling of self-reliance by allowing them to erect these institutes themselves."[169] From 1860, grants were made to mechanics' institutes and libraries for the purchase of books, but no grants were to be greater than £200, and the entire vote was only £2,000. The amount of each grant was in proportion to the amount raised by local subscriptions.[170] In 1863 the vote was raised to £3,000;[171] this sum, and the proportional method of allocating grants, was continued for some years, at least until 1872.[172] The Melbourne Institute, however, was explicitly excluded from obtaining such grants, and only one-sixth of the total allocated sum could be divided amongst institutes within ten miles of Melbourne.[173]

THE SPREAD OF THE INSTITUTE MOVEMENT

During the years 1856 to 1867 there was no government assistance for the building of mechanics' institutes at all,[174] and very little financial aid for the purchase of books. Yet there was a tremendous increase in the number of institutes formed, especially during and after the gold rushes. By 1855 there were institutes at Emerald Hill, Warrnambool, Castlemaine, Sandhurst, Kilmore and Collingwood. Information about further institutes formed after 1856 is in local histories and newspapers, but a study of the number and spread of grants made in 1861 indicates their rapid development throughout Victoria,[175] particularly in the gold-mining districts. They continued to spring up in most country towns, even the smallest ones.

This rapid and seemingly spontaneous formation of institutes throughout Victoria in the late 'fifties and 'sixties echoes the similar development in England during the 'twenties. But it is more inexplicable because there were not, in Victoria, people like Lord Brougham and Dr Birkbeck who inspired and encouraged their development. Certainly there were no politicians who held strong views on the value of mechanics' institutes; only Dr Owens persisted in bringing the matter to the House,[176] and even he did not seem particularly concerned. Nor do there seem to have been any efforts made by the Melbourne Institute itself or the people connected with it to form institutes in other places.[177] One can see from the newspapers that various people thought the institutes a good idea,[178] but few of them seem to have done anything very constructive in forming them. The conclusion might be that there was a spontaneous movement in each town to establish an institute. I think this is partly true; but there is one common link: in a number of cases, the original suggestion and impetus seems to have come from non-conformist ministers.

There has always been a close link between non-conformity in religion and "enlightenment" in social relations.[179] I would tentatively suggest that nonconformist ministers were particularly interested in mechanics' institutes, and that these institutes were quickly established on the gold-fields partly because 'mechanics' (in the broadest sense of the term) were concentrated there, and partly because of the influence of nonconformist religion there - Wesleyanism and Primitive Methodism in particular. There has not been time for me to give this idea anything but a cursory investigation, nor is the material readily available. However, a few examples are suggestive. Beechworth formed an institute in the 'fifties at the instigation of and through the efforts of the local Methodist Church. There were about nineteen Wesleyan churches in Ballaarat in the 'fifties and 'sixties, and the reading room of the Institute was situated in part of a Welsh chapel.[180] An early (unpaid) Secretary of the Emerald Hill Institute was the Reverend W Potter, a nonconformist minister,[181] and in Melbourne itself there was a complaint that "both the gentlemen of the Scotch Church are placed in office,"[182] while the Anglicans were unrepresented. It was Reverend W Moss of the Independent Church who called the meeting to establish the Prahran Institute and he was associated with Reverend W. Guiness (church unknown) in the opening ceremony.[183] Similarly in Kew, the foundation meeting was held at the Independent Chapel.[184]

Brian Hubber makes a similar point in his study of *Public Libraries and the Suburban Reading Public, 1850-1914*:

> Clergymen in their role of community patron and moral gatekeepers were often active supporters of the institute and public libraries.... Furthermore, many institutes traced their origins to dissenting denominations: the Collingwood Mechanics' Institute first met in the Independent Chapel, a Congregationalist minister established the Brighton Mechanics' Institute, and the Northcote Public Library was first housed in a Wesleyan schoolroom.[185]

In view of what Hubber calls "the traditional education fervour of dissenting religions,"[186] and the fact that dissenting churches - particularly the Wesleyans and Primitive Methodists - have historically been associated with mining areas,[187] an examination of the origins of the country institutes, particularly those in mining areas, is likely to disclose a vital link between them and the non-conformist churches.

CONCLUSION

One of the most striking things about Victorian country towns is that almost all of them, no matter how small, have an imposing building inscribed "Mechanics' Institute." Some of these buildings contain, or at least did until recent years, the remnants of a library, as at Yackandandah. It is in these buildings that lay the real importance and value of the Institute to the towns. As soon as an Institute Committee was formed, they generally set about building a hall in which to hold lectures and store their books. Usually this hall was the only one built in the small towns, and accordingly they became "the pivot about which public parochial business moved."[188] The Town Council, if there was one, met there, and local dances and public meetings were held there, sometimes church business was transacted there. The local mechanics' institute was the centre of parish life, not because it was particularly valuable to mechanics, only partly because its lectures and libraries satisfied a public need, but mainly because the hall provided a venue for the societies and associations which are the main interest in the lives of many.

Although the institutes in Victoria - and the Melbourne Institute in particular - may have failed in their espoused purpose of providing scientific and other 'useful' knowledge to mechanics, they can scarcely be judged a failure overall. Indeed, one must pay tribute to the enthusiasm and good intentions of the founders of the mechanics' institutes in Victoria. The Institutes in the colony were formed for a different purpose from those in England; they were concerned with popular knowledge on a wider scale and less exclusively for mechanics. The library became the most important feature to members, and for the community in general the institute hall was an essential part of social life. The institute movement is part of the great education movement of the nineteenth century; in a materialistic colonial society the recognition and dissemination of cultural values was of particular importance.

NOTES AND REFERENCES

1.Peacock, T.L. (1813/1969). *Nightmare Abbey: Crotchet Castle.* (edited and with an introduction by R. Wright). Harmondsworth, Middlesex: Penguin, p.103.

2.Hole, J. (1853). *An essay on the history and management of literary scientific and mechanics' institutions, and especially how far they may be developed and combined so as to promote the moral wellbeing and industry of the country.* London: Longman, Brown, Green and Longmans for the Society of Arts, p.6.
Webb, R.K. (1955). *The British working class reader, 1790-1848: Literacy and social tension.* London: Allen & Unwin, Chapter I, passim.

3.Webb, *ibid.*, p.23.

4.Webb. *op. cit.,* p.83. "The March of intellect...is a tune to which one day or the other a hundred thousand tall fellows with clubs and pikes will march against Whitehall." (Lord Eldon).

5.Lord Brougham. Quoted in Webb, *op. cit.,* p.15.

6.Christison, A. (1802). *The general diffusion of knowledge one great cause of the prosperity of north Britain.* Edinburgh: Peter Hill, pp. 9-11.
Irvine, A. (1815). *Reflections on the education of the poor, submitted particularly to the consideration of the landlords and principal manufacturers.* London: E. Lloyd, p.29.
The Society for the Diffusion of General Knowledge was started for this purpose.

7.Cavenagh, F.A. (Ed.). (1931). *James and John Stuart Mill on education.* Cambridge: Cambridge University Press, pp.61-2.

8.Dobbs, A.E. (1919). *Education and social movements, 1700-1850.* London: Longmans Green & Co., p.174.

9.Hole, *op. cit.,* p.8. Dr Birkbeck, when at Glasgow University, had given a gratuitous series of lectures on elementary philosophy to mechanics and artisans during the years 1800-1804. Hole. *op. cit.,* p.7.

10.*Edinburgh Review,* October 1824.

11.Hole. *op. cit.,* p.9. By 1825 there were Institutes in the following towns;

Aberdeen	Alnwick	Lancaster	Halifax
Dundee	Hexham	Portsmouth	Lewes
Leeds	Shrewsbury	Plymouth	Hull
Manchester	Bolton	Newscastle	Ashton
Birmingham	Dunbar	Ipswich	Lewth

12.Dobbs, *op. cit.,* p.174.

13. Dobbs, *op. cit.*, p.175. cf. a letter from Macvey Napier to J.R. MacCulloch in 1824, quoted in Mansbridge, A. (1920). *An adventure in working class education, being the story of the Workers' Educational Association, 1903-1915.* London: Longmans, p.2. "The populace are seeking excitement in the formation of Mechanics' Institutes and in the purchase of cheap periodical publications. I was the other night at the Institute there [i.e., London] with Brougham. There were about eight hundred persons present and I never saw a more orderly and attentive audience."

14. Birkbeck, quoted in Hole, *op. cit.*, p.15.

15. Hole, *op. cit.*, p.16.

16. Quoted in Dobbs, *op. cit.*, p.173.

17. Lord Brougham. Quoted in Mansbridge, *op. cit.*, p.3.

18. Hudson, J.W. (1851). *History of Adult Education.* Quoted in Mansbridge, *op. cit.*, p.3.

19. Hole, *op. cit.*, p.19.

20. Hole, *op. cit.* p.17.

21. Society for the Encouragement of Arts, Manufactures and Commerce (1853). *Report of Committee Appointed to Inquire into the Subject of Industrial Instruction.* London: The Society. Evidence before Committee, particularly pp.36, 37-9, 85, 102, 123, 131,138.

22. Quoted in Hole, *op. cit.*, p.21.

23. Report of the Yorkshire Union of Mechanics' Institutes. Quoted in Hole, *op. cit.*, pp.20-21.

24. Report of Committee of Society of Arts, *op. cit.*, p.82. "Do not imagine that meetings where the subscribers are at all times left to themselves, without teachers to point out the good from the bad, where lectures are few, given in a desultory manner, sometimes on one subject and sometimes on another, by fourth-rate lecturers, can ever be of real benefit."

25. *Ecclesiasticus, or The Wisdom of Jesus Son of Sirach,* 38:24-25.

26. Report of Committee of Society of Arts, *op. cit.*, p.37.

27. Hole, *op. cit.*, pp.25-26; Report of Committee of Society of Arts, *op. cit.*, pp.37-8.

28. Hole, *op. cit.*, pp. 35-36, 60.

29. Hole, *op. cit.*, p.33.

30. Hole, *op. cit.*, pp.26-27.

31. *Mechanics' Magazine,* 11 September 1824.

32. Report of Committee of Society of Arts, *op. cit.*
Evidence - by John Allen of Leskeard, pp. 86-87; by Prof. Johnston of Durham University, p.36.

33. Society for the Diffusion of Useful Knowledge (1841). *Report of the state of literary, scientific and mechanics' institutions in England: With a list of such institutions and a list of lecturers.* London: The Society, pp.28-29.

34. Mansbridge, *op. cit.,* Chap. I-II passim.

35. Shaw, A.G.L. (1946). *The economic development of Australia.* London: Longmans, Green, p.50.

36. Curr, E.M. (1883). *Recollections of squatting in Victoria: Then called the Port Phillip District, from 1841-1851.* Melbourne: Robertson, p.2.

37. Bonwick, J. (1856). *Discovery and settlement of Port Phillip: Being a history of the country now called Victoria.* Melbourne: Robertson, p.117.

38. Pratt, A. (1934). *The centenary history of Victoria.* Melbourne: Robertson and Mullens, p.59.

39. Westgarth, W. (1888). *Personal recollections of early Melbourne and Victoria.* Melbourne: George Robertson & Co. pp.19-21.

40. Bonwick, *op. cit.,* p.123.

41. Curr, *op. cit.,* p.2.

42. *Port Phillip Patriot,* 1839-1841, passim; *Port Phillip Gazette,* 1839-1841, passim.

43. Gartner, J. (1937). *Premier Victorian pamphlet.* Melbourne: Hawthorn House, p.1 of reproduction of pamphlet.

44. *Port Phillip Gazette.* 9 October 1839. The Society enumerated the trades of its members in an address of welcome to LaTrobe.

45. Editorial. *Port Phillip Gazette,* 28 September 1839.

46. *Port Phillip Gazette,* 28 September 1839.

47. *Port Phillip Gazette,* 12 October 1839.

48. *Port Phillip Gazette,* 6 November 1839.

49. *Port Phillip Gazette,* 16 November 1839.

50. *Port Phillip Patriot,* 7 November 1839, p.456. "This business is taken up with much vigour and spirit by the mechanics and appears so likely to be well supported by the monied interests, that nothing can cause its failure." Two donations of £50 were made, many of £25

and £10.

51.*Port Phillip Patriot*, 17 April 1839, p.61; *Annual Report of the Melbourne Mechanics' Institute* (hereafter cited as *Annual Report*), 1846.

52.*Port Phillip Gazette*, 12 October 1839.

53.*Port Phillip Gazette*, 6 November 1839.

54.*Port Phillip Gazette*, 7 September 1839.

55.*Port Phillip Gazette*, 6 November 1839; *Port Phillip Patriot, April 17, 1839, p.61.*

56.*Port Phillip Gazette,* 16 November 1839.

57.*Port Phillip Patriot*, 17 February 1842.

58.*Port Phillip Herald*, 18 March 1842.

59.*Annual Report*, 1840.

60.*Annual Report*, 1849, p.3.

61.*Hansard*, Volume II, 12 June 1857, p.797.

62.*Annual Report*, 1856; *Hansard*, Volume II, 12 June 1857, p.797.

63.*Port Phillip Gazette*, 16 November 1839.

64.*Argus*, 31 May 1854.

65.*Port Phillip Patriot*, 6 June 1842.

66.See lists of attendance in Minute Books.
Annual Report, 1849. President, Jas. Simpson: "The respectable tradesmen and mechanics of the city, most of whom are members of the Institution, having hitherto failed to take any legitimate share in the management" if they were on the Committee "with few exceptions their attendance at meetings has been so irregular, and the interest they have evinced so trivial, as to render their accession a virtual nullity."

67.Arden in a lecture on 'The Mechanical Agency of the Press in the Dissemination of Useful Knowledge' reported in the *Port Phillip Patriot*, 1 June 1840, praises the state in which "the degraded selfishness of rank and station were either unknown or suppressed by the mutual desire of every individual to contribute to the general good."
See also *Argus*, 2 June 1854: "It is therefore the especial duty of those who are placed in the better walks of life, and know how to appreciate the value of education, to endeavour to dispel the intellectual gloom which at present hangs over a large portion of our fellow colonists."

68.William Westgarth and James Simpson are excellent examples of this. See *Minute Book, Vol. I*, 18 May 1842; 3 February 1844.

69.*Port Phillip Patriot*, 2 March 1840. Fawkner condemns this restriction on the grounds "that men who have been toiling the livelong day at their different arduous vocations will (not) feel disposed to undergo mental fatigue at night in preparing their papers for the institute."

70.Special provision was made for the payment of dues by mechanics and tradesmen. An entrance fee of 10/- and an annual subscription of £1 were charged, but the levy of the entrance fee fluctuated during the years and "mechanics and respectable tradesmen" could pay their subscriptions quarterly. In view of the high wages prevailing in Melbourne, this does not seem to be a prohibitive amount for mechanics. See *Annual Report*, 1840, p.9.

71.*Annual Report*, 1849, p.3.

72.*Annual Report*, 1865, p.3.

73.*Argus,* 31 May 1854.

74.*Annual Report*, 1840.

75.*Port Phillip Patriot*, 1 June 1840.

76.*Port Phillip Patriot*, 7 December 1840.

77.*Port Phillip Patriot*, 5 August 1840.

78.*Port Phillip Patriot*, 13 July 1840.

79.*Annual Report*, 1850.

80.*Annual Report*, 1854.

81.*Annual Report*, 1855.

82.*Annual Reports*, 1843-1850.

83.*Annual Reports*, 1849-1859, passim. Scattered references in newspapers.

84.*Annual Report*, 1859.

85.F.D. Maurice. Quoted in Harrison, J.F.C. (1954). *A History of the Workingman's College, 1854-1954*. London: Routledge & Kegan Paul, p.xvii.

86.*Minute Book, Vol. I*, 30 April 1840.

87.*Minute Book, Vol. I*, 12 November 1839.

88.*Minute Book, Vol. I*, 27 March 1840.

89.*Minute Book, Vol. II*, 21 April 1856.

90.See Domestic Intelligence columns of newspapers.

91.*Annual Reports*, 1848-9.

92.*Minute Book, Vol. II*, 23 May 1856.

93.*Annual Report*, 1856.

94.*ibid.*

95.*Annual Report*, 1857.

96.*Annual Reports*, 1857, p.7.

97.*Annual Report*, 1857, p.8.

98.*Annual Reports*, 1858-59.

99.*Annual Report*, 1858.

100.*Annual Report*, 1860.

101.*Annual Report*, 1861, p.3.

102.*Annual Report,* 1858.

103.*Annual Report*, 1840, p.1; *Minute Book, Vol. I*, 1840, passim; *Minute Book, Vol, I*, 1 March 1844.

104.*Minute Book, Vol. I*, 22 December 1840.

105.*Annual Report*, 1845, p.11.

106.*Annual Report,* 1844, p.11

107.*Annual Report*, 1844, p.12; *Annual Report,* 1845, p.3.

108.*Annual Report*, 1848, p.5.

109.*Annual Report*, 1848, p.7.

110.*Annual Report*, 1848, *loc. cit.*

111.*Annual Report*, 1849, p.5.

112.*Annual Report*, 1854, p.6.

113.*Annual Report*, 1855, p.5.

PRACTICAL OBSERVATIONS

UPON THE

EDUCATION OF THE PEOPLE,

ADDRESSED TO

THE WORKING CLASSES

AND

THEIR EMPLOYERS.

BY

H. BROUGHAM, Esq. M.P. F.R.S.

FIFTEENTH EDITION.

LONDON:

PRINTED BY RICHARD TAYLOR, SHOE-LANE;

AND SOLD BY LONGMAN, HURST, REES, ORME, BROWN, AND GREEN,

PATERNOSTER-ROW,

FOR THE BENEFIT OF THE LONDON MECHANICS INSTITUTION.

1825.

Title page from Brougham's *Practical Observations upon the Education of the People*, 1825

Melbourne Mechanics' Institute, as originally built

Melbourne Mechanics' Institute, after 1853 additions

Healesville Mechanics' Institute, Vic

Smythesdale Mechanics' Institute, Vic

114.*Annual Report*, 1857, p.3.

115.*Annual Report*, 1860, p.5.

116.*Annual Report*, 1860, *loc. cit.*

117.*Annual Report*, 1861, p.4.

118.*Annual Report*, 1864, p.5.

119.*Annual Report*, 1864, *loc. cit.*
      Membership   512
      Circulation   13,312

120.*Annual Reports,* 1865-1872, passim.

Year	Membership	Circulation
1865	471	12,912
1866	480	13,102
1867	437	13,146
1868	458	13,249
1869	460	13,614
1870	510	- -

See Table. *Annual Report*, 1871, p.4.

121.*Annual Report*, 1866, p.5.

122.*Minute Book, Vol. I*, 30 April 1846; *Port Phillip Gazette*, 6 November 1839.

123.*Minute Book, Vol. I,* 7 May 1840.

124.*Minute Book, Vol. I*, 20 July 1840.

125.*ibid.*

126.*Port Phillip Patriot*, 26 October 1840. cf. LaTrobe's resignation of the office of Patron, the Committee's hostility towards his superior officer. *Port Phillip Patriot*, 10 June 1841; *Minute Book, Vol. I*, 3 June 1841.

127.*Minute Book, Vol. I*, 6 August 1840; 31 August 1840; 12 November 1840; *Port Phillip Patriot*, 14 December 1840.

128.*Port Phillip Patriot*, 24 September 1840.

129.*ibid.*

130.*Port Phillip Patriot*, 28 September 1840.

131.*Minute Book, Vol. I,* 31 January 1842.

132.In July 1840, a house in Bourke Street, formerly occupied by Captain McLachlan, was rented by the Institute at £1,000 per annum. The secretary, whose salary was £52 per annum, lived here rent-free. See *Minute Book, Vol. I,* 20 July 1840; 16 April 1840.

133.*Minute Book, Vol. I,* 10 August 1842.

134.*Annual Report,* 1845, p.3.

135.*Minute Book, Vol. I,* 16 January 1843.

136.*Port Phillip Gazette,* 3 September 1842.

137.*Minute Book, Vol. I,* 1 February 1843.

138.*Minute Book, Vol. I,* 5 July 1843; 29 August 1843. £771/13/0 was due in subscriptions but only £75 could be collected, the remainder was considered to be irrecoverable. *Minute Book, Vol. I,* 9 April 1844.

139.Report of Investigation Sub-Committee. *Minute Book, Vol. I,* 15 August 1843.

140.*Minute Book, Vol. I,* 15 August 1843.

141.*ibid.*

142.*Minute Book Vol. I,* 21 August 1843; 29 August 1843; 17 October 1843; 5 January 1844.

143.*Minute Book, Vol. I,* 5 January 1844; 29 August 1843.

144.*Annual Reports,* 1843, 1844.

145.*Minute Book, Vol. I,* 6 May 1844.

146.Westgarth's Report. *Minute Book, Vol I,* pages following entry dated 9 April 1844.

147.*ibid.*

148.*ibid.*

149.*ibid.*

150.*Minute Book, Vol. I,* 1 July 1844.

151.*Minute Book, Vol. I,* 13 September 1844.

152.*Minute Book, Vol. I,* 2 September 1844.

153.*Minute Book, Vol. I*, 2 December 1844. This was after a second petition to Gipps, following Westgarth's deputation had been made (*Minute Book, Vol. I*, 1 July 1844) and refused (2 September 1844).

154.*Minute Book, Vol. I*, 3 February 1845.

155.*Minute Book, Vol. I*, 1 June 1845; 5 May 1846.

156.*Minute Book, Vol. I*, 2 September 1846.

157.*Minute Book, Vol. I*, 22 July 1853.

158.*Annual Report*, 1855, p.4.

159.*ibid.*

160.*Minute Book, Vol. II*, 10 December 1854.

161.*Minute Book, Vol. II*, 2 July 1855.

162.*Minute Book, Vol. II*, 19 November 1855.

163.*Minute Book, Vol. II*, 21 February 1856.

164.*Minute Book, Vol. II*, 27 February 1856.

165.*Hansard*, Volume I, p.526; Volume II, 12 June 1857, p.797; Volume II, 17 November 1857, p.1376; Volume III, 14 December 1857, p.44; Volume III, 22 December 1857, p.87.

166.*Hansard*, Volume III, 14 December 1857, p.44.

167.*Hansard*, Volume III, 19 January 1858, p.144.

168.*Hansard*, Volume III, 22 December 1857, p.87.

169.*Hansard*, Volume IV, 2 November 1856, p.199.

170.*Hansard*, Volume V, 24 January 1860, p.397; Volume VI, 29 May 1860, p.1229.

171.*Votes and Proceedings of Legislative Assembly*, 1st Session 1866. Detailed Expenditure, p.37.

172.*Votes and Proceedings of Legislative Assembly, 1872.*

173.*Hansard*, Volume V, 24 January 1860, p.397.

174.See Estimate Debates and the *Votes and Proceedings, 1856-1867*. In 1867 £1,000 was voted to aid the building funds of free libraries in up-country areas. It is not known whether this category included mechanics' institutes. In any case the amount would have been small and was for one year only.

Votes and Proceedings of Legislative Assembly, 1867. I. p.301.
In 1870 the vote was renewed and extended to £2,000.
Votes and Proceedings of Legislative Assembly, 1870. Estimates p.17.

175.*Votes and Proceedings, 1860-1.* Schedule A.8.

176.*Hansard,* Volume II, 12 June 1857, p.297; Volume II, 17 November 1857, p.1376; Volume III, 22 December 1857, p.87; Volume III, 19 January 1858, p.144.

177.*Minutes and Annual Reports of the Melbourne Mechanics' Institute,* passim.

178.*Argus,* 31 May 1854; 1 June 1854.

179.Wearmouth, R.F. (1954). *Methodism and the struggle of the working classes, 1850-1900.* Leicester: Backus, Chapters I-III, passim.

180.Withers, W.B. (1870). *History of Ballarat.* Ballarat: Ballarat Star, p.167.

181.Daley, C. (1940). *The history of South Melbourne: From the foundation of settlement at Port Phillip to the year 1938.* Melbourne: Robertson & Mullens, p.234.

182.*Port Phillip Patriot,* 18 November 1839, p.48.

183.Cooper, J.B. (1912). *History of Prahran: From its first settlement to a city.* Melbourne: Modern Printing Co., pp.156-158.

184.Barnard, F.G.A. (1910). *Jubilee history of Kew: Its origin and progress, 1803-1910.* Melbourne:Hodges, pp.105-6.

185.Hubber, B.G. (1986) Public libraries and the suburban reading public, 1850-1914. *Unpublished M.A. Thesis.* Clayton, Vic: Graduate School of Librarianship, Monash University, p.39.

186.Hubber, *loc. cit.*

187.Wearmouth, *loc. cit.*

188.Cooper, *op. cit.,* pp. 118-119.

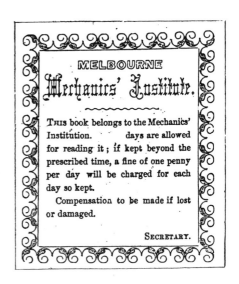

CHAPTER FOUR

THE ADVANTAGES OF MECHANICS' INSTITUTIONS: PART I[1]

Thomas Osborne

The Reverend Mr Osborne delivered, to a crowded audience, on Thursday evening [16 April 1840], an eloquent and appropriate lecture on the Utility of Mechanics' Institutions. The meeting was held in the Scots' School, and although the weather proved somewhat unpropitious, the overflowing house and the enthusiasm with which the talented Lecturer's discourse was received, sufficiently testified to the popular thirst after knowledge, the keen relish of the people for literary pursuits, and their determination amidst unusual difficulties to bring their project to maturity. Want of time leaves us no opportunity at present either for criticism or comment; to satisfy, however, the curiosity of those of our readers who were unavoidably absent, and to attract the attention of the neighbouring colonies to our happy achievement, we publish a few extracts from the manuscript before us, reserving its completion to a further number of the Gazette.[2]

Apologies upon such occasions as the present have become so common, that they have long since lost their intended effect, whether in silencing the Critic when resorted to by the really diffident, or in inducing a strange audience to expect little interesting from the speaker, and thereby securing for the Apologist that approbation which may not have been so much his desert, as the consequence of the auditory having been agreeably disappointed in their expectations. Confident of this fact, therefore, I forego all such Introductions, and would merely preface the following observations by congratulating the Originators and Supporters of the Port Phillip Mechanics' Institution, upon the gratification which the number and respectability of the present meeting afford as a reward for past anxieties, and the flattering omen which is thereby presented as a stimulus to future exertions. To its warm friends and its members generally, a full meeting like what I see before me, must be cheering; and whilst it must be to them at least equal to their anticipations, it carries with it more than a mere gratification of the personal and laudable ambition of a number of individuals, either separately considered or viewed as members of a committee. The meeting reflects credit upon the whole community of which we form a part, and I trust and am morally certain will in after-times be looked upon as the commencement of an important era in the literary annals of Australia Felix.

The pleasures and advantages of that Institution, in the first public organised meeting of which we have now assembled, will not only be felt and enjoyed by those within the immediate scope of its influence, but also directly and sensibly by our father-land; for in the present era when the nations of the earth are exerting themselves with a laudable energy in the field of discovery, and viewing with each other in introducing improvements into the Arts and Sciences, it cannot be a matter of slight gratification to Britain that in this -- one of the most distant colonies in her vast dominions -- a society is formed to assist in upholding her in that proud position which she has already attained - the first on the list of nations. Britain again, although the first and the most sensibly effected by the progress of such an institution as this, will not stand isolated, the solitary benefitted one amongst the mighty empires of the world, for by whatever name that may be called which aims at the promotion of useful knowledge and the extension of its consequence - personal and social happiness around the globe, every lover of his species, be he of whatever country or complexion, must hail its introduction with a spirit of philanthropic enthusiasm; such enthusiasm arising from that inherent natural sympathy of our common humanity, which I believe in a greater or less degree pervades the whole human race, and which reaps enjoyment in the conviction of the happiness of a fellow being. There is scarcely any country at the present day so rude as not to know that the friend of Science is the friend of man; and the practically ascertained truth that "knowledge is power," is approved by all and adopted as the motto and first principle of civilised legislation. Mark the illustration of this truism in respect of that country which appears but a speck upon the map of the world. Cast your eye to England, and ask - What is her original boundary? Compared with the extent of other nations she is far inferior; considered in point of physical strength and moral courage, her equal has not yet appeared. Resting with one arm upon the north and the other upon the south, with her fleets she sweeps and holds dominion of the seas, and with her armies she commands and obtains respect from pole to pole. This is owing to the spirit of her people thirsting after and anxious to communicate information. The number of her Scientific and Literary Institutions explains the mystery of her greatness, and we this evening proclaim that we are planting a slip of the old stock even amidst the wilds of nature, and far from the native soil, to vegetate and flourish on a future and no distant day, as the haunt of Genius, and to shelter with its branches the votaries of science.

*   *   *   *   *   *   *

Passing from a review of our climate and our soil, and this brief reference to the principles of our government, let us consider the constituent elements of our community, and we will discover other reasons to be satisfied that here a mechanics' institution must flourish, and its advantages be felt.

Within the limits of our infant colony may be discovered every quality that can render a nation prosperous and man happy. Although foreigners are not only not excluded, but invited to make their abode with us, we, as might be naturally expected, are principally English, or the former as well as present subjects of the British Crown. Whilst then we may occasionally meet with the characteristic peculiarity of other nations, we find in the greatest abundance the indomitable perseverance of the English, the shrewd intelligence of the Scot, and the quick thought and warm heart which characterise the Irish people. These are the rich ingredients of which our society is composed, and these are the stamina which would render any nation under heaven 'great, glorious, and free.'

*   *   *   *   *   *   *

The rising and future generations have every prospect of worldly independence; but alas without intellectual culture they will be unable to enjoy even what they themselves possess. In polished society they will not only be unable to participate in the pleasures of the passing scene, but they will find themselves in positive misery; unable to take a part in the various topics introduced, but feeling all the disquietude consequent upon a sense of intellectual inferiority, than which it is impossible to conceive a state of mind more unhappy. Their wealth in place of making them more respected, will act in a manner diametrically opposite, by rendering them more conspicuous, and therefore their ignorance more remarkable. The most stupid and the most dangerous works are frequently contained in the most costly bindings, and the most beautiful exterior and the richest plumage are frequently found upon the most dangerous quadrupeds of earth, or the fowls of heaven, and a parity of reasoning will hold good when applied to the human race. An individual or a community may at the same time be rich and miserable, either may be comparatively poor and happy. The one is by no means a necessary consequence of the other, for wealth is but the *means* not the *reality* itself; and in the seclusion of the world, with a bare competence, the man of letters and a polished mind can reap enjoyment in the survey of Nature's beauties around, or in the contemplation of the wonders of the Heavens where the God of Nature has registered his existence and written his attributes in the stupendous volumes of revolving worlds Even if the film of age has darkened his vision, or the infirmity of years confine him to his couch, he can turn inwards upon himself and live upon the past, or stretch forth his thoughts into the future and enjoy the anticipations of a holier and a happier home.

*   *   *   *   *   *   *

Respecting the description of lectures most appropriate to be delivered at this institution: some of its members may be disposed to advocate and encourage one class, and others another. I have heard some people when upon the subject of Mechanics' Institutions, disclaim against the title when applied to designate a society wherein the subjects treated of were of a varied character, and relating little, if any thing to Mechanics. To this I would briefly answer: - In the first place, at the great number of Mechanics' Institutions, the lectures are purely voluntary, and it cannot reasonably be expected that the weekly lectures of an entire session, should be continuously upon mechanics. Such would be too much to expect from two, three, or any small number of gentlemen; and if the usual number come forward, it is not probable that they could agree upon their respective parts, or even granting that they could, it is all but impossible they could so connect them as to make the whole a unique or consistent course. In the second place, even admitting that such were practicable, it is highly questionable whether such a course would be so popular, or so generally instructive as the usual system of voluntary lectures upon varied subjects at the option of the lecturers.

Mechanics' Institutions, unlike Universities or the usual places of education, are not solely for the purpose of communicating and receiving instruction, but for the two-fold object of pleasure and information. When, therefore, the lectures are varied, what may not be interesting to one may be so to another, as the tastes of men are as varied as the subjects of general literature themselves. In addition, I would also observe, that although many subjects may at first appear devoid of connexion with what may be termed the legitimate objects of this institution, still when viewed with an eye capable of discovering their varied tendencies, they may be seen to be the most important to be investigated, as forming the ground-work of Mechanics, or as tending above all others to elucidate by indirect application, some doubtful principles, upon the incontrovertible establishment of which, may depend that conviction of the mind, which will encourage the scientific enquirer to prosecute his researches into tracts untrod before, and to embolden him to try experiments which might terminate in results far surpassing those, the very discovery of which of late years has astonished the world, and the application of which to the uses of practical life has been marked by the increasing wealth, happiness, and peace of civilized nations. Lectures on history and biography, for example, may at first appear foreign to the objects of this institution; but if properly prepared, they may be of the most salutary tendency, in bringing before us the circumstances of the times in which men of mechanical genius lived, and the causes which produced their greatness. We may be informed by such lectures of men at particular eras, who in despite [sic] of every difficulty, arose from obscurity to eminence, and to be the preceptors of their superiors in rank and wealth. We may, for example, be informed, whilst attending to the origin of Russian greatness, how her most celebrated Emperor laid aside the emblems of royalty, and denied himself the ease and luxuries of state, to travel into distant countries, to learn the science of Mechanics, and become practically acquainted with the several trades of nations more advanced in knowledge and civilization than his own. From such information the meanest amongst us will be encouraged to exert his powers, and resist opposition; the greatest will perceive that Mechanics are not beneath their attention, whilst all will be directed to those Authors who have attained the greatest celebrity, and from whose writings they can obtain the most correct information to assist them in their studies. Lectures on Geology and Mineralogy will direct the mechanic in search of the best materials for his machinery. Lectures on Jurisprudence will teach us the laws by which the agricultural, commercial, and the mechanical communities are respectively governed, and thereby enable us to remonstrate against any legislative enactments which we may perceive detrimental to the interests of particular trades, or as having a deadly influence upon this advancement of science. Similar arguments may be used in reference to lectures upon many other subjects, few of which may not be so arranged as to be of the most useful tendency, and strictly consistent with, as forwarding, the objects of a Mechanics' Institution. At the same time, however, it must be desirable to have such varied lectures arranged as much in a system as possible.

In reference to the arguments brought against the applicability of the name 'Mechanics' Institution' to a general literary society, I have, however, heard an argument raised of the very opposite nature. I have heard it asserted, and that too by the intelligent and warm advocates of Mechanics' Institutions, that if the Lectures were purely upon the science of Mechanics, they would lose their interest, and our seats would in a short time become deserted. This, however, I consider a libel upon the community, of which we are members, and opposed in toto to the strongest probabilities deducible from facts. Is it probable, I would ask, that the kind of community which I have described, and of which we are members, would be more interested with what may be termed light subjects, than with those which address themselves to the understanding, and have for their object the advancement of science, and the welfare of man?

*   *   *   *   *   *   *

I may be told that my reasoning is just respecting the members of our Society, or those gentlemen who may as visitors occasionally honor us with their presence, but that it cannot be expected that the ladies, who we hope will grace our meetings, will feel an interest in the dry and abstruse theories of Mechanical or Mathematical Science - and that consequently they in a short time, will absent themselves and our Institution will begin to totter, and eventually go to wreck. This is indeed an alarming prophecy! Before, however, we give full credence to its truth, let us calmly enquire of ourselves upon what data it is founded, and we will perceive that it is based on the vanity of man, and a total ignorance of the strength and

Rev Thomas Hamilton Trail Osborne, 1806-1853
(reproduced by permission of the Corangamite Regional Library, Warrnambool)

capabilities of the female understanding. Cast a glance around you and you will find the nations of Europe and the enlightened members of the great western republic, throwing off the delusion in which for centuries they have been enveloped. You will perceive the higher branches of literature studied by females; and of the works which during the last half century have issued from the press, the names of female authors appear upon many a title page, and you will find therein depths of feeling and codes of political and moral science, equal if not superior to the most popular of the standard works of the present day, whilst in point of simplicity and beauty of style, they are surpassed by none. Throughout the continents of Europe and America, public meetings upon almost every occasion and subject are composed of females, who owing to the natural warmth of their feelings, are always found to take an intense interest in the proceedings. In Ireland, at least, I know that College Professors of Moral and Natural Philosophy, Botany, Chemistry, and other sciences, have each classes for ladies which are always attended both numerously and respectably. I have heard more than one Professor declare that they have perused essays handed in during the course of these lectures which would have done honor to any University. With these facts before us, let us proudly point to them in refutation of the insults I have mentioned, when offered to the female understanding.

*   *   *   *   *   *   *

In addition to the previous, many other advantages could be enumerated, but they are so plain that they can be easily perceived upon the slightest reflection. I would, however, take occasion in referring to a Laboratory, to suggest also what could be easily attained, and which would tend above almost every other means to advance the interests of this Institution - I allude to the publication of a Mechanics' Magazine. The same arguments which have been advanced to illustrate the unspeakable benefits which have accrued to the world by the invention of the Art of Printing, can also be advanced to a very great extent, in support of the establishment of a Magazine in connexion with our Institution. By being possessed of such a publication, the members can not only retain any valuable information, which we all trust will be great, for the purpose of being afterwards maturely considered by those who heard it, but also for the advantage of such as were either disappointed, or who had it not in their power to attend. This would also have a beneficial effect upon the lecturers themselves, by inducing them to pay a greater degree of attention to the matter and composition of their subjects, it being previously understood by them that their manuscripts should be handed in to the Committee for the purpose of being examined, and the portions considered advantageous or interesting, selected for publication. These manuscripts would of themselves form a nucleus of a library and after the present generation shall have passed away, will be interesting documents for the perusal of the curious on literary subjects.

I know comparatively nothing of the constitution of the literary societies of our metropolis, but from what my connexion with has enabled me to know of the Hobart Town Mechanics' Institution, I can fearlessly guarantee, on the part of its members, a hearty co-operation in the establishment of such a publication. It may be said, that neither Sydney, nor Hobart Town, nor Melbourne could individually support a Mechanics' Magazine, but let it not be said that united they would fail, were they but to make the attempt. Owing to the facilities of correspondence with Sydney, on account of a land post, and also the almost daily opportunities of intercourse with Hobart Town, this, for these reasons, as well as from it intermediate locality, is the place for the publication of such periodical. This is a suggestion thrown out and respectfully urged for consideration upon those gentlemen who hear me and who have shown a determined spirit that they will not allow their resolves of bringing this Institution into existence and maturity to be overcome by difficulties, however discouraging. They know better than I can, the literary resources they possess within themselves, and upon which they can draw; and in their correspondence with the Hobart Town Institution, they may rely upon receiving the urbanity of gentlemen, and the assistance of the learned.

* * * * * * *

I named the Press, that deadly foe of ignorance and oppression - that staunch friend and support of knowledge. To the Hobarton Mechanics' Institution the press has lent its valuable aid, and by that Institution has its assistance been sensibly felt and gratefully acknowledged. There the conductors of the press have advised of their lectures - there they have assisted by publishing to the world the operations of the body as a proof of its growing prosperity, and a call upon others to go and do likewise. To eulogise the good results of a well-conducted press, is above my humble abilities but it cannot, I hope, be considered presumptuous, to express a conviction, which I trust will be fully realised, that the Melbourne press will ever by ready to assist this infant Institution in its struggles, to enable it to overcome those difficulties against which it must have to contend, in its endeavours to obtain for the country of our adoption, a place and a name amongst the civilised nations of the earth. Within this body personal interests cannot have a place - here political strife cannot rage - here religious discussion cannot find an entrance - here then is common ground and a wide field for the philanthropist and the learned to exert their best abilities for the common good.

If properly conducted, and there is no reason to anticipate otherwise, the meetings of this Society will be anticipated by its members with pleasure, as presenting a relaxation from the duties and consequent cares of business, and affording an opportunity of meeting with each other as friends, and enjoying together the advantages obtained from the discussion of some literary subject. It has ever been found, that in a moral, as well as in a scientific point of view, Mechanics' Institutions have produced the most salutary benefits, by the simple circumstances of bringing men together. Although in our worldly intercourse with each other little jealousies will be engendered and petty dissentions [sic] will arise, yet there is some common object around which we can rally; there is something in which we have and can feel a common interest. When we meet on such occasions the mind begins to reflect and perhaps to discover that some blame belonged to self; that all should not have been placed to the debit account of him with whom we disagreed. If not this, we will at least be able to trace in each other's countenance some lineaments which indicate the existence of Mind, from which we insensibly pass to the reflection that there is also an Understanding to comprehend and a Heart to feel; and these granted, Nature proclaims that we should meet at all times upon the ground of our common humanity, and love each other as brethren of the same family.

I know, Ladies and Gentlemen, I have trespassed too long upon your time. I thank you for the attention with which you have honored me; and, hoping that the advantages to which I have alluded, will be fully enjoyed, I join with you in heartily wishing success to the Port Phillip Mechanics' Institution.

In continuing our extracts from Mr Osborne's inaugural lecture at the Mechanics' institute, we need hardly, we trust, use any arguments or pleading as incentives to the activity of the Managing Committee, in procuring for the now aroused desires of the people, a continuance of those intellectual entertainments. We may announce, we believe, that Mr Barry has consented to deliver the next lecture on the subject of Agriculture. As an appropriate subject for the third, we beg to suggest that both Mr Robinson, the Chief Protector, and Rev. Mr Tuckfield, Superintendent of the Wesleyan Mission Station at Geelong, be requested to lecture upon the habits, manners and language of the Natives, their intellectual capabilities for improvement, and an analysis of their several views in perfecting their civilization. This would be bringing the practical part of each side of the question before the public in the clearest manner.[3]

NOTES AND REFERENCES

1. This chapter was originally given as the introductory lecture to the Port Phillip Mechanics' Institution on 16 April, 1840 at Scots' School, Collins Street, Melbourne. It was originally published in instalments in the *Port Phillip Gazette*, 18 and 22 April 1840.

2. *Port Phillip Gazette*, 18 April 1840.

3. *Port Phillip Gazette*, 22 April 1840.

CHAPTER FIVE

'A SLIGHT ENCOURAGEMENT': THE COLONIAL BOOK GRANT AND THE VICTORIAN PARLIAMENT, 1857-1860[1]

Brian Hubber

INTRODUCTION

Nineteenth-century society was imbued with a philosophy espousing the perfectibility of the individual. The philosophy manifested itself in paradoxical ways. On the one hand society undertook an agenda which provided an environment for the development of the individual; this expressed itself in movements advocating universal suffrage, universal education, liberalisation of the press and access to knowledge. On the other hand individuals were thought to be ultimately responsible for their own development, and it was considered to be positively counter-productive for society to intervene. It was this latter belief which contributed to the practice of a version of "social Darwinism."

It was against the background of these competing beliefs that the first age of libraries developed in the colonial period. This chapter investigates the role of the Victorian colonial government in this nascent library movement, with special reference to the little known and little understood colonial book grant. The investigation focuses on the dominant ideologies as expressed in the parliamentary debates and in the conditions upon which the grants were made.

This chapter, in sum, attempts to show that the Victorian government, motivated by a philosophical commitment, made a substantial contribution to the development of a colonial library service, largely through direct support for mechanics' institute libraries. This contribution stalled in the depression of the 1890s, recovered to £10,000 per year in 1907/08, but again stalled during the years of the First World War. Library services subsequently decayed to the level so harshly criticised in the Munn-Pitt report of 1935.

Over the period from 1860 to 1900 the Victorian government expended some £308,400 on libraries, which is an average of £7,710 per annum. The peak years were in 1890-91 and 1891-92, when £20,000 per year was made available. According to the Retail Price Indexes in *Australians: a historical library: Historical statistics volume*, £20,000 in 1890 was worth about $500,000 in 1980. Therefore, the per capita outlay on libraries in 1890 - expressed in 1980 dollars - was approximately fifty cents. In 1980, the actual outlay was approximately $3.50.[2] Clearly the two outlays are not comparable, but in 1890, when there was no library profession, no library associations, and no organised lobbying for library subsidies, the government of the day was making a substantial investment in colonial library services.

THE BASES OF GOVERNMENT SUPPORT

The foundations of government support for library services in the colonial period were laid during the heady days of the goldrushes in Victoria in the 1850s. Accordingly, it is important to look at the arguments and philosophies which at that time were at the heart of the decision to implement a library grant. The most difficult task is in fact to identify any one dominant philosophy prevailing among colonial parliamentarians. Geoffrey Serle characterises Victorian politics at this time in the following terms:

> Instability was the leading feature of the history of Victoria's first two parliaments. The ideological assumptions of conservatives, liberals and democrats were overlaid by a confusion of complicating issues. Pastoral, banking, mercantile, agricultural, mining, manufacturing and other interests struggled for economic advantage. The established pre-gold pioneers resented the new men and new ideas which had overturned their society. Protestants feared an unaccustomedly large Catholic minority; Catholics themselves fell into two camps; a fervent Protestant minority placed the cause of voluntarism and the destruction of a potential Anglican establishment above all else. Some were elected with no intention but to serve the material needs of their locality; others had no views, or were prepared to adopt any to suit their personal ambition.[3]

In the parliamentary debates concerning the library grant there can be discerned strands of the various influences described by Serle, most notably a vehement parochialism and an antagonism between Town and Country.

The Ethos of Self-improvement

The philosophy to which conservatives, liberals and democrats all subscribed was the pervasive nineteenth century credo of self-help, or 'self culture,' as expounded in the works of John Stuart Mill, William Channing and others, and popularised by Samuel Smiles. In his book *Self-help*, first published in 1859, and a series of other 'improving' works, Smiles "captured perfectly the fashionable notion that the self-generated growth of the individual lay at the heart both of personal and societal progress and development."[4] His books were widely read in the colonies: they were frequently held in public and private libraries, and there are several personal accounts of their beneficial effect. For instance, Frederick Cato, in 1882, wrote in his diary, "I have finished Smiles on 'Thrift' ... it tends to do one a great amount of good."[5] Frances Bethune described her mother's role in socialising her children by reading aloud from the same work: "It is a fine book. Mama is reading it to us and every little while she will say, 'Now remember that children.' ... I must say I try to make a thrifty wife and not ruin my husband. It won't be Mama's fault if I do."[6] The opening paragraph of *Self-help* is the classic statement of the voluntarist philosophy, and one can assume that its impact on the millions who read it was considerable:

> 'Heaven helps those who help themselves' is a well-tried maxim, embodying in a small compass the results of vast human experience. The spirit of self-help is the root of all genuine growth in the individual; and, exhibited in the lives of many, it constitutes the true source of national vigour and strength. Help from without is often enfeebling in its effect, but help from within invariably invigorates. Whatever is done *for* men or classes, to a certain extent takes away the stimulus and necessity of doing for themselves; and where men are subjected to over-guidance and over-government, the inevitable tendency is to render them comparatively helpless. [original emphasis][7]

Government's Responsibility for Providing 'Social Goods'

Despite the persuasive precision of Smiles's statement, the voluntarist ethic was being eroded by policies which recognised that governments had a responsibility to assist society with those services which could not be provided by individual action. Even Mill saw that government had to assist the impoverished and alienated refugees from a *laissez-faire* economy; and free enterprise could not be relied upon to provide essential services such as water, sewerage, gas, health services, etc. Many argued that education was similarly a service essential for economic growth and a cohesive society, and nowhere did they argue this more effectively than in the Australian colonies, especially in the gold-rich colony of Victoria. In the nineteenth century Victoria was at the forefront of educational reform. In 1863 the government of the day involved itself in the previously voluntary system, establishing standards and inspectorates, and providing funds for the schools. In 1872 Victoria was the first state in the world to introduce free, secular and compulsory primary education.[8] Other areas of education similarly progressed: a grand public library and a university were established in 1854[9]; museums and art galleries were encouraged throughout the colony with grants of money and land, and in 1869 technical education (including the work of the mechanics' institutes) was the focus of a comprehensive inquiry conducted by Rev. John Bleasdale and sponsored by the government.[10] It is not surprising then that late in the 1850s there was a debate concerning state support for libraries and mechanics' institutes.

Of course, even by this time, there was a tradition of government assistance for literary institutions. In the case of the Australian Subscription Library - established in 1826 - it was simply a case of the élites "helping themselves"; but the Sydney Mechanics' School of Arts established in 1833, was also the recipient of generous grants of land and money from the New South Wales Legislative Council.[11] Following Victoria's separation from New South Wales in the period from 1851 to 1860, the Victorian government was equally generous to institutes in a number of locations including Melbourne (although this was later discontinued), Geelong, Prahran, Emerald Hill, Warrnambool, Castlemaine, Sandhurst and Ballaarat.[12] As can be imagined, the grant of money to one town made others envious, and created a precedent that others were quick to seize on.

VIEWS DISCLOSED IN PARLIAMENTARY DEBATES

In a debate early in 1857, Alexander Fyfe (MLA Geelong), moved that £750 be placed on the estimates for the Geelong Mechanics' Institute.[13] Fyfe argued that it was a state responsibility to support the institutes as they were "national blessings" which had "a tendency to improve the mental and social condition of the community." The truth, however, was somewhat different. The Geelong Mechanics' Institute had previously been offered a grant of £2,000 on the condition that a similar amount was raised locally. The institute was unable to do this and therefore had to settle for £1,500. Not to be deterred, the institute's committee proceeded extravagantly, and ran up debts of some £800. Things looked grim for the trustees who were personally liable for the institute's debts. Enter Fyfe into the parliament arguing for "national blessings," although to be fair he also argued that local gentlemen had contributed on the assumption that the government would keep its promise.

During this debate, several other members had their say and the contradictions in the philosophy of self-help were never more evident. J H Brooke, another member from Geelong, seconded Fyfe's motion, claiming that, as the grant was for adult education, it would complement initiatives in primary and university education. Brooke also expressed a hope that a more general grant might be formulated and, with a view to promoting the same, called for a discussion of the principle of state support. David Reid (MLA Murray) agreed with these sentiments and further claimed that "the cultivation of the intelligence of the masses would be effective in the prevention of crime." The motion received conditional support from Dr A F A Greeves (MLA East Bourke), who believed in the value of the institutes but did not think the state should be responsible for continuing support. The motion was eventually passed 24 to 6, though the amount of the grant was amended to £500, which was the balance of the original grant. The principle of state support was strongly opposed, however, especially - perhaps naturally - by the government. W C Haines, the Chief Secretary, agreed that the state might assist the establishment of institutes but that there should be no continuing support. George Harker (MLA Collingwood) and Archibald Michie (MLA Melbourne) believed the institutes should be self-supporting, though individual institutes might be able to make a special case. The arch conservatives, Thomas Embling (MLA Collingwood) and Peter Snodgrass (MLA Anglesey) opposed state support in any form and opposed this particular motion on the grounds that it would set a precedent.

Embling and Snodgrass were right. Within a few months, George Harker moved that £1,000 be granted to the Collingwood Mechanics' Institute, arguing that Collingwood, being a working-class suburb, was populated by those very artisans for whom mechanics' institutes were intended.[14] Although Harker did not support the practice of a regular subsidy he thought that Collingwood was at least as deserving as a number of other towns. The motion received little support however. Some sections of the legislature were fed up with the *ad hoc* nature of making grants to individual institutes. Several members expressed a belief in the socially beneficial character of the institutes and argued that they should be subsidised by more systematic means. Dr J D Owens (MLA Loddon) made the point most cogently when he stated:

> These mechanics' institutes were likely to become large educational institutions, and, as such, should be dealt with in a comprehensive spirit. He objected to the bringing forward of these solitary cases, and would rather that the vote now should be postponed, with a view to the introduction of a more organised plan.

Fyfe (MLA Geelong), Hughes (MLA Portland), Langlands (MLA Melbourne) and Goodman (MLA The Murray) supported Owens's call for a general plan of state subsidy, and therefore implicitly supported a philosophy of state encouragement for cultural institutions. The main opposition again came from the treasury benches: Haines pointed to previous debates and argued that state support was not a desired object; and Ebden, the Treasurer, stonewalled. The motion was withdrawn and Ebden pledged only to give the matter "fair consideration."

The government, then, had effectively tied the purse-strings. In December 1857 a question from George Horne (MLA Warrnambool) about a system of building grants drew a non-committal response from Ebden (MLA Brighton), who claimed to understand that the House was opposed to the principle of state support.[15] In January 1858 Dr Owens, probably in an attempt to demonstrate the *ad hoc* manner in which grants had been made, wanted to know which institutes had received money. Ebden tabled a return and there the matter rested.[16]

THE FREE LIBRARIES DEBATE

It rested for two years till 20 January 1860, when James McCulloch (MLA East Melbourne), the Treasurer in the new Nicholson government, moved in the Estimates debate that the sum of £2,000 be voted in aid of the purchase of books for free libraries.[17] Before this debate is looked at in more detail, it is necessary to examine the reasons for the delay in implementing a grant-in-aid to libraries.

If we refer to Geoffrey Serle's psycho-political analysis of the first parliament, it is clear that the members who supported the principle of state support for mechanics' institutes were generally of a radical-democratic temperament.[18] These men represented urban or goldfield constituencies and they had a common political cause in the Land Convention. Throughout the first parliament the ranks of these radical-democrats thinned considerably. In this period, when there were no parliamentary salaries - salaries for members of parliament were not introduced in Victoria till 1878 - the radical-democrats were particularly vulnerable. Vincent Pyke (MLA Castlemaine Boroughs) resigned in February 1857 for want of an income. Cameron (MLA Ovens) resigned in March the same year. Fyfe (MLA Geelong) resigned in November because he was insolvent. Charles Read (MLA Geelong) resigned in February 1858. Grant (MLA Sandhurst), Hummfray (MLA North Grant) and Owens (MLA Loddon) were often absent because they had to earn an income. The weakening of the democratic element was reflected in the actions of the government. O'Shanassy's ministry, which had promised electoral and land reforms, was disappointing. Niel Black, writing early in 1859, described the political opportunism which characterised the government: "More of the present ministry are now interested in squatting and if they are driven to revolutionary measures it will be for the sake of office."[19] The government survived till the end of the year because there was no alternative, but the 1859 elections brought about substantial changes to the parliament. Forty-three new members were elected, and the radical-democratic faction, though no more numerous, was more solidly knit under the banner of the Land Convention. The new Nicholson ministry was a mixed bag, being chiefly of a liberal temper, though including conservative and radical members. It was in this political milieu that the question of the grant-in-aid to libraries was again raised.

Returning, then, to the debate on McCulloch's budget which provided money for libraries, the original motion was as follows:

> That the sum of £2,000 be voted in aid of the purchase of books for free libraries, which are or may be established in the interior during 1860; grants to be made in equal proportion to sums collected by private subscription or local rates; no grant exceeding £300 to be paid to any one library.

The grant was apparently the result of lobbying by goldfield members because it was John Robinson Bailey, the radical member for West Ballarat and a minister in the O'Shanassy government, who was called on to explain and defend the motion. Bailey's life has received some attention in recent years, not because he was a parliamentarian, but because he was the uncle of Henry Handel Richardson and was the model for the character of John Turnham in *The Fortunes of Richard Mahoney*. Dorothy Green, in *Ulysses Bound: Henry Handel*

96

Prahran Mechanics' Institute, Vic. 1993
(still operates as a lending library)

Sandhurst Mechanics' Institute, Bendigo Vic. ca 1879
(Inset: Original canvas and timber building, 1854)

Sandhurst Mechanics' Institute, Vic, 1993

Ballaarat Mechanics' Institute, Vic
(photograph by Margaret Campbell)

THE LIBRARY.

ENTERTAINMENT HALL, WITH STAGE AND PROSCENIUM.

Ballaarat Mechanics' Institute, Vic

A CORNER OF THE SMOKE ROOM.

Richardson and her fiction, describes Bailey as a radical politician who was in favour of free selection, equitable reform of squatter's tenure of occupation, and the establishment of one national system of education. It is necessary, then, to see the introduction of state aid for library services as a radical innovation designed to provide educational opportunities for those with energy and perseverance, two of Bailey's most notable qualities.[20]

Bailey's speech might be paraphrased as follows: the object of the motion was to give the goldfields the advantage of public libraries of the same character as the Melbourne Public Library. As most of the towns in the interior had already been formed into municipalities it was thought that, if they received some slight encouragement, municipal bodies would be glad to vote a portion of their rates to the establishment of libraries. These institutions would not be of any great importance until after a certain number of years, but they would be a great improvement on the then current system.

The legislature appears to have accepted Bailey's premise that the state should support and encourage educational institutions. Of course, the provision that the grant would be made in proportion to the funds raised locally - either by subscription or local rates - is evidence for the continued belief in voluntary effort. Archibald Michie, described by Serle as a liberal (and, incidentally, a man with an interest in collecting early editions of Montaigne) thought that:

> the government was not called upon to supply books to any class of people. If books were such a desideratum, no doubt those anxious to obtain them would be able to save up money for that purpose... He did not think there was any necessity to coax and nurse the people, to induce them to read.

Michie, no doubt, had been irked by suggestions that a special service might be offered to itinerant railway workers. He had on other occasions supported mechanics institutes, but one gets the impression that he was at the end of his patience. Despite its eloquence, Michie's speech lacked persuasion: state assistance was unquestioningly accepted, and the debate concentrated instead largely on a number of practical points such as who would be eligible for the grant and the manner in which it would be administered.

There was a strong feeling in the parliament that the country districts were disadvantaged in respect of library services. The widespread perception was that the Melbourne Public Library was always generously funded, and the grant-in-aid under discussion represented an attempt to even the balance. Bailey (MLA West Ballarat) tried to restrict the grant to towns of the interior, but the motion was amended to "the colony," excluding municipalities within ten miles of Melbourne. The residents of Melbourne's suburbs, therefore, were doubly disadvantaged: they had access neither to the Melbourne Public Library nor to the library grant. R S Anderson (MLA South Melbourne) and George Verdon (MLA Williamstown) protested, but to no effect. It was not until 1863 that suburban institutions were included, and even then they were eligible for only one-sixth of the grant, a condition designed to prevent the metropolitan institutions from dominating the grant.[21] The initial exclusion of suburban libraries from the grant-in-aid appears to have resulted in the establishment of the Melbourne Public Library's travelling book-box service.

The second amendment to Bailey's motion related to the expansion of the number of eligible institutions, with the inclusion of the mechanics' institutes. The encouragement of voluntary organisations such as institutes sat better with the self-help voluntarist philosophy previously espoused by parliamentarians. However, this amendment was also essentially pragmatic: there were many institutes (more than thirty applied for the grant in 1860), but very few free public libraries (Prahran, Collingwood, Hawthorn, Castlemaine, Ballarat East, and maybe one or two others).

The concept of the free public library was not a new one in Victoria: the Melbourne Public Library had been operating for several years, and a section of the *Municipal Establishment Act* (1854) gave local governments the power to establish and fund public libraries - a clear echo of British Public Library legislation first enacted in 1850. While the concept of a public library was known, the reality was quite different. The Melbourne Public Library was a 'national' library with scholarly pretensions: indeed Archibald Michie compared it with the British Museum and the Bibliothèque Nationale. Furthermore, the provisions of the 1854 act were not used until 1860, when some local governments established libraries, probably anticipating the grant-in-aid. So, while Bailey's attempt to encourage public libraries was laudable, it was inevitable that a pragmatic legislature would attempt to build on existing providers such as mechanics' institutes, rather than create new ones. The pattern was set: local institute libraries were established by voluntary means and were subsidised by the colonial grant. Local government was not usually involved in this process unless the institution was in difficulty, an event which became increasingly common towards the end of the century. It is clear then, that in the colonial period local government was initially not involved with library services.

During the debate it was also suggested by O'Shanassy that the Melbourne Public Library could more efficiently manage the grant. This suggestion received some lukewarm support but was generally howled down by more parochial members such as Prendergast (MLA Maryborough), who thought it better to leave the purchase of books to those who wanted to read them, rather than a remote, centralised authority such as a 'national library.'

As a consequence of this debate, the final motion, passed by the Legislative Assembly, read as follows:

> In aid of the purchase of books for mechanics' institutes or other public libraries managed by local bodies which are already established or may be established in country districts; grants to be made in proportion to the sum already collected or to be collected by private subscriptions or local rates; no grant to exceed £200 to be paid to any one library provided that no grant be made to any such institution already established or to be established in Melbourne or within ten miles thereof.

Two important changes which found their way into the final motion, but which were not discussed in the debate itself, might be mentioned here. First, why was the maximum grant reduced from the originally suggested £300 to £200? Though there is no direct evidence, it appears that the reduction was the result of the amendment from "interior" to "colony," which effectively increased the number of eligible institutions by about one-fifth. There were several members who feared that, after the division of the grant, each institution's portion would be negligible. Other more radical members argued that the total amount of the grant should be increased so as to assist both the interior and seaboard towns. It is probable that this line of debate led the legislature to reduce the maximum grant so that the big institutions would not dominate the division of the grant.

The second point regarding the final form of the motion is that it changed the emphasis from the earlier initiatives of 1857: instead of being intended for establishing institutes - that is, a building grant - the grant-in-aid of 1860 was a grant for book purchases. Furthermore, it was not a one-off grant. Indeed, Dr Owens had argued that it would take several years before the institutes would fulfil their educational role, implying that any assistance would have to be continuing. If it is true that Bailey considered the grant to be continuing, then his innovation can be compared with a similar scheme in South Australia which appears to have been implemented about a year earlier. It might be assumed that the South Australian scheme influenced the Victorian legislators, but there is no documentary evidence one way or the other.

CONCLUSION

In conclusion, the grant-in-aid of libraries was a typical result of the legislative processes of the period, having its origins in parochial jealousies and Town versus Country antagonism. The grant nevertheless represented a pragmatic welding of prevailing voluntarist principles with a more radical vision in which the state had a role in establishing the cultural foundations of a society where energy and perseverance were rewarded. Although it did not go anywhere near as far as the highly centralised support and coordination of institutes in South Australia, at least it brought some measure of order and system to the previously haphazard development of mechanics' institute libraries throughout Victoria.

NOTES AND REFERENCES

1. This paper was first given at *Librarianship in Australia,* a seminar to honour Professor Jean P. Whyte, Foundation Professor of the Graduate School of Librarianship, Monash University, on the occasion of her retirement in 1988, 18-20 November 1988.

2. Price Waterhouse Urwick (1986). *A Strategy for local authority libraries: A discussion paper.* Melbourne: Price Waterhouse Urwick.

3. Serle, G. (1963). *The golden age: A history of the colony of Victoria, 1851-1861.* Carlton. Vic: Melbourne University Press; p. 315.

4. Candy, P.C. (1991). *Self-direction for lifelong learning: A comprehensive guide to theory and practice.* San Francisco: Jossey-Bass, p.28.

5. Frederick Cato to Frances Bethune, 10 April 1882. In Porter, U.B. (Ed.). (1981). *Growing Together: letters between Frederick John Cato and Frances Bethune, 1881 to 1884.* Carlton, Vic: Queensberry Hill Press, p. 89.

6. Frances Bethune to Frederick Cato, 23 March 1882. In Porter, *op.cit.,* pp. 110-120. This reference and that above are gleaned from Askew, M., and Hubber, B.G. (1988). The colonial reader observed: reading in its cultural context. In Borchardt, D.H., & Kirsop, W.

(Eds), *The Book in Australia: essays towards a cultural & social history*. Melbourne: Australian Reference Publications in association with the Centre for Bibliographical and Textual Studies, Monash University. For further work on the social history of colonial libraries and readers see Askew, M. (1982). 'The Diffusion of Useful Knowledge': Mechanics' Institutes in Nineteenth-Century Victoria. *Unpublished M.A. Thesis*, Monash University; and Hubber, B.G. (1986). Public Libraries and the Suburban Reading Public, 1850-1914. *Unpublished M.A. Thesis*, Monash University.

7. Smiles, S. (1859). *Self-help; with illustrations of conduct and perseverance*. London: John Murray, p.1.

8. Grundy, D. (1972). *Secular, Compulsory and Free: The Education Act of 1872*. Carlton, Vic: Melbourne University Press.

9. Kirsop, W. (1991). Barry's 'Great Emporium' in the twenty-first century: the future of the State Library of Victoria collections. *La Trobe Library Journal, 12*(46), pp. 49-59.

10. Bleasdale, J.I (1869). *Practical education: A brief review of its present condition on the Continent of Europe & in Great Britain*. Melbourne: Technological Commission of Victoria.

11. Whitelock, D. (1974). *The great tradition: A history of adult education in Australia*. St Lucia, Qld: Queensland University Press; Nadel, G.H. (1957). *Australia's colonial culture: Ideas, men and institutions in mid-nineteenth century eastern Australia*. Cambridge, Mass: Harvard University Press; and Roe, M. (1965). *Quest for authority in eastern Australia, 1835-1851*. Parkville, Vic: Melbourne University Press.

12. For reference to *ad hoc* grants to individual institutions see the following Appropriation Bills: 15 Vict. 7 (1851), 16 Vict. 30 (1852), 17 Vict. 7 (1853), 18 Vict. 35 (1854), 19 Vict. 18 (1855/56), 21 Vict. 44 (1856/57), 21 Vict. 46 (1857/58) and 22 Vict. 88 (1858/59).

13. *Victorian Parliamentary Debates*, 26 February 1857, p.526.

14. *Victorian Parliamentary Debates*, 12 June 1857, p. 796.

15. *Victorian Parliamentary Debates*, 14 December 1857, p. 44.

16. *Victorian Parliamentary Debates*, 19 January 1858, p. 144.

17. *Victorian Parliamentary Debates*, 20 January 1860, pp. 386-387; 21 January 1860, pp. 396-397.

18. Serle, *op.cit.*, p. 259.

19. Serle, *op.cit.*, p. 284.

20. It is distressing to find that Bailey, who was a spiritualist and who, on his death-bed, agreed to return from the other side, did not find everlasting peace. When he did return and was asked was he happy, he replied "No!," and when asked had he seen God, he did not answer.

Green, D. (1973). *Ulysses Bound: Henry Handel Richardson and her fiction.* Canberra: Australian National University Press, p. 365.

21.For the condition which made institutions within ten miles of Melbourne ineligible for the grant see Appropriation Bill 24 Vict. 98 (1859/60); for the condition which restricted the proportion of the grant available to institutes within ten miles of Melbourne see Appropriation Bill 27 Vict. 187 (1862/63).

CHAPTER SIX

CONFLICT, CONSENSUS AND CULTURE: THE GEELONG MECHANICS' INSTITUTE TO 1900

Marc Askew

INTRODUCTION

> Your committee cannot conclude their report without drawing the attention of the public to the high moral and intellectual influence which this institution has succeeded in obtaining in this town. During the past year a continual succession of lectures, concerts, soirées, &c., have enlivened its walls, and meetings of almost every description for the promotion of social and religious advancement, have taken place within its precincts.[1]

Mechanics' institutes, like the savings banks, building societies and friendly societies transmitted to the Australian colonies in the same period, were an institutional expression of the pervasive nineteenth-century ethic of self-improvement. Michael Roe, in his study of ideology and cultural institutions in pre-gold rush Australia, describes the complex of ideas prevalent in the early nineteenth century as an ideology (a 'new faith') of 'Moral Enlightenment,' with an emphasis on its relative coherence through being expressed in 'movements' of the period, such as scientific education and temperance.[2] Within the working-class movements of the late eighteenth and early nineteenth centuries, self-education and the associated virtues of self-discipline and thrift were a concomitant of political activity and part of the broader objective of working class mobilization.[3]

However, the mechanics' institutes and kindred organizations of various titles were a product of a broadly-based movement to popularize learning in the nineteenth century, and, not surprisingly, the objectives of such learning differed according to its advocates. Science, however important, was not the only form of knowledge considered essential to the process of mental improvement.[4] By the 1840s the emphasis and activities of the institutes had changed from an emphasis on science to a concern with general subjects of learning.[5] The take-over of institutes by professionals, shopkeepers and clerks was seen as the prime cause behind the dilution of the educational programs. Yet despite the general validity of criticisms levelled at the institutes in the 1840s, changes in activity and function were in some cases the result of realistic assessments of local conditions.[6]

The mechanics' institutes were not entirely the creatures of the British bourgeoisie, as argued by Frederick Engels in the 1840s.[7] The institutes were often used by working-class radicals for their own purposes.[8] It would be a mistake to apply a standard paradigm of British mechanics' institutes when analysing those which were founded in colonial Australia, yet this has been at the base of judgements of cultural historians such as Nadel, and more recently, historians of class relations in pre-goldrush Australia, such as Sullivan. The latter uncritically accepts Engels' characterization of the large urban institutes, largely through false assumptions about the comparability of class relations in Britain and the Australian colonies.[9]

That colonists should take to the idea so quickly, with the first institute established in Hobart in 1827, suggests that, while a concern with Science was uppermost, there was a fairly realistic view of the adaptability of these institutions to colonial conditions. To be sure there was, as Nadel and others have outlined, a particular focus on science in the pre-gold rush institutes in Hobart (est. 1827), Melbourne (est. 1839) and Sydney (est. 1833); yet their changes in function during the 1850s were not entirely a knee-jerk reaction to the demands of "an amorphous and democratically inclined multitude."[10] The attitudes of two prominent colonists of artisan origin, James Harrison of Geelong and Henry Parkes of Sydney, suggest the contrasting experiences and priorities of those immigrants who had belonged to institutes in Britain: Harrison concerned himself with scientific invention and criticised institutes for failing in science teaching; by contrast Parkes' great love of poetry and literature had been nurtured at the Birmingham Mechanics' Institute.[11] The seeds of change were already apparent in the Australian institutes before the gold rush immigration brought thousands of settlers who had some experience of the variety of institutes in their homeland. The functions of the institutes were seen to be appropriate in a newly settled society not so much for any specific economic purpose, but for a variety of needs, not least the general need to establish some level of cultural coherence. Demonstrating such a point takes care of one great indictment levelled by some historians of education; however, another dominant theme, developed both by radical historians of education and social historians, has been the functions of the institutes as instruments of bourgeois, or otherwise ruling-class ideological hegemony over a potentially challenging working class. Such a claim, it will be argued here, does little to further our understanding of either the mechanics' institutes or of colonial social structure. While the colonial 'bourgeoisie' dominated the mechanics' institutes, the institutes could never be a part of the world of the colonial working class.

Until relatively recently there were few attempts to seriously analyse the experiences of organizations in colonial settlements, taking into account the social structures and changes of the communities which surrounded them. It has been all too easy in the past for historians of all ideological stamps to assume, despite many indications to the contrary, that colonists were uncritical duplicators of British institutions, and that - despite significant levels of economic and social mobility - colonial class categories were rigid, and that class language was identical with that of the homeland. Of course, there were contradictions and tensions within colonial society: it is not surprising that the mechanics' institutes, like other organizations, would reflect such conflicts in their respective communities. It is argued here that the institutes were never capable of ideologically containing the colonial working class, and that support from the ranks of those who could afford to patronize the institutes was at best limited and at worst tardy. However, in the light of ethnic and religious diversity, and political conflicts within the ranks of the 'middling strata' of society (the professional, the white collar groups, the self-employed and the respectable artisans), the institutes were part of a framework of organizational affiliation which helped to define a cultural consensus in colonial society.

THE ORIGINS OF THE GEELONG INSTITUTE

This chapter takes as a case study the institute in Geelong, a provincial town in Victoria, situated some 70 km. south west of Melbourne.[12] The Geelong Mechanics' Institute, like many of its colonial counterparts, experienced some of the difficulties and dilemmas faced by British institutes, and like them, it was shaped by the ideals and demands of the social groups which supported it as well as by the socio-economic trends affecting the community as a whole. Moves to establish a mechanics' institute in Geelong in 1846 were greeted with acclaim and attracted a large measure of support, both from 'men of considerable influence' and artisans. The latter group was beginning to expand with the growth of the town's economic fortunes following the economic slump of the early 1840s, and the revival of assisted immigration.[13] Like other institutes founded in small settlements at the time (Geelong boasted a population of less than 2,000 in 1846) the movement in this infant wool town was premature, considering the lack of a strong base of economic support among its small group of patrons. Nevertheless, considerations of civic status were almost as important as those of accounting. The merchants and professionals who led this move were not the men to see their town - the "Naples of the South" - eclipsed by the pretentious elite of Melbourne across the bay, a group who had been conspiring to deny Geelong its rightful and prosperous role as a free warehousing and customs port and a self-governing municipality. By 1851 Geelong's population was to expand to over 8,000.

The two leading promoters of the institute had both been involved with schools of arts and mechanics' institutes in Scotland. James Harrison, although largely self-educated, had attended classes at Anderson's Institution (the precursor to the Glasgow School of Arts founded by Birkbeck), while the Rev. Andrew Love had been involved in the organization of the Kirkentillock Mechanics' Institute, near Glasgow.[14] Both men had been active in the Geelong Literary and Scientific Association, formed in 1844. This association was the preserve of the local elite.[15] These were the men who had been at the forefront of the early moves to establish churches and charity societies in the town. The Association was ailing when the mechanics' institute was mooted. The announcement of the new institution as a 'mechanics' institute' proclaimed a broader social function for activities which had hitherto attracted a relatively select group of participants.

Membership fees were set at £1 per annum, in line with the other institutes of New South Wales. In order to encourage workingmen to join, this fee could be paid in quarterly instalments of 5 shillings.[16] Although it depended on private subscriptions for its survival, the Geelong Mechanics' Institute was not regarded as an exclusive institution by its promoters. Like the institutes in Britain it was an organization which celebrated voluntarism, and moral commitment to culture and self-improvement was expected to be expressed through financial support. But it was the existence of membership fees which provided the most effective barrier to working-class involvement, and in the following years membership requirements were being continually altered in order to boost membership. The idea of a fee, however, was never abandoned. According to the rules, office-bearers and committee members were to be elected at annual meetings by paid-up members. Working-class involvement, in theory at least, was not discouraged. The Hobart and Sydney institutes, in deference to the precedent set by the parent institution in London, had stipulated that two-thirds of the managing committee should be drawn from the manual workers in the membership.[17] However, this rule was not promulgated in Geelong. The occupational profile of the office-bearers and committee members of the institute in the first four years of its existence shows that it was managed by a combination of professionals, merchants, smaller businessmen and self-employed tradesmen. Merchants, professionals and squatters dominated the offices of President, Vice President, Treasurer and Secretary, while the committee membership was shared with retailers and small masters.

Table 6.1
Office-bearers and Committee Members of
the Geelong Mechanics' Institute, 1846-1850

Occupation	Office-Bearers	Committee Members
Pastoralists	2	-
Merchants	2	2
Professionals	4	8
Business proprietors	1	11
Self-employed tradesmen	-	8
Clerical and lower professionals	-	1
Skilled and unskilled manual workers	-	-
Total	**9**	**30**

Source: G.M.I.M.B. Vol. 1., 1846-1850

The social character of the institute's support was generally consistent with that of other institutes established in the same period in Port Phillip and other colonies. The formal objectives of the institute, "the diffusion of scientific, literary and other useful knowledge" echoed the stated aims of its counterparts in other cities.[18] By "useful knowledge" was meant anything which would help to further the institute's goals: "To improve, elevate and refine the moral, social and intellectual character of the community."[19]

As with so many other institutes throughout the Australian colonies, the library was the most successful of the institute's departments. Until 1850, the collection was built on the donations of members. James Harrison's donations are particularly revealing in showing the wide range of titles considered useful and appropriate to the institute's functions. Among them were the *Life of William Hutton*, Ferguson's *Lectures on Astronomy*, *The Christian Reader* and *A Tour Through Sicily and Malta*.[20] The managers of the institute found it difficult to keep up with the literary demands of their members, yet at the same time they depended on the library to maintain the popularity of the institute. Because of this dependence, the Geelong Mechanics' Institute was not in a position to control the growth of its library collection, a condition that it shared with the Melbourne institute and many others at this time.[21] The strengths of the subject areas of the library collection in 1850 reflect the dominant reading tastes of the period. 'Novels and Romances' represented by far the largest single group of titles in the collection. Prominent among them were the novels of Walter Scott, Charles Dickens and James Fenimore Cooper, the standard moral fiction of the age. Other popular authors of fiction such as Bulwer-Lytton, Dumas and Marryat were also well represented. Among the 'miscellaneous' works were some of the most important 'improving' publications of the period - *Chambers' Edinburgh Journal* and the *Penny Magazine*. Arts and sciences, biography and history combined were almost equal to the number of fiction titles. Like the other categories they included works by most of the principal writers of the day, or earlier works by writers still considered important, such as Hume, Locke, Burke and Gibbon.[22] Martin Sullivan has correctly pointed to the importance placed on reading books by the promoters of the early Victorian institutes in Geelong and elsewhere: reading would inculcate habits of orderliness, reflection, temperance and discipline.[23] This reflected a widespread attitude.[24] However, to conclude from this that the managing committees rigorously attempted to reform the working class (as Sullivan seems to do) would be a mistake, as it would be to assume that there was a consensus within the elite about what constituted suitable reading material, when there was not.[25] As in Melbourne, the members of the infant institute had to tolerate a miscellaneous library collection which, in its preponderance of fiction titles of various genres and ages, was hardly calculated to impart any coherent moral message. Above all, the collection reflected the tastes of a broad reading public bent on using the institute to service its private reading needs.

The claims of the institute to be an effective agent of community enlightenment relied not so much on the library, as on those activities which encouraged active participation and social interaction. Without lecture courses and classes in various subjects, reading, although important, remained a private activity. Lecture courses were inaugurated in 1849. The first group of lecturers offered their services free of charge and they were all local identities. The Rev. Dr. Macartney (Church of England) delivered the opening lecture. He was followed by Robert Booley, ex-Chartist and temperance advocate, who gave three lectures on Phrenology. Dr. Forster Shaw followed him with two lectures on ventilation and the concluding lecture was delivered by James Harrison, the fiery editor of the *Geelong Advertiser,* who spoke on "self-education in science."[26] On the whole, these lectures were popular, but the programs depended on the availability of volunteer lecturers, and none was available in the following year.[27] Efforts to establish classes were hamstrung by the problem that the committee had devoted all available funds to the purchase of a building site, and could not afford to pay teachers. By the eve of the gold-rush in mid-1851, the institute was in debt and unable to afford to keep up the supply of English newspapers to its reading room.[28] Like many of the early colonial institutes, the Geelong institution foundered, largely perhaps because it was premature in such a small community Yet this in itself suggests the importance of the colonists' ambitions to help establish a civic culture.[29]

In the absence of detailed membership lists for the early period, the socio-economic basis of the institute's support is difficult to determine. However, the occupational profile of committee members probably reflects the major sources of its support. Given the membership fee of £1, a sum amounting to more than half the weekly wage of a skilled manual worker in the period, it is unlikely that this group was able, or willing, to participate in the institute's activities. Evidence of the committee's awareness of the unbalanced character of its support is shown in the change in membership qualifications; in 1849, a new rule was passed which provided that the sons and apprentices of members could be admitted as junior members at a reduced rate of five shillings per annum.[30] In an attempt to raise money for a building, the institute created two classes of members - proprietary and reading members. The former, being shareholders, were to be in effective control of the institute. It seems, however, that this measure did little, if anything, to enhance the popularity of the institution.[31] In 1846 the number of members totalled 106, whereas by 1850, when the town had more than quadrupled its population, the membership still numbered only 140, or one in 18 of all adult males between the ages of 21 and 60 years. Prior to the disbanding of the institute in late 1853 owing to the disruption caused by the goldrushes, the number of members had plummeted to 81, only 60 of whom could be relied upon to pay their subscriptions. By this time, the appropriateness of the institution's name was beginning to be questioned. It is important to note , however, that the institute had not been formed *for* mechanics alone, the promoters aimed rather to make the institution socially inclusive.[32]

A NEW INSTITUTE FOR A NEW ERA

In Victoria, the social dislocation brought about by the flood of gold immigrants had lent greater force to arguments supporting the creation of institutions which would promote social integration and the reformation of morals. In particular, the apparent disjunction between wealth and political and cultural capacity among the working class, and the severe imbalance of the sexes in the population, were seen as dangerous and destabilizing social phenomena.[33] The more optimistic of the contemporary commentators believed that the levelling of class distinctions would be beneficial, but only if material enterprise was leavened by the cultivation of learning.[34] Such reasoning lay behind the foundation of a range of cultural institutions in Victoria, among them the mechanics' institutes. If we are to accept the arguments of local cultural promoters at their face value (and there seems little reason not to), the motive for founding such institutions was less to do with controlling the working-class than with assuring a level of social stability in a volatile immigrant community.

Following an initial phase of inactivity among organized groups in Geelong during the demographically and economically unstable years of 1852-53, the period beginning in 1854 saw a renascence in the growth of voluntary organizations as society settled into a state of relative stability. Above all, the economic changes wrought by the gold rush had created further changes in the town's social fabric. In 1854, professional and clerical occupations now represented some 10 percent of the adult male work force. An expanded merchant community and a diffusion of wealth among smaller businessmen brought with it a greater capacity for civic patronage.[35] Demand for a revived mechanics' institute in Geelong grew from the early part of 1854. Some argued that a mechanics' institute was needed to counteract the evils of the public house and to bring the young unmarried men of the town into contact with the socially elevating influences of literature and learning.[36] Perhaps even more persuasively, the existence of a mechanics' institute was a measure of civic status, an essential part of the cultural inventory of any township with pretensions to greatness.[37] By 1854, the notion that the sole function of a mechanics' institute was to provide vocational education for the working-class had largely disappeared. The demand for mechanics' institutes was so general in local communities that the Victorian government acknowledged its strength by providing funds and land.[38] Regular grants for the purchase of books were to be made available from 1860.[39] At the first annual meeting of the revived institute in Geelong, the manifold advantages of the institution were outlined. The institute was accorded a significant role in reconstituting social relations. To the Mayor of Geelong, Dr W H Baylie (who owed his new-found wealth to property speculation, rather than to his profession), the lectures, library and reading room were intended not only to benefit "the better class of society" but also the "humbler classes." He added:

> Let them put aside the old fashioned notions of aristocracy, let people mingle together for their mutual improvement. People of all classes might meet together and deport themselves like ladies and gentlemen and yet each maintain their respective positions in society. The noblest way in which a man could employ himself was to encourage the enlightenment of his fellow man, and to endeavour to produce in him an internal improvement.[40]

Others considered the social, rather than intellectual character of the institute to be important. Young men in the colony were in danger of destroying their prospects through extravagant living and spending. The institute would provide opportunities for civilized recreation and moral reflection. Still others saw the institute as an instrument of social mobility and a training ground for future public men among the youth of the town.[41]

The new institute began with advantages not available to its forebear. The institute inherited the literary society's library and its lecturers - this group had been operating spasmodically since 1844 - and received a government grant of land and funds towards the erection of a building. The committee secured the services of Benjamin Wheatland, former secretary of the Borough Road Mechanics' Institute in London.[42] By 1854 there was a pool of educated people in the town qualified by education or vocation to deliver lectures, and an even larger base from which to draw donations and subscriptions. In 1855 the institute presented an impressive array of 17 lectures, rather ambitiously described as a "course." The series commenced with an opening lecture on the topic of 'Genius and its Applications,' followed by two addresses on 'Life, Health and Disease.' The scientific element did not persist, however; following lectures included the topics: 'Napoleon,' 'Humorous Poets and Poetry,' 'Modern Prose Literature,' 'Oliver Cromwell' and 'Thomas More.' In June 1856, the members approved a revision of the rules, which among other things, broadened the formal objectives of the institution and justified the introduction of entertaining and less rigorous activities.[43] Until the end of the decade the institute committee strove to increase the number of its activities, especially its classes, but rarely prescribed the intellectual content of these activities. As long as it provided a range of respectable diversions, the objectives of the institution were vindicated. The entertaining mix of lectures continued to be popular in the town, and no attempt was made to mould them into topically coherent programs.[44] So, too, classes on subjects such as Mathematics and Latin, beyond the pale of more fashionable skills such as drawing, elocution and vocal music, were short lived.[45] Those classes that were most successful, such as chess and discussion groups, were initiated by small bands of enthusiasts.

The prohibition on political and religious discussion which was imposed by the Melbourne institute did not take effect in Geelong.[46] In part, this was due to the existence of a strong Protestant elite whose hegemony was never threatened. The first list of debating topics was innocuous enough. The class restricted itself to broad moral issues: 'Whether poverty, ignorance or the struggle after wealth has had the greatest tendency to crime'; 'Ought Capital Punishment to be abolished'; 'Whether Shakespeare or Milton had the greatest moral influence on society.'[47] In the following year, while general moral issues such as 'Ought the sale of intoxicating drink to be prohibited?' were still debated, current political and economic concerns, such as state aid for education and protectionism, were appearing.[48] No list of members of this discussion class survives, but it is likely that the members were businessmen and professionals.[49]

Table 6.2
Geelong Mechanics' Institute,
Number of paid-up members, 1846-1900

Year	Members	Year	Members
1846	106	1877	604
1850	140	1878	n.a.
1852 (M.I. disbanded)	81	1879	594
1854 (M.I. re-formed)	127	1880	610
1856	342	1881	630
1857	438	1882	662
1858	502	1883	667
1859	485	1884	647
1860	433	1885	612
1861	443	1886	652
1862	402	1887	644
1863	372	1888	652
1864	415	1889	653
1865	405	1890	615
1864,65,66,67,	n.a.	1891	714
1868	534	1892	654
1869	523	1893	588
1870	578	1894	n.a.
1873	576	1895	720
1874	592	1896	531
1875	596	1897	644
1876	598	1898,99,	n.a.
		1900	575

Source: Geelong Mechanics' Institute, Annual Reports.

In 1859 the committee judged the institute to be a success. The comprehensiveness and frequency of its activities were its greatest claim to influence.[50] Membership fees were the same, although a greater level of accessibility was afforded by allowing members (still exclusively male) to introduce 2 ladies and to allow junior membership. The number of members had risen from 127 in 1854 to 502 four years later (See Table 2).[51] However, the numbers actually attending the various concerts and lectures probably far exceeded the membership figure.

The tendency of the institute to assume the character of a polite recreation club was already apparent in these years. By 1857 the building was already considered too small, and among the new rooms proposed for creation were coffee and conversation rooms.[52] Having succeeded in erecting a building by 1857, the institute was in a position to benefit from the local demand for meeting rooms, bazaars and benefit concerts. In part, this made the institute's prosperity less dependent on members' subscriptions which, by 1857, accounted for only 25 percent of total income.[53]

The management of the institute was in the hands of a coalition of some of the major activists in Geelong's organization life.[54] Clergymen played a prominent part in the management; between 1855 and 1860 there were never less than two clergymen among the office-bearers or committee, and towards the end of the period they increasingly tended to assume the position of Vice-President. The merchant presence was also strong on the committee. There were three among the twelve members in 1856, and five out of fourteen in 1857. The remaining committee members represented a broad range of business proprietors. The religious affiliations of these activists shows, as in many other groups, how the dominant Protestant elite was woven into the fabric of the town's associational life. Roman Catholic representation was minimal in the institute's management, although Father Dean Hayes maintained a strong interest in the institute during the 1850s. Like the welfare agencies, the mechanics' institute provided a way of uniting the leadership of the Protestant denominations and increasing their visibility.

Table 6.3
Occupations and Religious Affiliations,
Geelong Mechanics' Institute Management, 1855-1860:
Religious Affiliation

Occupation	Total	Angl.	Pres.	Wes.	Con. & Bap	Rmn	Unknown Cath.
Independent income or retired	2	1	1	-	-	-	-
Merchants & Bankers	15	3	4	1	2	1	4
Clergymen	9	3	3	1	1	1	-
Legal Profession	2	1	-	-	-	-	1
Medical Profession	3	1	-	-	-	-	2
Business Proprietors	14	1	3	1	2	-	9
Manufacturers & Self-employed Tradesmen	2	1	-	1	-	-	-
Non-Manual Occupations	2	-	-	-	-	-	2
Skilled Manual Occupations	1	-	-	-	-	-	1
Totals	**50**	**12**	**10**	**4**	**4**	**2**	**19**

Source: G.M.I. Annual Reports, Geelong directories, rate books, church records.

Notwithstanding the support of a large body of the town's notables, the next decade saw increasing criticism directed against the institute. In December 1860, James Harrison launched a scathing attack on the character of the colonial mechanics' institutes and the Geelong Mechanics' Institute in particular. He wrote:

Among the most notable failures of the age must unquestionably be classed the attempt to work educational wonders for the masses by means of mechanics' institutes...The mechanic has not been the individual who has to any great extent benefitted by the working of the mechanics' institutes. There have been very few, if any, instances of real laboring men having been developed into scholars by the appliances furnished at such institutions.[55]

Harrison considered the core of the problem to be the lack of any well-defined object or plan for the development of institutes' programs. His own definition of their objectives was far narrower than the contemporary one, for according to him, a mechanics' institute should be a working man's college. The present institutes failed to approximate to such a role - their library collections were too diffuse and non-specialized, the subjects of lectures "too frequently a mere jumble of varieties fortuitously grouped together in such manner as may best suit the convenience of a crowd of gratuitous, or only half paid lecturers."[56] In general, the aims of the libraries and lectures were to occupy rather than instruct the mind.

In 1860, perhaps as a response to Harrison's attack - but also quite possibly emulating an earlier project of the Melbourne institute - the committee attempted to establish evening classes in arithmetic, reading, writing, grammar, composition, algebra, French and Latin. John Bracebridge Wilson, headmaster of the Geelong Grammar School, offered to teach these courses. The attempt was a failure.[57] Although the economic recession of this period was partly responsible, more crucially, the institute had attracted a clientele that did not require such forms of education.[58]

Although the Geelong Mechanics' Institute justified its existence with a rhetoric that emphasized public utility and universal participation,[59] throughout the 1860s and into the 1870s it increasingly assumed the character of a private institution. This process was in large part determined by economic constraints and priorities which ultimately centred on the use of the institute's building, which was in high demand as a venue for activities of many organizations. Revenue from the hire of the hall and rooms constituted 37.8 percent of its income in 1860, 40 percent in 1861 and 43 percent in 1862.[60] Towards the latter half of the 1860s, as the local economy began to revive, members' subscriptions rose as a proportion of total income.[61] However, these changes do not reflect any reversal in policy. The economic slump of the early 1860s and the resulting decline in membership (and with it, income) convinced the committee that its major asset was its building, and, having survived this difficult period by capitalizing on this asset, the institute was unwilling to commit funds towards high-risk educational ventures. It was clear by the middle of that decade that whatever may have been the broader motives of its major supporters, the character of the institute was private, commercial and entrepreneurial.

The transformation was exemplified by changes in the promotion and nature of lectures and public entertainments. From the mid-1850s, public lecturing began to attract a small group of Melbourne-based professionals.[62] Articulate, entertaining and occasionally controversial, these men drew large audiences and charged high fees for their services, and offered a means of attracting members and boosting waning funds. It is not surprising then, that the committee invited Archibald Michie to give a lecture for the opening celebration of the newly renovated building in May 1860. "The returns," noted one member, "would be larger than by any other means that could be adopted."[63] One unforeseen consequence of this policy was that by employing professional speakers, the institute found that it had undermined the popularity of the local lecturers.

We know little of the social character of the concert and lecture audiences of the period. It would seem clear, however, that the town's working class was not strongly represented. As one local working man complained, admission prices to the entertainments staged at the institute - 1 shilling to 3 shillings - were generally too high for manual workers to take their families, especially in a period of low wages and irregular employment.[64]   Whenever lecture audiences were described, it was generally their "select," "responsible" or "fashionable" character that elicited comment.[65] The institute was used by ventriloquists, wizards and travelling groups like 'Woodruffe's Bohemian Troupe of Glass Blowers,' 'The English Glee and Burlesque Company' and 'Ethiopian Entertainers.'[66] These activities, while not demonstrably 'improving,' were nevertheless innocuous. They were accepted because at the very least they were 'respectable,' this status being conferred as much by the social character of the audience as by the nature of the entertainments themselves.[67]

In serving these functions it could be argued that the institution was conforming more closely to the varied needs of local society and hence expanding its public role. Yet contemporaries were aware that the institute was not performing an active reforming function in Geelong. Criticism reached its peak in 1865. In April that year, upwards of two hundred residents forwarded a petition to the Chief Secretary of the colony, protesting against "the manner in which the 'Mechanics' Institute is conducted in Geelong." More specifically, the petition objected to the staging of performances which were carried on solely for the benefit of the performers and not for the institute, or for charitable purposes.[68] This was followed by another protest in July which requested that the institute's theatrical licence not be renewed when it lapsed the following August. Again the institute's entrepreneurial role was attacked:

> The building has been used for purposes entirely inconsistent with the objects for which it was built, namely for theatrical representations, negro burlesque, stage dances and other performances peculiar to the stage of a theatre - held for the sole benefit and profit of the performers in the same manner as a licenced theatre.[69]

With the exception of several pastoralists and larger merchants, the bulk of the signatories were from the town's middling strata: clerks, retailers and self-employed artisans.[70] To some extent their motives were pragmatic, because from 1861 the local theatre had been closed.[71] The institute consequently had a monopoly on public entertainments and could charge fees at its discretion. But notwithstanding support in the business community for the promotion of an alternative venue for commercial entertainment, many people were acutely aware of the distinction between private and public institutions.

The most damning attack on the institute came from a number of working-class spokesmen. According to one of these critics the institute was "monopolized by a class for whom [it was] assuredly never intended, and if per-adventure any fustian clad artisan should in the reading room enter, between the wind and their nobility, he is saluted with a cold stare of astonishment, that quietly admonishes him that 'thus far shalt though go and no farther'."[72]
The visitor to the Geelong Mechanics' Institute, he went on, would see that it possessed a noble building and a magnificent hall, but on entering the reading room the observer would only see "the various pastors and masters of the town." The "regal hall" came in for equal criticism as a profit-making concern. In conclusion this critic wrote:

> And thus Mr Editor, in the reading room we speak of, may be found McParson, McClerk, McBanker, McMerchant, McSquatter, McDoctor, McDraper, but nae McChanics.[73]

Never had the patrons of the institute been identified in such detail. The committee of the institute replied lamely that the reading room did indeed attract "fustian clad" artisans.[74] One correspondent outlined the class discrimination pervading the institute. He had become a member so that he could read Kinglake's *History of the Crimean War*, Smiles's *Lives of the Engineers*, and other books too expensive for him to purchase. On attempting to borrow these books from the institute's library, he was told that they were out: "I was induced to ask the lad who had them? It was always the parsons, bankers, clerks, etc." He related how he was forced to wait behind the counter for his requested books to be located for him, while the town worthies, against all regulations of the library, "lift up the trap at the counter, and saunter through with the utmost sang froid, with their glass at their eye and pick and choose for their money."[75]

James Harrison, a proudly self-educated artisan (now editor of the *Register*), despite his earlier criticism of the institute, maintained that these outbursts suggested "a disposition to pull down the upper ten thousand, rather than to raise the million." Elevation, he stressed, should not be confused with levelling.[76] In reply William Stitt Jenkins, self-appointed town bard, temperance advocate, and champion of the "fustian clad mechanics," vowed that at the next annual meeting he would have a new committee elected.[77] Despite the threats there was no dramatic change in the composition of the institute's committee the following year, and no working men were elected.[78] It seems unlikely that Jenkins was able to mobilize the local working-class to participate in the elections, since voting rights were extended only to adult male members who had paid an annual or quarterly fee (£1 and 5s. respectively).

It is interesting that, despite the gradual decline in the town's population in the decade 1860-1870, the membership of the institute grew. In 1870 membership stood at 578, the highest since its establishment. One of the most significant changes in institute policy was the admission of women as members in January 1864. Until that time women were permitted to attend the institute lectures or the library only if introduced by members, but in 1864 they were admitted on the same basis as juveniles, on the payment of a ten shilling annual membership fee. They were, however, given no voting rights.[79] The increasing presence of women in the mechanics' institute was a trend apparent in other voluntary organizations during the period, most notably the welfare associations, churches and their auxilliary groups. But in a sense the mechanics' institute committee was making a calculated response to demographic reality as much as attempting to achieve social inclusiveness, because in the decade 1861-1871 women in the adult age groups increased significantly as a proportion of the adult population. This must have had a direct impact on membership;[80] in 1880 they represented nearly 25 percent of total subscribers (148 of total of 610).[81] Both as a response to the influx of women and as a means of encouraging more women to join, the committee built a separate Ladies' Reading Room in 1868. This measure was designed to enhance the social decorum of the institute's activities.[82]

The building of the Ladies' Reading Room was part of a comprehensive program which aimed towards structuring the internal space of the building so that it conformed to the character of a polite leisure and recreation club. Money was spent on elegant decorations and fittings. In the annual report for 1868 the secretary stated: "This alteration has had the effect of augmenting the popularity and attractiveness of the institute in a very marked degree, the number of subscribers being considerably in excess of what it was at any former period." [83] Library opening hours were extended and the price of tickets to lectures was reduced from one shilling to sixpence.[84] In 1868 a new chess club was formed in connection with the institute.[85]

In an effort to further popularize the institution, the committee launched a series of 'Penny Readings' in 1866, anticipating (correctly, as it turned out) that if such cultural activities were attracting attention in Britain they would prove successful in the colonies. The 'Penny Readings' had been initially developed by social reformers anxious to provide respectable and amusing entertainment for the poor. The organizers attempted to produce an atmosphere of family entertainment and, through this method, to more effectively diffuse culture among the working class.[86] Organizers were hopeful of the results and the readings enjoyed a brief period of success. One local writer observed:

> Nothing...has a more direct tendency to level class distinctions, and to promulgate a feeling of brotherly love and Christian charity than may be found in these social gatherings...'where the rich and poor sit down together, God being the Father of them all.'[87]

But by mid-1868 it was clear that the readings were little more than fashionable soirées of limited educational value; the original idea had become "smothered by intense respectability."[88]

The criticisms levelled at the Institute did not abate in the 1870s, but they tended to come from evangelical Christians protesting at the 'worldliness' of the entertainments. In 1871 a locally published jeremiad pointed to the institute as the major symbol of a complacent and material respectability which was perpetuating class distinctions and preventing the emergence of a truly organic, co-operative society tied by bonds of Christian fellowship. It was "the poor painted thing, that flaunts her tawdry finery before the eye of simple ignorance..."[89] This assailant saw the institute's indiscriminate approval for the promotion of theatrical performances as a moral danger to the young, and, just as serious, a threat to true *moral* respectability.[90] It was an overstatement of the power of the institute as a cultural agency; however, in pointing to the institute as a possible cause of moral laxity in the town, the pamphlet reflected a growing anxiety about the ability of religious groups to achieve social and moral integration in the community. "Fashion" and "worldliness," anathema to evangelical Protestants, were akin to the social decorum and material respectability which the institute represented in the estimation of its other opponents in the town. The institute had thus become shunned by both the working-class and the intensely religious groups in local society.

By the 1870s proposals for a free library posed a further threat to the institute's civic role. The establishment of a free library had been mooted as early as 1865, in the midst of the debate on the exclusiveness of the institute.[91] Until this time, the Geelong Mechanics' Institute had never been seriously threatened by a competing institution. As with other forms of leisure provision designed to uplift the working-class, free libraries were seen by their promoters as a possible alternative to the public house. It was suggested that the free libraries could be far cheaper than a police force in promoting social and moral order. In Britain the movement found expression in the *Public Library Act* of 1850.[92] In Victoria the *Municipal Institutions Act* of 1854 had given power to councils to enact by-laws for the establishment of public libraries, as well as museums and botanical gardens.[93] But few corporations chose to exercise this power during the 1850s, and there was no campaign to displace mechanics' institutes and establish rate-supported free libraries. By the late 1860s however, some parliamentarians were questioning the validity of granting funds to the institutes on the same basis as free libraries, since the latter were, in their opinion, the only institutions accessible to the working class. During the later 1860s and the 1870s increasing pressure was applied by governments to the institutes to establish free reading rooms as a condition of receiving grants.[94]

The promoters of the Geelong Free Library were drawn from the town's dominant groups - businessmen, professionals and manufacturers. Economically and socially, they were barely distinguishable from the supporters of the mechanics' institute and there was no consistent line of political cleavage between the two groups. One of the leading figures in the movement was Graham Berry, leading Victorian protectionist, democrat and working-class champion. He had arrived in Geelong in 1866, became part-proprietor of the *Register* and had been elected to represent West Geelong in the Legislative Assembly in 1869. He was already known as a promoter of free libraries in Melbourne.[95] Politically, he was opposed to George Belcher, Mayor of Geelong in 1873-74 and again in 1875-76, who was President of the mechanics' institute in the same years and became the MLC for the South Western Province in May 1875.[96] He was an ardent free-trader. The establishment of the free library in 1875 was an attempt on the part of a section of Geelong's élite to incorporate the socially marginal elements of the population more fully into the town's cultural life. The initiative was above all a recognition of the cultural divide existing within the social order. For a decade, the élite had witnessed the growth of conspicuous poverty in the town. Among the working class in the 1860s unemployment and underemployment were particularly severe. The increasing presence of deserted wives and children, the aged poor, "larrikinism" and prostitution posed a threat to the social fabric.[97] Political rhetoric in the period tended to stress sharp distinctions between the wealthy and the educated, and "the people." While this rhetoric oversimplified social boundaries, it is not surprising that cultural institutions, among them the mechanics' institute, were seen as reflections of this.[98]

The Geelong Free Library did not displace the institute, even though the latter had been embarrassed by the establishment of the free library. In 1876, the committee maintained confidently that "the institute with its well-furnished reading-room, its extensive library, now approaching 12,000 volumes, its classes, and other means of intellectual and social improvement, cannot but continue to be a source of attraction to the inhabitants of the town and district."[99] The institute's membership list for 1873 confirms the statements of its critics. The largest proportion were retailers and other business proprietors, representing 28 percent. The second largest group - merchants, larger manufacturers, bankers, financiers and woolbrokers - comprised 19 percent of the membership. Professionals, primarily physicians, solicitors and clergymen, formed the next largest grouping, with 16 percent. Non-manual occupations (including minor professionals) comprised 10 percent of the subscribers, almost equal to self-employed tradesmen and smaller-scale manufacturers who made up 13 percent. Wage-earners (skilled, semi-skilled and unskilled) formed less than 3 percent of the membership.[100]

With the foundation of its so-called 'School of Science' in 1870, the institute made what proved to be its final attempt to establish an educational role. The idea was not original. In 1869, the Victorian government appointed a Technological Commission to enquire into existing educational agencies and to promote technical education. It was a response to the growing anxiety about the colony's economic and industrial future, and paralleled the debates on elementary education. The Technological Commission attempted to encourage the development of Schools of Design in co-operation with educators, schools and mechanics' institutes in the colony. The committee had received a questionnaire from the Commission late in 1869 and, spurred by a sense of its shortcomings in the area of scientific education, announced its intention to establish a School of Science in the following year.[101] As a prelude to this event, the committee commissioned the sculpture of a statue of 'Science' and had it mounted in a vacant niche on the building's facade. The 'School' was a committee consisting of the town's leading amateur scientists, including several professional teachers, and also a number of the town's most prominent Protestant clergymen.[102] But the 'School of Science' did not organize classes as such, rather it established courses of lectures which combined novelty, spectacle and moral exhortation with information.[103] The School of Science gave local professionals and amateurs the opportunity to demonstrate their virtuosity. It also gave clergymen a chance to remind audiences of the divine plan which had ordered the world. No one objected when the Rev. T McKenzie Fraser spoke on the topic 'The Earth Geologically Designed for Human Habitation.'[104] At the inaugural meeting for the formation of the School, the Rev. C S M Price had been warmly applauded when he stated that science developed a love of truth and in doing so removed evil; if rightly conducted, scientific investigation was not only interesting but morally elevating.[105] For a time it appeared that the mechanics' institute had reclaimed its role as a popular educator, which is perhaps why many of the committee were so offended when the free library issue was raised. But the initiative lapsed in 1876.[106]

In the next decade increasing prosperity and a growth in population and industry encouraged renewed efforts to promote technical and vocational education, efforts which bore fruit in 1885 with plans to establish a technical college as a memorial to the imperial hero, General Gordon of Khartoum. The Gordon Technical College, officially opened in 1887, relieved the mechanics' institute of another of its traditional obligations. Closely modelled on the Melbourne Working Man's College, the Gordon College offered night classes in trade, commercial and language subjects.[107]

COLLEGE OR CLUB?

By the 1880s the name of the institution was the only remaining vestige of its claim to serve the town's working class. In 1889 Julian Thomas (alias 'The Vagabond') noted:

> My visit to the Geelong Mechanics' Institute impresses me with the fact that it is a most admirable institution, well managed and a credit to the town, but the 'mechanics', for whose use it was founded never enter its doors.[108]

Nevertheless it continued to satisfy the town's respectable and affluent citizens. Lectures were revived in 1883 and annual winter series were continued until the depression of the 1890s seriously affected the institute's finances.[109] Topics included contemporary issues such as education, marriage and the role of women, moral addresses (e.g., 'The Dignity of Man'), reminiscence of travel, and the contemporary literary biographies and renditions of poets such as Longfellow, Byron and Tennyson.[110] In sum, the character of the lectures conformed to the desires of the local colonial élite and middling strata to maintain a contact with the wider world and the affairs of the empire, to hear this group's concerns expounded and its moral attitudes confirmed, and to embellish its cultural tastes.[111]

Always loath to admit that the institute was an organization existing solely for the benefit of fee-paying members, the committee was surprised when government grants-in-aid of mechanics' institute libraries were withdrawn in 1887.[112] Despite protests, the government book vote was not reinstated.[113] It was the final public acknowledgment of the institute's private character.[114] In 1891 the committee announced with no trace of irony:

> We propose to popularize the library by making it more accessible to members during the whole of the day and by affording ample table space, with writing materials...we shall offer all the advantages of a well stocked free library in addition to the privilege at present possessed of borrowing books for home perusal.[115]

The ambiguity inherent in these objectives - to assume the appearance of a free institution but to continue in fact to be private - persisted until the turn of the century. In the same year the committee re-affirmed its "conviction of the value of the institute to the community at large."[116] In 1892 the members were asked to "regard the institute not merely as a place where certain rights and privileges are to be purchased, but as a club...in whose management each member has an equal voice."[117] To fund renovations to the building (including the extension of the stage and the purchase of stage scenery to encourage dramatic companies to hire the hall) the committee had floated debentures. By 1894 the management was seriously considering the advantages to be gained from incorporation. Such a measure would give the institute the power to mortgage its land (forbidden under the conditions of the original government land grant) and sub-let the building.[118] As an incorporated company, however, the institute could no longer pretend to be a public institution. In 1897 members finally began to discuss the appropriateness of the institution's name. The result was indecisive: "...the principal difficulty being to find a distinctive appellation to replace the present admittedly unsuitable one."[119] This was not a gesture of defeat or failure; rather, it was an attempt to re-define the cultural functions of the institute.

One of the major objectives of the institute had been to enhance social integration; to encourage an ethos of mutuality, cutting across lines of class and religion.[120] By the 1870s the membership shared a degree of homogeneity - since members shared a characteristic leisure style - by virtue of the alienation of the working class from the institute. Social and cultural uniformity had thus been achieved through a conformity to existing divisions in society. Notwithstanding this development, the institute still felt the need for active and collective modes of cultural participation among its members.

Among other attempts to achieve this mode of 'secular fellowship,' the establishment of the Literary and Discussion Class was the most successful. The class was formed in April 1868 with its formal object as "the mental improvement of its members by the delivery of Literary and Scientific Essays, Elocution and Discussion."[121] The first topic to be debated was 'Are Works of Fiction Beneficial,' a common debating topic of the period. In a spirited discussion, Mr Traill (clerk) won the debate by condemning the sensational writers of the day but upholding the usefulness of the novels of Dickens, Thackeray and Scott.[122] Debates were interspersed with the delivery of essays, readings and recitations, which were subject to the criticisms of members.[123]

Despite political and religious differences among members there were no violent schisms in the class. J W Wallace, active Catholic layman and President of the St. Patrick's Society, speaking at an annual dinner of the class of 1877, maintained that "no matter what religion they espoused, there was no distinction among the members of the class."[124] By this time the class included leading laymen of most religious groups in the town, among them Benjamin Hoare (Catholic) and G F Link (Wesleyan).[125] Speaking at the same gathering in 1877, Hoare outlined the character and benefits of the class. It was, he noted, "a source of genuine delight to minds of maturer views and riper knowledge, where the fruits of study and the acquisitions of culture could be unrolled...in a social and pleasant manner," and Hoare added that such activity "drew them closer together than the bonds of ordinary acquaintanceship and made them feel more to each other than their fellow citizens."[126] The class continued to operate until 1891. Its success was due primarily to its small size and the relative homogeneity in the occupational base of its membership - comprising professionals and other white-collar groups - and the fact that membership was drawn from among older members.[127]

The institute was not the only promoter of 'mutual improvement' in Geelong. It was only one effort (admittedly the most conspicuous) to translate ideas of improvement into an organizational form. By the mid-1860s, the three major improvement organizations in the town (aside from the Geelong Mechanics' Institute) were the Catholic Young Men's Society (established by 1863), the Geelong Wesleyan Religious and Literary Society, and the Geelong Presbyterian Young Men's Association (both established by 1865).[128] By the final decade of the century there was a plethora of groups in Geelong encouraging literary discussion, reading and elocution, as evidenced by the publication in 1896 of the *Geelong and District Societies' Federal Record* by J C Brownhill. The *Record's* aim was to publicize the activities of the many societies in the town and to encourage co-operation amongst them.

CONCLUSION

By the latter years of the nineteenth century, the multiple roles ascribed to the mechanics' institute - as a library, centre for formal technical and scientific education, promoter of respectable entertainment and haven of civilized leisure activities - had, to a large extent, been channelled into a number of more specific agencies. That such a multiplication of agencies for mental improvement should have taken place was not a symptom of the erosion of an ideal. It was instead a recognition of the limitations of certain institutional forms in achieving desired goals. However, the persistent espousal of a 'public' role and integrative social function in connection with 'mental cultivation,' and the limited success in achieving such goals, expresses one of the central contradictions in nineteenth-century colonial society. In spite of the rhetoric, these cultural practices tended to promote social closure. The institute represented some of the dominant cultural attitudes which were widely shared among the town's élite and middling strata, but it never functioned as an instrument of social control over the lower classes of the town. It can be argued that the institutes were poorly equipped to do so, given that they could never compel membership. Moreover, the expectations of most members was that the institute should serve *their* leisure needs. No doubt there was a lingering guilt about the lack of working-class support for an institute whose very name suggested something about its purpose, yet it is equally clear that the members were quite happy with the facilities provided. Far from imposing cultural values on those groups outside its membership, the mechanics' institute effectively reflected and reinforced the leisure patterns and moral ideals of Geelong's dominant socio-economic groups which we attracted to become members. For all intents and purposes it left the working-class to itself, in contrast to the charity agencies which dispensed aid with an explicit message. However, in its own way, the institute *did* reinforce distinctions between the respectable and the marginal. It was an institution which above all gave cultural coherence to the identity of the middling strata which in turn formed the backbone of its support.

NOTES AND REFERENCES

1. Annual Report of the Committee of the Geelong Mechanics' Institute, *Geelong Mechanics' Institute Minute Book* (hereafter cited as *G.M.I.M.B.*), 14 January 1859.

2. Harrison, J.F.C. (1961). *Learning and living, 1790-1960. A study in the history of the English adult education movement.* London: Routledge & Kegan Paul, pp. 43-57;
Altick, R. (1957). *The English Common Reader: A social history of the mass reading public, 1800 - 1900.* Chicago: University of Chicago Press, Chapters 5 and 6;
Roe, M. (1965). *Quest for authority in Eastern Australia 1835-1851.* Melbourne: Melbourne University Press in Association with the Australian National University, Chapters 7-9, passim.

3. Johnson, R. (1979). 'Really useful knowledge': radical education and working-class culture, 1790-1848. In Clarke, J., Critcher, C., & Johnson, R. (Eds.), *Working-class culture. Studies in history and theory.* London: Hutchinson, pp. 75-102;
Tholfsen, T.R. (1976). *Working-class radicalism in mid-Victorian England.* London: Croom Helm, chapters 2 and 3, passim;
Altick, *op. cit.*

4. Harrison, *loc. cit.* The London Mechanics' Institute, established in 1823, was the product of an uneasy alliance of reformers bent on teaching science and political economy to artisans, and articulate and assertive working-class spokesmen demanding a more autonomous and politically oriented educational institution run by artisans themselves. To achieve the official ends of instructing skilled workers in the principles underlying their crafts, classes of instruction, lectures, laboratory and reading room were planned. This was the model for later institutes.

5. Hudson, J.W. (1851). *The History of Adult Education.* London: Longman, Brown, Green and Longmans, p. 52.

6. For example, early in their development, the northern institutes had abandoned the teaching of science since their working-class members were often only barely literate - thus most of their energies were turned towards providing elementary training in reading and writing.   Other institutes inaugurated classes in vocational subjects such as bookkeeping and phonetic shorthand.   Some institutions set examinations for their class members, while others did not.
Inkster, I. (1976). The social context of an educational movement: A revisionist approach to the English mechanics' institutes, 1820-1850. *Oxford Review of Education, 2* (3), pp. 281-282;
Hemming, J.P. (1978). Some attempts at commercial education in the mechanics' institutes. *The Vocational Aspect of Education, 30* (75), pp. 41-42.

7. Engels noted of the institutes: "Here all education is tame, flabby, subservient to the ruling politics and religion, so that for the working man it is merely a constant sermon upon quiet obedience, passivity, and resignation to his fate."
Engels, F. (1892). *The condition of the working-class in England.* London: Allen and Unwin, pp. 264-265. (Originally published 1844 under the title *The condition of the working-class in Manchester*).

ᵟ   ·hester and elsewhere, working class groups seceded from employer-controlled institutes
      ᵻed their own institutions.

      . ₍1982). The division between 'mental' and manual labour: Artisian education in science
    ₋₋ᵤeteenth century Britain. In Buroway, M., & Skocpol, T. (Eds), *Marxist inquiries: Studies of
labor, class and states.* Chicago: University of Chicago Press.

9. Sullivan, M. (1985). *Men and women of Port Phillip.* Sydney: Hale & Iremonger, p. 266.

10. Nadel, G. (1957). *Australia's colonial culture: Ideas, men and institutions in mid-nineteenth
century eastern Australia.* Cambridge, Mass: Harvard University Press, p. 127.

11. *Australian Dictionary of Biography*, Vol. 1., p. 520.; Martin, A.W. (1980). *Henry Parkes: A
biography.* Melbourne: Melbourne University Press, p. 10. For a discussion of this concern to "build
a homogeneous society," see Roe, *op. cit.,* pp. 202, ff.

12. This analysis is part of a larger study of power and social relations in Geelong which formed the
author's doctoral dissertation: Askew, M. (1991). 'A Shapely and Benevolent Civilization':
Interaction and the social order in nineteenth century Geelong c. 1845-1900 *Unpublished. Ph.D
Thesis*, Monash University. Broader judgements rest on research drawn from my Masters' Thesis:
Askew, M. (1982). 'The Diffusion of Useful Knowledge': Mechanics' Institutes in Nineteenth
Century Victoria. *Unpublished Masters' Thesis.* Monash University. 1982.

13. *Geelong Advertiser,* (hereafter cited as *G.A.*) 19 March 1847; 2 April, 1847.

14. *ADB*, Vol. 1, p.520; Hughes, I.A. (1982). *Port Phillip Clergy.* Melbourne: I.A. Hughes, p.26.

15. Among its committee members were the merchants Frederick Champion, Thomas Sheppard,
William Timms and G.T. Lloyd, the leading squatters Edward Willis and William Roadknight and
the small group of local officials including E.B. Addis and Foster Fyans. *G.A.*, 19 December 1844.

16. *G.M.I.M.B.*, 9 December 1846.

17. Nadel, *op. cit.*, p.116.

18. See Nadel, *loc. cit.*; Stannage, C.T. (1979). *The people of Perth: A social history of Western
Australia's capital city.* Perth: Perth City Council, p. 76; Lawson, R. (1973). *Brisbane in the 1890s:
A study of an Australian urban society.* St Lucia, Queensland: Queensland University Press, p. 176.;
G.M.I.M.B. *loc. cit.*

19. *ibid.*, 10 January 1850.

20. *ibid.*, 9 December 1846.

21. *ibid.*, 23 July 1849.

22. Source: *Catalogue of the books in the library of the Geelong Mechanics' Institute, 1850* (Geelong,
1850).

23. Sullivan, *op. cit.*, p. 271.

Geelong Mechanics' Institute, Vic 1866 and 1915
(reproduced by permission of the Geelong Historical Records Centre)

24. For a discussion see, Askew, M. & Hubber, B. (1988). The colonial reader observed: Reading in its cultural context. In Borchardt, D.H., & Kirsop, W. (Eds.), *The book in Australia. Essays towards a cultural and social history*. Melbourne: Australian Reference Publications in association with the Centre for Bibliographical and Textual Studies, Monash University, pp. 110-138.

25. *ibid.*, pp. 114-115.

26. *G.M.I.M.B.*, 10 January 1850.

27. *ibid.*, 31 January 1851.

28. *ibid.*, 30 June 1851.

29. *ibid.*, 13 August 1852.

30. *ibid.*, 11 May 1849.

31. *ibid.*, 7 February 1848.

32. *ibid.*, 1846-50 passim; 13 August 1852.

33. àBeckett, W. ('Colonus') (1852). *Does the Discovery of Gold...deserve to be considered a national blessing, or a national curse?* Melbourne: Benjamin Lucas, printer;
Mereweather, J.D., (1859). *Diary of a working clergyman in Australia and Tasmania.* London: Hatchard, pp.26-34.

34. anon. (1857). The intellectual opportunities of the working-man in Victoria. *Illustrated Journal of Australasia, I*, pp. 169-170.

35. *Census of Victoria, 1854*, 'Occupations of the People.'

36. *G.A.*, 12 April 1854.

37. *ibid.*, 28 August 1854.

38. *Argus*, 24 February 1855.

39. Askew, M. 'The Diffusion of Useful Knowledge': Mechanics' institutes in nineteenth century Victoria, *op. cit.,* p.82.

40. *G.A.*, 16 January 1855.

41. *ibid.*

42. *G.M.I.M.B.*, 16 February 1855.

43. "The Geelong Mechanic's Institute has for its object the diffusion of literary, scientific and other useful knowledge, the intellectual advancement and recreation of its members generally." *ibid.*, 20 June 1856.

44. *G.M.I.M.B.* 14 January 1859.

45. *ibid.*, 4 September 1856, 17 September 1857, 3 February 1858.

46. Askew, *op. cit.*, pp.63-64.

47. *G.M.I.M.B.*, 4 September 1856.

48. *ibid.*, 16 January 1857.

49. Its chairman was G.M. Hitchcock, prosperous draper and active Wesleyan layman. *ibid.*, 17 June 1858.

50. *ibid.*, 14 January 1859.

51. Geelong Mechanics' Institute Annual Reports. In *G.M.I.M.B.*, 1854-1859.

52. *G.A.*, 1 December 1858.

53. *ibid.*

54. Among the merchants serving as office-bearers in the first five years were J.F. Strachan, M.L.C. Alexander Fyfe, M.L.C. James Balfour, George Board and James Guthrie. The professionals were well represented by George Belcher Sr. (solicitor), H.E. Combe (solicitor), Robert Pincott (surgeon), Dr. J. Strutt, Dr., V. Kilgour and J.S. Hill (accountant and actuary). Other prominent members included Vincent Giblin (bank manager) and Charles Sladen, M.L.A.

55. *ibid.*, 18 December 1860.

56. *ibid.*

57. *G.M.I.M.B.*, 11 January 1861.

58. *ibid.*, 13 January 1856, 12 January 1866, 11 January 1867.

59. *ibid.*, 11 January 1861.

60. Statements of Income and Expenditure. In *G.M.I.M.B.*, 1860-1865.

61. By 1874 subscriptions accounted for 58 percent of the institute's funds, with fees from the hire of the hall representing 21 percent.

62. Among them were Archibald Michie, leading barrister; David Blair, journalist; Dr. J. Bromby; Dr. John Macadam and Charles Smith.

63. *G.A.*, 25 May 1860.

64. *Geelong Register* (hereafter referred to as *G.R.*), 17 April 1865.

65. *G.A.*, 15 November, 11 December 1861, 15 October 1864.

66. *G.R.*, 6 April 1865, 15, 20 May 1868; *Geelong Evening Times,* 8 November 1871.

67. *G.A.*, 11 December 1861.

68. Petition having reference to the manner in which the 'Mechanics' Institute' is conducted in Geelong, 10 April 1865. (*Chief Secretary's Correspondence.* VPRS 3991/L3477).

69. *ibid.*, VPRS 3991/M6483.

70. *ibid.*, VPRS 3991/N9556.

71. It was reopened for a short time, but in April 1865 it was closed again. *G.A.*, 12 December 1861, 23 December 1861; *G. R.*, 3 April, 1865. For the business failure and subsequent suicide of the theatre proprietor, see Askew, 'A Shapely and benevolent civilization.' *op. cit.*, chapter 5.

72. *G.R.*, 6 April 1865.

73. *ibid.*

74. *ibid.*, 8 April 1865, 11 April 1865.

75. *ibid.*, 17 April 1865.

76. *ibid.*, 10 April 1865.

77. *ibid.*, 11 April 1865.

78. *G.M.I.M.B.*, 12 January 1865; 11 January 1866.

79. *ibid.*, 14 January 1864.

80. In 1861 females in the age cohorts 20-40 constituted nearly 19 percent of the population, while males in the same age groups represented 16 percent. By 1871, females in this age group in Geelong represented 14 percent and males only 9 percent of the total population. *Census of Victoria*, 1861, 1871, 'Ages of the People.'

81. *G.M.I.M.B.*, 19 January 1881.

82. *G.A.*, 13 January 1869; *G.R.*, 2 July 1868.

83. *G.A.*, 13 January 1869.

84. *G.M.I.M.B.*, 1 February 1861, 6 March 1863, 13 January 1865.

85. *G.R.*, 29 May 1868. In the following month it was reported: "These adjuncts are undoubtedly a great assistance to the Institute itself, for already some four or five gentlemen have become members of the Mechanics' Institute for the express purpose of joining the chess club." *ibid.*, 3 June 1868.

86. Meller, H.E., (1976). *Leisure and the changing city, 1870.- 1914*. London: Routledge & Kegan Paul, pp.134-137.

87. *G.R.*, 19 May 1868.

88. *ibid.*, 15 July 1868.

89. anon. (1871). *The spirit of the town*. Geelong: Henry Franks, printer, p.4.

90. *ibid.*, pp.7-8.

91. *G.R.,* 20 April 1865.

92. Allred, J.R. (1972). The purpose of the public library: the historical view, *Library History,*2(5) pp.185-204;
Bailey, P. (1978). *Leisure and class in Victorian England: Rational recreation and the contest for control, 1830-1885.* London: Routledge & Kegan Paul, p.39; The Melbourne *Argus* (9 April 1862) stressed that "For the maintenance of order and the guardianship of public morals, a library...is as efficacious as a troop of police."

93. *Municipal Institutions Act,* 1854 [Colony of Victoria] 18 Vict., No. 15. Section 28.

94. *Victorian Parliamentry Debates,* 1867, Vol. III, pp. 819-820, 834; Vol. IV, p.992.

95. *ibid.*

96. Thomson, K., & Serle, G. (1972). *A biographical register of the Victorian parliament, 1851-1900.* Canberra: Australian National University Press, p.16: As editor of the *Collingwood Observer* in the early 1860s, Berry had championed the establishment of a free public library in that Melbourne suburb. *Collingwood Observer,* 3 March 1862, 5 March 1864. These references to Berry in Collingwood were kindly supplied by Brian Hubber.

97. See Askew, 'A shapely and benevolent civilization,' *op. cit.,* chapters 5 and 12.

98. *ibid.,* chapter 13

99. *G.M.I.M.B.,* 14 January 1876.

100. Geelong Mechanics' Institute, subscription list for 1873. (*Chief Secretary's Correspondence,* VPRS 3991/74/998.) Occupations were identified through directories and rate books.

101. *G.A.,* 7 August 1870.

102. *ibid.*

103. The advertisement for a 'Scientific Conversazione' in March 1872, introduced the program by listing the mysterious scientific apparatus to be revealed: 'Microscopes, Pneumatic Apparatus, Electrical Machines, Galvanic Batteries, Induction Coils, Rotating Magnets.' The programme would begin with an address by the Rev. C.S.M. Price on 'Searching for Truth,' followed by an explanation of the electric telegraph. Following a musical interlude, Mr. Charles Kernot would conclude the conversazione "by the display of a variety of brilliant chemical experiments." *ibid.,* 15 March 1872.

104. *ibid.*

105. *G.A.,* 8 August 1870.

106. Annual Report 1876. In *G.M.I.M.B.*

107. Sillcock, K.M. (1982). G.F. Link: Early educationalist. *Investigator,* *17*(2), pp.55-59.

108. *Age,* 8 June 1889.

109. Among them the Rev. Charles Strong, S. McBurney and the Rev. Charles Clarke

110. *G.M.I.M.B.*, 10 January 1884, 14 January 1885, 10 January 1888.

111. *Belcher Diary*, 2 November 1874.

112. *G.M.I.M.B.*, 11 March 1887.

113. *ibid.*, 18 March, 7 October 1887.

114. Annual Reports and Balance Sheets. In *G.M.I.M.B.*

115. *G.M.I.M.B.*, 24 March 1891.

116. *G.A.*, 6 January 1891.

117. *ibid.*, 31 January 1892.

118. *G.M.I.M.B.*, 14 January 1894.

119. *ibid.*, 11 January 1897.

120. *G.A.*, 12 April 1854.

121. Geelong Mechanics' Institute Literary and Debating Society. *Minute Book*, 29 April 1868. (G.H.R.C. Ser. 113/1.)

122. *G.R.*, 22 May 1868.

123. In June 1868 the class was debating the question of the disestablishment of the Church of Ireland (the Chairman commended the class on the good feeling maintained), and in August it discussed payment of Members of Parliament. (G.M.I. Literary and Debating Society. *Minute Book*, 10 June, 17 June, 12 August 1868.)

124. *G.A.*, 31 January 1877.

125. *ibid.*

126. *ibid.*

127. G.M.I. Literary and Debating Society. *Minute Book*, passim. Directories and Rate Books. In 1889 Julian Thomas remarked that the members of the discussion class were "principally old citizens." *Age*, 8 June 1889.

128. *The Catholic Directory, and Almanac, for the Clergy and Laity in Victoria, 1863*. By authority of the Rt Rev Bishop of Melbourne. Melbourne: Michael T. Gason, publisher; Thomas Verga, printer, 1863; *G.R.*, 17 April 1865.

CHAPTER SEVEN

'RESPECTABLE' AND 'USEFUL': THE INSTITUTE MOVEMENT IN WESTERN AUSTRALIA

Peter Rose, Wendy Birman and Michael White

INTRODUCTION

The past decade has witnessed a growing interest in Australian library history among members of the library profession and the wider community. Four forums focussing on this theme have been held in recent years (Monash University 1984 and 1989; Canberra College of Advanced Education 1985; University of New South Wales 1987), and the published papers from these forums provide thought-provoking and interesting reading.[1] In addition, several other works contribute significantly to the literature in the field of library history: Jones's study of the State Library of New South Wales,[2] Levett's work on the Tasmanian State Library,[3] Bridge's history of the State Library of South Australia[4] and, most relevant to the present chapter, Cook's work on Public Libraries in Western Australia.[5]

In most parts of Australia, early library services were provided by churches and sunday schools, and through organisations variously referred to as mechanics' institutes, schools of arts, literary institutes, or in the case of South Australia, simply as 'institutes.' Orlovich,[6] Hubber[7] and Talbot[8] have written on aspects of institute libraries in New South Wales, Victoria and South Australia respectively.

While many of these authors' observations relating to the establishment and conduct of institute libraries in other states may apply equally to similar establishments in Western Australia, it appears that the institute movement was neither as widespread nor as successful there as in some other parts of the country. In his 1947 Report on Australian Library Services, McColvin - the City Librarian of Westminster, and Honorary Secretary of the Library Association (UK) - described library services in Western Australia in the following, less than flattering, terms:

> Very little has been done so far to provide library services in Western Australia. As already noted, there are no municipal libraries even in Perth and Fremantle; even institutes with all their shortcomings are less common than in, say South Australia or Queensland.[9]

One purpose of this chapter, therefore, is to explore the history of the mechanics' institute movement in Western Australia, and to consider why - at least as far as library services are concerned - the movement enjoyed only indifferent success there.

Perhaps more importantly, however, it is evident that the provision of library services was only one aspect of the social, cultural and educational role of the institutes.[10] Accordingly, a second major purpose of this chapter is to examine the foundation and functioning of Western Australian institutes within the broader context of 'progress' and 'self-improvement';

concepts that were so emblematic of the Victorian and early Edwardian eras, when the institute movement flourished.

Finally, it is evident that the colony's isolation and its early pattern of settlement and economic growth gave greater prominence to mining and agriculture than in other places. This in turn led to the foundation of other types of institutes and societies than the often-misnamed mechanics' institutes. Thus the third purpose of this chapter is to examine the emergence of alternative but nonetheless kindred organisations which served purposes similar to those of the mechanics' institutes in the western third of the continent.

THE EARLY INSTITUTES

The emergence of mechanics' institutes in Western Australia can hardly be considered one of the highlights of colonial history. The movement was neither led by an inspired educator like Reverend Henry Carmichael in Sydney,[11] nor did it arise as a result of grass roots pressure from a group of master tradesmen as at Hobart in 1827.[12] Instead it grew in a desultory and sporadic way, following the pattern of settlement and growth which itself was influenced by the unique circumstances of the colony's establishment.

Lacking either the systematic approach to settlement that characterised South Australia, or the government-supported infrastructure of the convict colonies, the early settlers were predicably preoccupied with the difficulties of nation-building in the harsh and unforgiving wilderness. As a consequence, the first three institutes appeared in the three earliest centres of settlement (Perth, Fremantle and Albany), more than twenty years after the first settlers arrived, and a further decade was to elapse before the movement spread to other towns and cities in the colony.

In this part of the chapter, the history of those three earliest institutes, which provided a model for subsequent developments, is detailed before passing on to a consideration of the spread of the movement.

The Swan River Mechanics' Institute[13]

The mechanics' institute in Perth was not only the first to be established, but also served as a prototype and model for many others that developed across the state. In his history of Perth, Stannage[14] describes the first attempt to establish a mechanics' institute as early as 1842, when Charles Foulkes, a painter by trade, called mechanics to a meeting at his house. By March, the new institute had acquired a library from either the Perth Book Society or the Western Australian Book Society, both gentry-run clubs which foundered at about this time. However, the institute did not appear to receive support either from the gentry - it was not, for example, offered land or financial support by the Government - or from artisans, and consequently it failed within a few months.

The next serious attempt to found a mechanics' institute occurred almost a decade later, by which stage the movement was well advanced in most other Australian colonies. On 28 January 1851, an inaugural meeting took place at the Perth Courthouse, for the purpose of laying down the rules for an association to be known as the Swan River Mechanics' Institute. On this occasion, according to Stannage, "the initiative came less from the artisans than from the gentry," in what he describes as "yet another attempt to preserve the social distinctions so necessary for the achievement of 'internal peace'."[15] Judging from the official support later enjoyed by the institute, Stannage's judgement is probably correct.

The Institute's object was clearly stated "to benefit the mechanics and young men of the colony, affording them an unobjectionable mode of recreation and improvement." This aim was to be achieved through the medium of weekly meetings at which discussions of literary, scientific or other useful topics were to be conducted. According to Stannage, the regulations required that the topics chosen for discussion in literary meetings should carefully exclude all questions "of controversial theology, party politics, or of an immoral tendency."[16] Classes for mutual instruction in useful branches of knowledge were to be arranged, likewise, and a wide range of lectures was to be given. In addition a museum was to be formed and a library developed; its reading room was to be open to all members and subscribers to the institute.

Officially, membership was unlimited, with nominees being selected by ballot without regard to their party, religion, nationality or residence, unless a person was generally known to be of immoral character. According to Stannage, the establishment of the institute in January 1851, less than a year after the arrival of the first convicts in Western Australia, was an attempt by the free artisans and builders of Perth to distance themselves from the bond men. Support for this view is to be found in the fact that bond men were not eligible to join the Institute. In June 1852 there was an unsuccessful attempt to persuade the office bearers to admit ticket-of-leave men, as it was considered undesirable for them to join another group - which did in fact eventually happen[17]. The annual subscription was ten shillings and the government granted a block of land valued at £10 on the corner of Hay and Pier Streets, Perth. On that site a single storey building known as the Mechanics' Hall was erected. After a mere three years, it appears that the gentry were well pleased with the progress of the Institute. An entry in *The Western Australian Almanac* for 28 January 1854 reads:

> Anniversary meeting of the Mechanics' Institute took place at their Hall, Perth, and was attended by most of the inhabitants of Perth, from the Governor downwards. This institute has done much towards improving the moral and intellectual character of the operative classes, and has achieved even more than could have been anticipated by its original supporters.[18]

In May 1854 the trustees, J S Roe, R J Scholl and G Shenton were notified that the Government had approved an additional grant of the adjacent block (Perth Building Lot 14). In 1860 the Legislative Council voted £200 towards a building which was opened at an anniversary luncheon on 11 February 1861, followed by a ball in the evening. Finally the legislature donated £48 to liquidate the building debt and £50 to allow for setting up a museum.

The Institute purported to serve the educational and recreational needs of the working class, but egalitarian principles did not extend to the governing body, whose composition reflected the normal social hierarchy. The executive consisted of community leaders (the Governor being patron and the Surveyor-General, John Septimus Roe, President) assisted by "so many Vice-Presidents as shall make a donation of money, books or articles of utility" (in 1864 the number of Vice-Presidents was fixed at four) and five committee members.[19]

Day-to-day administration of the Institute's affairs was left to a working committee whose members were mainly tradesmen; however, the President attended the Institute's annual general meetings and, by invitation, special meetings if difficulties arose. For instance, on 14 August 1854 the working committee was perplexed as to how to deal with Richard Birnie (the Advocate-General). Birnie wrote to the committee in strong terms saying that he would not be harassed by extortionate letters and threats, and that he was weary of a dull monotonous malignity and imputed selfish and unworthy motives.[20]

On the matter of leadership, one of the early men who from the first displayed a consistent interest in the mechanics' institutes generally, and the Swan River Institute in particular, was George Randell. Randell's position is especially significant because he not only played a leading role in education generally through membership of the Central Board of Education, but because in 1880 he took the first official steps to prod the Government into action on technical education. Later, as Minister for Education in the Forrest Government, he was actually to see his labours bear fruit in the form of the Perth Technical School, which was opened in 1900.

Probably the most stimulating educational developments at the Swan River Mechanics' Institute occurred in its earliest years. One of the key figures during the fifties was Joseph Thomas Reilly, who joined the Institute in 1854, and became Secretary in 1856. In his autobiography entitled *Reminiscences of Fifty Years' Residence in Western Australia*, he writes:

> I always felt a deep interest in the purposes of this valuable institution, and took full advantage of its excellent library and other facilities which it afforded for self-improvement. The discussion classes, in the early days, were a very attractive means for the diffusion of knowledge, and although its educational value was not of so much importance, still there can be no doubt that the 'discussion class' stimulated a desire for self-culture, and created a yearning to acquire a miscellaneous store of useful and practical information.[21]

Reilly goes on to mention a number of notable early supporters of the Institute:

> In the fifties, the institute was sell patronised by a number of gentlemen who had had a fair amount of mental training, and hence the various meetings never failed to prove deeply interesting. Among those who frequently attended the discussion class were Mr Johnstone, Mr Bernard Smith, Mr Michael Smith, Mr R Pether, Mr A Durlacher, Mr F Barlee (Colonial Secretary), and the Anglican Dean of Perth, the Very Rev G P Pownall. The Dean had an appreciable taste for literature, and his numerous lectures were specially noted for their ability, and were always largely attended. Indeed, no person worked so assiduously to promote the success of the institute as did Dean Pownall. His lectures on Tennyson were excellent, and his appreciation of the writings of the great poet did very much to make them familiar with the whole community. The Dean was also very fond of natural philosophy, and his numerous illustrations of the power and value of the microscope can be gratefully remembered ....

The Hon J S Roe (Surveyor-General) also took a warm interest in the institute, but his efforts on its behalf were more practical than literary. The Colonial Secretary, Mr F P Barlee, was a periodical lecturer, and the subjects he selected were always eminently practical as well as useful. Dean Pownall and Mr Barlee did not, however, agree on many points, and, as a consequence, the harmony of the meetings was often disturbed by a rencontre between the Dean and Mr Barlee ....

Mr A Durlacher was another popular lecturer, and his treatment of physical geography was always very much admired. The Rev J Johnston, Congregational minister of Fremantle, was also a warm supporter of the institute, and his lectures always drew large audiences. Another lecturer and ardent supporter of the institute was Mr Henry Trigg, one of the earliest settlers, whose name is closely identified with the early history of the colony.[22]

In addition to these relatively distinguished members, who did so much to give the Institute its reputation as a 'gentlemen's club,' there were many others who made a significant contribution to the early life of the organization. One such was H H Hughes, a compositor and one of the instigators of the Institute. He saw a need for classes in geography, mechanics and history and offered his services to publish the proceedings. Hughes departed in 1857.

Another of the first instructors was William Johnstone, a teacher sent to the colony by the Home and Colonial Church Society as a religious instructor in the convict ship, the *Dudbrooke*, in February 1853. Three months later he had become headmaster of Perth Boys' School, which was accommodated at the Mechanics' Hall until its own premises were ready.[23] Johnstone lectured to the mechanics on self-improvement and offered to give classes on physical geography. He also urged that speakers should be sought among the ordinary members instead of soliciting gentlemen to favour them with addresses.[24] The latter was not a new concept to the working committee which was still smarting with the memory of a debacle in August 1852, when Mr Burnell, a mechanic, lectured on phonography. On that occasion, the organisers received little encouragement because of "the absence of the officers, who, in common courtesy, ought to have supported any lecturer, whose services they accepted, and more particularly, when the lecturer was avowedly a member of the class for whose special benefit the Institute is supposed to be formed...Mr Burnell was certainly a competent master of his subject."[25] Johnstone left the colony under a cloud at the beginning of 1855, there having been several complaints of his cruel treatments of the schoolboys and his 'nasty temper.'[26]

The other lively mainstay of the Swan River Mechanics' Institute was Joseph Chester, a radical carpenter,[27] with an eloquent turn of phrase and a commitment to the advancement of the working man. A long time advocate of the basic principles of the mechanics' movement, Chester wanted technically-oriented classes. Elected chairman in 1856-7, he did not succeed in organising any vocational courses, but Monday evening discussions were regular events under his leadership. In fact, the discussion classes, or 'debates,' were a regular feature of the intellectual life of the Institute throughout its early years. The meetings were well attended, and they dealt with a great range of topics, both contemporary and historical. Between 1853 and 1855, for instance, members considered subjects such as whether the coloured races were, as alleged, inferior in intellect to white men; whether the coming of convicts had been as beneficial to the Colony as had been expected; whether death was the result of organic laws, or was the special Act of the Diety; whether there was any justification for capital punishment; and whether women do or would possess the same amount of intellect as men if they had the same advantages.

Not all the topics were controversial, some concerned erudite historical issues, but in either case, as Smith points out:

> The discussions were undoubtedly of educational value. A debate extended over a number of evenings, and between meetings the members prepared their arguments from books which they frequently quoted. Each speaker's argument was recorded in the minutes to ensure continuity of ideas. An imaginative secretary would be inspired by the scene before him to record not only the arguments advanced but the dramatic by-play of interjection and protest when passions were aroused, or the loud cheers that greeted a popular speaker rising to his feet.[28]

In her book of documents on Western Australian social history, *Westralian Voices*, Aveling reproduces lengthy extracts from three of these discussions. It is evident that the Minute Secretaries were not trained stenographers; the reports are mostly disjointed paraphrases of each speaker's contribution. Nonetheless, it is possible to gain a rare insight into the interests, understandings, prejudices, and beliefs of these "respectable, God-fearing men"[29] as they talked honestly and often passionately about a range of matters.

Interestingly, one of the books commonly invoked as a source of authority during the debates was the Bible, though on one occasion, when discussing women's intellect, Mr Farelly quoted from a 1784 encyclopaedia of philosophy, and during the same discussion, an extract was read from:

> a work entitled *Pursuit of Knowledge Under Difficulties*[30] showing that several characters among men of different occupations and generally arising from the humble stations had excelled (in a widely different sphere [from that] in which they were brought up in) as Poets, Musicians, Architects, Lawyers, etc., and in the various sciences among astronomers etc., while they were engaged in their various everyday pursuits, and that their humble circumstances did not prevent them overcoming great difficulties they had to contend with.[31]

This attitude towards self-improvement was a recurring motif in the educational endeavours not only of the Swan River Institute, but indeed of the mechanics' institute movement throughout the English-speaking world. In 1857, Chester went to Victoria, where he was soon involved in the working class movement and was much impressed by the achievements of the eastern mechanics. Disillusioned at the lack of spirit when he returned to Western Australia in October 1865, he was outspokenly critical of the Swan River Mechanics' Institute, which he considered had taken a retrograde step. There were no classes, discussion groups had lapsed, and the library had "become a Reading Room for gentlemen and could not now be considered to be a 'Mechanics' Institute'"[32]; indeed more books were borrowed by their wives than by working men themselves.

Chester continued pursuing his cause at Guildford, where he was a committee man and occasional chairman of the local institute. A minute of the Guildford Mechanics Institute aptly described the general attitude to adult learning in 1867:

> Upon the subject of classes your committee can say little, almost every attempt to establish such having fallen through. The Guildford Institute is not singular in this, regular classes such as the members of Mechanics' Institutes should form themselves into being rarely perennial. The minutes of preceding years inform us that this Institute possessed a creditable discussion class, which however, was allowed to lapse.[33]

Chester was right. Although intellectuals like Roe and his colleagues paid lip-service to the educational role of the Institute, they actually preferred "to spend a quiet evening with the books and newspapers, free of the distraction of a 'noisy discussion class'"[34] to keep themselves informed of developments in other parts of the world. During the 1860s, Roe and several other Honorary members did nothing to prevent the decline of the Institute into a gentlemen's reading room and, although Chester succeeded in reinstating the classes, it was only for a brief period. As often as not the sessions were cancelled for want of a quorum or because the speaker pleaded insufficient time to prepare his paper. One or two *ad lib* discussions on the state of the Colony bitterly reflected the sad situation of the artisan. It was said that there was no encouragement for a high class tradesman to pursue his craft in Western Australia - cabinet maker turned carpenter; carpenter became a shingler; the tin man believed himself a genuine plumber and some farmers were also importing merchants.[35] And so ended the heyday of the Swan River Mechanics' Institute, although, to a farewell deputation of its members, Governor Kennedy was pleased to commend the Institute's achievements, praising its activities and declaring that they provided a powerful antidote to the forms of frivolity and dissipation that would otherwise attract working-class men in their leisure hours.

Not only was the Institute largely the preserve of the well-to-do, but, as Spencer points out in her *History of the Library Movement in Western Australia*, it became increasingly undimensional, because "Gradually the library became more and more the main function ..., in 1860 it was regarded as one of the most attractive features of the institute."[36] She goes on to write:

> The library in this year was particularly well stocked and well used, with 3,600 volumes being issued during the year[37] (an increase of 900 over the previous year). A large number of books were added (chiefly scientific) so that in the collection, those in science, arts and manufactures maintained priority over fiction and those merely for amusement.

> It is noticeable that in the library at least, the main aim was still to educate the people, although in the other spheres of its work, the Swan River Mechanics' Institute was not quite so successful, virtually neglecting all other sections of the organisation. The reading room was also stacked with English and Colonial newspapers and gradually it developed into a nightly rendezvous for the members, who would read, or play chess or draughts. In 1861 a new building was added to serve as a museum, but this did not detract from the importance of the library.[38]

Despite the efforts of Joseph Chester, it is evident that "by 1868 most of the other activities had been overwhelmed by the library."[39]   Stannage concludes that by 1875, "The Mechanics' Institute became solely a literary and entertainment society, largely for men who moved in the best social circles."[40]   Ironically, not only did the institute attract criticism because of its socially-exclusive character, but even the quality of its library was questioned. According to Spencer, by the mid 1870s, the quality of the books had lapsed:

> the principal demand being for romances, novels and other light literature, and the institute had therefore declined considerably in its educational value.   Further criticism of the library itself appeared in the *Western Australian Times* in March 1876.   This article scornfully described the chaotic arrangement of the books, their dusty and dilapidated condition; while the reading room was mentioned as being dim, dusty and uncomfortable.   Such an unfavourable impression is gathered from this graphic account, that it must have had a considerable effect on the Colonists at the time.   The committee defended themselves by blaming a lack of enthusiasm on the part of the members.   Even so the library was still well patronised and filled an important part in the cultural interests of the city....

> In 1882 we find the mechanics' institutes being regarded purely as libraries, with no mention being made of other aspects of their work.   An article in the *Herald* that year discusses the Swan River Mechanics' Institute's library, considering it as an ill-assorted collection of books, of very little use to anyone.[41]   This chaotic selection was mostly due to the lack of knowledge on the part of the committee, who left the choice to the booksellers from whom they bought these books; in spite of this, the committee did their best, struggling against lack of knowledge and lack of financial aid.[42]

A year later, the Swan River Mechanics' Institute and other such institutes in the colony were still being roundly criticised for their failure to provide a proper educational service, or for that matter, even a suitably 'improving' library scheme:

> They were disdainfully marked down as poorly supplied circulating libraries that did nothing to encourage the reading of good literature; instead they pandered to the lowest tastes 'by supplying the public with sensational, nasty novels.'[43]   Yet in spite of all the criticisms, it was recognised that the mechanics' institutes were the only places in Western Australia that did provide libraries.   Even if they fell short of the condition of a public library, they were at least readily available to the majority of the people.[44]

A decade later again, things did not seem to have improved much.   Tacitly, the Swan River Mechanics' Institute seems to have taken on the role of a circulating library instead of public institution, but it was still held in low esteem.   This can be seen in this scornful description of the type of literature it contained: "You can get well-thumbed copies of *One-Eyed Dick*, or *Bill, the Murderer*, and books of that sort, but of really useful books, they are not there."[45]

Recognising the irrevocably changed nature of its clientele and its main activities, the institute's name was finally changed on 15 December 1909 to the 'Perth Literary Institute' to more accurately reflect its role. This represented for the Swan River Mechanics' Institute the final breaking of its traditional link with the working-class.

Despite the recurrent criticism over the years, about its élitism and lack of popular appeal, physically the Swan River Institute grew substantially. As previously mentioned, the Legislative Council in 1854 authorised an additional grant of adjacent land, and in 1860, it also voted £200 toward the cost of a new building. The second building was officially opened at the tenth anniversary luncheon on 11 February 1861, followed by a ball in the evening. The Government also donated £50 towards the cost of equipping a museum, the basis of which consisted of Roe's personal collection. After initial hesitancy donations were received from other colonists during the eighteen eighties. In 1886 the Government vested full rights, except the power to sell, over the land in the Institute and in 1896 the body was incorporated under the *Associations Incorporation Act* (1895), which was intended to encourage the development of "churches, chapels, and all religious bodies, schools, hospitals, and all benevolent and charitable institutions, mechanics' institutes, and all associations for the purpose of promoting and encouraging literature, science and art."[46]

The discovery of gold heralded an era of optimism throughout the colony; the Institute responded by commissioning William Wolff to design a new building. The foundation stone of the new structure was laid on 28 June 1898, and its final cost was £9,360. A brochure, published at the turn of the century, describes the Institute as possessing the best features of a club, but with other features of a more literary character. It boasted a large reading room, writing tables and requisite materials. Expansive balconies extended around the building and above a row of shops that were let to increase the Institute income. Facilities were provided for billiards, whist, draughts and chess. Lectures were undertaken from time to time and occasional socials were arranged to promote good feeling among the 1,000 paying members.

In the field of liberal adult education there was a slight resurgence of interest during the pre-war years. The establishment of a western university was imminent and in cooperation with the Perth Extension Committee, an offshoot of the University committee to administer public examinations on behalf of the Adelaide University, the Institute launched a series of lectures. Between 1908 and 1914, public lectures were given by G C Henderson, Professor of History at Adelaide and Chairman of the Extension Board, and later by the foundation Professors at the University of Western Australia, W Murdoch and A D Ross.

After the war a few lectures were again presented at the Institute, but interest lagged until, as an aftermath of the Institute's centennial celebrations,[47] a final effort was made in 1953. A course of lectures was then presented by the Adult Education Board of the University of Western Australia. The series cost £35 and it was stipulated that such expenditure would not be repeated "unless requested by members."[48] The course, however, was poorly attended; films from the visual education section of the Education Department proved more popular. On 30 June 1957, in accordance with the provisions of the *Library Act* (1951), the Perth City Council absorbed the Institute's collection in the city's free lending library.

Fremantle Mechanics' Institute

Although Fremantle was the second township in Western Australia to form a mechanics' institute, the concern to provide some sort of cultural stimulus can be traced back to the first few months of settlement. As early as 1831, "a literary society had been formed and an Agricultural Society was enthusiastically discussing the problems inherent in the cultivation of the soil in a new country."[49]

Not unexpectedly, the exigencies of trying to establish a viable settlement in this harsh and remote corner of Australia distracted the early settlers from such lofty pursuits as the study of literature, and it was not for a further twenty years, on 30 July 1851, that a meeting was held at Wellard's Hotel in Fremantle to form a mechanics' institute at the port. In the absence of the proposed President, R McB Brown, the meeting was chaired by Dr Shipton, the surgeon at the Convict Establishment. The Governor was invited to become patron and Mr Davey to chair the working committee. The usual aims were expressed and planning began on an inaugural series of lectures on mechanical and fine arts. Within a week, 32 men were admitted to membership.[50] The most significant difference between the Swan River and Fremantle institutes was that the latter admitted ex-convicts. But like Perth, in the mid-'fifties a hard core of working-class members from Fremantle drifted to the goldfields in other colonies and the Mechanics' Institute's activities tapered off to such an extent that it was obliged to go into recess in 1854. Resuming activities in 1857, it again dwindled until it too eventually degenerated into a gentlemen's reading room.[51]

In 1862 a breakaway group formed a Working Men's Association at Fremantle and, in 1863, because of its club-like role, the Government reduced the Institute's subsidy, withholding it entirely in 1864. The loss of the grant triggered an effort to revitalise the Fremantle Mechanics' Institute. It was decided to form two separate committees, one representing non-mechanics and the other the mechanics, to consider the position, and on 8 June 1864 a petition was forwarded to the Government seeking reinstatement of the grant. The report of the mechanics' committee points out just how different were the cultural objectives of the different classes in the community:

> The direction of the Fremantle Mechanics' Institute being at present greatly swayed by the upper classes, the lower do not feel for the Institute as theirs - thus antagonism or indifference spring up, producing apathy in those who stand aloof and discouragement in those willing to act.

> Experience teaches that the higher and lower classes never do work well together in the conduct of Public Affairs...An efficient mixed management by both classes is impossible, tastes differ, the action of an inferior in the presence of his superior becomes constrained and degenerates into mere patronage on the one hand, dependence on the other, resulting in indifference.[52]

The Committee of the reconstituted Institute was to consist, except for ceremonial positions, of members of the mechanic class, where the term 'mechanic' was redefined to refer to one "whose chief means of subsistence is derived from the labour bestowed on raw products of nature or the materials elaborated therefrom, and on the various workings up of the same, artistic or otherwise for the food, raiment, habitation, convenience and comfort of civilised life, whether as daily labourers therein or as the employers of such labour, in other words, as mechanics or master mechanics, also traders not being wholesale."[53] This also led to a reduction in the membership, only this time it was dissenting members of the upper class who withdrew from the Institute.[54]

135

For more than six years, the two groups - Working Men's Association and Mechanics' Institute - coexisted uneasily, but finally on 10 August 1868, the committee of the Fremantle Mechanics' Institute decided that it should join the splinter group. An advertisement in *The Herald* on 15 August 1868 advised the formation, on 31 August 1868, of The Fremantle Literary Institute, "being an amalgamation of the two cultural bodies existing in the town." Members of the existing organisations were to have access to their combined library facilities, however "NO BOOKS would be issued to members of late Mechanics' Institute or Working Men's Association in arrears of membership dues!!!"[55]

Initially, the Literary Institute occupied the premises of the old Association on the corner of Cliff and Dalgety Streets (later Croke Lane), Fremantle. However, during 1876-77 a new site for the Institute was selected on a triangular block of land bounded by Collie Street, Market Street and South Terrace; and "in 1879, the Institute erected its first premises..., reportedly erected at a cost of £1,000; this venue housed the society for twenty years."[56] Like so many similar organisations elsewhere in Australia, the Institute came under the acerbic notice of the local press, and was castigated for its ineffectiveness:

> *Fremantle Literary Institute* now 15 years old, noticeable for *intolerance and apathy of management*. It consists of a little cheap lending library and an untidy table strewn with periodicals of the nursery-maid type. During the past 12 months no new books had been purchased. In a community of 4,000 souls, 30 new members had been registered, together with 28 resignations! The Debit Balance at the National Bank amounted to £21/-/-. The Government grant was £50/-/-, plus, any Government publications that were issued. 1882 book issues 2369 and magazines 1258. Committee *promised* to do better in 1883![57]

Despite such criticism, the Institute - like its counterpart in Perth - continued to grow.

Perhaps buoyed by the discovery of gold, and its dramatic effect on the West Australian economy, and almost certainly spurred on by the opening of the new Institute building in Perth, the Committee of the Literary Institute announced a competition for the design of a new building. The competition was won by Wilkinson, Smith and Wilson, architects.

The new building was erected in South Terrace. It was an impressive two-storey structure, built on a corner site, and had an imposing façade. It was opened on 15 March 1899 by the President, Elias Solomon, who was also Member of the Legislative Assembly for East Fremantle. Originally the ground floor consisted of two shops and a main hall with an ante room. The library itself was located in the upper storey. This extract from the *West Australian* describes the accommodation:

> The public hall is recessed from the street with a portico in front. The dimensions of the hall are 40 feet by 20 feet with a raised platform at the back 13 feet 6 inches deep and the walls are decorated with dado and stencilling work. The entrance to the Library is on the right hand side of the hall, with a five foot passage to the staircase. The stairway is constructed of jarrah with turned balusters. On the upper storey there is the Library (23 feet 9 inches by 24 feet), the Librarian's quarters, a smoke and chess room (19 feet 6 inches by 21 feet 9 inches), a public reading room (27 feet by 45 feet) with ample light and ventilation, and a committee room (15 feet by 21 feet

9 inches). The whole of the first floor has been planned in such a manner that there remains very little waste space, and is a credit to the architects.[58]

For the next fifty years, the Literary Institute was a significant part of Fremantle's cultural landscape, but by 1948, the institute was struggling financially, and agreement was reached to vest the land, assets, and liabilities of the institute in the Fremantle City Council, which agreed to establish and conduct a free library service. In 1955, the Fremantle City Council resolved to join the Library Service of Western Australia.[59]

Albany Mechanics' Institute

The suggestion for the Albany Institute originated during a visit in 1852 by Dr Short, the Church of England Bishop of Adelaide. On 1st September 1852,[60] a public meeting was held, at which the sum of £27 was collected, and the following committee members were elected: President, Lt William Crossman; Deputy President, Lt George Egerton-Warburton; Treasurer, Ven. Archdeacon John Ramsden Wollaston; and Secretary, Arthur Trimmer. According to Stephens, in his brief history of the Institute:

> Mr Thomas Brooker Sherratt immediately placed his Octagon Church building at the service of the newly formed Institute free-of-charge and it began its long and useful life in the quaint eight-sided lath and plaster building which had been erected by its donor during 1835 for religious and cultural use of Albany citizens. This linked an earlier tradition with the new Institute. The Octagon building was used until the Institute erected its own building in October 1854.[61]

The aims and regulations of the new institute were very similar to those of its Perth counterpart, with the significant difference that it favoured the inclusion of ticket-of-leave men as members, although they were not eligible for office in the society. As elsewhere in Western Australia, a few committee members were 'mechanics' but most were yeoman farmers, businessmen, public servants, clerics, merchants and sea captains.[62]

Garden, in his history of Albany, suggests that the fact that two senior officers from the convict service held the senior positions in the Institute indicated its main purpose:

> It is obvious that the principal patrons of the institute were expected to be convicts and that its purpose was to teach them those ideas and attitudes which would reform them and make them 'respectable' and 'useful'. The Albany institute was to a degree unusual in its willingness to accept convicts as members, but it retained the safeguard that they were not eligible for positions on the committee of management... In August 1853 a block of land was granted... By August 1854 a neat brick building was constructed and a small library established.[63]

The block of land referred to was Albany Town Lot 187 on the corner of Vancouver and Collie Streets. The original trustees were Henry Camfield, Government Resident; Lt George Egerton-Warburton; and the Rector of St Johns Church. According to Stephens, the new building, which was formally opened on 18 October 1854, became the first section of the later Albany Municipal Library; it also served as the venue for the Albany State School until April 1857.

In 1858, the office of Secretary passed to the local schoolmaster, Thomas Matheson Palmer, who was to continue in that capacity for a quarter of a century, finally retiring on 20 November 1883. By 1860, the membership had grown to 44 under the Presidency of Captain John Hassell, and in 1866 Camfield's successor as Government Resident - Sir Alexander Cockburn-Campbell - took over the Presidency. In an article on Sir Alexander Cockburn-Campbell and his son Sir Thomas Cockburn-Campbell, published in the *Journal of the Royal West Australian Historical Society*, Hicks provides the following information:

> Sir Alexander was first elected president of the Albany Mechanics' Institute in 1866, and during his term a new reading-room and caretaker's rooms were added; the Institute was open from 9 a.m. to 9 p.m. The Institute was extremely popular with expatriates and colonials alike, a place of education which met a great need in the isolated colony. The Institute provided the small community with good literature, English and intercolonial papers and occasional cultural or scientific lectures.[64]

In the early 1880s, the whole town received a major stimulus in the form of the proposed construction of the Great Southern Railway. Under the Presidency of Dr Cecil Rogers, the committee made great plans for extending the Institute, and at the annual meeting held on 20 November 1883 the Patron - Government Resident R C Loftie - submitted detailed proposals to enlarge the buildings.

Early in 1884 the Legislative Council passed an Act (which had been drafted by Loftie) that vested the Institute site in the Institute itself, and gave it the power to mortgage its assets for additions to the buildings. A further two years were to pass, however, before the Annual meeting on 15 December 1885 actually authorised the committee to mortgage the property and to extend the buildings. At that same meeting, the Secretary/Librarian, John Norman, reported "a membership of 112 and a catalogue of books totalling 1,650."[65]

For a further thirty years the enlarged Institute continued to provide educational and cultural services to the town. Although Norman resigned in the closing years of the nineteenth century, and was replaced by Lewis Vaughan as Secretary, the Institute went on very much as before. However, like many other such organisations throughout Australia, its membership was severely depleted by the "cataclysmal First World War."[66] Finally, in February 1916, the dissolution of the Institute seemed unavoidable. President A H Dixon called a General Meeting on 16 August 1916, which attracted only 12 members. At that meeting a resolution directed "that the Institute and its assets be placed under the control of the Municipality of Albany" and "that Messrs A H Dixon, T J Harper and R McNie be appointed a committee to confer with the Council as to the details of the transfer." Stephens goes on to note:

> The proposal was considered by a special committee of the Municipal Council. On its recommendation the offer was accepted. A library committee of the Municipal Council was appointed on December 4, 1916. At the meeting of the Municipal Council held on February 26, 1917 the Library committee recommended "That the Mayor be asked to officially open the Library on March 1, 1917 and that an invitation be issued to ratepayers through the press."[67]

Thus the third oldest mechanics' institute in Western Australia formally ceased to exist sixty-five years after its foundation, yet in doing so, like its counterparts in both Perth and Fremantle, it laid the foundation for the provision of public library services in the town. Although the building itself was demolished in 1969, the spirit of its founders lives on in the Municipal Library which it spawned.

SPREAD OF THE MOVEMENT

Unlike Britain, where mechanics' institutes declined relatively early, in Western Australia they started rather later but continued to flourish into the twentieth century. As already described, the first longer-lasting institutes to be founded in Western Australia were in the three main areas of early settlement - Perth (January 1851), Fremantle (August 1851), and Albany (1852). Other institutes to follow included York (1861), Busselton (1861), Guildford (1862), Geraldton (1863), Northam (1864), Bunbury (1867), Katanning (1894), Kalgoorlie (1895), Midland Junction (1904), and Onslow (1912).

The rapid growth in the number of institutes between 1890 and 1905 (as indicated in the accompanying table) can be linked to the discovery of gold and the influx of wealth and population which was related to this. Between 1891 and the Census of 31 March 1901, the population of Western Australia grew from 53,285 to 184,124 - a 345 percent increase. In a list of 71 mechanics' institutes published in the *Statistical Register of Western Australia* in 1905, the dates of foundation of the institutes are given. These can be broken down as follows:[68]

Table 7.1
Establishment of Western Australia Institute, by years

1850-59	3
1860-69	6
1870-79	4
1880-89	6
1890-99	22
1900-05	19
Information not supplied	11
Total	**71**

Whereas in most Colonies the growth of the Institutes was haphazard and uncoordinated, in South Australia the pattern was rather different: the early establishment of the South Australian Institute in 1856 provided a model, as well as a mechanism, for sponsoring and coordinating the development of country institutes. In Western Australia, the Swan River Mechanics' Institute and, to a lesser extent, the Kalgoorlie Mechanics' Institute, performed this nurturing role. In the report already referred to - *A Century of Cultural Activity* - the following description of the Perth Institute's assistance to other organisations is provided:

On September 8, 1851, a reciprocal arrangement was approved by which members of the Swan River Mechanics' Institute and the Fremantle Mechanics' Institute were granted free participation in the benefits of both institutes. In 1857, when the Fremantle Mechanics' Institute had to go into recess, our own Institute offered to take charge of its remaining funds and books until the Fremantle Institute could re-establish itself. As time went on arrangements were made with other libraries for the regular subscription and received in return a consignment of books which were exchanged every three months. Libraries with whom these arrangements were made were Toodyay, Guildford, Busselton and Northam. The practice was discontinued when the smaller libraries were able to stand on their own feet, and the institute then introduced its system of country membership.[69]

In the following pages, the fluctuating fortunes of some of those country institutes are described; however, as it appears that the records of many of them have been lost, these descriptions are necessarily quite brief.

Busselton

Busselton, founded in 1861, had a distinctly upper class aura under the guidance of J G Bussell, who had earlier been associated with another cultural venture, The Thatched Roof Club (1832), at Augusta. Local politics were also very lively at Busselton; eventually the Reverend Henry Brown broke away to form a Working Men's Association on the Fremantle pattern.[70]

Guildford

On 14 March 1862, a meeting was held in the then newly completed Government School building at Guildford to form a Mechanics' Institute. Like so many similar organisations, its main objective was "to benefit the mechanics and young men of the district by affording them facilities for self-improvement and intellectual recreation." In particular, this was to be achieved through "Weekly meetings, at which to discuss subjects of a literary, scientific or other useful character; the formation of a Library; a Reading Room to be open to all members; and the delivery of lectures on interesting and useful subjects, to which all members shall be admitted."[71] The Institute got off to a flying start, with Governor Hampton as Patron, and William Locke Brockman ("whose contribution to the public life of the Swan district was so great, and over so long a period, that he has been referred to as the 'Father of the Swan'"[72]) as President. By 25 August, there were nine honorary members, including the Resident Magistrate S W Viveash, Justice of the Peace Dr A R Waylen and the Chaplain, Rev. W D Williams. There were also fifty ordinary members, including Joseph Chester who had been so prominent in the Swan River Institute in Perth, and George Throssell, who was to be very influential in the Northam Institute in later years.

As elsewhere, an early priority of the institute was to obtain its own premises, and the colonial government granted a site in Meadow Street, next to the Convict Depot hospital, and a £50 subsidy towards the cost of building.[73] In April 1865, a foundation stone was laid, and on 5 September that year the distinctive and attractive hall, built by John Welbourne using "bricks of local clay in flemish bond brickwork,"[74] was opened with a concert. "Among the items were a performance of songs by the 'Ethiopian Serenaders' of Perth, and piano pieces played by Mr Kochanovsky, a music teacher from Fremantle."[75]

From then on, the hall became an indispensable public facility in the town. As early as 1866 it was used as the venue for wine and produce judging for the Swan and District Agricultural and Horticultural Association Show,[76] and it also served as the unofficial town hall, as well as being a venue for a variety of lectures, musical evenings and other entertainments. On 10 September 1877 an amateur concert was held in order to raise funds to discharge a debt incurred by St Matthews' Church in replacing their building, the old one having been blown down by a hurricane.[77]

As in other places throughout Australia, a major function of the Institute was conducting a lending library and reading room, which served the local inhabitants for many years, until the establishment of a municipal library. In 1962, the centenary of the Institute was marked both through the acquisition of £250 worth of new books, and through "an evening at the institute" organised by the Swan-Guildford Historical Society on 4 June 1962, "performed in costumes suitable to the period."[78]

Even after the library moved to the Guildford Council Chambers, the old institute building continued its useful life, first as home to the Garrick Club (an amateur theatrical group) and then as headquarters and folk museum for the Swan-Guildford Historical Society. Subsequently, "in November 1991, an amateur theatrical group known as Oliver's Old Time Music Hall came to an arrangement with the Shire of Swan, whereby they are granted, on an annual basis, custodial use of the hall. They use it for rehearsals and the occasional performance, and they also encourage use of the hall by other community groups [such as the Guildford Association, Guildford Red Cross and the Arts and China Painting Clubs]. As 'rental,' they are responsible for the interior upkeep of the building"[79] Thus this tranquil building, "disturbed only by the sound of the horns of passing diesel trains, and the clanging of warnings at the railway crossing,"[80] continues to serve its community today as it has for almost 130 years.

Geraldton

In one sense, the history of the Geraldton Mechanics' Institute is very simple: it was formed in 1863 and within less than a decade it had ceased to exist, because of lack of support. This, however, is to greatly oversimplify the story of what is actually one of the more interesting institutes in Western Australia, one which in fact still exists albeit under a different name.

Available evidence suggests that the first Mechanics' Institute was formed in 1863, and that its premises were formally opened on 24 February 1864. Because of "indifferent support,"[81] however, the Institute did not last long, and collapsed within a few years. Despite this, there was still both a need and a desire for some sort of educational and cultural focus in Geraldton, and on 19 June 1868 the Geraldton Working Men's Society was formed. Within a matter of days the Secretary (Isaac Walker) had written to the Colonial Secretary (F P Barlee) seeking support in the form of an annual grant. At that time, Walker claimed, there were already "55 members, nearly all working men, who will take an interest in the progress of the Society."[82]

The resident magistrate reported that the principal objects of the Society appeared to be to provide a reading room, and books and papers. The Government responded quickly, granting the new Society both a £10 subsidy and a block of land, described as follows: "Lot 244 to be of three roods, more or less, bounded on the northwest by one chain of Marine

Terrace, on the southwest by five chains of Durlacher Street, on the southeast by one chain 50 links of Eleanor Street, and on the northeast by Geraldton Town Lot 245 measuring five chains." This was a prime location that in later years was to provide the Society (and its successors) with a steady income that helped it to keep going.

On 20 July 1870 the wife of the resident magistrate, George Eliot (who incidentally was one of the three trustees for the Society, the other two being Charles Crowther and Daniel Henry Scott[83]), laid the foundation stone for the Society's building. When the building had progressed to the satisfaction of the Government, the title deed was to be handed to the Society, and on 22 February 1871 Isaac Walker again wrote to the Colonial Secretary: "I have the honour to inform you that the Hall of the Geraldton Working Men's Society has been so far completed to allow of its being used, the plastering only being left.... I will feel thankful if you will forward me the Deed as early as possible ..."[84] This occurred on 7 October 1871, although the building was not completed for another three years, at a cost of some £400. In that year, 1874, despite finishing the building, the Sixth Annual Report revealed that the Society "had barely existed recently and might suffer the same fate as the Mechanics' Institute."

Eight years later, in 1882, the Society seems to have been in much better shape. According to an editorial in the *Victoria Express*, its membership had reached 130, while its property was worth "not less than £700" and the Society was "well supplied with English and Colonial papers and periodicals"[85] as well as quite a range of books. Through judicious management its overdraft with the WA Bank had been reduced to about £13, against which there was some £20 of subscriptions in arrears.[86] Interestingly, the same editorial recommended the construction of an addition to the Society's premises, because "it is, to say the least, inconvenient that the hall, the library, and the reading rooms should be in one...."[87] It would seem that it was some years before the Society took this advice, however; according to Norris, it was not until about 1897 that "a new library was built [on the Institution's block of land] facing Greenough Road [Durlacher Street] and the other one was let as a hall...."[88] At around this same time the institution changed its name to the 'Geraldton Mechanics' Institute,' perhaps because it had already been operating as one, or perhaps to take advantage of Government Grants to such organisations.

On 18 January 1900, at around 7.25 in the morning, the alarm was raised: the recently built Mechanics' Institute library - which Norris describes as "a small wooden building with an iron roof"[89] - was ablaze. Although the fire brigade arrived within minutes of the alarm, "it was too late to do other than save an adjacent building.... The Institute was thoroughly gutted but some books, and a good quantity of the furniture belonging to the caretaker, Mrs Pead, were saved."[90]

This was a serious, though fortunately not a fatal, blow to the Institute. Although the losses were only partially covered by insurance,[91] the committee wasted no time in establishing a new library. Within months of the fire, the Government had provided a subsidy of £50 to support book purchases, and the Municipal Council had provided premises in the form of the disused terminal building of the Northampton to Geraldton Railway (Town Lots 76 and 77) on Marine Terrace. With its new premises, the Institute leased its own property on Town Lot 244 for commercial purposes which, as previously mentioned, provided it with an independent source of income.

On 8 August 1900 the new library - believed to be the first free public library outside Perth - "was formally opened by the Mayor...in the presence of a number of ladies and Gentlemen."[92]   This arrangement was formalised on 9 July 1909 when the Municipal Council granted a thirty year lease at a peppercorn rental on the old Railway Station, on the understanding that a second storey be added. By 1911 the second floor had been added to form a "dignified two storey building on the ocean side of western Marine Terrace."[93] Years later a long-term resident was to recall that the library itself was on the ground floor, while the upstairs level had contained "a reading room well stocked with a wide variety of newspapers and magazines [as well as] a billiard room, gents only of course,"[94] and also that "The verandah was a great place [from which] to watch yacht races."   A list of books available around this time is provided in a printed catalogue dated 31 August 1910.[95]

For the next half century, the Institute operated essentially as a lending library, much like its counterparts in other parts of Australia, with the exception that its property holdings insulated it to some extent against financial difficulties.   In 1957 renovations were made to the library building, and in 1960 a significant change occurred when the Institute changed its name to the 'Geraldton Cultural Trust,' with the following objects:

(i)   to promote and provide monetary assistance for the spread of useful cultural and rational mental recreation particularly among the people of the town of Geraldton and the Victoria district;

(ii)   to maintain and/or conduct a lending and reference library and a reading room for members; and

(iii)   the management, control and development of the Trust property as a perpetual endowment and/or centre for the [other] objects...[96]

In the furtherance of these aims, especially the last, the Trustees embarked on an ambitious program of development, so that by 1968 the whole of its land was covered with buildings of varying ages facing the three street frontages of Marine Terrace, Durlacher Street and Eleanor Street. In 1975, it was decided not to renew the lease on the old Railway Station, and the library's 10,000 books "were transferred to the Trust's own property in Durlacher Street,"[97] where they were to remain for a further seven years. In 1982 the Trust took over another historic Geraldton building for use as a library and Arts and Craft centre. 'The Residency,' described as a "pleasant and typically colonial stone bungalow," had formerly been the official home of the Government Resident, and is now rented by the Trust from the W.A. Ministry of Works at a peppercorn rental.

In April 1983 the Trust's links with its early history were substantially obliterated when fire raced through the old Geraldton Arts and Craft Centre, formerly the original Working Men's Society Hall in Marine Terrace. The iron-roofed stone building was gutted by the fire, and afterwards remained boarded up until 1986, when it was demolished to make way for a new commercial development on the site. By 1993, the Trust controlled 23 tenancies, with a capital value in excess of $1.7 million, from which its income was derived. According to the Managing Secretary of the Trust, "The proceeds of these tenancies are used for the maintenance and upkeep of the Residency building, the combined expenses of the library - both reading and video - the general improvement and maintenance of the Trust buildings, and free accommodation and grants to the various arts and craft groups in the Victoria district."[98] In this way it provides support for a diverse range of local educational and cultural activities in the best tradition of the mechanics' institute movement.

Northam

The Northam Mechanics' Institute was founded in 1864, for the promotion of literary, scientific and other useful knowledge. It owed its existence largely to the efforts of a prominent citizen, George Throssell, who for a short period in 1901 served as Premier of Western Australia after Sir John Forrest retired to stand for Federal Parliament. Evidently his support for the Institute developed from his earlier encounter with the Swan River Mechanics' Institute in Perth:

> Throssell epitomises the nineteenth century ideal of the self-made man of humble origin who rose in the world by hard work and sober devotion to duty and self-improvement. Taking a job with a Perth merchant, George spent his evenings reading newspapers and listening to discussions at the Swan River Mechanics' Institute. In later life he acknowledged the large debt he owed to the principles and knowledge which were imbibed at the Institute.

> Soon boasting a membership of thirty-four, the institute hired books from the Guildford Mechanics' Institute until it could afford its own, and held regular lecture nights and discussion evenings. At first, the institute was housed in the new school building, but in 1866 the Government granted a block of land and contributed £50 towards an institute building, which was ultimately opened in 1867. Public subscriptions paid for most of the rest of this building, with Throssell contributing the balance.[99]

Although its earliest records were destroyed by fire, all indications suggest that it was one of the dullest institutes.[100]

Bunbury

Like Northam, Bunbury also had problems. When the foundation stone was laid for a mechanics' hall in January 1868, it was "regretted that efforts are not made to have regular series of lectures but we suppose those who came forward on previous occasions have had their ardour dampened by having to talk to empty benches."[101] Hardly an auspicious beginning!

Katanning

The story of the Katanning Mechanics' Institute is one which, with minor variations, probably reflects the growth and decline of numerous institutes in the late nineteenth century throughout rural Western Australia. In *A Place to Meet: A History of the Shire of Katanning,* Bignell outlines the origins of this institute:

> Some less sportsminded men craved for the more reflective subjects such as reading, debate and lectures so the idea of establishing a mechanics' institute was mooted as

early as August 1892. A novel evening, a calico masked ball, was arranged to raise funds for the venture.[102]

The town's mechanics' institute was officially inaugurated in October 1894. Until such time as a suitable building could be erected, it was given free use of a hall belonging to a local merchant and Member of Parliament, F Piesse (MLA Williams):

> The institute's founding was celebrated with a concert and ball, the display of musical drill by the schoolchildren, under the direction of their teacher, Miss F. Williams, being voted the most outstanding item of the night.[103]

In October 1896 the mechanics' institute held a fancy dress ball (which lasted until five the following morning) to raise funds for their library. At about the same time the building committee for the town's agricultural hall arranged for the foundation stone to be laid. On the day, it was publicly stated that the building was to be for the sole use and benefit of the agricultural community - words which were to cause much concern to future committees, when, through a proliferation of organisations, the town gradually developed an identity separate from the farming community. The conflict was clearly evidenced in the affairs of the mechanics' institute, which in 1899 had amalgamated with the Agricultural Hall to form 'The Mechanics' Institute and Public Hall.' As this name was considered too cumbersome, moves were made in 1903 to have it changed to 'Mechanics' Institute (Incorporated)':

> The meeting ended in a deadlock and for the next few weeks the subject was discussed widely in the streets and the open columns of the *Great Southern Herald....* The discussion which ensued ... practically turned into a fight between town and country members. The town members however were too strong numerically and the name of 'Mechanics' Institute (Incorporated)' was allowed to stand.[104]

The mechanics' institute continued to have an influence in the town, and in 1943 the Eleanor Roberts Youth Library was set up in the mechanics' institute building in commemoration of a much-loved teacher who had introduced three generations of Katanning families to reading and writing.[105]

Midland

In 1906 a library of eight hundred books was set up in the Midland Junction Mechanics' Institute. An application to the Carnegie Foundation for a grant of £1,500 to build a new library was successful, and the building opened in May 1912. This was the only Carnegie Library to be built in Western Australia and one of only four in Australia. The library was not successful, however, being described by Ralph Munn in 1935 as one of the worst he had seen. It was demolished in 1966, leaving Midland for some years as the only Western Australian metropolitan local government authority not to have a local public library as part of the Library Board joint agreement. The reason for the failure of the library is unclear. Cook suggests that there might have been an antipathy towards Carnegie and his libraries in a strongly-unionised railway town, and that it might have been unable to compete with the larger Midland Junction Railways Institute Library.[106]

145

KALGOORLIE AND THE EASTERN GOLDFIELDS: A SPECIAL CASE

Partly because it was so late in being established, partly because it took its lead from Adelaide and Sydney rather than from Perth, and partly because of its strong affiliations with the Labor movement in Western Australia,[107] the story of the Kalgoorlie Mechanics' Institute was a little different. Founded in 1895 as the Kalgoorlie Miners' Institute, it changed to Mechanics' Institute on becoming an incorporated body in 1905. The Institute's objects were cultural, educational and recreational and, until the outbreak of the 1914-18 war, it retained an enviable reputation for its lively programs. The link between Kalgoorlie with Sydney and Adelaide extension movements was not accidental. The Institute's secretary, Andrew McClintock had been trained at the Fisher Library at Sydney University and had been associated with the Working Men's Technical College at Melbourne, and the father of the President (E H Irving) was a professor at Melbourne. The other members of the committee were Dr A R Wallace (scientist), A Price (accountant), M Rosenberg (Mayor), A T Lassock (headmaster) and G Hall (sportsman and elocutionist); all were interested in education. Furthermore, McClintock was also secretary for the Adelaide University's Committee in Kalgoorlie and it was through his offices that Kalgoorlie became the recognised centre in Western Australia for the University of Sydney's Extension Board.

The Institute Committee was concerned that lectures should be educational but not dull or pedantic. It also endeavoured to offer a series of related talks rather than spasmodic, unconnected addresses. In this way a subject could be treated in depth and continuing study would be encouraged. The lectures were given both by local citizens and by visiting scholars such as G C Henderson and Darnley Naylor from Adelaide, Dr Chapman, Dr S A McClintock and Professor Woolnough from Sydney, Professors Irving from Melbourne and Cole from London. Later, speakers were brought from the University of Western Australia. Favoured topics tended to be scientific or related to the local industry of gold-mining.

Under McClintock's guidance the library policy was broadly based; the old moralistic tomes were gone, and instead an array of literature on a wide range of subjects filled the shelves. McClintock, who closely followed American developments in the library field, spelt out his policies in the *Kalgoorlie Record and Institute Journal*. He tried to persuade the Government to establish a free lending library on the goldfields but was disappointed. Nevertheless, he maintained a free reading room at the Institute and never ceased to press for government grants to improve the reference section and upgrade the scientific and technical collection. In 1913, shortly before he left to work in Perth, he arranged for reciprocal loans with the library at the newly established Chamber of Mines.[108]

Small institutes mushroomed in the tiny settlements scattered through the goldfields - Lake Austin, Bonnievale, Day Dawn, Bardoe, Broad Arrow, Bulong and others, many long since forgotten. None had the prestige of Kalgoorlie, but some like Boulder, Southern Cross and Coolgardie had bursts of activity between 1897 and 1902. The significance of the institutes lies not so much in their own educational functions, although these were important for the people concerned, but more for their effect in raising the level of expectations in communities lacking access to formal educational facilities. In the larger centres - Coolgardie and Kalgoorlie in particular - there are clear links between the mechanics' institute movement, the need for trained men in the gold-mining industry, and agitation for the establishment of schools of mines in Western Australia.

Meanwhile, McClintock attempted to introduce into Western Australia some new ideas which drew heavily upon developments in other places. At the beginning of November 1904, he succeeded in organising what came to be regarded as the first library conference in Western Australia.[109] It was, in fact, an inaugural conference of W A Institutes' Secretaries and Librarians which gathered at the Swan River Mechanics' Institute. Heavily supported from the goldfields, representatives came from thirty institutes and the sessions were chaired by the WA Public Librarian, J S Battye. McClintock's contribution to the conference involved three papers, one on how to popularise mechanics' institutes, the second on library procedures, and the third on the introduction of billiards. Another conference was planned for Albany in 1905, but it did not eventuate.

OTHER KINDRED INSTITUTIONS

Although mechanics' institutes played an important role in Western Australia's cultural and educational history, they arguably had a lower profile than in other states, and were by no means the only institutions which performed this sort of broadly educative role. By 1906[110] there were 56 mechanics' institutes, 48 miners' institutes and 87 agricultural halls in Western Australia. Which amenity occurred in a particular town or village depended on the predominant occupation in the locality - pastoral, mining or service industry. The small town of Greenbushes featuring all three (the mechanics met in the Timber Corporation Hall) was a rare exception.

The next part of this chapter is therefore devoted to a consideration of three other types of non-formal educational organisation dating from the second half of the nineteenth century: working men's associations, agricultural halls, and the Railways Institute.

Working Men's Associations

As in other parts of Australia, one of the recurrent early criticisms of the West Australian mechanics' institutes concerned their middle-class bias, and consequent failure to meet the needs of their ostensible constituents - the working class. In several places, this led to the establishment of breakaway groups, specifically aimed at the enlightenment of artisans and tradesmen.

The first meeting of the Fremantle Working Men's Association took place on 5 January 1862 in the Boys' School Room. It was established with Governor Hampton's blessing, and was guided by the local Congregational Minister, Reverend Joseph Johnston, and the Anglican rector, Reverend George Bostock. The Governor, the Comptroller-General of Convicts, the Anglican Bishop and the Colonial Secretary all gave influential patronage to the Association with its declared intention to improve the minds of working men. Even so the new society had a mixed reception from the public - "Some with warm heart and generous mind, anxious to do good, helped, others remained neutral lacking courage." Many opponents prophesied publicly "that this association arising like a fungus from an unhealthy soil, would only appear upon the surface of society for a brief space presently to sink into its original obscurity."[111] But Johnston and Bostock, assisted by G B Humble, headmaster at the Fremantle Boys' School, knew what they were about and despite gloomy prognostications the Working Men's Association survived. As mentioned previously, it was joined by the Mechanics' Institute in 1868 to become the Fremantle Literary Institute, in which form, with less of the club atmosphere and a more community-oriented policy, it served the port until it ceded to the State Library Board in 1955.

At Perth, a Working Men's Association was formed on 20 January 1865. It was hoped that it would be fostered on the same 'protestant basis' as Johnston and Bostock had nurtured at Fremantle.[112] In addition to the widening gulf between 'mechanics' and the middle-class, religious discussion had caused certain members to resign from the Swan River Mechanics' Institute. There had been an internal rift and it was rumoured that because of papist elements in the executive committee, some gentlemen had withdrawn their support.[113] Archdeacon James Brown, formerly the Anglican Chaplain at the Convict Establishment during its most enlightened educational period, and who retained a lifelong commitment to learning, was inaugural president of the Association. As soon as possible it was accepted that the society should be managed by the class whom it was designed to benefit.

There were signs of a slightly more political motivation in the Perth Association than elsewhere. Lectures on more contentious issues, such as "our Association or an appeal to the working classes," were arranged. Yet most members were still too apathetic to take an active part in discussion groups, and there is no remaining suggestion of any vocational classes. As at Fremantle, 'Penny Readings' were popular. Although the official records of the Perth Working Men's Association have disappeared, reports were sometimes published in the contemporary press. For instance, on 28 May 1883 a meeting was held, whether of the Association or in its rooms hired for the occasion is not clear, for the purpose of forming a Labor League. Led by T Donelly, "an importation from the other side," the league's objects were the cessation of immigration and introduction of an eight hour week. However, after the Labor League registered as a Friendly Society in August 1884 it functioned as little more than an employment society.[114]

During April 1886 an acrimonious discussion took place as to whether or not the Association should adopt a political platform.[115] Significantly, a typographical society to improve the social, moral and intellectual standards of its members was formed about the same time. The first stable union, two branches of the English Amalgamated Society of Carpenters and Joiners, had been previously formed at Fremantle and Perth (1884). By 1888 the Perth Working Men's Association had fallen into disfavour with the establishment and was being castigated by the press as a practical failure: On 23 February 1888 an editorial in the *Daily News*, headed 'Ropes of Sand,' stated that the association had been of no value in deciding issues between capital and labour, and that its members had fallen out amongst themselves on the issue of unions.

Although a few other short-lived working men's associations appeared in country towns, notably Geraldton, Bunbury and Busselton, it could scarcely be claimed that the movement thrived in Western Australia. The south west towns were influenced to follow the Fremantle model by the Reverend Joseph Johnston, who regularly visited the area in the course of his pastoral duties. After a dramatic break with Bussell and his committee, the Busselton Working Men's Association was established on a site in Queen Street by the Reverend Henry Brown in 1863. Before the century closed it was apparent that the impetus for both mechanics' institutes and working men's associations had declined. The movement never attained anything like the high intellectual aims with which it was conceived. Despite the generally greater sympathy of ideals between organisers and members,[116] a broad lack of direction, or of cohesive leadership, and an absence of a strong body of skilled artisans combined to contribute to the failure.

Agricultural Halls

Apart from the mechanics' institutes, another non-formal facility which in a very broad sense could be described as 'educational,' was the Agricultural Hall. The Royal Agricultural Society supported the idea of halls being established in country areas, to serve not only as social meeting places but also to provide the focus for agricultural shows and competitions, and also lectures on relevant subjects. The colonial Legislative Council, heavily representative of landed interests at the time, gave what little financial support it could in the form of 'grants-in-aid'; however it appears that the 'educational' value of the halls was greatly over-estimated. The annual 'show' was about the only time when farmers in the locality concerned actually had the opportunity of seeing (and of learning from) the judging of livestock and produce. On the other hand, the shows and other functions organised around the hall as the venue added to the consciousness of farmers and fuelled their growing agitation, late in the nineteenth century, for the establishment of an agricultural college.

Some impression of the range of institute and agricultural halls functioning in 1900 is provided below in Table 7.2. While many of the halls listed outlived their usefulness, and simply disappeared, others passed over to the control of local shires under various pieces of legislation.

In the long term, of course, schools and colleges, as well as activities launched by various government departments gradually supplanted the work which the institutes and halls were designed - at least in part - to fulfil. The institutes and halls, in the event, gradually drifted out of existence, either to find a new role within the state library system during the twentieth century, or to become derelict structures in decaying towns long since abandoned. On the latter point, the then State Librarian, F A Sharr in a letter dated 6 August 1962 suggested to the Coolgardie Shire that:

> A representative collection of the sort of books which were found in the Goldfields Mechanics' Institute in the heyday of the Goldfields is an extremely interesting project and will in time become quite valuable as far as this State is concerned. It will be the only record of the sort of books which Goldfields read, or at least bought.[117]

The Railways Institute

One aspect of library provision in Western Australia to receive at least faint praise from Lionel McColvin in his 1947 report on libraries was the service provided to its members by the Western Australian Railways and Tramways Institute. McColvin wrote:

> If one must be honest, the best general country library service in Western Australia appeared to be that provided by the Western Australian Railways and Tramways Institute with headquarters in Perth and several branches from which books are sent out by rail to individual members (railway employees) in outlying places. The books distributed are frankly mostly recreational, though some technical works are also circulated. The Institute is supported partly by members' subscriptions, partly by

Table 7. 2 STATE GOVERNMENT OF WESTERN AUSTRALIA
ESTIMATES OF EXPENDITURE FOR THE YEAR ENDING JUNE 30TH, 1902.

	VOTE FOR 12 MONTHS ended 30th June	1900-1901 EXPENDITURE FOR 12 MONTHS ended 30th June
Public Buildings — continued	£ s. d.	£ s. d.
Grants in Aid for Mechanics' Institutes and kindred Buildings — £1,500.		
Grants in Aid (in accordance with regulations) for Construction of and Additions to Mechanics' Institutes, Miners' Institutes, and Agricultural Halls	—	—
Armadale Mechanics' Institute	250 0 0	250 0 0
Belmont Agricultural Hall	100 0 0	100 0 0
Boyanup Agricultural Hall	50 0 0	50 0 0
Bulong Miners' Institute	125 0 0	125 0 0
Boulder Mechanics' Institute	300 0 0	300 0 0
Brunswick Agricultural Hall	50 0 0	50 0 0
Bonnievale Miners' Hall	150 0 0	150 0 0
Bridgetown Mechanics' Institute	200 0 0	200 0 0
Bunbury Mechanics' Institute	500 0 0	500 0 0
Busselton Municipal Buildings, Additions	250 0 0	250 0 0
Colliefields Miners' Institute	250 0 0	250 0 0
Coogee Agricultural Hall	60 0 0	60 0 0
Claremont Municipal Buildings	225 0 0	225 0 0
Cookernup Agricultural Hall	50 0 0	50 0 0
Coralup Agricultural Hall	250 0 0	—
Derby Mechanics' Institute	250 0 0	350 0 0
Donnybrook Agricultural Hall, Conversion into Mechanics' Institute	100 0 0	100 0 0
East Fremantle Town Hall	250 0 0	250 0 0
Field's Find Miners' Institute	100 0 0	50 0 0
Guildford Municipal Buildings	150 0 0	150 0 0
Goongarrie Miners' Institute	100 0 0	100 0 0
Geraldton Fire Brigade Building	150 0 0	150 0. 0
Greenbushes Miners' Institute	250 0 0	250 0 0
Helena Vale Mechanics' Institute	150 0 0	150 0 0
Jandakot Agricultural Hall	30 0 0	30 0 0
Kalgoorlie Trades Hall	300 0 0	300 0 0
Kanowna Public Library Building	200 0 0	200 0 0
Kookynie Miners' Institute	250 0 0	250 0 0
Kojonup Agricultural Hall	250 0 0	150 0 0
Katanning Mechanics' Institute	150 0 0	250 0 0
Lennonville Mechanics' Institute	250 0 0	250 0 0
Menzies Municipal Buildings	250 0 0	500 0 0
Mount Sir Samuel Miners' Institute	250 0 0	250 0 0
Mulline Miners' Institute	250 0 0	250 0 0
Mundaring Agricultural Hall	250 0 0	250 0 0
Narrogin Agricultural Hall	150 0 0	150 0 0
North Fremantle Municipal Buildings	500 0 0	500 0 0
North Greenbushes Mechanics' Institute	150 0 0	150 0 0
Northam Town Hall	250 0 0	250 0 0
Paddington Mechanics' Institute	100 0 0	100 0 0
South Perth Mechanics' Institute	200 0 0	200 0 0
Wagin Mechanics' Institute	250 0 0	250 0 0
Walkaway Agricultural Hall	250 0 0	250 0 0
Wedgecarrup Agricultural Hall	250 0 0	250 0 0
Weeloona Miners' Institute	250 0 0	250 0 0
Wonnerup Agricultural Hall	35 0 0	35 0 0
Woodanilling Agricultural Hall	250 0 0	250 0 0
York Mechanics' Institute	500 0 0	500 0 0
Bulong Amalgamated Workers' Hall	—	100 0 0
Capel Agricultural Hall Improvements	—	50 0 0
Cookgardie Mechanics' Institute	—	250 0 0
Cue Workers' Association Hall	—	200 0 0
Kanowna Workers' Hall	—	100 0 0
Morning Star Miners' Hall	—	100 0 0
Nannine Miners' Institute	—	100 0 0
Paddington Workers' Hall	—	100 0 0
Sons of Gwalia Workers' Hall	—	200 0 0

Source: Estimates for 1902, VPWA 1902, pp. 124-125.

150

the State Railway Commissioners, who pay a subsidy at the rate of 10/- per member. I am not suggesting that this organisation can compare with the average British county library service; to make such a comparison would be to ignore the differing functions of the two types of service. But I do suggest that it demonstrates the virtues of centralised administration. Certainly in one town where I saw both a local council-run subscription State-free-subsidy library and a Railways Institute Branch, the latter was immeasurably more active and better provided.[118]

From 1881, when the Fremantle-Guildford rail line was opened, the spread of the rail system throughout Western Australia was arguably the single most influential factor in the development of transportation and communication. The government railways were a large employer of labour, and substantial railway establishments were created in many regional centres and towns. The railways were a major feature in the economic development of the state during the 1890s, but in his annual reports for 1895 and 1896 the Chief Engineer in John Forrest's administration, Charles Yelverton O'Connor (who also served as Manager of the Railways), pointed out that:

> unless opportunities were created locally for the training of professional and skilled workmen, Western Australians would miss out on all the jobs being generated as the then colony grew quickly as a consequence of the gold rushes.[119]

In 1897, the Education Department commenced evening classes for railway apprentices employed at the Fremantle Railway Workshops, but by all accounts these were poorly attended. In the same year the Inspector for the Chief Traffic Officer and Safe Working, J W Shaw, called a meeting at Perth with the object of founding an institute specifically geared to the needs of the railways. According to White, Shaw found ready support for his idea: not only was it enthusiastically endorsed by those at the meeting, but "the Government willingly gave a grant of £200 and a gift of some rooms."[120]

The institute opened its doors in 1898, with much the same rhetoric about mental and moral improvement as the mechanics' institutes before it, emphasising, as White puts it, "the twin virtues of self-help and occupational advancement." The first issue of the *W A Railway Gazette* carried the following exhortations:

> By punctuality, perseverance, trustfulness and sobriety, he (the railwayman) may attain the highest position in his particular department. We should like to impress upon all what is required in Railway life, as in other spheres of labour, is an 'aim' and 'ambition,' a 'goal,' for which we strive might and main ... Let us rise like one man -- the younger ones to make themselves proficient in their duties; the indifferent to arouse and stir up their activities in the interests of themselves, the Department and right; the ambitious to acquaint themselves with the principles which control railway work, and so make themselves indispensable to the service.[121]

The Institute provided a range of classes on safe-working, shorthand and typing, bookkeeping and accounts, as well as technical aspects of railway engineering. In 1899, the Institute also offered classes in first-aid, and by 1908 the offerings included telegraphy, vacuum brake and even Esperanto! Over succeeding years the range of subjects offered, especially in technical and engineering areas, increased considerably, and a number of branches of the Institute opened throughout Western Australia.

Aside from its pivotal role in the development of Technical Education, the Railway Institute also provided a library service to serve the needs of railway employees and their families. Bigger towns, such as Midland Junction, Merredin, Narrogin, Bunbury Kalgoorlie, and Northam were large enough to have their own branch of the Institute (complete with library), while smaller centres of employment (twenty to thirty families), such as Pinjarra, would have a "book cupboard," the key to which was held by the Deputy Station Master. The stock was replenished every three months. Staff at smaller stations and sidings had to rely on book parcels railed out from the central library in Perth on request.

The Western Australian Railways Institute continues to operate a lending library to the present day, in manner and substance not very dissimilar to that described by McColvin in 1947. Perhaps the most interesting sidelight on this is that today the most popular library service of the Institute is an exceptionally well-stocked VHS videotape lending library. The most recent addition to the library collection has been compact discs (CDs). The Institute still maintains branch libraries in the larger country centres, and despatches material in response to requests received from country members through the Perth Branch.

CONCLUSION

Although the mechanics' institute movement itself does not seem to have taken root as quickly or as deeply in Western Australia as in many other parts of the country, the fact remains that they - and other kindred organisations - made an invaluable contribution to the growth and development of the state. As elsewhere, the institutes were intended largely for the working class and lower middle class, but also as elsewhere, the leadership tended to come substantially from the colonial élite - the pastoralists, farmers, civil servants and professional people - who acted out of a mixture of motives. The earlier institutes drew upon the liberal tradition, buttressed by moral and corrective objects, but as the century progressed, these were overtaken by more utilitarian goals and objectives.

By the end of the nineteenth century, the discovery of gold - first in the north and then later in the eastern parts of Western Australia - had unleashed enormous developmental forces. The attendant growth in commerce, industry, agriculture and the public service all gave rise to a demand for skilled employees, and the old institutes were, for the most part, superseded by other educational providers: miners' institutes became schools of mines; agricultural societies led to agricultural colleges; technical schools took over vocational preparation from mechanics' institutes and the railways institute; and evening classes, university extension and the Workers' Education Association - all launched in the early years of the twentieth century - usurped the 'educational' functions of the institutes.

This left them as libraries and recreation centres, functions which they served - and even continue to serve - as part of the fabric of municipal and community facilities. Despite the disparaging comments on library services in Western Australia made by Munn and Pitt in 1935, and McColvin in 1947, there are many Western Australians who have fond memories of one or more institutes or similar subscription libraries throughout the State, and the memories of these libraries stand to remind us of the special role accorded to libraries and the perceived benefits they bestow on a society, even when the contents of the collections are

Guildford Mechanics' Institute, WA, ca 1870
(reproduced by permission of the Battye Library, Perth, WA)

Original Swan River Mechanics' Institute, Perth Wa, ca 1857
(reproduced by permission of West Australian Newspapers Ltd.)

Fremantle Literary Institute, WA
(reproduced by permission of the Fremantle City Library, WA)

Kalgoorlie Mechanics' Institute, WA
(reproduced by permission of the Goldfields Historical Society)

deemed to be largely recreational and ephemeral. Further to this, the institute libraries also established the important principle of direct government financial aid to libraries, which was to have a profound influence on the subsequent development of library services in Western Australia.[122]

Overall, Western Australians owe an enormous debt of gratitude to the far sighted pioneers who, amidst the difficulties of creating a new society in one of the remotest and most isolated parts of the English-speaking world, laid the cultural and educational foundations that subsequent generations were to build upon.

NOTES AND REFERENCES

1.Morrison, E., & Talbot, M. (Eds.). (1984). Books, libraries and readers in colonial Australia. *Papers from the Forum on Australian Colonial Library History, Monash University, June 1-2, 1984.* Clayton, Victoria: Graduate School of Librarianship, Monash University.

Biskup, P., & Rochester, M. (Eds.). (1985). Australian library history. *Papers from the Second Forum on Australian Library History, Canberra, July 19-20, 1985.* Canberra: College of Advanced Education.

Rayward, W.B. (Ed.). (1988). Australian library history in context. *Papers from the Third Forum on Australian Library History, University of New South Wales, July 17-18, 1987.* Kensington: University of New South Wales.

Upward, F., & Whyte, J.P. (1991). Peopling a profession. *Papers from the Fourth Forum on Australian Library History, Monash University, September 25-26, 1989.* Melbourne: Ancora Press.

2.Jones, D.J. (1968). *A source of inspiration and delight: The buildings of the State library of New South Wales since 1826.* Sydney: Library Council of New South Wales.

3.Levett, J. (1988). *The origin of the State Library of Tasmania, 1849-1850.* Hobart: Tasmanian State Committee of the Australian Library Promotion Council.

4.Bridge, C. (1986). *A trunk full of books: History of the State Library of South Australia and its forerunners.* Adelaide: Wakefield Press in association with the State Library of South Australia.

5.Cook, J. (1985). Information, enrichment and delight: Public Libraries in Western Australia. *Occasional Paper No. 35.* Halifax, Nova Scotia: School of Library Service, Dalhousie University.

6.Orlovich, P. (1985). The decline of schools of arts libraries in New South Wales. In Biskup, P., & Rochester, M.K. *op. cit.*, pp. 50-60.

7.Hubber, B.G. (1986). Public libraries and the suburban reading public, 1850-1914. *Unpublished M.A. Thesis.* Clayton: Graduate School of Librarianship, Monash University.

153

8.Talbot, M. (1988). Origins of the Institutes Association of South Australia Inc. In Rayward, W.B. (Ed.). *op. cit.*, pp. 129-138.

9.McColvin, L.R. (1947). *Public libraries in Australia: Present conditions and future possibilities*. Melbourne: Australian Council of Educational Research, p.46.

10.Biskup, P. (1960). The Library of Western Australia, 1886-1955. *The Australian Library Journal, 9* (1), p.3.

11. Whitelock, D. (1974). *The great tradition: A history of adult education in Australia*. St. Lucia: University of Queensland Press, p.84

12.Nadel, G. (1957). *Australia's colonial culture: Ideas, men and institutions in mid-nineteenth century Eastern Australia*. Cambridge, Mass: Harvard University Press, p.181.

13.A detailed treatment of the early history of the Swan River Mechanics' Institute is to be found in Smith, B.J. (1961). Early Western Australian literature: A guide to colonial and goldfields life. *Unpublished MA thesis*. Perth: Department of History, University of Western Australia, especially chapter two.

14.Stannage, C.T. (1979). *The people of Perth: A social history of Western Australia's capital city*. Perth: Perth City Council, p.76.

15.Stannage, *loc. cit.*

16.Smith, B.J. (1961/2). Early Western Australian literature: A guide to colonial life. *University Studies in History, 4* (1), p.47.

17.*Inquirer*, 8 September 1852.

18.*The Western Australian Almanac for the Year of Our Lord 1856*, p.38.

19.*The Perth Literary Institute, RN 422*. BL.

20.S.R.M.I. Minutes, 24 Aug. 1854.

21.Reilly, J.T. (1903). *Reminiscences of fifty years' residence in Western Australia*. Perth: Sands and MacDougall, p.35.

22.Reilly, *op.cit.*, pp. 35-36.

23.Ewers, J.K. (1947). *Perth Boys' School, 1847-1947*. Perth: W.H. Wyatt, Government Printer.

24.S R M I Minutes, 19 June 1853.

25.*Inquirer*, 4 August 1852.

26.Ewers, *op.cit.*

27.Smith, *op. cit.*, p.49.

28.Smith, *op.cit.*,p.48.

29.Aveling, M. (Ed.). (1979). *Westralian voices: Documents in Western Australian social history*. Perth: University of Western Australia Press for the Education Committee of the 150th Anniversary Celebrations, p 135.

30.Craik, G.L. (1830). *The pursuit of knowledge under difficulties*. London: Society for the Diffusion of Useful Knowledge.

31.SRMI Minutes, 17 October 1853.

32.SRMI Minutes, 29 January 1866.

33.CSR 517/169-171. 1862--.

34.Smith, *op.cit.*, p.52.

35.S R M I Minutes, 10 August 1866

36.Spencer, L. (1957). A history of the library movement in Western Australia. *Unpublished Research Project*. Perth: Graylands Teachers' Training College, p.16.

37.*Inquirer*, 25 January 1860.

38.Spencer, *loc. cit.*

39.Spencer, *op. cit.*, p.17.

40.Stannage, *op. cit.*, p.184.

41.*Herald,* 11 March 1882

42.Spencer, *op. cit.*, pp. 18-19.

43.*Inquirer*, 14 March 1883.

44.Spencer, *op. cit.*, pp.18,20.

45.*Parliamentary Debates, 1893 Vol. IV. N.S.*, 14 August 1893, p.316.

46.White, M.A. (1981). *The community and post-school education in Western Australia: An historical study of institutional response to community demand.* Perth: Technical Publications Trust, p.37.

47.Perth Literary Institute (1951). *A century of cultural activity - the first hundred years of the Perth Literary Institute*. Perth: Perth Literary Institute.

48.Perth Literary Institute Minutes, 1953.

49.Ewers, J.K. (1971). *The Western gateway: A history of Fremantle.* (2nd ed.) Perth: University of Western Australia for the Fremantle City Council, p.14.

50.*Fremantle Mechanics' Institute Register of Members 1851.* Fremantle City Library Local History Collection Series No.020.

51.CSR 549/240/63. BL.

52.CSO Societies. Memorial of Fremantle Mechanics' Institute to Governor, 8 June 1864.

53.Fremantle Mechanics' Institute Report No.1 CSR 549/240/63. BL.

54.Smith, *op.cit.*, p.54.

55.*Herald,* 15 August 1868.

56.Kerr. W. (1973). Architecture in Fremantle, 1875-1915. *Unpublished B.Arch Thesis.* Perth: Faculty of Architecture, University of Western Australia.

57.*Herald*, 3 March 1883.

58.*West Australian,* 17 March 1899, p.7c.

59.Birch, J. (1967). *Notes on the Fremantle Library Service.* Fremantle: Fremantle City Library, p.1.

60.*Inquirer*, 1 September 1852.

61.Stephens, R. (1953). Albany Mechanics' Institute, 1852-1952: Centenary of Albany's Municipal Library. *Albany Advertiser*, 31 March 1953.

62.*Inquirer,* 18 October 1854.

63.Garden, D.S. (1979). *Albany: A panorama of the Sound from 1827.* Melbourne: Nelson, pp.118-119.

64.Hicks, B. (1967). Sir Alexander and Sir Thomas Cockburn-Campbell. *Early Days, 6* (6),p.77.

65.Stephens, *op.cit.*

66.*ibid.*

67.*ibid.*

68.Cook, *op.cit.*, p.3.

69.Perth Literary Institute, *op. cit.*, p.6.

70.*Inquirer*, 20 February 1867.

71. Guildford Mechanics' Institute (1900). *Rules of the Guildford Mechanics' Institute - Founded March 14th 1862; Revised at a Special Meeting November 2nd 1900.* Perth: R.W. Davis, printer.

72. Bourke, M.J. (1987). *On the Swan: A history of the Swan District of Western Australia.* Nedlands: University of Western Australia Press for the Shire of Swan, p.205.

73. *ibid.,* p.216.

74. Guildford Study Group (1981). *Guildford: A study of its unique character.* Guildford: The Study Group, p.65.

75. Bourke, *loc.cit.*

76. Bourke, *op.cit,* p.207.

77. Tanner N.H. (Hon Secretary, Swan-Guildford Historical Society), *personal communication,* 29 March 1993.

78. Swan-Guildford Historical Society (1962). *Handbill advertising the centenary celebrations.* Guildford: Historical Society.

79. Warren, L. (Guildford Public Librarian), *personal communication,* undated - March 1993.

80. Cogan, M. (1976). *Bassendean and Guildford Sketchbook.* Adelaide: Rigby, p.34.

81. *Herald,* 11 July 1874.

82. I. Walker (Hon. Sec. Geraldton Working Men's Society) to Colonial Secretary, 29 June 1868.

83. Grant of Land to Geraldton Working Men's Society, 28 October 1868

84. I. Walker (Hon.Sec. Geraldton Working Men's Society) to Colonial Secretary, 22 February 1871.

85. *Victoria Express,* 21 June 1882.

86. *ibid,* 28 June 1882.

87. *Victoria Express,* 21 June 1882.

88. Norris, C. (1989). *Memories of Champion Bay or Old Geraldton.* Geraldton: Soroptimist International of Geraldton, p.101.

89. Norris, *op.cit.,* p.24.

90. 'Fire in Geraldton: Mechanics' Institute burned down.' *The Express and Murchison and Yalgo Goldfields Chronicler,* 19 January 1900.

91.*ibid.*

92.'Opening the Geraldton Free Library.' *The Express and Murchison and Yalgo Goldfields Chronicler,* 10 August 1900.

93.'Trust to end lease of old library.' *Geraldton Guardian,* 25 June 1975.

94.Woodward, M. 'No mention of former name.' Letter to the Editor, *Geraldton Guardian,* 7 February 1989.

95.Geraldton Mechanics' Institute (1910). *Rules and by-laws: Adopted at a General Meeting held on September 20 1900 and registered in the Supreme Court, Perth, with additions and alterations to 31 August 1910; Library catalogue, revised to 31 August 1910.* Geraldton: Geraldton Mechanics' Institute.

96.Geraldton Cultural Trust Inc. (1984). *Rules as altered and amended by Annual General Meeting held 22 August 1984.* (typescript & mimeo). Geraldton: Cultural Trust.

97.'Trust to end lease of old building.' *Geraldton Guardian,* 25 June 1975.

98.N.J. Curnick (Managing Secretary, Geraldton Cultural Trust), *personal communication,* 24 March 1993.

99.Garden, D.S. (1979). *Northam: An Avon Valley history.* Melbourne: Oxford University Press, p.72.

100.Northam Mechanics' Institute PR3471. BL

101.*Perth Gazette,* 10 January 1868.

102.Bignell, M.(1981). *A place to meet: A history of the Shire of Katanning in Western Australia.* Perth: University of Western Australia Press, p.109.

103.Bignell, *op. cit.,* p.127.

104.*ibid.,*p.215.

105.*ibid.,*p.272.

106.Cook, *op.cit.,* pp.45-46.

107.Laurent, J.A. (1988). Mechanics' institutes and the labor movement: A case study of the West Australian goldfields, 1895-1917. *Melbourne Studies in Education, No.29,* 81-98.

108.Kalgoorlie Miners' Institute. 1900-64. PR3996. BL.

109.*West Australian Librarians' and Institutes' Journal 1,* November 1904.

110.Col. Sec. Dept. 1178/06. List of Mechanics' Institutes, Miners' Institutes and Agricultural Halls etc., in W A. See also Stat. Reg. 1905.

111.Fremantle Working Men's Association Minutes. (1867). *Fifth Annual Report*. Fremantle: Working Men's Association.

112.*Perth Gazette*, April 1864

113.*ibid*.

114.*West Australian*, 29 May 1883.

115.*West Australian*, 5 May 1886, pp.3 & 6.

116.Smith, *op.cit.*, p.56.

117.F A Sharr to Shire Clerk, Coolgardie, 6 August 1962. Cons 4854 Libraries Board of Western Australia, *State Librarian Correspondence File T1 C10*.

118.McColvin, *op.cit.*, p.47.

119.White, M.A. (1984) Historical aspects of railway training in Western Australia. *Railways Institute Magazine*, February, p.7.

120.White, *op.cit*, p.7.

121.quoted by White, M.A. (1981). The community and post-school education in Western Australia, *op. cit.*, p.36.

122.Biskup, *op.cit.*, p.3.

CHAPTER EIGHT

THE EDUCATION OF ADULTS IN SCHOOLS OF ARTS IN COLONIAL NEW SOUTH WALES

Michael Whiting

ORIGINS OF THE MOVEMENT

As Whitelock points out in his history of Australian adult education - *The Great Tradition* - prior to the advent of the mechanics' institutes in New South Wales, "organised education for adults in the colony, where it existed at all, was but a feeble embryo of a movement."[1] This was all to change, however, with the formation in March 1833 of a committee to establish the Sydney Mechanics' School of Arts.

So began the movement for adult education in the colony of New South Wales. Characterised by a mixture of moral and practical appeal, it sought to capture the pragmatic aspirations of the immigrants and be itself an instrument to reconstruct colonial life, and culture. That first decade saw all the seeds sown of success and failure, but primarily it was an era for the movement of practical and moral inspiration.

One of the first tasks of the committee was to create a precedent for which the movement throughout the nineteenth century would be grateful. They petitioned Governor Bourke for a building site, in the following terms:

> It does not seem to your Memorialists to be possible for Your Excellency to exercise your discretionary power in this respect, or any other occasion, or for any other purpose, more likely to produce permanent and solid advancement of Australia - than by granting to the Sydney Mechanics' School of Arts an Allotment of disposable ground in some central or otherwise eligible situation in or about Sydney.[2]

Not only did Bourke concur (by the February of 1834, the institution had a home of sorts) but he influenced the Legislative Council to grant £100 a year. By 1837 buildings were completed on the institution's own block of land in Pitt Street, but by 1859, the Sydney Mechanics' School of Arts had been rebuilt on government land, and that building continued until very recently as the Sydney School of Arts.

From the start, the mechanics' institute movement overcame a perennial barrier to adult education in this country, that of initial costs and finding suitable premises. The entire movement in the colony was aided by government grants of land often in the centre of towns, and generous capital grants to erect buildings and buy equipment. However, once this barrier was surmounted, the realisation came that the edifice was not all. The voluntary nature of the movement demanded special efforts to maintain impetus, and soon the question of who were the 'volunteers' had an ominous ring.

Rev. Henry Carmichael became a leading lecturer at the Sydney institution, as the movement grew in membership, reflected in its activities and subscriptions. The Report of the Committee of Management in 1835 expressed confidence in the future of the institution's work:

> Although the School of Arts has not yet arrived at the termination of its third year, it has made that progress and attained that character in the opinion of the public, which authorises them to indulge in the most flattering prospects of its future success. Taking into account our limited population, in connection with the apathy to literary and scientific pursuits which pervades our society, the Institution may be considered as having already surpassed the expectations of its original projectors - and as the colony continues to advance in wealth and intelligence, there can be no doubt that the importance and usefulness of the Mechanics' School of Arts will become the more appreciated.[3]

Despite this early outward success, however, the realisation grew that the mechanics and young workers were not coming in the numbers envisaged. In fact, the Sydney Mechanics' School of Arts was attracting a predominantly middle class group - clerks, merchants, lawyers, shopkeepers and others. When one examines the activities of that first decade it is not difficult to see why the mechanics were absent. Lectures offered included 'Philosophy of the Atmosphere,' 'Application of the Sciences,' 'Banking,' 'Intemperance,' and 'Strength of Colonial Timber.'[4] Others were 'The Law as Applicable to the Social Condition of the Working Classes,' by R Windeyer; 'Poetry,' by W A Beckett; 'Painting,' by Mr Bowers; 'Ancient Oratory,' by R Therry; and 'Palaeography,' by Rev. T Saunders.[5] In 1838 lectures ranged over chemistry, poetry and drama, natural history, architecture, phrenology, mechanical philosophy, political economy, and the use of celestial and terrestrial globes.

Obviously such activities tended to appeal to the already-educated members of the middle-classes, but were lost on the mechanics who generally were without any elementary education whatsoever. The knowledge which could have enabled them to derive full advantage from the lectures was not provided. The mechanic had specific educational and practical needs of instruction; instead he was usually offered prosaic and theoretical 'gentlemen lectures.' The movement was discovering early the need in adult education, with its dependence on voluntary interest and attendance, for an education to be offered on the terms of those to be educated, rather than the educators. The mechanics of Sydney stayed away out of indifference to lectures unrelated to their needs. In fact, the mechanics were not to come in great numbers until the 'seventies, when technical classes, in specific and needed courses, were established.

The 1837 Report lamented the absence of the mechanics and their "apparent indifference to their own improvement as well as to the benefits which accrue to their posterity from the full establishment of so philanthropic an institution."[6] The breast-beating of the well-intended!

The problem lay not so much in the absence of truly 'useful knowledge,' relevant to a mechanic's tasks in the colony, but that this took second place to the social and moral emphases. Carmichael, in his outline general aims, had mentioned the function of the mechanics' institutes in combating the colony's geographic isolation by stimulating interest in general scientific, especially geological and botanical, research. Successive Governors, patrons of the Sydney Mechanics' School of Arts, kept the utility of practical knowledge alive by lecturing in science, surveying and engineering. Governor Denison, in the 'fifties, lectured on 'The Advantages to be Derived from the Employment of Machinery.'[7] But the utility of educating men in terms of the colonial economy and manufactures remained less important than the moral and social consequences of the popular diffusion of knowledge.

An added feature of those early years, which helped to account for the minor place accorded to instruction in the natural sciences for mechanical and industrial processes, was that these processes in the colony had not yet reached anything near the proportions prevailing in England. The immigrant culture, which transplanted and sustained the institution, had not yet realised the difference in need in the new community. As Nadel observes, "the founders were not scientists, pastoralists, or agriculturalists. They were society-builders and generally conceived of colonisation less in terms of exploitation of the resources of the land than of the spread of culture and education."[8]

In 1841, a record number of lectures was delivered, and 812 members were paying £577 in subscriptions. In 1842 a government subsidy of £200 a year was assured; it was also a peak year for immigration. It was becoming apparent, however, that the Sydney Mechanics' School of Arts, as a form of adult education, had failed to define its educational function to suit its aims. The specific education of mechanics was already being forsaken in favour of education and amusements for the middle-classes.

Indeed the 'forties were a difficult period for the developing mechanics' institute movement as a whole. The colony suffered a severe commercial depression from 1841 to 1843, and the dislocation and dismay in connection with this had much effect on institutions aiming for popular support. T H Brain, in his 1848 history of the colony, records how the Legislative Council of New South Wales, on 3 October 1843, resolved:

> that this Council will make good any sums, not exceeding £2,500...in giving employment to distressed mechanics and labourers, having families in Sydney, during the remainder of the present year;

and a month or so later, on 15 November, resolved:

> that a sum not exceeding £500 be appointed to enable a number of the unemployed labourers, at present in Sydney, to proceed with their families to the districts of Moreton Bay, Hunter's River, Bathurst, Goulburn, Yass, Illawarra, and other country districts where they are likely to find employment.[9]

Returning times of prosperity did not, however, mean revival of membership or interest; in fact, 1847 saw a decline in numbers. The Committee of Management of the Sydney Institute reflected ruefully in its *Fifteenth Annual Report* of that year:

> Some diminution in the number of members has taken place...Many of them have removed to different parts of the colony... not a few from that increase of occupation which returning prosperity necessarily brings with it, have found themselves unable to devote any time to the pursuits of literature and science; while a third, but not a very numerous class, having skimmed over our limited stack of works of fiction, without deriving from them that taste for more solid reading...have abandoned

themselves to the inglorious charms of inactivity...[10]

and continued on a theme so often repeated in the immigrant society:

> the truth is that however it may be desired, it cannot be reasonably expected that any large proportion of time should be devoted to pursuits not directly remunerative, in a community all classes of which are to a greater or lesser degree affected by the spirit of commercial enterprise...[11]

J B Laughton, delivering a lecture at the opening of the Bathurst Mechanics' School of Arts in 1855, remarked in a familiar way that:

> in the year 1849, the Member's Roll of the Sydney Mechanics' School of Arts did not include more than twenty Mechanics properly so called; the other members were clerks, shopmen or gentlemen who subscribed to obtain light reading for their wives and daughters at a cheap rate.[12]

The editor of *The Empire* believed that the Institute was not fulfilling its role because it did not have working-class support. If the support was encouraged then the Institute would have a Committee of Management more faithful to its objectives and, by extending education facilities, lead the lower classes "to a state of social happiness and moral influence."[13]

At mid-century, therefore, the fortunes of the Sydney Mechanics' School of Arts, and the movement generally, were doubtful. The city middle-class had arrived in the lectures and the reading room, and were influencing the choice of literature for the library. As the population of the colony grew in the wake of the goldrushes, the pressure for a sense of community was more urgent than ever. The advocates of culture knew how national sentiment would be forged by literature and political knowledge, and the mechanics' institute movement still held out the best means of that education for adults. Carmichael had said in 1833:

> the living world of the mind we have quitted although we still may glance at the panorama of its movements, as reflected in the literary and scientific publications of our 'beloved fatherland.' Yet if we mean to rise in the scale of nations, we must possess a literature and science of our own.[14]

For the apostle of the Enlightenment, these appropriate words of the 'thirties were still relevant in the 'fifties. As colonial life and culture were dislocated by the challenges and changes of the goldrushes, many still had this faith in the mechanics' institute movement as the best means of educating the community in its sense of unity and harmony.

The movement followed the people with the foundation of mechanics' institutes at Newcastle in 1835, Maitland in 1839, Patrick's Plains (Singleton) in 1845, and in the 'fifties at a sequence of settlements such as Goulburn, Bathurst, Mudgee, Windsor, Braidwood, East Maitland, and Armidale. In each case:

> The pattern was generally the same. A group of educated men would band together, sometimes at the instigation of a person with experience of the movement in the

mother country and sometimes simply to take over or extend activities of a previously existing library association, debating club or reading room.[15]

For Instance, *The Maitland Mercury* reported in April 1845 that at Patrick's Plains "a few gentlemen are interesting themselves in a movement to get up a society for the diffusion of useful and interesting knowledge in the shape of a Mechanics' Institute." The first three lectures emphasised the immigrant middle-class presence. On 12 May, J J Davies gave "a luminous account of the advantages that had been derived from the mechanics' institutes in Britain," on 26 May, Henry Bailey spoke on 'Poetry and Drama,' and two weeks later again, on 9 June, Dr Stolworthy addressed a large audience on 'The Theory of Digestion,' which was described as "being of great benefit to the community."[16]

The Society supporting the Institute reported proudly in 1846 that the first annual meeting of the Patrick's Plains Mechanics' Institute was held at Cox's Inn on 4 May. It was stated that:

> during the first year 12 lectures had been given and that the library now contained 216 volumes comprising various of the arts and sciences and some polite literature, all which have been extensively read. There were 58 members during the first year. The receipts of the year amounted to £38/12/3 of which £9/3/- represented donations.[17]

However, by 22 January 1848, membership was down to 13, and shortly thereafter, to three. The impetus for this adult education endeavour seemed about to ebb altogether, however by 5 May 1852, *The Maitland Mercury* was reporting a new committee and a fresh lease of life:

> Your committee regrets that for the last three years your institution has been in abeyance arising from the prostrate condition of the colony generally and the adverse condition in which every member of the community has been placed. But a brighter era is now opened before us, and they now look forward with confidence not only to an improvement in wealth but a more extended and beneficial development of our social condition...

> The library contains 230 volumes, the greater number of which are first-class standard works, and the remainder known as works of light reading. The first are in very good condition and the latter in a rather dilapidated state. The funds in the hands of the treasurer amount to £13/5/3½.[18]

Still the reprieve was brief and within the year the Institute was to go the way of so many of its contemporaries: "this is a rather dull portion of the year...we have no lectures now, the Mechanics' Institute having shrunk into a subscription library."[19] Patrick's Plains, it seems, was too small and too isolated. Once the gentlemen scholars of the district had given an original lecture in their particular field ("Dr Glennie lectured on Electricity in the Court House in June 1852, when there were upwards of 200 persons present")[20] the absence of educated teachers was only too apparent. The fact that the Library continued, as it did in so many settlements, was more an indication of the need for entertainment than desire for learning. In most cases, as will be explored later, the library and reading rooms, or museums, became the springboard for a revival of 'our defunct Institute' in the 'seventies and 'eighties.

Meanwhile, what of the classes of instruction adults were opting for? McDonald reports that in 1846, at the Sydney Mechanics' School of Arts, 49 persons had indicated their wishes:

> to enrol in classes in arithmetic (6), writing and grammar (2), mechanical and architectural drawing (4), figure and landscape drawing (4), French (11), Latin and Greek (8), chemistry (5), and music (9). These numbers were, the Committee of Management believed, insufficient to warrant classes being formed, although action was being taken to begin classes in French, which soon failed for lack of support.[21]

The mechanic had little here to attract support or stimulate interest, while the better educated were aroused by the prospect of French and music.

Classes at a higher level were persisted with, but the gold fever so affected several members of the instrumental section of the music class that they departed for the diggings. Classes were discontinued. In 1855 a revival was attempted, and Henry Parkes gave the clarion call: a person enrolling in classes, he wrote:

> would have the satisfaction of knowing that [he was] improving his mind, whilst obtaining some relaxation from the monotonous and engrossing toils of the day. At all events it would be a decided improvement on the theatre and the tavern, and cheaper to boot.[22]

But an elementary educational tenet, so important to the psychology of adult learning as we know today, had then still to be understood. The classes were so arranged as to discourage any systematic study under a teacher in any particular topic. Good intentions were not enough, and many students, having to brave a haphazard and disjointed series of lectures, reluctantly or otherwise gave in instead to the 'theatre or tavern.'

In a familiar vein, the Class Committee at the Sydney Mechanics' School of Arts was concerned in 1858 that the classes offered by the Institute were "entirely inadequate to the encouragement of middle-class education."[23] It was obvious the working-class had long since disappeared from view.

This was not the only failure becoming apparent by the mid-'fifties. Patrick's Plains' lamentable story found a corollary in the sometimes ineffective and bad leadership of the Sydney Mechanics' School of Arts. Most institute affairs fell to the responsibility of a secretary, who also functioned as librarian. At the Sydney Institute, a decline of members to 296 by 1851 caused a committee of investigation to be created to ascertain "the extent of the defalcations of a former secretary-librarian."[24] Classes were already beginning to lose their attraction; lectures were few in number, so the fact that the library had been allowed to "sink into a condition of disgraceful and culpable neglect containing a considerable number of inferior works wholly unworthy of the institution"[25] encouraged no-one. Obviously the movement needed an impetus. While the prosperity and growth of the period ensured that the immigrant culture would at least carry the colony's only form of adult education to its growing rural settlements, somehow, the spirit was dissipated. Encouragement was needed.

Crusaders were found. In common with other countries, adult education in Australia has relied, at most stages of its development, on a handful of visionaries: secular missionaries, who offered adults relief from the material toil surrounding them. New educational blood was surely needed in the early 'fifties, and it was the establishment of a fellow educational institution - the University of Sydney - that bought to the colony a group of men whose life was thinking, teaching, and sharing knowledge. At the same time, that companion of popular education, popular journalism, gained considerable expansion with the colony's growth. It was in such newspapers as *The Empire*, under Henry Parkes' care, that popular education received press encouragement.

The proponents of popular education for adults usually held the dual assumptions "that society had witnessed a revolution, and that education made men moral."[26] The revolution was in the role of education and was continuous, creating knowledgeable men (especially in the colony with adult male suffrage and the proposed secret ballot), and the educational institutions at least provided a civilised haven to encourage a moral community. Popular education was inextricably linked with the cultural responses of a growing society to new social and political mores, as well as to scientific and industrial change.

Dr John Woolley, arriving as Principal of Sydney University and its foundation Professor of Logic and Classics, soon joined the Sydney Mechanics' School of Arts (in 1853), and gave the opening address in 1854 for the year's series of lectures, in which he stated his views on education and on adult learning in particular. Not just popular education, but intellectual training set the working man free, Woolley believed. Adult education was most favourably promoted by high standards in teaching, a little bookwork, and as much dialogue as possible. Knowledge not only made the individual happy, and society virtuous by its diffusion, but it enhanced social harmony and egalitarianism.[27]

Speaking in 1860, again at the Sydney Institute, Woolley was in tune with the social egalitarianism of his new culture: "certainly we have learnt that popular education is a revolution and that it does unfit the great body of our people for that moral serfdom to which they were not long ago degraded."[28] His echo was the chairman of the inaugural meeting to form the Deniliquin Mechanics' Institute in 1864, who overruled an objection raised to the term 'mechanics' institute': "What was he but a mechanic? We had no aristocracy in this country (cheers). We had left them behind in the Old Country."[29]

Social egalitarianism was one advantage of the mechanics' institutes which Woolley claimed the movement had not realised. Everyone in New South Wales could reach for intellectual improvement and knowledge - the fault of the 'fathers' had been their singular cry for the general diffusion of knowledge; the challenge to the present generation was to find ways of utilising that knowledge. A proper sense of the utility of knowledge, not just its communication, must result in social improvement.

The institutes were the community's means of interpreting to the popular mind the knowledge of the thoughtful scholar. In this egalitarian oasis, a University was not the preserve of an aristocracy, but the instrument of the masses. However, if most obstacles to social advance had been overcome, was not the utility of knowledge only a material one? Had not the

166

diffusion of knowledge become a weaker social force as it left behind the morality of the Enlightenment and the defiance of public ignorance?

Woolley's answer, if indeed he was aware of these questions easily posed in retrospect, was that the effort of understanding the principles of the sciences and humanities was enriching in itself. The uneducated person could discover this in the institutes, where teaching by the learned could be had - not just through isolated lectures and by borrowing books, but through classes of instruction.

After 1855, classes at the Sydney Mechanics' School of Arts widened considerably, and a Woolley-inspired emphasis on liberal and general studies prevailed. Woolley himself conducted the classes in Greek, logic, and political economy. In 1858 the Class Committee found that the classes:

> were not only actively supported...and recommended that 'immediate steps - be taken to stimulate the ambition and sustain the perseverance of students by honours and awards.' They proposed that examinations be held annually in all the subjects in which the classes had been given during the year and that medals, certificates, or other prizes be awarded to recommended students. The prizes would be presented at the Annual General Meeting of the Institution and the names of successful candidates embodies in the Annual Report.[30]

This more formal and determined attempt at class instruction suffered the fate that such adult education courses often did: there was little formal academic discipline (the uneducated were also the uninitiated), no particular line of study could be enforced or recommended, and attendance had to be voluntary, as was the case with any written exercises. There is no doubt that, significantly, Woolley's pioneering of this method had its sequel later in the intensive class programs operated jointly by Sydney University's Department of Adult Education and the Workers' Education Association.

Even though the classes at the Sydney institute came in for criticism in the Letters columns of Sydney newspapers from time to time, *The Empire* was often the most vocal.[31] Popular education received much support from newspapers generally. Henry Parkes, while editor of *The Empire,* feared that material prosperity would interfere with the moral and ethical growth - let alone the intellectual inclinations - of adults in the community. Parkes believed that the development of an adult's ethical personality was the greatest safeguard against temptation and moral lapses. Ignorance, he knew, was the greatest danger to human progress, for "an ignorant people infuriated by sense of wrong, would wreck the social structure education is destined to strengthen and improve."[32]

It was this emphasis on the social and reconstructive function of adult education which found Henry Parkes in harmony on the topic with John Woolley. Ironically, it was *The Empire* and other newspapers which were becoming 'competitors' of the mechanics' institutes for the attention of the working classes.

Woolley felt the institutes had a second function besides the merely educational. They provided a means of bringing people together for worthwhile activities during periods of leisure. "The spread of social sympathy" was a real contribution to the development of true communal harmony in colonial life. Speaking at Wollongong School of Arts in 1861 Wolley said, "I am so firmly convinced that the habit of meeting is itself a priceless good, that it would be worthwhile to come [to the Institute] if only to shake hands and go home again."[33]

Here Woolley was highlighting a factor of the community role of the mechanics' institutes that became particularly strong in rural areas as the century progressed. Not exactly educational perhaps, but this social function of the institutes was undoubtedly one of their most important and successful contributions to nineteenth century cultural and social life.

For Woolley the happiest consequence of the 'Volunteer movement' was the way it operated as an "antidote against social misunderstanding...by removing the only cause of misunderstanding, mutual ignorance and isolation; by giving us work to do together, in which the chief praise is awarded to no artificial pre-eminence but belongs to him who labours most zealously and effectively in the common cause."[34] This was complimented, nevertheless, by the:

> primary mission of the Australian Schools of Arts. They are, if wisely used, no less than Palladiums of our Nationality. Some have lamented the extension which has been given to the original design of these Institutions, which were only ever intended by the founders to teach Mechanics the scientific principles of their trades. But our wants are not those of England thirty years ago: we require not only skill in a section of our people, but education for all; not more art-culture but preparation for the general duties of society. To balance the drawbacks of colonial life there is always this advantage. A colonist cannot be a mere instrument; he is not a living part of some stupendous machinery; he must think and act for himself...
>
> Our object is not so much to teach, as to stimulate thought and promote self-training.[35]

DEVELOPMENT OF THE MOVEMENT

As rural settlements spread after the 'fifties there were many continuing causes of social misunderstandings, one being sectarian disputes regarding childhood education. These divisive factors often encouraged the educated few in a settlement to promote a mechanics' institute or a school of arts, as a community interest free from jealousies and as a means of creating refinement in an often difficult and crude environment. The local institute would offer an "education (which) is not knowledge, but the habit of thinking...(for) mental like bodily activity is the reward of regular and daily exercise; it is not the fruit of occasional effort."[36]

Just what would be the educational nature of these institutes as they became elegant or humble additions to a rural town's 'public amenities'? Would it be 'education of adults,' seeking in the broadest sense to provide facilities for an impact on the adult mind, or would it be 'adult education,' providing activities which were decidedly educational by intent? An informal or formal education? It was an argument that was quickly solved in the growing colony as far as the institute movement went. The institute movement opted in most cases for the informal and socially-based ideal of 'education of adults.'

In the *Lithgow Mercury*, some years after the turn of the century, a certain 'C C J' reminisced that at Mitchell's Creek the School of Arts was one and everything to all people, and a success at that:

> In Mitchell's Creek with a population of not more than five hundred our Mechanics' Institute boomed splendidly, and was praised by all who visited the place. There were two pubs, and beyond these there was no other place for the young men to go of an evening after work. We changed all this by renting an old store; knocking several rooms into one, thus making a good-sized room for concerts, debates, dancing (we were not straight-laced, and did not affect puritanism), athletic exercises, including boxing and fencing. And here we met - or, some of us did - every night in the week, and so we arranged the nights to suit all parties, and to please all tastes. The first Monday in every month we gave a social dance to which every man and women on the creek was invited (and persons of no character were in a big minority, and we were thus on safe ground.) One of the publicans, Mr McLaughlin, assisted us materially by supplying 'soft stuff' on dance nights, and in other ways. Books, magazines, and newspapers were sent to us from all parts, and by 'all sorts and conditions of men' - some of whom also sent us money, believing as they said, that we were doing good - as indeed we were. We formed a good band, we had a fine minstrel troupe; we taught rough uncouth young men to dance, and generally conduct themselves as respectable men. We instilled in them a love of reading, a liking for discussion, for music, for games, for innocent enjoyment - of which, heretofore, they had had none.[37]

It was this spirit, a social and wider cultural - but still educational - role for the institutes which began to prevail over the more formal and narrow educational provision of earlier years. Perhaps it was the middle-class making entertainment, or wanting to reform 'the uncouth young men'; or, perhaps in a more philosophical vein, it was a struggling community attempting to give itself a heart that would overcome the social divisions of colonial life and prepare for nationhood. Most definitely it was a belief that an educational institution was the ideal instrument for social reconstruction.

Adults, it might be argued, needed this focus in the last decades of the nineteenth century in New South Wales. In any event, every town boasted of its mechanics' institutes or school of arts, and each settlement was to have its own variation. Braidwood, for instance, felt the need first for a 'subscription library':

> A letter dated 29th October, 1857, and signed by seventeen of the town's most prominent citizens was addressed to Mr William Essington King, Police Magistrate of Braidwood, requesting him to call 'a meeting of the inhabitants to take steps for establishing a subscription library in the town of Braidwood'...in due course, Rules and By-laws were formulated and the title of Literary Institute was suggested...The concluding paragraph from the minutes of the meeting held on 26th November, 1857 merits quotation in full:
>
>> 'Your Committee cannot close their pleasing duties without congratulating the Inhabitants of the District on the dawn of what to them appears an auspicious future as the establishment of such a Society cannot fail to have a most beneficial effect on all classes, tending as it must do to elevate

the tone of Moral and Intellectual attainment in the minds of all members of the community, and would therefore urge the cordial and hearty cooperation of every well-wisher of his adopted or native land.'

...(In 1858) with a view to 'raising the intellectual tone of the community,' lectures were delivered by prominent citizens at intervals in the Library Room. It was unanimously decided, 'that children under ten should not be admitted to these lectures!'....

In January, 1862, the Library contained approximately 400 books. At the meeting of 29th May, 1862, it was decided to conduct a Public Subscription Ball at the Commercial Hotel to raise funds to match the Government Grant of £100 towards the cost of a new building...
Success followed the efforts of these early culture-minded citizens, because a fine building was later erected bearing the uplifting title of the 'Braidwood Literary Institute.' The front room was a Reading Room, also provided (was) on its ground floor a two-table Billiard Room. Upstairs a fine Hall became the centre of social life in the district...

As the years passed, enthusiasm for 'Moral and Intellectual uplift' as the pioneers phrased it, must have waned considerably, because the Library slowly lost its popularity and gradually reached a stage of stagnation. The Billiard Room also had its decline and finally became a meeting place for a few old faithfuls who often played cards instead of using the tables.[38]

Despite the fortunes, and eventual misfortunes, of the Braidwood Literary Institute, it was with wistful glances that the folk of Queanbeyan looked upon the events involving their Braidwood contemporaries:

After the collapse of the Mechanics' Institute (six months into 1859), the Church of England Reading Room was revived, and a discussion class was inaugurated, but this degenerated into a mere debating society and failed to gain much support.

The Queanbeyan Mutual Improvement Association, operating from J J Wright's branch store in Macquaid Street, was only a slight improvement mixing recitations of poetry with abstract debates. A second Mechanics' Institute, lasting from the late 'sixties until 1880, throve fitfully and was able to establish both a library and lecture program. It was finally split asunder in one of the recurrent rows involving W G O'Neill who, as landlord of three rooms rented to the Institute, first let one room to the newly established Bank of New South Wales, and then evicted the Institute from the other two, seizing goods and chattels for unpaid rent. But for the clash of personalities on organising committee the Mechanics' Institute might have survived, particularly as it was in its later years receiving a Government subsidy on a 10s. in the £ basis. A Literary Institute formed at Braidwood at the same time lasted for the best part of a century and was able to erect a most imposing building which still serves as a community centre.[39]

Indeed, the institute movement, particularly in rural areas such as these, where numbers were always relatively small and personalities so important, suffered the pitfalls most voluntary adult education movements were (and still are) prone to. Management had usually to be part-time, and thus often inefficient, funds were never sufficient, permanent premises were either non-existent or in being built took too much of the Committee's time and attention, and, such a community project left itself vulnerable to all sorts of faction fights. Such a circumstance occurred at Armidale over the Mechanics' Institute, when the running of it was turned into

> an arena for the trial of denominational strength. In 1865 a meeting of certain members of the school was held to protest against alleged false elections, and against an alleged slight to the President, a Roman Catholic priest, at a previous meeting. The Institute's hall was refused for the meeting, with the result that the protesting faction, when wishing to hold a second meeting, occupied the hall at least 48 hours in advance to ensure that it would be available. But, despite this display of energy, the previously elected committee, not one of whom was a Roman Catholic, remained in office. If this spirit of sectarianism was at all normal, and we may assume it to have been in evidence at least for a time both before and after the events of 1865, the School's lack of success is not difficult to understand.[40]

Many Committees were left in no doubt as to community attitudes about the running of the local Institute. In the mid 'sixties, one indignant citizen wrote to the *Albury Banner*:

> Sir - Can you tell me whether or not there is such an adjunct to the machinery of the Mechanics' Institute as a Secretary; and if so, when, where, and how he performs the trifling duties pertaining to the office? I ask, because for months I have seen a parcel of books, given to the Institute, lying on the floor, and, although the shelves contain hardly a score of books, time has not yet been found to cut the string of the said parcel. A great inducement this to others to make donations of books, while the subscribers are most anxious for fresh reading. Again, there is a sort of farce of filing the papers pretended to be gone through. If you, Sir, will look you will see it is a farce and no more. I think the last *Sydney Herald* or *Argus* filed is dated about August last! I am glad to see the new building progressing, but can you tell me why there was no little ceremony about laying the foundation stone which ceremony could easily have been made the means of bringing £20 or £50, or perhaps more, to the funds? It is public building of the town and such a proceeding should not have been neglected. If a little more energy cannot be shown in carrying out the arrangements, it will be better to appropriate the building to some other purpose and sink the notion of an Institute which no one appears to think it worthwhile to look after or think about -
>
> Your obedient servant, A SUBSCRIBER.[41]

The *Maitland Mercury*, on 3 August 1865, advised the public that:

> We have been favoured with an inspection of the plan for the new Mechanics' Institute (at Singleton), drawn by Thomas Rowe, Esq., architect, of Sydney. The architect, who seems to be a devoted admirer of the Gothic, has allowed this style of architecture to prevail in the plan, and however desirable the Gothic style may be for churches, or even hospitals, the introduction of the gloomy Gothic in the erection of a building under whose roof it is intended to advance the acquisition of the liberal arts

and the intellectual progress of the community generally is, we think, totally unsuitable and uncalled for...[42]

Needless to say, Mr Rowe's 'gloomy Gothic' was unanimously rejected!

A happier note was struck a year later. The foundation stone was laid for the new and redesigned Singleton Mechanics' Institute. The President of the Institute, The Reverend Mr White, in the presence of the Governor of the Colony, Sir John Young, unconsciously emphasised a tension between the educational and prestigious role of an Institute in many rural settlements, when he was reported as saying:

> It had been said that the building they were about to erect was too large and fine a one for Singleton, but they must thank themselves or the exceeding liberality of the donors of the sites of land and the subscribers to the funds for that. The contributions of several gentlemen had been most princely.... When the Committee found themselves so nobly supported by these gentlemen, they were enabled to erect a more handsome building than was at first designed, and when completed it would be a credit to their town... He proceeded to advert to some of the advantages of mechanics' institutes. And first he said they were a protest against mammonism, of which there was great danger in the colony, from the fact that men were not only engaged in the ordinary ways of making money, by means of commerce, but also in digging it out of the bowels of the earth. In the lifetime of man there was higher results to be achieved than the mere acquisition of wealth. Then, again, these institutions were a protest against sectarianism, and in carrying on the affairs of that institution, he said that it was a gratifying fact that representatives of all religious denominations had been emulous of seeing who could do the most good work. Moreover, such an institution was a refutation that slanders that had been uttered against the people of the colony were wrong, that they were mammon-worshipping people.... Mechanics' Institutes were a great desideratum in the colony, for there were hundreds and thousands of persons in it whose education had been neglected, and who could not avail themselves of the infant school on the one hand, or the university on the other. To such persons the mechanics' institutes afford great facilities for self-improvement, and would enable many such persons to obtain a position in the literary world. Such institutions as these could afford a means of rational amusements also. He strongly advocated the desirability of working men taking part in the government of these institutions, as this was one of the elements of their success.[43]

That the institutes would offer a means of 'rational recreation' became an imperative feature of planning by every institute committee. In a sense they were using an educational medium to satisfy what they considered a community need. A Committee called together in Broken Hill in 1888 to initiate steps to establish a library and reading room pragmatically suggested that:

> It was thought better to erect a room first of all, and endeavour to fill it with books afterwards. The establishment of such a place would serve to keep the young men out of the public houses, so that they could enjoy themselves rationally instead of spending money foolishly.[44]

These were echoes of Dr John Woolley's words at Maitland: "and the School of Arts would deserve well of the community, if it did no more than offer to a few artisans an employment for the leisure hours which might counteract the attraction of our deadly and implacable enemy - strong drink."[45] This moral tone, never far below the surface of a committee's reports, obviously did not go unnoticed by the working men urged to come and learn, and participate. The 'mechanics' were reluctant to respond to an education offered in so didactic a manner, and usually alien to their cultural aspirations. When they did come, it was, more often than not, to play billiards.

The pioneering communities tended to follow a customary immigrant pattern: the more precarious and challenging life became, the more tenaciously the old institutions were clung to. The absence of the working-classes from the institutions designed for them was a sign that something needed revision. Otherwise, what was intended for the working-class would become the preserve of the middle-class instead.

There was, in the colonial community, a great social generosity towards education, but the colonial culture was also characterised by a willingness to give over to the government responsibility for providing community services. The growing prosperity and self-assurance of colonial governments in New South Wales in the latter half of the nineteenth century - governments often conspicuously imbued with a strong sense of social egalitarianism - meant that government action both aided and hindered the community role of the institutes. The library facilities of the mechanics' institutes and schools of arts were strengthened and enlarged by government action, but these government subsidies were to strike at the very real voluntary feature of the movement. The creation of a Board of Technical Education was to finally provide, outside the institute movement, the disciplined and practical courses of study that working men had been led to think were available at the local institute. The very social success of the institutes in many towns meant that the educational emphasis tended to be broadened, especially in a community where all were receiving some elementary education, and a few, secondary education. Providing debating clubs was a distinct triumph of the movement in the 'eighties and 'nineties, but by then the trade unions and political parties had become an equally significant forum.

RENEWED EMPHASIS ON TECHNICAL EDUCATION

As the change in character of the mechanics' institutes became apparent, it was hoped that special schooling for working men would be provided, if not at the institutes, then elsewhere. The idea of popular education had been based on the social benefits of the diffusion of knowledge, whether in moral improvement or social amelioration. But the mechanic held out for a systematic and relevant education.

John Woolley, in 1860, proposed a Working Men's College which would meet in a more determined and organised fashion the day-to-day needs of working people; and in 1865 and 1869 evening classes for mechanics did begin at the Sydney School of Arts.

Between 1865 and the late 'seventies, the Sydney Mechanics' School of Arts considered many plans for the establishment of technical classes, and in 1873 a recommendation was made to the Government that steps be taken to establish classes in applied mechanics, physiology, practical drawing, chemistry as used in the arts and manufactures, mensuration, practical geometry, algebra and trigonometry. By 1878 the Government was willing to provide the finance for the building of classrooms and laboratories, and the School of Arts raised the rest by public subscription.[46] On 19 May 1879, the buildings were opened:

> Members may with some pride claim the first conception and introduction of technical education into New South Wales. But while saying this much for themselves, they must not overlook the important pecuniary and other assistance they have been afforded by the Government of the colony in giving effect to the idea. It cannot at present be predicted what may hereafter be the precise relation between the New South Wales Government and the important matter of technical education. Four hundred and seventy-eight students have availed themselves of its educational advantages during the year.[47]

From 1879, a Working Men's College grew, using the Sydney Mechanics' School of Arts facilities, and by 1881 it had about 2,000 participants. By 1883 Parliament had contributed £3,000 towards the cost of this new direction of the institute.[48] Thus, with the aid of a State subsidy, the Sydney Mechanics' School of Arts was playing a very prominent role in broadening adult education in the 'seventies and 'eighties, and probably by the *ad hoc* nature of the provision and organisation proved receptive to new ideas and trends.

At this time came a crisis which was to indicate one of the reasons for the desertion of the institute by those involved in technical education. The Sydney Mechanics' School of Arts was under an Act of Incorporation which strictly limited its power, it being unable to allow outside organisations to have any direct voice in its councils. Adult education institutions, to be properly understood and supported, need wide, and free, access to them by interested associations and adults. (The Workers' Education Association was to prevent a repetition of this error in the twentieth century, but the lesson had still to be learnt in the 'eighties.) Though the Act was changed, the School of Arts, with only a year-to-year grant of around £1,500 from the Government, could not even be sure of paying lecturers, let alone providing employment for permanent officers to run the college.

It was a clash, however, with the liberal imagination basic to the School of Arts' view of itself that led in 1889 to the Technical Education Board being dissolved and the Technical College being brought under direct state control. Mr W C Windeyer, fifty years after the Rev. Henry Carmichael had given his inaugural lecture at the School of Arts, lamented that any separate technological institutions would create prejudice between 'trade' and 'less material' occupations. Academic and practical labour were not distinct, for they served the same end.[49] The skilled mechanic possessed more dignity in his labour than the clerical worker. As well, the academically skilled needed, by the diffusion of knowledge, to justify their social roles. Here, Windeyer was returning to that popular education based on the social benefits of the diffusion of knowledge. By the 'eighties, however, the institute movement was obviously not retaining this adult education role, and nothing emphasised this more than the formal break with technical education.

Some adult education needs to be highly systematic, and skilfully prepared and delivered. In the end, the *ad hoc* appointment of lecturers, the absence of organised syllabuses, a view of science and technology too broad and lacking particular application and reference, and the inability of all interested parties to take part in the planning and conducting of courses combined to frustrate the role which mechanics' institutes could fulfil.

It had been an effort to impose technical education from above (not a method conducive to the voluntary nature of adult education) which, nevertheless, encouraged and awakened a community interest in science and technology. Stephen Murray-Smith contended that:

> On the credit side...it can be said that the mechanics' institutes performed an educational service that has been unfairly depreciated...they placed emphasis on design, and popularised the idea of science and the concept of individual responsibility in learning. Above all, from the example of educational initiative they set, did come an organisational core which had a direct link with the subsequent development of technical education.[50]

A feature of the School of Arts' endeavours in the technical education field (and which has managed to plague Australian adult education to this day) was the necessity for adults to study at night and on a part-time basis. Likewise, in the purely technical field, there was not satisfactorily established that relationship between scientific instruction, useful knowledge, industrial efficiency, and the job, which the working adult sought and needed.

THE COMMUNITY DEBATING FORUM AS A STIMULUS TO CULTURAL DEVELOPMENT

When the Government had moved in 1884 to transfer the Technical College to a Board of Technical Education this meant an end, in one way, of the Sydney School of Arts as a 'mechanics' institute.' Yet this applied only to the formal courses; that working-class activity and vital sign of popular education entitled "classes for mutual improvement" continued with the School of Arts being used as a debating forum for radical politics. In this sense, both the founding institution and its numerous offspring throughout the countryside of New South Wales kept alive for twenty or more years a form of adult education - socially beneficial and communally progressive - that has rarely been seen since.

The report of the Sydney Mechanics' School of Arts for 1840 voiced deep concern lest the then being proposed Debating Classes encouraged "angry sectarian discussion" and allowed the organisation to develop as a "political debating club."[51] By 1853, the *Sydney Morning Herald* was reporting the view of William T Cape, senior Vice-President, that the debating classes were, on the contrary, of considerable value:

> With their own perseverance in such efforts as circumstances placed in their power; with kindly feelings towards each other in all differences of opinion, all with the co-operation of older members, especially in maintaining the usual proprieties, there would be little doubt of the complete success - and good reputation of the class as well as its value to the young men of Sydney.[52]

And indeed, the classes flourished in the following decade, with debates upon the more popular questions engaged in, under Cape's enthusiastic guidance. Cape was a typical member of 'respectable' society - a philanthropic reformer, of conservative political views and liberal social persuasions, who saw such an adult education movement as the mechanics' institutes as a legitimate arena for personal social leadership. He was typical of that

175

generation and class who, for a variety of motives, reached out in the immigrant and colonial community to the working men. This nexus of the liberal middle class and the working class (based on a whole variety of moral, intellectual and political reasons relating to the education of the masses being an obligation and necessity) was to be broken, particularly in the urban areas in the last decades of the nineteenth century, because of the organised growth of Unions and the Labor Party. The debating clubs of the institutes paved the way for the working class organisations, and ironically, the severing of a bond which had given vitality to the educational aims of the institutes.

In many cases it was the local debating society (just as it was the library in other places) that was the precursor of the local mechanics' institutes. Such was the Windsor Debating Society, which, before the Mechanics' Institute grew out of it, was debating such topical questions as protective tariffs and land sales. During the 'eighties and 'nineties many aspiring politicians used their institute debating floor for initiation and practice. The wish of the founders - that the proper function of popular education in colonial life was a search for unity through culture - came to the fore at the Sydney Mechanics' School of Arts in 1886, when 1,200 people attended 41 meetings of the debating club, and young men such as W A Holman led in public controversy then, and in the 'nineties, amidst depression, strikes, Federation and the growth of the working man's own political party.[53]

At the Queanbeyan School of Arts in 1891, a Literary and Debating Society had been established as an adjunct to supplement a normal lecture program with practical discussion on topical questions. It was symbolic that the first debate discussed whether women should be allowed to vote![54]

WOMEN IN THE INSTITUTE MOVEMENT

John Woolley, when lecturing on *The Social Uses of Schools of Arts* in 1860, had mused "that the nearest approach which our school [the Sydney institution] affords to this practical education, is the debating society or 'class of mutual improvement'.... One thing they give us: they humanise thought." He in turn showed his humanity when he forecast the topic of Queanbeyan's School of Arts' first debate in his comments regarding the role of women in society, in particular, their place in the institute movement:

> But I have one serious fault to find both with this [debating society] and the only other social element in our institution - the Reading room. They are, whether from necessity of not, confined to the male sex....
> The School of Arts may do something, however little, by way of example. They may even, perhaps, [by permitting women to take part] be the cloud no bigger than a man's hand which poured at last richness and fertility over the dry and blasted land. In this effort, married people ought to bear their part. It is their interest as well as their duty. Domestic affection, like other talents, is given not for ourselves alone. Selfishly hoarded it corrupts like stagnant water: for our sakes as well as for others it should be diffused abroad. The family is indeed the unit of civilisation; isolated it leads back to barbarism... The heart of the young longs for wider sympathies, and demands new associations.[55]

Woolley set the trend by having permission extended for women to attend classes and use

Sir Henry Parkes, 1815-1896

Braidwood Literary Institute, NSW, 1986

the reading room at the Sydney School. Small institutions followed suit, and as the institutions' value as an important, and often only, community centre grew, so women played an increasing role. Indeed, the program for the Initial Concert of the School of Arts at Port Macquarie in 1913 listed women on the Committee of Management, and 11 items on the program were to be performed by women.[56]

As the institutes, more often in country towns, became more social in purpose, so they provided for the women of the community - isolated already by distance and social customs - facilities where they could meet and promote a feminine view on community affairs. There is little doubt that the wider educational growth of women in the immigrant colonial life owed much to the efforts of the local institute. In this the institutes were being faithful to their inspiration by stimulating cultural growth and harmony through giving a new role to women.

CONTRIBUTION OF THE INSTITUTES TO POPULAR EDUCATION

During the latter part of the nineteenth century - in those lively decades of the 'eighties and 'nineties - schools of arts, mechanics' institutes, literary institutes, and the rare athenaeum, spread throughout the countryside of New South Wales. Their aims were now a mixture of enlightenment and entertainment; 'intellectual recreation' become the common term. Often one of the most handsome buildings in town, and very likely on a prime block of land, with extensions often called the 'Town Hall,' they existed in greater numbers than ever. But the lectures and classes were becoming minor attractions - musical evenings, the odd play, occasional debates, regular and enthusiastic evenings of billiards and card playing were now the preoccupation of members.

One suspects that the infrequent lecturer, perhaps from the University, was invited mainly out of some deference to the original objectives and to ease the consciences of the Committee of Management - as Sydney University's Extension Board (established in 1892) frankly commented in 1912: "It seems certain that some institutions asked for lectures chiefly because they believe that some educational work would be required of them when they apply for the state subsidy."[57] If it was by 1901 more entertainment than education in the institutes, what had happened? Why the apparent failure of so ambitious an attempt to educate the great numbers of adults?

Organizationally, the enthusiastic lecturers and classes of instruction of the first generation of institutes were too carelessly conceived. It was not until the 'eighties that it was realised that lectures and classes were too spontaneously organised, often simply on a whim, or the hoped-for presence of the lecturers and teachers. Simultaneously, there was little skilled and educated planning of how to overcome the technological and scientific ignorance of the mechanics. The absence of planned and consecutive courses of study only highlighted the fact that the courses of instruction were rarely in accord with people's needs in this new land.

The fatal weakness of the institutes' educational work in the towns and cities was their failure to attract the so-called responsible sections of the urban working-class, including the youth, for whom they were designed. In the rural areas, too, insufficient efforts were made to cater for the working-classes. Few institutes fulfilled the wishes of Birkbeck: that the people for

177

whom the institutes existed ought to run them. One major New South Wales town in 1865 had but one mechanic as a committee member of about a dozen.[58] John Woolley believed that the lack of working class support lay in the poor facilities - the "mean building, whose incommodious library and uninviting lecture hall" contradicted the "enjoyment and advantages of membership" so confidently advertised.[59]

It was obvious that in town after town, the 'respectable' members of society, with their own prejudices of middle-class behaviour and standards, committed many institutes to a tone and reputation which alienated the mechanics. At the same time, many of the mechanics for whom the "improvement of their minds" was thought a foremost priority by others demonstrated that they could become successful and influential men of importance in their communities by devoting their efforts to more profitable activities. The institutes' adult education efforts confronted the same realities of the colonial economy and immigrant culture that elementary education was to: the general unimportance of education for economic and social advancement, a dispersed population, and a recurrent shortage of labour. The desire for social cohesion and a sense of community on the part of many adults in colonial New South Wales just did not involve a profound commitment to education, most certainly not after a day's hard physical labour. With the leisured middle-class, perhaps, but not the labourers. It is apparent, with hindsight, that the institutes may have been more successful had members of the Committees of Management recognised the needs of the working-classes for more elementary education of a practical nature, and obtained facilities and personnel to that end.

The original intentions of the supporters and founders of the institutes in the colony, when they espoused "the diffusion of knowledge, scientific and useful, among the mechanics," were a misjudgement. Political and social growth of the immigrant working-class could not be surrounded by such cultural influences and the high standards (or, rather expectations) of education be maintained at the same time. The spread of culture in such a haphazard and moralistic manner was to be contradicted by its quality and presentation. The popularity of fiction in the libraries, and the search for entertainment, perhaps emphasises this point most strongly. Rather than popular education becoming a driving force in cultural development and social amelioration, for the great majority of adults it clearly became an adjunct to such improvement as took place. Consequently, once specialised educational facilities become available - primary and secondary education, technical education, free municipal libraries, a multiplicity of independent clubs and societies - popular education, with the institute as the community's intellectual centre, could largely be dispensed with. Perhaps it is true to say that most working people, because of the educational 'failure' of the institutes, remained constricted by the material and mundane demands of life, demands from which 'knowledge' had once promised to free them.

Nevertheless, if the institutes failed by strictly educational means to emancipate the working classes, in a wider sense they were obviously successful as community centres, educating adults in a variety of ways. There was a sense, most perceptibly, in which these buildings and their facilities established in the popular mind a close relationship between educational endeavours of adults in the community, and social and cultural activities. There was a sense in which, by insisting that knowledge was the prerequisite of freedom and that it belonged to all in the society and not to caste or privilege, that the institutes gave the cause of Australian egalitarianism and social democracy an added positive meaning. It cannot be without some significance that the period of New South Wales' greatest social and democratic advances in the lives of ordinary working people coincided with the remarkable growth of the institutes. Even if it is accepted that the institutes were only fulfilling, in the end, "the primary (and secondary sometimes) and practical wants of our community...the opportunity for refined and innocent recreation,"[60] then they provided a form of education allowing adults the "collision of minds and intellectual activity" which the more formal education precluded.

CONCLUSION

A lesson gathered from the history of the mechanics' institutes and schools of arts in New South Wales was that adults were still being educated even if they only met and became less "atheists in their social relations." For many adults, knowledge was neither an end in itself, nor a means to moral improvement; it was, rather, either of utilitarian value or a means for the meeting of minds. For the colonist, 'good' resided in the social and moral qualities of an individual, and if knowledge served to display those qualities then this was good also. If not, then one may as well play billiards.

The achievement of the institute movement was in making apparent the needs of technological and scientific change. It pioneered the idea of community educational initiative, and created an organisational core of which the most obvious legacies in New South Wales were technical education, and community libraries. Above all, the institutes in their final years were distinct social successes, combining a spirit of self-help and community responsibility.

The philosophy underlying adult education is not wholly an intellectual one - as the institute movement discovered. It is more a philosophy for social betterment and social activity. The adult who spends most of his or her time gaining a livelihood seeks to balance this with imaginative, moral and intellectual development. The institute movement came to realise that adult education did not mean students merely listening to words of wisdom as they fell from the lips of great scholars, but was more an activity whereby adults were involved in learning more about themselves and those around them. The institute movement, by 1901, had realised that adults sought knowledge as an adjunct to practical life; but the realisation came too late for the movement to adapt.

Adult education, or continuing education, should give adults not only a wider and deeper satisfaction in life, but it should also give the community more wisdom and depth. At some time, to many people, the local institute or school of arts did this. Henry Parkes told the audience at West Maitland in 1870: "Education commences when the child first looks upon its mother's face, and ceases when the eyelids are closed for ever. Education goes on every day from the cradle to the grave, under all circumstances, in all societies, at home and abroad."[61] He was speaking about lifelong learning. While the institute movement may have failed to provide formalised instrumental education, it was most definitely Australia's first attempt to establish a form of continuous or lifelong education. For a long time, and for many, it succeeded in providing access to learning in the widest sense of the word.

NOTES AND REFERENCES

1. Whitelock, D. (1974). *The great tradition: A history of adult education in Australia.* St Lucia: University of Queensland Press, p.85.

2. Nadel, G. (1957). *Australia's colonial culture: Ideas, men and institutions in nineteenth century Eastern Australia.* Cambridge, Mass: Harvard University Press, p.116.

3. *Third Annual Report of S.M.S.A.*, p.7.

4. McDonald, D.I. (1968). The diffusion of scientific and other useful knowledge. *Journal of the Royal Australian Historical Society, 54* (2) p.182.

5. Warburton, J.W. (1963). Schools of arts. *Australian Quarterly, 35*(4), p.74.

6. *ibid.*

7. Warburton, *op. cit.,* p.73.

8. Nadel, *op. cit.,* p.123.

9. Brain, T.H. (1848). *A history of New South Wales.* London: Richard Bentley, pp. 314-316.

10. *Fifteenth Annual Report of the S.M.S.A. for 1847*, Sydney, 1848, p.5.

11. *ibid.*

12. Laughton, J.B. (1855). *A Lecture delivered at the opening of the Bathurst School of Arts.* Sydney, p.16.

13. *The Empire*, 14 February 1851.

14. Carmichael, H. (1833). Introductory discourse delivered at the opening of the Sydney Mechanics' School of Arts. *New South Wales Magazine, I*(2), p.78.

15. Nadel, *op. cit.,* p.43.

16. *The Maitland Mercury*, 19 April 1845.

17. *The Maitland Mercury*, 9 May 1845.

18. *The Maitland Mercury*, 5 May 1852.

19. *The Maitland Mercury*, 21 May 1853.

20. *The Maitland Mercury*, 5 June 1852.

21. McDonald, *op. cit.,* p.184.

22.*The Empire*, 2 June 1855.

23.Minutes, *Meeting of the Committee of Management of the S.M.S.A.*, 4 March, 1858.

24.Warburton, *op. cit.*, p.75.

25.*ibid*.

26.Nadel, *op. cit.*, p.161.

27.Woolley, J. (1862). *Lectures delivered in Australia*. Cambridge: Macmillan, p.370.

28.Woolley, J. (1860). *The social uses of schools of arts*. Sydney: Hanson & Bennet, p.14.

29.McDonough, M.E. (1935). Down the Years. *Deniliquin School of Arts catalogue of books*. Deniliquin: School of Arts, p.3.

30.McDonald, *op. cit.*, p.187.

31.*The Empire*, 15 February 1857.

32.Smith, S.H., & Spaull, G.T. (1925). *History of education in New South Wales*. Sydney: George Phillips, p.114.

33.Woolley, J. (1861). *Schools of arts and colonial nationality*. Sydney: Reading and Wellbank, p.23.

34.*ibid*, p.17.

35.*ibid*, p.18.

36.Woolley, J. (1857). *The Inaugural Address delivered to the members of the Maitland School of Arts*. Supplement to *The Northern Times*, 10 April, 1857, p.4.

37.*Lithgow Mercury*, 18 September 1912.

38.*Back to Braidwood* (1966). Braidwood: Back to Braidwood Executive Committee, p.55. (Cited in correspondence from Mrs L.P. Lyons, Braidwood & District Historical Society, October, 1973).

39.Lea-Scarlett, E. (1968). *Queanbeyan: District and people*. Queanbeyan: Queanbeyan Municipal Council, pp.125-126.

40.Duncan, R. (1951). Armidale: Economic and Social Development, 1839 - 1871. *New England College Research Magazine, No. 6*, p.134. For further information on this dispute, see Raszewski, C. (1988). The Armidale School of Arts or Mechanics' Institute, 1859-1871. *Armidale and District Historical Society Journal, 31*, pp.35-52 (especially pp.46-50).

41.*Albury Banner*, 3 January 1863.

42. *The Maitland Mercury*, 3 August 1866.

43. *The Maitland Mercury*, 30 August 1866.

44. Coulls, A. *Broken Hill Municipal Library*. (Cited in correspondence from L. Gough, City Librarian, Broken Hill, October, 1973).

45. Woolley, Inaugural address at Maitland, *op. cit.*, p.3.

46. Warburton, *op. cit.*, p.76.

47. *Annual Report of the S.M.S.A. for 1879*. Sydney, 1880, p.9.

48. Windeyer, W.C. (1883). *Commemorative Address on the Celebration of the 50th Anniversary of the S.M.S.A.*, Sydney, p.3.

49. *ibid*.

50. Murray-Smith, S. (1965). Technical education in Australia: Historical sketch. In Wheelwright, E.L. (Ed.), *Higher education in Australia*. Melbourne: F.W. Cheshire, p.174.

51. *Eighth Annual Report of the S.M.S.A. for 1840*. Sydney, 1841.

52. *Sydney Morning Herald*, 20 August 1853.

53. Warburton, *op. cit.*, p.78.

54. Lea-Scarlett, *op. cit.*, p.127.

55. Woolley, The social uses of schools of arts, *op. cit.*, p.20.

56. Program of Port Macquarie Choral and Musical Society, for *Initial Concert of the School of Arts, Port Macquarie, July 28, 1913*. (Cited in correspondence from M.R. Howell, Hastings District Historical Society, August, 1973).

57. Warburton, *op. cit.*, p.79.

58. Lee-Scarlett, *op. cit.*, p.134.

59. Woolley, The social uses of schools of arts, *op. cit.*, p.20.

60. *ibid*, p.23.

61. Smith & Spaull, *op. cit.*, p.149.

CHAPTER NINE

SOME ASPECTS OF THE ROLE OF THE INSTITUTES IN TECHNICAL EDUCATION IN NEW SOUTH WALES 1878 - 1916

John Laurent

INTRODUCTION

The important place of mechanics' institutes and kindred institutions in the beginnings of technical education in Britain (originating with the Edinburgh School of Arts in 1821 and the Glasgow and London Mechanics' Institutes in 1822-3) has been well documented in the literature, beginning with Hudson's classic 1851 account[1] and continuing through to the more recent studies of Tylecote, Harrison, Kelly, Armytage, and most lately Inkster.[2] Unfortunately - with notable exceptions (e.g., Inkster) - the received opinion generally on these institutions seems to have been that first argued by Hudson, namely, that they had 'failed' in their founders' (usually prosperous factory owners) original intention of bringing 'useful' knowledge to working people and became little more than entertainment centres for a more middle-class clientele. Writers of a radical persuasion - beginning with Engels in 1844[3] - also regarded these institutions as failures, in that the working classes for whom they were intended saw through their bourgeois aims and simply stayed away.

But however one views the role of mechanics' institutes and schools of arts in their country of origin, there is no doubt about their importance in Australia's social and educational history. At the height of the mechanics' institutes and schools of arts 'movement' in Australia (between about 1880 and 1910) there were, according to one writer (Whitelock), "over 1000" institutes functioning in this country, with over 250 in New South Wales alone.[4] In this chapter I will not attempt to present a comprehensive history of the place of mechanics' institutes and schools of arts in the history of technical education in New South Wales, but rather will focus on aspects of this role which tell us something more about the institutes in terms of their *social and cultural* function in the community. It will be argued, basically, that the kinds of scientific and technical studies pursued in these institutes often tell us as much about the intellectual and even ideological *interests* of their *clientele* as about the New South Wales government's policies of the time; indeed the latter can, to a considerable extent, be regarded as a reflection of the former.

Beginnings

What *were* these institutes in Australia? Firstly, their origin was somewhat different from that of those in Britain, in that they looked much more to state support - in the era of what Butlin[5] has called 'Colonial Socialism' in Australia - and there was usually more dependence on the initiative of clergymen for their establishment than on wealthy industrialists: Australia being very largely a primary-producing country at the time. The first mechanics' institute founded in the Australian Colonies was the Hobart Mechanics' Institute, founded by a clergyman, Dr James Ross, "and other prominent citizens of Hobart Town"[6] (Whitelock says "master tradesmen"[7]) in 1826. The next, and more enduring (it still exists as a subscription lending library) institution to be established was the Sydney Mechanics' School of Arts (SMSA), in 1833, by another clergyman, the Rev. Henry Carmichael.

It was at the latter that what are usually regarded as the first 'technical education' lectures were given in Australia (in mechanics, geology and natural history[8]), and by 1842 the SMSA had in its library 39 books on 'mechanical arts', 24 on natural history, 20 on 'mathematics, astronomy and education,' 13 books on chemistry and 10 on medicine.[9] The writer of the article from which this information is taken considers that "any enthusiasm for science could now be cultivated."[10] Be this as it may, by the mid 1860s formal classes in mechanical drawing, geology and mineralogy, and slightly later, chemistry, were being conducted[11] and it was not many years afterwards - in 1878 - that these classes were formally taken over by the New South Wales Department of Public Instruction. It is with developments from that date onwards that this chapter will be primarily concerned, but before taking up this subject further, something more should be said about the peculiarities of Australian, and more specifically New South Wales, mechanics' institutes and schools of arts.

It was mentioned that these institutions differed from their forebears in Britain in that they received much more government support from the start. In fact, land was usually granted (at a time when most land belonged to the Crown). At Kincumber (near Gosford) for instance, the site which was eventually 'confirmed' in 1911 as that for a school of arts building (erected in 1914) had originally been part of a block set aside as early as 1847 for a 'village pound' and had remained crown land.[12] (This School's ms. 'Inventory,' still housed in the building, shows that the money expended on transference of the land to its committee - £5 - was the same as that outlaid for construction of a fence around it.[13]) Similarly, at Bathurst, a government grant of half an acre of land in William Street enabled the establishment of a 'Mechanics' School of Arts' (later simplified to 'School of Arts') in 1855.[14] In addition to grants of land, a building subsidy of £1 for every £1 raised locally by mechanics' institutes and schools of art committees was later made available, under legislation of 1893, and a subsidy of 10 shillings in the pound on members' subscriptions was available thereafter for general running costs (maintenance, purchase of books for the library, etc.). Earlier, such subsidies had been on an *ad hoc* basis. Special grants could also be obtained for the initial setting up of libraries and class rooms. Exceptionally, the entire building could be provided by the government, as at Leeton (see below).

The Beginnings of Formal Technical Education in New South Wales: The Sydney Mechanics' School of Arts, 1878-1888

The taking over of the SMSA's technical education classes by the Department of Public Instruction in 1878 is usually taken as the beginning of formal technical education in New South Wales. And already, this move by the State tells us something about the attitude of the Australian public towards this subject. Stephen Murray-Smith has remarked that while the mechanics' institutes marked the most determined effort to improve technical education from above, "it would be wrong to ignore the effect of general awakening of interest in science and technology, which saw the birth [in the mid- to late-nineteenth century] of numerous agricultural, scientific and 'philosophical' societies."[15] Michael Cannon has looked at this subject of interest in science and technology 'from below' in Australia also;[16]

and there is reason to believe that this interest influenced the more 'practical' concerns of skilled workers keen to acquaint themselves with the new technologies which bore upon the trades. In any event it was largely due to initiatives from the Sydney Trades and Labour Council that the above move was made. In 1877 a Mr W H Edmunds of the Couriers' Union formed a Technical Education Committee within the Council, which was shortly afterwards called upon by members of the SMSA's committee (who had read of the TLC's interest in technical education in the press);[17] and it was as a result of representations from these two bodies that the New South Wales parliament voted £2,000 towards the cost of establishing classes at the SMSA, and a further £2,500 towards extensions to the SMSA building in Pitt Street, the latter being named a 'Working Men's College.'

In 1879, these classes were extended following a Technological Conference under the chairmanship of the former Birmingham artisan and staunch advocate of technical education, Sir Henry Parkes, and by 1880, 1,047 students were attending these SMSA classes, some of the largest enrolments (out of 21 subjects) being in writing and arithmetic, freehand drawing, 'chemistry and physiology' (the latter having the second highest enrolment after writing and arithmetic in the second quarter of that year).[18] Besides formal classes, a number of 'Popular Science Lectures' were given at the SMSA free of charge, "several of which," the Working Men's College Committee was claiming in its 1881 report, "were attended by between 500 and 600 persons."[19] Titles of some of these lectures in 1882 included 'Coal, Limestone, and Fossils,' 'Coal: Its History, Uses and Formation,' 'Natural Phenomena,' 'Light and Its Nature,' 'A Walk in the Zoo' and 'Human Physiology.'[20] A short series of lectures on 'The Place of Physiology in Education' also appears to have been offered at the SMSA around this time.[21]

By 1883 the administration of technical education in New South Wales had passed to a Board of Technical Education under the Chairmanship of Norman Selfe, a former engineer at Mort's Dock who had started the first classes in mechanical drawing at the SMSA in 1865,[22] and in 1889 administration came under direct control of the State as the Technical Education Branch of the Department of Public Instruction. In the meantime, as accommodation in the SMSA building was becoming a problem, the classes moved into new premises in the Temperance Life buildings in Pitt Street, in 1888. With this move, the SMSA's direct involvement in State funded technical education virtually came to a close (apart from library subsidies). However, this was far from the end of involvement of New South Wales schools of arts and mechanics' institutes in technical education. On the contrary, this involvement was to *expand* over the next two to three decades, mainly in centres outside Sydney (but also in a number of suburban centres). This involvement of non-metropolitan mechanics' institutes and schools of arts will now be looked at under three headings: lectures; classes; and libraries, museums etc.

COUNTRY MECHANICS' INSTITUTES AND SCHOOLS OF ARTS

Lectures

Non-metropolitan schools of arts and mechanics' institutes had actually been involved in 'technical education' of one kind or another for some time. At the Goulburn Mechanics' Institute (founded in 1853 - the fourth relatively durable institute in present-day New South Wales after Sydney, Newcastle and Maitland) for instance, the purchase of chemical apparatus and an 'electrifying machine' for science lectures was one of the first committee's first activities.[23] Similarly at Bathurst, at a somewhat later date, an interest in science and technology manifested itself. In 1881, this School's committee organised an 'Industrial Exhibition' which proved an outstanding success (netting a profit of £900), and in 1883 the committee turned its attention to more formal educational activities. It is not clear how these activities were connected with the Board of Technical Education (I have found no reference to them in the Board's records -but these are very incomplete), nevertheless, according to an 1893 *Guide to Bathurst*: "Geological specimens and various scientific appliances were procured, and for some years technical lectures were delivered in class rooms fitted up below the stage.... In 1886 a splendid collection of geological specimens and minerals was presented to the institution by Mr L S Bensusan who was elected a life member as a mark of appreciation and esteem."[24]

One important means by which mechanics' institutes and schools of arts could play a role in the Board's and later Branch's efforts to spread a knowledge of technical education was as venues for visits by itinerant lecturers. In the 1880s and early '90s especially, such lecturers were employed by the New South Wales government to travel to country districts, and the local school of arts hall - being the centre of a town's social and cultural life[25] - was usually the logical place to address an audience. A printed document on 'Technical Education' issued in 1889 by the then Minister of Public Instruction, J H Carruthers, in connection with the changeover in administration from the Board to the Branch of Technical Education, refers to the suitability of "Public School buildings and class-rooms in Schools of Arts"[26] as a means for bringing country areas within the reach of the Department, and an obvious way of achieving this was through the visiting lecturer. Angus Mackay, author of the Board's (and later Branch's) textbook, *Elements of Australian Agriculture* (1885) was a strong advocate of such lectures. In 1890, for instance, Mackay wrote to the Branch's first Superintendent of Technical Education (Frederick Bridges) explaining that:

> During the year since the last annual report thirty-four lectures have been given in country districts at the request of and at the cost of Agricultural Societies, Progress Committees, Schools of Art [sic], Literary Societies and other public bodies...[D]iscussions have followed on many occasions, during which most valuable information has been made available, information which could not easily be got by other means than the opportunities afforded by meetings in the districts and amidst the industries immediately concerned.[27]

A fair idea of the kind of lecture given can be gauged from a newspaper report on a lecture given by J H Maiden, Curator of the Sydney Technological Museum (and later Superintendent of Technical Education and eventually Government Botanist), on 'Our Native Timbers' in June 1890 (in this case at a public school, but more than likely repeated at schools of arts). Maiden set out by saying that "New South Wales has been foremost of the Australian colonies in disseminating information in regard to the properties and uses of our native timbers," and he went on to talk about such things as "the native orange (*Capparis Mitchelli*) of the dry west [which] is a timber which deserves more notice than is usually taken of it [and which] grows to a good size and is a fair substitute for box in wood-engraving."[28]

In 1890, also, travelling lecturers in geology (Rev. J Milne Curran) and Horticulture (Albert

Gale) were appointed.[29] On one excursion to the Bathurst-Orange district in October that year, Gale lectured on subjects like 'A Flower and its Parts,' 'How Seeds Grow,' 'How Plants Feed' and 'Bee Culture' in various centres, including Orange, Lucknow, Millthorpe, Stradforth, Blayney, Carcoar and Eglington, sometimes at schools of arts and sometimes at public schools. At Lucknow, Gale noted in his handwritten report, the "audience were very eager for information," while at Millthorpe, notwithstanding "a dark night, muddy roads, and falling rain," the people "came in from all parts to the number of upwards of 150."[30] Some idea of the flavour of Gale's lectures can probably be gained from the following passage from a chapter on 'How Plants are Fed' in Mackay's *Elements of Australian Agriculture:*

> The sap taken up by the roots, being water holding in solution the various ingredients necessary for building the plants, is carried along the cells or chambers, until it is further enriched by contact with the gases absorbed by the leaves - the process as a whole being much akin to the blood circulation system in animals.[31]

The Rev.Fr. J Milne Curran's lectures on geology were always well attended, it seems - whether for their practical value to miners, prospectors and others, or possibly also, simply for the inherently interesting nature of their subject matter. Henry Lawson begins one of his stories with a quote which reads in part: "There's nothing quite so interesting as Geology, even to common and ignorant people, especially when you have a bank or the side of a cutting, studded with fossil fish and things;"[32] and it is easy to see how this could be so. In the United States, adult education had its origins in the lyceum movement earlier in the nineteenth century, which had been started by an obscure Yale geology student who had found that talks which he gave on geological topics in towns while on field trips were always well received.[33] In any event, a perusal of minute books of schools of arts testifies to Curran's popularity as a lecturer: In 1893, for instance, the secretary of the Parramatta School of Arts wrote to Curran asking for a lecture, adding: "believe me you are sure to have the gratification of a crowded house."[34] An earlier lecture by Curran on "An Evening with the Microscope" (Curran did early important work on thin sections[35]) in the Granville School of Arts had been "well attended and much appreciated."[36]

In February 1897 the secretary of the Jamberoo School of Arts wrote to the Department of Public Introduction asking for a lecture from Curran on "the Geology of the District,"[37] which was particularly appropriate since from about this time Curran periodically took parties of students from the Sydney Technical College on geology excursions to the Kiama district.[38] Curran's assistant on these occasions was Carl Sussmilch, a later lecturer at the Sydney Technical College and eventually Superintendent of Technical Education. Sussmilch, too, was a popular lecturer in Schools of Arts in later years. In March 1909 for example, Sussmilch gave a lantern lecture on 'Earth History' at the Kiama School of Arts (erected 1902), treating of such subjects as "the fossil remains of labyrinthodont and ichthyosaurus" and the "volcanic material and fertile soil ... which in that permo-carboniferous period made material to support the luxuriant growth of vegetation which went to form the rich coal measures of the Illawarra."[39]

These juxtapositions of subject matter neatly illustrate the fascinating amalgam of intriguing and practical information one can find in a subject like geology. Much of this material may have been beyond the audience; nevertheless, the local press referred to the "interest and imagination" excited by the lecture,[40] and this is understandable, the Illawarra being a coal

187

mining district and coal-bearing strata being a rich source of fossils with which colliery workers would have had some familiarity. Similarly, while audiences were apparently attracted to Curran's lectures at least partly out of curiosity (this must surely be the explanation for the popularity of his 'Microscope' lectures), there were, no doubt, frequently more down-to-earth motivations as well. Thus, in 1902, a Mr. Travers Jones, a former MLC, wrote to D J Cooper, then Superintendent of Technical Education, requesting Curran's services as a lecturer to the Abercrombie District. "I have just made a tour of various mining districts," Jones explained, "and on every field I have met with a request to get Rev. M Curran to visit the localities." "Your lecturer will have a hundred men to listen for every one student in the [Sydney] College class," Jones went on to claim.[41] (Curran's previous services in the Peak Hill gold-mining district had apparently been much appreciated.)[42]

Classes

In his 1890 letter to Superintendent Bridges about the possibilities for agricultural education in New South Wales, Angus Mackay wrote, under the sub-heading 'Agricultural Classes in Country Districts':

> A class has been in operation at Granville since July, another has been organised at Hornsby Junction to commence with the 1891 session. Efforts for the establishment of classes are being made at Goulburn, Maitland, Mudgee, and other centres.[43]

The response of the local population to the classes at Granville over the next few years - which were held at the 'School of Arts and Working Men's College' (established in 1883 along the lines of the SMSA at the time) - can be gauged from the fact that combined enrolments there in the Elementary and Advanced Agriculture classes in the third term of 1894 (45) were nearly three times that for the second most popular subject, chemistry (18) out of the eight subjects then offering.[44] And that the subject was apparently of *general*, and not just instrumental, interest, to at least some students is indicated in the occupations of students enrolled in the subject a few years later (1902-9 - the earliest years for which such information is available). There were numerous orchardists, farm labourers, etc; but among them were people like an eighteen year old moulder (probably, like most others of similar occupation, an employee of the Clyde Engineering Works), a thirty-nine year old painter, a fifty year old signalman, a forty-seven year old machinist, a twenty three year old cement-burner, a twenty-three year old clerk, a thirty-eight year old boiler maker, a fifty-three year old boilermaker, a twenty-one year old carpenter, a fifty-year old ironmoulder, a seventeen-year old bootfinisher, and a fifty-four year old plumber.[45] J H Maiden took a personal interest in these classes at Granville, it seems: in 1897 for instance (by which time he was Government Botanist), he was present at the School's annual prize-giving evening.[46]

A Technical Education Branch manuscript - *Return of Buildings used for purposes of Technical Education in Sydney suburbs, and Country Districts* - from March 1890 shows that, among other centres, classes were being conducted at the Singleton Mechanics' Institute, and the Newcastle, Lambton, Morpeth, Granville, Parramatta and Kogarah Schools of Arts.[47] (By 1912, 42 mechanics' institutes and schools of arts were being utilised.[48]) Geology appears to have been another popular subject among these classes. In 1889 geology had attracted the second highest enrolments at the Singleton Mechanics' Institute[49], and by 1894, by which time this subject was being offered at the Goulburn Mechanics' Institute, it

188

had the fourth highest enrolment (out of 16 subjects) at that Institute also.[50] Curran's *Geology of Sydney and the Blue Mountains* was one of the textbooks for this subject from its date of publication, in 1898.[51]

By the early 1900s classes had been established at numerous other locations in these and a wide range of other subjects offered by the Technical Education Branch. In Blayney in 1904, for instance, as a result of conversations between the local School of Arts Committee and an officer from the Branch, it was being "proposed to form classes in geology, chemistry and agriculture, but of course other subjects would be added when the necessary number of students were obtained."[52] In 1910, in an effort to further spread the work of the Branch, Acting Superintendent George Hooper made a tour of the northern part of the State meeting schools of arts committees and similar groups and giving public addresses on the subject of technical education in schools of arts halls and other suitable venues. At Maclean, for example, Hooper met the Mayor, the Secretary of the local School of Arts and the President of the Agricultural Association, and in the evening addressed a public meeting in the School of Arts at which the attendance was "good." At Lismore, "The School of Arts was filled, and the people ... most enthusiastic." The classes decided upon were Veterinary Science, Dressmaking, Millinery, Carpentry, Art and Cookery (the order as listed by Hooper).[53]

Libraries, Museums, Etc.

Mechanics' institutes and schools of arts also played an extremely important role in the diffusion of scientific and technical knowledge through their libraries. The prominence of scientific and technical literature in the library of the SMSA as early as 1842 has already been mentioned, and similarly, a library catalogue included with the Goulburn Mechanics' Institutes' first *Report* - from 1855 - shows that of the 201 titles there listed, at least 43 (I am not familiar with some of them) can be classed as scientific and/or technical works. Examples of these are: Ure's *Chemical Dictionary*, Hugh Miller's *Old Red Sandstone* and *Footprints of the Creator* (a book about fossils), Linnington's *Astronomy*, Chambers' *Education Course - Mechanics, Economy of Vegetation*, Lyell's *Principles of Geology* (two copies), *Faculties of Birds*, Robinson's *Mechanical Philosophy*, Wilson's *Trigonometry*, and ten volumes of the *Mechanics Magazine*.[54]

For a later period, there simply is no question about the prominent place of scientific and technical works in the libraries of country mechanics institutes and schools of arts, notwithstanding the undoubted fact that such libraries often primarily catered for readers of fiction.[55] Thus, after fiction, the Gunnedah School of Arts had more books listed under 'Natural Philosophy, Science and the Arts' in its 1909 catalogue than under any other category (out of nine sections); and this is even after publications like Turner's *Forage Plants of Australia*, Von Mueller's *Subtropical Plants*, Ogilby's *Edible Fishes of New South Wales*, *Geology of the Hunter River Coal Measures* and *Scientific American* were listed under 'Works of Reference, etc.' and works like J H Maiden's *Sir Joseph Banks* were classed as 'Miscellaneous'.[56] Likewise, the 1914 library catalogue for the Orange School of Arts has only slightly less books listed under 'Science and Art' (just under seven pages) than under 'Miscellaneous' (7 1/4 pages), the second largest section after fiction out of eight categories; and this is after books like Grant Allen's *The Evolutionist at Large*, T H Huxley's *Lay Sermons, Addresses and Reviews*, Lubbock's *Beauties of Nature*, Kropotkin's *The Conquest of Bread* and Ware's *Educational Foundation of Trade and Industry* are listed as 'Miscellaneous.'[57]

Some further example of titles in these catalogues will give some idea of their frequently strong bent towards science and technical education. Thus, in the Gunnedah School of Arts' 'Natural Philosophy, Science and the Arts' section we find volumes like Curran's *Geology of Sydney and the Blue Mountains, Australian Sheep and Wool*, by A. Hawkesworth (another Technical Education Branch textbook), Darwin's *Origin of Species* and *A Naturalist's Voyage Round the World*, Saleeby's *Organic Evolution*, Lyell's *Principles of Geology*, Lubbock's *The Sense, Instincts and Intelligence of Animals*, Hooker's *Botany*, Lockyer's *Astronomy*, Tyndall's *Eight Lectures on Sound*, and A R Wallace's *Man's Place in the Universe*.[58] In the Orange School or Arts' 'Science and Art' section are books like Curran's textbook, Johnston's *Chemistry of Common Life*, Fream's *Elements of Agriculture*, French's *Destructive Insects of Victoria*, three volumes by Darwin (*Origin of Species, Descent of Man*, and *Expression of the Emotions in Man and Animals*), A R Wallace's *Geographical Distribution of Animals* and *Contributions to the Theory of Natural Selection*, Von Mueller's *Select Tropical Plants*, Wilson's *Timber Trees of New South Wales*, 'Technical Education' (2 vols), Grassby's *Principles of Australian Agriculture*, Jaquet's *Notes on Gold Dredging*, T H Huxley's *Vertebrated Animals*, Knight's *Dictionary of Mechanics*, Charles Lyne's *Industries of New South Wales* and Laing's *Modern Science and Modern Thought*.[59]

Unfortunately most schools of arts and similar institutions did not produce printed catalogues, so one must try to gauge the kinds of books and other publications that they had in their libraries from occasional mentions of purchases in minutes or annual reports or, if one is lucky, from a look through surviving collections. In the following account, then, I will give some examples of titles I have either seen in collections or have found reference to in the sources indicated.

One of the first journals subscribed to by the Jamberoo School of Arts after its opening in 1896 was the *Australian Technical Journal* (at 2/6[d] per annum), published by the Department of Public Instruction from the Sydney Technical College.[60] No doubt this had something to do with the new institution's desire to secure the New South Wales government subsidy (and this School's committee was unusual in that it had purchased its block of land in private sale, and was hoping for "some consideration" from the government on that account).[61] Nevertheless, the subscription is worth noticing, especially since, as will be seen, this journal was an important means of communicating scientific and technical information to which readers could turn should they wish to follow up material touched on in lectures.

This latter point was true also for the *New South Wales Agricultural Gazette*, an attractive (some of its plates of birds, insects, etc. are now highly sought after) and informative monthly published by the NSW Department of Mines and Agriculture and available *gratis*. The Mudgee Mechanics' Institute and the Kangaroo Valley School of Arts were receiving this journal in 1900 and 1903 respectively for example,[62] and among other institutions receiving it a few years afterwards were the Orange, Bathurst, Cowra, Young, Coolamon, Bowral and West Maitland Schools of Arts, the East Maitland and Narrandera Mechanics' Institutes, the Hay Athenaeum, and the Cootamundra, Grenfell, Hornsby and North Ryde Literary Institutes.[63] Other journals and government publications containing scientific and technical information mentioned in minutes and annual reports include the *Review of Reviews* (which has regular reviews of the latest scientific literature), the *New South Wales Year Book*, *Life* (which contained a section on 'New Things in Science'), *Hawkesbury Agricultural Journal*,

The Engineer, Forestry Journal, Australian Industrial and Mining Standards, Nineteenth Century (in which people like Huxley, Wallace and Kropotkin first published), *Scientific American, Scientific Australian, Stock and Station Journal* and *Farmer and Grazier*.[64]

Besides such regular acquisitions, scientific and/or technical educational material is often mentioned as having been donated or especially procured. Thus in its 1909 *Annual Report* the Bathurst School of Arts made special mention of its having recently acquired Moore and Silcock's *Sanitary Engineering*,[65] and in June the same year the Forbes School of Arts committee at its regular monthly meeting instructed its secretary to write to Angus and Robertson "*re* Lieut. Shackleton's expedition" (i.e., *The Heart of the Antarctic*, in which Professor T Edgeworth David of Sydney University - a member of the expedition - has a long chapter on the expedition's scientific results, including intriguing references to the discovery of coal and "sandstone with fernlike markings").[66] The Forbes School of Arts' secretary was also asked to "obtain a copy of Mr Turner's work on Technical Education"[67] - i.e., *A Quarter Century of Technical Education in New South Wales*, published by the Technical Education Branch, of which J W Turner was then Superintendent.

Earlier that year (1909) *The Wonderful Century*, by Alfred Russel Wallace (co-discoverer of natural selection with Charles Darwin - the book is a wide-ranging account of scientific discovery and invention in the nineteenth century) is mentioned in the *Forbes Times* as having been acquired by that town's School of Arts.[68] In 1915 the West Maitland School of Arts and the East Maitland Mechanics' Institute expressed thanks in their *Annual Reports* to the Engineering Institute of Newcastle for the booklet, *On the Use of Electricity in and about Coal Mines*,[69] and the committee of the Hay Athenaeum "desire[d] to record our appreciation of Mr McLean's donation of two handsome volumes of Mawson's *Home of the Blizzard*." (Mawson's work, an account of the Australian Antarctic Expedition of 1911-14, also refers to the finding of "carbonaceous shales and coaly strata").[70]

Very little seems to exist in terms of surviving collections of books from schools of arts libraries, unfortunately. Where one does discover them, they are usually from a later date (older books having fallen into disrepair, or if more valuable, found their way into private collections). The most interesting collection I have located is a small remnant of 67 volumes from the Muswellbrook School of Arts library which has been collected by the town's present librarian, Mrs Una Garland. Of these 67 volumes, eight are scientific and technical works, viz: Charles Darwin's *Descent of Man and Selection in Relation to Sex* (an 1871 copy) and *Expression of the Emotions in Man and Animals* (1872), T H Huxley's *The Crayfish* (1880), Maeterlinck's *The Life of the Bee* (1901), Johnston's *Chemistry of Common Life* (1885), E Ray Lankester's *Science from an Easy Chair* (1910), Dr. Karl Schezer's *Narrative of the Circumnavigation of the Globe by the Austrian Frigate 'Novasa'* (1862), and R T Baker's *Australian Flora in Applied Art* (1915), published by the Department of Public Instruction from the Sydney Technical College as its *Technical Education Series No. 22*. There are some books remaining from the Wentworth Falls School of Arts library (opened 1915) still in the building. While most of these are novels from a later period, there is the occasional older volume, among which is Turner's *A Quarter Century of Technical Education in New South Wales* (1909).[71] A number of schools of arts and mechanics' institutes (for example Blayney, Molong, Mudgee and Narrandera) had at least second-hand (frequently donated) sets of the *Encyclopaedia Britannica* in their libraries at this time[72] - frequently the famous

9th edition, with contributed articles from people like T H Huxley, A R Wallace and the geologist Geikie - which of course contained an enormous amount of scientific information. In the case of the Narrandera Mechanics' Institute (established 1886), the set is still housed in the building, which is now the Narrandera Shire Library.

While these books were *in* the libraries, one may legitimately ask, were they being *read*? This question will be looked at below.

Besides libraries, another extremely valuable function which mechanics' institutes and schools of arts could perform in terms of the dissemination of scientific information was as accommodation for exhibitions and more permanent museums. Mention has been made of an 'Industrial Exhibition' at the Bathurst School of Arts in the early 1880s, and the acquisition of a geological and mineral collection in connection with 'technical lectures' given at that School from 1883 onwards. Similarly, at the Goulburn Mechanics' Institute, classes (such as geology, as noted previously) were held, and in 1890 a government funded 'Technology Museum' (later transferred to the Goulburn Technical College on completion of the latter in 1901) was established at the Institute by J H Maiden.[73] In May 1903 the secretary of the Mudgee Mechanics' Institute wrote to the Superintendent of Technical Education (D J Cooper) asking whether he would be willing to "send up a Technical Exhibit (Telegraphy preferred) for the Fine Art Exhibition in connection with the Institute on 3rd, 4th and 5th June," adding as an incentive: "As there has [sic] been additional rooms built my committee thought by your acceding to their request that it might prove an incentive to the formation of Technical Classes in town, and that was one of the principal reasons for writing to you to make the request."[74]

Other examples of temporary and more permanent exhibitions at schools of arts and mechanics' institutes were: at Cowra in 1903, where "A very good idea has been put into practical operation by the School of Arts committee... A prize is offered for the best collection of minerals, fossils, and rocks, not less than 10 varieties; also a prize for the best collection of wheat, oats, barley, rye, etc"[75]; at the Granville School of Arts in 1912, where, at a 'Conversazione' organised by the School's Student Association, among other things, "Mr J B Brown [the School's 'Resident Master'], Miss Mackay and Mr Swan kindly lent microscopes and supplied specimens for the audience to look at through the microscope"[76]; and at the Narrandera Mechanics' Institute in 1915, where a display case was set up for the preservation of a collection of sheaves of 23 varieties of wheat, six of barley, twelve of oats, two of rye and "samples of almost every class and variety of grain that can be grown in the district," which had been sent by the Department of Agriculture.[77]

UNIVERSITY EXTENSION

Scientific and technical lectures in New South Wales mechanics' institutes and schools of arts were not restricted to those which the Board and Branch of Technical Education were able to provide. Notwithstanding the generally held view that, in terms of scientific and technical education, the mechanics' institutes and schools of arts were a 'failure,' their clientele preferring billiards and novel-reading, or perhaps 'light entertainments' (musical performances, recitations etc.), there is good evidence that University Extension lectures on scientific and technical subjects were readily responded to. Moreover, audiences seem to have frequently been *more* interested in lectures of this sort than in, say, literature or more 'cultivated' subjects; and it is easy to see how this could be so: working people being used to dealing with the physical world around them - the domain of science. And this was, of course, the 'heroic' age of scientific discovery, when science seemed to hold out the hope of a better world based on an understanding of nature's laws.

University extension had been started in Britain in the 1870s, and by the 1890s had become a very active facet of the life of Oxford and Cambridge Universities, and the new 'Civic' universities at Leeds, Manchester and Liverpool.[78] The University of Sydney's Extension Lectures Board was also active from the latter decade, and by the early 1900s, especially the period around 1907-10, was particularly vigorous, mainly due to the energetic input of a remarkable group of academics at the time - notably Professors Mungo MacCullum (History), Edgeworth David (Geology - the same who, as noted above, had been a member of the Shackleton Antarctic expedition) and Anderson Stuart (Physiology). There is no doubt that cultural and intellectual life in New South Wales, especially in country districts, was greatly enriched for a time by the lectures delivered by these people and others in the State's mechanics' institutes and schools of arts and other venues. Some examples of these lectures are as follows:

In 1907-8 a course of six lectures on mixed "literary, historical, geographical, commercial, chemical and geological" subjects at the Newcastle School of Arts attracted an average audience of "over 100" and "generally gave evidence of sustained desire that the work of the Board shall continue" in the district. Responses to courses of similar length in West Maitland (the same as in Newcastle) and at the Singleton Mechanics' Institute (Physiology and History) were also gratifying, the Extension Lectures Board noting in its *Report* for that year the West Maitland School of Arts' "very good library and other advantages for University Extension." A course of three lectures at the Goulburn Mechanics' Institute that year, on 'The Chemistry of Air, Water, and Foods' by Acting Professor J A Schofield, drew a "good, regular attendance," while at Helensburgh a course of "scientific, historical, and literary" lectures at the Workmen's Literary and Social Club brought together "a large audience, almost entirely of working miners, who have shown themselves very keen and appreciative hearers."[79]

The following year a course of lectures on 'Electro-Magnetic Induction,' by O U Vonwiller, and another on 'Timber: with Special Reference to the requirements of New South Wales Railways' by J H Maiden and G A Julius at the Railway Institute in Redfern attracted audiences of "more than a hundred"; and further courses, "mainly scientific in character" given by Professors David and Welsh, and Dr. H G Chapman, assistant Lecturer in Physiology, at the Newcastle, West Maitland and Singleton centres mentioned above again drew gratifying audiences: over 200 on one occasion at the West Maitland School of Arts. At Helensburgh in 1909 a mixed scientific and literary course at the same venue once more drew audiences averaging "over a hundred" - that at Edgeworth David's lecture being one of the "exceptionally large" attendances attracted by this speaker that year, no doubt partly owing to the widespread press coverage devoted to his and Mawson's Antarctic exploits.[80]

A course of lectures by W G Woolnough, D.Sc. (a geologist) at the Inverell School of Arts in 1909 - on 'The Building of New England,' 'Artesian Water' and 'Earthquakes' - attracted audiences "running from 100 to 130 and including people from the country around as well as from the town"; and another course at the Wyalong School of Arts by H G Chapman on "scientific subjects" was similarly successful.[81]   Examples of extension lectures in 1910 include a further mixed historical, geographical and geological series by Drs. Woolnough and F A Todd, and Mr C Hedley, F.I.S. at the Newcastle and West Maitland Schools of Arts and the Singleton Mechanics' Institute; a similar series at the Tamworth Mechanics' Institute; a series of mixed "historical and scientific" lectures at the Scone and Muswellbrook Schools of Arts (by Woolnough, Hedley, Todd, Vonwiller and A W Jose); a geological series at both the Casino (average attendance 256) and Murwillumbah Schools of Arts by Woolnough; a mixed "geographical, historical and anatomical" series at the Helensburgh Club by Edgeworth David, F A Todd and S A Smith (average attendance 243); and mixed "scientific, historical and literary" and "scientific and literary" series at the Katoomba and Blackheath Schools of Arts by Woolnough, R C Teece, J P Madsen and E R Holme, M.A.   Earlier that year, also, a special series of two free 'Agricultural' lectures by Professor R D Watt was given to rural workers in a shearing shed at North Yanco.[82]

Further Evidence of Interest in Science and Technology at Mechanics' Institutes and Schools of Arts

As already shown, ample opportunity existed for members of mechanics' institutes and schools of arts to follow up an interest which may have been stimulated by such lectures with further reading in their libraries. But did people read the kind of books referred to above? There are two sets of evidence which suggest that they did: one circumstantial, and one direct (and strong). These two sets of evidence will now be looked at in turn.

With regard to circumstantial evidence, it can be pointed out that, firstly, at least some of the numerous scientific and technical books in mechanics' institutes and schools of arts libraries would in all probability have been purchased in response to member's requests. Many (perhaps most - I have only been able to find the library rules of a limited sample of institutions) schools of arts, mechanics' institutes and similar institutions made provision for readers to be able to suggest titles for addition to their libraries. The Kiama School of Arts, for example, had written into its Library By-Laws in 1910 that "Any member may propose books for addition to the library on entering the titles, prices and other particulars in a book to be kept for that purpose in the library"[83]; and similar provisions obtained at, for example, Mudgee, Young, Narrandera and Kangaroo Valley.[84]   In the case of the Kangaroo Valley School of Arts, an interesting sidelight into the workings of the suggestion-book system is provided by a newspaper report of that School's annual general meeting of July 1903, which reads:

> The [librarian's report] having been received, a member complained at length that the past two committees had shown him scant courtesy in not procuring two books he had suggested.

> The matter was argued, and the member in the end seemed to be satisfied that everything had been done to procure the works he wanted.[85]

The fact that a substantial proportion of acquisitions *were* scientific and technical works -at the Bathurst School of Arts, for instance, the fourth (out of nine) largest category of volumes added to the library in 1914-15 was 'Science'[86] - supports the view that at least a proportion of these books would have been requested by readers, and therefore would probably have

194

been read by them.

But the strongest evidence that these books were read - and read seriously - consists not only in the tattered condition in which one finds those that have survived (as at Muswellbrook), but also in the numerous marked passages, marginalia, etc., that one frequently finds in these volumes. In the Muswellbrook School of Arts' copy of Darwin's *Descent of Man and Selection in Relation to Sex*, for example, the following passage has been marked in pencil by a reader:

> Those naturalists... who admit the principle of evolution, and this is now admitted by the greater number of rising men, will feel no doubt that all races of man are descended from a single primitive stock; whether or not they think fit to designate them as distinct species, for the sake of expressing their amount of difference. With our domestic animals the question whether the various races have arisen from one or more species is different. Although all such races, as well as the natural species within the same genus, have undoubtedly sprung from the same primitive stock, yet it is a fit subject for discussion whether, for instance, all the domestic races of the dog have acquired their present differences since some one species was first domesticated and bred by man; or whether they owe some of their characters to inheritance from distinct species, which had already been modified in a state of nature. With mankind no such question can arise, for he cannot be said to have been domesticated at any particular period.[87]

It is impossible to know, of course, what exactly prompted the reader to take particular notice of this passage. But one can surmise possibilities, and one plausible explanation, I would suggest, relates to Darwin's association of the concept of human evolution with the evolution of domestic animals through human intervention - or artificial selection - a subject with which working people in rural areas frequently had considerable first-hand knowledge and could relate to. We should now turn to look at what I consider to be a very important element in the appeal of late nineteenth and early twentieth-century science to members of mechanics' institutes and schools of arts in rural districts: an interest in evolutionary theory.

EVOLUTION - A LINKING THEME

In 1890, after attending a Summer Meeting at Oxford, England, in connection with that University's Extension program, a 'North-Country Student' wrote:

> If there was a connecting thought which could be traced through the varied teaching of the summer meeting this year, it was distinctly optimistic in tendency -the idea of development, of evolution, of a rise from the lower to the higher; from the idea of mere individual life, to the wider one of the well-being of the species and a higher realisation of social life.[88]

This paragraph encapsulates the thinking of many people at this time. Darwin's theories were only by then reaching a wide audience through improvements in basic education over the previous couple of decades (following, for example, the Forster and Mundella Education Acts of 1870 and 1880 in Britain; and Henry Parkes' 1880 Compulsory Education Act in New South Wales[89]), the proliferation of newspapers intended for a working-class audience

195

(made possible not only by improvements in literacy, but also by technological advances in printing, paper-making techniques, etc.[90]), and for a variety of other reasons - including a decline in the influence of traditional religion amongst working people following the inroads of Marxist and other radical ideas. Evolution, for many people, epitomised science's triumph over ignorance and superstition, and somehow represented a liberating force to be harnessed for the building of a better society. As Alfred Russel Wallace wrote in *The Wonderful Century* (which, as we have seen, was in schools of arts libraries), at the beginning of his chapter 'Evolution and Natural Selection': "We now approach the subject which, in popular estimation, and perhaps in real importance, may be held to be the great scientific work of the nineteenth century - the establishment of the general theory of evolution."[91] Further on Wallace wrote: "What was a 'great heresy' to Sir John Herschel in 1845, and 'the mystery of mysteries' down to the date of Darwin's book, is now the common knowledge [Wallace is writing in 1898]... of every one who reads even the newspapers."[92]

It is easy to illustrate Wallace's point about the frequency of appearance of articles about evolution and related subjects in newspapers. From a decade later (1909) for instance (Australia being somewhat behind Britain in this respect), one can read articles in the pages of the *Forbes Times* like 'Darwin and His Publisher' (an interview with the younger John Murray[93] - it contains some remarkable insights into Darwin's character not available anywhere else, so far as I am aware), or 'This Year's Copley Medalist' (A R Wallace himself, who "was honoured by the Linnean Society for his share, fifty years ago, in Darwin's great work"),[94] or numerous items on geological, palaeontological, etc. subjects, such as one headed 'Ancient Fossils,' another 'Fossil Remains,' another 'More Mammoths Found,' and so forth.[95] A lengthy feature article on the Wellington Caves contains the following kind of information apparently considered of interest to readers:

> Special scientific interest attaches to these caves, owing to discoveries of large numbers of fossil bones in the various caverns. Some of these fossils bear evidence to the enormous development, both in size and numbers, of the marsupials of the period. Among the most important fossil remains are those of the *Diprotodon Australis*, the *Thylacoleo*... and several other extinct animals and birds.[96]

As seen above, many of the most popular educational lectures from both the Technical Education Branch and the University of Sydney's Extension Lectures Board were on geological and related subjects, and, given this apparent widespread interest in evolutionary theory, it is not difficult to appreciate how this could be so, and how newspaper articles on geology, etc. could also be read with interest. But as well as articles like these, there are also many articles on subjects bearing on evolutionary theory which would have been of *direct* interest to farmers and other people involved in the agricultural and pastoral industries - the majority of people in country districts like that around Forbes. An example of this kind of article would be that in the *Forbes Times* of 10 March 1909 on the 'Science of Wheat Culture,' about William Farrer's experiments. It reads in part: "There is scarcely a grain grower in this and the sister state [Victoria] who, if not an actual producer of the new wheats introduced by Farrer, has not yet determined at the first opportunity to adapt them, or some of them, to his own particular use." That the last part of this sentence refers to wheat farmers conducting their own experiments with wheat varieties, to determine those most suitable to their own particular climatic and soil conditions, etc., seems to be implied. In any event, horticulturists, wheat farmers, sheep raisers and other rural producers had of course been employing 'artificial selection' techniques for centuries (indeed, Darwin depended very heavily upon this knowledge for the formulation of his theory).[97] So Darwin's theory of *natural* selection would have been meaningful to these people and would have struck a chord with them.

Further articles in country newspapers similarly attest to this quite sophisticated knowledge of the basic principles of selection among rural working people. An item in the *Molong Express* (all of these newspapers were in Schools of Arts reading rooms) of 4 August 1906, for instance, headed 'An Australian Burbank,' reads in part as follows:

> Probably every reader of current literature has heard more or less of that wonderful American wizard Luther Burbank, who has worked wonders in the propagation of improved varieties of fruit and vegetables. If the following from the 'West Macquarie' can be taken as correct, Burbank appears to have a prototype in Blayney:-
>
> Mr 'Johnny' Fitzgerald, of Brown's Creek, brought for our inspection this week a small plant of the common elderberry variety, which he claims to, after seven years experiment, have converted from a deciduous to an evergreen type. The specimen that he showed us was covered with full green leaves, and as it has withstood the severe frosts of the past few days it must be something out of the ordinary. 'Johnny'... claims also to have done the same for a quince tree, and doubting ones are at liberty to inspect his results.[98]

Darwin's theories, then, would have made perfect sense to people on the land, and one can appreciate how they would have responded readily to such views. An interest in evolution may or may not have been a factor in the response of locals to lectures on some of the more theoretical aspects of agriculture and horticulture by Gale and others in the 1880s and '90s, but there is good reason for believing that such an interest was becoming influential in the years leading up to the First World War. Apart from the range of related material in local newspapers, and the attendances at university extension and other lectures on subjects related to evolutionary theory in general, one can cite lectures at schools of arts and similar institutions specifically on the relevance of evolution to the agricultural and pastoral industries. In June 1911, for example, a Mr Frank McCaffrey of Kiama lectured at the Kangaroo Valley School of Arts under the auspices of the local Agricultural Society on 'Cattle and Their Origin.'[99] The text of the lecture does not appear to be extant, unfortunately, but one can probably gain a fair idea of its contents from articles like 'The Origin of our Domestic Cattle,' in the October 1901 *Australian Technical Journal* (which, as noted above, was in the nearby Jamberoo School of Arts reading room), and which in turn is based largely on Darwin's chapter on 'Cattle' in *The Variation of Animals and Plants under Domestication*.[100] Some lines from this article indicate the kind of follow-up reading available to those interested:

> Did the thought ever occur to your minds when a herd of neat cattle - or even a solitary bullock or cow - has come under your notice, whence have they sprung? Have they all originated from one common ancestor of special creation, or have they reached their present conformation by natural selection through a long succession of evolutionary changes?

The question is of great interest, not only to the naturalist, but to every veterinary and agricultural student...

According to the authority of that great scientist Geikie, the first traces of the ox family are found in the more recent formations of Europe - in the Pliocene of the Tertiary epoch. Of course, in making this statement, I wish it to be clearly understood that the skeleton of a fossil ox of the Pliocene period differs vastly in the eyes of a comparative anatomist to that of a champion improved shorthorn or Hereford...

... From the middle ages there were men who took an interest in the well-being of their live stock. But it is not till nearing the end of the 18th century that the different breeds of the country had as a result of environment, and circumscribed selection in breeding, reached a fixity of character... Towards the close of this century several gentlemen, imbued with a love and interest in the improvement of their livestock, began to give their attention to the industry. Foremost amongst these early pioneers who laid the foundation of Great Britain's fame as a cattle breeding nation, are such men as Bakewell, the brothers Collins, Benjamin Tomkins, Francis Quartly, and Hugh Watson, etc... [B]y acute discernment, attentive study, indefatigable and judicious exercise of scientific methods in selection... they succeeded in establishing an ideal type.[101]

With regard to sheep, a lecture at the Kiama School of Arts on 'Technical Education' by George Hooper, by then Superintendent of Technical Education, only a few days earlier had included some discussion on "the breeding of sheep for wool and meat to command the highest commercial value" which had "passed from the experimental to the scientific stage."[102] The *Kiama Independent* report on this lecture also referred to Hooper's lantern slides showing "the evolution of the sheep of early days to the finished wool product of to-day," which "was interesting."[103]

And people who wished to follow up Hooper's lecture with further reading could do so in articles such as that on 'The Evolution of the Cross-bred' in the February 1912 *Agricultural Gazette*,[104] or in books like Alfred Hawkesworth's *Australian Sheep and Wool* which, as noted above, was in schools of arts libraries such as Gunnedah's and was also the Technical Education Branch's textbook for the Sheep and Wool course (which was offered at the Cowra School of Arts, for example).[105] Hawkesworth's book has chapters on such subjects as 'The Natural History of Breeding,' which contain a considerable amount of information of evolutionary interest. The following passage is an example:

Every animal organism possesses the power to transfer to its descendants all its inherent qualities, both the individual and the race... With the changes upon the earth's surface were changed of course the life-conditions for the animal world. They were themselves subjected to constant change. Produced from the one original form, they were bound to comply with the many different conditions, and adapting themselves to different circumstances, continue to exist. Now began the struggle for existence in which the strongest individuals always came off conquerors...

[With the intervention of man] through attentive care in providing food for them, as well as shelter against inclemency of the weather, weaker domestic animals find their struggle for existence a less burden to themselves. The artificial choice of brood animals has taken the place of the natural, inasmuch as man makes use of those animals only which suit his purpose best for the propagation of the race.[106]

That such aspects of sheep and cattle raising *were* of interest to people in rural New South Wales is indicated in trade publications like the 1916 *Sheepman's Diary*, for example, which contains much information about the genetic history of breeds, such as: "The Border Leicester is a distinct type of sheep from the Leicester. It was formed by crossing the latter with the Cheviot in the eighteenth century"; and goes on to explain that "[S]uccess [in breeding] consists in a system of 'evolution by selection.' By selection and combination the historical flocks of Australia were established."[107] In his lecture in the Kiama School of Arts, Hooper also wished to pay tribute to "the farmers of the South Coast who had done so much for the dairying industry for the improvement of types for the diary cow"[108] (the south coast being, of course, the home of the Australian Illawarra Shorthorn).

Agricultural and General Scientific Education, 1911-1916

An interest in evolution amongst agricultural workers (and country people generally) is an instance of how 'technical' (or 'vocational') and 'general' education might overlap. In his 1988 White Paper, *Higher Education - A Policy Statement*, Mr John Dawkins, then Federal Minister of Employment, Education and Training, remarked that "It is likely that there will be further convergence between the traditional concepts of 'general' and 'vocational' education."[109] This process would appear to have begun a long time ago in New South Wales. As was explained above, part of the *general* fascination with science in the late nineteenth and early twentieth centuries stemmed from the fact that science purported not only to provide an understanding of nature's laws - that is to say, to provide answers to some of the most fundamental questions known to mankind (the physicist John Tyndall once declared, in a lecture to a general audience: "We claim, and we shall wrest, from Theology the entire domain of cosmological theory"[110]) - but also to make possible the building of a better society in which all would share in the greatly increased utilisation of nature's resources. This latter aspect of the widespread faith in science characteristic of the time shows through clearly, for instance, in the following lines taken from an address by a Mr. O'Donogue, from the local branch of the Railway Workers and General Labourers Union, at the Leeton School of Arts in the evening of the town's Eight Hours' Day holiday in October 1913. O'Donogue told his audience:

> Scientists contend that the work of the world can be done by men working six hours a day only. Machines had enormously increased the earnings of capital since the eight hours a day system was inaugurated over 50 years ago. The workers should now participate a little more in the improved economic conditions brought about by machinery.[111]

The Leeton School of Arts hall had been one of the first buildings constructed (in 1912) by the McGowan and Holman Labor government's Murrumbidgee Irrigation Trust in connection with the government's ambitious irrigation scheme for the area;[112] and the public's

199

enthusiastic response to this scheme (as evidenced in its willingness to take up leaseholds) is a good illustration of this same faith in the applications of modern science and technology. And just as officers from the Trust and the NSW Department of Agriculture saw the School of Arts (another was built at Yanco about the same time) as the logical place to speak to settlers on various aspects of agriculture and stock raising, so too was the local populace willing to attend these lectures. Among these lectures at the Leeton School of Arts, then, were one on 'Fruit Growing,' another on 'Dairying,' another on 'Pruning and Spraying,' another on 'Fruit Pests,' and another on 'Co-operation.'[113] A library was set up and subsidised on the same basis as with other schools of arts, and government journals and pamphlets were supplied *gratis*.[114] And again, the contents of this literature underline the convergence of 'technical' and 'general' education that is part and parcel of agricultural education, with its concern with fundamental natural processes. An item on the 'Law of Heredity' in the Trust's *Irrigation Record* is worth quoting as an example of this overlap:

> Professor R C Punnett, of Cambridge University, in referring to Mendel's theory regarding the law of heredity in plants and animals, says that the problems to which Mendel found the key have had the attention of Professor Bateson of Cambridge. Poultry was one of the first subjects of experiment by Bateson, and during the past ten years much has been learned of the transmission of various characters. Offering as they do a number of features showing sex-linked inheritance, poultry are of importance for gaining an insight into the nature of sex, and of studying the peculiar influence of each sex in the transmission of hereditary properties. Several of these sex linked characters are now under investigation at Cambridge.[115]

An example of a more 'practical' lecture in the same subject area - heredity in poultry - would be that by a Mr. Bradshaw from the Department of Agriculture at the Wetherill Park School of Arts in 1912, on 'Utility Poultry-keeping.' The following lines are from a summary of this lecture in the *Agricultural Gazette*:

> Like produces like under natural laws and conditions. A capacity for producing for laying 200 eggs per year by a hen is an acquired character, and if mated with a male bird of a like prolific family, will but rarely transfer this trait to the progeny. It may be transmitted in a slightly increased degree to one or two of the specimens, but the overwhelming number of the progeny will fall far short of the parent's records. There is a continual effort to revert to the original wild fowl's laying of twenty or thirty eggs in the year. Hence to maintain, much less to improve, the heavy laying trait, there must be continual selection and mating of the best layers, otherwise the flock's record will soon revert to very ordinary production.[116]

Other examples of lectures by officers from the Department of Agriculture and the Murrumbidgee Irrigation Trust over the period 1911-16 include the following: A lecture by G McKeown, Manager of the Wagga Experimental Farm, at the Wagga School of Arts on 'Take-all and Whiteheads in Wheat'; another lecture on 'Noxious Weeds and Plants' at the same institution; another by a Mr. Palgrave, a veterinary surgeon, on 'Foaling and Mortality among Foaling Mares' at the Burraja School of Arts; another on 'Up-to-date Poultry Farming' at the North Ryde Literary Institute; another by a J Aspery at the Sackville School of Arts on 'Maize Culture'; an unnamed lecture at the Cundletown School of Arts by a veterinary officer from the Department of Agriculture; a lecture on 'Agricultural

Fig. 1.   Dun Devonshire Pony, with shoulder, spinal, and leg stripes.

Fig. 4.   Old Irish Pig, with jaw-appendages.   (Copied from H. D. Richardson on Pigs.)

Illustration from Charles Darwin's *Variations of Animals and Plants under Domestication,* 1835

Molong School of Arts, NSW

Bondi-Waverley School of Arts, NSW

Mudgee Mechanics' Institute, NSW

Singleton Mechanics' Institute, NSW

Leeton School of Arts, NSW, ca 1917

Experiments' at the Bonville School of Arts by Inspector G Marks; a paper on 'Water Conservation,' read by a Mr. R H Lalor at the Blacktown School of Arts; a lecture on 'Contagious Abortion in Cattle,' by C J Sanderson, another veterinary officer with the Department (this lecture is printed in full in the *Agricultural Gazette*) at the Kiama School of Arts, and another on 'Conformation and Unsoundness in Horses' at the Jamberoo School of Arts; and lectures on the Murrumbidgee Irrigation Scheme at the Liverpool, Kogarah and Epping Schools of Arts and the North Ryde Literary Institute.[117]

As well as these, other lectures of a scientific and technical nature given at schools of arts and similar institutions over this period included one on the Franco-British Exhibition (of 1911) at the Kiama School of Arts, a series of three (unspecified) lectures at the Tenterfield School of Arts by a Dr. Anderson of the Australian Museum (under the auspices of the Sydney University Extension Lectures Board), another unspecified series by members of the Maitland Scientific Society in the West Maitland School of Arts, and two lectures on Astronomy - one on 'The Moon' and another on 'The Majesty of Creation,' by a Walter Gale and a J Clement Wragge respectively - at the Bathurst School of Arts.[118]

SUMMARY AND CONCLUSIONS

This chapter has attempted to trace certain aspects of the role of mechanics' institutes and schools of arts in the beginnings and early growth of technical education in New South Wales, particularly in rural New South Wales. It has been argued that these institutions did indeed play a significant part in the spread of technical education to country districts, especially agricultural education, and especially following the appointment of itinerant lecturers by the Board and Branch of Technical Education in the 1880s and 1890s. As well as serving as venues for lectures, mechanics institutes and schools of arts were also utilised by the NSW Technical Education Branch as accommodation for classes, particularly after around 1900; and throughout this period libraries in these institutions fulfilled an extremely important role not only as an educational support system, but also in stimulating an interest in scientific and technical subjects among these institutions' clientele in the first place. Museum collections and exhibitions, too, no doubt played an important role in stimulating and supporting an interest in technical education in rural New South Wales throughout the period looked at in this chapter.

The University Extension movement, particularly around the period 1907-10, provided educational authorities with increasing evidence of a widespread fascination with science and technology amongst the New South Wales rural and mining population, including in terms of demand for lectures in these subject areas at mechanics' institutes and schools of arts and in attendance figures for these lectures. These lectures, in turn, very likely further stimulated and fostered an interest in technical education, as was probably partly reflected in the continuing interest in scientific - particularly connected with agriculture - lectures in mechanics' institutes, schools of arts and related institutions in later years.

An important theme in this chapter has been the explanatory power of evolutionary theory in providing a common thread to the various subject interests apparent amongst those attending mechanics' institutes and schools or arts for a variety of reasons - whether pursuing formal courses of study, or attending lectures largely out of general interest, or simply using the library. This interest in evolution will be taken up further in my final chapter. In the present chapter I have argued that this apparent coalescence of interests around evolutionary theory provides compelling reasons for believing that the dichotomy one frequently finds between 'technical' and 'general' education was not a conspicuous feature in the educational work of New South Wales mechanics' institutes and schools of arts. At the same time, the contention one frequently encounters - that in terms of providing 'useful' education for the working-classes, the mechanics' institutes and schools are arts were a 'failure' - has been found to be not appropriate for New South Wales for the period studied in this chapter.

NOTES AND REFERENCES

1. Hudson, J. W. (1851). *The history of adult education*. London: Longman, Brown, Green and Longmans.

2. Armytage, W.H.G. (1961). *A social history of engineering*. London: Faber and Faber; Harrison, J.F.C. (1961). *Learning and living 1790-1960: A study in the history of the English adult education movement*. London: Routledge and Kegan Paul;
Kelly, T. (1970). *A history of adult education in Great Britain*. Liverpool: Liverpool University Press;
Tylecote, M. (1957). *The mechanics' institutes of Lancashire and Yorkshire before 1857*. Manchester: Manchester University Press;
Inkster, I. (Ed.), (1985). *The Steam Intellect Societies - Essays on culture, education and industry circa 1820-1914*. Nottingham: Department of Adult Education, University of Nottingham.

3. Engels, F. (1844/1958). *The condition of the working class in Manchester in 1844*. Oxford: Basil Blackwell, pp. 271-2.

4. Whitelock, D. (1970). A brief history of adult education in Australia and an outline of current provision. In Whitelock, D. (Ed.), *Adult education in Australia*. London: Pergamon, p.12. Since writing this, discussions I have had with Pam Firth, present owner of the Healesville Mechanics' Institute building in Victoria, suggest that the total number of institutions at the time of their greatest extent was probably closer to 2000.

5. Butlin, N.G. (1959). Colonial socialism in Australia, 1860-1900. In Aitken, H.G.J. (Ed.), *The state and economic growth*. New York: Social Science Research Council.

6. Reeves, C. (1935). *A history of Tasmanian education: Vol. 1. State primary education*. Melbourne: Melbourne University Press, p.18.

7. Whitelock, *op. cit.* p.10.

8. Sydney Mechanics' School of Arts, *Third Annual Report*. Sydney: Henry Bull, printers, 1836. In 1835, the full program of lectures was: one on 'The Benefits and Advantages of Scientific and Useful Knowledge' (Rev. Henry Carmichael), one on 'Landscape Gardening (T. Shepherd), one on 'Banking' (Mr. Hipkiss), one on 'Intemperance' (Mr. Kemp), two entitled 'Introductory to a Course of Natural Philosophy' (Rev. Henry Carmichael), two on 'The Application of the Sciences' (Dr. Charles Nicholson), one on 'Botany' (Dr. Charles Nicholson), one on 'Animal Physiology' (Mr. Robert Band), two on 'The Steam Engine'

(Mr. W.J. Edwards), two on 'Natural History' (Dr. J Lhotsky), three on 'Geology' (Dr. Charles Nicholson), four on 'Philosophy of the Atmosphere' (Mr. Robert Band), and one on 'Strength of Colonial Timber' (Edward McDonald).

9.anon. (1988). A Land Where Beasts Lay Eggs and Birds Cannot Fly. *Ascent, 15*, p.11.

10.*ibid*.

11.Turner, J.W. (1909). *A quarter century of technical education in New South Wales*. Sydney: W.A. Gullick, Government Printer, p.83.

12.Kincumber School of Arts. (Typescript history framed in Kincumber School of Arts building).

13.Kincumber School of Arts, MS Inventory, 1914, housed in Kincumber School of Arts building.

14.Bathurst Progress Committee. (1893). The Bathurst Mechanics' School of Arts. In *Bathurst guide, embracing particulars of the rise and progress of the city and its public institutions*. Sydney: Bathurst Progress Committee, p.14.

15.Murray-Smith, S. (1965). Technical education in Australia. In Wheelwright, E.L. (Ed.), *Higher education in Australia*. Melbourne: Cheshire, p.175.

16.Cannon, M. (1978). *Australia in the Victorian age: Life in the cities*. Melbourne: Nelson, chs. 7-9.

17.Edmunds, W.H. (1890). Letter to the Hon. The Minister for Public Instruction, received 11 January 1890 (NSW State Archives).

18.Sydney Mechanics' School of Arts. (1881). *Report from the Committee of the Technical College at the Sydney Mechanics' School of Arts to the Honourable, The Minister of Public Instruction of New South Wales*. Sydney: Samuel Edward Lees.

19.*ibid*, p.18.

20.Sydney Mechanics' School of Arts. (1883). *Annual Report to the 31st December, 1882*. Sydney: Jarrett & Co., printers, 1883.

21.Field, E.P. (1883). Letter to Under Secretary, Education Office, received 11 January 1883 (NSW State Archives).

22.anon. (1983). *Spanners, easels and microchips - A history of technical and further education in New South Wales, 1883-1983*. Sydney: NSW Council of Technical and Further Education, p.11.

23.Wyatt, R.T. (1941). *The history of Goulburn, NSW*. Goulburn: The Municipality of Goulburn, p.228.

24.Bathurst Mechanics' School of Arts, *op. cit.*, pp.15-16.

25.Crane, A.R., & Walker, W.G. (1957). *Peter Board: His contribution to the development of education in New South Wales*. Melbourne: Australian Council for Educational Research, p.164.

26.Carruthers, J.H. (1889). *Technical education*. Sydney: Charles Potter, Government Printer, p.3.

27.Mackay, A. (1890). Letter to Superintendent of Technical Education, n.d. (1890) (NSW State Archives).

28.*Sydney Morning Herald*, 19 June 1890.

29.Turner, J.W. *op. cit.* p.87.

30.Gale, A. (1890). General Report on a Visit to the Orange and Bathurst Districts, 1 November 1890 (MS, NSW State Archives).

31.Mackay, A. (1885). *Elements of Australian agriculture*. Sydney: John Sands, printer, p.60.

32.Lawson, H. (1896). The geological spieler. In Lawson, H. *While the billy boils*. Sydney: Angus and Robertson.

33.Brubacher, J.S. (1947). *A History of the problems of education*. New York and London: McGraw Hill, p.376. See also Bode, C. (1968). *The American Lyceum: Town Meeting of the Mind*. Carbondale and Edwardsville, Ill.: Southern Illinois University Press.

34.Parramatta School of Arts, *Letter Book*, 15 June 1893.

35.See, e.g., Curran, J.M. (1899). *The geology of Sydney and the Blue Mountains: A popular introduction to the study of geology*. (2nd ed.). Sydney: Angus and Robertson, pp.30-4.

36.Granville School of Arts, *Annual Report*, 3 February 1893 (newspaper cutting in Granville School of Arts Minute Book, Parramatta Central Library).

37.Jamberoo School of Arts, *Minutes*, 20 February 1897.

38.See, e.g., Larcombe, C.O.G. (1901). Notes of a geological excursion to the Illawarra District. *Australian Technical Journal*, 30 March 1901.

39.*Kiama Independent*, 6 March 1909.

40.*ibid.*

41.Jones, T. (1902). Letter to J.D. Cooper, Superintendent of Technical Education, 6 June 1902 (NSW State Archives).

42.*ibid.*

43.Mackay, A. (1890). *op. cit.*

44.Technical Education Branch (1894). *Suburban and country technical classes.* (bound register, NSW State Archives).

45.Granville Technical School, *Admission Register* (MS.), (Granville Technical College Library).

46.*Australian Technical Journal*, 31 May 1897.

47.Technical Education Branch (1890). *Return of buildings used for purposes of technical education in Sydney, suburbs, and country districts* (MS.), 14 March 1890 (NSW State Archives).

48.Board, P. (1912). Printed memorandum on schools of arts, Department of Public Instruction, 21 August 1912.

49.Sydney Technical College (1889). *Country Branch Technical Schools, Return No. 2.* (printed and MS, NSW State Archives).

50.Technical Education Branch (1894). *op. cit.*

51.Technical Education Branch (1902). *Calendar, 1902.* Sydney: W.A. Gullick, Government Printer, p.31.

52.*Blayney Advocate*, 19 November 1904.

53.Hooper, G. (1910). Northern portion of state - recent tour. *Typescript memorandum,* 3 March 1910 (NSW State Archives).

54.Goulburn Mechanics' Institute (1855). *Report of the Goulburn Mechanics' Institute with a catalogue of the books, and a list of officers and members.* Goulburn: The 'Herald' office, printers.

55.See, e.g., Penglase, B. (1988). Hunter Valley readers and adult education in the nineteenth century. *Australian Journal of Adult Education,* 28 (2), pp. 39-42.

56.Gunnedah School of Arts (1909). *Catalogue of the Library.* Gunnedah: T.B. Roberts and J. Longmuir, printers.

57.Orange School of Arts (1914). *Catalogue of the Orange School of Arts.* Orange: 'Western Daily Advocate' Office, printers.

58.Gunnedah School of Arts, *op. cit.*

59.Orange School of Arts, *op. cit.*

60.Jamberoo School of Arts, *Minutes,* 17 September 1896.

61.*ibid.*, 19 March 1897.

62. *Mudgee Liberal*, 2 August 1900; *Kangaroo Valley Times*, 21 July 1903.

63. Bathurst School of Arts, *Report*, 1915; Bowral School of Arts, *Annual Report*, 1915; Coolamon School of Arts, *Annual Report*, 1915; Cootamundra Literary Institute, *Annual Report and Balance Sheet*, 1916; Cowra School of Arts (later Literary Institute), *Annual Report and Balance Sheet*, 1915; East Maitland Literary Institute, *Annual Report*, 1915; Grenfell Literary Institute, *Report and Balance Sheet*, 1915; *Riverina Grazier*, 23 July 1915 (re Hay Athenaeum); Hornsby Literary Institute, *Annual Report*, 1915; Narrandera Mechanics Institute, *Annual Report and Balance Sheet*, 1916; North Ryde Literary Institute, *Annual Report*, 1915; Orange School of Arts, *Annual Report*, 1915; West Maitland School of Arts, *Half-Yearly Report*, December 1914; Young School of Arts, *Annual Report*, 1914-15.

64. *Blayney Advocate*, 2 April 1904; Bowral School of Arts, *Annual Report*, 1915; Coolamon School of Arts, *Annual Report*, 1915; Cootamundra Literary Institute, *Annual Report and Balance Sheet*, 1916; Cowra School of Arts, *Annual Report and Balance Sheet*, 1916; *Forbes Times*, 2 July 1909; Glebe Workingman's Institute, *Half-Yearly Report*, 1916; Goulburn Mechanics' Institute, *What do you Read?* (undated leaflet, ca. 1900, in possession of Goulburn Historical Society); *Mudgee Liberal*, 2 August 1900; Mungindi Mechanics' Institute, *Annual Report*, 1916; Orange School of Arts, *Annual Report*, 1915.

65. Bathurst School of Arts, *Annual Report*, 1909.

66. *Forbes Times*, 7 July 1909; Shackleton, E. (1910). *The heart of the Antarctic: Being the story of the British Antarctic expedition, 1907-1909.* London: Heinemann, pp. 194, 255.

67. *Forbes Times*, 7 July 1909.

68. *Forbes Times*, 17 March 1909.

69. East Maitland Literary Institute, *Annual Report*, 1915.

70. *Riverina Grazier*, 23 July 1915; Mawson, D. (1915). *The home of the blizzard: Being the story of the Australasian Antarctic expedition, 1911-1914.* London: Heinemann, Vol.2, p.294.

71. I am grateful to John McIntyre of the Faculty of Adult Education, University of Technology, Sydney, for this information.

72. *Mudgee Liberal*, 16 August 1900; *Blayney Advocate*, 2 August 1902; *Molong Express*, 3 August 1907.

73. Wyatt, R.T., *op. cit.*, pp. 229, 376. Government museum staff also provided other services. In the 1880s, for example, curators at the Australian Museum undertook the naming and arrangement for exhibition of the collections of a number of Schools of Arts throughout the State. (See Pitts, J. [1990]. Science and Public Museums: Some nineteenth-century connections. *Unpublished B A. [Hons.] Thesis.* Griffith University, p.43.)

74. Secretary of Mudgee Mechanics' Institute (name indecipherable). (1903). Letter to D.J. Cooper, Superintendent of Technical Education, 27 May 1903 (NSW State Archives).

75. *Blayney Advocate*, 23 December 1903.

76. *Granville Technical College Journal*, 20 July 1912.

77. *Agricultural Gazette of NSW*, 2 July 1915.

78. On the British background to University Extension see, Welch, E. (1973). *The peripatetic university*. Cambridge: Cambridge University Press. See also, Jones, D. (1988). *The Origins of Civic Universities: Manchester, Leeds and Liverpool*. London: Routledge.

79. University of Sydney (1908). *Report of the Extension Board for the Year 1907-8*. (University of Sydney Archives).

80. *ibid*. 1908-9.

81. *ibid*.

82. ibid., 1910; Whitelock, D. (1974). *The great tradition: A history of adult education in Australia*. St Lucia: University of Queensland Press, p.165.

83. Kiama School of Arts (1910). *Catalogue of books in the library and library by-laws*. Kiama: J. Weston, printer.

84. *Mudgee Liberal*, 13 October 1900, *Kangaroo Valley Times*, 21 July 1903; Narrandera Mechanics' Institute, *Annual Report and Balance Sheet*, 1916; Young School of Arts, *Annual Report*, 1914-15.

85. *Kangaroo Valley Times*, 21 July 1903.

86. Bathurst School of Arts, *Report*, 1915, p.7.

87. Darwin, C. (1871). *The descent of man and selection in relation to sex*. London: John Murray, Vol.1, p.229.

88. *Oxford University Extension Gazette*, October 1890.

89. Crane & Walker, *op. cit.*, p.163.

90. See Laurent, J. (1984). Science Education, Evolution Theory and the British Labour Movement, 1860-1910. *Unpublished PhD Thesis*. Griffith University, ch.4.

91. Wallace, A.R. (1898). *The wonderful century: Its success and its failures*. London: Swan Sonnenschein & Co., p.134.

92. *ibid.*, p.141.

93. *Forbes Times*, 4 December 1909.

94.*ibid.*, 13 February 1909.

95.*ibid.*, 27 February, 5 June, 3 July 1909.

96.*ibid.*, 9 October 1909.

97.See, Darwin, C. (1891). *The origin of species by means of natural selection.* London: John Murray, ch.1 ('Variation Under Domestication').

98.*Molong Express*, 4 August 1906.

99.*Kiama Independent*, 3 June 1911.

100.Darwin, C. (1885). *The variation of animals and plants under domestication.* London: John Murray, Vol.1, pp.82-97.

101.*Australian Technical Journal*, 31 October 1901, pp. 273-9 (273, 278).

102.*Kiama Independent*, 31 May 1911.

103.*ibid.*

104.*Agricultural Gazette of NSW*, 2 February 1912.

105.Cowra School of Arts, *Annual Report and Balance Sheet*, 1915 and 1916.

106.Hawkesworth, A. (1911). *Australasian sheep and wool: A practical and theoretical treatise.* (4th ed). Sydney: William Brooks & Co. Ltd., pp.34-5.

107.*The sheepman's diary, 1916.* Sydney: Wm. Cooper & Nephews, 1915, pp. 26, 60.

108.*Kiama Independent*, 31 May 1911.

109.Dawkins, J. (1988). *Higher Education - A Policy Statement.* Canberra: Australian Government Publishing Service, p.69. On this question of 'general' and 'vocational' education, see also Hager, P. (1990). Vocational Education/General Education: A False Dichotomy? *Studies in Continuing Education, 12*(1), pp.13-23.

110.Tyndall, J. (1874). Presidential Address. *Report of the Forty-Fourth Meeting of the British Association for the Advancement of Science; held at Belfast in August 1874.* London: Murray.

111.*Irrigation Record*, 15 October 1913.

112.Maguire, M. (1985). *Where sheep once grazed.* Leeton: The Author, p.73.

113.*Irrigation Record*, 1 October 1913; *Murrumbidgee Irrigator*, 7 May, 4 June 1915; *Agricultural Gazette of NSW*, 2 June 1915. In 1916 Premier Holman appointed his old friend (see Chapter 19) Henry Lawson as a publicist for the scheme. See Prout, D. (1973). *Henry Lawson: The grey dreamer.* Adelaide: Rigby, chapter 19.

114.*Murrumbidgee Irrigator*, 7 May 1915.

115.*Irrigation Record*, 15 October 1913.

116.*Agricultural Gazette of NSW*, 2 October 1912.

117.*ibid.*, 2 November 1911; 2 March, 2 April, 2 July, 2 August 1912; 2 March 1915; *Kiama Independent*, 8 February, 22 March, 1911; Epping School of Arts, *Ninth Annual Report*, 1915; Kogarah School of Arts, *Annual Report* (typescript), 1915; Liverpool School of Arts, *Annual Report*, 1914-15; North Ryde Literary Institute, *Annual Report*, 1915.

118.*Kiama Independent*, 12 July 1911; Bathurst School of Arts, *Report*, 1912; Tenterfield School of Arts, *Annual Report and Balance Sheet*, 1914-15; West Maitland School of Arts, *Half-Yearly Report*, December 1914.

CHAPTER TEN

THE MOVEMENT'S CONTRIBUTION TO THE VISUAL ARTS: THREE NEW SOUTH WALES CASE STUDIES

Jean Riley

INTRODUCTION

> They persist in standing, scores of stone edifices and wooden halls, which were once temples to reason and art and beacons of Britishness and Colonial philanthropy.[1]

These are the opening words of an article in the *National Times* by Edward Howard entitled 'Crumbling Temples' describing the "failure" of the school of arts movement, and claiming that "success spoiled them." It is not exactly clear what Howard meant by this statement, for any success the movement achieved was hard earned, and the generally superficial nature of his article highlights how little is known by the community, in general, about the schools of arts.

Before proceeding, it is necessary to make a comment about nomenclature, as there is some confusion regarding the correct name or title for these institutions: whether a school of arts is the same as a mechanics' institute or a literary institute. From the very first meeting, the association in Sydney was referred to as the Mechanics' School of Arts, and the Regulation read at the public meeting on 22 March 1833 and again on 23 April (as recorded in the minutes) states: "An association shall now be constructed under the title of 'The Sydney Mechanics' School of Arts'."

Later publications also refer to the association as the 'Sydney Mechanics' School of Arts.' In New South Wales and Queensland most suburban and country institutions were termed 'schools of arts,' usually preceded by the name of the suburb or town. Some, however, were known as mechanics' institutes or literary institutes. Sometimes, the name changed as the function of the institution changed. Now known as the Taree Literary Institute, the name on the front of the building concerned indicates that it was originally known as the Taree School of Arts. In Victoria, Western Australia and Tasmania they were more often termed 'mechanics' institutes' and in South Australia simply 'institutes.' The name of the institution is a simple matter of preference, but the objects (as set out in the Rules), were invariably the same: to provide intellectual, social and/or moral improvement for the members, by the cultivation of literature, science and art.

There is no definitive history of the movement and, except for George Nadel's *Australia's Colonial Culture*[2] and Michael Talbot's recent history of the institutes in South Australia,[3] printed sources are frequently slight and incomplete, misleading or inaccurate. Nadel, however, does look briefly at the history and development of the Sydney Mechanics' School of Arts (as well as at the movement generally), and he gives a short overview of the lecture program of the Sydney School. He concentrates mainly on the 1840s and, writing as a social historian, examines the original aims of the School, i.e., "the diffusion of scientific and other useful knowledge throughout the Colony of New South Wales."[4] He sees the movement as a failure from as early as 1842, when "critics denounced the so-called Mechanics' School of Arts as devoid of any benefits to the mechanic."[5]

Membership of the school, however, appears to have been open to all who could afford to pay the annual subscription of 12/-, and the Rules and Regulations never restricted membership to the 'mechanic' class. The term mechanic seems to have been used in a more general sense in the Colonies than in England, and covered many unskilled as well as skilled occupations. But it was unlikely that unskilled workers would have become members, at least until 1851 when wages trebled, for in that period 12/- represented approximately a week's wage. On the other hand, from the emphasis on the diffusion of "scientific knowledge," it would seem that the benefits of the school *were* meant primarily for the mechanic.

When arguing that the movement was a failure, Nadel does not speculate on the causes, except to say that the institutions were "caught up in the general failure of Mechanics' Institutes," both here and overseas.[6] He quotes Bishop Nixon's address of 1865, which attributed the failure of the schools to the fact that their "benevolent founders" failed "to ascertain the conscious wants of the working classes."[7] This comment, however, was made well before the Sydney institution started the Technical or Working Men's College, which opened in May 1879.[8]

When speaking of failure, both Nadel and Nixon are suggesting that the social benefits to be derived from education for the working classes were not realised by either the Sydney Mechanics' School of Arts, or by mechanics' institutes as a whole. If the institutions were meant exclusively for the mechanics and working classes, there would be a great deal of truth in this suggestion, but even then the blame for not realising their full potential cannot be laid entirely upon the institutes. Of enthusiasm they were rarely short, but voluntary organisations such as mechanics' institutes lacked sufficient funds to finance an effective educational program, especially for people on lower incomes.[9] This situation was exacerbated, because building programs commonly took first priority. Thus, in the case of the Sydney Mechanics' School of Arts, while the Governors were willing to become Patrons of the institution, the niggardly official attitude of governmental authorities towards financial assistance for a new and ambitious venture in a new country must bear a large share of the responsibility for the failure to achieve the original aims of the institution. In fact, such sums as were allocated frequently took months to arrive.

There is no doubt that the first consideration of a Committee of a newly formed school of arts was usually to find suitable premises, and the popularity of the movement is evidenced by its vigorous building program. Howard's article, already referred to, states that there were "more than 150" schools of arts in New South Wales alone. In fact, a list of such institutions in New South Wales (i.e., Literary, Mechanics' Institutes or Schools of Arts) receiving government subsidies in 1928 places the figure as high as 434 institutions, and recent field studies in Victoria indicate that there could have been as many as 1,000 kindred organisations there as well. This chapter argues, therefore, that in spite of claims of failure, which may be justified in many cases, the school of arts movement *overall* made a positive contribution to the cultural history of New South Wales through its libraries, lectures and involvement in adult education. As well, the movement made a contribution to the visual arts in two areas: art education, and architecture.

The extent of the contribution cannot be judged fully, as only the Sydney, Parramatta and Taree Schools will be examined. However, additional information regarding other schools will be introduced to support these claims.

THE SYDNEY MECHANICS' SCHOOL OF ARTS

The aims of the Sydney School were outlined at a public meeting held at the Sydney Court House on 23 April 1833, by the Reverend Henry Carmichael, one of the driving forces behind the School of Arts.[10] Nadel claims that Carmichael's aim was to instruct mechanics "in science rather than in art."[11] He believes therefore, that Bernard Smith "errs in interpreting a call for a School of Arts to raise the Colony's productive and manufacturing skills, as a reference to the place of fine arts in commerce."[12] Nadel is quite correct in claiming that Smith errs. The attempt to 'marry' commerce and fine art was the aim of the British Schools of Design set up as a result of the British Government's *Report on Design and Industry* in 1835. The Sydney Mechanics' School of Arts pre-dates that inquiry, as well as other British Design Schools such a Summerly's Art Manufacturers of 1847. However, Nadel too, is incorrect in suggesting that Carmichael's reference to art was exclusively in the context of "useful arts," for example "engineering and applied mechanics."[13]

The original Regulations were prepared by Henry Carmichael,[14] and Regulation No. 3 stated: "The objects shall be accomplished...by engaging for the benefit of members, teachers and lecturers of the various branches of Science and *Art*." The Revised By-Laws of 1890 also state that "literature, science and *art* shall be promoted." These By-Laws also list as part of the library, 500 books on fine art, 300 on architecture and 1,790 on other arts.

Major Thomas Mitchell, Surveyor General of the Colony, and the institution's first president, in his address on 22 March 1833 delivered at the Sydney Court House, spoke of the "power of art" and the "light of science" as two separate elements, which together are able "to extend the dominion of civilised man across regions peopled hitherto only by savages."[15] This evidence suggests that the Fine Arts were seen as positive sources for fostering moral and social improvement, and that education in the Fine Arts was a conscious objective of the Sydney Mechanics' School of Arts from its inception.

Origins of the School[16]

Following a discussion with the Governor, Sir Richard Bourke, Rev. Henry Carmichael called a meeting on 1 March 1833 to consider the establishment of an "association for the diffusion of scientific and other useful knowledge among the mechanics of New South Wales."[17] The meeting was chaired by Carmichael and was attended by twenty people, including the Rev. J D Lang, himself a noted educational activist, who had brought Carmichael, among others, to the Colony to set up his 'Australian College.'[18]

Two public meetings were subsequently held on 22 March and 23 April at the Sydney Court House. The first meeting was addressed by Thomas Mitchell. As a result of the encouraging response at this meeting, Carmichael delivered the Inaugural Address and presented the Regulations of the Sydney Mechanics' School of Arts at the second meeting. Major Mitchell became the Institution's first president and Carmichael took the position of vice-president. It is noted from the minutes however, that Major Mitchell was frequently absent from Sydney for long periods, because of his work, and almost without exception meetings were chaired by Carmichael. To Carmichael, then, must go the credit for putting the institution on its feet and arranging for the erection of its first building.

Following the April meeting, the Committee sought the services of Committee members and other members to deliver lectures or to take classes. Several gentlemen consented to give lectures, including one on 'The Rudiments of Architecture.' Who offered the lecture and whether it was actually delivered was not recorded in the minutes. Among the courses of instruction proposed was a class in drawing and one in music.

Contribution to Art Education

The frustrations of obtaining a building in the first years after its foundation occupied the attention of the Committee, and held back any educational programs that they may have envisaged. Once the building was obtained, however, lectures were held regularly and were remarkably well attended.[19] In 1841, a peak year admittedly, forty-three lectures were delivered, which included three on 'Principles of Drawing,' by John Skinner Prout, four on the 'Principles of Taste,' by John Rae and one on 'Printing' by a Mr J Kemp. Prout gave further lectures on drawing, and from June 1843 conducted art classes at the institution. Fees were fifteen shillings per quarter for non-members and ten shillings for members. This was a fairly substantial fee, and may explain why large numbers were not attracted to the class. Prout also attempted to organise an art show in Sydney, but without success. He left shortly afterwards for Hobart,[20] where he continued his association with the institutes by lecturing at the Van Diemen's Land Mechanics' Institute.

The mid to late 'forties were difficult times for the institution. Preoccupation with building problems as well as administrative problems caused its other activities to languish, offering critics evidence of failure. In 1848 the secretary was dismissed, but the new Secretary, Mr Bellingham, suggested the formation of a Mutual Instruction Class to fill the gap left by the closure of the other classes. Thirty-two members enrolled in what was to be the first attempt to form adult education classes in New South Wales.

The Fine Arts played a part in reviving the institution's educational program, the first lectures on this subject being organised by a Mr Gilfillan. Among the classes to be re-formed was one for instruction in drawing, which began with nine pupils.[21] By 1851, the institution was again having administrative problems and classes terminated again on 30 June that year. A dispute between the secretary of the institution, the librarian and several committee members concerning the secretary's terms of employment was hotly debated. A special meeting was called on 30 July 1851 to consider the management of the institution, as a result of which the honorary secretary and treasurer resigned.[22] This event apparently cleared the air and, although still preoccupied with attempts to secure a new building site or at least more adequate premises, classes and lectures were resumed. In August 1854, Joseph Fowles offered his services and was engaged as a drawing teacher by the institution, a post he held for several years. Classes were now more efficiently run and the Committee appointed an art examiner.

Apart from performing his teaching duties, Fowles assisted the Secretary, Mr Joseph Dyer, to organise a major Fine Art exhibition in January 1857. Held in the institution's hall, the exhibition consisted mainly of European paintings of both contemporary and old masters, eg. Bonnington, Gainsborough, Claude, Rembrandt, Caravaggio, Titian and Velazquez. Local artists S T Gill, J Fowles and W Dexter were represented among the 336 works lent by members and friends for one of the earliest art exhibitions in the Colony.[23]

Under Fowles, the standard of the drawing class improved, and when he retired from the position he was succeeded by Edmund Thomas, and then by Mr F Nixon. The appointment of art examiners was also an attempt to maintain a standard, and Mr F C Terry[24] and Mr J Kemp both held this post. In 1869 Nixon formed the first ladies' drawing class at the institution. Apparently the drawing classes before this were attended only by males, as prizes presented to students after this date list the prize for the ladies' drawing class separately.

In June 1870 a proposal to commence a School of Design was quickly adopted. Rules were drawn up, and Mr Thomas Hodgson, in accordance with a system of instruction he had learned in New Zealand, became head of the school.[25] The students presented an exhibition of their work in the School of Arts hall during December, and prizes were awarded to the best students. Apart from three drawing classes, a water colour class was held, which proved so popular that a second class was commenced in 1871. However, in 1874, in spite of good attendance, it was decided to suspend the School of Design, as Mr Hodgson was frequently absent from classes. An attempt by Mr Hodgson to remove the classes to his own home drew a strong letter of rebuke from the Committee.

Miss Marsh, the institution's first female teacher, began a ladies' drawing class in August 1874, which proved successful enough for the Committee to approve the formation of a second class under her tutelage.

There were two offers to form life drawing classes, the first in 1874 by Mr Anivitti (who later became a teacher at the NSW Academy of Arts), and the other from a Mr Sidgfield, in March 1880. Both these offers were referred by the Class Committee to the General Committee, but no decision was ever made to take up either offer, and although no reason was stated in either case, it no doubt reflected a particular prejudice of the committee.[26] The number of drawing classes, however, continued to increase, and besides the two ladies' drawing classes, prizes in 1877 were also awarded for mechanical and architectural drawing.

Soon afterwards, the Technical or Working Men's College commenced and, apart from writing and arithmetic, the drawing classes were the best attended. Mr Lucien Henry, an extremely competent and versatile teacher, was the Principal of the Art School and a detailed outline of the classes available under his direction was provided in the 1881 *Calendar of the Working Men's College*.

In September, the Committee of the Technical College advised the Committee of the School of Arts that in order to secure a knowledge of drawing, modelling and design (on the system adopted by the Science and Art Department at South Kensington) for the pupils attending the primary schools in the City, it was proposed to form a special class for teachers and pupil-teachers employed under the Council of Education. The classes would be held on a Saturday morning at a cost of 5/- per quarter. These classes were still operating in 1883, for teachers at both public and private schools. By 1883 the Technical College was also offering a good variety of art classes six days a week for persons who wanted instruction in art other than for trade purposes.

The general success of all the art classes held at the Technical or Working Men's College, particularly the high standard of instruction, is reflected in the award of a gold medal for the collection of drawings from the freehand, architectural, mechanical and ladies' drawing classes forwarded from the School of Design to the Melbourne International Exhibition in 1881. This set a high standard for the Board of Technical Education to follow when, at the request of the School of Arts Committee, it took over the Technical or Working Men's College in 1883 - including the non-technical art classes.

Criticism of the work of the Technical or Working Men's College expressed by Nadel, at least as far as the School of Design is concerned, seems somewhat unfair.[27] From minutes kept by the College, it would appear to have been run in an efficient manner, with an obvious spirit of co-operation between Committee and staff, and concern for the maintenance of standards in both instruction and examinations.

PARRAMATTA SCHOOL OF ARTS[28]

It is ironic that the Sydney Mechanics' School of Arts should begin its decline at about the same time that suburban and rural schools were opening in increasing numbers. In 1886, Lord Carrington, Governor and Patron of the Sydney Mechanics' School of Arts, opened the new building of the Parramatta School of Arts in Macquarie Street, Parramatta, near its intersection with Marsden Street. Featuring a rather severe form of the Italianate style, the new brick building replaced an earlier building on the old barrack Square, beside the Lancer Barracks, on the corner of Macquarie and Taylor (now Smith) Streets. The earlier building had been opened by Sir John Hay in May 1867,[29] but the site had been resumed by the government in 1879 for a sum of £1,620 for the proposed new public school. From 1879 to 1885 the School of Arts occupied premises in George Street, owned by Mr W C Burge, where it continued to conduct its library until the new premises were opened. Built on land purchased in 1884, the new building provided a large library and reading room downstairs and a large lecture hall upstairs, with a small committee room at the rear. It was constructed by Messrs Hart and Lavors.

The first addition to the premises was a small cottage built at the rear of the building in 1896 by Mr John Smith for the resident caretaker. Then in November 1900, following inquiries made to several country institutes regarding the estimated income and running expenses of a billiard room, the Committee requested Mr Hill, architect, to prepare suitable plans. A billiard room was built by a local builder, Mr Gazzard, on the ground floor immediately behind the library. In spite of restrictions imposed (e.g., strict prohibition of gambling and no game to commence after 10.40pm), the game proved so successful and so profitable that a second table was purchased, and ping-pong was made available for the lady members.

However, the main object of the institution, as stated in its Rules and By-Laws, was the intellectual and social improvement of the members by the cultivation of literature, science and art. The Parramatta School of Arts did attempt to give consideration to each of these areas. Like the Sydney School, its library was usually popular and apparently technical classes were held in the building for several years after the opening. The minute book is missing for the period 1886-1894, but the President's report delivered at the Annual General Meeting in July 1901 declared:

> The recent election cry of all parties and candidates for an extension of technical education in the State, makes your Committee almost hope that the Parramatta technical classes, formerly held in this building may, at an early date, again be rightly available for our town and country students.

The only class of a vaguely technical nature that the School offered at this period was a shorthand and typing class, which began in 1896. It closed after a few years because of lack of support, no doubt influenced by the fact that the School had insufficient typewriters to be really effective.

The School had much more success with its classes in the arts however. Elocution and singing classes were popular, as were woodcarving, drawing and painting classes. Mr J Salvana and Mr M Booker both conducted drawing and painting classes, while a Mr Bastings conducted a drawing class in which students' work was examined by a teacher from the Sydney Technical College. For many years prizes were awarded to the most proficient advanced and elementary students. These were presented at the Annual General Meeting, along with a display of students' work. In 1895, the prizes awarded were:

> School of Arts prize for senior student - Three of Ruskin's works on art;
> Mr Bastings prize for elementary student - The Complete Works of Tennyson.

Lectures in Parramatta were usually popular and the School of Arts frequently made use of the Sydney University Extension Board's lecture program. Frequently during the early 1900s, however, local lecturers were more popular than those provided by the university, and the Committee assumed that the latters' subject matter was not relevant to the townspeople. The quality of local lecturers and their subject matter, however, also left much to be desired. Nevertheless, lectures overall were successful and interesting, as the 1911 program offered by the University Extension Board indicates:

- Shakespeare's Heroines
- Buried Cities of Herculaneum & Pompeii
- Modern Greece.

This association with the Sydney University Extension Board (later the Tutorial Class Department) continued until 1959, just before the Parramatta School of Arts was wound up. The topics of the above lectures, along with one entitled 'The Potter's Art,' given by Mr John Shorter, an authority on Doulton ware, indicated a strong interest in lectures on artistic or historic subjects. It also indicated that the audience was no longer of the 'mechanic' class, reflecting a trend in many schools of arts. The Committee clearly regretted this fact, and at the Annual General Meeting of 1897 Archdeacon Gunther, while expressing pleasure that much of the program sketched some years earlier had been realised, nevertheless regretted that the artisan classes did not avail themselves of the advantages of the institution.

The Parramatta School of Arts was close enough to Sydney to be influenced by that institution's adult education program. However the influence was of limited effect; in 1900 Parramatta was also sufficiently remote from Sydney - having regard to contemporary modes of travel - for its inhabitants to seek recreational activities near home. Consequently, recreation was an important function of the Parramatta institution. Therefore a chess and draughts club, as well as the library and billiard room, were well patronised, and an entertainment committee organised a variety of functions, including a bazaar, flower show and ball, with the secondary purpose of raising funds.

In spite of a small government subsidy of approximately £60 per annum, the institution was rarely out of debt. It made several attempts to consolidate its debts and, at the same time, to borrow enough funds to convert some part of its premises into shops, as the Sydney Mechanics' School of Arts had done. In 1936, Mr L J Buckland advised on the addition of shops to the front of the building and submitted plans and specifications in October 1939. However, neither these plans, nor the ones submitted by Messrs W Kenwood and Sons, were ever realised. Unable to raise funds to alter the premises, they remained unchanged until December 1946, when the Parramatta District Co-operative Building Societies Ltd. leased part of the premises and carried out, at their own expense, the necessary alterations to conduct their business.

Even leasing its premises did not solve the financial problems of the Parramatta institution, which was suffering the same fate as many other suburban schools of arts; namely, being left behind by progress and competition, because there was no longer a demand for the few services it could offer.

TAREE SCHOOL OF ARTS

By contrast, the Taree School of Arts, or as it is now called, the Taree Literary Institute, experienced a new lease of life and is still today exceptionally prosperous. Apart from being financially secure, with a healthy bank account and a valuable commercial property in a prime position on the corner of Manning and Victoria Streets, it still runs a free library for its members and contributes liberally to local cultural and charitable organisations. Its major contributions are centred on literary activities, but it also supports the performing arts, through donations to the local Arts Council and prizes for the local eisteddfod. The Institute encouraged interest in the visual arts in 1979, when, in conjunction with the Department of Education, it invited students from 43 local schools to submit an essay, painting or sculpture on the theme of 'The Year of the Child,' offering $1,500 in prizes. At the time this chapter was originally prepared (1982), Professor Ken Cable of Sydney University had been commissioned to write a history of the Manning Valley, and to this end $3,000 had been set aside by the Taree Institute for research.

The life of the Taree Institute had not always been marked by the same measure of affluence and success, however. Although the library and reading room were well supported, billiards had provided the main source of income. By 1957, the building was in a very dilapidated condition and the committee considered the redevelopment of the site. It sought advice regarding the possibility of erecting a building of one storey, incorporating several shops, with foundations strong enough to carry a second storey at a later date. In May 1958, the committee met with a firm of Sydney architects, Messrs Hodgson & Sons, who prepared plans for a new building.

The trustees sought a loan of £8,000 from the Commonwealth Bank, but encouraged by the manager of the bank, the committee boldly undertook the construction of the present building of two storeys. Built by local builders, Messrs Schmitzer and Burg, the building cost £18,500 and was completed in June 1960.

A new constitution was drawn up in 1974,[30] because the old one could not be located in spite of inquiries to the Department of Education. In the absence of a formal constitution defining its objects and confirming its status as a non-profit making organisation, its income may have been liable to taxation.

An earlier Constitution, which came to light in the Mitchell Library during the course of this study,[31] stated the purpose of the establishment of the School as the "mental and moral improvement and rational recreation of its members." According to an 1897 census of schools of arts and kindred organisations in New South Wales[32], the Taree School of Arts began its activities in 1887. On 13 May 1901, the trustees purchased the present site from Walter Plummer, executor of the estate of Samuel Plummer, for £190.[33] The land was originally part of an allotment containing two roods, purchased by Samuel Plummer from Samuel Gibson on 9 February 1865 for £25, described as Lot 1 Section 6. On Samuel Plummer's death, his executor sold part of the land to Alphons Frederick Rose for £190. This land, facing Manning Street, adjoined the land shortly afterwards acquired by the School of Arts. On 7 October 1901 the School of Arts purchased a two-foot wide strip of land between the two properties from a Mr Rose for £10. The original minute book has been lost, but the cash book, which refers to the financial year ending June 1903, lists the purchase of a billiard table for £82-19-6d, which realised an income of £116-16-9d. The cash book also shows an amount of £853-11-10d standing in the building fund, although only £504-5-6d was received that year.[34] These facts, along with the absence of any record of a building program, other than repairs, in the early years from 1902 onwards suggests that the School of Arts acquired an existing building. (Whether this building may have been the private residence of the Plummer family or a commercial building is unknown). The style of the building, however, supports this hypothesis. Built in the Early Victorian style, it featured narrow columns, which supported the upper verandah with a cast iron balustrade. It was constructed of timber, with a galvanised iron roof. The fact that by 1927 most of this roof needed replacing also suggests that the building dates from before the turn of the century.

The peak of the school of arts movement is well illustrated by the number of institutions in the Taree area at the turn of the century. These included: Killabakh, Krambach, Marlee, Mitchell's Island, Landsdowne, Upper Landsdowne, Tinonee, Harrington, Coopernook, Cundletown, and Wingham. Without exception, each of these School of Arts buildings occupied a prime position, either in the main street of a town or village, or in some other similarly accessible and central position; but when surveyed in 1982, some were active, some deserted, and some were serving other purposes. At Mitchell's Island, for instance, a dairy farming community approximately 10-12km from Taree, the School of Arts was the only public building, apart from a church. Apparently unused and derelict, with broken windows and badly in need of paint, the building, like most of the other schools of arts in the area, featured a rectangular hall of generous size for a small community, timber cladding and galvanised iron roof. There can be little doubt that it was once the centre of communal activity. Coopernook School of Arts, on the other hand, with the date of its opening displayed prominently above the door (8 May 1901), was newly painted, in excellent condition and still occupied an important place in this small community, approximately 20km north of Taree. Its design is almost identical with the School of Arts building at Landsdowne, even to the finials on the front of the building. The comparison ends there, however, for the latter building was even more neglected than the one on Mitchell's Island. Branching out from Coopernook to the coast lies the beach resort of Harrington. The School of Arts there was still operating its library in 1982, and the hall behind, which is now a Soldiers' Memorial Hall, still provided recreation for residents and holiday makers. The same situation applies to the Cundletown School of Arts, situated approximately 6km north of Taree. Designated a Soldiers' Memorial Hall, the fact that an Art Show was in progress in 1982 indicates that only the name had been changed, with the community still making use of its old School of Arts hall in much the same ways as it always had.

The Cundletown hall appears to have been reclad with concrete blocks. Otherwise all the buildings are very much in keeping with their surroundings and typical of the timber and iron buildings of mid-north coast dairy farming communities. Even the Taree Literary Institute, sitting today in the main commercial part of the town, is an integral part of its surroundings, with its downstairs shop fronts. It proclaims its existence, however, to every passer-by going north on the Pacific Highway with the name Taree Literary Institute prominently displayed on the upstairs corner facade.

It can be seen therefore, that schools of arts enjoyed varying degrees of success and that each one worked according to the needs of its own community. The idea of the city institution, to create educational opportunities for the mechanic class, was given little attention in Parramatta and, if Taree is typical, no attention at all in some rural areas. Libraries, lectures and recreation were the focus of the suburban schools, while the library and a greater emphasis on social and recreational pursuits typified the rural institutions. Almost clubs for men, the Schools were dominated by them and, although they had no rules to exclude women - indeed many accepted female members with varying privileges - they did not at their peak accept women into positions of authority. Over the years this had changed, however, for at the time of writing, the Taree Literary Institute had a female president and the committee was dominated by women.

THE DEMISE OF THE MOVEMENT

When considering the overall demise of the school of arts movement, the fact that the Taree Literary Institute and several schools of arts operating in the Taree area continued to provide venues for community activities as well as an occasional library service, indicates that rural or even semi-rural schools of arts could still be reasonably active. For instance, the fine building belonging to the Richmond School of Arts, in West Market Street (opened in 1867), still provides a meeting place for several lodges and clubs in the district.

Suburban schools were not so fortunate and few still exist, even as buildings. Standing on valuable commercial sites, they were quickly grabbed for redevelopment as they were wound up, as was the case with the Parramatta School of Arts, now the site of an insurance company's multi-storey building. Had the Parramatta School of Arts managed to raise the funds to incorporate shops into its building, it too may have struggled along. Valiant efforts were made after the second world war to keep the institution going, including plans to resite the School on a cheaper block of land. The institution was heavily in debt to the Parramatta Council for unpaid rates and in early 1956 it was proposed that the building be transferred to the Council. The trustees delayed making a decision and approached the local State Member for Parramatta to inquire of the Minister for Education on their behalf about the possibility of assistance in connection with the payment of the rates. The Minister, Mr Heffron, whose Department administered the schools of arts, replied that the Parramatta School failed to meet the necessary requirements of the *Local Government Act, 1919* regarding exemptions from rates. By 1959, as articles in *The Parramatta and Hills News* indicate, the Council was running out of patience. The trustees continued to delay the final decision to transfer the property until the Council made an undertaking to employ the institution's librarian in a suitable clerical position, and to allow the subscribers to the School of Arts library who lived outside the Parramatta Council area the right to join the Council library. The Council agreed to these conditions and the building was finally handed over to the Council on 15 June 1961 under the provision of Sec. 357A of the *Local Government Act*.

The long, arduous process to effect the transfer indicates the degree of personal involvement the trustees and committees frequently had with the institutions, and emotions could run high. In April 1982, the Holroyd Council closed the Wentworthville School of Arts, and the secretary spoke with some bitterness about what he felt was a hasty decision. The Wentworthville School of Arts, as it appeared in 1982, offered a graphic picture of the demise of a School of Arts. Standing in Station Street, padlocked, with paint peeling, it looked very dilapidated. The Council notice, beside the Auction notice, read:

> Hall Closed to Public - by Council Resolution 6.4.82.
> FOR SAFETY REASONS - Alternate accommodation
> has been arranged for ALL users
> I. Wilson Town Clerk
> Holroyd Municipal Council

Whether the lodges, or the various dance and karate instructors, whose notices still adorned the walls on the School, took up the Council's offer of accommodation is not known, but at the auction held on 12 August 1982 the building was passed in, possibly a sign of the then current economic climate.

For its part, the Sydney Mechanics' School of Arts in 1982 occupied only a very small area of its premises. The subscription library, which was still operating, and vied with the Melbourne Athenaeum for the title of the largest subscription library in the country, was located, together with the secretary's office, on the ground floor at the rear of the building, where once the chess room was located. The hall, which once occupied the full depth of two floors, had a mezzanine floor installed, and the institution occupied the top half. It was still an attractive and well proportioned room, and was kept in good order. The only other part of the building which showed decorative features, which may survive from Bibb's time, was the hall in the centre of the building. Altered slightly by Backhouse, by narrowing the lower end, the decorative features under the pilasters placed at intervals along the upper half of the wall were stylistically similar to those designed by Bibb, which were placed above each window in the upper storey of the façade. The rest of the building, at the time of writing, was occupied by shops and offices and it was impossible to locate the original library, reading rooms or other accommodation. While rentals allowed the library to continue to operate, expenses including rates and maintenance were high, and the stonework on the upper storey of the façade was showing marked signs of wear and tear.

The building has since been sold, though the School of Arts library still offers its services from a location in George Street, Sydney, facing the main entrance to the Queen Victoria Building.

CULTURAL CONTRIBUTION OF THE INSTITUTES

Within the limits set by this study, it is evident that at least some vestiges of the school of arts movement are still active, particularly when one considers such instances as the library of the Sydney Mechanics' School of Arts, and the participation of the Taree Literary Institute in the cultural activities of the Taree community. The negative approach of critics of the movement thus needs comment.

Recent critics, generally writing as social historians, have accepted and agreed with the contemporary critics of the mid-nineteenth century that the institutions were a failure. Their studies are mainly concerned with whether or not the mechanics' institutes succeeded in attracting and catering for the mechanic or working classes, and whether or not their libraries, lectures and other activities were of a suitably 'improving' nature. (Even Anthony Trollope commented unfavourably "that Mudgee shepherds certainly prefer novels" after his visit to Mudgee Mechanics' Institute library.[35])

To establish more accurately whether the aims of the Sydney Mechanics' School of Arts were realised, the establishment of the Technical or Working Men's College has to be taken into account. Clearly Nadel's study was not intended as a comprehensive history of the school of arts movement, and accordingly some areas have not been investigated in full. Furthermore, in general, there is a concentration on the "diffusion" of science, to the exclusion of art.

When reading the minutes of the Sydney Mechanic's School of Arts, one is conscious that in the mid-nineteenth century Australia was very isolated from the rest of the world, and that the pioneer spirit was still a necessary component of life in Australia. Distance is still a problem for Australians, but the delay in completing the purchase of the original site for the building in 1848 due to the death of the vendor, who lived in London, indicates how long it took even for news to reach the Colony. Distance was no less a problem within the Colony, and Major Mitchell, the first President of the Sydney Mechanics' School of Arts, was frequently absent from Sydney for months. A report in *The Australasian* on 26 February 1836 regarding Major Mitchell's departure from Sydney on his way to an expedition in the direction of the Swan River reveals how little of the Colony had been explored. The dangers in opening up this vast land are recorded in the minutes of the Sydney Mechanics' School of Arts in March 1865, when a request was made for an allocation of funds to search for Dr Leichhardt, who had lectured at the School some years earlier. (The institution displayed a bust of Dr Leichhardt among a collection of busts of eminent Australians.)[36] The distance, as well as the danger inherent in the voyage to England, was recorded the following year, when the institution mourned the death of its former president, Dr Woolley, who had been lost at sea when the ship on which he was returning to England foundered in the Bay of Biscay. Even as late as 1910, the Parramatta School of Arts requested the Extension Board of the University to consider it a country school for the purpose of its lecture program.[37] The difficulties that had to be overcome should be given more attention when considering the contribution of the school of arts movement to the cultural history of New South Wales.

Because the movement spread its influence into the social life of its members, particularly in the suburbs and country towns, a social/historical methodology is useful. Apart from the usual examination of documents necessary for historical research, in line with modern sociological methods, a large amount of statistical evidence (e.g., classes, number of students, classes offered, patterns of library usage, comparison with similar institutions, etc.) is needed to more accurately assess any contribution. In recent years there have been some excellent studies, both of individual institutes and comparisons between them, which show that the success of the 'movement' depended largely on the extent to which a particular school met the needs of the community of which it formed a part, particularly in rural areas.

The random, rather than selective, nature of this study does indicate that each school developed its own characteristics, and the influence and benefits of the movement went beyond the provision of libraries and lectures. The halls provided the only meeting place for a variety of civic activities in small communities. The Granville School of Arts, for example, provided a meeting place for the local Council from 1883 to 1889. Similarly in Richmond, a metal plaque on the front of the Richmond School of Arts records that:

> Local Government commenced in Richmond with the Incorporation of the Borough Council 18 June 1872. The School of Arts was used until 1913 for the meeting of the Council, and this plaque, installed 25 November 1972 to commemorate the commencement of local government 100 years ago, records with appreciation the participation of many Richmond citizens.

A review of the activities of the Sydney Mechanics' School of Arts shows that it introduced many firsts into the community, and established a tradition of activities that still exists. Lectures and the mutual instruction classes begun in 1848, in particular, were among the first attempts at an adult education program. The tradition was carried on by the Sydney University Department of Adult Education and Workers' Educational Association classes, and more recently by the Sydney Centre of Learning for Adults.

Lectures on architecture and the Fine Arts, some of the first in the Colony, no doubt helped to create a public awareness of art and to promote the success of the early art classes held by the institution. Several early teachers and examiners at the institution, such as J Fowles, J Kemp and F C Terry, are important figures in the early art history of New South Wales. During Terry's time as art examiner, he awarded first prize in drawing to William Macleod, who later was the "first artist engaged for the *Picturesque Atlas* and for the *Bulletin*."[38] In 1886 he became the manager of the *Bulletin*, and from 1891 to 1926 was the managing director. Later art classes, both technical and non-technical, which commenced at the Technical or Working Men's College in 1879 under the management of Lucien Henry, trained many artists, both painters and sculptors, some of whom went on to become instructors at the Sydney Technical College and, like G H Aurousseau (who taught at the

Technical College from 1885 to 1929) influenced generations of later art students.[39] Another of Henry's students from the Technical and Working Men's College to achieve success was G.W.L. Hirst, who won the Wynne Prize for Sculpture in both 1907 and 1923. The modelling class, which Henry formed at the Technical and Working Men's College in 1881, and in which W.P. MacIntosh also trained, was the first such class in Australia.[40] During his time as Head of the School of Design at the Working Men's College, Henry also strenuously promoted the use of Australian flora in design, and he is acknowledged as the artistic discoverer of the waratah, which he introduced as a motif in wallpaper designs. Stained glass windows which he designed for the Town Hall Sydney and the Hotel Australia feature also some of the work of his student Aurousseau, who inherited his instructor's love of Australian native flowers.[41]

Realising the success and importance of the non-technical art classes, the Sydney Mechanics' School of Arts urged the new Board of Technical Education to continue its operation. The Board agreed, and education in the visual arts continued under the Department of Technical Education at East Sydney Technical College and later at suburban Technical Colleges until the beginning of 1976, when the last students in the Diploma of Art transferred to Alexander Mackie College. In 1975 the Department of Technical and Further Education began a 2-year certificate course in the visual arts, which in due course was planned to become a 3-year certificate, thus continuing the unbroken tradition of education in the visual arts set by the Sydney Mechanics' School of Arts. An exhibition of students' work at the end of the year is still a tradition and an important conclusion to a year's work in all New South Wales art schools.

The attempt to improve drawing instruction in the schools, by introducing Saturday morning classes in drawing principles for teachers untrained in this discipline, was an important innovation. A primitive form of professional development, these popular conversion classes operated from 1878 till 1883.

Although many school of arts buildings are quite undistinguished, some have made a significant contribution to the architectural history of New South Wales. The National Trust has classified the facade of the Sydney Mechanics' School of Arts, as well as the former Yass Mechanics' Institute, designed by Thomas Rowe, and the Nowra Mechanics' Institute and School of Arts, designed by Cyril Blacket. Other Schools of Arts to come from the Blacket office were those at Lismore, Corrimal and Rockdale. A further building classified by the Trust is the Windsor School of Arts, and the Trust has a list of 15 other schools or former schools considered worthy of classification. The school of arts movement, therefore, afforded architects an opportunity to use their talents. The high standard and number of entries in competitions for plans run by the Sydney institution further indicates that architects considered schools or arts to be significant public buildings, worthy of their attention.

Moreover, with considerable foresight, no doubt to provide convenience and accessibility for members, the committees invariably chose prime positions for the sites of their schools. This contributed in no small way to the progress and prestige of the town, and to the prosperity of the commercial centre. Thus, when the Parramatta School of Arts was sold in September 1961 it realised £75,015 (compared with an original outlay of £2,715). A display table in the entrance area of the Parramatta City Library bears a plaque commemorating the acquisition of the 'Parramatta School of Arts and Mechanics' Institute' by the Council. The new central library, where the display table stands, was opened on 28 November 1964, and was financed, along with three other libraries in the area, from the proceeds of the sale. This represents a final but lasting contribution by the Parramatta School of Arts to the cultural history of Parramatta. No doubt other schools of arts - like organ donors whose bequests help others to live - have already provided, or in the future will provide, lasting benefits of a cultural nature to local residents.

Apart from these major contributions to cultural history and the visual arts, the school of arts movement contributed to the visual arts in a more minor way, by providing printers, designers and lithographers with a great deal of work in the preparation and printing of annual reports, library catalogues and constitutions. As well, the Sydney Mechanics' School of Arts, like others, used the visual arts to commemorate important occasions for the School. Portraits were commissioned of both Dr Woolley (copied from an existing portrait, after his untimely death), and of Mr Stenhouse. Mr James Dalgarno's retirement as President of the institution on 11 April 1889 was marked by the presentation of an illuminated address, decorated with a border of native flowers and birds and surmounted by a drawing of the School of Arts. It was printed by Messrs John Sands & Co. Photographs of the building were also used as presentations.

What the school of arts movement provided, and is still providing in Taree, is an opportunity for communities to decide their own cultural needs. Activities that the institute supports are well patronised (e.g., contribution to the performance of the Queensland Ballet Company in Taree), and often ambitious, such as the first ever regional conference of the Australian Society of Authors - sponsored by International PEN (poets, playwrights, editors, essayists and novelists) and to a 'Meet the Authors' conference at Taree attended by local and international authors and film writers.

CONCLUSION

When the Sydney Mechanics' School of Arts was approaching the celebration of its 150th anniversary, in 1983, it established a new era of association with the visual arts. On 12 October 1982 the Sydney Artists' Cooperative held its first exhibition in the Henry Carmichael Room, which had been converted to a gallery. The gallery was situated immediately above the library, in the rear of the building. One of the artists associated with the venture also had a studio in the building, which he acquired by chance when he answered an advertisement offering studio accommodation. As explained in a conversation with the author, he had previously known nothing of the existence of the building, or of its history. He admired, however, the decoration of the studio, which was once the smoke room designed by John Smedley in 1888. It have previously formed a part of the reading room designed by Benjamin Backhouse. At the time, the artists in the Co-operative considered the location of the building, in the heart of Sydney, a highly suitable venue for an ambitious new gallery.

Through a study of three institutes, and reference to the work of others, it is considered that this chapter has supported the contention that the school of arts movement has made and continues to make a positive contribution to the cultural history of New South Wales, including a contribution to the visual arts, and that the movement has had lasting effects in both art education and architecture.

Sydney Mechanics' School of Arts, NSW

Parramatta School of Arts, NSW

Taree Literary Institute, NSW, ca 1914

NOTES AND REFERENCES

1.Howard, E. (1981). Crumbling temples. *National Times*, 27 December 1981, p.33

2.Nadel, G.H. (1957) *Australia's colonial culture: Ideas, men and institutions in mid-nineteenth century eastern Australia.* Cambridge, Mass: Harvard University Press.

3.Talbot, M. (1992). *A chance to read: A history of the institutes movement in South Australia.* Adelaide: Library Board of South Australia.

4.*S.M.S.A Minute Book*, Vol. 1.

5.Nadel, *op. cit.*, p.143.

6.*ibid.*, p.182.

7.Nixon, F.R. (1865). Self Help. *Inaugural Lecture at the Hobart Town Working Men's Club, 1865.* Cited in Nadel, *op. cit.*, p.182.

8.Classes actually started in 1878, before the opening of the College.

9.Funds available for the work of the S.M.S.A. could be compared with
i.   funds supplied from private sources for other similar institutions, such as church schools, and
ii.   funds supplied by the government for institutions such as the Australian library, museum, art gallery, university and railway institutes.

10.Henry Carmichael was a keen educationist. He arrived in the Colony to take up the post of Master of Classics at the Australian College, but he fell out with Lang and founded the Normal Institution, a College based on the proposed Irish National System of education. The Normal Institution was designed to be a training ground for teachers as well as a model on which they could base their teaching methods. As further evidence of a strong interest in education, W.T. Cape, a foundation member of the S.M.S.A., after a quarrel with the trustees over funds spent on buildings rather than education, started his own school at Paddington in 1841. It flourished till his death in 1858. (Jordens, A.M. (1979). *The Stenhouse circle: Literary life in mid nineteenth century Sydney.* Carlton: Melbourne University Press, p.103)

11.Nadel, *op. cit.*, p.12. See also Smith, B. (1975). *Documents on art and taste in Australia.* Melbourne: Oxford University Press, p.87.

12.Nadel, *op. cit.*, p.285

13.Nadel, *loc. cit.*

14.*S.M.S.A. Minute Book*, Vol. 1 , 7 and 8 March, 1833 records a Vote of Thanks to Henry Carmichael for constructing and arranging the Proposals for the Constitution.

15.*S.M.S.A. Minute Book*, Vol. 1 (Appendix 1) records Major Mitchell's speech.

16. The most detailed account of the foundation, and subsequent early history of the S.M.S.A. is contained in Johnson, R.I. (1967). *The history of the Sydney Mechanics' School of Arts from its foundation in 1833 to the 1880s. Unpublished Master's Thesis*, Canberra: Australian National University.

17. *S.M.S.A. Minute Book*, Vol. 1. All information, unless otherwise indicated, regarding the Sydney Mechanics' School of Arts, comes from the Minute Books.

18. Child, A.C. (1936). Studies in the life and work of John Dunmore Lang: Part II - Education. *Journal of the Royal Australian Historical Society*, 22 (3), pp. 208-228.

19. Nadel, *op. cit.*, p.133

20. Moore, W. (1934). *The story of Australian art: From the earliest known art of the continent to the art of today*. Sydney: Angus and Robertson, p.215.

21. Other proposed classes were music, arithmetic and mensuration, practical geometry and algebra.

22. Nadel and Jordens refer to a special inquiry into the affairs of the School of Arts in 1851, as though it were the subject of outside investigation. The dispute was an internal one and was investigated by a special meeting of the management committee. Nadel, *op. cit.*, p.143; Jordens, *op. cit.*, p.40.

23. Exhibition Catalogue, priced at 1/- ML 1857/2.

24. Terry, F.C. (1973). *New South Wales Illustrated*. Sydney: Lansdowne Press. (Originally issued under the title, *The Australian keepsake*. Sydney: Sands and Kenny, 1855.)

25. Rules of the School of Design required pupils to be over 14 years of age. Classes held 2 hrs for 2 nights @ 1/- per week. Examinations to be held quarterly under direction of 3 committee members, work to be inspected by head of the committee. Pupil teacher certificates to be issued to those who pass 1st and 2nd grades. Pupil teachers may be called upon to conduct classes.

26. The first life class would appear to be that started by the Society of Artists (later Royal Art Society) on 26 August, 1880. The Society was formed in 1880 and in 1886 listed their classes as

Life classes	Tues. & Wed. Evening
Antique class	Mon. & Fri. Evening
Painting	Sat. afternoon. under direction of Julian Ashton.

27. Nadel, *op. cit.*, pp. 180-181. The extent of the work that went into the formation of the Working Men's College and the quality and quantity of the advice is outlined in the *Report*.

28. All details in this section are from the Minute Book of the Parramatta School of Arts, unless otherwise noted.

29. Entry for May 26, 1867 from Journal of Rev. J. Watkins. M.L. A835, p.262: "On Wednesday eve we had a grand occasion for Parramatta. The Mechanics' Institute was opened. A Member of Parliament delivered the opening address. What poor speakers these Parl. mem. are as a rule, Mr H. is one of the best of our set. A good tea. Meeting at night. Music, singing, recitals and speeches." 'Mr H.' was the Hon. John Hay, then MLA for Central Cumberland and speaker of the House, later to become Sir John Hay KCMG., President of the Legislative Council). Arundel, J. (1911). Culture in Parramatta. In Wharton, J.C. (Ed.), *Jubilee History of Parramatta: in commemoration of the first half-century of municipal government, 1861-1911*. Parramatta: Little & Richardson, p.156.

30. Taree Literary Institute (1974). *Constitution and by-laws of the Taree Literary Institute.* Taree: The Institute.

31. Taree School of Arts (1906). *Rules and Regulations of the Taree School of Arts.* Taree: T.B. Boyce, printer.

32. Library Association of Australasia (1898). Appendix: Finances and number of members of schools of arts, mechanics' institutes &c., for 1897. In *Proceedings of the Sydney Meeting, October 1898* (reprinted in facsimile by the Libraries Board of South Australia, *Occasional Papers in Librarianship, No. 8*, 1969). Sydney: Hennessey, Campbell & Co.

33. Details from Old System deeds at Registrar General's Dept. Sydney.

Conveyance	No.	835 Book 91	Gibson to Plummer
	No.	309 Book 674	Executor Plummer to Rose of part land
	No.	674 Book 688	Executor Plummer to Trustees S/Arts
	No.	702 Book 702	Rose to Trustees S/Arts

34. Details of the Taree School of Arts/Literary Institute from Minute and Case Books, unless otherwise indicated.

35. Cannon, M. (1973). *Australia in the Victorian age, Vol 2: Life in the country.* Melbourne: Thomas Nelson.

36. A record of what happened to the collection of busts, as well as old photographic views of Melbourne and original portraits of Dr Woolley ad Mr Stenhouse, portrait photographs of Lord and Lady Carrington and among other items the library, which included a copy of Gould's *Birds of Australia*, for which the School declined an offer from the Museum to purchase 31 parts for £60, may be contained in later minutes books.

37. Minutes of the University Extension Board indicate charges for lecture program in March, 1890 were 10 lectures for Fifty pounds. Attendance fee set at 5/-, printed material supplied and exam at end of course. From October, 1893 fees charged were as follows:

Suburban Schools	£30 for 10 lectures
	£18 for 6 lectures
Country Schools	£20 for 10 lectures
	£12 for 6 lectures

Schools fixed their own admission fee.

38. Moore, W. (1934). *The story of Australian art. From the earliest known art of the continent to the art of today.* Sydney: Angus & Robertson, Vol. 1, pp.200-201.

39. McCulloch, A. (1968). *Encyclopaedia of Australian art.* Richmond, Vic: Hutchinson, p.52.
Aurousseau was the author of two journal articles and one book: Aurousseau, G.H. (1907). *The analysis of inanimate form or object drawing illustrated and explained.* Sydney: Angus & Robertson.

40. McCulloch, *op. cit.*

41. Moore, *op. cit.*, Vol 2, p.215.

CHAPTER ELEVEN

FOUNDATIONS AND FORTUNES OF THE MECHANICS' INSTITUTES AND SCHOOLS OF ARTS IN NEW SOUTH WALES

Tessa Raath

INTRODUCTION

Although every individual institution has its own history and indeed its own 'personality,' the fact remains that the mechanics' institutes and schools of arts spread throughout Australia (and indeed throughout the British Empire and beyond) like seeds carried on the winds of expanding settlement. While lacking, perhaps, the centralised agency of a church, they became so widespread and so commonplace, especially in the nineteenth century, that one could be excused for assuming that some sort of secular evangelism was at work.

This chapter represents an attempt to explore the extent and development of the institute movement throughout colonial New South Wales. Drawing on *Statistical Registers* and other documentary sources, the chapter shows the growth of the institutes, and their progressive spread from Sydney to the most distant and remote parts of the state. The chapter then surveys the diverse range of buildings - from humble to ornate - that housed the institutes and represented their public face at different times and in different locations. Finally, the chapter switches to the present day and, through a field survey of towns in south-eastern New South Wales - in the vicinity of Canberra - records the appearance and current use of some twenty-five institute buildings. In this last part, the enduring impact of the institute movement on the physical and cultural landscape is highlighted.

SITE DISTRIBUTION PATTERNS AND ECONOMIC ANALYSIS, 1833-1899

From 1875 until 1914 lists of mechanics' institutes, schools of arts, literary institutes and other organisations such as Free Public Libraries were published in the *New South Wales Statistical Registers*. Various categories of information were compiled from returns received by the Government Statist from individual organisations.[1] A few of these original returns, and some from a later date, have survived and are located in the New South Wales State Archives.[2]

The published format was not maintained consistently from year to year, but the *Statistical Registers* provide a useful and presumably fairly reliable official source on which to base a 'site register' of schools of arts and mechanics' institutes in New South Wales. The present study is based primarily on data extracted from the 1897 *NSW Statistical Register*. Additional information on dates of establishment and the value of buildings was taken from the 1904, 1905 and 1912 Registers.

In the 1897 *Statistical Register*,[3] 261 voluntary institutions were listed alphabetically according to the name of the place in which they were founded and by title. There were 192 schools of arts, the most popular title, 51 mechanics' institutes and 18 literary institutes or similarly named organisations. (Free Public Libraries were excluded from this analysis).

Spread of the Institutes

Based on dates of establishment derived from official sources, the general trend in the growth rate of institutions from the 1830s to the 1890s was able to be assessed. The institutes which survived for relatively short periods were not accounted for. For instance, the Gulgong School of Arts, established in 1872, disappeared from the records in 1880. A similar case holds for the Mechanics' Institute at Young, established in 1877, but not listed as having been founded in 1877. Attempts were made to resolve chronological details relating to the intermittent existence or changes in titles of some institutes by recourse to other published documentary sources, however these were not always successful. For instance, details of the official record of the Parramatta Mechanics' Institute/School of Arts compared with published accounts by Jervis[4] and Charles[5] exemplify the problems. Since this is intended as a survey of trends rather than an exhaustive study, it is not considered that any omissions and inaccuracies which may have inadvertently occurred will greatly affect the overall profile of the growth and development.

After the establishment of the Sydney Mechanics' School of Arts in 1833, and disregarding the rise and fall of a few scattered institutes such as those at Newcastle, Maitland and Singleton in the meantime, twenty years were to elapse before the Goulburn Mechanics' Institute was formally established in 1853. The lapse between the 1830s and 1850s can be partly accounted for by the economic depression of the 1840s, and partly by the conditions affecting the process of founding townships in the colony. According to Governor Darling's town planning regulations of 1829, the founding of towns was officially restricted to the Settled Districts except for Gundagai and Albury, which were laid out as safe places on the route to Port Phillip. When the restrictions were relaxed in 1842, the spread of towns gradually caught up with the advance in pastoral occupation.[6]

At the end of 1859 the total number of institutes in New South Wales was 13. By this time country towns such as Bathurst, Goulburn and Braidwood had experienced population and economic growth following the gold rushes of the 1850s and townspeople were settling down to a more ordered existence. Indeed, the establishment of a school of arts or mechanics' institute in a particular place was often significant, in that it indicated a stage of development in the history of settlement at which a community had managed to attain a certain level of stability, cohesion, and permanence. Goulburn, for example, was initially settled in the 1820s, but the mechanics' institute was not founded until 1853.[7]

From 1860 to 1869 the growth rate almost doubled, with the addition of 25 institutes, followed by 35 in the next decade. The pace accelerated further from 1880 to 1890, with the establishment of 75 institutes, and the trend was maintained from 1890 to 1899 with another 102. The highest number of institutes founded during any one year was 16 in 1895 and again in 1897. The dates of establishment of 11 institutes listed in 1897 were not published in the official records, however by a process of elimination, it was found that most of these had come into existence between 1880 and 1897. From 1900 the upward trend continued, and by 1912 the total number of schools of arts and mechanics' institutes in New South Wales was 433.[8]

A series of site distribution maps (see Figures 11.1-11.5) was drawn up to illustrate the extent of the spread of the institutes in New South Wales from 1833 to the 1890s. (The maps do not show every recorded site.) A number of trends complementing the profile of the rate of growth are revealed in the spatial patterns. In general, the distribution patterns reflect the growth of settlement in New South Wales. In the initial phase, development was fairly slow and restricted to the main centres of population. With the exception of Albury, Armidale and the Sydney suburb of St. Leonards, institutes were established in towns which had been founded in the Nineteen Counties within the Limits of Location proclaimed in 1829. Most of these originated as government townships, although West Maitland was a private township and Stroud was founded by the Australian Agricultural Company in 1834.[9]

There are several interesting features in the growth pattern from 1860 to 1869. The cluster of sites near Newcastle coincided with development of mining and industrial activities in the area and the extension of the railways from Newcastle to Singleton from 1855 to 1862. This made for a substantial increase in the working-class population. The Bulli and Woonona School of Arts (1863), a joint venture, was also established when collieries were opening up in the Illawarra. The location of Bulli and Woonona on a trade thoroughfare also stimulated urban growth.[10] In and around Sydney, schools of arts were established in Botany (1867) and in Richmond and Windsor (1861). The institute at Grafton (1865) was founded when this town was a major port in coastal trade, although little evidence of these activities has survived.[11] The establishment of institutes in towns along major western routes reflected the consolidation of urban settlement at these points which were important service centres in relative isolation from one another.

Between 1870 and 1879 the number of sites near Newcastle increased markedly. Most of these were certainly linked with the continued development of mining townships. They are individually cited in Shaw's *Newcastle Directory*,[12] where it is noted that the colliery managers in Wallsend and Minmi acted in the capacity of both president and secretary at their local institutes. Another characteristic feature of the mining townships was the establishment of Masonic Lodges, Oddfellows' Halls, Friendly Societies and Nonconformist churches. These partly reflected the social background of the migrant mining population as did the replication of many place names in this area. The most isolated institutes at this stage were at Bourke (1872) and Brewarrina (1878), which were then important ports on the Darling River. The Bega School of Arts (1878) was the first of many in the south coastal region. The Moruya School of Arts was founded in 1880.

Mechanics' institutes continued to proliferate in the Newcastle area over the next twenty years. Their direct links with the colliery towns are clear for the 1870s, but the situation changed from the 1880s with the decline of coal mining in the area and the changing pattern of urban growth. As Newcastle expanded and new suburbs were formed, the incentive to establish new schools of arts was stimulated as in metropolitan Sydney. Further development was also typical in the Wollongong area, with a number of new institutes being established in mining townships. Clifton, for example, was founded in 1877 by a mining company[13] and supported a school of arts by 1880.

The pattern of growth from 1880 to 1889 shows a more even distribution of sites in the eastern half of New South Wales. In the far west the institutions had almost reached their westerly limit at Wentworth (1884), Menindie (1883) and Wilcannia (1884), another

231

important river port at the time. By 1891 Broken Hill had a mechanics' institute and this was followed by White Cliffs in 1895.

During 1880 to 1889, a period of economic upsurge, 75 institutes were established. They were followed by an even greater number in the next decade, a period of depression. This suggests that the overall rate of proliferation was not directly affected by economic conditions, nor did the government withdraw its subsidies at this stage.

By 1897 the institutes had penetrated to the boundaries of settlement and into towns of all types, irrespective of their origins. The distribution pattern revealed in Figure 11.5 indicates the intensification of settlement in the eastern half of New South Wales, particularly in the south-east and along the coastal region. The highest concentration of sites in the Newcastle area persisted. It was only overtaken by the establishment of a considerable number of schools of arts in metropolitan Sydney after 1900.

The *similarity* between the spread of the institutions in colonial New South Wales and in England consists in the initial stimulus stemming from the capital city. In New South Wales the impetus then moved to the major centres of population growth in the provincial towns such as Goulburn and Bathurst, where development preceded that of smaller settlements such as Windsor and Richmond. Expansion in Sydney was relatively slow in comparison with the rapid increase in Newcastle. The links with mining and industry were maintained in many places but were not essential to the ongoing development of the movement. Eventually the institutes were a common feature in all towns and villages.

The main *difference* between the spread of the institutions in New South Wales and in Britain was that in New South Wales the movement reached a peak period of activity in the 1890s. There was an even greater number of institutions established in the next decade, a period of continued depression, and they continued to flourish long after the movement had passed its hey-day in England.

Support for the Institutes

A measure of the importance of a mechanics' institute or school of arts at the local level may be gained from an examination of the funds which were invested in the buildings. Although often incomplete, itemised accounts of the cost of erecting buildings together with the amount of public subscriptions and government subsidies towards the building and maintenance funds were published intermittently in the *Statistical Registers*. In New South Wales, buildings were subsidised on a £ for £ basis.[14] Funds were usually accumulated by individual institutes over several years before a sufficient amount was raised to construct a building. The 1912 *Statistical Register* contained the most up-to-date record of building costs, which were tabled as the 'value' of buildings. By cross reference, it appears that the term 'value' was substituted for 'cost' as no adjustments for appreciation or depreciation appear to have been made.

This accounting system is useful because it provides an indication of the proportion of institutes that had buildings. The range of values recorded also provides a basis from which the joint investment, by public subscription and government subsidy, can be analysed and compared on a broad regional level. The Statistical Divisions of New South Wales are a convenient way of classifying the sites for this purpose. The Divisions were designed to be relatively homogeneous regions with identifiable social and economic links between the inhabitants under the overarching influence of one or more major cities or towns, although these links have not always remained static and invariable.

The following analysis is relatively crude as neither the cost nor type of building materials was recorded in the NSW *Statistical Registers*. In addition, a standardised comparison of other cost components, for example maintenance, alterations, extensions and labour, is difficult to make for the period concerned. Nevertheless, the comparison was considered worthwhile as an illustration of the widespread community commitment to the institutions.

The Government, of course, had a substantial share, as a 'sleeping partner,' in this total building stock. On face value, the total building subsidy over 60 years was about £125,000 (Table 11.1), a relatively insignificant amount compared with the total annual expenditure on public works itemised in Sait;[15] but in many instances it proved very useful and economical. For example, in 1883, the New South Wales Government introduced a scheme to extend the scope of the Free Public Libraries by granting an annual subsidy for library purposes to the mechanics' institutes and schools of arts in proportion to the amount of monetary support provided by public subscription.[16] Many institutes became involved in this system, partly by having subscription library services in operation but also by having ready-made and conveniently located premises for the purpose.

This system continued until 1932,[17] by which time most institutes had either passed into the control of local government agencies in accordance with provisions in a series of Local Government Acts and Public Acts of New South Wales, or were made entirely dependent on public support, or had come to serve other purposes. Their buildings were an important asset in all these instances.

By 1897, 196 mechanics' institutes and schools of arts committees had erected their own buildings at some stage. This represents a high proportion (75 percent) of the total of 261. A small percentage (3 percent) had received building funds by 1897, but were not listed in the official records again. The remaining institutes (22 percent) operated from rented premises.

Table 11.1 shows the number of institutes established, the number of institute buildings and the sum of the value of buildings by statistical division. The number of buildings and their value are expressed in absolute terms and as percentages of the totals (196 and £247,555 respectively).

In examining this table, it is evident that there are significant regional differences in both the penetration of the institute movement, and the resources devoted to institute buildings. The Hunter is obviously outstanding in terms of both the number and value of its buildings. The Newcastle School of Arts alone, however, was valued at £18,600 in 1897, a figure far in excess of any other, its closest rival being Bathurst at £9,739. By comparison, the Sydney Mechanics' School of Arts' value of £4,000 is meagre, although this was offset by the highest maintenance figure of £29,000.[18]

Table 11.1

Number and value of institute buildings, by Statistical Division - 1897

	Statistical Division	Total Number of SAs/MIs	SA/MIs Buildings		Value of Buildings	
			Number	% of total	(£s)	% of total value
1	Sydney	28	22	11.2	28,700	11.6
2	Hunter	57	41	21.6	56,083	22.6
3	Illawarra	18	16	8.2	15,407	6.2
4	Richmond-Tweed	13	9	4.6	16,088	6.5
5	Mid-north Coast	21	17	8.7	10,290	4.2
6	Northern	22	18	9.2	28,451	11.5
7	North Western	18	12	6.1	13,600	5.5
8	Central West	17	13	6.6	20,740	8.2
9	South Eastern	28	22	11.2	22,855	9.2
10	Murrumbidgee	17	13	6.6	16,507	6.9
11	Murray	18	11	5.6	16,584	6.7
12	Far Western	4	2	1.0	2,250	0.9
	Total	261	196	100.0	247,555	100.0

At the other extreme from the Hunter is the Far Western region. Wilcannia supported an Athenaeum (1884) of £2,000 value whereas the Broken Hill Mechanics' Institute (1891) cost £250. By comparison with the average cost of houses (£40) and hotels (£300 to £400) in the settled area of the mining camp in Broken Hill in 1886,[19] the Mechanics' Institute represents a fairly substantial investment.

Between these two extremes, the descending order of values (%) column suggests significant regional differences in the distribution of wealth. For instance, although the Illawarra and mid-north Coast regions had almost the same number of institute buildings erected between 1860 and 1899 (16 and 17 respectively), the gross difference in their value was over £5,000. It is calculated that on average each building in the Illawarra cost 30 to 40 percent more than those in the mid-north Coast. One likely explanation is that, in general, the Illawarra was a wealthier area, and according to membership lists, numbers in the Illawarra towns exceeded those of the mid-north Coast. But other factors relating more specifically to local circumstances, such as building costs, may well have contributed to the apparent differences.

Averages, however, are quite deceptive and can mask major variations *within* regions. As already indicated, a single institute in the Hunter Region - the Newcastle School of Arts - accounted for almost one third of the total value of all institutes in the Region. In the same way, many other Regions also boasted more costly institute buildings which, as might be expected, were in the most important towns.

Table 11.2
Most valuable buildings in various statistical Divisions - 1897

Statistical Division	Institution	Value (£s)
Illawarra	Nowra School of Arts	2,962
Richmond	Casino School of Arts	5,776
Northern	Glen Innes School of Arts	4,500
	Tenterfield School of Arts	4,500
North-Western	Mudgee School of Arts	3,040
South-Eastern	Goulburn Mechanics Inst.	5,350
Murrumbidgee	Hay Athenaeum	4,300
	Wagga Wagga School of Arts	3,000
Murray	Albury Mechanics Institute	6,174

To gain an overall picture of the expenditure of funds on institute buildings, all 196 institutes were divided according to an arbitrary classification of values ranging from less than £100 to more than £4,000. The results of this survey showed that the majority of the buildings cost less than £1,000 (in fact more than 30 percent of them cost less than £500); with 22 percent in the range from £1,000 to £1,999, 12 percent in the £2,000 to £3,999 range and only 6 percent in the highest bracket of £4,000 or more.

Efforts to raise building funds were based on locally sustained initiatives, and it is interesting, judging by the high proportion of institutes in very small country towns, that so many managed to achieve this goal. In the 1880s and 1890s, when most of these institutes were established, the minimum amount required for a building by public subscription was about £100. Today this would not even buy the timber framework for a small shed.

The official record of the pounds, shillings and pence raised by communities throughout New South Wales in support of this cultural enterprise represents much more than the statist's requirement for accountability. It testifies to the determination of people for over 80 years to maintain a tradition and to construct their own buildings for community use, albeit with government assistance. The next part of the chapter illustrates how community values were expressed in built forms within the financial constraints imposed upon them.

SURVEY OF INSTITUTE BUILDINGS BASED ON DOCUMENTARY SOURCES

The intention in this part of the chapter is to describe and illustrate examples of mechanics' institutes and schools of arts based on evidence derived from a literature survey. References are scattered through a diverse range of publications dating from the 1830s to the 1980s. The survey produced a number of examples which have been selected in order to show the range of buildings that have represented mechanics' institutes, and how the public image of the institutes has changed through time. In part, the image reflects the history of the institutions over the period of their popularity and decline. Some institute buildings have been resurrected as worthy items of historical and cultural significance.

Sydney Mechanics' School of Arts

As New South Wales' first, and oldest surviving institute, the Sydney Mechanics' School of Arts has received a good deal of attention from researchers. The most comprehensive study of the early history of the institute is Robert Johnson's MA Thesis,[20] though it also features significantly in Michael Whiting's research at the University of Sydney.[21] Architecturally, the most detailed study is Jean Riley's research for her honours degree in Fine Arts at Sydney University,[22] and there is also a useful treatment of its architectural history in Ross Thorne's research into colonial theatre buildings in Australia.[23]

Stylistically, the original Sydney Mechanics' School of Arts was typical of the colonial version of Georgian domestic architecture characterised by symmetry and order. The entrance provided a focal point of interest, with its pedimented portico extending over the doorway and the suggestion of an ornamental fanlight over the door. In comparison with the centrally grouped features (ornamental gateway, imposing entrance and inscribed entablature) drawing attention to the Independent Chapel next door, it appeared to be a compact, modest and respectable-looking edifice.

This basic structure gave way to a second, more elaborate version. Following the routes mapped for strangers to Sydney by Waugh (1861), one would have confronted a "massive structure recently erected"[24] in Pitt Street. The Palladian facade of this building, attributed to John Hilly, is described as restrained and simple.[25] It was very much in keeping with the times in displaying an appropriately dignified classical style.

By 1861 the Independent Chapel had moved, and its former site was purchased by the School of Arts in 1855 and converted into a hall. Plans of the development of the site[26] indicate that the new façade was built on the street alignment, thus providing space for extensions and making use of expensive land in Pitt Street. The depth of the sandstone façade and the extent of the encroachment were revealed in 1987, when the adjacent buildings were demolished. Behind the solid and respectable front, but away from public view and for economic considerations, plain brick walls on the side elevations were a common feature where buildings abutted. For obvious reasons, added expense was incurred on corner sites, which were frequently occupied by banks because they offered greater opportunity to display solidity and wealth by the use of appropriate materials and design features.

Prompted by the extensive additions and alterations to the Sydney Mechanics' School of Arts in 1877-79, Gibbs and Shallard[27] said that its future was contemplated without fear. The plans in Thorne[28] show the addition of the Working Men's College to the rear and interior rearrangements to accommodate a Ladies' Reading Room. The hall, used mainly for theatrical performances, was leased to the government from about 1880 to 1887 for strictly educational purposes which, it was claimed, "rid the [School of Arts Committee] of an element of perpetual annoyance to many members."[29]

Contemporary sketches of the interior of the Sydney institution[30] show ample provision for comfort in the library, the furnishings in the Ladies' Reading Room being more refined in style. Judging by their clothing and stance, the library was frequented by fashionable (top-hatted, slim-trousered) gentlemen. A working man (cloth cap, crumpled trousers) is notable for his presence among the gentlemen posing in front of display cabinets in the College hall.

The hall reverted to use as a theatre in 1887 because the Technical College was in the process of moving out.[31] The front of the building then acquired a new look.[32] A flimsy, ornamental porch was erected over the entrance. Billboards were attached to the uprights to advertise current theatrical fare. The porch was surmounted by lamps and a decorative centrepiece consisting of a jewelled crown flanked by faunal emblems of an emu and kangaroo. While this may have constituted a fitting celebration of the Queen's jubilee, it was nothing compared with the scale of opulence and extravagance displayed on many other buildings at the time.

Bathurst and District

Tourist guides and directories were instrumental in promoting the idea to visitors and readers at 'Home' (Britain) that modern civilisation was emerging in the wilds of Australia, a point made quite explicit in the *Bathurst and Western District Directory* (1886). Re-creating familiar urban institutions was in itself a civilising act. As townships evolved, the replacement of temporary structures with buildings of a more substantial nature and more durable materials gave an impression of permanence and added credence to the notion of progress and achievement. Centrally located public buildings were indispensable adjuncts in this regard, and they provided visible and tangible evidence to substantiate this view.

In 1886, schools of arts in many towns in the Bathurst district were active. The Orange School of Arts was reported to have one of the finest halls in the colony, and that of Molong a fine brick hall built in 1879.[33]

Bathurst itself, however, was one step ahead of the others, as might be expected of such an important provincial town. The first School of Arts was built on the corner of William and Howick Streets in 1860-61. Although a solid and imposing two storey building, it was not adequate to the needs or to the burgeoning status of the town, and so in 1874-75 a much larger hall was built next door. Designed by Edward Gell, and built at a cost of £4000,[34] it claimed to be "the finest and most commodious hall in the colony - if we except that of the Sydney University."[35] In about 1882, an enclosed balcony, supported by cast iron columns, was built on the two street frontages of the original building, creating a verandah at ground floor level. In the opinion of Middleton and Maning,[36] it was the finest building of its kind in the town, with a spacious reading room supplied with works of art, pictures, newspapers and periodicals, a library and a lecture hall. By the 1920s, this building had been converted for use as a picture theatre.

Meanwhile the adjacent hall fronting Howick Street underwent considerable refurbishment. In 1881 a horseshoe gallery or dress circle was added to the previously flat-floored hall, increasing the seating capacity and acoustic quality of the auditorium. Later, modifications were made to the lighting and the stage, and a sliding roof was installed to improve ventilation. Eventually "the Hall was adapted for a cinema and was known as the 'City Theatre,' but live shows and concerts were also staged there from time-to-time."[37] In 1938, an illustration of the façade of the building appeared in *150 years of Progress in New South*

Wales, showing a horizontal cantilevered awning, and above that a two-tiered balcony which, with its darkened windows and external ventilators, was probably the projection box. The only intact feature denoting the former function of the building was the pediment, aptly inscribed 'School of Arts.'

As a sad footnote, sometime after the last film screening in September 1972, the hall was demolished.[38] In a rare fit of candour, an officer of the Bathurst City Council contacted during this research stated that the building was missed by residents and its demolition greatly regretted.

Newcastle and District

Probably no region in Australia has received such concentrated attention to its institutes as that of Newcastle and the lower Hunter Valley.[39] Although not specifically architectural in focus, several of these studies include extensive illustrations and attention to the changing appearance of the respective buildings.

As with the Bathurst District, similar claims about the many fine school of arts halls in the Newcastle area were made by Shaw.[40] Wallsend, for instance, was said to have had a fine building, second to none in the colony outside Sydney. Many claims were probably exaggerated, but it was typical of towns to boast of their accomplishments and actively compete for recognition.

The Wickham School of Arts, established in 1881 and notable for its connection with Henry Lawson (see Chapter 19), is one example of a building that was reputedly the town's finest and largest when it opened in 1882;[41] in the 1950s it served as the Police Boys Club and later as a gymnasium. The building is typical of façade architecture, with an ornamental front masking a very plain double-storeyed structure. Details of the façade - the urns, niched parapet, quoins and window labelling - conformed, in general, to stylistic trends in High Victorian architecture. However, this building exhibits none of the excesses of stuccoed ornamentation and elaboration that was evident on many shops, hotels and banks in the 1880s.

The New Lambton Mechanics' and Miners' Institute, which re-opened in 1900,[42] presents an entirely different picture to the Wickham School of Arts. The weatherboard structure, valued at £500, [43] is essentially domestic in character, but by comparison much larger than the miners' cottages depicted in the colliery villages by Turner and Sullivan.[44]

Young Mechanics' Institute

Illustrated views of country towns were often published as collections of vignettes in newspapers and journals in the late Victorian period. They provide a perspective on developments in country towns which cannot be appreciated from directory listings. Scenes of Young in 1880 for instance depicted the wide main street leading to hilly country, the cottage-style hospital complete with garden, the post office with attached residential quarters and the picket fencing which all lend a country atmosphere to the scene. In these surroundings the Mechanics' Institute looks quite grand. It was a large costly brick building, architecturally conventional in style. The Institute opened in 1877 but was in severe financial straits by 1886 and was bought by the Council. In 1889 it was officially opened as the Town Hall.[45] The building, which is extant, has retained many of its 1877 features, whilst a number of its contemporaries in Young disappeared during a concentrated phase of demolishing and rebuilding in the late 1880s and 1890s.

Moree School of Arts

The photograph of the Moree School of Arts adjacent to the Town Hall appeared on a postcard found by chance.[46] Old postcards are a valuable pictorial source for studying certain aspects of public buildings, albeit with a biased perspective towards the front. Of course, it was exactly the intention to show the best buildings in town.

The foundation stone of the School of Arts was laid in December 1884 and the building dates from 1885; the Town Hall was built c. 1891-92.[47] The buildings were destroyed by fire in 1917 and the site in Albert Street is now occupied by the RSL Club.[48]

The buildings are notable for their large size and weatherboard construction. Of necessity, timber was the most commonly used building material in the area, which is on black soil plains devoid of other building materials such as stone. A vaguely 'classical' style in timber was achieved with the Town Hall.

The verandah attached to the front of the School of Arts lends a domestic appearance to the building. In Peter Freeman's opinion,[49] this feature was of particular interest in its regional context because it bears a very close resemblance to verandahs more commonly associated with housing in tropical Queensland.[50] The street has a neat appearance enhanced by the picket fences.

Discussion

Evidence from these examples supports the view that mechanics' institutes and schools of arts were considered important and necessary for urban life. As such, they were appropriately situated in central locations. Pitt Street is highly significant in this respect because it exposed the Sydney School of Arts to the world.

In general, the buildings were unpretentious and stylistically conventional, befitting their role in Victorian society. In essence, they tried to keep up with the times and certainly did not display any unusual or bizarre forms.

Based on external appearances alone, no two buildings were identical. In general they represent a heterogeneous collection, but two broad categories are distinguishable. The first is characterised by the 'classical' capital city type (Sydney, 1861) with the façade formally rendered in durable stone. Variations on this theme were typical of the larger provincial towns. The second category, showing a decreasing degree of formality, is the residential type, represented by a large 'house' in a country town and a cottage-style variant in a village.

The public image of the mechanics' institutes and schools of arts faded when their educational and library facilities were superseded by those provided by public authorities. A fossilised form of the institutes is evoked by Lynravn's comment that they had become cemeteries of old and forgotten books.[51] The recreational activities of the institutes were scorned by some, and this attitude has been perpetuated in an article in the *Australian Encyclopedia* in which it is asserted that most institutes eventually became merely recreational halls.[52]

It is worth pointing out that heated, and sometimes acrimonious, debates in many institutes arose concerning the question of whether billiards represented an appropriate form of recreation for institutes to offer. On the one hand, traditionalists frequently derided billiards as a lightweight and inappropriate digression from the serious 'improving' and edifying educational and cultural work of the institutes. Others, however, recognizing the reality that institutes faced stiff competition from theatres, public houses, music halls and billiard parlours, argued pragmatically that billiards was a relatively innocuous pastime, and that if young men could be entertained by the institutes through billiard competitions, they were at least being kept out of more serious trouble, while at the same time the finances of the institutes were enhanced from the income derived.

Independent of the encumbrances attendant on arguments about 'higher' education, the village institutes often thrived and became a significant part of the local cultural infrastructure. This notion is conveyed in the artist's impression of a 'typical' village streetscape on the dustcover of a book entitled *The Australian Countryside in Pictures*[53], where the Mechanics' Institute dated '1873' is open and in good repair.

The theme of age and decay persisted, however, with descriptions of the schools of arts (by Warburton, for example)[54] as old-fashioned buildings in city streets, broken down halls in country towns, an occasional town hall and little shacks of unpainted wood and rusty iron in the middle of nowhere. But each in its own way was a monument to cultural enterprise, even if not always perceived as such now. The examples of the former Mechanics' Institute at Jerilderie and the former School of Arts at Taralga illustrate this point. These buildings are basically plain rectangular boxes, one brick, one weatherboard, with corrugated iron roofs. The 1881 date on the Jerilderie Mechanics' Institute is interesting. It is not consistent with the official date of establishment of 1891. But, although 1881 does not necessarily testify to the date of establishment, construction or completion of the building, it is nevertheless an important component of the building's fabric.

An attempt was made to impress a 'classical' style onto the cement-rendered façade by moulding 'pillars,' labelling the windows and entrance and adding urns and scrolls to the arched parapet. Architects nowadays tend to regard these seemingly crude attempts with contempt. Nevertheless, the buildings represent a form of vernacular architecture significant in its time and place partly because of these contrivances.

This style of building was aptly named the 'Bush Classical' by Wesson,[55] who devised what he described as a semi-facetious typology of mechanics' institutes based on the architectural styles represented by examples of institutes in Victoria. The 'Bush Classical' represented a variation on the most common type identified by Wesson,[56] namely the 'Chapel Cheapie', which was a "minimum-priced box with a gable roof." These were executed in a variety of materials according to financial constraints and the builder's expertise. Priestley's comment[57] on these mock classical styles is that, "like churches and the best hotels, they displayed a town's concern with what were considered the decencies of life."

The Taralga School of Arts, established 1899,[58] and valued at £120,[59] does not feature among the sites recommended for tourists in a locally produced pamphlet dated 1987. Attention is naturally drawn instead towards the stone buildings which characterise this small town. They were built from local basalt and sandstone, and the practice of combining these materials in various ways resulted in a number of interesting colour patterns. By comparison, the former weatherboard School of Arts building appears quite insignificant. The local basalt incorporated in the foundations is visible in the front of the building only.

Local informants assisted in verifying the site as that of the former School of Arts. It bore no inscriptions or other features by which it could be positively identified. However, the projecting porch and the interior, consisting of one room only, signified its use as a meeting place. The site had been deteriorating for some years but according to the locals it had been purchased (July, 1987) with a view to renovation for private use.

During the 1970s the cultural status of the mechanics' institute and school of arts buildings was perceived in a different light. They were no longer just remnants of a defunct institution; in effect, the buildings emerged with a new role in education, particularly in the context of local history. For instance, Barcan et al[60] used examples as a guide for secondary students seeking suitable material for investigating the past.

Published case histories of mechanics' institutes in Australia are rare. One exception is Cusack's history of the Bendigo Institute of Technology, which grew out of the Sandhurst Mechanics' Institute established in 1855.[61] The book *Canvas to Campus* traces the evolution of the institute, from its humble beginnings as a temporary canvas pavilion erected for an Industrial Exhibition to the architect-designed structure of the 1880s. The final result displays aspects of the elaboration and excessive ornamentation associated with the display of opulence typical of the 1880s.

Coming full cycle to guided tours in *Sydney's West*, Proudfoot (1987) makes the point quite explicitly that the buildings he selected for description were not so much because they were considered worthy of preservation, but because their inclusion may help in understanding how localities evolved. Therefore, in view of the socio-cultural activities formerly associated with the movement, the inclusion of the Fairfield School of Arts, (built c. 1901), the Windsor School of Arts, (converted for use as a factory in 1947), and the Richmond School of Arts[62] may be read in the context of their contribution to community and civic development. The Windsor and Richmond Schools of Arts buildings are both listed on the Register of the National Estate.

The ongoing importance of the Sydney School of Arts to a concerned yet increasingly cynical public was made obvious by Leo Schofield in 1987:

> OK, COP this latest bit of monorail madness. You know Bondy has bought the Hilton site. Well, he proposes to re-orient the hotel and get rid of that horrendous ramped entrance for which we should all join in a collective hallelujah, as it is possibly one of the most horrible sights in Sydney. However, a related proposal is truly obscene, for there is a plan afoot to put a monorail station *inside* the beautiful Sydney School of Arts building next door at 275-277 Pitt Street. This building represents a most important link with our colonial past and is a symbol of our cultural growth. It has stood on its

241

present site since 1837, making it one of our city's longest-surviving buildings. Its Palladian facade is intact, as are several important rooms inside, including the former reading and smoking rooms and John Verge's Independent Chapel, which was incorporated in the later 1862 building. However, they will not remain intact for much longer if this outrageous proposal is allowed to proceed. During the week surveyors were inside the building, deciding where to locate the monsterail's platform. So much for a permanent conservation order.[63]

In fact, the proposed alterations did not take place. But it is more remarkable that this building in Pitt street has survived at all when so many of its contemporaries have fallen prey to developers. The School of Arts is noticeably dwarfed by its former Bond Corporation neighbour, but by contrast has gained stature by virtue of its age and associations. Its survival was due to the fact that the Sydney School of Arts Subscription Library, the oldest in Sydney, was still operating and had managed to retain the premises by deriving income from renting rooms.

FIELD STUDY OF EXISTING SITES

On the basis of the results obtained from the analyses of official sources, in conjunction with evidence from other published documentary sources, and taking into account provisions for surrendering mechanics' institute and school of arts buildings to local government authorities, it was considered likely that a high proportion of institute buildings was likely to be extant.

Accordingly, as explained above, a field survey was undertaken primarily for the purpose of determining the number of extant sites and their current use. The survey was conducted in the southeast region of New South Wales and was restricted to places within a reasonable distance of Canberra. The area included towns on the Southern Tablelands, the Shoalhaven and Illawarra. The most westerly point was Young.

The results of the field survey were rewarding in that twenty-five sites (Table 11.3) were positively identified in the survey area. It was evident from occasional visits elsewhere and on advice from others that mechanics' institute buildings are still in existence in many other New South Wales towns, for example, Byron Bay, Inverell, Pilliga, Mudgee (possibly the oldest intact Mechanics' Institute building in New South Wales) and many towns on the New England Highway.

In general, no problems were encountered in locating the institute buildings. Indeed, many of them were found to be familiar landmarks. Two examples are the former Braidwood Literary Institute, now the Tallaganda Shire Council Chambers and Public Library, and the former Goulburn Mechanics' Institute which now houses the Public Library on the first floor and commercial premises on the ground floor.

Positive identification of sites was based on material evidence incorporated in the fabric of the building. Each site was verified by recourse to documentary evidence. In cases where evidence from the history of an institute - for example the Nowra School of Arts[64] - indicated that the process of acquiring land and building premises was undertaken more than once, only the most recently occupied site was recorded.

SITE NAME		DATE ESTD	DATE BLDG	DATE BLDG STREET FRONTAGE	ORIGINAL FABRIC OR PART EXTANT	CURRENT USE
1 Goulburn	MI	1853	1858	from 1881	?	LGA/PL
2 Yass	MI	1857	1869	from 1869		O
3 Braidwood	LI	1858	1869	1869/1891	✓	LGA/PL
4 Young	MI	1870	1875	from 1875	✓	LGA/PH
5 Milton	MI	1871	1872	1872	✓	LGA/PL
6 Bombala	LI	1872	opened 1872	c.1872	✓	O
7 Harden	MI	1881	1909	1909	✓	LGA/PH
8 Nowra	SA	1885	1891	1891	✓	LGA/PL
9 Robertson	SA	1886	1886 1936	1936	✓	O/CP
10 Queanbeyan	SA	1887	1926	1926	✓	LGA/PA
11 Bungendore	SA	1888	1891	1926	at rear	O/CP
12 Burrawang	SA	1889	1886	from 1883	✓	O/CP
13 Berry	SA	1890	1906	from 1906	✓	LGA/PA
14 Moss Vale	SA	1890	1891	1891	✓	LGA/PL
15 Gundaroo	LI	1894	c.1895	c.1895	✓	O/CP
16 Crookwell	SA	1895		1953	?	LGA/PL
17 Pyree	LI	1895	1894	1894	✓	O/CP
18 Taralga	SA	c.1900	c.1900	c.1900	✓	O
19 Jerrawa	SA	1902	c.1902	c.1900	✓	O/CP
20 Bibbenluke	SA	1903	c.1903	c.1903	✓	O/CP
21 Nelligen	MI	1903	1903	c.1903	✓	O/CP
22 Murrumburrah	SA	c.1910	1912	1912	✓	O
23 Binalong	MI	1912	1912	1912	✓	O/CP
24 Tomerong	SA	1926	c.1920	from 1920s	✓	O/CP
25 Wingello	MI	1926	c.1926	c.1926	?	O/CP

Key to abbreviations:

LGA =	Local Government Authority		O =	Other
PL =	Public Library		CP =	Community Purposes
PH =	Public Hall		PA =	Public Amenity

The most obvious feature of the institute buildings denoting their former use is the title - 'Mechanics' Institute,' 'School of Arts' or 'Literary Institute' - variously inscribed and usually on the upper level of the centre front. Village institute buildings are sometimes unlabelled or less formally labelled. In these cases the degree of corroborative evidence for

243

identification becomes increasingly important. Site recognition was facilitated by a growing familiarity with the range of built forms and stylistic conventions associated with institute architecture.

The 1891 façade of the Moss Vale School of Arts, for example, exhibits characteristic features of the High Victorian period, but with restraint in the degree of elaboration. The stuccoed brick façade is divided into three bays and the main entrance and windows are labelled and decorated with plaster keystones. The central bay rises to the dated entablature and triangular pediment. Twin orbs provide the final flourish. There are obvious similarities between the Moss Vale and the 1891 Nowra buildings, but Nowra's is much larger and was more than twice the cost. The recessed central bay is made more important by having a balcony for special occasions. The Braidwood building also featured a small balcony in the 1891 extension. The 1890s witnessed a substantial increase in institute building, and Moss Vale, Braidwood (1891 extension) and Nowra (second building) all display expansionism at the local level. Judging by their relative sizes, Nowra was forging ahead in local development.

A notable difference between the three buildings is the effect achieved by paint. The Nowra building, in white, is starkly clinical in contrast to the other two dressed in fashionable 'heritage colours' to delineate certain features, but not their redundant titles.

Two different types of village institute were identified in the survey area. The majority are minimum-priced boxes with gable roofs, or 'Chapel Cheapies.'[65] The 1903 Nelligen Mechanics' Institute is a typical example: decoration is minimal except for special touches such as the finials and bargeboards. The second type of village institute basically resembles a country cottage. The Gundaroo Literary Institute on two acres of land was a gift to the society in 1897 from the local dignitary, William Affleck.[66] Unlike most domestic dwellings, however, there is no back door, and the interior consists of one room only.

Based on the range of dates of establishment (Table 11.3) for the sites (1853 to 1926), the sample is interesting because it includes one of the earliest institutes established outside Sydney, namely Goulburn (1853), through to the most recent example of Wingello (1926). Eight sites (nos. 18-25) entered the *New South Wales Statistical Register* records after 1897. With the exception of Murrumburrah they are all in small villages or sparsely populated localities.

As a rule, the dates of establishment do not coincide with the dates of building construction; there was often a lag of two or more years before building commenced. Efforts were made to verify a date or dates associated with the construction of each site. In some cases, particularly in larger towns, it was less difficult than others. Institute establishment was a ceremonial affair and laying foundation stones was all part of the tradition, with the result that there is usually at least one firm indicator relating to a part of the original fabric. But in complex sites, such as Goulburn, which have been subject to frequent structural changes, it was not possible to ascertain whether any part of the 1858 building is intact.

The foundation stones of Nowra and Moss Vale testify to the association of these buildings with very important persons; namely, the Premier and Governor of New South Wales. Henry Parkes, a great supporter of the institutes (and an autodidact who had received his own education through evening classes at the Birmingham Mechanics' Institute in England), had been opening their buildings since 1866 (Richmond). He also gave has famous Federation speech in the Tenterfield School of Arts, but he was unavoidably absent from Nowra on 3 October 1891 and the Minister of Works, the Hon. J.H. Young MLA, performed the honours instead.[67]

Current ownership and use of the Institutes

It was found that ten former institute buildings (40 percent) are under the control of local government agencies. Ranked according to their dates of establishment, they include most of the earlier sites in the sample. This follows logically from the 'spread' data, discussed earlier in this chapter. These buildings are used for various purposes, but each building is associated with providing a public amenity, such as a public library and/or a public function hall.

The premises of another four former institutes (16 percent) are also used for a variety of purposes. One is the Harden-Murrumburrah Museum run by the Harden-Murrumburrah Historical Society; another is a commercial business, F.L. Kelly Stock and Station Agent, Yass (privately owned); a third is a furniture storage depot, formerly the Bombala Literary Institute (privately owned); and the fourth, the Taralga School of Arts, was unoccupied at the time of the survey.

Eleven institutes (44 percent) are those typically found in small country towns and villages. This group constitutes the highest proportion of the total. They are mostly viable concerns, and continue to function as community centres. Some maintain small libraries. It was ascertained that nine have retained their independence and are run by local voluntary organisations.

Broadly classified, the sites now represent either those pressed into service by municipal or shire councils (40 percent) or those that are independent (60 percent). Several examples from each class have been selected to illustrate the different ways in which the institute buildings contribute to the urban fabric, in terms of their past and/or present associations in the local context.

It was found that the majority of buildings taken over by councils exhibit part of the original fabric to a greater or lesser degree at the main street frontage. The exception is Crookwell, where the 1954 Art Moderne extension had seemingly obliterated or encapsulated the former School of Arts façade.

Direct links with the role of the Goulburn Mechanics' Institute in the development of technical education are evident in the 1886 structure (built to accommodate classrooms) at the rear of the main complex. It is now the tourist information office. Conversely, the Milton building has been extended at the rear, to accommodate TAFE.

Extant fabric of the Young Mechanics' Institute (1877) consists of a series of stages that became physically locked into Young's advancement, and the building thereby retains a role as an important civic structure. The foundation stone and commemorative stone, now covered in calcemite, document the early stages. It is notable that 'C A Cranfield, Mayor' (actually George A Cranfield[68]) is more boldly inscribed than W J Watson Esq. (whose standing in the community presumably increased in 1880-82, when he was elected MLA).

In wider perspective, the former Mechanics' Institute now recognisably constitutes the right wing of the Town Hall, a monument to the boom-style architecture of the 1920s. The left wing was designed to complement the existing building,[69] but although the overall effect has been achieved, the wings are in fact asymmetrical. The central feature of the Town Hall extension (1924) is the War Memorial. It incorporates a niche for the statue of a digger, symbolising the local contribution to national heroism, a tall tower complete with clock - an almost essential element for a town hall - and a dome; in sum, the epitome of achievement in municipal affairs. In 1989-90 the Young Shire Council, in keeping up with the fashion, gave the Town Hall a face lift and dressed its façade in 'heritage colours.'

The Harden-Murrumburrah Museum (independent) is a good example of a local, poorly-funded museum that provides a valuable service to the public. But in terms of local developments the building may be viewed in a different light. According to the Minutes and Records of the Murrumburrah School of Arts (held at the museum), the Government refused to subsidise the building because Harden already had a Mechanics' Institute (1909) and Harden-Murrumburrah is officially one town. Not to be deterred, the Murrumburrah supporters acquired land and built their own School of Arts. This explains why there are two institutes within 4km of each other. The case has been interpreted by Littlejohn[70] as one of intense socio-political rivalry partly due to the fact that Harden became an important railway centre from 1877, and Murrumburrah was left behind.

Both the Harden, and Harden-Murrumburrah buildings display the polychrome banded effect popular in Federation style architecture; in each case it was limited to the street frontage. On the museum, the effect was achieved by the lavish use of cream paint and in Harden by the combination of tinted cement rendering and light cream paint.

The museum gives the immediate, but false, impression of being three storeys high, or higher than Harden. The top of the building is highlighted with cream paint, decorated ventilators and a vaguely castellated effect on the projecting bay. In the light of events described above, it could be seen to be competing with Harden and in this instance it is interesting that it retained its independent status.

None of the buildings in the survey area resembled a broken down hall or little shack, but three appeared to be in the process of decline - Taralga, Bombala and Bungendore. The Bungendore School of Arts (a double-fronted weatherboard cottage) has been used for meetings, a creche and other community purposes, but less and less frequently. A likely explanation for this is that a large multi-purpose function centre was built in 1986 and the cottage was inadequate for current needs.

The former Bombala Literary Institute (c.1872) is showing signs of considerable deterioration. The rendered Italianate façade was disintegrating and was also affected by sooty mould. Its continued use for storage only is likely to contribute to the overall process of decline. The locked front doors added to the bleak appearance of the building, suggesting its abandonment and making the Bombala Literary Institute - the only surviving example of relatively early age (c.1872) in the survey area - one which most obviously reflected a faded public image of a defunct institution. It is ironic that the Bombala Shire Council offices constructed in 1986 are located on the adjacent block.

The state of this building partly reflects the status of towns in the survey area. For example, towns on the Hume Highway are highly significant for their historical role in the spread of settlement in New South Wales. This, among other reasons, has provided the incentive to attract tourists. It is important, therefore, that towns maintain a high profile which means clean, tidy, well-maintained and eminently presentable buildings.

The former Yass Mechanics' Institute is the most striking contrast to Bombala in this respect. The building has gained high cultural status as an item on the Register of the National Estate, and its owner has taken the matter seriously. It now exhibits pride of place in the town, and is a salutary gesture to its former self, especially within its faunal emblem, the only example in the survey area with such a distinctive embellishment. Bombala, however, cannot compete with towns like Yass, partly for the reason that it is simply out of the way.

At the other extreme are the viable 'independents.' Their significance lies partly in the fact that a high proportion have survived. The immediate impressions gained from their appearance are, firstly, that the buildings are well maintained, and secondly, that their large size - often being the largest single building in a village or locality - is seemingly out of proportion to the mass of residential accommodation and by inference to the presumed needs of the population.

The Bibbenluke School of Arts, 20km north of Bombala, and the Jerrawa School of Arts, 2km north of the Hume Highway midway between Gunning and Yass, are two examples of these kinds of buildings. According to local informants at Jerrawa, support for the institution is drawn from the whole district, and not just the village itself, which is in a process of decline, having lost its function as a postal village and railway station. The former post office and associated postmaster's residence has reverted to use as a private residence, and the railway station has been physically removed (1985/86) leaving a blank platform.

The Pyree Literary Institute (1894) is a good example of village-hall culture wrapped in a red tin box with a gable roof. I am indebted to Mr D M Watts for confirming the existence of the Institute on this site since 1894 and for providing documentary evidence of the changing nature of its social significance to the community over many years. The building is in a commanding position at the junction of Greenwell Point Road and Pyree Lane, 12km east of Nowra. It is set in the midst of flat pastureland which was once part of the Alexander Berry Estate. A sportsground and clubhouse are on the adjacent block. The scene is distinctly pastoral and Pyree is best described as a locality.

The basic structure is a plain corrugated-iron building set on sandstone blocks, possibly chosen because the low-lying pastureland has a tendency to become water-logged. No concessions were made to ornamentation, with the exception of the finial, centre front. An unevenly sited window towards the rear of the building denotes the use of that end of the hall for a stage. Evidence of the currently popular activity at the hall is reflected in the brilliant red paintwork, the result of a face-lift in 1982, which has a visually compelling effect in the green pastureland setting. As a viable concern in relative isolation from habitation, this basically ordinary structure is an outstanding feature in the landscape. In the context of the local development, however, the activities associated with the Institute accentuate its significance as an important element in the built environment.

CONCLUSION

The arrival of the Mechanics' Institutes in Hobart and Sydney, each with its particular cast of principals, set the scene for a wave of enthusiasm which, notwithstanding an absence of mechanics, eventually extended throughout much of Australia, reaching its most distant parts. The official records have assisted in establishing facts and figures - and thereby dots on the map - so that the rate of growth of the institutes in New South Wales could be shown to be related to the spread of settlement. This study has also attempted to demonstrate that mechanics' institutes and related institutions were common to all types of towns, with distinct clusters of activity in, but not limited to, the industrial and mining areas and later in metropolitan Sydney.

A literature survey produced evidence of a heterogeneous array of sites, but more importantly, it allowed the identification of a number of variations on the theme, from unpretentious country cottages to more elaborate structures in important towns, and the 'classical' façade of the Sydney institution.

It was interesting to find that the decline of the institutes had not resulted in a complete dearth of buildings. On the contrary, there are a substantial number of extant schools of arts and mechanics' institutes in New South Wales. The field survey results incorporated in this study also showed that in larger towns the buildings were frequently occupied by the local government authority. In many cases, the buildings have retained their distinctive features but have lost their identity and now look as though they were provided by local government in the first place.

The functioning village institutes are particularly interesting. In contrast to the original small institutes in England, they represent the highest proportion of the total. Moreover, 'village-hall culture' has been and is likely to remain an important aspect of community life in Australia, which is why the social and recreational function of the mechanics' institutes have survived more than a century and a half of evolutionary change.

NOTES AND REFERENCES

1.*New South Wales Statistical Register*, 1875, p.4.

2.Laurent, J. (1989). *personal communication.*

3.*New South Wales Statistical Register,* 1897, pp.610-616.

4.Jervis, J. (1961). *The cradle city of Australia: A history of Parramatta, 1788-1961.* Parramatta: Council of the City of Parramatta, p.124.

5.Charles, M. (1986). *Old Parramatta.* Sydney: Arrand Pty Ltd, p.77

Growth of Institutes in NSW

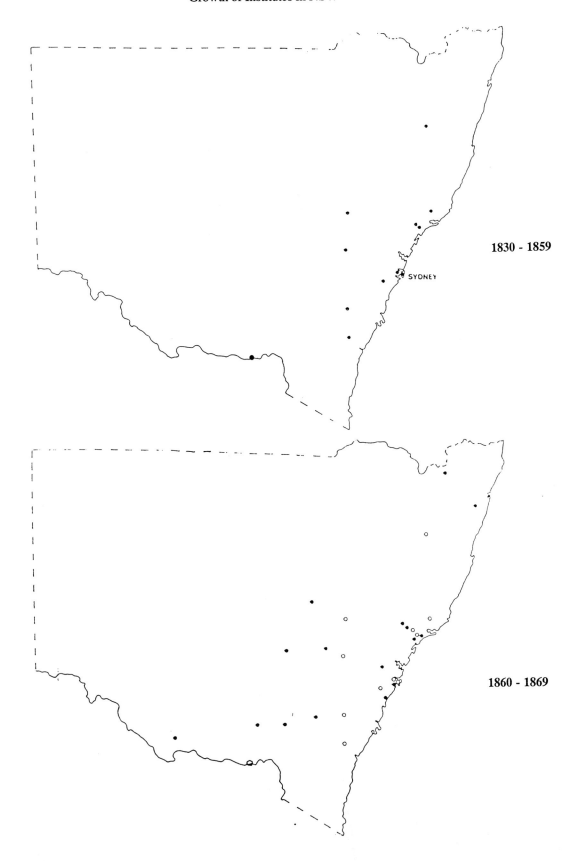

1830 - 1859

SYDNEY

1860 - 1869

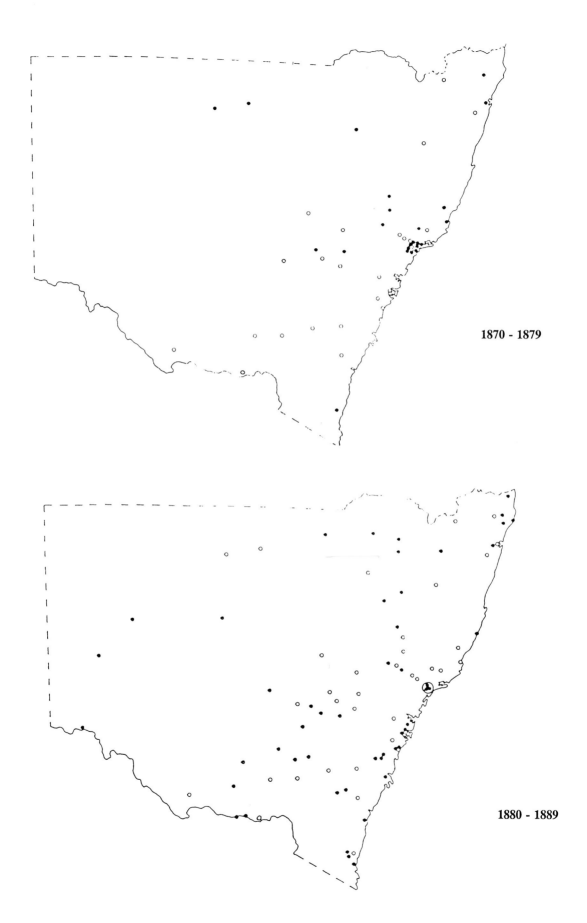

1870 - 1879

1880 - 1889

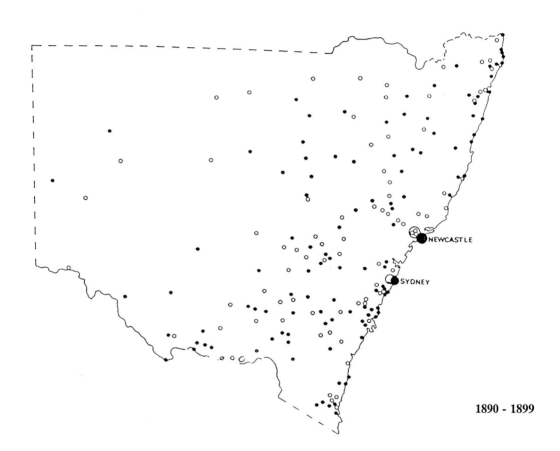

NEWCASTLE

SYDNEY

1890 - 1899

Harden School of Arts, NSW, 1986

Murrumburrah School of Arts, NSW, 1986

Moree School of Arts, NSW ca 1910

Goulburn Mechanics' Institute, NSW

Nelligen Mechanics' Institute, NSW, 1989

Bombala Literary Institute, NSW, 1989

Bibbenluke Hall, NSW 1989

Yass Mechanics' Institute, NSW, 1989
(currently used as a Real Estate Agent's office)

Murrurundi Literary Institute, NSW, 1987

Bathurst School of Arts, NSW, ca 1875
(reproduced by permission of the Bathurst District Historical Society Inc.)

Bathurst School of Arts, NSW, ca 1923
(reproduced by permission of the Bathurst District Historical Society Inc.)

Newcastle School of Arts, NSW, May 1899
(reproduced from the Snowball Collection, Newcastle Region Public Library)

6.Jeans, D.N., & Spearritt, P. (1980) *The open air museum*. Sydney: George Allen & Unwin, p.39.

7.See Hopcraft, P.J. (1978). Notes towards a history of the Goulburn Mechanics' Institute, 1853-1946. *Unpublished paper*. Goulburn: Southern Tablelands Joint Library.

8.*New South Wales Statistical Register*, 1912, p.40.

9.Jeans and Spearritt, *op. cit.*, p.39

10.Bolton, K.R. (1977). Urban beginnings - development of the colliery towns of Northern Illawarra, 1858-1905. In Robinson, R. (Ed.), *Urban Illawarra*, Melbourne: Sorrett Publishing Company, p.72.

11.Jeans & Spearritt, *op. cit.*, p.74.

12.Shaw, W. (1881). *The Newcastle directory and almanac for 1880* (reprinted in facsimile by the Library of Australian History, Sydney, 1978), pp.50-65.

13.Jervis, J. (1942). Illawarra: A century of history, 1788-1888. Part I. *Journal of the Royal Australian Historical Society*, 28 (2), p.98.

14.*New South Wales Statistical Register*, 1894, p.736.

15.Sait, J.E. (1989). Public building and town planning: The first 100 years. In Coltheart, L. (Ed.), *Significant sites: History and public works in New South Wales*. Sydney: Hale & Iremonger, p.39.

16.Coghlan, T.A. (1888). *The wealth and progress of New South Wales*. Sydney: New South Wales Statistician's Office, p.577.

17.*Official Year Book NSW*, 1933, p.448.

18.Some of these apparent anomalies can only be understood by tracing the building history of individual institutes. Those of both Sydney (Thorne 1971:134-136) and Newcastle are complicated, and matters of expenditure on building/rebuilding and/or alterations and extensions are not easily resolved.

19.Solomon, R.J. (1959). Broken Hill: The growth of the settlement, 1883-1958. *Australian Geographer, 7*(5), p.183.

20.Johnson, R.I. (1967). The history of the Sydney Mechanics' School of Arts: From its foundation in 1833 to 1880s. *Unpublished MA thesis*. Canberra: School of General Studies, Australian National University.

21.Whiting, M. (1973). The education of adults in the mechanics' institutes of the colony of New South Wales, 1833-1901. *Unpublished major paper*. Sydney: Department of Education, University of Sydney.

22.Riley, J. (1982). The mechanics' school of arts movement in New South Wales. *Unpublished BA(Hons) thesis.* Department of Fine Arts, University of Sydney.

23.Thorne, R. (1971). *Theatre buildings in Australia to 1905. Vol. 1.* Sydney: Architectural Research Foundation, University of Sydney.

24.Waugh, J.W. (1861). *The stranger's guide to Sydney.* (Reprinted in facsimile by the Library of Australian History, Sydney, 1978) p.33.

25.Australian Heritage Commission (1981). *Heritage of Australia: The illustrated register of the national estate.* Melbourne: Macmillan, 2/108.

26.Thorne *op. cit.,* Plate 45.

27.Gibbs, Shallard & Co., (1882). *An illustrated guide to Sydney.* Sydney: Gibbs Shallard & Co. p.42.

28.Thorne, *op. cit.,* Plate 45.

29.Thorne *op. cit.,* p.135.

30.Gibbs, Shallard & Co., *op. cit.,* pp.41,62,66; Thorne, *op. cit.,* Plate 46.

31.*ibid.,* p.135.

32.*ibid.,* plate 44.

33.Middleton, A., & Manning, F.B. (1886). *Bathurst and western district directory and tourist's guide and gazetteer.* Bathurst: J. Virtue & Co., p.7.

34.Tighe, W.H. (1989). *The man whose name was left off: A study of John Copeman, architect of Bathurst's Boer War Memorial.* Bathurst: The Author, p.10.

35.*Bathurst Daily Times,* 27 January 1875.

36.*ibid.,* p.3.

37.Tighe, *op.cit,* p.14

38.*ibid,* p.14.

39.Rabbitt, M. (1984). The development and history of the Lambton Mechanics' and Miners' Institute. *Unpublished M Ed thesis.* Newcastle: Faculty of Education, University of Newcastle.
Heaton, B. (1985). Aspects of the school of arts movement with particular reference to the Newcastle institution. *Unpublished BA(Hons) thesis.* Newcastle: Department of History, University of Newcastle.
Preston, G.D. (1990). A comparative evaluation of the aims and achievements of the mechanics' institute movement, with particular reference to the Lower Hunter Valley, 1800-1914. *Unpublished MEd thesis.* Newcastle: University of Newcastle.

40. Shaw, *op. cit.*

41. Turner, J.B., & Sullivan, J. (1980), *Photos of old Newcastle: From Stockton to Minmi.* Stockton, NSW: Hunter History Publications, p.24.

42. *New South Wales Statistical Register*, 1900, p.314.

43. *New South Wales Statistical Register*, 1912, p.418.

44. Turner & Sullivan, *op. cit.*, p.44.

45. Bayley, W.A. (1977). *Rich earth: History of Young, New South Wales.* Young, NSW: Municipal Council, pp.81,109.

46. The postcard was printed in Germany, presumably before World War 1.

47. Jervis, J. (1963). Exploration and settlement of the North-Western Plains. *Journal of the Royal Australian Historical Society*, *48*(6), p.449.

48. Mahaffey, M. (1986). *personal communication.*

49. Freeman, P. (1986). *personal communication.*

50. Refer to Steve Kellermeier's chapter in this book about the Architecture of Queensland Institutes.

51. Lynravn, N. (1948). *Libraries in Australia.* Melbourne: F.W. Cheshire, p.16.

52. *The Australian Encyclopaedia.* The Grolier Society, 1965, Vol. 6, p.17;1983 Vol. 6, p.228.

53. anon. (c.1950). *The Australian countryside in pictures.* Melbourne: Colorgravure Pub.

54. Warburton, J.W. (1963). Schools of arts. *Australian Quarterly*, *35*(4), p.72.

55. Wesson, A. (1972). Mechanics' institutes in Victoria. *Australian Journal of Adult Education*, *12*(1), p.9.

56. *ibid.*, p.8.

57. Priestley, S. (1984). *The Victorians: Making their mark.* Melbourne: Fairfax, Syme & Weldon Associates, p.78.

58. *New South Wales Statistical Register*, 1900, p.714.

59. *New South Wales Statistical Register,* 1912, p.419.

60. Barcan, A., Blunden, T., Dwight, A., & Shorten, S. (1973). *Shaping our heritage: Survey and depth, 2.* Melbourne: Macmillan, p.252.

61.Cusack, F. (1973) *Canvas to campus: A history of the Bendigo Institute of Technology.* Melbourne, Hawthorn Press.

62.Proudfoot, H. (1987). *Exploring Sydney's West.* Kenthurst, NSW: Kangaroo Press. pp.66, 142, 153.

63.*Sydney Morning Herald*, 6 June 1987.

64.Antill, R.G. (1982). *Settlement in the South.* Kiama, NSW: R. Anthill, pp.143,147,150.

65.Wesson, A., *op. cit.*, p.8.

66.Lea-Scarlett, E. (1972). The improbable culture of Gundaroo. *Canberra and District Historical Society Journal, 1*, p.5.

67.Antill *op. cit.*, p.152.

68.Bayley, *op. cit.*, Civic Record.

69.Bayley, *op. cit.*, p.163.

70.Littlejohn, R.A. (Curator, Harden & Murrumburrah Museum) (1986). *personal communication.*

CHAPTER TWELVE

THE ARCHITECTURE OF THE INSTITUTES: SELECTED EXAMPLES FROM QUEENSLAND

Steve Kellermeier

A TYPOLOGY OF INSTITUTE BUILDINGS

Queensland developed a style of architecture peculiar to the State. Much has been written and said about timber, tin, stilts and verandahs, mainly in relation to residential construction. However most of those idioms are also applicable to the architecture of schools of arts.

Mention of such buildings conjures up images of derelict, barn-like structures. Among those whose memories are beginning to fade, recall varies, and descriptions range from small single room structures sheeted on one side only and roofed with sheet iron, to much larger and more elaborate buildings. In people's memories, large dance halls are prominent, containing stages, ante-rooms, libraries and reading-rooms, with such buildings being thoroughly finished throughout. Verandahs are commonly mentioned in the latter type, often running the full length of the building on one or both sides. Some people even talk of ornate brick or stone institutions with imposing facades and extensive facilities.

The fact is that while the memory does play tricks, all these sorts of school of arts buildings did - and to a considerable extent still do - exist in Queensland. Indeed, one of the enduring legacies of the school of arts movement as a whole is the buildings that they left behind, and it is therefore possible to study and write about the schools of arts on the basis of the size and complexity of their premises.

As indicated, schools of arts buildings appear to fall into three major categories. While it is true that each separate institution could be described in terms of its own particular design, type, size, materials, and decoration, generally speaking, division into the following three broad categories suffices:

Table 12.1
Typology of Queensland School of Arts Buildings

TYPE I Building	-	basic single room structure, some with one ante-room
TYPE II Building	-	large dance-hall buildings with ante-rooms and verandahs
TYPE III Building	-	permanent masonry construction.

In other states, a similar three-way classification is also possible, with variations to account for differences in building materials and climate. In Victoria, for instance, Wesson proposed three "semi-facetious titles, in the hope that they will be more memorable."[1] First are the "Chapel Cheapies" which he defined as "the minimum priced box with a gable roof."

According to Wesson, this is "the commonest style, one which was used all through the institute-building period... Over half of all institutes were built like this."[2]

The second style, perhaps analogous to Type II buildings, were the "Bush Classical,"[3] which, in more ways than one, covered a multitude of sins. Wesson writes, "the functional architecture of the early institutes continued for a generation, but...with extra money to spend,...most trustees talked themselves...into adding some ornamentation to the basic building. The usual style was Classical Greek and Roman, filtered through the Renaissance, European Neo-classicism,...and the aspirations of local designers...[It even included] an occasional lovely, homogeneous building - like the Bairnsdale institute."[4]

Finally, there were the elaborate and often flamboyant institute buildings, many of them built by nouveau-riche communities after the goldrushes, and accordingly dubbed "Goldrush Glorious." Wesson claims that this category divides into two subsections, "one of which I rejoice in, and another which I dislike. The first consists of building in honest, and graceful stone; Benalla and Portland illustrate it well. The second sub-style went for conspicuous consumption, as at Ballaarat and Bendigo; the Ballaarat institute cost £12,000..."[5]

In Queensland, masonry construction was by far the least common. Although often employed in public buildings within municipalities, brick was rarely used in schools of arts. However, some fine masonry examples do survive, notably: Bundaberg, Maryborough and Rockhampton. Much more prevalent were the smaller, single-room structures. A statistical survey undertaken in 1910 revealed that, of 162 known institutions in Queensland, 58 had an estimated value of £100 or less. To this must be added 48 libraries at stations and sugar mills which were valued at an average £68 each.[6] Thus, while Rockhampton boasted the most valuable structure at £5,578, more than half of the 210 institutions were housed in buildings worth less than £100.

Simply because these modest structures predominated does not automatically provide a wealth of information. In fact, only a basic history can be constructed for a limited number of them. For instance, the plan of a proposed structure for the Kaimkillenbun School of Arts, founded in 1910, and built for about £350, is available, and could be used as an example of the Type I school of arts. However, very little other information is extant for that particular institution. Conversely, records of the larger schools of arts are relatively common. Large memberships, and hence greater sums of money involved, meant that a comprehensive account of their activities had to be kept. From such records, it is possible to determine much of the history and development of those institutions. Two of the most extensively documented of these larger institutes are those at Brisbane and Rockhampton.

The remainder of this chapter consists of several case studies of different schools of arts - two to illustrate each architectural type.

TYPE I BUILDINGS

North Tamborine

Mention has already been made of the difficulties encountered in obtaining information in connection with Type I buildings. However, the North Tamborine School of Arts is one of the best documented of this class, and is discussed for that reason.

The origins of this institution can be traced to a general public meeting which was called for 9 October 1925 to establish a School of Arts for Tamborine Mountain and district. It was therefore a late beginner, which, as circumstances would later prove, was ill-timed. However, the meeting did go ahead and it was decided to proceed with the proposal. By February 1926, the library was in operation, on a site described as Subsection 2, Portion 100A, Country of Ward, Parish of Tamborine.[7] All real property of the institution was vested in three Trustees appointed by the Committee.

The first elected chairman of the institution was Mr Abraham Hartly, who was also chairman of the North Tamborine Progress Association, a position he held from its inception in 1915.[8] He was one of the best known characters in the district, having been a member of the Tamborine Shire Council for sixteen years. As Chairman, he continued to serve until, in 1929, the first woman, Mrs Walmsley, was elected to the committee as President.

Clause 2 of the by-laws adopted on 30 June 1927 declared the aims of the institution. They read very much like those of any other school of arts, and are in harmony with the aims of similar southern institutions:

> The object of the institution shall be the establishment and maintenance of a Library and Reading Room; the recreation and entertainment of members by games of skill, and generally by the diffusion of knowledge and the promotion of intellectual amusement.[9]

Actually, the by-laws discriminated against women to a certain degree. This was not unique, as many other schools of arts originally included a rule such as Clause 3c, which defined Family Members, one of the three classes of membership, as follows:

> The wife, or child under 16 years of age, of any member may become a family member for the then current year by the payment, in advance, of the relative subscription of 2/6.[10]

At least they were able to borrow books for half the price of ordinary members!

Support was strong for the first few years, but with the 1930s Depression, the institution's sound financial position was shaken. Fund-raising activities were wide and varied until then, including a Dramatic Party in 1927, a Wireless Concert in 1926 and Garden Parties in 1929, 1930 and 1931.[11] The July 1931 Garden Party raised £22/14/1 but Government aid, paid at the reduced rate, was only £2/15/4 for that year.[12] One year before, the subsidy had been £25/16/6.[13]

By September 1938 the institution had almost ceased to exist, with an all-time-low membership of 13 subscribers. Only three of the 1937 committee were still financial members, and this lack of a driving force would have reinforced the decay that was being manifested.

It would appear that the institute was in recess throughout the whole period of the second world war, however, a revival meeting was called for February 1951 which was attended by twenty-two people. It was decided then that the School of Arts should attempt a comeback.

Shortly afterwards, the building was moved to a new site, although the genesis of this move actually dates back to twenty years before. A committee meeting on 23 March 1932 had voted to accept a donation of approximately 1,000 square metres of land at Eagle Heights from a Miss McDonald.[14] It was at that time proposed to erect a new building on the site, but due to financial difficulties, no action was taken at the time. However, on 14 April 1951 the existing structure was transported to the site, and later that year, a porch was added at a cost of £38/8/6.

The School of Arts never really thrived, but did survive, mainly through affiliation with the School of Arts Association, and its book lending scheme. By the late 1960s, however, it was realised that the peak of popularity was well past, and so it was taken over by the Beaudesert Shire Council after a general meeting of subscribers in June 1970 decided that the institution should cease to exist.

Gin Gin

Opened on 30 June 1883, Gin Gin School of Arts was typical of the Type I buildings, as indicated in the photograph (Plate p. ?). It was a small weather-board building, valued at £42/10/- in 1910.[15] Basically a rectangle with a small, well protected entry porch, the building was the hub of all social activities in the very small community that existed when it was first established. In fact, in 1910 only 20 local residents were members.[16]

Popularity can be gauged from the endowments received from the Government, but these are only available for the years 1910, 1921, 1930 and 1931. In 1910, private subscriptions and contributions amounted to £14/16/6, while Government aid was £10/5/9; but the library held a relatively high number of volumes - 1,307 - on its shelves.[17] That is an average of 65 volumes for each member, which compares with a state average for schools of arts of 21 volumes in 1910.[18] By 1921, the state subsidy had risen to £31/15/4,[19] only to fall in 1930 to £24/3/5,[20] and when the Government reduced its total grant, Gin Gin received a mere £3/0/4.[21]

As with many other similar institutions, television has been cited as the main cause for loss of popularity, which, until that time, had apparently been very high for such a small community. With assistance from the Association's book-lending scheme, the School of Arts struggled on for a few years until, on the motion of the Chairman, the library and contents were handed over to the Kolan Shire Council in the late 1950s, to be administered as a free public library, with the building itself being demolished.

TYPE II BUILDINGS

Boonah

Boonah is nestled in the Fassifern Valley, where agriculture is the main industry. It is a picturesque area of intense farming which at one time was dense scrub and wilderness. Following initial settlement, the district prospered and as in so many other parts of Queensland, if not Australia, the School of Arts "stood out prominently as a barometric indication of the unchecked rise and progress of that flourishing township."[22]

In 1982, the Boonah School of Arts was one of the select few still operating under its original name in Queensland. *The Directory of State and Public Library Services in Queensland, 1980*, published by the Library Board of Queensland, listed the others as Ayr, Buderim, Clayfield, Goondiwindi, Home Hill, Howard, Julatten, Mackay, Meandarra, Morningside, Tansey, and Yangan. It was also distinctive because it controlled and operated its own cinema. The Teviot, as it was known, had to battle with growing competition from radio and television, but was still operating at a marginal profit.

The progress of the Boonah School of Arts followed the general trend of other such institutions in Queensland. It is not certain, but all available information points to the fact that the idea emanated from the Dugandan Draught and Chess Club. The formation of the latter is dated 29 February 1888, according to the first minute book, which also refers to a suggestion by Messrs L Blumberg and Thos Griffiths at a committee meeting on 27 April concerning the building of a School of Arts. A subsequent meeting on 9 May 1888 decided to call a public meeting to consider the proposal.

No records are extant for the following six years. However, a grant of land was made by proclamation in 1889, being Reserve No. 263, Allotment 1 of Section 3, Town of Dugandan proclaimed in *Government Gazette* 1889.1.1306.[23] The area of land was 1,846 square metres, and its acquisition made way for the erection of a building to house the institution.

The photograph (Plate p. ?) is purported to be that of the earliest structure. On the reverse of the original photograph is the information that it was built in 1890 at a cost of £103/17/-, and measured 7.2m x 4.57m (25' x 15'). As a style, it would fall into the Type I Class, being a small room displaying minimum decoration. A small entry porch at the left of the picture is reminiscent of many of its type, and even some of the larger Type II buildings. It is, however, one of the few known to have been sheeted internally, leaving studs and bracing exposed. As recently as 1982 it still survived in Boonah (no longer the property of the School of Arts) but as is the case with so many others, had been clad externally.

Additions and alterations were made from time to time in keeping with the town as it progressed. By 1910, the value had increased so that the Queensland *Social Statistics* for that year listed the value of the building at £350 and the library contents at £125, being for 888 volumes which catered for 98 subscribers.[24]

The Boonah School of Arts Land Mortgage Act of 1911 was assented to on December 14, 1911, in order to

> Enable the Trustees of a certain Parcel of Land in the Town of Dugandan used for the Purpose of Boonah School of Arts, to Mortgage the Land, together with the Buildings erected thereon, and to Devote the Moneys raised to the Enlargement and Improvement of the School of Arts Buildings and the Furnishing and Equipment thereof.[25]

The Act enabled the four Trustees to obtain a mortgage, the total sum not to exceed £800. It was perhaps fortunate that the district boasted a Parliamentary representative like Mr A Weinholt, described as "self-sacrificing" and as one who would "devote the whole of the emoluments of his office to the funds of that institution."[26]   Mr Weinholt had been instrumental in getting the enabling bill through Parliament.

Plate p. ? illustrates the material result of the Act. Opening of the new building proceeded with as much fanfare as was witnessed in connection with the much larger and more prominent North Brisbane School of Arts. To celebrate the occasion, the committee promoted a fair, which extended over two days. Maximum revenue was anticipated for a minimum outlay, one of the amusements being a sports program. During the evening, a fancy-dress ball was held in the new hall, with a grand concert the following day. For subsequent information, the source of reference is the *Queensland Times*.

No background is provided on money-raising ventures undertaken before the official opening. The Hon W H Barnes, Treasurer of Queensland, opened the building on 31 January, at which time he expressed the hope "that in a very few years, the institution would be free of debt."[27] Together with the provisions of the Act, those words support the conjecture that a loan was actually raised to secure the necessary finance.

The local populace felt great pride in their new building, which was described as "commodious and pretentious, the exterior presenting an appearance in keeping with the best of the extensive business premises which have been erected in recent years."[28]

The cost of the building was quoted as being between £1,200 and £1,300, providing seating for some 800 to 1,000 persons. This structure easily falls into the Type II category as dimensions were in the order of 21.3m x 12.4m (70' x 41'). Several internal rooms were contained at the rear, while a 3.6m (12') wide verandah ran the full length on the Southern side, providing access to the hall through three doors. Decoration was kept to a minimum, being little more than a plain, shaped parapet, not uncommon for the period. Roof ventilators provided in the original building have since been removed, the reason for which is unknown, although during subsequent re-roofing, they were perhaps felt to be unnecessary.

Comparing the photograph taken on opening day with that taken in 1980 reveals a low-profile deep fascia that can be seen in the left of the latter photograph beside the Teviot Theatre. It belongs to the modern-day library, erected as a joint project with the Boonah Shire Council, and completed on 30 September 1973. A small plaque attached to the library wall credits James Birrell and Partners as architects. At the rear of the library is a small hall, the first function held there being a wedding reception.

Credit must go to successive committees, for it is obvious that the building has been well maintained, and seems capable of serving its purpose for many years to come.

Mount Morgan

Founded formally on 11 September 1891, the Mount Morgan School of Arts was twice burned to the ground, a fate that was experienced by several other mechanics' institutes and schools of arts throughout Australia[29]: establishment of these institutions was difficult enough without the disruptions of fire which completely destroyed the work done.

Because of the fires, all records held were destroyed, resulting in a lack of knowledge concerning the early history of the buildings and of the people involved. It is known that the original building was erected prior to 1891, probably on land purchased or donated for the purpose. In 1889, Gilbert Parker visited Mount Morgan, which he described as "one of the quietest places I have ever visited."[30] No description of the building is forthcoming, but he does indicate that Mount Morgan was progressing, as he reported:

> ...many evidences of thriving and sturdy life. Churches were springing up in three places, a fine School of Arts was in full swing and the public school gave token of such a settled life as rarely comes so soon to a mining centre.[31]

The date of the first fire is not recorded, but it is reasonable to assume that it was before 1895, since it was in that year that land was proclaimed as a School of Arts reserve, being Reserve No. 21, Parish of Calliungal, proclaimed in *Government Gazette* 1895.1.1168.[32] (see Townplan of Gooroolba showing School of Arts reserve - Eds.)

This second school of arts would be the same building which was valued at approximately £250 in 1910.[33] At the time, subscribers numbered 240, while the value of library contents was £353, representing 3,612 volumes.[34] Whereas Government aid was £93/9/- for 1910, in 1920 it had dropped to £86/12/9, suggesting that the School or Arts had reached its peak and may actually have been in decline when the fire of 1923 wiped it out.[35]

Information on the second structure is also sparse. It was erected some time after the first was destroyed, but in this case, the date of its destruction by fire is known to be 25 April 1923. A publication produced by the Mount Morgan Historical Society provides much of the information concerning events subsequent to the fire.

Speedy action was taken following the loss of the second building. Next day, 26 April 1923, a special meeting of the committee decided to approach the Government for a loan and to canvass the public for subscriptions. Time would be required to raise the funds and erect a new home, but the public was not to be inconvenienced to a great degree. The committee rented St. Mary's institute hall for 15/- per week for the purpose of continuing the library service.

Gold mining at Mount Morgan must have been a profitable business, as the manager of the company, Mr A A Boyd, "...arranged to have £500 worth of books imported from London for the library."[36] He also offered to have his company draw plans for a new building, free of charge.

True to his word, Mr Boyd presented the plans for tender, two of which were received, being for £5,091 and £5,088 respectively.[37] As collusion is unlikely, it is fair to infer that the plans and specifications were quite detailed, conferring all the more credit on the mining company for the support it gave. Naturally, the cost was beyond available resources, and the building was eventually erected by R A Ames and W Butcher who were appointed on a day-labour basis. The final cost was paid for mainly by a loan of £3,000 granted by the Treasury.[38] The library and reading room were opened to the public on 24 April 1924, one year after the fire. A Grand Ball was held on the occasion of the official opening on 20 August of the same year.

Though repayments to the Treasury were only £188/5/- per annum, the committees still found it impossible to meet the repayment schedule, due to the effects of "industrial strife and an underground fire [which] forced closure of the mine."[39] The mine remained closed until 1932, when it reopened as an open-cut mine. The effect of the closure and the Depression meant that "there was a mass migration of townspeople seeking work elsewhere,"[40] and by the late 1920s there were only 50 subscribers; in 1930 Government aid amounted to only £47/14/6.[41] After the Depression, however, the School enjoyed a new lease of life. New books enticed a large number to enrol, and subscriptions grew to a high of 400. Within a short time the outstanding debt of £1,135 owing to the Treasury was repaid. Television and the advent of book exchanges are blamed for the steady decline in patronage, which by 1969 had fallen to about 100 subscribers. In 1976, the Mt Morgan Shire Council took over the administration of the School, with the consent of the Committee and Trustees.

At the original time of writing this chapter, in 1982, the building was the largest hall in Mount Morgan, where most of the civic and social functions were conducted. A photograph of the building held by the National Trust, Queensland Division, indicates the proportions of the structure. Due to its high position in Morgan Street, it is one of the major landmarks of the town. It is a timber building and one of the largest schools of arts erected in Queensland. A large stage, designed by Alan Wilkie, a Shakespearian actor of the 1920s, is housed at the rear under an elevated section of the gabled roof. Roof ventilators are prominent along the ridge, and together with the fenestrations along the side, provide for a well ventilated building. Symmetry to the street is obvious and the formal opening for light and ventilation contrasts with the interesting side elevation.

In 1968, the Rotary Club raised $6,000 to repaint the exterior and carry out other repairs, thus keeping the building in a good state of preservation. Today, it is frequently mentioned in tourist promotion literature as one of the main attractions in this interesting, but faded, mining community.

TYPE III BUILDINGS

Bundaberg

The Bundaberg School of Arts was founded in 1871 and survived for over one hundred years, before it was finally transferred to the control of the Bundaberg City Council on 1 January 1979.

The chances are that this institution had a tardy awakening, as almost nothing of its origin remains. Clauses 3 and 4 of a petition to the Legislative Assembly in 1887 refer to the then existing building as being of wooden construction, erected in 1881 and extended as demand required. The petitioners considered it no longer suitable, and not worthy of a town of Bundaberg's importance.

Apparently that was the second structure, the first being described by a later President, G H Bennett, as a "miserable weather-board barn-like structure."[42] Built in 1871, it had contained "a moderately equipped reading-room and a library composed mostly of fiction."[43]

Unlike the Boonah School of Arts, no facts exist concerning the initial steps or proposals that led to the establishment of the institution. It is known that Mr W E Curtis, one of the petitioners referred to earlier, was instrumental in forming the institute. Apart from being granted life membership in recognition of his tireless work for the institution, he was also elected President in 1885, 1898, 1903 and again in 1908.

A list of Presidents from 1878 to 1947 reveals that in those seventy years, only three men presided for two or more consecutive years. While Rules and Regulations pertaining to the School of Arts have not been sighted, it is likely that the tenure of office may have been controlled by a rule similar to that of North Brisbane in 1899, the purpose of which was evidently to limit the term of office to one year, after which the President would retire. This frequent change of presidency indicated the competition for this position that apparently existed within successive committees. In seventy years, the institution's constituents elected forty-six different men to the honoured position of President. Such competition suggests that the coveted title carried with it substantial prestige in the community.

If such a situation did exist, as it almost certainly did, it may reasonably be assumed that the School of Arts not only survived, but prospered. Bundaberg itself progressed quickly from a small agricultural community, and as is evidenced today, the rising affluence was reflected in the enlarged ideas of architecture which prevailed. Thus the wooden sheds that had earlier served were deemed unworthy of a respected institution such as a school of arts. Although successive committees recognised the deficiencies and limitations of their ward, to erect a satisfactory edifice required more funds than could be raised through standard procedures, such as fundraising bazaars and appeals for public subscription to a building fund.

As it was inconceivable that the School of Arts could ever make full use of the total area of its reserve (approximately 3,000 square metres), and as, in any case, the building itself was inadequate to requirements, an Enabling Act was petitioned for which would sanction the committee's proposal to divest itself of the unwanted portion, and use the money thus raised to build a substantial institute building. The consequence of the petition was *The Bundaberg School of Arts Land Sale Act* of 1887.

No sooner had the desired Act been Gazetted than a portion of land was sold for £3,400. Competitive designs were immediately invited, the successful architect being a Mr Hettrich. Tenders were called on his drawings, with a bid of £3,150 by a Mr Calvert being accepted. Work was commenced on 2 June 1888, and the Trustees took possession on 16 April 1889. Satisfaction was obvious, as the builder was praised for the manner in which he completed the contract. Upon the opening of the building to the public, the President, Mr G H Bennett, expressed his delight by commending it as a "building of which, as a School of Arts, any city or town in the colony would be proud."[44]

As is often the case, drawings of the original building are not in existence today. However, the Bundaberg City Council possesses plans of the building in its present state, while J Walker described the internal spaces. Accordingly, this description, together with the existing plan, provides a basis for the illustration appearing in these pages.

Several suites of offices occupied the ground floor, intended to supply a permanent annual income. The result of that venture cannot be ascertained, but the idea is similar to that used in the case of North Brisbane, which, twenty years before, had failed so miserably due to depressed circumstances. No record of tenants is available, so it can only be wondered what effect the depression of the 1890s had on these office suites in Bundaberg.

Sir Thomas McIlwraith appears in the list of life members. His exact connection with the institution is not known, but one reason for the honour bestowed upon him can reasonably be surmised. In 1880, the then Mr McIlwraith forwarded a collection of books to the School of Arts from London at a personal cost of £100. The donation consisted of three cases of English classics, a great boost to the embryonic library. These were supplemented by 1,400 volumes purchased by the Book Committee and placed on the shelves on taking possession of the new premises.

It remained the only library in Bundaberg until the 1970s, when the council conducted a feasibility study with a view to establishing a free public library. The press report of the study upset the members of the Bundaberg Historical Society Committee. Cr H J Strathdee, President of the Society, saw the object of the council as being "to get a new library as cheaply as possible, regardless of the destruction of this piece of early Bundaberg architecture."

The *Bundaberg News Mail* report (2 February 1972) of the Historical Society meeting during which this claim was made is not altogether accurate, as it also claimed that the building had been financed originally by public subscription, which, as has been shown, is incorrect: the means actually employed to raise the money was a loan.

As a result of the efforts of Bundaberg's Historical Society, the building has been retained. On 1 January 1979 the Trustees for the School of Arts transferred the land, building and assets to the City Council. In doing so, they endowed the Council with "land valued at $100,000, a building worth about $200,000 and $40,000 worth of books."[45]

While retention of the building itself is commendable, the methods of advertising its occupants at the time of writing left a lot to be desired. Billboards sitting on the footpath and peering out of windows clearly detracted from the building. The architecture would be described as Australian Victorian and, although originally a free-standing structure, it now nestles into a continuous, interesting streetscape. Attractive details require sensitive treatment if they are not to be completely overpowered. Careful decoration, together with considerate design and placement of signs, would restore the building's outward appearance to an acceptable standard.

Maryborough[46]

The first successful attempt to settle in what was to become Maryborough was in 1848. During the 1850s cotton and sawmilling were the major industries, and the Wide Bay Cotton Association was formed in 1859. In the same year Maryborough became an important Port of Entry to the colony of Queensland. Sugar became a major product during the 1860s, while in 1861 Maryborough was declared a Municipality.

Agitation for a School of Arts began in Maryborough some time during 1860. Support must have been significant, as by late 1861 the first building, a small brick structure, was complete. The Queensland *Social Statistics* for 1910 puts the date of foundation as October 1861, making it the fourth School of Arts in the Colony of Queensland, and the second to be established following separation from New South Wales.

The photograph presents the original building as a fine example of early Maryborough architecture. It is by no means Queensland in conception, being somewhat reminiscent of an English cottage. Planning, though, does appear to have been similar to many of the Type I institutions. Steps up from the footpath led to a small hall, through which access was gained to a compact library and reading room. Unusual is the fireplace, the chimney of which is visible at the rear of the building.

Decoration is limited. Shingles cover the gable roof which is terminated by a shaped barge board. The weather mould over the windows and doorway is repeated in the gable end, capping what appears to be the name of the institution. These features produce a continuity of design.

Gympie's gold rush boosted the city for some time. After James Nash's discovery of gold in 1867, money drifted north for provisions, timber and clothing. Together with the demands of the rural industry, Maryborough became a major manufacturer of heavy machinery. These influences decided Maryborough's fate. As it happened, the city thrived and, as with Bundaberg, some imposing structures were built, among them the second School of Arts. That building still survives today, being occupied by the Maryborough Historical Society. The photograph of this second building, taken in 1924, shows what was "regarded as one of the finest and most up-to-date institutions of its class in the Commonwealth."[47]

The original building was erected on land described as Reserve No. 132 (as a grant to elected Trustees), being Allotment 4 of Section 85, Town of Maryborough.[48] Two later bills enacted by Parliament in 1879 and 1884 respectively sanctioned the wishes of the Trustees to sell part or all of the land in order to secure funds - for additions in the first instance, and for rebuilding in the second. It seems certain that the land and buildings were actually disposed of and a new Hall was erected on a more convenient site. Today it stands in Kent Street, opposite the Town Hall.

During an inspection of the building prior to National Trust ratification on 29 October 1979, I Sinnamon described it as "an imposing two storey Classical Revival Structure."[49] Built in 1887, it is of brick construction, being two storeys with cement render finish. To determine the size, reference was made to the Queensland School of Arts Association annual reports. In 1947, the School of Arts had "made application to the Board [the Library Board of Queensland] for £2,000 for the erection of an addition 80 ft. x 36 ft. which would given them a building 135 ft. x 36 ft. on one floor for the library."[50] In 1910, the value of the building had been estimated at £3,821/18/4.[51]

Notable features, as depicted in the photograph (Plate), are the circular windows at ground floor level and semi-circular arched windows at the first floor. Corinthian capitals on pilaster shafts support a simple entablature. Below the architrave and between the pilasters appear some basic mouldings. There is a central arched entrance at ground level "whose keystone features a sculptured and painted head of the goddess Minerva."[52] This was an excellent choice, as Minerva was the Roman goddess of wisdom and originally also of handicrafts.

263

In Greek mythology, she was referred to as Athéne, who gave her name to the Athenaeum, a title by which a number of institutes throughout Australia were also known.

CONCLUSION

There are two methods of assessment available to judge the success, or otherwise, of Queensland's schools of arts. The first concerns the original objects of the institutions; the second is to consider community support, numbers established and the duration of their survival.

With respect to the original objectives of the schools of arts, the rules of the Brisbane institution cited the objects as being "the establishment of a Library and Reading Room for the use of its members, and the advancement of the community in literary, philosophic, and scientific subjects."[53] Quite clearly, that rule was not structured to cater for the working-classes.

At the foundation of the Brisbane institution in 1849, many members of the working-class could not read or write. Philosophy was well outside their realm of understanding and interest, while science frequently had little to do with the elevation of their standard of work, even if they had been able to comprehend the matters placed before them. The result was that members came mainly from the middle-class; those that were interested in the range of subjects available. Such people could identify more easily with the espoused aims of the School of Arts.[54]

Over time, illiteracy became less of a problem, but works of an uplifting nature and volumes on general and technical knowledge tended to take second place to fiction. As such, the provision of libraries and reading rooms did fulfil a useful, if less lofty, function than that originally intended.

Before the turn of the century, the objects were altered to included "the recreation and entertainment of its members by games of skill, and generally the diffusion of knowledge and the promotion of intellectual amusement." Even these aims, however, did not fulfil the requirements of the working-class. It was not until the introduction of technical education in the cities that working people were properly catered for. There they could learn their trade from professional tutors or add to their previously acquired knowledge.

With respect to the actual achievements of the movement, it appears that approximately 350 such institutions were founded in Queensland alone, some in the most remote parts of the State (for example Thursday Island and Longreach). Without exception, persons with a sense of responsibility for the welfare and advancement of the community were involved in the establishment of those institutions. Indeed, the major reward was the satisfaction of knowing that fellow men and women were provided with an outlet to help overcome boredom and to provide harmless - if not always instructive - amusement.

Although the major role was officially the provision of a library, many buildings became the home of community and social gatherings. In country areas, those halls associated with the library were often the largest structures available for social events. It would appear that, in many cases, the library was incidental to, and a by-product of, the erection of a community

Mt Morgan School of Arts, Qld, 1992

Bundaberg School of Arts, Qld

Gin Gin School of Arts, Qld

Original Maryborough School of Arts, Qld, ca 1861

Official Opening of Boonah School of Arts, Qld, ca 1912

hall. Whatever the priorities may have been, the whole community gained by their establishment.

What survives today are, primarily, basic halls. Often disguised under altered nomenclature, schools of arts have largely been forgotten, their roles taken over by a range of other organisations. But the halls and institutes that remain - whether austere or ostentatious, whether shabby or lovingly maintained, and whatever their present use - provide a tangible link with the past, and a constant reminder of the sense of community and spirit of self-help that characterised our forebears.

NOTES AND REFERENCES

1.Wesson, A. (1971). Mechanics' institutes in Victoria. *Victorian Historical Magazine, 42*(3), p.614.

2.*ibid.*

3.*Wesson, op. cit.,* p.615.

4.*ibid.*

5.Wesson, *op. cit.,* p.614.

6.*Queensland Parliamentary Papers (Q.P.P.),* 1911-12, Vol. I, pp.1305-1306.

7.Eriksson, J. (1978). History of the Tamborine Mountain Library, 1925-1978. *Unpublished research project.* Adelaide, SA: School of Library Studies, University of Adelaide, p.8.

8.Eriksson, *op. cit.,* p.4.

9.Eriksson, *op. cit.,* Appendix p.4.

10.*ibid.*

11.Eriksson, *op. cit.,* p.12.

12.*Q.P.P.,* 1931, p.327.

13.*Q.P.P.,* 1930, p.316.

14.Eriksson, *op. cit.,* p.11.

15.*Q.P.P.,* 1911-12, Vol.1, p.1305.

16.*ibid.*

17.*Q.P.P., op. cit.,* pp.1305 and 1307.

18.*Q.P.P., op. cit.,* 8L.

19. *Q.P.P.*, 1921, p.306.

20. *Q.P.P.*, 1930, p.316.

21. *Q.P.P.*, 1931, p.327.

22. *Queensland Times*, 1 February 1913.

23. Archives, File A/16157.

24. *Q.P.P.*, 1911-12, pp.1305-1309.

25. *Public Acts of Qld.*, pp.5253-5255.

26. *Queensland Times*, 1 February 1913.

27. *ibid.*

28. *ibid.*

29. Ashworth, D.W. (1988). *The Walhalla Mechanics' Institute and Free Library, 1865-1988: From the ashes third time lucky*. Walhalla, Vic: The Walhalla Mechanics' Institute.

30. Parker, G. (1892). *Round the compass in Australia*. London: Hutchinson & Co., p.312.

31. *ibid.*, p.313.

32. Archives, File A/16157.

33. *Q.P.P.*, 1911-12, Vol. 1, p.1306.

34. *Q.P.P.*, *op. cit.*, p.1308.

35. *Q.P.P.*, 1921, p.306.

36. Mount Morgan Historical Society. In National Trust, File - Mount Morgan.

37. *ibid.*

38. *ibid.*

39. Chardon, N.F. (1982). The Mount Morgan School of Arts. In Chardon, N.F., & Golding, F.L. (Eds.), *Centenary of the Town of Mt. Morgan, 1882-1982*. Mt. Morgan: District Historical Society, p.47.

40. *ibid.*

41. *Q.P.P.*, 1930, p.316.

42. quoted in Walker, J. Y. (1890). *The history of Bundaberg: A typical Queensland agricultural settlement*. Bundaberg: Aitken, p.203.

43.*ibid.* p.202

44.*ibid.,* p.204.

45.*The Telegraph*, 11 November 1978.

46.Since this chapter was written, an exhaustive and extensively illustrated history of the Maryborough School of Arts has been prepared as part of a conservation study for the City of Maryborough: Riddel, R., & Hill, S. (1992). *Maryborough School of Arts conservation plan.* Brisbane: Robert Riddel Architect.

47.Lennon, J. (comp). (1924). *Maryborough and district, Queensland, 1842-1924.* Maryborough: Alston & Co., p.31.

48.Archives, File A/16157.

49.National Trust File - Maryborough School of Arts.

50.John Oxley Library, File OM71-25.

51.*Q.P.P.*, 1911-12, Vol. 1, p.1306.

52.National Trust Files - Maryborough School of Arts, *op. cit.*

53.Brisbane School of Arts (1849). *Rules and By-laws of the Brisbane School of Arts.*

54.see Cleary, J.T. (1967). North Brisbane School of Arts, 1849-1899. *Unpublished BA(Hons) thesis.* University of Queensland.

CHAPTER THIRTEEN

GROWTH AND DECLINE OF THE QUEENSLAND SCHOOLS OF ARTS, 1849 - 1981

Carole Inkster

INTRODUCTION

This chapter is a study of the interacting forces which led to the development, maintenance and decline of schools of arts in Queensland. Each Australian state tended to produce an individual pattern of institutional development and Queensland is no exception. The major forces which predominated throughout the colony and later the state were social and demographic patterns, environmental conditions, economic trends and colonial and state Government policies. The exact degree to which each modified the Queensland process is treated only by inference in this account, it being impossible to deal adequately with all the many factors involved. It is clear, however, that some were of greater import than others, when compared with developments in other colonies or states at the same time.

Initially, each community established its school of arts independently, following closely the objectives laid out by Dr George Birkbeck for the mechanics' institutes in Britain. These objectives were often embodied in the respective schools of arts rules; however, for many, this printed version was as far as Birkbeck's ideas went. The reality of community demands took precedence over the lofty ideals the rules contained, but this did not detract from the contribution that each school of arts made to its local community. For many communities, because of their isolation or size, the school of arts provided the only source of cultural contact to which they had ready access. In other instances, such as in Brisbane, the school of arts also promoted the establishment of adult and technical education as well as the expansion of library services.

During the latter part of the nineteenth century, the school of arts movement enjoyed a period of growth in keeping with national and international trends of economic expansion and educational promotion. However, by the early twentieth century, this pattern of growth had reversed in Queensland and, in order to consolidate those schools of arts still operating, the Queensland Schools of Arts Association was established in 1927. Though their decline was retarded by this central organisation, it was not halted. The principle of free public libraries was gaining momentum, and many of the other functions performed by the schools of arts either fell into disuse or else were taken over by other organisations. It is these contributions that this chapter identifies and comments on in the course of describing the evolution of the school of arts movement in Queensland.

PHASE 1.　ESTABLISHMENT

The Brisbane School of Arts was not established until 1849, and was the product of a different phase in the development of the British movement than was the case with the earlier colonial institutes. Between the 1830s and 1840s, mechanics' institutes in Britain had become, in many instances, the leisure vehicles of the middle-classes, with works of fiction rather than reference becoming the major items in demand in the libraries and with concerts and clubs utilising the facilities. Derek Whitelock notes that:

> Even in the 1830s many mechanics' institutes were obliged to depart from the severely scientific curriculum prescribed by their original rules...[and]...later in the century, that the institutes competed with places of amusement and light entertainment.[1]

Further to this, in Australia in the 1830s, sales of land had begun, the proceeds of which were supposedly to be channelled back into the immigration schemes, either to assist passages or to subsidise other land subdivisions. As Blainey has stated, "the problem of attracting working people to Australia was crucial,"[2] and it was easier and cheaper to offer passage to the already deprived Irish, who would fit the bill as workers, than to encourage others to emigrate. Thus in the early years of Queensland, there were increasing concentrations of Irish Roman Catholics being absorbed by the colony.

The Rev. Dr J Dunmore Lang, in his self-appointed task of trying to redress the imbalance that the influx of Roman Catholics was claimed to be causing in the population, selected over 600 Scottish protestants to immigrate to Brisbane in the year 1849. He insisted that it was properly the duty of the colonial legislature to expend a good part of the land revenue on the promotion of immigration. According to him, the failure to do so represented "a gross act of injustice and [was] perpetrating a grievous wrong upon the people of England."[3] The revenue from land sales should have been used to attract "a large emigration of reputable and desirable emigrants"[4] (the Irish being excluded) Dr Lang contended, and he considered the Scottish mechanics to be just such a group. His views are now variously described in the literature as 'conservative,' 'respectably bourgeois,' 'radical' or 'sectarian.'

With this concentrated influx of Scottish immigrants into Brisbane, the town's population nearly doubled. Lang's immigrants also gave rise to a pronounced unevenness in the distribution of people of Irish and Scottish descent throughout colonial society, the Irish settlers being absorbed mainly in New South Wales and Victoria. The effect of this on the life of schools of arts in different states was clear. Those in New South Wales were, by that time, not catering for the less educated Irish workers and accordingly were not attracting a growing proportion of the population, whilst those of Queensland very ably met the needs of their Scottish founders. The colonial population may have had common origins in the British Isles and a common use of the English language, but it is generally held, as stated by Ward in *The Australian Legend*, that "the Irish convicts and immigrants became unskilled labourers in Australia while a very high proportion of Scotchmen, even those who landed with little or no capital, became rich or at least successful."[5]

The Scottish succeeded for a number of reasons: the relatively few Scottish convicts transported, the usually middle class affiliations of the Scots (which corresponded well with the state of the schools of arts in the 1850s, when mass migration to Queensland was under way), the much higher average standard of education of the Scottish over both the English and Irish, and the Protestant ethic of 'work rewarded by success.' This latter reason is echoed in the words of a welcoming poem to the 'Fortitude' pioneers (Lang's immigrants):

Here, far from poverty and factious broil,
Plenty and peace repay the labourer's toil:-
He reaps himself the harvest of his hands,
Industrious care, well paid, by wide spread lands.[6]

Against this background, the (North) Brisbane School of Arts was established, which heralded the Queensland movement. As Cleary demonstrated in his study of that institute,[7] it had the backing of a largely middle-class, well-educated, Protestant community, a trend which was to be replicated throughout the State. In fact, such middle-class domination became a public issue in Bundaberg in 1876. The editor of the then newly-established *Bundaberg and Mount Perry Mail* accused the town of local cliquism, and the School of Arts committee, in particular, of being "conceited, self-important, incapable and self-elected."[8]

The controversy that ensued revealed a situation common in many Queensland settlements at that time: that the members of the school of arts committee were frequently elected to every office that wanted filling in the town. As one commentator observed:

> It is not surprising that a small new community struggling against many difficulties ...should find a difficulty in obtaining the services of even six or seven of their number capable of even decently managing the affairs of a literary institution... nor [is it surprising] that in such circumstances they should frequently be found filling the same offices from year to year.[9]

The subscribers to the schools of arts in Queensland were trying to preserve the literature and lifestyle they had known before emigrating. One example of this was the totally unsuitable, cold climate attire that they retained, even in the Queensland tropics. Less obviously, but no less significantly, is the emotional link that the schools of arts provided with the homeland of most of the immigrants. Their patronage, however, was simultaneously establishing the divergence that become evident in the growth of the institutes throughout the colony, a patronage that was to determine the unique direction, extent and continuation of their development in each colony.

PHASE 2.   PERIOD OF GROWTH

The next phase in the spread of schools of arts in Queensland, their period of growth, was the direct result of the gold discoveries and the consequent increase in population. In the increasing numbers of gold prospectors, the most influential factor for the schools of arts was the influx of large numbers of middle-class immigrants. Ward asserts that:

> There can be little doubt that the average standard of educational attainment was much higher among the newcomers than it had been among the pastoral workers prior to the discoveries... [L]arge numbers of educated and professional men [were] among the motley crowds that swarmed to the diggings, and it was only after the Gold Rush that observers began to remark on the high standard of outback literacy.[10]

The higher educational standards of these people obviated the need for the type of intellectual and moral "elevation" that had initially been the objective of the institutes. Instead, there was a greater need for the establishment of recreational facilities that would provide both enjoyment and amusement. While these attitudes had already been important at the establishment of many Queensland institutes, there was certainly an added need for such amenities with the onset of the gold rush. Lectures were often abandoned, whilst the library function increased, providing the users both with a wider selection of fiction and, through subscription to the major periodicals and papers of the time, with much sought-after news from the other Australian colonies and from overseas. Nadel, in *Australia's Colonial Culture*, expressed this change in priorities when he stated: "the amusement function first challenged and finally ignored the loftier aims still printed in the rules."[11]

The adaptation of the institutes to becoming the social and cultural centres of outback communities, whilst distorting the original aims, nevertheless played an important role in those communities, one which has perhaps been ignored or denigrated. For instance, in Mackay, the School of Arts "soon came into being as the cultural centre of the community,"[12] and in Bundaberg, "almost from the first, Protestant groups conducted united services...in the School of Arts building, the town's only public hall for some years."[13] And though it was initially a "miserable, weather-boarded, barn-like structure,"[14] it served as "the only meeting place for some for a variety of purposes."[15] In Ravenswood, "the erection of the School of Arts Hall and Library fulfilled a vital role in the social, cultural and recreational activities";[16] and in Brisbane, "from 1849-1879 the North Brisbane School of Arts was the focal institution for the ideas and aspirations of English and Scottish migrants."[17]

The recreational function, whilst perhaps having little in common with Dr Birkbeck's original objectives in Britain, did promote the use of the institutes by a wider spectrum of the population. In doing so, it not only brought in subscription fees but also advanced the consolidation of the community.

Throughout the nineteenth century, the constant influx of immigrants, with their equally constant desire to retain homeland literary and leisure heritages, contributed to the school of arts movement wherever these people settled. The great surge of immigrants to the goldfields merely accentuated this process. As a result, the 1870s and 1880s were the most expansive periods of growth for schools of arts. In Queensland this growth was encouraged by Government legislation and policy in a number of ways.

Soon after separation from New South Wales in 1859, the Queensland Government passed an Act which provided a bonus of thirty acres of land to every adult person paying his own passage out. Lang records the results of such a move by comparing the relative population growth of Queensland and New South Wales. He noted that,

> at the period of its separation the population of Queensland was 25,146; but through the land system and, no doubt, the attraction of gold...the population of the colony had more than quadrupled itself before the close of the first decade of its existence, for in December 1869 it amounted to 107,000.[18]

In New South Wales, however, the increase in population from immigration for the same period was only 34,817, about a tenth part of the population at the beginning of the same decennial period.

A second factor which influenced the growth of schools of arts was *Local Government Act No. 8* of 1878, which gave local authorities the power to establish local libraries and to charge fees for their use.[19] This effectively laid the burden of providing such facilities on each individual locality, though aid of sorts was given in many cases, with a crown land allotment being set aside for the school of arts in the initial surveying of proposed settlements. Prior to this, in 1875, the question of establishing free libraries throughout the colony along the lines of the *New South Wales Municipalities Act No. 12* of 1867 (which transferred schools of arts to local council administration and provided a Parliamentary subsidy for their conduct) was considered, but it was felt by the Colonial Treasurer to be "his duty to oppose motions of this kind." He went on to observe that "...of course there were a great many things they would like to have but they could not afford to have everything..."[20]

Grants were, however, made to building funds for schools of arts when the grant was matched by local fund-raising. The Government members of the time felt, as J P Bell (MLA Dalby) expressed it in 1877, that "there was no better way of expending money than by voting it for Schools of Arts...[and that]...these institutions and Savings Banks were the two most useful institutions for the working portion of the Community."[21]

This could of course have been political 'sweet talk,' since Bell was at the time applying for improvement funds for the Dalby School of Arts. Two years later, in 1879, the reverse opinion was expressed by the Colonial Secretary when he stated that, "in his experience, Schools of Arts were meant for small cliques in towns and nobody else derived any benefit from them.[22]

This statement seems equally as sweeping as Bell's, and such accusations had been defended and refuted in Bundaberg, as has been mentioned. The Colonial Secretary was also denying the wide support that schools of arts enjoyed and the benefits they provided, especially in the mining towns; and though this support turned out to be mostly transitory, such statements appear unnecessarily harsh. It was more than likely a product of the Colonial Secretary's obligation to protect the Government purse.

Like so many facets of colonial life, the institutes were particularly susceptible to economic trends, and the boom of the 1870s and 1880s was reflected in the rapid growth of schools of arts throughout Queensland and elsewhere in Australia. It was at this time, however, that Government subsidies for them were severely cut in Queensland, the demand for expenditure in other areas (e.g., railways, telegraph services, roads, shipping facilities, etc.) being much greater than the available funds could satisfy The effects of this expenditure were clearly felt by even the most well-established institute libraries. For instance, the Brisbane School of Arts, at its quarterly meeting in April 1880, announced that "since the beginning of the year the institution has not been paying its way; [and] that the expenditure has exceeded the income at the rate of fully £1 per week."[23]

Its membership at that time, however, was increased by 12 from the previous quarter to 653, so the community was, in part, helping to allay these effects. By the 1890s, the economic downturn had compounded an already difficult situation, and many schools of arts were forced to close because of financial problems.

An indication of the reluctance of the Queensland Government to take the initiative in the development of its cultural heritage is evidenced by the comparatively late establishment of its State ('Public') library, fully forty years after its counterpart in Melbourne was opened, and even ten years after that of Western Australia. As Balnaves and Biskup have remarked: "it was not only the latest, but also the least adequately supported of the State Libraries...it did not begin any significant development until 1943."[24] Indeed, in 1878, the Government's attitude was summed up by J Macfarlane (MLA Rockhampton) when he said that "he hoped the day was not distant when towns would not come to the Government cap-in-hand for grants for their schools of arts and public gardens."[25] From the late nineteenth century there was a growing trend for schools of arts to be taken over by local government authorities, but at that time only when financial difficulties demanded such a transfer of responsibility. Such was the case with the Ipswich School of Arts, one of the first to be managed by a local council, with the authority to do so under the *Municipal Institution Act* of 1864.

Whereas the decline of schools of arts in other States - especially in Victoria, New South Wales and Tasmania - accelerated into the twentieth century, those in Queensland remained relatively stable. In 1908, there were 181 schools of arts in the state and, though this figure inevitably fluctuated, there was not the massive reduction that some of the other states experienced. A number of factors were at work to maintain this situation, most importantly the lack of Free Library legislation, although such legislation in South Australia (in 1898) appeared to be ineffectual. Another factor was the lack of a centralised organisation or country lending service from a central government-funded library. Even where the country lending service existed only as the 'box of books' system, if it emanated from government controlled sources or a central public library the next step was usually the development of a public library system. Country services were established in Victoria in 1860, in New South Wales in 1883 and in Western Australia in 1903, and all three States continued to build their public library systems on these small beginnings. Perhaps for Queensland, the most important factor was the sheer size of the State. Whilst Western Australia may have been greater in area, its population was more concentrated; but when the area and spread of population of Queensland is paralleled with that of South Australia (where institute libraries were also maintained well into the twentieth century), the magnitude of the distances involved might be seen to have encouraged the school of arts movement. In these States, regional public library services would have been that much more difficult to maintain. As Metcalfe has written: "It is the right and certainly the most amicable conclusion that each pursued a line of its own, best suited to its own conditions."[26]

Metcalfe goes on to comment that the concentration of populations in a few capital and coastal cities meant that the development of city library systems outside the capitals was not feasible because there were no sizeable cities, and also, "even if these towns [i.e., those outside the capital] could maintain adequate libraries, the presence of an institute...has presented a good enough excuse for inaction."[27] And when that institute was successful in providing for the needs of the community, a replacement was neither a practical nor a credible suggestion.

A concession to a city system was proposed by the Minister of the Queensland Department of Public Instruction in 1908, when it was suggested that "the School of Arts Library in each area should be approached to hold and issue library books for all school children in the area."[28]

The obvious advantages in such a plan for a combined school/community library service can be seen in the rationalisation of both acquisitions and services. Rejection of the proposal at the time, despite the Department's offer of an annual endowment for each participating institute, was mainly because the institute libraries were already preoccupied with the problems of providing a service to a particular portion of the community that taxed both the voluntary labour and the available accommodation. The idea was also rejected because it was seen that the Department of Public Instruction viewed this as a cheap way out of building new school libraries at a time when only a few schools had libraries which were regarded as satisfactory. The suggestion was even made that this was perhaps a Departmental manoeuvre to reduce the endowments for the adult libraries, whilst the Crows Nest School of Arts added the unexpected objection that, "At State School age, a too close attention to literature might go to build up a neurotic man instead of a man having the *Mens Sana in Corpore Sana.*"[29]

PHASE 3. CENTRALISATION

A third phase in the history of Queensland schools of arts occurred in the early decades of the twentieth century when, because of rising costs of both materials and running expenses, a School of Arts Association was established in 1927 to co-ordinate as many aspects of the running of member institutes as possible from a central point. In the minutes of the first meeting of the Association, one of the advantages to be derived "by the formation of an association" was seen to be the "interchange and wholesale purchase of books."[30] To allay any suggestions that schools of arts were not properly utilising the Government subsidies then being paid to them, J McKenna (Director of Education) stated, at the First Annual Conference of the Queensland Schools of Arts Association, that this subsidy was to be devoted mainly to the purchase of literature "and very close investigation was occasionally necessary to see that the social side did not overwhelm the educational."[31] Concessions were, however, made as to the type of literature purchased. With regard to works of fiction, McKenna pointed out to the Association that, since the proportion of readers who concentrated on science was small and the majority wanted light reading, then

> if a list of about two hundred of the best novels written within the past ten years were supplied for general information...you would render signal service to country institutions, [because by doing so] you would popularise them and you would do a service in promoting the reading habit.[32]

It is indicative of the popularity of the Association's aims and services to the various member institutes that it continued to increase its membership throughout the depression of the 1930s even though Government subsidies had ceased altogether during this period. The Association constantly lobbied Parliament for the renewal of subsidies, so that by 1935 the Government was ready to acknowledge that a central library for the schools of arts would mean that many

> would get volumes which otherwise would not be available to them. It would enable them to build up a much better reference library; works of a higher educational value could be bought and forwarded to various institutions...and generally a demand would be created for a better class of literature and technical books.[33]

Whether or not this was prompted by the release of the Munn-Pitt Report on library services in January 1935 is only supposition. Certainly the School of Arts Association must have wondered whether it had done the right thing in supporting the survey that led to the Munn-Pitt Report. Earlier, the Library Association of Victoria had written to the Queensland Schools of Arts Association,

> and other libraries of this state, to cooperate with them in forwarding a joint invitation...to the Carnegie Corporation of New York to make a survey of the Australian Libraries which it is hoped would be of great advantage not only form an advisory but practical point of view.[34]

The invitation was accepted, but the practical benefits that the Queensland libraries had hoped for appear to have been gained in only a minimal sense, unless the criticism of the whole Australian system could be construed as having prompted the Government action described. The Report was scathing in its criticism of the contemporary library system of Australia when it observed that;

> Australia was better provided with local libraries in 1880 than it is today. Almost every city and large town now contains a decadent institute or School of Arts, many of which give evidence of having had a former period of real usefulness...[35]

The schools of arts in Queensland, in both large and small towns, were, however, still providing useful services; and although in Brisbane control was totally with the local Government, the schools of arts were still being utilised, giving little indication of the decay that the Munn-Pitt Report had suggested. By 1937, the Central Library of the Queensland Schools of Arts Association was in full swing. The Association was a bulk subscriber of the Brisbane School of Arts, the subscription fee being 3d. for fiction and 4d. for non-fiction per volume. It had already begun to send out boxes of twenty-five books at quarterly intervals, the ratio of fiction to other literature being four to one. Whilst from 1921 to 1930 the Government subsidy to schools of arts had averaged out at £8,767,[36] from 1931 to 1936 no subsidy was paid; and with the mere £500 subsidy paid to the Association after that year, it endeavoured to supply outback centres and other towns with books to take the place of those which had been purchased with the former subsidies. The effect of this, together with generally improved economic circumstances both state- and nation-wide, might be seen in Maryborough for example, which, in 1939, had a membership of 420 whilst two years previously the membership had been only 110.

Not only was the book supply service made available, but the Association endeavoured to answer members' queries in many other areas, such as the sale and exchange of old books, the position of trustees of institutes, insurance problems, questions relating to Government policy and regulations, and various other legal and technical queries. The bulk-buying scheme which operated effectively first required the separate school of arts committees to compile lists of favourite authors suitable for their libraries. These were then forwarded to the London agents by the Association and, when a book was published by any of the authors listed, it was sent directly to the institution. By this arrangement no time was lost after publication, and bulk-buying kept prices down. Books purchased under the scheme with a published price of 7/6d were landed at the institutes at 4/11d each, whilst the 8/6d publications were a little more costly. This was often cheaper and quicker than purchasing through an Australian wholesaler, the cost of purchases being debited against an account kept by the Department of Public Instruction for each library taking part in the scheme. Invoices from the English publisher, William Dawson and Sons Ltd., were then made out to the Department and paid from the combined trust account it administered. For these services the Association charged an annual subscription fee of just one guinea.

Books sent between the Association and institute libraries were allowed half parcel rates by rail on both forward and return journeys, but even so, the huge distances involved in meeting some requests made these costs very high. At the Association's Twelfth Annual Dinner and Conference in 1939, the representative for Esk, Mr T Chaille, said that "the freights are killing what we are trying to do... [Indeed]...in many instances the freight is more than the subscriptions."[37] He also noted that, at that stage, whilst the Queensland Government was providing a subsidy of £500 to their Association, the equivalent South Australian Association was getting £7,000.

The secretary of the Queensland Schools of Arts Association, Mr R J Linnet, in a letter to the Premier and Chief Secretary on 20 October 1939, put forward the Association's protests at the rail charges made, especially for the very distant schools of arts. In summarising their position he stated:

> Up to date the Association has purchased 3,160 books of high class literature, of which 88 percent are other than fiction, and, for the sum of 2/-, boxes of twenty-five books are selected for the respective Schools of Arts. On these boxes of books the Association pays the freight outwards and the School of Arts pays the return freight. Should the School of Arts desire a second box of books for the same three months, this is supplied at a cost of 3/- but the School of Arts must pay freight both ways as the amount at our disposal will not permit of the Association undertaking this expense... [O]n several occasions members of the Executive of the Association have waited on the Railways Department as a deputation and urged a reduction in freight charges...[38]

Such requests were consistently refused, even though it was pointed out that the Department of Public Instruction, when sending out books for State School libraries, paid only quarter rates, while the Queensland Country Women's Association was allowed to send books by rail freight-free.

At that time, the Government Statistician's Office in Brisbane calculated that there were 185 schools of arts in 1938, while the Queensland Schools of Arts Association was able to calculate 290 with the proviso that "even allowing for those that have closed there must be at least 200 operating today." Those that were closing down were doing so mainly for lack of community support, while those not renewing Association membership were often dissatisfied with book selection. Goondiwindi wrote that

> the main reason [for non renewal] is that books have to be chosen from a 1936 catalogue, books listed therein appear to us to be somewhat out of date... Many if chosen are found to be in a dilapidated state, savouring of the unhygiene. On the other hand many forwarded books comprise subjects really too weighty for the average reader.[39]

PHASE 4. DECLINE

The final phase in the school of arts movement in Queensland can be dated from the beginning of World War II. The War not only promoted a substantial growth of urban centres and regionalization of public services, but it also made demands on the time of many potential and actual subscribers for the 'war effort.' As well, a *Library Act* was passed in 1943 providing for the establishment of the Queensland Library Board which was to promote a public library movement, whilst for many ageing schools of arts there had been a general deterioration of both buildings and books.

World War II marked for Australia the "transition from its traditional role as echo and image of Britain...and the emergence of a new era when...heredity ceased to be so powerful [and] when Australians ceased to have nearly all their emotional, commercial, financial and human ties with Britain." It also marked the transition for many schools of arts from successfully operating centres to eventual closure. The *Libraries Act No. 39* of 1943, whilst allowing grants to be made to schools of arts, also exacerbated their declining situation by providing the Free Library movement as a spearhead to promote and encourage similar activities. As stated above, provision was made for the establishment of the Queensland Library Board which was to control the Public Library of Queensland and was to offer assistance to the libraries under such conditions as it saw fit. There was no limit to the subsidy that might be paid by the Board, either to existing libraries or to any local authority which decided to establish a library under the Act or to take over an existing school of arts "if it deems it desirable for the general betterment...of the inhabitants."[40]

This last clause provoked much argument and distress in those situations where the local council *demanded* to take over the school of arts against the wishes of both the committee and the members. This was the position faced by the Bowen School of Arts in 1945, when the Bowen Council passed a resolution to take over the School of Arts. The Council attempted to pressure the committee by stating, through the local newspaper, that a State Librarian would be sent to investigate the position of the institute. Had there in fact been a State Librarian at that time (there was not), he or she would have discovered that "at no time has the Institution been unfinancial. In 1934 the sum of £900 was spent on renovations and extensions to the building," and the library had 6,359 books and 120 subscribers.[41]

The uncertainty that surrounded schools of arts at that time is further seen in Bundaberg School of Arts correspondence to the Association requesting information:

> I refer to the Government's plan to subsidise the schools of arts 10/- in the £ towards the purchase of books. Could you please advise whether this applies to all schools of arts...and would acceptance of this subsidy in any way jeopardise the position as regards taking over the institution...is it meant to be the thin end of the wedge towards the objective of ultimately Government supervision of ALL schools of arts?[42]

The Association Secretary replied that, in his opinion, the scheme was drifting towards free libraries controlled by Municipal Councils and subsidised by the Government. This was indeed the Government's intention, even if initially unstated. The Secretary for Health and Home Affairs, in discussing the Wilston School of Arts in 1943, said that:

the whole position of these institutions needs looking into...since the war the position has grown much more difficult...[and]...property that has been acquired at heavy cost may fall into disrepair or be wrongfully used.[43]

The Secretary also noted that dances were not paying in the suburbs and smaller towns on account of the shortage of young men, and that consequently revenue had fallen; whilst many of those left behind were working long hours and were in patriotic movements which left them very little time for 'recreational pastimes.' Increasingly, as more and more schools of arts went unsupported and eventually became unfinancial, the pattern for either closure or takeover was set, though many others remained popular and active throughout. E B Maher (MLA West Moreton) commented during the Wilston debate:

> While there are a number of stagnant schools of arts throughout the State, I am proud to say that there are others that operate very well indeed. It gives me a feeling of pride to go through them, to see the fine books, the splendid buildings, and the care that is shown.[44]

With the passing of the *Libraries Act* it was hoped that the Government would move decisively in the matter of establishing libraries, since it was suggested that a national library scheme could not be attained by subsidising small country committees. A certain amount of ignorance was also shown about the extent of schools of arts at that time when it was suggested, by G F R Nicklin (MLA Murrumba), that "a provision for circulating libraries [be set up] and the machinery by which these people in the distant parts of the State will have the opportunity of enjoying the advantages of a Library service."[45]

It was recognised, however, that if a State-based scheme of free libraries was to be the objective, it could not be realised overnight. As a result, the Library Board continued for many years to subsidise both public libraries and schools of arts libraries. This guaranteed the continued existence of the schools of arts, such that by 1959 there were still 96 members of the Queensland Schools of Arts Association.

Dissension was growing, however, over the equality of subsidies that schools of arts shared with free public libraries. To some, the "continued government support of purveyors of cheap fiction on a commercial basis on equal terms with rate-supported public libraries is probably our greatest shame."[46]

A differential subsidy was introduced in 1968, which increased that for free public libraries by 12½ percent whilst that for schools of arts remained static. The tenor of criticism during the 1960s included many florid descriptions of the institutes, such as that in 1963 which described them as "old fashioned buildings in city streets, broken-down halls in country towns or a little shack of unpainted wood and rusty iron perched in the middle of nowhere... [In these circumstances]...one would not be straining credibility in thinking of these places as dumps for the local bottle-oh."[47]

While criticism of the schools of arts took many forms, and much was made of the free public libraries, the mere existence of a free library gave no indication of the quality of its service. This is seen in the *Twenty Third [Annual] Report of the Library Board of Queensland*, which stated that of seventy-three local authorities conducting free library services, only four employed a qualified librarian in charge and only six others employed a librarian who was partly qualified.[48] When the *Report of the Committee of Inquiry into Public Libraries in Australia* (Horton Report) was made public in 1976, it stated that the "service provided by subscription libraries...is characterised generally by lower aspirations and expertise in the service..."[49] In an Australia-wide comparison, overall the Queensland and South Australian populations were rated the most disadvantaged. The Committee had been informed by the Queensland Branch of the Library Association of Australia (Submission No. 10) that, with regard to Queensland,

> Where it exists at all, library service for those living in country areas varies from the merely inadequate to the abysmal...[and that]...visits to centres from remote areas are too irregular or expensive to allow systematic library use...[50]

The situation would appear to be largely self-inflicted, since the Library Board was effectively stifling even such meagre services as some of the remote country areas had at all. This strategy seems to have been almost totally successful for, as far as it was possible to ascertain, by 1981 there appeared to be only one remaining active School of Arts in Queensland, that of Julatten,[51] which served the parishes of Riflemond and Garioch and whose membership was approximately fifty.

CONCLUSION

Schools of arts enjoyed a prolonged existence in Queensland in the absence of any other organisations which could offer the same range of services. They managed to reach, at various times in their history, some of the most remote of the Queensland populations. During this extended period the schools of arts not only contributed useful library functions, but also vital community services where none had existed before, and it was these needs that kept them operating well into the 1970s in Queensland. Their wider contribution to State systems of both adult education and public library schemes cannot be underestimated, and though for a long time Queensland lagged behind most of the other States in the development of adequate library services, it would be even further behind had it not been for the schools of arts.

NOTES AND REFERENCES

1.Whitelock, D. (1974). *The great tradition: A history of adult education in Australia.* St Lucia: University of Queensland Press, p.26.

2.Blainey, G. (1966). *The tyranny of distance: How distance shaped Australia's history.* Melbourne: Sun Books, p.152.

3.Lang, J.D. (1875), *The fatal mistake, or How New South Wales has lost caste in the world through misgovernment in the matter of immigration.* Sydney: Maddock, pp.21-22.

4.*ibid.*, p.22.

5.Ward, J.M. (1965). *The Australian legend.* (2nd ed.). Melbourne: Oxford University Press, p.35.

6. 'Frederick'. (1849/1980). *Moreton Bay Courier* (Brisbane), 24 February 1849. In Crowley, F. (Ed.), *Colonial Australia, 1841-1874: A documentary history of Australia, Vol. 2*. West Melbourne: Nelson, pp.150-151.

7. Cleary, J.T. (1967) The North Brisbane School of Arts, 1849-1899. *Unpublished BA (Hons) thesis*, University of Queensland.

8. Walker, J.Y. (1890). *The history of Bundaberg: A typical Queensland agricultural settlement*. Bundaberg: Aiken, p.85.

9. *ibid.*

10. Ward, *op. cit.*, p.127.

11. Nadel, G. (1957). *Australia's colonial culture: Men, ideas and institutions in mid-nineteenth century eastern Australia*. Cambridge, Mass: Harvard University Press, p.127.

12. Nilsson, J. A. (1963-64). Mackay in the Nineteenth Century. *Journal of the Royal Historical Society of Queensland, 7*(2), p.366.

13. Nolan, J. (1978). *Bundaberg: History and people*. St Lucia: University of Queensland Press, p.81.

14. *ibid.*, p.82.

15. *ibid.*, p.84.

16. Hogan, J. (1978). *Building Queensland's heritage*. Brisbane: National Trust of Queensland, p.164.

17. Cleary, *op. cit.*, p.223.

18. Lang, *op. cit.*, p.28.

19. Though this Act was repealed by No. 19 of 1902 (s. 17), these same provisions were made regarding libraries.

20. *Queensland Parliamentary Debates (QPD)* Vol. XIX (1875), p.736.

21. *QPD*, Vol. XXIV (1877), p.1353.

22. *QPD*, Vol. XXVI (1879), p.1602.

23. *Brisbane Courier*, 16 April 1880, p.3.

24. Balnaves, J., & Biskup, P. (1975). *Australian libraries*. (2nd ed). Sydney: James Bennett, p.59.

25. *QPD*, Vol. XXV (1878), p.73.

Nudgee School of Arts, Qld, ca 1914

Longreach School of Arts, Qld

Original North Brisbane School of Arts, Qld, ca 1866
(Corner of Queen and Creek Streets, Brisbane)

South Brisbane Mechanics' Institute, Qld

26.Metcalfe, J. (1934). Public library systems in Australia. *Library Association Record*, 4th Ser. I, p.8.

27.*ibid.*

28.Clyde, L. (1978). The magic casements - 1909. *Journal of the School Library Association of Queensland, 10* (3/4), p.15.

29.*ibid.*, p.17 (Letter 9533, 20/5/1909. Dept. of Education Records, Library Various File 1).

30.Queensland School of Arts Association. *Minutes and Reports, 1927-1945*, 9 August 1927.

31.*ibid.*, 16 August 1928.

32.*ibid.*, 16 August 1928.

33.*ibid.*, 24 August 1935. Press Release by the Minister for Public Instruction.

34.Queensland School of Arts Association, *op. cit.*, 7 July 1933.

35.Munn, R., & Pitt, E.R. (1935). *Australian libraries: A survey of conditions and suggestions for their improvement*. Melbourne: Australian Council for Educational Research, pp. 24-25.

36.Queensland School of Arts Association, *op. cit.*, 18 August 1939, Twelfth Annual Dinner and Conference.

37.*ibid.*, 18 August 1939.

38.Queensland School of Arts Association. *Correspondence, 1939-41*, E-D 20 October 1939.

39.Queensland School of Arts Association. *Correspondence, 1939-1941*, E-D 10 March 1939, Goondiwindi.

40.*Libraries Act, No. 39* of 1943.

41.Queensland Schools of Arts Association. *Correspondence, 1944-1949*. A-G 6 October 1945, Bowen.

42.*ibid.*, 24 July, 1945, Bundaberg.

43.*QPD*, Vol CLXXX (1942-43), p.1558.

44.*ibid.*, p.1559.

45.*QPD*, Vol CLXXXI (1943), p.1274.

46. Huish, G. (1967). Country libraries in Queensland - Praise and an apologia. *Australian Library Journal, 16*(3), p.99.

47. Warburton, J.W. (1963). Schools of Arts. *Australian Quarterly, 35*(4), p.72.

48. Library Board of Queensland (1968). *Twenty-third Annual Report*. Brisbane: Government Printer, p.1.

49. Horton, A.R. (Chair). (1976). *Public Libraries in Australia: Report of the Committee of Inquiry into Public Libraries*. Canberra: A.G.P.S., p.12.

50. *ibid*, p.44.

51. This information clashes with the claims by Kellermeier in this Volume that there were twelve schools of arts still operating in Queensland at this time, but in either case the dramatic reduction in the number of schools is still impressive - Eds.

CHAPTER FOURTEEN

THE ROCKHAMPTON SCHOOL OF ARTS LIBRARY AND MUSEUM IN THE NINETEENTH CENTURY

Wayne Murdoch

"A BUSH LIBRARY..."

Introduction

"Your primary object in establishing a School of Arts has been to procure a good spacious room where access could be had to the best periodical literature of the day."[1] When these words were spoken by John Douglas (MLA Port Curtis), President of the Rockhampton School of Arts at the opening of the School's original building on 25 February 1865, he summed up in a single sentence the thoughts of many of the School's early subscribers: the School's aims were the moral and intellectual elevation of its members, and the main means of achieving this goal was the establishment of a morally and intellectually elevating library collection.

The establishment of a library and reading room was undoubtedly the main task to be tackled by the School of Arts Committee at its inaugural meeting on 30 June 1861. The first item of business on the agenda at that meeting, after accepting the School's constitution, was to authorise the Treasurer, Mr Larnach, to "send for periodicals and newspapers for the use of the institution."[2] Just over a month later, on 4 August, the *Morning Bulletin* announced: "The Rockhampton School of Arts would commence with a reading room containing newspapers of the colony, together with the leading papers of Sydney, Melbourne, and Great Britain. It would also contain some of the first-class periodicals and literature of the day. Other publications would be introduced when funds permitted."[3] The reading room was opened, with prayers by the Reverend Samuel Kelly, in the temporary court house later the same month.

In its first twelve months, the reading room and library appear to have contained little more than current newspapers and journals (as well as chess and backgammon sets). In his annual report in January 1862, the Secretary, Den Taafe, suggested that the lack of books in the library was probably due to the fact that the School did not possess its own building: "Well wishers of our institution have refrained from making donations of books etc. until they know that there is a proper place to receive them."[4]

The small collection of newspapers and magazines that constituted the School's library collection at the Court House was dispersed during the institution's dormant period of 1863-4, and the re-formed School Committee of August 1864 faced the prospect of re-establishing the library collection from scratch. Their first step was to call for donations of books from subscribers and members of the public in March 1865. A month later, the Library Subcommittee suggested that £25 be spent on books from Brisbane suppliers. By July the committee was able to report the following:

In forming the nucleus of a library, by voluntary contributions, the appeal of your Committee has been met with numerous responses by donations of books, amounting in aggregate to 250 volumes; and the liberality of the donors merits public acknowledgment.

The Honourable, The Colonial Secretary, has also forwarded (unsolicited) Pring's *Statutes of Queensland* - in three volumes.

Your Committee have recently ordered a selection of first class works in light literature to the extent of £25. A portion of this order has already been supplied and is now on the shelves for issue and it is hoped the selection will meet with approval...[5]

Development of the Library Collection

By the end of its six months of existence, the School of Arts Library had laid the basis of its acquisitions and supply policy - books were to be obtained through donations, individual purchases and bulk orders from library suppliers. Although at first the library was forced to rely on the generosity of members' donations for its book stock, it quickly switched its main source of supply to bulk orders from library suppliers, especially Mudie's of London. As will be shown, this acquisitions source was to play a major role in determining the structure, content and nature of the School's collection, and it is therefore important to discuss the involvement of Mudie's Circulating Library with the Rockhampton School of Arts.

Mudie's Circulating Library was established in 1842 as a subscription library and, by the mid-1850s, was the largest such library in Great Britain, and indeed the Empire. Its main branch in New Oxford Street, London, housed approximately one million volumes for loan and a fleet of delivery vans covered the London suburbs picking up and dropping off customers' orders. As well as running a lending department and a bindery, the New Oxford Street headquarters also housed Mudie's large second-hand book selling department:

Although definitely subsidiary to the lending department, bookselling ... was a profitable adjunct. First, of course, it provided a market for some of the many volumes of three-decker novels that had run their course in the library... Besides selling individual titles, Mudie offered books in large lots, for example 100 volumes, for small provincial libraries.[6]

Not only provincial British libraries drew on Mudie's as a source of their book stock: "One thousand boxes, carrying 10 to 100 books each, were dispatched weekly to country and colonial subscribers, many of whom were provincial or colonial libraries..."[7] The Rockhampton School of Arts Library received its first order of second-hand books from Mudie's in July 1866, having placed an order late the previous year.[8] The Library was to continue a regular standing order with Mudie's until 1893, when the Committee decided that the selections arriving from London were "inferior,"[9] and the standing order was replaced by regular orders of requested titles. After 1893 many of the Rockhampton School of Arts Library's books were bought locally or in Brisbane.

However, for almost thirty years, between 1866 and 1893, the School of Arts Library regularly spent £100 or more every year at Mudie's. A regular standing order for journals was also established in 1866 with Richardson and Co. of Cornhill, London, heralding the beginning of another business relationship which was to last several decades.[10]

Placing a regular standing order with Mudie's was, in many ways, a sensible course of action for the School of Arts to take. It meant that boxes of a hundred or more reasonably cheap, popular, current and attractively presented books arrived regularly at the Library. Standing orders were also the only way for the Library to obtain large numbers of books and multiple copies, as local booksellers usually tended not to stock many multiples of individual works. In addition, local booksellers were often accused of being expensive and offering a limited range of stock. Consequently, the Library only bought from Rockhampton bookshops if a particular work was required at short notice.

However, the Library's standing order with Mudie's did present some problems. Mudie's book boxes tended to dictate the content of the library's collection to a very great extent. Mudie's Library was renowned for the high moral tone of its stock, especially its fiction stock:

> Mudie carefully excluded certain books for 'moral reasons.' No longer would the head of a Victorian family need to waste his time scanning circulating library works to see whether they were suitable for his daughters; no longer would the daughter, like Lydia Languish, have to throw her book behind the sofa at the entrance of her parent; the Mudie novel ... lay on the parlour table, ready for any member of the family circle to read aloud.[11]

Whilst Mudie's practice of excluding "unsuitable" works did prevent his shelves from becoming clogged with a large amount of allegedly substandard literature, it also meant that many works of merit were excluded simply because they were thought unfit for ladies and children to read. Consequently, Mudie's was accused of pandering to the lowest common denominator of middle class intelligence - authors, critics, and publishers complained again and again that Mudie's acquisitions policy made for a collection that was safe, predictable, stifling and unchallenging.

By placing standing orders with Mudie's, the Rockhampton School of Arts Library laid itself open to accusations of poor collection development. One subscriber went so far as to say at the 1887 Annual General Meeting that "several standard works were not ordered [for the library] because Mudie could not supply them,"[12] whilst others commented on the number of "green backs"[13] in the fiction collection and complained that "the proportion of standard works was very small indeed [and] very little attention was being paid to the library [collection] ..."[14]

Unfortunately, the root of the problem of poor collection development can probably be laid at the door of the School's Library sub-Committee and the Librarians' lack of an acquisitions policy. No collection policy was ever formulated during the period from 1865 to 1894, apart from the Library refusing to stock religious material, thereby making the collection's development dependent on reader's requests, standing orders, and donations. The Rockhampton School of Arts Library was not alone in this situation however. Formal collection policy statements are very much a twentieth-century development. As well as a haphazard approach to purchasing, it also appears that very little culling of the collection took place, apart from the disposal of volumes that were damaged, dirty or otherwise deemed unattractive. It was also (unofficial) Library policy to accept any donation and any reader's request, provided they were morally inoffensive and in good condition. Such a state of affairs meant that the Library's collection soon grew to contain a wide array of diverse material and quite a few items which had no real reason for inclusion.

Using its three main sources of book stock - donations, standing orders and individual purchases - the School of Arts Library grew steadily in size from 250 volumes in 1865 to 1,170 in 1868, 2,361 in 1872, 4,300 in 1878, and 5,630 in 1890.[15]

Analysis of the 1872 Library Collection

Of course, the important point to bear in mind when evaluating the worth of a library collection is not so much its size, but the quality and range of the material it contains. In order to gain an idea of the contents of the nineteenth century collection of the Rockhampton School of Arts, it is necessary to examine the Library's catalogues. Fortunately, two of the three printed catalogues which the Library published during the period are extant.

The Rockhampton School of Arts Library published its first catalogue in 1872, when the collection contained 2,500 volumes. (It appears that a handwritten catalogue of sorts had been compiled before this date, but unfortunately it no longer exists.) The 1872 catalogue covered the complete monograph, journal and pamphlet collections of the Library and tells us a great deal not only about the collection itself, but also about the institution to which it belonged and those who used it.

The catalogue was compiled by the School's first librarian, William James Cumming, who had been appointed in 1868. Cumming, like all nineteenth century Australian librarians, had no formal library education and acquired his skills on the job. That he, as an untrained person existing in isolation from other libraries and librarians, was able to compile a catalogue of any kind is probably a remarkable feat, but his lack of library training and his lack of professional contact is obvious when one examines his cataloguing system.

Cumming divided the Library's collection into fifteen subject classes, designating each with a letter of the alphabet. Each title within a subject division was given a running number and, as the collection did not become an open access system until the 1880s, the system worked reasonably well. The Catalogue sets out the subject classes as per Table 14.1:

One is immediately struck by the fact that fiction is by far the largest single class in the catalogue, accounting for 71 percent of the collection, whilst the largest non-fiction subject categories are 'Voyages & Travels,' 'Miscellaneous Sciences & Arts,' 'History,' 'Miscellaneous Works,' 'Biography' and 'Poetry & Drama.' The subjects with the smallest representation in the collection are 'Astronomy,' 'Geology,' 'Zoology,' 'Botany' and 'Theology.' The differences in the number of volumes in these categories can be attributed largely to the varying degrees of inclusiveness of individual categories; for example, 'Astronomy' is a relatively small subject category, whilst 'History' is an extremely large one. It follows, therefore, that there will be more works in the latter category. Bound periodicals

Table 14.1
Library Holdings by Subject, 1872

CLASS	SUBJECT	NUMBER OF TITLES
A	Astronomy	8
B	Geology	17
C	Zoology	25
D	Botany	3
E	Miscellaneous Sciences & Arts	98
F	History	84
G	Biography	78
H	Voyages & Travels	106
I	Works of Fiction	1,778
K	Essays Reviews & Speeches	51
L	Miscellaneous Works	82
M	Poetry & Drama	75
N	Theology	26
O	Bound Magazines	34
P	Works of Reference	35

The overwhelming amount of fiction in the School of Arts' collection, the predominance of biographies, histories and travels in the non-fiction collection, and the meagre number of titles in the sciences raises the question: Was the School of Arts' collection a "good" collection in terms of providing the School's members with access to useful, informative and current non-fiction works? Or did the library's role as a provider of information and education suffer as a result of its concentration on entertaining its subscribers with fiction and light reading? These questions can probably best be answered by discussing and evaluating the actual content of the fiction and non-fiction collections.

The fiction collection

It has been said that the nineteenth century was the great period of the novel - Anthony Trollope commented in 1870: "We have become a novel reading people, from the Prime Minister down to the last-appointed scullery maid ... Poetry also we read and history, biography and the social and political news of the day. But all our reading put together hardly amounts to what we read in novels."[17] Trollope's words underline the point, and one can begin to understand the Victorians' love of the novel. It was perhaps only to be expected that the Rockhampton School of Arts' fiction collection would overpower its non-fiction collections. What, then, were the School's members reading? What were they able to borrow from the School's fiction collection?

According to the 1872 catalogue, the library possessed most of what have now come to be regarded as 'the Classics' - the works of Dickens, Trollope, Dumas, Thackeray, Goëthe, the Brontës, Bulwer Lytton, Henry Fielding, Wilkie Collins, Kingsley, Fenimore Cooper, Irving, Defoe, Disraeli, George Eliot, Swift, Mrs Gaskell, Cervantes, Hawthorne, Victor Hugo, Melville, and Scott. However, at the time, many of these authors did not enjoy the respect they do today; instead, they were regarded as popular writers, which is precisely what they were. The library also held a great many of the complete works of other popular contemporary writers who are not usually as well remembered today: Harrison Ainsworth, Mrs Henry Wood, Mrs Oliphant, Charles Lever, Florence Marryatt, Miss Mallock, and Miss Edgeworth. Whilst the works of some of these writers were undoubtedly of an acceptable literary standard to meet with the approval of some of the library's critics, many of them were of an ephemeral nature.

One can surmise the nature of the work of some of these 'forgotten' authors by reading the titles of their works: Ainsworth's *Lancashire Witches, Miser's Daughters* and *Spendthrift*, Robinson's *Anne Judge, Spinster,* Fenn's *Bent, Not Broken*, Mrs Braddon's *Lady Audley's Secret* and *Run to Earth*, Hayward's *Diaries of a Lady of Quality*, Mrs R J Green's *Cushions and Corners*, Riddell's *Far Above Rubies*, Lady Black's *Helen's First Love*, and Cannibal Jack's *Run Away from Home*. Whilst it has to be admitted that the works cited are among some of the slightest, the most sensational, and the most ephemeral, it is fair to say that approximately 75 percent of the fiction collection consisted of comparable works of light fiction. Only about a quarter of the fiction collection as catalogued would be worthy of being called 'The Classics' today. A number of gaps are also evident in the 1872 fiction catalogue; for example, there was a complete lack of Jane Austen's works. Happily, this gap was filled by the time the next surviving catalogue was published in 1890.

The non-fiction collection

The predominance of fiction in the Library's collection makes one wonder about the quality of the Library's non-fiction collections. As it happened, the Rockhampton School of Arts' non-fiction collections, although small, seem to have met the often high expectations of its users, some of whom were familiar with the great libraries of Britain and Europe. Whilst these users realised that a library in a frontier town in one of the Empire's newest colonies could not hope to match the established libraries of the old world, they did use their experience of good libraries to build a series of small, concise collections of some quality.

The library's newspaper, journal and periodical collections, both in the reading room and in the bound volumes in the Library, show a wide coverage of both subject matter and geographic area. Among the periodicals to be found on the table in the reading room were *Blackwood's Journal, The Art Journal, Harper's New Weekly, London Society, Chambers' Journal, Tinsley's, The British Quarterly Review, The Saturday Review, Punch* and *The Edinburgh Review*; whilst the newspapers included *The Illustrated London News, The Spectator, The Weekly Freeman* (Irish), *The Weekly Scotsman* and *The New York Herald*, as well as *The Australasian, The Sydney Morning Herald*, and *The Sydney Illustrated News*. Queensland newspapers were also well represented, as would be expected: eleven colonial papers were held, including *The Brisbane Courier, The Darling Downs Gazette, The Ipswich Observer, The Toowoomba Chronicle* and two local papers, *The Rockhampton Morning*

Bulletin and *The Northern Argus*. Even more periodical titles were to be found if one went into the Library's stacks and examined the bound volumes of journals stored there. They included: *Mechanic's Magazine* (holdings from 1865), *Broadway* (1868 - 1870), *Athenaeum* (from 1865), and *The Westminster Review* (from 1866), to name just four of the thirty-four bound journal titles in class O - 'Magazines and Reviews.'

As far as the non-fiction monograph collections were concerned, the subject coverage was generally as wide as in the journal collection. Some subject classes, such as Astronomy, Botany and Geology were too small to provide any decent coverage, but on the whole, the choice of works in the non-fiction classes compensated for the small size of the collections. It is easy to find works of great worth and quality in the non-fiction collections - class C 'Zoology' contains Darwin's *Origin of the Species, The Descent of Man* and *Variation of Animals and Plants under Domestication*; as well as other important works including Bennett's *Gatherings of a Naturalist in Australia* and several 'popular' works suitable for supplying answers to reference queries and allowing interested readers to understand the subject.

The conglomerate labelled class E - 'Miscellaneous Sciences and Arts' contains, as its title suggests, works on anything from the English Constitution and Chartism to chess, dominos, the electric telegraph, geometry and elocution. Among the important works assembled in Class E are Miss Mallock's A Woman's Thoughts About Women, Faraday's *Lectures on the Chemistry of a Candle*, Carlyle's *Chartism*, and *Past and Present*, most of J S Mill's works, including *Subjection of Women, Liberty, Logic, Moral and Metaphysical Philosophy* and *Representative Government*, and Schlegel's philosophies of *History, Life* and *The Human Mind*. All in all, the ninety-eight works of 'Miscellaneous Sciences and Arts' represent a cross-section of nineteenth-century political, social and philosophical thought, combined with a fair sprinkling of odd items for which Cumming could find no other category.

Class F of the catalogue - 'History' - begins with two works on the recently-ended American Civil War, or "The American War" as it was known to most Britons at the time, and continues as a standard collection of British and Imperial histories. Titles include Allen's *Battles of the British Navy*, Hallam's *Constitutional History of England*, H Murray's *History of British India* and Stanley's *Memorials of Westminster Cathedral*. Of the eighty-four works in Class F, thirty-seven refer directly to British history or the history of colonies other than the Australian colonies, twenty-seven refer to European history and six to North and South American history. The collection contained no books on Asian nations apart from those which were Imperial colonies. However, perhaps surprisingly for the period, the collection contains half a dozen works on Australian history: Westgarth's *Australia - Its Rise, Progress and Condition*, Bennett's *Australian Discovery and Colonisation*, Flanagan's *New South Wales*, J D Lang's *History of New South Wales* and *History of Port Phillip*, and Wentworth's *Australia*. These early works on the history of the Australian colonies are today rare and valuable, and at the time the Rockhampton School of Arts collection was being built, they represented some of the best works available on the subject. Needless to say, works on Australian history were not common in the early 1870s, especially in a frontier society which saw itself as not being old enough to have a history.

The Library's collection of biographies contained works on most of the nineteenth century's

289

imperial heroes (e.g., Nelson), notable statesmen (e.g., Bismarck, Bonaparte, Mazzini), royalty (the Prince Consort, the Georgian Kings), artists (Hogarth, Michelangelo), scientists (Faraday, Stephenson, Newton) as well as such notable works as Pepys' *Diary*, Carlyle's *Lives of Schiller and Stirling*, De Quincey's *Autobiographic Sketches from 1790* and *English Opium Eater*, Rousseau's *Confessions*, Boswell's *Life of Johnson*, Thackeray's *The Four Georges* and Macaulay's *Biographies*.

The biographical collection consisted overwhelmingly of works on Britons (and mainly British men at that, although several works on notable British women were available, for example, Julia Kavanagh's *English Women of Letters*, Holt's *Royal Ladies*, Agnes Strickland's *Lives of the Queens of England* and Lady Morgan's *Memoirs*; non-British women only received notice in Wrathall and Wehrhau's *Memoirs of Queen Hortense* and Julia Kavanagh's *French Women of Letters*). Very little of the collection was concerned with European or American lives (sixteen and one respectively, of a collection of seventy-eight) and only two Asian, or rather "Middle-Eastern," personalities were deemed worthy of inclusion - Saul of Tarsus and Mahomet.

However, one should not be too hasty in judging the School of Arts Library for the coverage (or lack of it) of its biographical collection. Its content was due not only to the conscious imperial bias of the Committee, the members and the Librarian, but also to the availability of works and the types of works being published in Britain at the time. One has to bear in mind that biographies of women and of non-British personalities were not written in great numbers in Britain during the nineteenth century, nor were English translations of European biographies readily available. It was probably due to the presence of a German, a Dutchman, and a Frenchman on the early Committee that any sort of Continental representation was made in the collection at all.

The nineteenth century fascination with travel and exploration was probably the main reason why the School of Arts' collection of 'Voyages and Travels' was so large (106 works, or 14 percent of the non-fiction collection), so varied, and why it contained works on practically every part of the globe, from Abyssinia to Iceland, Paris to China and to Australia.

Although much of the collection focussed on British possessions, a great deal more of it covered Europe, the Americas and those parts of Africa and Asia not under British rule. The breakdown of the subject matter is as follows;

Works on -

Britain	4
British Possessions (Not Including Australian Colonies)	16
North America	14
South America	3
Asia	20
Africa	8
Europe	18
Miscellaneous	10
Australian Colonies	10

The ten books which have been labelled 'Miscellaneous' for the purpose of this brief survey contain a varied mixture of sea voyages and three works on the life and voyages of Christopher Columbus. However, it is readily apparent that the largest group of works in the collection was that dealing with those parts of Asia not under British rule - China, Japan, Indo-China and parts of the Middle East - followed by works on Europe, Imperial possessions, North America, the Australian colonies and miscellaneous voyages. The remaining small groups, those dealing with South America, non-British Africa and Britain itself, take up very little space in the category; only fifteen works altogether.

The Australian content of this particular subject category is interesting: C H Allen's *A Visit to Queensland*, W J Wills *Burke and Wills Expedition, Captain Grey's Travels in North Western and Western Australia*, Cook's *Voyages*, Landsborough's *Expedition, Leichhardt's Expedition 1844-5*, Mitchell's *Tropical Australia*, Munday's *Our Antipodes*, Stuart's *Australian Expedition* and S Sydney's *The Colonies of Australia*. These works represent a fairly typical collection of contemporary Australian 'Travels' - the deeds of the explorers for the most part; only Sydney's *The Colonies of Australia* and Munday's *Our Antipodes* stand out in this collection as being works of contemporary description, capable of telling those overseas or in other colonies what the continent was really like. Oddly enough, another work of great interest for its contemporary descriptions and social insights of Victorian and Tasmanian life (made all the more so for being written by a woman) - Louisa Meredith's *Over the Straits* - was banished to Class I - 'Fiction'!

Some of the Library's most interesting works were to be found in Classes K and L - 'Essays, Reviews and Speeches' and 'Miscellaneous Works.' The former group contained mainly works of philosophy and sociology, whilst the latter consisted mainly of those works which couldn't be allocated a place in any other subject category.

'Essays, Reviews and Speeches' contained, among others, Cicero's *Orations*, Emerson's essays on *Nature* and *Representative Man*, Ruskin's *Selections, Ethics of the Dust, Lectures on Art*, and *Crown of Wild Olives*, Macaulay's *Speeches* and *Essays*, J S Mill's *Inaugural Address*, Carlyle's *Critical Essays, Illustrations from the German of Musaeus, Tieck and Richter* and *Shooting Niagara and After*, and Arnold's *Celtic Literature*.

It is remarkable that this category, Class K, although small in size (fifty-one works), contained a wide cross-section of nineteenth-century thought and opinion, and managed to cover, albeit briefly, most of the social, moral and cultural philosophy of the mid-Victorian era. A wide variety of political views were also represented in Class K's collections of Speeches - from Bright to Brougham, to O'Connell and Macaulay - a reasonably wide spectrum of political opinion which probably would have been unavailable in any private collection in Central Queensland at the time.

Class L - 'Miscellaneous Works' appears as a glorious mixture of subjects and titles, from *Aesop's Fables* and *Curious Myths of the Middle Ages* to *Gold Deposits in Australia, Brand's Popular Antiquities* and *Brigandage in South Italy*. There is little one can do in attempting to describe or qualify a subject division such as this one assembled from the left-overs and cast-offs of the rest of the collection. At best one can quote a few of the more outstanding or well-known titles, in the hope of outlining the scope of the category. Of course, it must be admitted here that, although this subject category was in effect the cataloguer's "Too Hard" basket, it did contain many valuable, useful and important works, for example, Disraeli's *Curiosities of Literature*, J D Lang's *Freedom and Independence of the Seven United Provinces of Australia,* Hawthorne's *American Notebook*, Mayhew's *Dogs and Their Management*, Daunt's *Ireland and Her Agitators*, Longfellow's *Prose Works*, A Steinmetz's *Romance of Duelling*, Swift's *Works*, Stern's *Works*, Coleridge's *Table Talk, The Confederate Secession*, Trollope's *Travelling Sketches*, Timbs' *London* and, oddly enough, the *Sydney University Calendar 1859-60*!

If Classes K and L present the reader with a tangled (and in the case of Class L, extremely so) list of works and subjects, Class M - 'Poetry and Drama' - presents no such problem.

The Rockhampton School of Arts' Library's Poetry and Drama collection is a simple, although worthy, sample of what the nineteenth century saw as the best in *English*-language literature.   The 'Classic' English-speaking poets and dramatists are represented - Burns, Byron, Coleridge, Cowper, Elizabeth Barrett Browning, Keats, Sheridan, Dryden, Chaucer, Whitman, Longfellow, Milton, Moore, Southey, Pope, Edmund Spenser, R W Emerson, Swinburne, Tennyson, Shelley, Wordsworth, George Eliot and Shakespeare. Translations of some of the more respected European writers such as Goethe, Heine, Schiller, Dante and Bon Gaultier also appear, and it goes without saying that Homer's *Iliad* also found its way into the collection.   Unfortunately, however, not one Australian poet appears in the catalogue, a situation which eventually led one member to complain that "The Committee had performed the task of selecting books for the Library very badly. They had not acquired poems of the three Australian poets - Gordon, Kendall and Brunton Stephens..."[18]

The penultimate subject class in the 1872 catalogue - Class N, 'Theology and Religious Literature' - is one of the smallest. It was a reasonably standard collection of theological texts, sermons and religious histories, with an almost exclusively Protestant Christian content, although Young's *Cicero on the Nature of the Gods* and Romanoff's *Graeco-Russian Church* are two of the exceptions.

At times the Library's theological collection proved to be something of an embarrassment to various Committees due to their repeated stand on the matter of not having religious journals and papers in the Reading Room. It was School policy not to support any particular religious point of view, and some members saw this policy as being at odds with the collection of religious works in the Library. Successive Committees had taken the line that "of all controversies, those on religion were the most to be deplored and avoided. It was for that reason...that the Committee had refrained from having any religious opinion in the Reading Room and he (the President) hoped that they would be the last to stir up religious controversy in the town."[19]   Possibly as a result, the Library's theological collection remained a largely unwanted and unused part of the whole Library collection, added to only when a religious text or book of sermons was donated to the Library by a well-wisher.

Finally, Class P - 'Works of Reference' - included some of the Library's most useful and valuable material - the latest edition of the *Encyclopaedia Britannica*, French/English and German/English dictionaries, *Blackie's Imperial Dictionary, Burke's Peerage, 1863, Consolidated Statues of Queensland, Gazetteer of the Australian Colonies,* Graham's

Domestic Medicine, Hayden's *Dictionary of Dates, Journals of the Queensland Legislative Assembly*, Lloyd's *Register, Men of the Times: A Dictionary of Contemporaries*, Pring's *Statutes of Queensland, Queensland Post Office Directory, Votes and Proceedings of the Queensland Legislative Assembly, Queensland Government Gazette* (1862 to date), Roget's *Thesaurus, Specimens of Ancient and Modern Sculpture, Stateman's Year Book* and Ure's *Dictionary of Arts and Sciences*.

Essentially, the collection of the Rockhampton School of Arts Library as it existed in 1872 was a typical 'gentlemanly' collection, similar to many others to be found in Schools of Arts, private homes, public institutions and gentlemen's clubs throughout the Empire. It possessed a very strong Imperial and British bias and had a heavy slant towards the arts and humanities in its non-fiction collections, characteristics typical of middle-class collections throughout the British world. The ever-observant William Archer noted that private libraries in Queensland at this period usually consisted of

> An encyclopaedia, Shakespeare, Macaulay's *England* and *Essays*, Mill's *Political Economy*, one or other of Darwin's works and a few books of household medicine, farriery, etc. - this is the sort of ground work upon which a bush library is generally built. Pope, Goldsmith, Byron, and Carlyle are often to be had. Buckle's *History of Civilisation*, Livingstone's or Baker's travels, are frequently met with. Among novelists again Anthony Trollope is to all appearances more popular than even Dickens or Thackeray, but that is probably because his recent visit [in 1871/2] to Australia has given an unnatural impetus to the sale of his books. Lord Lytton's works are scattered broadcast over the colony. George Eliot is, I have observed, unpopular, but the same cannot be said of Wilkie Collins, Miss Braddon and even - alas - 'Ouida.' Most popular of all, perhaps are the Americans; Bret Harte and Mark Twain, and even the more scholarly but not less amusing Lowell and Holmes are pretty well known in the bush.[20]

The School of Arts Library was, therefore, essentially an expanded version of what was to be seen on the shelves of private homes throughout the district in the 1870s. It is in the size and character of the Library's fiction collection that one can clearly see the School adjusting to the wants and expectations of its subscribers - "The reason light literature predominated was because it was asked for..."[21]

Analysis of the 1890 Library Collection

By the time the next surviving catalogue of the School of Arts Library was published, in 1890, several changes had taken place within the Library and the collection. There had been several changes of Librarians, the collection had grown to over 7,000 volumes, many of the gaps in the collection's subject coverage had been filled and the Library had been operating as an open access system for several years, thereby making it necessary to develop a new cataloguing system.

Like Cumming, Newton Molyneux Montgomery Davidson, who catalogued the collection in 1890, had no formal training in librarianship. However, he managed to develop a workable catalogue with little more to use as a model than Cumming's 1872 and the (no longer extant)

1885 catalogues. Davidson's catalogue maintained the subject divisions of Cumming's catalogue, although in a more refined form, as per Table 14.2.

As with the 1872 catalogue, one is struck by the vast size of the fiction collection compared with the non-fiction collections, although the difference was not as great as it had been eighteen years before. One is also struck by Davidson's refinements of Cumming's subject classes - 'Philosophical Works' had been added to 'Theological works,' 'Geology', 'Botany' and 'Zoology' became 'Geology and Physical Geography' and 'Natural History and Biology,' whilst much of the material which had once been found in the 'Miscellaneous Science and Arts' class formed the basis of a new subject division, 'Chemistry and Physics.' 'History,' 'Biography' and 'Voyages and Travels' remained the same in content but increased dramatically in size, and 'Miscellaneous Works' was renamed 'General Literature' - still an amalgam of works unable to find a home elsewhere, but which were gradually being shaped into a literary collection.

Table 14.2
Library Holdings by Subject, 1890

	CLASS	NUMBER OF VOLUMES
A	Astronomy	27
B	Geology	63
C	Natural History and Biology	166
D	Chemistry and Physics	33
E	Miscellaneous Sciences and Arts	133
F	History	420
G	Biography	289
H	Voyages and Travels	382
I	Novels Arranged Alphabetically According to Titles / by Author	4,583
K	General Literature	420
L	Philosophical and Religious Literature	116
M	Poetry	139
O	Reviews, Magazines and Illustrated Papers (Bound and kept in the Library)	48 Titles
P	Works of Reference, Newspapers, Reviews, Magazines, Pamphlets, etc. in the Reading Room	208 Titles

Essentially the content of the School of Arts Library's collection changed little between 1872 and 1890; Davidson's catalogue still reveals a middle-class British collection with a heavy emphasis on the arts and humanities. However, some changes had taken place. The introduction of technical education classes at the School of Arts fostered the growth of the scientific collections, as did the vital part played in the life of the School by the Natural History Society, which was founded in 1885 and pressured the School's Committee to buy works on the biological sciences, as well as keeping its own collection of monographs and journals in the Library.

If one examines the catalogue closely, it is noticeable that the Australian content of the collection had grown markedly during the 1870s and '80s. Works on Australian history increased in number and included Bonwick's *First Twenty Years of Australia*, Rusden's *History of Australia*, Favenc's *History of Australian Exploration*, Curr's *The Australian Race*, Deven's *Our First Century*, Russell's *Genesis of Queensland* and Bull's *Early Experience in South Australia*. Australian 'Voyages and Travels' were in evidence; the collection of 1872 being supplemented by such works as Davis's *McKinlay's Tracks Across Australia*, Cassell and Co.'s *Our Own Country*, Butler's *Wild North Land*, and six works on New Guinea (by 1890 a Queensland possession). Its also gratifying to note that Louisa Meredith's *Across the Straits* had been rescued from fiction and placed in its rightful place.

The 1890 catalogue included Australian poetry for the first time, with Samuel Harpur's *Australia and Mnason* [sic], Sladen's *Australian Poems* and *A Summer Christmas*, and Kendall's *Poems*; while Australian fiction was represented by Miss Murray-Prior's *An Australian Heroine*, Rosa Campbell-Praed's *Black and White, Band of Wedlock*, Miss Jacobsen's *Chance, Moloch, Nadine* and *Policy Passion*, Marcus Clarke's *His Natural Life*, and H. Smart's *Pride of the Paddock*, among others.

One of the most useful and valuable collections to be found in the 1890 catalogue was the newly-formed Pamphlet collection, part of the Reference collection. Titles in the pamphlet collection include the *1890 Handbook of Information, Queensland Parliamentary Papers, Some Account of the Mt Morgan Gold Mine, An Improvement in the Process for Creosoting Timber, On the Antiseptic Treatment of Timber* and *The Customs Compendium*, as well as four Queensland almanacs and business directories.

The Library's newspaper collection had also grown, from twenty-four titles in 1872 to forty-four in 1890, and included *The Auckland Weekly News, European Mail, Glasgow Weekly News, Licensed Victuallers' Gazette, The Mail* (London), *The Melbourne Argus, The South Australian Register, The Tasmanian Mail, The Times* and *The Cape Times* (Capetown), as well as eighteen Queensland newspapers and each of the three dailies and one weekly that were published in Rockhampton at the time.

A Survey of Users

Having discussed the Library's collection, we need to consider the collection's users to decide whether or not it adequately met the needs of its clientele. Unfortunately, no lists of School of Arts members exist for the 1861 - 1894 period, so one is unable to define accurately the educational, professional or class backgrounds of most of the School's ordinary members. However, one can make assumptions regarding the composition of the membership based on information derived from several sources, viz., Committee lists, personal details in published accounts of meetings, and the high price of subscriptions. The composition of the Library collection and the Library's loans statistics also help to assemble a picture, albeit one based on educated guesswork and suppositions, of the type of people attracted to the Rockhampton School of Arts and its Library.

The School of Arts' ordinary membership tended to be cast in the mould of the School's Committees - Protestant, professional, Anglo-Saxon or Scot, possessed of a better than average education, and socially mobile (the School of Arts was always seen as one of Rockhampton's more socially superior institutions). Although the School imposed no religious barriers to membership, very few Catholics joined, a fact possibly due to the strong social and educational opportunities offered by the Catholic Church in Rockhampton. Though the School was a predominantly middle-class institution, some working-class men did become members and two of the School's Presidents, John Ferguson (President 1887-88 and 1890-98) and William Pattison (President 1888-90), started life as a carpenter and a butcher respectively. However, Ferguson and Pattison had each made fortunes in land or mining speculation and had entered the Queensland Parliament before becoming School of Arts presidents.[22]

The Library's loans statistics (available for the period 1872 - 1893) paint a picture of a Library which was well used by its members, especially as a source of fiction:

Table 14.3
Membership and Circulation Statistics Selected Years

Year	Membership	Collection	Loans	
			Fiction	Non-fiction
1865	40	250	-	-
1866	121	750	-	-
1867	152	820		-
1868	134	1170	-	-
1869	138	1505	-	-
1872	195	2470	5494	1579
1873	212	2411	7182	1943
1875	231	2711	-	-
1878	-	4300	4297	2126
1879	-	4358	4058	2358
1880	-	4500	4067	1985
1881	210	4500	-	-
1882	270	4500	-	-
1883	295	4727	6278	3495
1884	-	4874	7349	4787
1885	-	5200	9224	4084
1886	380	5630	6589	3287
1893	-	-	8435	5363

School of Arts Library users were also quite vocal in their praise, or condemnation, of the Library and were often forthcoming with suggestions about the Library's management and collections. Annual meetings were forums for open discussions about library policy. For example, in July 1866, it was noted that "Mr Rea inquired if any extension might not be made in the time during which the members might remain in possession of books - there were many out of the town who would no doubt become members if such an alteration were made. He had asked a squatter to become a member, and he urged that very ground [sic].

The Chairman [John Douglas MLA] said that the matter had not been spoken of, but he considered the number of books [750 volumes] was too small to allow such an alteration."[23] The Library's borrowing period at this time was fourteen days. An infraction of this rule was dealt with quickly and severely: the 1872 Catalogue stated, "The time which members shall be allowed to keep books shall be fourteen days for each book; and every member keeping books longer than the time specified shall forfeit sixpence per week until the book is returned."[24] The length of the Library's borrowing period was to remain an issue that would arise at intervals over the next three decades, although the period was never extended beyond the two weeks allowed in 1866.

Acquisitions and collection development was another Library issue which drew much criticism and suggestion over the years. It was Library policy to have "a book left on the Library table, in which members may enter, affixing respectively, their names to the entry, the title of any work they may wish to have in the Library, together with the price and publisher's name if possible. These entries shall be examined every month by the Committee, who shall decide upon the reception or rejection of each book so proposed."[25]

The Librarian, and the School's Committee, often came in for harsh criticism if a member's proposal was rejected as being unsuitable or too expensive, or if the Library collection was found to be otherwise inadequate; one member went so far as to call the Committee "a lot of old fossils"[26] during a heated debate in 1887, whilst several others at the same meeting "pointed out the almost total absence of Irish and American papers...[and]...the exclusion of all journals save those of a Conservative tendency."[27] These last two complaints also highlight the tendency of the Library's collection towards a middle class, Protestant, Anglo-Saxon and Scottish bias.

The question of Library policy regarding religious material was also an issue which members saw fit to comment on at annual meetings. The subject was first raised in July 1888, when "Mr F. Hopkins [a well-known local Quaker and teacher] pointed out that all the papers and magazines in the Reading Room were of a secular nature, and expressed an opinion that the Committee should place in the list papers, magazines & representative of all religious creeds, published in Australia. The proposition was not seconded and consequently fell through."[28] Three years later, on 16 July 1891, the Reverend J Williams asked the annual meeting's Chairman, Sydney Williams, if the Committee objected to allowing certain newspapers to be placed on the tables in the Reading Room. The following exchange then ensued:

THE CHAIRMAN - 'We do exercise a direction in what papers or books we allow in the institution. ... MR WILLIAMS - Is it true that religious papers are refused to be placed on the tables? THE CHAIRMAN - I don't think you would find any what you call religious papers there. MR WILLIAMS - That is not the point. Does the Committee refuse to allow religious papers on the tables? THE CHAIRMAN - They don't do it. They don't allow any religious papers there. (Laughter and applause) ... Mr Williams said he had been in a great many schools of arts in Queensland, and in the other colonies, and this was the first that had refused to permit religious papers to enter the reading-room. Still, there were papers that expressed religious opinions - and in much stronger terms than any religious paper would do - that were allowed in, the Sydney *Bulletin* for instance. While it was perfectly right the [Sydney] *Bulletin* should be put on the tables, he thought that religious papers that expressed opinions on the other side should be there also. (Applause) If the Committee took a stand against religion, it should take it on both sides. In his opinion it was a decided mistake to exclude religious papers - Mr R Kelly said he had been a member of the institution for nearly twenty years, and they had got on very well without religious papers. If anyone wished to read those publications, let him buy them.

The institution was better without them. The Sydney *Bulletin* was not a religious paper, and whether it should be admitted or not was for the subscribers to decide.[29]

The religious newspapers issue was also to resurface periodically in the future, but subsequent Committees held firm, and religious magazines and newspapers never found their way into the Reading Room, even though the Sydney *Bulletin* was to remain.

As one can see, the School of Arts Library was supported by a vocal group of users who were not afraid to tell the School's Committee, or the Librarian, what they thought of the service they received. It must have taken a special breed of Librarian to cope with such a demanding clientele. One wonders how the School's early Library staff fared, given that they had little or, more often, no library training, were isolated from professional contact, and operated on a strict (and small) budget under a demanding Committee. A brief examination of the lives and work of the four men who ran the Rockhampton Library from 1861 to 1894 may answer some of these questions.

Portraits of the Librarians

Unfortunately, few biographical records survive on the early librarians. Newspaper reports on the School's activities and meetings carried a great deal of information on committee members, who were usually civic worthies; but the School's librarians, being only "paid servants"[30] of the Committee, rarely rated a mention. Consequently, large gaps exist in most accounts of the lives of the early Library staff.

Prior to 1867, the School of Arts' library was maintained by the Secretary for the Committee. As a collection cannot be said to have existed and the Library was not officially opened until 1865, this arrangement seems to have worked fairly well. The Secretary, with help from the Committee and members, made decisions on the books that the School would buy for the collection, and an assistant was employed for £67/13/6 per annum to attend the Reading Room and Library during opening hours, to collect subscriptions and to act as a general caretaker and cleaner.

By March 1867 the Library was serving 152 members with a collection of approximately 820 volumes. The Committee decided to take a bold step and employ a full-time Librarian to oversee the collection. On 16 March they appointed William James Cumming at a salary of £118/21/1. The services of the assistant in the Library were dispensed with, although he remained on the payroll as a caretaker/cleaner.

Nothing is known of Cumming's early life, his educational qualifications, or his personal life, apart from the fact that he was a keen rifleman and was unmarried. He certainly had no formal library training, but he appears to have been an educated man, a tireless worker, and to have had a love for his job and a fanatical zeal for improving the Library's services and collection.

Cumming inherited a two-year old collection which had never been catalogued, possessed a very small budget and was controlled by a Committee which desired not only a morally and educationally elevating collection, but demanded one that would attract paying members.

During the ten years that Cumming was Librarian of the School of Arts, the collection grew in size from 850 volumes to approximately 3,000, and a great deal of reorganisation was required. To this end, Cumming devised his cataloguing system and compiled the 1872 catalogue. He also assisted with the School's early plans for establishing a museum, as well as continually haranguing the successive Committees to spend money on the Library.

Cumming was so highly thought of by the Committee of 1872 that they discussed the possibility of converting the old Reading Room into a flat for him. A shortage of funds prevented this project from going ahead in 1872, but the following year a detached residence was built behind the School for Cumming's use.[31]

Two years later the membership of the School's Committee changed dramatically and Cumming found himself at odds personally with his new masters. Under the leadership of John Headrick, a prosperous local importer and agent, the new Committee's first act was to abolish the post of Honorary Secretary and insist that the Secretary's duties be taken over by the Librarian. Cumming kept his position for a further two years, juggling the duties of Committee Secretary, Librarian and Museum Curator, whilst still campaigning for his Library and its users. Nevertheless, he was dismissed by the Committee in 1877 for being too "irascible."[32]

The School of Arts could not, however, rid itself so easily of such a vocal thorn in their side as Cumming. He remained a member of the School until well into the twentieth century and would often attend annual meetings to harangue the Committee and complain bitterly that the Library was being neglected. He was a formidable opponent in a public discussion, always being well armed with facts and figures, as he proved at the 1891 annual meeting:

> Mr Cumming remarked that he had been through the books of the Institution for some years past and found from 1876 to 1883 the income amounted to £4,000, and the expenditure on the Library account was equal to 29 percent of the revenue. Between 1883 and 1889 the revenue was £8,000, and the outlay on the Library was only 18 per cent showing that the income was increasing very rapidly, and the expenditure on the Library decreasing as rapidly. In the present year [1891] for instance, when the Institution had received the largest income it had yet in a year, the Committee had expended on the Library only 15 percent out of the total receipts. More than that, the Library contained only 7,000 volumes at the present moment, or almost 2,000 volumes more than 1876... Very little attention was being paid to the Library, which in his opinion, was the most important branch of the Institution.[33]

Cumming was replaced as librarian by George Pilcher B.A., an Oxford graduate who had taught for a time at Eton. Pilcher brought his classical education to the Librarian's post, which probably helped him in building up some areas of the non-fiction collection. However, he was to stay in the position for only three years, leaving in December 1881 to start a private school in Rockhampton. The school folded less than twelve months after opening and Pilcher dropped from local sight.

In January 1882, George Potts Jnr., a popular and respected teacher at the Rockhampton Central Boys School (where his father was headmaster), resigned his post and became Secretary/Librarian/Museum Curator at the School of Arts. Potts was to remain in the position for seven years, during which time he published a new catalogue of the collection (1885), and pushed for the Library's stacks to be open to the members for browsing.

As Secretary/Librarian, Potts received free accommodation in the Librarian's residence and an annual salary of £91/13/4. In addition, the Committee employed a full-time Library Assistant, E C Master, at £32 per annum. However, free accommodation, a living salary, and the help of a full-time assistant were not enough to keep Potts in the Library. He resigned in July 1889 to go into business and left the School with the hearty good wishes of the 1889 annual meeting:

> They [the Committee] were indebted to their energetic Secretary for the able manner in which he had carried out his work (Applause). He [the Chairman - Sydney Williams] had been on the Committee for a great many years and he had never heard one single word of complaint at the manner in which he had performed his duties. (Applause) That was a wonderful thing because the patrons of a public institution were sometimes a little hard to please ... He hoped Mr Potts would be successful in his new sphere, and he thought he was wise in trying to put himself in a better position. At any rate, he admired his pluck and energy in trying to get on. (Applause)[34]

Potts' place was filled by N M M Davidson, one-time dispenser at Rockhampton's General Hospital, who was to act as Secretary/Librarian until 1910. Davidson's term as Librarian saw a great deal of activity and change in the Library. His first major task was to recatalogue the collection and then to publish his new catalogue (in 1890). The demolition of the School's old building and the construction of a new one in 1893-4 called for the temporary relocation of the Library collection in rented premises and the storage of the Museum's collection. When the new building opened in March 1894, Davidson, and his staff of two, were faced with the task of reorganising the collections and reopening the Library and Museum to the School's subscribers. The upheaval of the collection caused by relocating to the new building made it necessary to completely recatalogue the collection again in 1900.

Davidson, although not trained as a librarian, was a book lover with a particular interest in Australiana. He "succeeded in procuring a fine collection of early Australian Travels, Discovery and Explorations, also first editions of many early poems and Australian tales, making a very fine collection of Australian literature."[35] Happily, much of Davidson's collection of Australiana is still in the possession of the Rockhampton Municipal Library which developed from the School of Arts Library in 1946.

Davidson was also a supporter of the School's technical education program which began in

1890 and later (in 1914) developed into the Rockhampton Technical College and, later still, the Rockhampton TAFE College. He resigned from the Library in 1910 - sixteen years after the original School of Arts building had been demolished - and returned to his post as dispenser at the General Hospital, and later retired to Fiji. His term as Librarian covered not only the end of the old School of Arts, but the beginning of the new, as well as the dawning of a new century, in which the Librarians of the Rockhampton School of Arts and the Rockhampton Municipal Library would cease being little more than gifted amateurs with an interest in books and would become professional managers.[36]

Because the early librarians of the School of Arts had no formal training in librarianship, one is inclined to dismiss them lightly. However, formal library education did not exist in the nineteenth century and most librarians were trained on-the-job or had served as booksellers' apprentices. Cumming, Pilcher, Potts and Davidson were all educated men who had an interest in their work, a concern for their collection and its users, and a love of the School of Arts Library. They each devoted long hours under a demanding Committee to give their users the best library service possible in the circumstances. They operated on small budgets, with no professional contact or support, and often without adequate staff. The incentives of a salary and free accommodation may have existed, but they were hardly enough to keep anyone but the most devoted in the position. The Rockhampton School of Arts committees and members owed a great debt to their librarians, a debt which was not often recognised.

The Rockhampton School of Arts Library flourished until 1946, when it was taken over by the Rockhampton City Council. Its collection formed the basis of the Rockhampton Municipal Library's collection, and Miss Grace Perrier, the School of Arts Librarian (a member of the Library staff from 1900 to 1952) became the Municipal Librarian. Today, the Rockhampton Municipal Library system encompasses the main Town Library, a branch, and a hospital and nursing home service - a far cry from the two hundred and fifty volumes that the School of Arts' Library started with in 1865.

"THE MUSEUM OF THE CENTRAL DIVISION"

> A want has been lately felt in town for a room, suitable to receive specimens of various productions indigenous to the colony, and as this is the centre of a large mineral district, the time has come in which some special effort should be made to commence such a collection as will form the nucleus of a museum [at the School of Arts]. For the present the Librarian could attend to it without any extra cost, and... [the]... Committee will be in a position during the next year, to advance £150 towards erecting two rooms at the rear of the present buildings... One of these could be used as a Library, the other as a Museum, and we have no doubt that an appeal to the inhabitants of Rockhampton will have the effect of raising the other £150 required to carry out this most desirable object."[37]

This "want" of a museum of natural history, however, did not materialise with its announcement in the *Morning Bulletin* in July 1869. In fact, it had been felt in some quarters for a fairly long time.

Some Early Enthusiasts

It appears that the main instigator of the Rockhampton Museum project was one Anthelme Thozet, a French botanist-turned-publican who had arrived in the district with the Canoona Rush of 1858. Thozet had busied himself from his first days in Central Queensland with collecting and studying the local flora. He had been a collector for Ferdinand Von Mueller of the Melbourne Botanical Gardens, and as early as 1862 had exhibited a collection of timber specimens from the Rockhampton area at the London Exhibition.

In 1866 Thozet published his *Notes on Some of the Roots, Tubers, Bulbs, and Fruits, Used as Vegetable Food by the Aboriginals of Northern Queensland*, a sixteen-page booklet dedicated to Von Mueller and selling for sixpence. Thozet also announced that "Any profits arising from the sale of this Pamphlet will be placed to the credit of the 'Rockhampton Museum Building Fund',"[38] thereby recording the first interest in forming a museum for Rockhampton.

Public support for a museum grew throughout the 1860s, due largely to Central Queensland's involvement in international exhibitions and the work of several visiting zoologists and botanists. Thozet's booklet, along with specimens of the plants it listed and many other samples of Central Queensland products, were sent to the 1867 Paris Exhibition, and when the entire collection of local material was displayed in Rockhampton prior to its dispatch, "it inspired the public to 'more than ordinary feelings of pride and satisfaction'."[39]

When reports of the Paris Exhibition filtered back to Rockhampton, those feelings changed to anger, for Thozet and Rockhampton itself had felt themselves slighted by the title 'Queensland Exhibits' on their display. According to Rockhampton's historian, L L McDonald:

> The *Rockhampton Bulletin* described this as a 'piece of shabbiness' on the part of Brisbane and as yet another attempt to 'smother' a Rockhampton man and 'to exalt a Brisbane pet'. The Brisbane pet was Walter Hill, Curator of the Botanic Gardens. There were genuine grounds for dismay, for not only was Thozet's name omitted from both the Paris and London catalogues, but a large collection of his timber specimens were listed under Hill's name. In addition, of the $4,000 voted by the Queensland Parliament to finance the project, Rockhampton did not receive one cent.[40]

Rockhampton contributed a much smaller number of items to the 1872 London International Exhibition due to "gross mismanagement on the last occasion."[41] The work of Thozet and other professional scientists and collectors during the 1860s did much to draw the attention of the Rockhampton public to the natural wonders of Central Queensland and to promote the need for a museum in the town.

Amalie Dietrich (1821-91) arrived in Rockhampton in 1864 from Germany and spent two years in the Rockhampton district assiduously collecting and skinning mammals and birds, mounting and drying plants and insects, and collecting shells and coral for a private museum in Hamburg. In McDonald's words, "this rare emancipated woman, in an age when most of her sex were denied lives of their own, revelled in her freedom as a collector in the district where she was able to stride across the wide plains, cross rivers and lakes in a small canoe, and ...'collect-collect-collect'."[42]

John O'Shanesy (1834-99) and his brother Patrick (1839-84) arrived in Rockhampton from Ireland in 1864 and 1866 respectively. John had been trained as a scientific gardener and after arriving in Queensland worked as a collector for Von Mueller before establishing a nursery. He also wrote many articles on botanical subjects for the Rockhampton press and, along with Thozet, assisted in establishing the Rockhampton Botanic Gardens in 1869. Patrick O'Shanesy, a Fellow of the Linnean Society of London, had also collected specimens for Von Mueller, as well as writing prolifically on botanical subjects.[43]

The Museum Movement Gathers Momentum

Public interest in establishing a museum began to grow in mid-1869, when Thozet presented the profits of *Roots, Tubers, Bulbs and Fruits* [£10] to T.S. Hall, manager of the Australian Joint Stock Bank. A few days later, the *Rockhampton Bulletin* carried the following report on attempts to form a museum:

> The arguments...for the establishment of a Government museum in Rockhampton, are answerable, if we look at the question in its bearing on mineral discovery. We do not dispute the expediency of having a museum at Brisbane; but there it will be simply a congeries of collections and specimens - objects of interest and possibly of study to the dilettanti mineralogists of Brisbane, but of very little practical benefit to the working miners... The idea of founding a museum in Rockhampton , has originated with Mr Thozet; and we trust that the people of the town and district will support it. The advantages of such an institution to the district are self evident; and though the Government had scoffed at the idea of a museum for Rockhampton, we believe that there is sufficient public spirit amongst us to realise the project... The establishment of a museum in Rockhampton by ourselves, and with our money, would be practical protest against the injustice and narrow-minded economising of the Government, and would be an effectual means of placing before the public of Australia and Great Britain, a truthful representation of the mineral wealth and the agricultural capabilities of Northern Queensland.[44]

When it became obvious that the Brisbane-based government was not going to support a Rockhampton museum, the School of Arts stepped into the breach and offered to establish one. Donations for the collection began pouring in almost immediately. In November 1869, Richard Daintree, the Government geologist, donated a large collection of local minerals, and the *Rockhampton Bulletin* noted: "They [the School of Arts Committee] may collect a large quantity of specimens before their [museum] building is erected."[45] The School of Arts continued to build a museum collection without progressing far towards the completion of a building in which to house it. In September 1870, the project's supporters were informed that "The museum project seems to be indefinitely postponed, on account, we believe, of the extreme poverty of the Government, which makes the concession of a money grant very problematical."[46] A Government grant was eventually made and a new Library and Museum wing was added to the School of Arts building early in 1872.[47]

The partial completion of the Museum wing added impetus to the project, for on 8 August it was announced that:

> Among the things not generally known is the fact that Mr Cumming, Librarian of the

School of Arts, is unobtrusively collecting specimens for the future museum. These specimens, which are open to public examination at all times, embrace the following:-
PRECIOUS STONES - Yellow and White Topaz, Turquoise, Beryl, Sapphire, Garnets Onyx, Opal.
MINERALS - Sulphuret of Mercury or Cinnumbar, Plumbago, Galona, Argentiferous Galona, Native Silver, Antimony, Crystals of White Cobalt, Copper Ore, Grey and Black Oxides of Manganese, Native Bismuth, Stream Tin, Sulphuret of Tin, and Oxides of Tin; sixty-four specimens of Native Metals and Metalliferous Minerals; seventy-two specimens of Minerals which are either the components of rocks, or frequently found embedded in them; twenty-six specimens of Aeidiferous earthy Minerals.

These are examined almost every day, and the Committee will be exceedingly obliged for any specimens sent. The Reference Library also contains works having articles on almost all known minerals, with their assays and methods of reduction.[48]

However, the Museum was not to be opened for another twelve months. The annual meeting of 1873 noted that: "A number of contributions have been received for the Museum, and more are promised. Cases to receive these have been ordered but owing to the skilled labour in town being fully employed, the work has not been completed. It is expected, however, that in a short time the Museum will be open. Contributions of specimens of natural history, minerals, etc. will be gladly received by the Librarian."[49] True to the promise of the Committee, the Museum was unobtrusively opened late in 1873, and almost immediately suffered a severe lack of funding. In January 1875 it was found necessary for:

a number of ladies and gentlemen...[to give]... an amateur concert in aid for the Museum funds. The sum realised was £27/4/6, which amount the Committee made application to the Government to supplement, but were unsuccessful. The matter has been entrusted to the advocacy of the Member for the town, who, it is to be hoped, will be able to induce the Government to grant a small annual sum in furtherance of such a useful object.... The Museum, although in connection with the School of Arts, is free to all, and has therefore the greater claim to public support.[50]

Dust and Disorder

Two years later, the lack of financial support for the museum was hailed as a prime factor when allegations of neglect were made in the local press:

Above the Reading Room in the School of Arts is a mysterious region whose recesses are rarely explored even by the most determined sight-seer; and yet it is a place to which one would naturally expect strangers to be attracted. This is the Rockhampton Museum. The term 'museum' raises a picture before one of the large hall, around the walls of which are placed polished mahogany cases with glass covers, full of gorgeous birds, gleaming metals, and strange fantastic fossils; and at the door of which one expects to be accosted by a bland servitor and requested to inscribe name and address in a book, in order, possibly that the visitor may be captured if he attempts to pocket the ostrich or Irish elk. But a visit to the Rockhampton Museum speedily dispels such old world ideas.

Original Rockhampton School of Arts, Qld, ca 1865
(reproduced by permission of the Capricornia Collection, University of Central Queensland)

Second Rockhampton School of Arts, Qld, ca 1895
(reproduced by permission of the Capricornia Collection, University of Central Queensland)

Around the reading-room of our School of Arts, then, runs a broad gallery, reached by a flight of steps in the corner. Proceeding up these stairs, which are kept scrupulously clean, I found myself in a gallery about six or eight feet broad.... In the gallery are four cases such as are generally found in museums.... Underneath [the first case] are huddled together a few pieces of timber, probably specimens of local woods, but sadly in want of arrangement. The next case is the only one in the Museum which is neatly arranged. It contains minerals, and appears to be a very fair collection. They are almost all neatly numbered, and a guide book lying on the case gives the names of all the specimens. In the corner nearby, is a mass of papers and magazines, which may be the nucleus of the Museum Library, but it is certainly not an ornamental exhibit.

On the other side of the gallery are two more cases and a long wooden table. The table is interesting, as it excites one's wonder as to what it can possibly be there for. It is a scrupulously clean, long, narrow table. Nothing is laid on it. There it stands, a mystery. The case beside the table contains a collection of corals and shells, some beetles, and a piece of Queensland tin. The shells are neatly ticketed with their names and classes.[51]

Unfortunately, this critical article brought forward no great changes or improvements in the Museum, apart from the repainting of the interior and the installation of some new shelving in 1879.[52]

Accusations of neglect resurfaced in 1881 with the publication of another article in the *Morning Bulletin*:

A meeting of the School of Arts was held on Thursday evening, at which the attention of the Committee was called to the state of the Museum. It is not at all to the credit of the Committee that they should not have been better able to meet Mr Potts' reflections. As an educational agent and interesting place of resort, the Museum is comparatively worthless. We went up the other day to see the articles which had been returned from the Melbourne Exhibition. The cases of birds are very pretty, but the names of the specimens are not given. In like manner, the timber specimens, very nice and attractive, are set up against the wall without attempt at order or arrangement. It is no doubt the duty of the Curator to attend to the Museum, but when it is obviously being neglected, the Committee should not render it incumbent on ordinary members to call attention to the matter. Parliamentary papers, moreover, are useful and interesting and, when placed where they may be easily seen and read, their value becomes apparent. They are not, however, when placed on a shelf and covered with dust. A little more energy and determination on the part of the Committee is most desirable.[53]

Subsequent Committees appear to have pulled their socks up in the Museum department, as it was commented in 1883: "The Museum is advancing steadily, several additions to the collection having been made during the last year..."[54]

The Museum received a further boost in August the following year when the School of Arts Committee decided to hold an Exhibition of local products, akin to the Melbourne Exhibition of 1880. The Committee later decided that the "exhibition...proved in every way a thorough success, the number and quality of exhibits being exceedingly good, also the attendance of visitors, and shows that such exhibitions are productive of much good. On the success of the...exhibition, your Committee has decided to hold one annually in August, and have every reason to believe that they will be quite successful in the future, as in the past [sic]." Unfortunately, the Exhibition program lasted only until 1886, when it was abandoned due to lack of public support. However, the success of the 1884 Exhibition boosted the Museum's public image and led to a sharp increase in the number of donations of specimens, and to a short-lived increase in the number of visitors.

The Museum's first purchase of material was made in 1885, when a collection of twenty birds' skins, at a cost of £2/15/-, was ordered from a southern supplier. The following year the Librarian (Potts) invested in a microscope worth £50 and a telescope for £25 for the Museum, justifying the expenditure by stating: "There are plenty of good works in the Library, but they merely taught students what would never be put into practice, unless by the aid of the instruments referred to."[55]

At around the same time, the Museum began to encourage visits by school children, and the Committee was told by its Chairman that "Mr G Potts Snr., headmaster of the Central State School for Boys, had applied for the use of the geological specimens, and they had been granted to him. The same privilege would be conceded to others if they guaranteed to return the specimens."[56] One wonders whether the fact that Mr Potts was the Librarian's father had anything to do with this special privilege.

For the next eight years the Museum progressed steadily, if slowly, accepting donations and making some small purchases of material and fittings for the collection. However, by 1894, when the new School of Arts building was opened, the Museum was referred to as merely "a nucleus."[57] It was thought by some optimists that "not very long hence it might be desirable to erect a separate building for it - for what might become the Museum of the Central Division, in the mould of the Brisbane Museum."[58]

The Museum Stagnates and Dies

Unfortunately, the museum was to remain very much 'a nucleus' even after it was transferred to its permanent home in the new building and it was never a very large or healthy part of the School of Arts' structure; it certainly never became the Museum of the Central Division. It was eventually closed in 1946 and its collection, which had grown to be an eclectic mixture of stuffed animals, metallurgical specimens, coral, shells, "the hat of a Chinese Mandarin and the sword of a Chinese executioner,"[59] aboriginal and pioneering artefacts, as well as samples of timber and local primary products, was dispersed.

Why, then, was the School of Arts Museum so sorely neglected, thus failing to be "an educational agent and place of resort"?[60] There are a number of reasons. Firstly, it is possible to assume that the School of Arts Committees either were not fully supportive of the Museum project from the start, or that they soon lost interest in it. A natural history museum in Rockhampton was essentially the dream of a small number of influential and vocal original School or Arts members, headed by Anthelme Thozet. Thozet was undoubtedly the leading light in the push for the establishment of a government-supported museum in Central Queensland, and he devoted a great deal of his own energy, time, and money to the project.

When the Government of the day rejected Rockhampton's request for a natural history museum, Thozet, as a member of the School of Arts Committee, convinced the School to establish its own Museum. This was done, and Thozet would have been the Museum's most ardent supporter. Unfortunately, his early death in 1878 (from a fever contracted whilst on a collecting expedition), less than five years after the Museum was established, robbed the Museum of its leading supporter and another was never found.[61]

Consequently, the School was left with a Museum it had possibly never really wanted and which it was ill-prepared to care for. During the whole of the period from the opening of the Museum in 1873 to the construction of the new building in 1894, the School of Arts Committee received no direct funding for the Museum from successive Queensland governments, even though the Museum was open free of charge to the public. Without government funding or revenue generated by such means as admission charges, the Museum was effectively a drain on the School's resources, and every Committee in the School's early history was unwilling to spend money on enlarging or improving the collection, or to employ curatorial staff to supervise it.

Post Mortem

Without an adequate source of funding it was impossible to implement a responsible or substantial collecting policy, as the Museum was unable to make regular purchases of material for the collection or for museum fittings. The Museum was forced to rely on donations for the bulk of its collection, and while a great deal of valuable and interesting material was donated, for example Richard Daintree's mineral samples and the material sent from Central Queensland to the Melbourne Exhibition of 1880, the almost total reliance on donated material, and the reluctance of successive Committees to veto contributions for fear of offending the donors, meant that the Museum became little more than an eclectic jumble of other people's rubbish. The haphazard collection of material which was accumulated through donations was of little value or use, to either the School or the citizens and students of Rockhampton, who voted with their feet and stayed away from the Museum in droves.

Added to the complications caused by a non-existent collection policy, a nearly total lack of funding, and a collection of donated curios and cast-offs, was the problem of staffing the Museum. Of course, experienced Museum staff were thin on the ground in nineteenth-century Queensland and, due to its reluctance to spend money on the Museum, the School of Arts never employed a Museum curator, or attendants, qualified or otherwise. It was always perceived to be the Librarian's duty to keep the Museum in order, to supervise its users and to develop its collection. Clearly this was an impossible task; the Librarian had to devote most of his time to his first responsibility - the Library - as well as acting as Secretary to the Committee (in the period after 1874). It was a physical and mental impossibility for the Librarian to run the Library, the Committee and the Museum. Something had to suffer; one of the departments had to be neglected. The School's *un*wanted, and financially unproductive, Museum was apparently considered the obvious choice.

307

NOTES AND REFERENCES

1.*Rockhampton Bulletin,* 25 February 1865.

2.*Morning Bulletin* (Rockhampton), 23 February 1932. This article, which has been quoted extensively in this chapter, directly quotes original *Bulletin* articles which are no long extant.

3.*ibid.*

4.*ibid.*

5.*ibid.*

6.Griest, G. (1970). *Mudie's Circulating Library and the Victorian novel.* Newton Abbott, Devon: David and Charles, p.30.

7.*ibid.*, p.29.

8.*Rockhampton Bulletin*, 14 July 1866.

9.*Morning Bulletin*, 15 April 1893.

10.*Rockhampton Bulletin*, 14 July 1866.

11.Griest, *op. cit.,* p.18.

12.*Morning Bulletin*, 22 July 1889.

13.*Morning Bulletin*, 21 July 1893.

14.*Morning Bulletin*, 17 July 1891.

15.*Rockhampton Bulletin*, 15 July 1865, 11 July 1868, 13 July 1872; *Morning Bulletin*, 12 July 1878, 16 July 1890.

16.*Catalogue of the library of the Rockhampton School of Arts.* Rockhampton: Rockhampton School of Arts, 1872.

17.Trollope, A., quoted by Griest, *op. cit.,* p.3.

18.*Morning Bulletin*, 23 July 1886.

19.*Morning Bulletin*, 20 July 1888.

20.Archer, W. (1977). *Tourist to the antipodes - William Archer's Australian journey, 1876-77.* St Lucia, Qld: University of Queensland Press, p.33.

21.*Morning Bulletin*, 17 July 1891.

22. McDonald, L.L. (1981). *Rockhampton: A history of city and district.* St Lucia, Qld: University of Queensland Press, see index entries.

23. *Rockhampton Bulletin*, 14 July 1866.

24. *Catalogue*, (1872).

25. *ibid.*

26. *Morning Bulletin*, 19 July 1887

27. *Morning Bulletin*, 10 July 1888

28. *Morning Bulletin*, 20 July 1888

29. *Morning Bulletin*, 17 July 1891.

30. McDonald, L.L. (1989). Conversation with W. Murdoch - July 1989.

31. *Morning Bulletin*, 3 July 1872; McDonald, Rockhampton: A history, *op. cit.*, index entries.

32. McDonald, *op. cit.*, p.402.

33. *Morning Bulletin*, 17 July 1891

34. *Morning Bulletin*, 19 July 1889.

35. McDonald, *loc. cit.*

36. Perrier, G. (1964). *A short brochure on Mr N.M.M. Davidson - During the years 1889 to 1910* (typescript) n.d. [circa 1964].

37. *Rockhampton Bulletin*, 10 July 1869.

38. Thozet, A. (1866). *Notes on some of the roots, tubers, bulbs and fruits used as vegetable food by the aboriginals of Northern Queensland.* Rockhampton: A. Thozet, p.1.

39. McDonald, *op. cit.*, p.405.

40. *ibid.*, p.405.

41. *ibid.*

42. *ibid.*, p.408.

43. *ibid.*, p.407.

44. *Rockhampton Bulletin*, 8 July 1869.

45. *Rockhampton Bulletin*, 16 November 1869.

46. *Rockhampton Bulletin*, 24 September 1870.

47. *Rockhampton Bulletin,* 13 July 1872.

48. *Rockhampton Bulletin*, 8 August 1872.

49. *Rockhampton Bulletin,* 13 July 1873.

50. *Morning Bulletin,* 9 July 1875.

51. *Morning Bulletin*, 27 April 1877.

52. *Morning Bulletin,* 18 July 1879.

53. *Morning Bulletin,* 15 October 1881.

54. *Morning Bulletin,* 20 July 1883.

55. *Morning Bulletin,* 17 July 1885.

56. *Morning Bulletin,* 23 July 1886.

57. *Morning Bulletin*, 7 March 1894.

58. *ibid.*

59. *Morning Bulletin*, 23 February 1932.

60. *Morning Bulletin*, 15 October 1882.

61. McDonald, *op. cit.*, p.406.

CHAPTER FIFTEEN

A TALE OF TWO CITIES: MECHANICS' INSTITUTES IN HOBART AND LAUNCESTON

Stefan Petrow

INTRODUCTION

Although Hobart was settled in 1803, some fifteen years after Sydney's foundation in 1788, it is to Hobart that the record must go for establishing the first mechanics' institute in Australia, in 1827. Given that this was a mere six years after the foundation of the first such institute in Glasgow, and only four years after the inauguration of the famous London Mechanics' Institute, this is a remarkable achievement for such a small, remote, and young part of the British Empire. Yet this, the earliest of Australia's institutes, did not live a full fifty years, and its history has never before been recorded.

The Launceston Mechanics' Institute, on the other hand, was founded some fifteen years later again, in 1842. Although its progress was neither smooth nor uninterrupted, it at least survived under its own name until well into the twentieth century, and in 1992 its successor - the Launceston Public Library - sponsored special celebrations to recognise the 150th Anniversary of its foundation.

What is it that accounts for the dramatically different fortunes of these two Tasmanian institutes? It is the purpose of this chapter to compare and contrast the origins, aims and progress of both institutes. Their respective attempts to educate the working-classes through lectures and classes and to develop library collections will be discussed, and I will end by analysing the reason for the collapse of the Hobart Mechanics' Institute and the survival of the Launceston Mechanics' Institute.

Before 1850 the dominant secular creed of colonial society was, as Michael Roe has argued, "moral enlightenment."[1] This creed grew out of the eighteenth-century enlightenment and stressed "individualism, rationality, the importance of the temporal world, and man's power to solve its problems." Predominantly egalitarian, it fused the utilitarian preoccupation of "the greatest good for the greatest number" with the "romantic belief in everyman's perfectibility," which would be achieved through "self-respect, self-discipline, and self-improvement." Heavily imbued with moral rhetoric, the creed put great faith in the spread of temperance, science, culture and education (i.e., knowledge) as elevating, progressive and unifying influences in society. The mechanics' institutes of Hobart and Launceston both contained definite traces of moral enlightenment ideals.[2] This will become clear in what follows.

THE VAN DIEMEN'S LAND MECHANICS' INSTITUTE - HOBART

First settled in 1803, by the 1830s Hobart was not only the administrative centre of Van Diemen's Land but also "the main port, a manufacturing centre, and the cultural and religious capital of Tasmania."[3] The population was about 6,000 in 1830, growing rapidly to 15,000 by 1841. In Hobart, "authority unmistakably flowed from above" and the preferences of the élite tended to outweigh the preferences of other classes. This was illustrated by the establishment of the Van Diemen's Land Mechanics' Institute, which became known as the Hobart Town Mechanics' Institute in February 1857.

After an initial meeting in 1826, the *Colonial Times* reported that a mechanics' institute had been formed on 2 January 1827 by "many of the most respectable master tradesmen."[4] However, later reports indicate that it was established on 20 March 1827 at a meeting attended not only by all "the operative mechanics," but by most of the Justices of the Peace and many other gentlemen.[5] Dr James Ross, teacher and editor, chaired the meeting and George Augustus Robinson, builder and philanthropist, was described as the founder of the institute.

The aims of the institute were to promote "useful and scientific knowledge" by "the voluntary association" of mechanics and others.[6] A library, reading room and museum of "machines, models, minerals and other objects of natural history" was to be set up as well as "an experimental workshop and laboratory." It was intended that lectures would be arranged on natural and experimental philosophy, practical mechanics, chemistry, literature and the arts, and that classes would be held on arithmetic, algebra, geometry and trigonometry and their different applications, particularly to perspective, architecture, mensuration, and navigation. The *Hobart Gazette* praised the institute. Too often in newly formed countries and colonies, it stated, energies were concentrated on "the actual business of settling" to the neglect of "the mind and its acquirements."[7] Van Diemen's Land, it hoped, would form "an exception to this precedent and the desire of getting knowledge as well as money will prevail." On 20 June, at a quarterly meeting, it was announced that the Chief Justice, J L Pedder, would be President supported by two Vice-Presidents, a Secretary and twenty committee members.[8] Half the committee (not two-thirds as originally proposed) would be mechanics.

From the start the Van Diemen's Land Mechanics' Institute attracted criticism. One critic called 'Numskull,' a mechanic but not a member, claimed it was "not an institution of and for mechanics" but rather "of and for gentlemen;....public officers and rich men, merchants and others, exclusively, who have assumed to themselves all the power and control of the institution": the presence of a "superior" was the only way to "keep the fellows in subjection," one Vice-President was heard to say.[9] The gentlemen should have become Vice-Patrons, not Vice-Presidents, leaving mechanics with "power in their own hands." This would have "created gratitude and respect from the poor men," but their action had "only occasioned a general jealousy and disturbance throughout the Society." 'Numskull' denied that mechanics had called for the support of their superiors. He alleged that "a number of individuals who know by property and by the offices they hold, that they can *command* sway," came "*en masse*," and wrested the management of the institute "out of the hands of *those who founded it on its present basis*." They proposed and elected themselves office-bearers "in direct opposition to the rules and laws." Any "apparent cordiality" between gentlemen and mechanics was based on "the TERROR OF POWER": Mechanics did not oppose the gentlemen and public officers for fear of giving offence, and thereby losing work which it was perhaps in their "gift" to offer.

Unable to recover from this inauspicious start, over the next ten years the Van Diemen's

Land Mechanics' Institute languished and then was reorganised on a regular basis. It was held back by the lack of government support under Governor Arthur and minimal public support because of the existence of an "exclusive and narrow spirit" in the management.[10] The institute was kept alive mainly by the efforts of James Ross. He argued that in "the absence of a university or college," a mechanics' institute where lectures were "periodically delivered on useful and scientific subjects" was crucial to "the character and reputation of the colony."[11] According to Ross, the mechanics' institute would enliven and enlarge "the powers of the mind," ameliorate "the social habits and affections," add to "the mechanical power of man by the acquisition of important and powerful truths," and enable "us to extend the general sphere of human enjoyment." It would also add to "the numbers of the honest, the industrious, the temperate, the respectable and the contented classes of the community." In 1833 Ross made his new reading rooms in Collins Street available to the institute for lectures and for depositing the library and scientific apparatus.

When Sir John Franklin became Governor in 1837, intellectual pursuits in Van Diemen's Land were given a new lease of life.[12] In March 1838 Franklin, who agreed to be patron, promised to vote £100 per annum to the institute.[13] Much to the chagrin of colonists, the British government did not sanction the grant until February 1841; however, it remained a mainstay of the institute until its withdrawal in 1863. Another mainstay was the Presbyterian, Rev. John Lillie, who was President from 1839 to 1855 and who often opened or closed the lecture season to large audiences: his lectures "reached the high-water mark of learning publicly disseminated" in the colony.[14] In 1840 Lillie's introductory lecture on the advantages of classical knowledge in forming the mind so greatly impressed the Glasgow Mechanics' Institute that it intended to print an edition for its members.[15] Lillie supported mechanics' institutes because of the "moral and social benefits which naturally arise from bringing together the different classes of the community in connection with an intellectual and liberal object," a clear expression of moral enlightenment ideals.[16]

After using temporary accommodation for its activities, in 1841 the institute secured the old Wesleyan Chapel in Melville Street at a rent of £50 per year.[17] Subsequent management committees discussed ways of raising funds for their own building but felt that during the 1840s depression the expense was beyond them. In 1845 the committee decided to take out a twenty-one year lease on the Wesleyan Chapel and to spend £500 on alterations.[18] The alterations provided members with "a commodious and well-adapted hall" for lecturing and for housing the scientific apparatus, museum collection and library: A reading room was also established. Despite being granted a number of sites by various governments, the remodelled hall remained the home of the institute and no serious attempt to raise funds for a building seems to have been made by 1871.[19] In Hobart the members and management committees apparently relied on various governments to grant them money for a building, while in Launceston, as we shall see, striking efforts by many residents were made to raise building funds.

Although the Hobart Mechanics' Institute became firmly established in the 1840s, it still attracted criticism. In June 1841 the *Courier* claimed it was not a mechanics' institute but "a society for the promotion of the literary and scientific tastes of the public, without reference in any degree to classes of society."[20] Accordingly, it argued, the Hobart Town Literary and Scientific Association would be a more accurate designation. In January 1845, 'Tasmaniensis' noted that "few of the humbler class take any interest" in the institute, and "many of the more elevated station [lend] support only in the condescending style of sanction and patronage." 'O.P.Q.' alleged that the needs of mechanics had been "too much overlooked" and much of what was done was "better adapted to please the 'respectable' than to improve the mechanic." The Committee of Management responded to such criticisms by allowing mechanics to pay quarterly subscriptions of 2s 6d from 1845, but mechanics remained aloof, leaving membership to the "salaried officer," who loomed large in Hobart Town.[21]

In the 1840s mechanics were particularly critical of the fact that they had no control over the management of the institute.[22] Clear manifestations of dissatisfaction were the appearance of rival organisations. In February 1845 the Tasmanian Society for the Acquisition of Useful Knowledge was formed but did not survive for long.[23] In 1849 the Tasmanian Public Library first emerged as a subscription library and lasted until 1870, when it was taken over by the government and the Hobart Municipal Council.[24] Finally, in March 1850, the Hobart Town Mechanics' School of Arts was formed and staggered on until November 1853 when it disbanded, handing over its books and property to the mechanics' institute.[25]

After seeing off its rivals, the institute reached its most flourishing phase in the 1850s. But it depended on the government grant, which was increased to £250 in 1856 and kept the institute from being devoured by debt.[26] Not enough revenue was generated by subscriptions as membership was low - 172 annual members, and 252 members who paid at least one quarterly instalment.[27] Perhaps mechanics could not stomach the paternalism of an institute which saw its mission as "cultivating their minds, improving their general intelligence and information, making them at the same time better workmen, better artists, better members of society, and better men."[28] If mechanics still did not 'adequately' support the institute, who did join and why? In 1858 the *Mercury* thought that the

> largest proportion of subscribers were those who joined for the advantage of reading the light literature contained in the Library; many others subscribe for the purpose of spending an hour in the Lecture Room viewing it as a place of fashionable resort; some again subscribe because they deem it a duty to patronise such an Institution; a few, and but very few, join with the object of gaining practical instruction in the Arts and Sciences.[29]

It could not discard its reputation for being "an exclusive and an aristocratic institution, a fashionable lounge for the educated and wealthy rather than a school for the humble and poor."[30] The managers were "not working men, and they have not intimate associations with that class." In 1860 a number of mechanics, no longer able to tolerate an unsympathetic and unqualified management, attempted to grab control but failed.[31] Thereafter membership began to fluctuate, usually downwards, attendance at lectures and classes dropped, and from 1864, after the government grant was withdrawn under heavy protest, the closure of the institute was yearly debated.[32]

Perhaps the most serious threat to its long-term viability was the formation in October 1864 of the Hobart Working Men's Club, which was designed for "the exclusive benefit" of and was managed by working men.[33] Recreation was given a higher priority than learning in the club, which also intended to establish a provident fund and a savings bank. A donation of £1,600 by the wealthy businessman W A Guesdon enabled clubrooms to be built in

Liverpool Street, a piece of good fortune which contrasted starkly with the mechanics' institute's risible inability to raise funds for a building.[34]

The formation of the Hobart Working Men's Club acted as a spur, and the appointment to the mechanics' institute's committee of "younger and more ardent" workers helped stop the institute sliding quickly into oblivion.[35] In desperation, efforts were made to popularise the institute by limiting the number of scientific lectures and arranging concerts and readings "to bend to what may ... be called the frivolous tastes of the public."[36] But this also had mixed success, and the institute finally closed in November 1871.[37]

THE LAUNCESTON MECHANICS' INSTITUTE

In Launceston, on the other hand, the mechanics' institute was beginning to consolidate and prosper by the 1870s, its early history having not been a tale of progress. Founded in 1806, Launceston began to develop economically in the 1820s and 1830s, was held back by the depression of the 1840s, but after 1850 began to rival Hobart as a commercial centre.[38] As "the heartland of colonial nonconformism," Launcestonians believed in the philosophy of self-help and, as a town with "a narrow social scale," businessmen and shopkeepers "participated to a much greater extent in community life" than in Hobart: Launceston was "possibly less class-conscious" and had a "more democratic character" than Hobart.[39] This was the kind of town in which a mechanics' institute should flourish.

According to the Congregationalist minister, Rev. Charles Price, the idea of forming a mechanics' institute arose from discussions at the Launceston Book Society, formed in 1841.[40] Its members decided that a mechanics' institute should be open to all residents at a moderate cost. On 8 March 1842 the Launceston Mechanics' Institute was established at a meeting presided over by Police Magistrate, W H Breton, R.N., and attended by a large audience, comprising many mechanics and operatives, who were apparently enthusiastic in their support.[41] The Rev John West, another Congregationalist minister and a leading intellectual, was a prime mover and the meeting passed his resolution that the objects of the mechanics' institute be "the promotion of science and the arts, combined with the diffusion of general literature." The meeting agreed to form a mechanics institute to promote "the intellectual culture of the operative classes": "mechanics and workmen of all classes" were invited to become members. Fifty people in an estimated population of over 6,000 enrolled immediately. As in Hobart, the Launceston Mechanics' Institute would conduct lectures and classes and build up a library, museum, and a laboratory: a provisional committee was set up to further these objectives.

Support came from many quarters. The *Examiner*, at that time edited by West, believed a mechanics' institute would have an elevating influence: "pernicious amusements and intemperate habits among the mass of mechanics" would disappear because the institute would open up "a field of more rational pleasure."[42] The paper hoped that "every moral and intelligent inhabitant" of Launceston would not only join but assist by "active exertions." The mechanics' institute would, it was envisaged, unite the various classes and sects, the artisan and the employer, the scholar and the tradesman. Similarly, the *Launceston Advertiser* thought that the mechanics' institute would help improve "the moral and social condition of the people," especially of "the indifferent and indolent youths" of Launceston.[43] Inculcating "a taste for literary pursuits amongst the rising generation" would be an important function of the institute. On 10 May 1842 the governing body was formed. Breton was President and he was assisted by a Board of Managers of twenty, two secretaries, a treasurer and five trustees.[44] The *Examiner* claimed that the office-bearers were taken from "every sect" and the lecture list embraced "men of every colonial party." Governor Franklin was patron.

Despite the *Examiner's* view, it would be a mistake to convey the impression that there was complete support for the mechanics' institute, as correspondents to the *Cornwall Chronicle* quickly made clear. 'An Operative' alleged that everyone in Launceston "who from their education, profession or pretensions might be expected to afford any valuable literary aid" to the mechanics' institute stayed away from the first meeting.[45] Another correspondent called 'A Mechanic' thought that the provisional committee was unrepresentative, contained too few mechanics, and intended to cram the by-laws of the institute "down the throat" of mechanics. Unless mechanics ran the institute, it would fail to achieve its aims. Mechanics should withhold their membership fees until they were satisfied that the mechanics' institute would promote science and not provide books for members of the Book Society, whose members dominated the provisional committee. The gentry should be told that the mechanics of Launceston were "not illiterate idiots in the arts and sciences" - many were "more conversant" with those subjects than the lecturers, who must attain a more superior "intellectual standard" than they had hitherto demonstrated. In April 1843 the *Cornwall Chronicle* noted that "the leading portion of the community" and mechanics studiously kept away from the institute, despite the absence of other attractions "to divide public attention, divert their thought, or gratify particular inclinations."[46]

In part, the lack of support can be explained by the Launceston mechanics' dislike of paternalism imposed by their superiors, but there are other reasons. The mechanics' institute became embroiled in disputes between temperance and anti-temperance forces and contending sects within Launceston society fighting for control of various philanthropic and commercial bodies.[47] Faced with opposition and disputes, the management board tried in vain to further the educational objectives of the institute. Classes seem not to have lasted very long and attendance at lectures was invariably low into the 1850s.

The year 1856 was a turning point for the Launceston Mechanics' Institute. By 1856 the excitement and confusion engendered by the gold discoveries on the mainland had subsided and prosperity was becoming more widespread.[48] The Board of Managers made a concerted effort to raise money to construct a building on land at the corner of St John and Cameron Streets granted by the government in 1846. When the foundation stone was laid on 24 June 1857 by the Congregationalist-turned-Presbyterian Rev. R K Ewing, who was mainly responsible for reviving interest in the institute, the day was declared a public holiday and banks, public offices and shops were closed.[49] In an impressive example of communal self-help, the board of managers of the Launceston Mechanics' Institute, with the indispensable help of Launceston women, raised some £5,896 between 1857 and 1860.[50] Parliament chipped in to vote £3,000. The new hall was opened on 9 April 1860 and was followed by a bazaar comprised of ten stalls, an art exhibition, and a concert, which raised another £1,300 before it closed on 14 April 1860.[51] Charles Price, one of the early members, thought it was "the dawn of a new era" in the history of the institute because of the unprecedented nature of the support given by all members of Launceston society.

Again, after a period of enthusiasm, attendance at lectures and classes dropped and membership - especially of mechanics - was discouragingly low by the mid-1860s. It seemed to the Board of Managers that the operatives and workmen had "stood aloof" from the services offered by the institute because they perceived "an exclusive spirit in the management."[52] The managers, however, disavowed any élitism, stressing that the institute was a democratic body open to all Launcestonians, but they were shouting into the wind. Moreover, the government refused to renew its grant-in-aid in 1863 because the institute was regarded as a place of "amusement" which did not warrant "support from the general fund."[53] As in Hobart, there is no compelling evidence to suggest that the membership was other than predominately middle-class or lower middle-class males, and this was indisputably true of the Boards of Management, which bemoaned this sad fact with exasperated regularity in their annual reports. The mechanics' institute simply did not meet the needs of the Launceston working classes. As one worker wrote in the mid-1860s: the mechanics' institute was "very useful in its way but not for the working man."[54] As in Hobart, some of the recreational needs of working men were supplied in the Launceston Working Men's Club, which was formed on 10 July 1865.

From the 1870s, and in common with many other institutes throughout Australia, the most important department of the Launceston Mechanics' Institute was the library.

LECTURES

The core aims of mechanics' institutes were to disseminate useful information of a scientific nature and to educate working men through lectures, classes, and a well-stocked library. How successfully were these aims achieved in Hobart and Launceston? Prior to 1837, lectures on a variety of subjects, mainly scientific, were held irregularly by the Van Diemen's Land Mechanics' Institute. From 1838 to at least 1862 the annual number of lectures averaged around twenty-one. In the 1840s most lectures were on physical science, and those "accompanied by attractive illustrations" (on electricity, electrometallurgy, electromagnetism and entomology) were "highly popular."[55]

In the 1850s tastes changed: most lectures tended to be on literary subjects and were "highly relished."[56] However, as some argued that such lectures were "incompatible" with the aims of the institute, the committee arranged "more scientific and mechanical" lectures in 1860, but these were not "generally appreciated."[57] The 1860s saw an "almost irresistible demand for light and comic amusements," "a great name," or "a very uncommon subject," otherwise audiences stayed away.[58] Lectures were commonly attended by the young of both sexes, "interspersed with a sprinkling of older seekers after intellectual excitement."

In a small community the number of capable lecturers was small. Too often the same lecturers, most of whom were volunteers, were required, and repetition was not unknown. Apart from Lillie, the only time that lecturers of "a learned and instructive character met with due appreciation" from the public occurred when Inspector of Schools J J Stutzer lectured on history and literature.[59] His success was due to "a great command of language, combined with a remarkable faculty for word-painting and the novelty of being personally new to Tasmanians." Periodically it was suggested that a paid lecturer should be obtained from Melbourne or Sydney. In 1853 an advertisement was placed in Melbourne papers without success, but most agreed that the institute could not afford a paid lecturer anyway, and doubts were expressed about the success of such an "experiment."[60] For variety, the Hobart and Launceston institutes sometimes exchanged lecturers.

Prior to 1860 the Launceston Mechanics' Institute arranged lectures on a broad range of subjects - natural and experimental philosophy, astronomy, chemistry, natural history, literature, political economy and the arts. Initially enthusiasm was high, but as the novelty of lectures wore off, attendance of members and the public began to diminish. In 1849, in order to regain public support, Ewing persuaded the Board of Management to admit the public free to lectures on a trial basis.[61] Numbers immediately increased from between twenty and fifty to between two hundred and four hundred, but this success was not sustained and numbers again started to become discouragingly low in the 1850s.

In 1860 the Board of Management in Launceston departed from tradition by paying two lecturers of "established repute" rather than relying on the voluntary efforts of enthusiastic individuals.[62] Stutzer's lectures on history were "a brilliant success," but not so Rev. F W Quitler's on chemistry, which, despite having "such immediate practical bearing" were not received well. Attendances at lectures waxed and waned in the next three decades. The number of lectures averaged six per year, ranging from twelve in some years to none in others. As in Hobart, most lectures were on literary and historical subjects, while scientific lectures, with few exceptions, were attended "worst of all."[63] Attendance was high only at those lectures which were of "daily interest and concern" to citizens. From the mid-1860s lectures lost out in the popularity stakes to musical and dramatic presentations, penny readings, and spelling bees, which were held in front of packed audiences. Launcestonians would prefer to pay a shilling to see a play rather than sixpence to hear a lecture.[64]

CLASSES

Class instruction at both institutes suffered a similar fate to lectures. Disillusionment was greater, however, because more was expected of classes. Class instruction was "the soul" of the mechanics' institute: without "the foundation of systematic knowledge to build upon," the information gained from libraries and lectures did not become "fixed in the mind."[65] Until 1864, the only successful attempt to run a class at the Van Diemen's Land Mechanics' Institute was Lillie's maths class, which attracted twelve students in 1842.[66] In 1846 classes on natural history and drawing attracted pupils, and there were plans to introduce chemistry and architectural drawing classes.[67] The Committee of Management anticipated "a gradual introduction of classes in the most useful branches of Science and Art," which would "ultimately place this Institute on equal ground with some of the most efficient Mechanics' Institutes of our Native Land."

This laudable aim was not realised. Over the next decade or so, only the drawing class and singing and music classes were consistently held. Mechanics, maths and chemistry classes were planned but failed to eventuate. In 1855 the failure of class instruction was attributed to the "apathy and indifference" of the public, and to the difficulty of getting and keeping teachers with "a competent knowledge of their subjects" and with "an aptitude for conveying instruction."[68] Buoyed somewhat by the success of the chemistry class taught by Edwin Pears in 1856 and 1857, the Committee of Management sought to introduce classes of "systematic instruction" in 1858.[69] They planned to arrange classes on arithmetic and bookkeeping, languages (Greek, Latin, French and German), English etymology, composition, literature, and drawing, especially related to mechanics and human physiology. A number of teachers were secured, but the plans foundered because the number of pupils was too low. In later years the institute, while not establishing its own classes, encouraged their formation by an "independent agency," granting the rooms, light, and fuel free of charge.[70]

In the 1860s classes were held on history, English literature, grammar and composition, drawing, elocution and singing, but interest was never strong.[71] One member, Josiah Pratt, noted that "apathy extended itself to all their Hobart Town Institutions" and was "observable in politics as well as educational matters."[72] Apathy was a convenient explanation, but it was more likely that working men saw little use in what was on offer and made a conscious decision not to support the institute's classes. On the other hand, between 1884 and 1887 artisans enthusiastically supported William Charpentier's more relevant School of Arts, often called the Technical Art School, which conducted drawing classes in the old mechanics' institute building.[73] The success of Charpentier's classes paved the way for the establishment of the Hobart Technical College in 1888.

In Launceston high expectations for class instruction were similarly dashed. Class teaching was regarded as "more efficient in promoting education than either lectures or mere reading."[74] Early attempts to sustain classes were not successful, but in 1860 a speech by the Governor - Henry Young - inspired fresh attempts.[75] Young strongly advocated evening classes for citizens "whose primary education had been neglected." The classes would supply "a great desideratum," as in Tasmania "many men even now of respectability, intelligence, and prosperity" were "scarcely acquainted with the rudiments of writing and arithmetic." In 1860 the institute found tutors to conduct classes in elocution, algebra and geometry, music, artistic and mechanical drawing, stenography, and general instruction in arithmetic, English grammar, and composition.[76] Some tutors were paid; others gave their services voluntarily. As elsewhere however, after one year the "zeal of the pupils" attending classes "rapidly died away," and only the elocution class run by Ewing was successful.[77] Various classes (French and phonography were two new ones) were begun and then disbanded from year to year until 1876, when the last attempt to start a reading and elocution class failed to attract any students.[78] Though often mooted, no systematic attempt was made to present classes again. As in Hobart, technical education was brought to Launceston in 1888 and was well received by working men.

LIBRARIES

As ways of disseminating practical, scientific information, lectures and classes had limited effectiveness. A third way was by building up a library of scientific works, but here too, the institutes fell short of their aims. The Van Diemen's Land Mechanics' Institute library grew very slowly: by 1852 it contained 1,900 volumes and regularly received seventeen periodicals and thirteen newspapers.[79] In the 1850s the most popular categories of books were fiction and light literature, history and biography, voyages and travels, and literature and fine arts.[80] Books on science and philosophy were amongst the least popular. The *Hobart Town Advertiser* was particularly savage in its assessment of the library: it was "more than half full of trashy American novels" and had "a remarkable dearth of books of standard merit."[81] It catered for young men and women novel readers, but was useless for anyone "pursuing a course of study and anxious to consult the authorities upon it." The withdrawal of the government grant and a persistent debt in the 1860s severely affected the library which, after forty years, could only boast 4,500 volumes.[82]

The Launceston Mechanics' Institute library also grew slowly and by 1860 contained 2,430 volumes.[83] In the 1860s other expenses diverted funds from the library, which, except for donations, languished, with only one-third of subscription fees being spent on books, newspapers, and periodicals.[84] It was not until around 1874, after the librarian's residence was extended, that the library collection was steadily developed. With 5,990 volumes and about fifty-four colonial, British, and American newspapers and periodicals, the library committee consciously sought to build up the collection. Its policy was "while meeting present tastes and wishes, to place in the library works of permanent value,...representing various schools of thought in theology, philosophy, and history."[85] Notwithstanding this aim, the library was sometimes criticised for containing "too large a proportion of light literature," but this was what most members wanted. Light reading circulated most and "good and recent works" in biography, history, travel, and natural history were in "considerable demand."[86] As in Hobart, the demand for "purely scientific works" was "comparatively small" and, as they were "so costly" and rapidly became outdated, few were purchased. Periodicals like *Scientific American* were relied on for modern scientific information.

By 1889, James Coulter, long-time member, could say unequivocally and without contradiction that the library was "the chief feature" of the institute, comprising "a very valuable collection" of some 14,161 volumes.[87] The attention lavished on building the library collection paid dividends in an increased membership which, by that year, had reached 512 subscribing and about 37 life members in an estimated population creeping over 20,000. In 1890 the mechanics' institute took over the funds and books of the defunct Launceston Public Library in exchange for opening the library and reading room for the use of the public, thereby consolidating its role as the largest library at the time in Tasmania.[88] As the Launceston Mechanics' Institute and Public Library, it was known as "the home of literature in Northern Tasmania."[89] The last vestiges of its origins were discarded in 1929, when the words 'Mechanics' Institute' were dropped and it became the Launceston Public Library.

Despite limited funds, the library was so shrewdly added to that in 1934 Munn and Pitt, in their survey of Australian libraries, pronounced the Launceston Public Library to be the finest library in Australia outside the capital cities, with an especially impressive general literature collection.[90] In 1945 control of the library was transferred to the Launceston City Council and it became a fully-fledged free public library, remaining under municipal control until 1964, when the State Government assumed control.[91] In 1971 the gracious old mechanics' building was pulled down in an unconscionable act of State government vandalism. The tradition of library service to the community , however, was continued in the new building housing the Northern Regional Library.

CONCLUSION

The founders of mechanics' institutes in Hobart and Launceston were high-minded and sincere in their belief that imparting scientific and other useful knowledge to mechanics would benefit the economy of the colony, would unite the classes, and would direct the

Hobart Town Mechanics' Institute, Tas

Launceston Mechanics' Institute, Tas

energies of mechanics to moral ends. It soon became clear that mechanics did not share these ideals and in fact were repelled by the exclusivity and the paternalism that characterised both institutes. Very little science of practical utility was imparted to mechanics through classes, lectures or the library. Elementary instruction was similarly a lost cause.

In the failure of their original aims, we have an obvious point of comparison. The striking difference is, of course, that the mechanics' institute in Hobart passed away in "ignominious silence," while the Launceston institute lived on as the city's public library.[92] We can explain the demise of the Hobart institute in a number of ways. One reason was the emergence of strong rivals. In 1870 the Tasmanian Public Library was strengthened by its transfer to the control of the municipal council and state government, and became "a formidable competitor for public patronage."[93] The "attractions" of the subsidised public library "considerably damaged the usefulness" of the mechanics' institute. Other competitors included various mutual improvement and young men's associations of "a semi-religious and semi-literary character," the Hobart Working Men's Club and the Royal Society of Tasmania, all diverting either members or patrons.[94]

A second reason was the supineness and inefficiency of the various Committees of Management and Vice-Presidents, too many of whom wanted the cachet of the position without throwing themselves into the affairs of the institute.[95] This was particularly true in the later 1860s, when, "as rats desert a sinking ship, so those who should have shown themselves the staunch supporters" of the mechanics' institute "left it to its fate."[96] The most egregious error committed by the management committees was not to strive to build a new mechanics' institute building in a more central location, which would have given the institute an aura of permanence. The third and final reason why the Hobart mechanics' institute was disbanded was financial. From the mid-1850s the institute was burdened with persistent debts of varying amounts, which ensured that caution and economy were more central to the concerns of managers than initiative and expenditure. Debt weakened the foundations, but the withdrawal of the government grant "pulled out the key stone of the arch" and the institute collapsed.[97]

In Launceston, the mechanics' institute succeeded; firstly, because it had fewer rivals. It subsumed the Launceston Public Library and no branch of the Royal Society existed in Launceston: mutual improvement and young men's associations (fewer in number than in Hobart) and the Launceston Working Men's Club probably attracted some potential members, but they could not match the institute's library collection. Secondly, most of the leading citizens and businessmen served on the Board of Managers or as Vice-Presidents and generally spent much time furthering the interests of the institute. True to the spirit of self-help that characterised Launcestonians, the institute's office-bearers showed much initiative and drive in raising funds for a building, while their counterparts in Hobart waited for the government to spare them this effort. The erection of an imposing, even noble, building gave the institute and its members confidence in a prosperous future. Finally, the Launceston Mechanics' Institute was rarely dogged by debt because of the financial skill of the managers and the ability to raise money from bazaars, concerts, and other entertainments rather than relying on government aid. By eventually channelling funds into the library, the managers satisfied the needs of the reading public and attracted their support. They thus ensured the viability of the Launceston Mechanics' Institute and bequeathed to future generations a valuable library and intellectual resource.

NOTES AND REFERENCES

1.Roe, M. (1974). 1830-50. In Crowley, F.K. (Ed.), *A new history of Australia*. Melbourne: William Heinemann, p.112;
Roe, M. (1965). *Quest for authority in eastern Australia, 1835-1851*. Melbourne: Melbourne University Press, part three.

2.Very little has been written on these institutes. For Hobart see Bolger, P. (1973). *Hobart Town*. Canberra: Australian National University Press, pp. 121-2, 173-5, 188; and Atkinson, A., and Aveling, M. (1989). (Eds.), *Australia 1838*. Sydney: Fairfax, Syme and Weldon Associates, pp. 254-60. For Launceston see Petrow, S. (1992). The Launceston Mechanics' Institute 1842-1871. *Launceston Historical Society Occasional Papers*, forthcoming.

3.Rimmer, G. (1989). Hobart: A Moment of Glory. In Statham, P. (Ed.), *The origins of Australia's capital cities*. Cambridge: Cambridge University Press, pp. 97-9, 107-8, 114.

4.*Colonial Times* (Hobart), 5 January 1827.

5.*ibid*, 23 March 1827, *Tasmanian,* 22 March 1827.

6.*Tasmanian,* 23 November 1827.

7.*Hobart Gazette,* 23 June 1827.

8.*Tasmanian*, 21 June 1827.

9.*Colonial Times*, 20 July, 10 August 1827.

10.*Tasmanian,* 26 June, 17 July 1935; *True Colonist*, 13 March, 12 June 1835.

11.*Hobart Town Courier*, 8 June 1832; *Colonial Times*, 7 May 1833.

12.Robson, L.L. (1983). *A history of Tasmania: Volume 1 - Van Diemen's Land from the earliest time to 1855*. Melbourne, Oxford University Press, Vol. 1. Chapter 16.

13.*Tasmanian and Austral-Asiatic Review*, 6 April 1838; *Colonial Times*, 9 June 1840; *Hobart Town Courier*, 23 February 1841.

14.Nadel, G. (1957). *Australia's colonial culture: Ideas, men and institutions in mid-nineteenth century Eastern Australia*. Cambridge, Mass: Harvard University Press, p.131.

15.*Hobart Town Courier*, 3 July 1840, 12 March 1841.

16.Lillie, J. (1854). The Advantages Derivable from Mechanics' Institutes. *A lecture presented at the Van Diemen's Land Mechanics' Institute, 24 October 1854.* I thank Phil Candy for sending me a typescript copy of this lecture, which is reproduced in full as a chapter in this book.

17.*Hobart Town Courier*, 11 June 1841.

18.*ibid.*, 19 April 1845; Mitchell Library, *Van Diemen's Land Mechanics' Institute Minute Book*, 29 January 1846, 29 January 1847; *Annual Report of the Van Diemen's Land Mechanics' Institute, 1846*.

19.*Mercury* (Hobart), 7 October 1862; Archives Office of Tasmania, Colonial Secretary's Department 4/43/588 and CSD 8/326.

20.*Hobart Town Courier*, 11 June 1841, 28 January and 30 January 1845.

21.*ibid.*, 4 February 1845, *Colonial Times*, 10 February 1846.

22.*Colonial Times*, 30 January, 6 February 1849.

23.*ibid.*, 8 February 1845 letter by J. Morgan.

24.Levett, J. (1985). The Tasmanian Public Library in 1850: its members, its managers and its books. In Morrison, E., & Talbot, M. (Eds.), *Books, libraries and readers in colonial Australia*. Clayton, Vic: Graduate School of Librarianship, Monash University, pp.11-21.

25.*Colonial Times*, 19 March, 4 June 1850; *Hobart Town Courier*, 20 January 1854.

26.*Van Diemen's Land Mechanics' Institute Minute Book*, 17 January 1856.

27.*ibid.*, 20 February 1857.

28.*Annual Report of the Van Diemen's Land Mechanics' Institute*, 1855.

29.*Mercury*, 15 April 1858.

30.*ibid.*, 31 January 1860; *Hobart Town Advertiser*, 27, 28 February 1860.

31.*Mercury*, 1 March 1860.

32.CSD 4/43/588; *Mercury*, 10 March 1865.

33.*Mercury*, 6 October 1864, 15 February 1865.

34.*ibid*, 21 February, 29 October 1867.

35.*Mercury*, 22 March 1869.

36.*ibid.*, 6 January 1872, Letter by S.H. Wintle.

37.*ibid.*, 29 November 1871.

38.Beever, E.A. (1972). *Launceston Bank for Savings, 1835-1970*. Melbourne: Melbourne University Press; Dyster, B. (1981). The Port of Launceston before 1851. *The Great Circle*, *3*, pp.103-124.

39.Rimmer, *op. cit.*, p.114; Robson, *op. cit.*, pp.176, 491.

40. *Launceston Advertiser*, 10 March 1842.

41. *ibid., Examiner*, 12 March 1842.

42. *Examiner*, 12 March, 16 April 1842.

43. *Launceston Advertiser,* 10 and 17 March 1842.

44. *Examiner*, 14 May, 9 July 1842.

45. *Cornwall Chronicle*, 12 March, 23 April, 28 May 1842.

46. *ibid.*, 29 April 1843.

47. For details of these disputes see Petrow 'The Launceston Mechanics' Institute,' *op. cit.*

48. *Examiner*, 10 April 1860.

49. *ibid*, 27 June 1857.

50. Whitfield, E. (1910). *A History of the Launceston Mechanics' Institute and Public Library*, Launceston: The Examiner, p.9.

51. *Examiner*, 17 April 1860.

52. *ibid.*, 22 January 1861.

53. *ibid.*, 31 January 1865; CSD4/41/546.

54. *Launceston Times*, 15 January 1866.

55. *Annual Report of the Van Diemen's Land Mechanics' Institute*, 1847.

56. *Mercury*, 5 July 1860 letter by R. Worley.

57. *ibid.*, 16 March 1861.

58. *ibid.*, 28 October 1868; *Hobart Town Advertiser*, 27 and 28 February 1860.

59. *Mercury*, 6 January 1872, letter by S.H. Wintle.

60. *Van Diemen's Land Mechanics' Institute Minute Book*, 1 April, 6 May 1853; *Annual Report of the Van Diemen's Land Mechanics' Institute*, 1855.

61. Button, H. (1892). *Jubilee of the Launceston Mechanics' Institute*. Launceston: The Examiner, p.10; *Cornwall Chronicle*, 10 October 1849.

62. *Cornwall Chronicle,* 23 January 1861.

63. *Examiner*, 20 January 1876, 28 January 1864.

64.*ibid.*, 22 August 1874, letter by 'Chacun à son goût.'

65.*Mercury*, 4 March 1857.

66.*Van Diemen's Land Mechanics' Institute Minute Book*, 14 February 1843.

67.*Annual Report of the Van Diemen's Land Mechanics' Institute*, 1846.

68.*ibid.*, 1855.

69.*Mercury*, 4 March 1857; *Hobart Town Advertiser*, 1 March 1858; *Tasmanian Weekly News*, 24 April 1858.

70.*Annual Report of the Hobart Town Mechanics' Institute*, 1859.

71.*Mercury*, 16 March 1861, 13 March 1863, 28 February 1868, 17 March 1869.

72.*ibid.*, 26 February 1864.

73.Waters, J. (1988). *The cultured mind - The skilful hand: A Centenary History of the Hobart Technical College*. Hobart: Hobart Technical College, pp. 8-9.

74.*Examiner*, 22 January 1861.

75.*ibid.*, 17 April 1860.

76.*ibid.*, 1 November 1860.

77.*ibid.*, 22 January 1861.

78.*ibid.*, 20 January 1877.

79.*Van Diemen's Land Mechanics' Institute Minute Book*, 29 January 1852.

80.*ibid.*, 20 February 1857.

81.*Hobart Town Advertiser,* 27 and 28 February 1860.

82.*Mercury*, 17 March 1869.

83.*Cornwall Chronicle,* 23 January 1861.

84.*ibid.*, 24 January 1872.

85.*Examiner*, 20 January 1876.

86.*ibid.*, 20 January 1877, 29 January 1881.

87.*ibid.*, 24 January 1889.

88.*Examiner*, 22 September 1890, letter by W.F. Wathen.

89.*ibid.*, 9 March 1892.

90.Munn, R., & Pitt, E.R. (1935). *Australian libraries: A survey of conditions and suggestions for their improvement*. Melbourne: Australian Council for Educational Research, pp. 87-8.

91.For the period after 1929 see Petrow, 'The Launceston Mechanics' Institute,' *op. cit.*

92.*Mercury*, 23 December 1871, letter by S.H. Wintle.

93.*ibid.*, 24 January, 24 February, 24 March 1871.

94.*ibid.*, 7 March 1872.

95.*ibid.*, 23 December 1871, letter by S.H. Wintle.

96.*ibid.*, 2 January 1872.

97.*ibid.*, 23 December 1871, letter by S.H. Wintle.

CHAPTER SIXTEEN

THE ADVANTAGES OF MECHANICS' INSTITUTIONS: PART II

John Lillie

This chapter was originally presented as a lecture at the Hobart Town Mechanics' Institute, on 24 October 1854. It has never before been published, and is reproduced here by kind permission of the Trustees of the Wellcome Trust. The original manuscript is located in the Wellcome Institute for the History of Medicine, London.

We are naturally led, on an occasion like the present, to ask ourselves what are the advantages which we may expect to obtain from meeting together at the lectures of a Mechanics Institute - or what is the good we may reckon on as an equivalent for the time and attention consumed? The most obvious answer to such a question is that the information communicated is in the first place calculated to give pleasing and salutary exercise to our mental faculties - to gratify that strong and generous appetite which is innate in the human mind for knowledge on its own account; and thus to strengthen and rejoice the intellect with the precious food which its Maker has ordained for its nutriment.

Or we may, on the other hand, consider the information referred to in its relation to the practical purposes of life - as directly useful to the mechanic, for example, by throwing light on the principles of his craft - not only elevating him in the scale of being; by developing and expanding his capacities of intelligence - but, by the vantage ground on which it places him - aiding him in the performance of his manual operations - enabling him to work with greater independence and effect, leading him to his object by a nearer or better way, or imparting to that object itself characters of higher utility and value.

Such we say would be the more obvious reply to the question of what use is it to attend the lectures of a Mechanics Institute - and such accordingly is the reply which has often been given and by which the value and importance of such institutions have been demonstrated, and their claim to public countenance and support vindicated and upheld.

But besides these direct and evident advantages there are others of a less obvious character, which on account of their great importance are entitled to special consideration in every estimate of the value of such institutions. We refer to the moral and social benefits which naturally arise from bringing together the different classes of the community in connexion with an intellectual and liberal object.

The elucidation of these benefits with reference to the peculiar character and circumstances of our own community is the proposed subject of this lecture.

Human society has a natural tendency to arrange itself in a gradation of ranks or classes. When we go back even to the ruder periods of its history, we at once discover the elements and conditions of such an arrangement. One man excels his fellows in physical or mental endowments. He is a stronger or a braver man - or he possesses in an eminent degree those qualities which fit him for bold adventures and arduous exertion. Or he may be distinguished for those higher abilities which are requisite for directing the operations of others, for planning and adjusting a scheme of difficult achievements; and by the fertility and readiness of his invention, and the sagacity and wisdom of his counsels conducting its execution through the complication and embarrassment of contingent events and untoward circumstances, to a successful issue.

Such personal distinctions naturally command the respect and admiration of mankind, while their direct and powerful adaptation to the security and aggrandisement of society gives them a hold on deeper and more permanent feelings. The individual therefore, who in any community has been favoured with these qualities, is marked out by nature, as a person of consequence. He takes a higher place and becomes invested with greater influence and authority than his less gifted fellow-citizens.

And all this, naturally and as a matter of course, and independently of positive institutions or artificial laws. The authority emanates from the *personal qualities* themselves and exerts itself inevitably on the natural apprehensions and instinctive passions of men. And hence that equality and uniformity of condition which political theorists have sometimes aimed to introduce are rendered practically impossible by the very distinctions which men bring with them into the world. The elements of society are graduated, so to speak, in their first formation, and assume their relative position by the necessary tendencies which the hand of their maker has impressed on them.

But besides this, there is another source of inequality in the great diversity with which *wealth* is usually distributed among the different members of the community. In all well regulated societies, men are allowed the free use of their natural talents and advantages. No restriction is put upon individual industry or enterprise, so long as it does not interfere with the rights of others, or the public good.

In such circumstances and with the different degrees of ability and skill, as well as of outward advantages with which men start in the race of competition - they cannot but be very unequally placed in relation to the goal towards which they are all moving. Multitudes through calamity, and still more through misconduct, break down at the outset and sink into comparative obscurity and indigence. Many under happier auspices or with higher principle, attain a mediocrity of condition alike removed from the gloomy shades of poverty and want and the gaudy and perilous elevation of super-abundant affluence and power. While only a few by a rare combination of fortunate circumstances, and now and then as the reward for resplendent abilities in beautiful alliance with integrity and virtue - retire from the contest laden, but not always blest, with the golden spoils of victory and conquest.

This great difference in the amount of worldly possessions which fall to the lot of different individuals, leads the capacity to a corresponding distinction in their social position. Wealth when rationally used and enjoyed, always confers influence. It gives its possessor a superior command over the conveniences and luxuries of life, and it puts it in his power to contribute in many important ways to the well-being and happiness of his fellow-men. When such uses are made of it, credit seldom fails to be given for them in the high estimation and respectful deference with which he who makes them, is regarded.

The weight which belongs to it in a political point of view also, is manifest from the fact that

Rev Dr John Lillie, 1806-1866
(reproduced by permission of the State Library of Tasmania)

property is the basis on which this modern system of representative government is founded and the standard by why its privileges are measured and ascertained.

Birth is another of these general causes which are usually regarded as producing diversity of rank in society - since a man naturally bequeaths not only his external goods but in some degree his character and reputation, together with his place and influence in the community to his offspring. Birth in this sense therefore does not so much originate distinctions in society, as it serves to continue and keep up these that previously existed.

There is indeed a great difference between what a man is born *with* and what he is born *amongst* - between the circumstances of wealth and grandeur which surround him when he comes into the world, and the capacities - whether of body or mind - with which nature has endowed him. We have already seen that the latter are the primary fountains from which social distinctions are derived. But while the natural powers of the individual give a most important impulse and direction to the events of his life, these events on the other hand, and more especially the circumstances under which a man is born and brought up, powerfully *react* on his natural capacities, and have therefore a great deal to do with the position in which these capacities finally place him.

While each receives a nature having a peculiar stamp and value of its own - which may and often does, triumph by its own inherent energy over all external disadvantages - the outward circumstances nevertheless in which each enters on his career and particularly the character, manner and position of his parents, tend, in all ordinary cases, to give a specific formation to his individual nature, and perpetuate in some degree in him, what had belonged to them. The strong instinct of natural affection makes any man anxious to convey to his children whatever advantages he may have acquired - so that they as it were set out from his level; and supposing their natural ability equal, they may be expected to describe a course in its general relation analogous to his.

Beside these general causes of distinction, which we have now considered - there are others of a more limited range of influence - such as the *various trades and professions* which are found in all civilised communities, and which though they do not always coincide in their effects, with the former, have yet a tendency on the whole to form so many separate groups or classes, each having a distinctive character as well as a peculiar mark of its own. Men of the same profession have common pursuits, and are conversant about common objects. Their thoughts flow in the same channel - their views and opinions naturally harmonise and they are usually united together by a bond of common interest. They thus form a separate association and have a line of demarcation - more or less distinct - drawn between them and the rest of the community.

Trades and professions, moreover, on account of the different degrees of capital or skill required to prosecute them, or the diversified estimation of the ends to which they are respectively subservient, are arranged, in a principle of subordination and relative importance which makes one superior, in public opinion, to another.

There is another class of distinction which has been very conspicuous and important in its effect on modern society - we mean those which are founded on a *difference of opinion* in regard to political and religious subjects. We do not refer at present to the marked

329

professional diversities which both of these subjects have given rise to in the arrangement of society where we have, in the one case, the necessary distinction between Ruler and Subject, and the whole organisation of the ruling process; from the Chief Officer as its head, through all the various functionaries of its subordinate departments - and in the other, the division of the whole community into the two orders or classes of laity and clergy. And a distinction of office and authority among this latter more or less complicated according to the peculiar system of each.

The consideration of these obvious and important distinctions has been anticipated in what has been already said, relating to birth, wealth, natural ability and profession. The distinctions we have at present in view are those, flowing from a particular class of sentiments, or abstract opinions in regard to the subjects in question and which have had the effect of dividing men into parties - sects or denominations. The opinions of every man, whether political or religious, when honestly entertained, have a value in his apprehension, in proportion to the magnitude of the interests they embrace; and necessarily create a strong bond of sympathy and union among all who participate in them. The intrinsic worth of every opinion is its *truth* and the degree in which it is applicable to the good of mankind. And as there is no absolute or infallible standard for determining the worth of opinion, but every man naturally regards *his own*, as the true one - no opinion can of itself be considered as a ground of precedence or as entitling him who holds it to take up a superior social position.

But while every man is bound to show that respect for the opinions of another which he claims for his own, this does not hinder the different systems of opinion from becoming so many centres of attraction and combination, drawing the members of a community into a variety of groups irrespective of external condition and by the force of mental conviction alone.

Such is the manner in which human society is classified and divided; and such the causes by which this effect is produced. We have not time, nor does it fall within our immediate aim to discuss at any length the benefits which accrue to society from this distribution of its parts.

We may briefly observe however that a larger amount of the social good obtained from the arrangement referred to, depends on the principle of the division of labour. Instead of having all the offices of citizenship shared equally among the individual members of a state, they are, by this arrangement, distributed in separate portions, among the different classes of society. The result is that these offices are on the whole far more effectively performed and higher degrees of individual excellence attained. This admits of a clear illustration in the case of the mechanical arts.

Suppose for example, that a few families were living together, in some similar situation - They would soon find that by making one man confine his attention to one set of operations their common wants would be more perfectly supplied, than by dividing the different kinds of work indiscriminately among all. It would be a far better arrangement to have one man a carpenter and nothing else - another man a blacksmith and nothing else - another a shoemaker and nothing else, than to have each of the three, as shoemaker, blacksmith and carpenter. One man by limiting his attention to one kind of work would acquire a facility and expertness in performing it which would add immensely both to the quantity and value of the work done. This is so well understood in practice that where there is an adequate demand for the product the division of the operations necessary to produce it, into so many distinct branches of trade has been carried to an astonishing degree of minuteness.

The effects proceeding from this gradation of society are analogous to these, and derive their efficacy from a similar principle. The different classes have all their respective Offices in relation to the common weal.

The human mind receives a particular education and takes a definite and specific form in each. Each has its own peculiar views and feelings - its own independent motives and principles of action and each therefore acts in subordinance to its own salient purposes and ends. But further the organisation of the social body by presenting a succession of conditions each surpassing the other, in the amount of comfort and convenience belonging to it - in the splendour and magnificence of its accommodations - or in the elegance and refinement of its tastes and manners and more than all in the degree of power and influence which it confers - holds forth so many prizes all tempting men to exertion, and inspiring an upward movement in the whole society.

Every station in life thus becomes a point of excitement and attraction to those who are beneath it. It sets all their faculties to work in order to rise to it. And when society is left free to obey its own natural laws and the wise and beneficial arrangements of Divine Providence are not defeated by the folly or the wicked ways of human interference, it affords scope for development and discovery of superior talents. Minds of a high order which are not limited to any one class of the community - but are scattered indiscriminately, though sparingly throughout the whole - always rise, by their own innate powers of exertion when not compressed and held down by extraneous forces.

The distribution of the parts of society which we have been considering, supplies the conditions under which such minds unfold their capacities and attain their proper place and office in the system. The eminence to which they naturally aspire not only prompts them to exertion and calls out their powers - but the efforts they have to make in order to reach it, strengthen and mature their faculties for the elevated position they are destined to hold.

It may be proper here to observe that the distinctions to which our attention has been called, have reference only to the *outward* form and state of society. They belong to what may be denominated its material and visible organisation. They are the distinctions which birth, wealth and natural talents bestow. Besides and independent of these, however, there are distinctions of a finer nature and higher form. There is a scale of character and moral worth which has no necessary or natural connexion or coincidence with the mere gradation of rank and outward condition. Men are arranged and estimated on this scale not by the accidental and extrinsic circumstances of birth, or fortune or talent - but by the intrinsic merits of their actions - by those characters and features of their moral being over which every man has a voluntary control - and for which therefore, every man is directly and properly responsible.

Rank according to this measure of value, does not depend on the place which a man occupies - but on the manner in which he performs its duties. It is not in the ornaments, or splendour of the outward vehicle in which his spirit passes on to its destiny - but in the permanent lineaments and characteristics of the spirit itself. By such a standard the man who discharges the most menial offices of society with integrity and uprightness is exalted and ennobled;

while he who fills the world's eye and excites the world's astonishment with the pomp and grandeur of his station but who has no regard for truth or principle in his conduct is consigned to degradation and contempt. Thus may the beggars take precedence of the monarch.

It is on this ground that whatever tends, like the lectures of this Institution to assemble the different grades and sections of society under the same roof and fixing their thoughts together on the same intellectual subjects contributes especially to the harmony and social condition of a community. In a course of such lectures a very considerable amount of information is supplied on various subjects of natural science. The attention is withdrawn from the interests and passions of active life, and directed on the laws and mechanisms of the universe the very grandeur and vastness of which make us feel our own littleness and insignificance.

But it is not so much the absolute value or character of these objects which are brought before us, as the relationship in which we stand to them and the community of thought and feeling with which we regard them. It is from these latter sources that the benefit we have in view is derived.

When we investigate the wonderful properties and relations which exist among the physical elements and the beautiful laws by which they unite in forming the various objects of nature; When we trace the steps of geological discovery and the new and interesting views it has given of the history of our globe and the immense periods of time which that history embraces; When we contemplate the beautiful and varied forms of vegetation and animal life, or inquire into the laws and operations from which such forms are derived; When we survey the wonders of astronomy, the magnitudes and distances of the heavenly bodies, the teeming multitude of worlds which occupy the boundless dimensions of space, and the regularity and harmony which characterise all their movements and operations, we are not only called to contemplate things which are intrinsically great and interesting but things also which with all their interest and grandeur we are *all alike* privileged to contemplate. We are thus thrown back on the ground of that common intellect which belongs to us as men - outward distinctions, how useful so ever in their place, are here of no value and must be left out of view. We have taken a position whose proper office is to *think* or to use our understandings. If we fail in discharging this office we consciously sink in our own estimation and lose caste by that standard which measures the rank and dignity of men as intelligent beings. But if on the other hand we apply our intellectual powers to the subjects that are brought before us - the consciousness that there are others around us whose outward circumstances, it may be, contrast widely with our own who are exerting the same high faculties and reaping the same reward and elevated satisfaction as ourselves - must impress us with respect for them as partakers with us of the same precious endowments of intelligence and must proportionally crush in us every unworthy tendency to arrogance or presumption on the mere ground of outward show or accidental circumstance.

We are aware indeed that outward things have an invidious sway over the minds of the great mass of men, so great that some may be inclined to think that the views we have been unfolding of the powers of intellectual sympathy for producing social good are too refined and speculative to have any influence in practice. But we are nevertheless persuaded that it is as accordant with real observation and experience as it is true in theory that a number of persons belonging to the different conditions of society cannot be brought together under the circumstances supposed without being mutually benefitted - without having their best and most kindly feelings aroused and strengthened and all acrimony and asperity proportionally weakened and overcome.

There is a natural tendency to union, a kind of spiritual affinity, strong and invincible which makes minds go together and confess their kindred origin whenever they are placed in circumstances to bring it forth. Let any great event occur to rouse some strong passion in a community; let the foot of the invader plant itself on their soil and threaten danger to their country and presently you shall see them rise up as one man animated and knit together by one intense feeling of patriotism to beat back the aggressor and vindicate their common liberties.

Or let some dire calamity such as pestilence or famine sweep with the indiscriminate fury of a tempest over a community. The ordinary landmarks and distinctions of society are for the time torn down and carried away in the wide-spreading desolation. Outward advantages of fortune or station lose all their power to protect or save. Rich and poor, high and low, stand on the same ground of helpless humanity - subject alike to the same stirring necessity and exposed alike to the same fatal blow. The sentiment of awful apprehension which pervades and agonises all hearts, levels any fictitious distinctions and extorts the confessions of a common nature and equal liability to a common doom. Men come out of such a situation with their pride chastened and subdued and their hearts disposed to look kindly and compassionately on each other.

It is on the same principle that the meeting together of all classes of society on selected occasions for the hallowed purposes of Divine worship has had such a beneficial effect throughout Christendom. Apart altogether from the specific instruction or peculiar offices of the occasion.

The fact of all degrees of rank and condition associating within the same walls for the one great purpose of prostrating themselves before one almighty being in relation to whom they are all naturally equal and on whom they alike depend for the countless blessings of the present life and brighter hopes of immortality cannot but exert the most salutary influences on society. It is a standing memorial and a weekly demonstration to the highest and haughtiest of mankind that, however wide the interval which divides them in respect of outward condition, they are in regard to all the great and fundamental relations of their past, their present and their future being, on an absolute level with the poorest and the meanest of their species. He must have renounced the sympathies of humanity and triumphed over the strongest laws of his nature who can place himself in such circumstances and yet steel his heart against all the impressions they are calculated to make or fail to learn some of the lessons they so obviously teach.

Here is one common ground on which laying aside our separate peculiarities we can all meet, without any compromise either of practice or opinion to exercise those noble capacities of understanding, which, short of moral qualities, are the highest distinctions which man can possess. No jealousy of caste or profession, no sectarian fastidiousness, need prevent us from meeting together on the ground of an institute in a place suited to the examination of the glorious work of our common creator and the improvement of those exalted faculties, the seeds of which are sown liberally in all minds and the high cultivation of which confers the honour and dignity common to rational beings.

The facilities which the state of society in modern times is thus presenting for the free intercourse of man with man hold forth the brightest hopes for the destinies of mankind. Its direct and immediate effect is to destroy that strangeness and cold alienation of the heart which separation unquestionably tends to produce, and to bring men into the situation of realising the warm and generous sympathies of their kindred being. But indirectly and by its negative operation it paves the way for the demolition of prejudice and the growing predominance of truth. Thought comes advantageously into comparison or collision with thought. The artificial props and buttresses on which false opinions are too often sustained themselves gradually give way. The circle of narrow and illiberal views with which the individual mind had surrounded itself and within which it had cherished and brooded over unkind and undesirable thoughts is broken in upon and defeated by interchange of thought and feeling with other minds. The number of minds that thus think in unison and take part with a great principle against partial and isolated views is gradually increased.

Men in their haughtiness, and their pettiness and exclusiveness may stand aloof, and long seek to destroy the intellectual and moral advancement of society. But however long delayed, truth must achieve its victory at last. So have we seen a number of giddy boys seeking in their foolish phantasies to repel the rising tide by heaping up their mounds of sand. As break after break is made, it is as eagerly sought to be repaired - but it is all in vain. Wave follows wave in the destructive assault. Embankment after embankment tumbles down, some one may stand longer than the rest. But while its little occupant is exulting in his fancied security, the whelming waters have risen upon him and compel his retreat.

And so it is with the exclusive views and the false systems of opinion that have gained a footing in the world. The great ocean of truth which has its fountains deep in the eternal law of human thought and the unchangeable nature of things, is daily rising through the enlightened conviction and the accumulating intelligence of man - and by its ceaseless surges it is breaking down the sandy fabrics which human ignorance or human folly have placed in its way - Where our beautiful reasonings have failed - by a noted example[1] - we have seen that observation and experience have carried conviction and vindicated the right of liberty and truth. And so, may we confidently anticipate, will truth - under the Empire of an infinitely wise and merciful and beneficial God - proceed, till at the consummation of his mysterious plan, it is universally and for ever triumphant.

NOTES AND REFERENCES

1. This almost certainly refers to the short-lived Van Diemen's Land Mechanics' School of Arts, which was set up in March 1850 but petered out towards the end of 1853. It was established by some ex-members of the Van Diemen's Land Mechanics' Institute, which was felt to be to inefficient and unsuitable for mechanics (*Colonial Times*, 19 March 1850). Sir Richard Dry gave the inaugural address on 29 May (*Colonial Times*, 4 June 1850). By April 1853, it had some 100 members, but it did not last out the year (Stefan Petrow to Philip Candy, personal communication, 27 April 1992).

CHAPTER SEVENTEEN

A CLOSE AFFILIATION: COORDINATION OF INSTITUTES IN SOUTH AUSTRALIA

Michael Talbot

INTRODUCTION

South Australia has had a very strong institute tradition, imported from Britain by the earliest settlers, and not finally disbanded until 1989. Principal reasons for this longevity have been government support for what was originally envisaged as a local self-help movement, and the early formation and continued existence of a central organisation providing services to institutes affiliated with it. This chapter examines the models influencing the planners during the formative years of the 1850s and 1860s and the system that they developed. The essential elements of this system proved durable, but changes in the central administration at several key points are examined, as are changes in emphasis on the various services offered. Interstate interest in the South Australian system is also discussed.[1]

The progression of bodies beginning with the South Australian Literary and Scientific Association formed in London before settlement has been well documented.[2] The original body was supplanted in turn by an Adelaide Mechanics' Institute, the South Australian Subscription Library, a revived Adelaide Mechanics' Institute, and a combined organisation known as the South Australian Library and Mechanics' Institute. Each experienced the financial difficulties attendant on establishment in a small, new colony. These groups should be seen in the context of a variety of other cultural groups which also emerged in the 1840s and 1850s, and which, as often as not, sank back into oblivion.

A brief sampling of other cultural and educational bodies would include the South Australian School Society, defunct by 1843,[3] the Adelaide Philosophical Society formed in 1853 and still in existence as the Royal Society of South Australia,[4] and the still functioning Royal South Australian Society of Arts, which first met in October 1856.[5]

Newspapers and directories of the time reveal the existence of debating societies, mutual improvement groups and a number of choirs. Book clubs, subscription libraries run by individuals as businesses, and libraries attached to various religious groups attempted to satisfy a need for reading matter.

These groups were widely echoed, though on a smaller scale, in the country and suburbs. Confining ourselves to mechanics' institutes - or simply "institutes," as they became known in South Australia - a survey listed ten of them in August 1857.[6] A similar number had come and gone - perhaps to be reinstituted later.[7] All experienced the struggle to attract a large enough membership at a sufficiently high subscription to be viable.

In a community where issues of government funding for religion and education were hotly debated, the South Australian Library and Mechanics' Institute was unusual in receiving several grants to buy books.[8] But irregular injections of government funding did not ensure its stability. In January 1853 an inquiry into its situation found that:

> Your Society in its present condition is able only to defray...the cost of binding your books as they fall out of repair...and it is quite unable to carry out what have always been its main objects namely the formation of a complete National Library and of a Mechanics' and General Scientific Institute.[9]

In an attempt to carry out this aim, the South Australian Library and Mechanics' Institute established a committee to lobby for government support in return for public ownership and access to the book stock.[10]

OVERSEAS PRECEDENTS

In bringing this plan to fruition by establishing the South Australian Institute, the organisers drew on a number of distinct models. One was to focus arts and science bodies in Adelaide on one site combining economies in staff and accommodation with the convenience of similar services being co-located. Another was to provide a central focus for the growing number of country and suburban institutes. As the South Australian Institute developed, different degrees of emphasis were given to these different elements, producing a unique South Australian organisation.

The proposal by the South Australian Library and Mechanics' Institute to lobby for a new approach involving some government funding, was led by successive Committee secretaries Benjamin Herschel Babbage and John Howard Clark. Both were keen supporters of cultural and scientific organisations in the colony and had co-operated in this necessarily small community. For example, Babbage had been one of the organisers of the Adelaide Philosophical Society and Clark its first secretary. Clark was an active lecturer at the growing number of country and suburban institutes and was one of the founders of an institute near his home. He brought to his undertakings the energy and dedication of his Dissenting, Unitarian background.[11]

Babbage drew Clark's attention to a series of articles in the British weekly *The Athenaeum* which the latter used in supporting their recommendations to government.[12] In 1846 *The Athenaeum* distinguished between well endowed bodies such as the Royal Society, and the majority forced to spend their income "in working the mere machinery" and unable to concentrate on their real objects. It was argued that these societies, "utterly beggared in their solitary independent action," should unite and benefit from the economies of "One house...one general secretary, one general librarian, and a clerk to each Society..."[13]

The Athenaeum returned to the topic in 1852 to discuss moves by the Society of Arts, and by the Royal Society, to group a variety of kindred organizations together. Again, the stress was on co-operation to reduce running expenses, but "leaving to each Society, as at present, its independent action, and the independent conduct of its own affairs." Their separate libraries "would become, by being brought under one roof, virtually part of a general Library of Science, and would be available for reference in a far greater degree than in their present dispersed state."[14]

A second article supported proposals to use the surplus revenue from the Great Exhibition of 1851 to found an Industrial University. Nearby, the "Government should erect a new National Gallery - as well as a new home for the Royal Society, the Society of Antiquaries, the Geological and Astronomical Societies- all of which are threatened with expulsion from their present lodgings in Somerset House:- a suggestion which it is said the Government of the day is quite willing to entertain."[15]

A CENTRAL INSTITUTE

Clark quoted these 1852 articles and it is evident that they influenced the design of the South Australian Institute. When established in 1856, the South Australian Institute was "to comprise a Public Library and Museum, and, by means of lectures, classes, and otherwise, to promote the general study and cultivation of all or any of the branches or departments of art, science, literature and philosophy." Societies with similar aims might become incorporated with it, retaining their own identity, constitutions, and subscriptions, but having the use of rooms and the services of officers of the Institute at agreed times. In return they were to contribute agreed sums towards the Institute's working expenses, and their property was to be vested in the South Australian Institute and made accessible to the public.[16]

The Act provided for a government contribution of not less than £500 a year to pay salaries, defray running costs, and add to the library and museum collections. Those wishing to borrow from the library or to join the incorporated societies would subscribe - the money going to support the particular facet of the Institute's work for which it had been paid. The idea of housing a number of affiliated bodies economically and in a way that focussed their efforts, was the aspect given most emphasis in formal submissions and in the legislation; but there was also a recognised need for the South Australian Institute to serve the whole colony. In its editorial on the establishment of the Select Committee in 1854, *The Register* newspaper - John Howard Clark was its editor - believed the South Australian Institute would form a central body to draw the literary and scientific taste of the colony towards it: an educational focal point, it would, it was asserted, lead to practical scientific advances to benefit all. The good arising from the central institution in this way would percolate through the whole colony.[17]

When the legislation was before the Legislative Council, Richard Hanson, the Advocate-General, and a member of the 1854 Select Committee that recommended establishment of the Institute, said:

> ...a vast amount of good might reasonably be expected to accrue to the colony at large....If, however, the House looked upon the Institution as one which would benefit the inhabitants of Adelaide only, they could not of course expect that any Government aid should be granted towards its establishment and support.[18]

This vague central role was not referred to in the legislation, but the needs of local institutes for advice, supplementing the bookstocks of small institute libraries, provision of lectures, and a government subsidy on local subscriptions were all quite well known and recognised.

Nathaniel Hailes, Secretary of the South Australian Institute from 1856 to 1859, reported applications from institute secretaries for assistance[19] and tried to meet their needs. He published two articles in the *Educational Journal of South Australia* giving constitutional details of the South Australian Subscription Library and the South Australian Library and Mechanics' Institute which, with local modifications, might form models for institutes seeking advice on their form of rules.[20] He also found lecturers and lent books to institutes on an individual and unstructured basis.[21] With only a few institutes in existence this was possible, but as their numbers grew, some kind of systematic approach was necessary. Rapid development occurred after Clark was elected to the Board in 1857 and his friend and fellow Unitarian, Robert Kay,[22] succeeded Hailes as Secretary. With Clark providing ideas and Kay efficient administration, a travelling book box library and a lecture scheme were soon implemented.

After Clark joined the Board in late 1857, Hailes was ordered to develop a scheme for circulating books to country institutes, and to order about 400 volumes for circulation. The books were ordered, and arrived in February 1859, but nothing else seems to have been done until after his replacement by Kay.[23] Kay brought to the administration a sense of method and direction lacking during Hailes' period as Secretary. He developed the practical details, ordering boxes to contain the books, and drawing up the necessary regulations. Six institutes participated in the first loans in September 1859.[24]

This scheme narrowly pre-dated a similar one in Victoria,[25] but the idea was not a colonial invention. The 1849 House of Commons Select Committee on Public Libraries, and other publications during the 1850s, mentioned "itinerating" (or travelling) libraries in Britain.[26] As close observers of life "at Home," some colonists would have been familiar with the concept. The final details were only worked out after the arrival of a text on institute management which gave details of such schemes.

In 1858, the South Australian Institute Board became aware of W H J Traice's *Hand-book of mechanics' institutions, with priced catalogue of books suitable for libraries*, published in 1856. This work was prepared as a handbook for the Yorkshire Union of Mechanics' Institutes - the largest of a number of such unions in Britain. Twenty-six pages dealt with the objects and management of mechanics' institutes and gave a set of model rules. The catalogue provided a buying guide for committees, while an appendix gave the rules the Yorkshire Union Itinerating Village Library.[27] The South Australian Institute bought two copies which were in use by February 1859, and Clark had his own. In 1862, thirty copies were ordered for distribution among country institutes. Traice's handbook formed a useful and practical manual not only for local institutes, but for the South Australian Institute as it was establishing its services.[28]

After the book box scheme was firmly established, the Board moved to introduce a lecture scheme. Initial funding came from money granted by the government to subsidise institutes. In 1859 a round sum of £500 had been voted for subsidies, but claims fell short of this figure. By applying for the unexpended balance in this and succeeding years, the Board was able to fund, first, the book boxes and, later, the lecture scheme.

Attending lectures was a popular pastime in the period before the cinema and other forms of mass entertainment. While country towns might be able to persuade local clergymen, doctors, teachers and the like to provide some lectures, such a pool of talent would be quickly exhausted. Accordingly, both Hailes and Kay helped to find lecturers for country institutes.[29] In 1861 the Board compiled a list of lecturers together with the distances they were prepared to travel and the titles of their lectures, and sent copies to each of the 23 active institutes.[30]

Institutes selected their own lecturers and negotiated directly with them. The idea of a detailed course of lectures was never adopted - these were single appearances intended as a popular but improving form of entertainment. The South Australian Institute paid the lecturers' standard fees and travel costs, recouping half the amount from the individual institutes. Thus institutes had a choice of willing lecturers, and the South Australian Institute simply had to compile and circulate its list once a year, and collect and pay fees.[31]

The Board required proof of competence from its lecturers.[32] Although lecture topics were frequently biographical, literary or to do with travel, various aspects of popular science were also in the repertoire and the Board had some apparatus to illustrate scientific talks. The scheme was appropriate for its time and quickly proved popular. Four to six lectures a year seems to have been typical for an active institute, but small or distant ones might have been able to afford only one or two.[33] As with other services, there were British precedents.

Issues of *The Athenaeum* also contained a series on 'The popular institutions of the United Kingdom' which dealt with proposals for obtaining lecturers for mechanics' institutes and similar organisations. These articles again referred to the work of the Yorkshire Union of Mechanics' Institutes and the Society of Arts Union, both of which ran lecture schemes.[34] An editorial in *The Register* in October 1857 recommended that the South Australian Institute adopt the system employed by the Yorkshire Union, but with government funding.[35] Traice's handbook reproduced the rules of the Yorkshire Union and the affiliation of institutions with the Society of Arts.[36]

The novel aspect of both the South Australian book-box and lecture schemes was government funding. As with the lectures, the contents and major administrative costs of the travelling box library were met centrally from government funds: institutes merely had to pay the cost of carriage of the books to their next destination to ensure regular exchange. The British schemes were self-supporting.

The South Australian Institute also developed services to offer advice to institutes and to dispense the government subsidy. In the early period, institutes seeking advice on their form of rules were provided with suggestions such as those contained in Hailes's articles or Traice's handbook; but as numbers increased, and as the government had a greater stake in them by way of the subsidies and grants provided, the system became more rigid. A set of model rules and a form of trust deed were drawn up by the end of September 1867. Existing institutes were encouraged to adopt them: the rules of new institutes wishing to participate in the benefits of affiliation had to be in the approved form. The rules allowed local variations in matters like subscription rates and numbers on committees, but prevented restrictive membership conditions and ensured that property was adequately protected.[37]

The South Australian Institute and its successors could not intervene directly in the working of any institute; but various policies - such as a ban on card playing for a time, specific audit requirements, or provision of certain statistical returns -could be enforced by making payment of the government subsidy conditional on their observance.[38]

From 1858 subsidy conditions were publicised in the *Government Gazette* and institutes were invited to apply. While at this early stage the South Australian Institute had no role in apportioning the grant, it provided information both to the government and to the institutes. Nathaniel Hailes advised several institutes on who to approach, and also notified them that grant conditions had been gazetted.[39]

Initially grant applications were handled by the Chief Secretary's Office, but Kay soon realised that the South Australian Institute would naturally receive inquiries about grants. He therefore sought information so that he could answer these inquiries directly. Later his board offered to receive and consider grant applications for final approval by the Chief Secretary's Office. In this process more lenient grant conditions were negotiated to benefit smaller institutes most in need of help and encouragement.[40]

Dealing with a disinterested government department placed all the onus on the applicants. Consequently, Kay distributed copies of the gazette notice and also encouraged institutes to apply.[41] The South Australian Institute advised on the wording of the annual gazette notices, collected applications and drew up an apportionment of the grant for the Minister's approval. In 1869 the Board also accepted responsibility for paying out the grants.[42]

After the South Australian Institute had been in existence for some time, its established structures began to change as it redefined its role and responded to changes occurring around it. Few societies had taken advantage of the opportunity of incorporation with the Institute. Other agencies, such as the University of Adelaide, established in 1874, took on some of its teaching functions. An inquiry into the South Australian Institute in 1874 led to the establishment of a reference library whose books were not to circulate. In 1884 legislation split the organisation into a Public Library, Museum and Art Gallery, and an independent Adelaide Circulating Library which continued to charge subscriptions and lend books. It is not the purpose of this chapter to follow the Public Library, Museum and Art Gallery's own development, but rather to follow its role in relation to the institutes. On the surface, these remained substantially unchanged.[43]

The lecture scheme had already faded towards the end of the 1860s, attributed at the time to lack of new blood in the lecturing staff, financial depression around 1870, and possibly to a change in public taste.[44] While these factors were no doubt influential, it is also likely that they served as an excuse for the Board to move towards a greater concentration on its own role as a 'national' library for South Australia. In depressed times, economics was a consideration: the only possible saving in the lecture scheme was to cut back on the number of lectures, whereas the travelling library could at least run on its own momentum for some time before it was absolutely necessary to replenish the bookstock. Whatever the reasons, the lecture scheme died away after 1873,[45] even though lectures themselves remained popular in the community. The Travelling Box Library continued to expand as the following table shows:

Table 17.1
Growth of the Book Box Scheme, Various Years

YEAR	NO OF INSTITUTES	NO OF BOXES IN CIRCULATION	NO OF BOOKS IN BOXES
1859	18	8	320
1870	57	60	1,961
1880	106	144	4,511
1890	137	189	6,018
1895	154	199	6,454

German language boxes were introduced in 1875 and formed 17.5 percent of the number of boxes in 1896.[46] This service was allowed to fall into disuse after 1900, but was not finally phased out until the Institutes Association took over the administrative role in 1910.

The South Australian travelling box library scheme differed from those introduced in Victoria and New South Wales in that much of the bookstock was fiction - bought secondhand from Mudies in London. In 1898 the librarian justified the high proportion of fiction by saying, "We wish to get readers at almost any price and we afford them the opportunity of spending their time perhaps, over harmless works of fiction."[47]

The fiction content was offset after 1897 by the establishment of a small lending collection of reference material. Institutes could place subject requests which might be satisfied if they were considered of sufficient general interest to warrant spending from the small budget allotted to this service.[48]

By the 1890s the system developed by the South Australian Institute and subsequently taken over by the Public Library, Museum and Art Gallery was showing signs of wear. The Librarian and Secretary had both been in their posts since the very early days of the South Australian Institute, and while both were efficient, they were now elderly and somewhat set in their ways.[49] Increasingly, the organisation was concerned with its own functions rather than its services to institutes. An important catalyst for change arose through the Board's passive reaction to erosion of the subsidy level to institutes.

FORMATION OF THE INSTITUTES ASSOCIATION

A Parliamentary Committee for institutes was established as a watchdog group after a dramatic campaign led by the Librarian of the Port Adelaide Institute, F E Meleng (later long-time Secretary of the Institutes' Association of South Australia) to return the subsidy level to that prevailing in the mid 1880s. This group moved to form an Institutes Association of South Australia in the late 1890s.[50]

This Institutes Association provided a range of extremely practical services to institutes, including a bulk buying scheme for periodicals that brought an immediate reduction in costs for those that joined. An Association lobby helped protect the subsidy level. Port Adelaide

Institute, in collaboration with the Association, started a scheme whereby institutes that bought large numbers of popular journals could resell them on a regular subscription basis, a month old, at half price to smaller institutes with smaller budgets. The Association published the *South Australian Institutes Journal* from August 1900 to 1964. Enough institutes joined the Association to make it a significant lobby. By contrast, the Public Library, Museum and Art Gallery appeared to have a very passive relationship with the institutes.

Institute Association representatives or supporters gained places on the Public Library, Museum and Art Gallery Board, where they were able to press their cause. Definite factions developed on the Board representing those who favoured the functions of the central body and those who represented the interests of the institutes.

The signs that the Institutes Association believed itself to be the best representative for institutes were clearly developing before a catalyst for drastic action emerged in the shape of the Morgan Thomas Bequest. Dr Morgan Thomas left his residual estate of some £65,000 to the Public Library, Museum and Art Gallery in 1903. The institutes lobby sought a share of the bequest, but were prevented from doing so by an argument that services were provided as a matter of administrative convenience to government and were separately paid for - institutes were not in any sense regarded as a part of the Public Library, Museum and Art Gallery and therefore were not entitled to any share. Thus rejected, the Institutes Association mounted a strong campaign to have institutes put under the aegis of a body whose sole purpose was their welfare. A brisk campaign brought this to fruition in 1910.

INCORPORATION OF THE ASSOCIATION

The Institutes Association of South Australia, Incorporated, was set up by *The Public Library, Museum, and Art Gallery, and Institutes Act* of 1909. This completed the process of turning South Australia into a virtual union of institutes with a central body whose sole purpose was to look after their interests. Under the able and entrepreneurial administration of its Secretary, F.E. Meleng, the Institutes Association Council carefully overhauled the services it had inherited from the Public Library. Meleng, as noted, had been librarian of the Port Adelaide Institute - South Australia's largest - and he had been Secretary of the Association since its inception. When the post became a salaried position, he was appointed to it and resigned from Port Adelaide. Meleng was continually questing for improvements and new developments until the time of his death in 1930.[51]

One of the Association's first actions was to review the travelling box library. Most institute collections were largely fiction. The new Act precluded direct intervention in the affairs of any institute. The Council could not dictate buying policy but decided to set institutes an example and not provide fiction in the boxes. The box library was expanded, with boxes of 60 volumes replacing the older boxes of 30. The government was persuaded to provide a healthy grant for book provision and a rapid modernisation of the collection took place, during which fiction was replaced with general literature - travel, biography, history and general science. A percentage of juvenile books was introduced as part of a general encouragement for institutes to provide for children.[52]

The old system had had fewer books and they had remained in circulation longer. Some withdrawn books had been given to institutes but gifts were most frequently to new institutes and were not as a part of any general distribution. The new policy was to turn the contents over more rapidly, and to present the contents to institutes in a much more systematic way.

By 1914 nearly £2,000 had been spent on books for the boxes and, with a predicted annual expenditure of about £600, it was felt the presentations could begin. The 210 then affiliated institutes were divided into groups of 30. Gifts of 60 volumes were made to each institute, a group at a time, at four monthly intervals until each of the seven groups had been covered - a gift to each institute being worth about £13 or £14.[53]

Three gifts were possible during the 1920s. The addition of 60 volumes of non-fiction to collections of a few hundred or thousand books, every few years, was intended to gradually increase the quality of the state's libraries.[54]

Following a postal referendum on its future, the Institutes Reference Library was retained intact[55] and promoted in various ways.[56] Its organisers made genuine attempts to answer inquiries, but a low level of use was endemic - partly owing to the fact that the 1909 catalogue compiled by staff of the Public Library was never updated. Furthermore, the presence of an intermediary provided yet another barrier to those seeking information.[57] If material had to be bought in answer to an inquiry this might take several months. Items considered cheap enough for institutes to afford, or too esoteric and expensive, were not bought. Material was only lent on the request of an institute. The collection was finally returned to the Public Library when it established its Country Lending Service direct to users in 1938.[58]

A concerted policy of praise and criticism was used to try to encourage provision of public reading rooms where non-subscribers could use institute materials.[59] Increasingly, the government felt that as it provided funding to institutes they should make a reasonable effort to provide services to the public in general. This was not a universally popular policy, but one which was encouraged by the Association.[60] During the later 1920s the Minister of Education took a definite interest, and matters nearly reached the stage where minimum standards were to be required as a condition for subsidy. However, the total withdrawal of the government subsidy as a Depression measure in 1931 removed the basis of the argument, and many institutes closed their separate public reading rooms as a necessary economy.[61]

One of the original proposals - that of appointing an inspector of institutes - proved too threatening to institutes jealous of their independence and was dropped when the legislation was being prepared. The secretary of the Association was charged merely with visiting institutes and offering advice.[62] Meleng was instructed to make his first visits at the end of 1910,[63] and these were to become a regular feature of the Association's work.

After visiting each institute, the secretary produced a short paragraph highlighting good and bad points and any advice offered. Edited versions were published in the *South Australian Institutes Journal*. The conclusions to Meleng's reports show that, although he felt the constraints of the Act in not being able to interfere directly in the affairs of institutes, he continually sought ways of providing services and meeting changing conditions.[64]

During its early period, the incorporated Association reintroduced the subsidised lecture scheme in much the same form as in the 1860s. This lasted into the 1920s.[65] There was also continued support for educational classes - especially at remote institutes where there were no other facilities. Approved courses were subsidised until the Depression.[66]

The keynote of the Institutes Association's administration was gradualism. There were no sudden upheavals, and the casual observer could be forgiven for thinking the transfer in 1910 had had very little influence. But inherited services were carefully examined and reformed as necessary. In the areas where it could not interfere, indirect pressure for reform was applied. Meleng, as Secretary, was continually alert for new ideas to improve the standard.

During and after the First World War the Association continued to work to introduce new benefits. One area was to negotiate the best group deals possible for insurance and taxation. Exemption from the Federal entertainment tax introduced in 1916 was relatively quickly won.[67] State entertainment taxes were introduced the same year, but only partial concessions were achieved, and then only in 1929.[68] When performing rights charges were introduced in 1926 the Association negotiated a reduction of 15 percent on fees if they were paid through the Association's office.[69] Later, in 1926, Meleng attended an interstate conference on performing rights and succeeded in negotiating even better terms: a flat rate of 5s per institute compared with amounts ranging from £1/5s to £7/7s for normal licences.[70]

In 1930 institutes running their own movie businesses were said to be ordinary commercial ventures which should pay accordingly, but even here the Association managed to negotiate fees that were significantly less than the cost of a normal licence. For its part, the Council assisted by continuing to collect and forward fees to the Performing Right Association. This system lasted until 1954, when the Institutes Association was able to obtain a single licence covering all its members.[71]

Insurance for institutes could be effected through the Association. Meleng was accredited as an insurance agent in recognition of the quantity of business transacted, and the commission was put back into institute work. Even until the early 1980s the volume of business gave the Association enough bargaining power to gain worthwhile discounts.[72]

World War I forced up the cost of living - including a significant rise in the price of books and periodicals. In general, however, institutes did not put up their subscription rates. To assist them in keeping costs as low as possible, Meleng designed a subscription system to help provide the light reading most wanted by subscribers. In its original form, launched at the 1920 annual meeting, participating institutes received a different box of 30 works of fiction every two months: 180 volumes a year at a rental of less than ten pence each compared with purchase costs of three to four shillings. The last box of each subscription became the institute's. This also ensured the boxes were continually refilled with fresh material.[73] Part of the contents were bought locally or interstate[74] - probably as remainders rather than the latest new fiction which was imported directly from the Association's London agents.[75] This, and a similar juvenile subscription box scheme,[76] proved extremely successful and were continued by the Association until it finally wound up all its services in 1988.[77]

344

INTERSTATE CO-OPERATION

As early as 1900, a vision of a federal body to carry the advantages attained by co-operation in South Australia to the whole Commonwealth was voiced by the Association's father figure, Thomas Burgoyne, at the Library Association of Australasia's Adelaide meeting. Although this was probably just rhetoric,[78] surprisingly quickly after the Association gained administrative control over the centralised aspects of South Australian institutes, the idea of a federal association resurfaced.[79] In 1913, Meleng was sent on the first of a number of eastern-states buying trips. He used the visit to gauge interstate reaction to the idea, and subsequently reported interest in other states for introducing legislation similar to South Australia's and in ultimately federalising the movement.[80]

Other states were also still heavily dependent on subscription libraries. The existence of the Institutes Association made the South Australian system more organised and offered advantages not available interstate. Legislative recognition gave an appearance of greater government support for institutes, and there is considerable evidence that other states looked to South Australia as a possible model and leader.

Probably no state patterned itself more explicitly on the South Australian model than Western Australia. Shortly after the turn of the century,

> The First Conference of the Librarians and Secretaries of the many different city, suburban, and country Institute Libraries [in Western Australia] was opened in the presence of a large and representative gathering, at the Swan River Mechanics' Institute, Perth, at 2.30pm on Thursday, November 3rd, 1904.[81]

The conference, "which was inaugurated by the secretaries of the Kalgoorlie and Swan River Institutes, was convened for the purpose of discussing means for improving Institutes and extending the Library Movement generally."[82] Over the next two days, delegates discussed subjects such as 'Government subsidies,' 'How to manage and popularise institutes,' 'Modern fiction,' 'On the mission of libraries,' 'How the WA Public Library can assist country institutes,' and 'Mechanics' institutes and the introduction of billiards.'

Perhaps the conference's greatest achievement, however, was the formation of an association "to be known as the West Australian Institutes' Association,"[83] and the decision to publish a journal, the *West Australian Librarians' and Institutes Journal*. Despite the promise of this initiative, however, it seems that enthusiasm for the Association soon petered out. There is no evidence that projected annual meetings to be held "in the first week of November in each year"[84] ever eventuated, and the interesting and informative *Journal* seems to have ceased publication after just one issue in November 1904.

The Literary Institutes Association of New South Wales had its origins in billiard competitions organised each year from 1909 to 1913 with the aim of bringing metropolitan schools of arts in touch with each other. A definite association including all similar institutes in New South Wales, formed in April 1914, invited Meleng to visit.[85] This New South Wales body attempted to gain legislative status similar to the Institutes Association and sought further details from South Australia in preparing its case.[86] However, W H Ifould, the Chief Librarian at the Public Library of New South Wales, argued against giving it official status.[87] Eventually it salvaged what it could of the South Australian model by becoming a limited company able to trade in books and other library requisites, buying books in bulk at lower prices for New South Wales schools of arts.[88]

Alfred McMicken, librarian of the Prahran Free Library in Victoria, was the prime mover behind a Library Association of Victoria started in 1912, which lapsed during World War I, and was then revitalised in the late 1920s. McMicken saw considerable advantages in the South Australian structure.[89]

During the 1920s the Institutes Association of South Australia provided the impetus for an interstate library conference. The idea was adopted by the Institutes Association's 1922 annual meeting[90], but progress was slow. A meeting proposed for 1923 was postponed several times[91] and it finally took place in Adelaide in 1926. Representatives from Western Australia, Victoria, New South Wales and Tasmania attended the conference which was combined with the Institutes Association of South Australia's annual meeting. The meeting voted approval for formation of a Federal Association and called into existence a committee of South Australian library officials to draft a constitution for consideration at a future conference in one of the eastern states.[92]

Some South Australians clearly saw the proposed federal association in terms of their Institutes Association: a huge bulk buying scheme providing for the reading tastes of subscription library members around Australia. These proposals had to be jettisoned as the institutes officials from South Australia came up against the the library professionals from the eastern states.[93] In particular, Ifould had met with H M Green of the University of Sydney Library, and C G Bertie of the Sydney Municipal Library in October and November 1926, and agreed they would have nothing to do with a library association that included other than professional librarians as full members, although others might be accommodated in associate or honorary membership categories.[94]

The meeting in the eastern states did take place - in Victoria in 1928[95] - with a strong feeling of optimism present in the reports of the meeting. Ifould's previous doubts seemed to have been assuaged, and he even moved to give the South Australians Sowden, Meleng and the Public Librarian H R Purnell the inaugural places on the executive of the Australian Library Association.[96] From a South Australian viewpoint this was a high point in which Institutes Association of South Australia influence had brought about an Australian Library Association. But once set up this association was able to achieve little.

Its full existence depended on state associations joining the national body.[97] The 1926 meeting had helped create an interest in State Associations. McMicken was able to bring the Library Association of Victoria to life again in 1927.[98] Early in 1928,William Sowden, president of the Institutes Association of South Australia, visited Hobart and discussed the possibility of a Tasmanian Association with E Morris Miller. Miller had been a member of the Library Association of Australasia in 1902, and had assisted McMicken in the first establishment of the Library Association of Victoria in 1912 before accepting an academic post in Hobart, where he also became Honorary University Librarian and Chairman of Trustees of the Public Library of Tasmania. While the Tasmanian delegate to the 1926 meeting had been cautious about the idea of an association, Miller took the matter to his fellow trustees and by March 1928 had promoted establishment of a Tasmanian association.[99]

Queensland had not been represented at the 1926 conference, but correspondence with the principal library authorities seems to have been the catalyst for the establishment of a Queensland association.[100]

New South Wales had not yet formed an Association. Ifould was evidently moving in this direction, but too slowly, and his initiatives were cut short by the Depression. Any national meeting of the Association had to be postponed until the depression lifted, by which time the situation had changed.[101]

The Institutes Association of South Australia's action in inviting interstate representatives to the 1926 conference caused interest (or a resurgence of interest) both at the level of state structures, and in the idea of a federal association. If nothing else, the heightened interest and debate were worthwhile achievements in themselves.

It should also be remembered that the *South Australian Institutes Journal* was the only genuine library journal in Australia between the demise of the short lived *Library Record of Australasia* in 1902 and the establishment of McMicken's *Library Journal*, first published by the Library Association of Victoria in 1937 (apart from the one-off *West Australian Librarians 'and Institutes' Journal* of November 1904). From about 1915 onwards Meleng included such interstate news as he could obtain, and built up a circulation for the journal especially in Victoria and New South Wales.[102]

THE CURTAIN LOWERS

Two events in 1930 removed much of the dynamic nature of the Association: Meleng's death,[103] and the temporary suspension of subsidies to institutes. Meleng was succeeded by H J Emslie, who had joined the Association staff in 1917 as a boy of fourteen.[104] An efficient administrator, he was neither a librarian nor the restless entrepreneur Meleng had been. Nevertheless he maintained traditional services and retained the Institutes Association as a formidable lobby during his term as Secretary from 1930 to 1968. He also undertook various reforms to disaffiliate inactive institutes and, from the early 1940s, gradually began to acclimatise local governments to the idea that they should contribute to institute funding. Despite his best efforts however, it became evident following the Munn-Pitt report that institutes could no longer be considered at the forefront of library provision, and Emslie's long administration only staved off the inevitable demise of the institute system.[105]

Suspension of grants in response to the Depression in 1931 also signalled the end of the institutes as a dynamic force in South Australia. The total subsidy, amounting to £10,271/18/- in 1929, was cut to zero for three years. Reinstated in 1932-33 at £2,600 - less than a third of the previous amount - the grant did not again exceed £10,000 until 1957-58.[106] Without raising their subscriptions dramatically, and without the significant levels of pre-depression government support, the Institutes Association of South Australia and individual institutes could hope to do little more than partially satisfy a desire for light reading and continue to provide social centres through their halls and other amenities. However, the close affiliation between the central body and local institutes, based on the mid-nineteenth century concept of unions of mechanics' institutes in the United Kingdom,

347

strengthened in South Australia by the addition of government funding, proved remarkably durable. This unique system retained its essential elements until June 1988, only a year before dissolution of the last South Australian institute.[107]

NOTES AND REFERENCES

1.This chapter is based on research for the author's official history, *A chance to read: A history of the institutes movement in South Australia* (Adelaide: Library Board of South Australia, 1992), prepared for the Institutes Association of South Australia.

2.Bridge, C. (1982). South Australia's early public libraries, 1834-56. *South Australiana*, *21* (1), pp.80-86.

3.Pike, D. (1967). *Paradise of dissent: South Australia 1829-1857*. (2nd ed). Melbourne: Melbourne University Press, p.487.

4.*Register* (Adelaide), 30 January 1854, p.3; *The Australian encyclopaedia, vol. 7*, (1965) Sydney: The Grolier Society, pp.512-513.

5.*Register*, 16 October 1856, p.3; *The Australian encyclopaedia, Vol. 1, op. cit.*, p.261.

6.Hailes to Private Secretary, 8 August 1857, Public Record Office of South Australia [hereafter PROSA] GRG19/14/1 pp.35-28.

7.Institutes known to have been started before 1856 (not necessarily an exhaustive list) are Hindmarsh & Bowden (1847), Gawler (1848), Strathalbyn (1850), Port Adelaide (1851), North Adelaide (1851), Mount Barker (1851), Port Lincoln (ca 1852), Clarendon (1853), Glen Osmond (1854), Port Elliott (1854), Willunga (1854), Stepney & Norwood (1855), Woodside (1855). Only Stepney, Willunga, and North Adelaide were listed by Hailes in 1857. (Talbot, *The institutes movement in South Australia*, chapter 3.)

8.Grants to the South Australian Library and Mechanics' Institute were: 1850 - £200; 1851 - £200; 1853 - £300. Bridge, C. (1986). *A trunk full of books: History of the State Library of South Australia and its forerunners*. Adelaide: Wakefield Press in association with the State Library of South Australia, p.23, note 33, citing PROSA GRG19/30.

9.*South Australian Gazette and Colonial Register*, 23 April 1853, p.3, quoted by Le Duff, G. (1980). Adult education and the institute movement in South Australia, 1836-1890. *Unpublished M.Ed thesis*. Adelaide: Flinders University, p.121.

10.Bridge, *op. cit.,* chapter 3, pp.24-31; Le Duff, *op. cit.,* pp.121-130.

11.*Australian Dictionary of Biography*, vol. 3, pp.65-66, 404-406; Bridge, *op. cit.*, p.25. For the East Torrens Institute which Clark help to found see, e.g., *Register*, 8 May 1856, p.1 (advertisement), 13 May 1856, p.3. As examples of Clark's lecturing activities see *Register*, 30 November 1855, p.3; 22 March 1856, p.3; 18 August 1856, P.2; 11 October 1856, p.2 and 19 December 1856, p.2.

12.South Australia (1854). Report from the select committee of the Legislative Council of South Australia to report if it be expedient that a bill to establish a National Institute should be introduced, *South Australian Parliamentary Papers No. 80*, p.5.

13.Anon. (1846). The literary and learned societies. *The Athenaeum*, 1 April 1846, pp.372-373, from which the quoted passages are taken, and debate in succeeding issues.

14.Anon. (1852). The learned societies of London. *The Athenaeum*, 17 July 1852, pp.773-774.

15.Anon. (1852). New Industrial university. *The Athenaeum*, 14 August 1852, p.872.

16.*An Act to establish and incorporate an Institution to be called 'The South Australian Institute'*, 1855-56 (No.16).

17.*Register*, 5 September 1854, p.2.

18.*Register*, 9 May 1856, p.2.

19.Hailes to Private Secretary, 8 August 1857, PROSA GRG19/14/1 pp.25-28.

20.Hailes, N. (15 August 1857). Institutional dawnings in South Australia. *Education Journal of South Australia, 1* (1), pp.3-4; Hailes, N. (15 September 1857) Institutional progress in South Australia, *Educational Journal of South Australia, 1* (2), p.13.

21.For lectures see e.g., Hailes to Rev G.D. Mudie, 16 June 1857, PROSA GRG19/14/1 p.16, Hailes to Nesbit, 2 July 1857, PROSA GRG19/14/1 pp.17-18; Wilshire to Hailes, 9 June 1858, 26 July 1858, PROSA GRG19/1/Sturt. For lending books see e.g., Wilson to Hailes, 19 May 1857, PROSA GRG19/1/Sturt; Hailes to Wilson, 23 May 1857, PROSA GRG19/14/1 p.12; Hailes to Isaacs, 25 January 1859, PROSA GRG19/14/1 pp.95-96.

22.Bridge, *op. cit.*, pp.40-42.

23.*Minutes, South Australian Institute* [hereafter SAI] *Board*, 20 October, 3 November 1857, 9 February and 9 April 1858, PROSA GRG19/355/1; Hailes to Private Secretary, 22 September 1858, and Hailes to Smith, Elder & Co., 26 February 1859, PROSA GRG19/14/1 pp.79 and 96-97, 100.

24.*Minutes, SAI Board*, 15 June, 9 and 13 July, 17 and 31 August 1859, PROSA GRG19/355/2; Kay to Messrs Cadd & Twigg, Adelaide, 15 June 1859, PROSA, GRG19/14/1 p.116; 'Substance of replies received from Country Institutes to circular of July 1859 respecting circulation of boxes of books &c &c,' in *Register of statistical returns from country and suburban institutes*, 1 July 1859 - 13 November 1906, PROSA GRG19/76 Vol. 1, p.2 and facing page.

25.Boys, R.D. (1898). Travelling libraries. In *Library Association of Australasia, Proceedings of the Sydney meeting, October, 1898. With three appendices:- the programme, guide to the loan exhibition, and library statistics of New South Wales,* [Sydney: Hennessey, Campbell and Co., 1898]; also republished in facsimile as *Occasional papers in librarianship*

No. 8, Adelaide: Libraries Board of South Australia, 1969, [hereafter L.A.A/sia 1898], pp.33-38.

26.Great Britain. House of Commons. *Report from the select committee on public libraries...*, 1849 No.548, see index under 'Itinerating libraries,' among those giving evidence was Rev. J.C. Brown, son of Samuel Brown who introduced such libraries into East Lothian in 1817; other important works to mention itinerating libraries in the 1850s were Hudson, J.W. (1851). *The history of adult education ...* London: Longman, Brown, Green & Longmans; and Hole, J. (1853). *An essay on the history and management of literary, scientific, and mechanics' institutions...* London: Longman, Brown, Green & Longmans.

27.Traice, W.H.J. (1856). *Hand-book of mechanics' institutions, with priced catalogue of books suitable for libraries. Prepared for the Yorkshire Union of Institutes*, London: Longman, Brown, and Co.

28.*Minutes, SAI Board*, 15 June 1858, PROSA GRG19/355/1; Hailes to Secretary, Nelson Institute, NZ, 26 February 1859, PROSA GRG19/14/1 pp.101-103; Kay to Willson, Yankalilla, 22 August 1859, PROSA GRG19/14/1 pp.147-151; *Minutes SAI Board*, 14 July 1862, PROSA GRG 19/355/3.

29.For Hailes see references in note 21 above. For Kay see e.g., Willshire to Kay, 18 January, 6 February 1860, PROSA GRG19/1/Sturt; Kay to Willshire, 3 February 1860, PROSA GRG19/14/1 p.216.

30.Kay to Chief Secretary, 3 September 1859, 9 February 1860, PROSA GRG19/14/1 pp.157-158, 218-219, 25 June 1861, PROSA GRG19/14/2 pp.238-239; *Minutes SAI Board* 14 September 1859, PROSA GRG19/355/2; *SAI Annual Report, 1859-1860*, section 17, published in *Register*, 13 October 1860, p.3; *SAI Annual Report, 1860-61*, p.[2].

31.*Minutes, SAI Board*, 8 April, 29 July, 19 August, 2 September 1861, PROSA GRG19/355/2; *Register*, 9 April 1861, p.1; Kay to Chief Secretary, 25 June 1861, PROSA GRG19/14/2 pp.238-239; *SAI Annual reports, 1860-1* p.[2], *1861-2* p.[2]; Kay to ten possible lecturers, 30 July 1861, PROSA GRG19/14/2 P.251-255; List of Country Institutes sent notices about Lectures, 11 September 1861, PROSA GRG19/14/2 p.291.

32.See for example the case of Mr Caire, who was accepted for his descriptive topics on China, African Travel and Switzerland but not for his scientific topics, and was then removed from the list after complaints from institutes. (*Minutes, SAI Board, 28 June 1869, 13 September 1869, 27 September 1869, 8 November 1869, PROSA GRG19/355/4 pp.347-349, 373-377, 378-380, 395-397.)

33.The pattern can be ascertained from the column for each institute headed 'Lectures in last Six Months' in *Register of statistical returns from country and suburban institutes*, 1 July 1859-13 November 1906, PROSA GRG19/76.

34.Anon. (1852). The popular institutions of the United Kingdom. *The Athenaeum*, 24 July 1852, pp.799-800; 7 August 1852, pp.845-846.

35.*Register*, 10 October 1857, p.2.

36. Traice, *op. cit.*, pp.81-83; 85-89.

37. *Minutes, SAI Board*, 12 and 26 August, 30 September 1867, PROSA GRG19/355/4, pp.125-129, 130-133, 145-147. The issue had arisen in 1864 out of the Board's concern to protect institutes' property by appropriate trusteeship provisions, see *SAI Annual Reports, 1864-65* to *1866-67*; and Benham, R.S. (1896). A brief account of the country institutes of South Australia. In *Library Association of Australasia, Account of the proceedings of the first Australasian library conference held at Melbourne on the 21st, 22nd, 23rd, and 24th April 1896; together with the papers read, lists of delegates, etc., and the constitution and office bearers of the Library Association of Australasia.* [Melbourne: Government Printer, 1896]; also republished in facsimile as *Occasional papers in librarianship No. 7*, Adelaide: Libraries Board of South Australia, 1969, pp.61-65, which also contains a printed copy of the model rules current in 1896.

38. For example, card playing see *Minutes, SAI Board*, 4 and 18 March 1881, PROSA GRG19/355/7 pp.489-493, 494-499, 8 April 1881, PROSA GRG19/355/8 pp.15-21.

39. For example, Hailes to Turner, 18 February 1858; Hailes to Talbot, 7 April 1858, PROSA GRG19/14/1, pp.53-54, 58.

40. Kay to Chief Secretary, 27 July 1959, 5 August 1859, 31 August 1859, PROSA GRG19/14/1 pp.133, 140, 152; *South Australian Government Gazette* [hereafter *SAGG*], 8 September 1859, pp.816-817.

41. e.g., Kay noting he had written to Mitcham and Noarlunga Institutes, 29 September 1859, PROSA GRG19/14/1, p.173.

42. *SAI Annual Report, 1868-69*, p.3.

43. Bridge, *op. cit.*, chapters 5 and 6.

44. *SAI Annual Report, 1868-9*, p.3 and successive annual reports.

45. See the 'Accounts Passed' section for individual meetings in *Minutes, SAI Board*, PROSA GRG19/355/5.

46. Benham, *op. cit.*, for both the table and German language content.

47. Adams, J.R.G. (1888). The Circulation of book boxes amongst country institutes in South Australia. In *L.A.A/sia 1898*, pp.38-44.

48. Adams, *op. cit.*

49. The Librarian was Richard Somersal Benham, appointed in 1858: Bridge, *op. cit.*, p.66, 73-75.

50. Unless otherwise stated, the early development of the Institutes Association and its campaign to take on the central role towards institutes is drawn from Talbot, M. (1988). Origins of the Institutes Association of South Australia, Inc. In Rayward, W. B. (Ed.), *Australian library history in context: Papers for the Third Forum on Australian Library*

History, University of New South Wales, 17 and 18 July 1987. Sydney: University of New South Wales School of Librarianship, 1988, pp.129-138; Bridge, *op. cit.*, pp.75-85 also deals with the Morgan Thomas bequest and the institutes' campaign for independence from the Public Library, Museum and Art Gallery Board.

51. 'Mr F.E. Meleng.' *South Australian Institutes Journal* [hereafter *SAIJ*] 1,9; 20 April 1901, pp.160-161; Meleng to Secretary, Port Adelaide Institute, 11 March 1891, applying for the position of Assistant Librarian, Port Adelaide Institute Correspondence - letters received 1873-1946, PROSA GRG58/170/4; Sowden, W. (1930). Frederick Edward Meleng - gentleman. A memoir. *SAIJ* 18,12: 31 August 1930, pp.5-9.

52. Institutes Association of South Australia, Incorporated [hereafter IASA], *Annual reports* 1910-11 to 1913-14, particularly but not exclusively the 'Annual report of the Literature Committee.'

53. 'Valuable assistance for institutes'. *SAIJ* 13,5: December 1914, p.589; IASA, *Annual reports* 1914-15 to 1916-17.

54. 'Annual report of the Literature Committee.' In IASA, *Annual reports* 1920-21 to 1931, passim; Leading lights. A valuable gift to institutes. *SAIJ* 19,5: 30 June 1931, p.6, claimed the process about to begin would be the fifth gift of its kind.

55. 'Institutes' Association annual meeting,' *SAIJ* 11,1: 24 October 1911, pp.289-300; 'Annual report of the Literature Committee; in IASA, *Annual Reports 1910-11, 1911-12*; Minutes, 2 October 1911, IASA Council Minutes 1910-1922, pp.63-64 PROSA GRG58 unprocessed material; *Minutes*, 9 November 1911, 1 March 1912, IASA Literature Committee 1910-1929, PROSA GRG58 unprocessed material.

56. Various means of publicity were used. For publicity in the journal see e.g., 'Various views. Institutes reference library,' *SAIJ* 13, 8: June-July 1915, p.681; 'Books recently added to the institutes reference library,' *SAIJ* 14,9: January 1919, pp.348-49; 'The Association's reference library,' *SAIJ* 19,11: 30 June 1932, pp.34. For publicity in annual reports and annual meetings: IASA, *Annual Reports 1910-11* to *1937-38*, and see also motions in agendas published in annual reports for e.g., 1914-15, 1916-17. For publicity by Meleng speaking at ceremonies and institute visits see e.g. IASA, *Annual Report, 1928-1929*. For publicity by posters sent to institutes for display see e.g., *Minutes*, 5 March 1917, *IASA Council Minutes* 1910-1922, pp.243-244, PROSA GRG58 unprocessed material; 'The Associations reference library,' *SAIJ* 20,12: 31 August, 1934, pp.29-30.

57. A summary of policy is in 'Leading lights. The reference library,' *SAIJ* 19,4: 30 April 1931, pp.5-6.

58. *Minutes*, 30 November 1937, IASA Literature Committee 1929-1972, PROSA GRG58 unprocessed material; *Minutes*, 6 and 16 December 1937, 7 February, 7 March 1938, IASA Council Minutes 1936-1944, pp.51-53, 54-56, 57-60, 61-63, PROSA GRG58 unprocessed material; IASA, *Annual Reports 1937, 1938*.

59. Earliest interest in this policy is documented in 'Agenda' in IASA, *Annual Report, 1910-11*; 'Institutes Association annual meeting,' *SAIJ* 11,1: 24 October 1911, pp.289-300.

Port Elliot Institute, SA
(courtesy of Goolwa and District Historical Society)

Port Pirie Institute, SA

Crystal Brook Institute, SA
(photograph by Margaret Campbell)

Sorting new books for the circulating boxes and fiction lending department of the SA Institutes Association, 1923. From left: H J Emslie, junior clerk, F E Meleng.

Frederick Edward Meleng, 1866 - 1930
(reproduced by permission of the State Library of South Australia
- SSL:M:B17821)

60. Argument for and against the issue is typified in debate at the 1924 annual meeting: 'Institutes Association of South Australia, Incorp.,' *SAIJ* 16, 11: October 1924, pp.385-393.

61. 'Leading lights. The Hon. the Minister of Education and institutes,' *SAIJ* 18, 4: February-March 1929, p.143; 'Leading lights. Reading rooms,' *SAIJ* 18, 6: July 1929, p.238; 'Leading lights. A play on names and a purpose,' *SAIJ* 18, 7: September 1929, p.275: IASA, *Annual Reports 1928-29* to *1930-31*. The Minister had been in correspondence with the Council: *Minutes,* 28 February, 6 June, 30 July, 29 August, 26 September 1929, *IASA Institutes Committee 1924-1946,* pp.71-72, 76-77, 80-81, 82, 83-84, PROSA GRG58 unprocessed material.

62. The original concept shows in meeting reports, e.g., 'The Institutes Association. The annual meeting,' *SAIJ* 6, 8: 24 March 1906, pp.151-156; the skeleton bill is reproduced in 'Before the Public Library Board,' *SAIJ* 8, 8: 24 March 1908, p.155; the resulting legislation is *The Public Library, Museum, and Art Gallery, and Institutes Act, 1909* (No. 986).

63. *Minutes,* 3 October 1910, *IASA Council Minutes 1910-1922,* pp.34-35, PROSA GRG58 unprocessed material.

64. e.g., 'Institutes' Association of South Australia (Incorporated),' *SAIJ* 13, 4: October 1914, pp.561-565; 'Extracts from the Secretary's report on his visits to institutes, 1922-3,' *SAIJ* 16, 7: December 1923, pp.245-246.

65. *Minutes,* 2 and 29 March 1911, *IASA Institutes Committee Minutes, 1910-1924,* pp.14-15, 16-17, PROSA GRG 58 unprocessed material; *Minutes,* 6 March, 3 April 1911, *IASA Council Minutes 1910-1922,* pp.42-43, 44-46 PROSA GRG58 unprocessed material; 'Report of the Literature Committee; in IASA, *Annual report, 1911-12* lists lecturers and their topics. Organised lectures were discontinued in 1927: *Minutes,* 29 March 1927, IASA Literature Committee 1910-1929, PROSA GRG58 unprocessed material; 'Leading lights. Lectures for institutes,' *SAIJ* 17, 8; April 1927, p.299.

66. From 1916 the subsidy was only paid for subjects on the syllabuses of the School of Mines or the School of Art: IASA, *Annual Report, 1915-16.* Avoidance of duplication with other agencies was a concern: e.g., in a speech by J.G. Bice, Chief Secretary reported in 'Ninth annual report of the Institutes Association, Incorporated' [in fact the report of the meeting], *SAIJ* 15, 1: October 1919, pp.5-11. For removal of subsidies: IASA, *Annual Report, 1930-31; The Institutes Association of South Australia Incorporated. 1910-1960,* [Adelaide, The Association, 1960], p.10.

67. Paech, P. M. (1969). Cinema in Adelaide to 1945. *Unpublished BA (Hons) thesis.* Adelaide: University of Adelaide, p.1; *Minutes,* 3 August 1917, IASA, *Institutes Committee Minutes, 1910-24,* PROSA GRG58 unprocessed material.

68. IASA, *Annual Report, 1928-29.*

69. *Minutes,* 19 and 29 July 1926, General Purposes Committee 1912-56 PROSA GRG58 unprocessed material.

70. 'Leading lights. The Australasian Performing Right Association and Institutes,' *SAIJ* 17, 8: April 1927, p.300; IASA, *Annual Report, 1926-27*.

71. 'The Performing Rights Association and the Institutes Association,' *SAIJ* 18, 9: January-February 1930, p.396; IASA, *Annual Report, 1932-33; The Institutes Association of South Australia Incorporated. 1910-1960*, p.12.

72. *The Institutes Association of South Australia Incorporated. 1910-1960*, p.12; 'Ninth annual report of the Institutes Association, Incorporated,' *SAIJ* 15, 1: October 1919, pp.5-11; *Minutes*, 27 November 1919, IASA Finance Committee 1910-1930, PROSA GRG58 unprocessed material; IASA, *Annual report, 1919-1920;* information from R.J. Broad, IASA Executive Officer from 1975 to the winding up of the Association.

73. 'Annual conference,' *SAIJ* 15, 6: November 1920, pp.222-225.

74. e.g., *Minutes*, 1 December 1921, 21 February 1923, IASA Literature Committee 1910-1929, PROSA GRG58 unprocessed material.

75. *Minutes*, 2 and 31 March, 1 September 1922, IASA Literature Committee 1910-1929, PROSA GRG58 unprocessed material; *Minutes*, 6 March 1922, *IASA Council Minutes 1910-1922*, pp.359-360, PROSA GRG58 unprocessed material; 'Leading lights. The fiction lending department,' *SAIJ* 15, 9: September 1921, pp.325-326; 'The fiction lending department,' *SAIJ* 15, 12: June 1922, p.460.

76. *Minutes*, 2 November 1923, 31 January 1924, *IASA Literature Committee 1910-1929*, PROSA GRG58 unprocessed material; IASA, *Annual Report, 1923-24*.

77. Information from R.J. Broad.

78. Burgoyne, T. (1900). The Institutes Association of South Australia. In *Library Association of Australia, Transactions and proceedings of the Library Association of Australasia at its third general meeting, held at Adelaide, October 9th, 10th, 11th, and 12th, 1900*. [Adelaide: Government Printer, 1901], also republished in facsimile as *Occasional papers in librarianship No. 9*, Adelaide: Libraries Board of South Australia, 1969, pp. xviii-xx.

79. Typescript pasted in with Minutes, 1 August 1913, *IASA Institutes Committee 1910-1924*, p.64 PROSA GRG58 unprocessed material; 'First annual conference of institutes. Held at Mount Barker on Saturday, September 6, 1913,' *SAIJ* 12,12: September-October 1913, pp.394-395; *Minutes*, 4 August 1913, *IASA Council Minutes 1910-1922*, pp.121-123 PROSA GRG58 unprocessed material; 'Annual meeting of the Institutes Association,' *SAIJ* 12,12: September-October 1913, pp.392-394.

80. 'The library movement in Australia,' *SAIJ* 13, 2: February-March 1914, pp.459-460; press clippings one nd, one annotated 2/3/14, loose in *IASA Council Minutes 1910-1922*, between pp.144-145, PROSA GRG58 unprocessed material.

81. anon. (1904). Librarians' conference: Auspicious opening. *West Australian Librarians' and Institutes' Journal, 1,* p.8.

82.*ibid.*

83.*ibid.*, p.22-25

84.*ibid.*, p.22

85.'Various views. The Literary Institutes' Association of New South Wales,' *SAIJ* 13, 6: February 1915, p.609; 'Various views. Institutes in New South Wales,' *SAIJ* 13, 6: February 1915, p.610; Minutes, 30 July 1914, *IASA Institutes Committee 1910-1924,* PROSA GRG58 unprocessed material.

86.'Personal and particular,' *SAIJ* 14, 4: August-September 1917, pp.131-133.

87.W.H. Ifould, Memoranda relating to the Conference concerning Literary Institutes' Association, 25 March 1916, contained amongst unsorted correspondence in Mitchell Library, ML Uncat MSS, Set 358.

88.'Leading lights. A co-operative scheme for the purchase of books,' *SAIJ* 15, 11: February 1922, p.398; 'The Literary Institutes Co-operative Society of New South Wales, Ltd,' *SAIJ* 15, 12: June 1922, p.464.

89.Redmond, L. (1989). Alfred Ernest McMicken, 1972-1963: Innovator and pioneer in library development. *Unpublished MA minor thesis*. Clayton: Monash University, chapter 2.

90.'Institutes Association of South Australia (Incorporated). Annual Meeting,' *SAIJ* 16, 2: October 1922, pp.65-69; 'Personal and particular. A federal association,' *SAIJ* 16, 2: October 1922, p.46.

91.'Leading lights. Sydney's librarian,' *SAIJ* 16, 4: March 1923, p.116; 'Leading lights. An interstate conference of librarians,' *SAIJ* 16, 4: March 1923, p.117; 'Leading lights. Big things ahead,' *SAIJ* 16, 6: October 1923, pp.191-192; 'Leading lights. Interstate conference of library officials,' *SAIJ* 16, 7: December 1923, p.229; Minutes, 5 May 1924, *IASA Council Minutes 1922-1936* pp.43-44, PROSA GRG58 unprocessed material.

92.Most of the November 1926 issue of the *SAIJ* was devoted to the conference, in particular 'Conference of state and interstate library officials and annual meeting of the Institutes Association of South Australia (Incorporated),' *SAIJ* 17, 7: November 1926, pp.246-280.

93.'Institutes Association of South Australia (Incorporated). Annual meeting,' *SAIJ* 16, 2: October 1922, pp.65-69; 'Library Federation of Australia and New Zealand,' *SAIJ* 17, 7: November 1926, pp.290-291.

94.'Leading lights. Mr W.H. Ifould, O.B.E.,' *SAIJ* 11, 12: May-June 1928, p.495; Whyte J.P. (1985). From ALA to LAA - the Australian Institute of Librarians. In Biskup, P., and Rochester, M.K. (Eds.), *Australian library history: Papers from the Second Forum on Australian Library History, Canberra, 19-20 July 1985*. Canberra: Canberra College of Advanced Education, pp.122-133, referring to correspondence between Ifould and Green, 4 November 1926, LAA Archives.

95.*Proceedings of the Australian library conference held at the University of Melbourne, August, 1928*. Melbourne: Government Printer, 1928.

96.Whyte, *op. cit.*, pp.124-125; *Argus* (Melbourne), 23 August, 1928, p.7; 'Australian Library Association,' *SAIJ* 18, 3: December 1928 - January 1929, pp.104-105.

97.Whyte, *loc. cit.;* 'Australian Library Association,' *SAIJ* 18, 3: December 1928 - January 1929, pp.104-105.

98.Redmond, *op. cit.;* her thesis findings support the central role of the Institutes Association of South Australia in the events leading to the resuscitation of the Library Association of Victoria.

99.Miller, E. (1985). Some Public Library memories, 1900-1913. (Edited and introduced by Derek Drinkwater). *La Trobe Library Journal 9*, (35), pp.49-88: *Minutes*, 6 February 1928, *IASA Council Minutes 1922-1936*, pp.129-130, PROSA GRG58 unprocessed material; 'Leading lights. The library movement,' *SAIJ* 17, 11 March 1928, p.453.

100.'A Queensland view of the proposed Library Federation of Australia and New Zealand,' *SAIJ* 17, 9: July 1927, pp.348-349; 'Leading lights. The library movement,' *SAIJ* 17, 11: March 1928, p.453; 'Queensland Library Association,' *SAIJ* 18, 6: September 1929, p.274.

101.Whyte, *op. cit.*, pp.125-126.

102.IASA, *Annual Reports, 1914-15* to *1926-27, 1928-29* to *1930-31, 1932-33*; 'The second annual report of the Library Association of Victoria for the year ending 30th June, 1929,' *SAIJ* 18, 7: September 1929, pp.309-310.

103.Sowden, *op. cit.*, pp.5-9.

104.'New secretary of the Association Mr H.J. Emslie,' *SAIJ* 19, 1: 31 October 1930, pp.10, 13; 'Mr H.J. Emslie's farewell,' *IASA Newsletter* No. 17, September, 1968, p.7.

105.Talbot, *op. cit.*, passim.

106.'Leading lights. Government subsidies,' *SAIJ* 18, 11: May-June 1930, p.465; Photocopy of a table of government grants to the Association from 1910-11 to 1939-40 (original attached to Minutes, 26 October 1939, *IASA, Finance Committee Minutes 1930-1943*, PROSA GRG58 unprocessed material) updated to 1987-88 from institute sources by R.J. Broad, in the author's possession. The figure of £10,428/1s/4d for 1957-58 includes a new component, an amount based on local government contributions to institutes as well as the normal subsidy on membership fees.

107.Information from R.J. Broad. The last institute was dissolved in June 1989, the last meeting of the Institutes Standing Committee was held in July 1989, and the provisions of the *Libraries Act Amendment Act, 1989* (No. 40), which removed all references to institutes from the legislation were proclaimed in *SAGG* 28 June 1990, p.1710, to take effect on 28 June 1990.

CHAPTER EIGHTEEN

'IMPROVEMENT' AND 'PROGRESS': THE SOUTH AUSTRALIAN INSTITUTES AFTER WORLD WAR I

Amanda Bettesworth

INTRODUCTION

The First World War represented a major watershed in Australia's history. It has been described as the end of the age of innocence and, with our wholesale commitment to the British war effort, it was also the end of the age of isolation. Few parts of the Australian social fabric escaped the effects of the war, and not surprisingly, the institute movement was also directly affected by those momentous events so far away. Many institutes across the country suffered reversals of fortune. This affected long-established groups as well as those founded in the first few years of the new century.

First and most obviously, there was a sharp decline in membership, as thousands of young men enlisted to serve in the armed forces. Naturally, this exodus affected the subscription base of many institutes, and their finances were further eroded when those who were left behind turned away from the social and educational life of the institutes towards the sober and serious business of fighting a war. Government subsidies also diminished, and even when local communities gathered for fundraising events, the institute halls rarely benefited: the halls were often hired out for a nominal sum, while the proceeds were diverted to patriotic efforts such as supporting the war-ravaged people of Belgium.

To the extent that the institutes relied on voluntary labour for their maintenance and upkeep, the absence of able-bodied men in many areas led to a general deterioration in the physical appearance and amenities of many institute halls. Furthermore, their libraries and other facilities fared little better; in a number of places it was treated as frivolous, if not downright unpatriotic, to channel resources away from the war into providing diversions for those left at home.

All in all, the institute movement came out of the war in a rather rundown condition, and once it was over, there was much to be done to rebuild local communities, to re-establish social and educational programs and, perhaps most immediately, to commemorate those who failed to return.

However, regaining lost revenue and membership was only one concern of South Australian Institutes in the immediate post-World War I period. In fact, two major themes dominated institute activities after the war and before the depression of the 1930s: 'improvement' and 'progress.' For example, the Robe Institute, which in common with several others had been relatively inactive during the war, was 'resurrected' in 1920. There was a resurgence of activity as fund-raising drives were held in order to buy more books, bolster the Institute's depleted funds and reduce the £90 debt on the building. Regular working bees were held to improve the appearance of the land surrounding the building, with other bees being planned to make seats for the hall from timber and iron already purchased by the committee. It was also the committee's intention to recatalogue the books in the library.[1] At Truro, an "institute improvement scheme" was implemented, with similar aims to those of Robe.[2] At the Cockburn Institute in 1920 the committee members themselves made several improvements to the building, reconstructing the stage and installing a new jarrah floor and a 'Delco' electricity plant. Committee members carried out this work free of charge, with only the materials being paid for out of institute funds.[3]

Indeed many country and suburban institutes carried out renovations on buildings which had been allowed to fall into disrepair during the war. In one single issue of the *Institutes Journal* it was reported that the Gawler, Hoyleton, Kalangadoo, Kensington and Norwood, Morphett Vale, Mount Barker, Port Lincoln, Whyalla, Kapunda, Murraytown, Port Noarlunga and Tarcowie Institutes were all at various stages in renovating buildings or erecting new ones, mostly in the form of soldiers' memorial halls.[4] In addition, new institutes were being founded, particularly in towns on the Paringa and Peebinga railway lines in the Riverland,[5] and in other river towns such as Barmera[6] and Wood's Point.[7] The number of institutes which became affiliated with the Institutes Association continued to grow steadily throughout the 1920s, from 220 in 1920 to 282 in 1925, and to 305 in 1929.[8]

INCREASING MEMBERSHIP

To boost institute membership, traditional methods including dances, concerts, strawberry fêtes and bazaars were usually employed. But an innovation of the 1920s was the 'Institute Night,' or 'President's Evening.' A report on Strathalbyn's highly successful President's Evening on 25 May 1920 appeared in the *Institutes Journal*. It was held for the purpose of recruiting new members, and three hundred invitations were sent to local residents, attracting a good response. Frederick Meleng delivered a speech on the advantages of institute membership, the president's wife supplied the supper and a program of musical and elocutionary items followed. This included an "amusing parody" by nine young ladies of "Three Blind Mice" and musical items by Miss Gwen Neil and Messrs Frank Johnston and Keith Marsh. All were called upon for an encore, which Mr Marsh had to decline because of his heavy cold. The local orchestra played a selection of music "in a capable manner" and there was an hour's dancing to round off the night's entertainment. The whole evening was pronounced "an unqualified success in every respect."[9] Other institutes, such as Lyndoch and Beachport, followed Strathalbyn's example and were equally successful in attracting new members.

Still on the themes of 'improvement' and 'progress,' in 1924, Mr S J G Davey from the Council of the Institutes Association made some suggestions in the *Institutes Journal* which he hoped institutes would take up. (Some of his ideas had already been adopted by various institutes in South Australia). With regard to the educational and cultural side of institute life, Davey suggested the extension of juvenile scholarships and more juvenile libraries with special management committees composed of boys and possibly girls, who would be expected to make recommendations to the institute executive committees. He also made suggestions concerning the beautifying of institute premises, and the provision of book wagons (as well as motorised library services) for people in outlying districts, isolated farms or construction and mining camps. On the social side, he recommended the formation of dramatic societies, billiards clubs, gymnasiums, boy scout groups and even swimming clubs. "Institute Welcome Committees" could be formed to make contact with visitors and new settlers in districts for the purpose of making known the town's (and particularly the institute's) advantages, and newcomers could be presented with free membership tickets. "An institute should be the centre of culture, and no effort spared to render the culture complete as far as circumstances permit," urged Davey. His expectations for institutes were realistic, as he recognised that often it was not possible to make the institute's work of an "advanced character." But it was, he claimed, often possible to make an institute more effective than it already was on the "lower planes."[10] The main object of country institutes, Davey explained, was to provide anything of an educational or social character to make life in the country more attractive for the young people in particular, and so to stop the drift to the city.

EDUCATIONAL ACTIVITIES

By the post-war period, the educational function of institutes was seen by some people as being undermined by the Workers' Educational Association (WEA). This adult education movement had been formed in England in 1903 to enable people from educationally disadvantaged groups - mainly working class men and women - to receive further education. The WEA tutorial classes and courses, run by university lecturers and tutors, proved to be highly successful and rewarding for both teachers and students.[11] In South Australia, the WEA had begun its operations by 1914 and was immediately successful, attempting to form country branches wherever possible. As in England, study groups, classes, educational excursions and a wide variety of interesting public lectures and short courses were offered.[12] Notwithstanding the concerns of some people, institutes responded to this challenge in their usual pragmatic way, turning the situation to their advantage by hiring out their halls and rooms for WEA activities. After all, as the editor of the *Institutes Journal* assured his readers, the WEA recognised the value of institutes as "intellectual outpost[s] carrying the light of learning into the country", and the WEA wished to work *with* institutes in furthering education in the community.[13]

Many institute committees thought that a local branch of the WEA on institute premises would encourage people to join their institute. One such institute was Thebarton. Here the WEA was granted the hire of rooms in which to conduct lectures from July 1919 onwards. The Institute committee organized the printing and circulation of admission tickets, and enrolment forms for WEA classes were placed in the library.[14] Subjects of early WEA lectures at Thebarton included 'Australian Literature,' 'Industries of the Back Blocks' and 'The Industrial Revolution.'[15] In 1920 the Thebarton Institute became affiliated with the WEA, which meant that for the annual fee of one guinea the Institute could have a representative on the WEA Council and receive all notices and pamphlets for the year, as well as copies of reports, lectures and booklets published by the WEA, to be placed on reading room tables.[16]

In general, country institutes were equally enthusiastic about the WEA. At Clare, for example, the local branch of the WEA ran an English literature class, while at Freeling the WEA ran weekly classes with Mr Mackay, assistant lecturer in economics at the University of Adelaide, as the tutor.[17] In 1927, the Council of the Institutes Association decided to discontinue the series of travelling lectures which had been so popular during the war, partly as a result of successful WEA activities in institutes, and partly because, as the *Institutes Journal* correspondent for the council explained, "the old-time educational lecture, illustrated with lantern slides, has been superseded by the movies." In addition, the ever-increasing use of motor cars meant that even people from some rural areas were now able to travel to Adelaide regularly for education and entertainment.[18]

TECHNOLOGICAL CHANGE

There were further signs of post-war 'progress' in institutes during the 1920s. For example, many suburban and country institutes replaced their acetylene gas lighting with electricity plants, in particular the 'Delco' brand. Gas generators could be dangerous, as some institute members discovered: In 1923, Mr G Boyce was killed while attending to a faulty acetylene gas generator at the Kingston Institute,[19] while at another (unnamed) country institute the town's mayor miraculously escaped the same fate, receiving only badly singed whiskers when he lit a match to investigate the cause of a broken-down acetylene gas lantern.[20] The popularity of these 'Delco' electricity plants in institutes prompted Frederick Meleng, editor of the Institutes Journal, to suggest that a good slogan for progressive institutes of the 1920s might be "Let there be light!"[21]

Another innovation was the telephone. The Terowie Institute, for example, paid for one to be installed in the home of its secretary, Mr A Kenner, in 1924. The "wireless set" was yet another piece of new technology to be introduced to institutes. At the remotely situated Honiton Institute on 31 July 1924, the first public "wireless concert" on southern Yorke Peninsula was held. The hall was packed that evening with an eager audience of all ages who listened with silent anticipation as Mr Mel Osborne, amateur wireless enthusiast of Murdock Bros, Yorketown, attached his home-made receiving set to the aerial and earth wires. He soon picked up another amateur in Adelaide, who obliged by sending some music across the airwaves. Eventually, just before eight o'clock, Mr Osborne was able to pick up 2FC, a farmers' broadcasting station in Sydney.[22] A clear voice came across the airwaves announcing that a "first-class concert" had been arranged. The announcement of each item was also distinctly heard, even by those at the back of the hall. Those who were present in the Honiton Institute that night marvelled at the way in which Mr Osborne's small, home-made receiving outfit was able to pick up, with such clarity, music from a concert being given hundreds of miles away in Sydney. It was certainly a novel way of arousing local interest in the institute.

By 1929, institute committees regarded radio broadcasting as having the potential to play an important part in the "uplift of the people." At one unnamed institute in the South-East of South Australia, a dance had been arranged to coincide with one being held in Adelaide. With the aid of a receiving set, "people three hundred miles away fox-trotted to the music of a well-known band performing in the City." The Council of the Institutes Association was already considering the possibility of a broadcasting scheme for institutes. But as usual, the 'popularisers' versus 'improvers' argument had to be resolved. Broadcasting facilities, claimed the Council, would not be intended solely for social activities such as those already described, but would "enable lectures and news items to be heard by thousands who do not possess a wireless outfit."[23]

It was surely appropriate that institutes should take advantage, as far as possible, of new technology such as electricity, automobiles, telephones and radio broadcasting. After all, one of the chief aims of institutes had always been to bring communities together and to attempt to alleviate geographical isolation as best they could. But these were not the only ways in which institutes adapted to modernity during the 1920s.

360

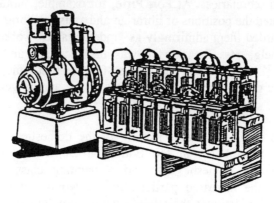
361

THE INCREASING ROLE OF WOMEN

Another new development was the increasing prominence of women in institute affairs. The participation of women in institute activities had hitherto usually been restricted to ladies' committees or individual fund-raising efforts, both of which - while essential to the survival of institutes - usually attracted little official recognition. Throughout the war years and then during the 1920s, however, women increasingly occupied places on institute committees, usually as librarians and secretaries. At Port Pirie, for example, mother and daughter Mrs and Miss Bensley occupied the positions of librarian and assistant librarian respectively. The Institute committee regarded them admiringly as "indefatigable" workers in the interests of the Institute. At Glenelg, Mrs B Atkinson was the secretary and librarian, and Miss Campbell her assistant.[24] Also during the 1920s, for the first time, a few women were elected by their institute committees to be delegates at the annual general meetings of the Institutes Association.

Women also conducted institute classes, usually in the domestic arts. At the Riverton Institute, for example, Miss Paget of the Education Department conducted classes in dressmaking, millinery and domestic art, and a painting class was taught by Miss Longbottom.[25] Despite the increased participation of women in executive positions on committees, fortunately for institutes their fund-raising activities did not diminish. At the Macclesfield Institute, for example, the post-war financial difficulties were alleviated substantially by the efforts of the public-spirited Miss Nicholas. In 1924 she formed a glee club with local residents for the sole purpose of raising funds for a new Institute piano. When this was purchased, Miss Nicholas offered the services of her glee club to assist with fund-raising for other improvements to the Institute. Naturally, the Institute committee readily accepted her offer, allowing the glee club free use of the hall for their practice sessions and concerts. The glee club then paid for repairs and tuning of the new piano, and for a new dressing room which was built at the back of the hall in 1928, at a cost of £57. Miss Nicholas also offered a quantity of crockery to the committee on behalf of the local Methodist church for £3. It was purchased and hired out at socials and meetings held in the Institute.[26]

DECLINING ECONOMIC CONDITIONS AND RESPONSE

This spirit of co-operation, expansion and improvement was not experienced by all institutes. In the *Institutes Journal* of March 1921, it was claimed that institutes on Yorke Peninsula were having a bad time owing to a "general depression." Those worst hit included the Moonta Mines and Wallaroo Mines Institutes. After the war, the mines were intermittently closed and re-opened every few months because of falling world copper prices, limited ore reserves and severe shortages of coal due to a series of strikes in the eastern states.[27] In October 1923, the Wallaroo and Moonta Mining and Smelting Company went into voluntary liquidation and the mines were closed permanently.

Because the Company had been the main source of revenue for these two institutes, between 1920 and 1930 annual reports from the Moonta Mines Institute contained details of severe financial hardship and depleted membership as the Company's financial aid was withdrawn and subscribers were forced to leave the district in search of work. Of those who remained, many lost interest in the floundering institute as they had more pressing personal problems.

In 1924, the ailing Moonta Mines Institute was itself threatened with closure. The committee decided to hold off the liquidators by selling first its billiard tables, which by now were hardly ever used, and then its gymnasium equipment. The library of mostly old, dilapidated books now became this institute's first priority. Other assets, including furniture, were gradually sold off to keep the library going until the Institute was forced to close in 1944.[28] It was that tough, enduring quality associated with institutes in general which kept the Moonta Mines Institute going for a further twenty-one years after the mines closed permanently.

It was generally accepted by those connected with institutes, in whatever capacity, that the movement was flourishing through the 1920s. New institutes were becoming affiliated with the Institutes Association every year and the building activity which had begun so enthusiastically after the war continued throughout the decade. At the same time, however, behind the appearance of progress there was evidence of organisational weakness. One example of this was the way in which some institutes arranged public lectures by visiting speakers. The Institutes Association received complaints from lecturers who visited country institutes in particular, who claimed that they were often treated with a lack of courtesy by institute committees. They were invited to lecture in order to raise funds for these institutes and so they expected and received only very nominal fees. However, when a lecturer arrived in a town, almost invariably no preparation had been made by the local committee for his stay. (Travelling lecturers were almost always male). Frequently he had to find his own way to the institute from the railway station and inquire where a meal and bed could be found and, according to an unsigned report in the Institutes Journal, a lecturer sometimes found that he was also expected to set up and take down unaided the screen for lantern slides. In one instance, a visiting lecturer was refused admittance to the institute until he paid his admittance fee at the door. When he protested that he was, in fact, a lecturer, the doorkeeper replied, "I can't help it sir. You can't hear the lecture unless you pay!" These are some of the reasons why, as mentioned previously, the Institutes Association decided to discontinue the travelling lecture series in 1927.[29]

A further sign of weakness in institutes is revealed in the criticism levelled at institute library literature, especially fiction. This criticism became even stronger during the 1920s. At Brighton, the Institute committee was proud of its well-stocked library. At a men's "smoke social" in 1920, a Dr Torr had described the Brighton Institute library as one of the best classified in South Australia, containing over three and a half thousand books with no "rubbish" among them. However, in a letter to the editor of the *Glenelg Guardian* seven years later, the bookstock of the Brighton Institute was criticised thus:

> ...what it lacks in quality of literature it makes up in quantity. New fiction of any standing being so rare that by the time the books arrive at the "outer" circle they are back numbers.[30]

The *Register* was a little kinder, claiming that fiction found in institutes "is at least morally innocuous, even if much of it may fail to convey a serviceable lesson or any enlightenment to the reader."[31] In addition, even the reviewer of books in the *Institutes Journal* scoffed at some of the institutes' most popular authors: *Love's Pilgrim*, by J D Berresford, was described as "Tentative sallies of an over-sensitive young man who for a time believes the right girl will never come along. Harmless." And then, of *Tetherstones* by Ethel M Dell, the reviewer wrote: "The villain is, as usual, a real villain and the hero a real hero; but we do wish the heroine didn't faint at every crucial moment."[32]

By 1929 the effects of the depression to come were being felt in all parts of South Australia. Institutes generally found that they were not financially secure enough to remedy their deficiencies, if indeed they considered that they had them. But even in 1930 Frederick Meleng, in his capacity as editor of the *Institutes Journal*, affirmed his belief that despite the depression and general unemployment there was likely to be much continued activity in institute building and renovating in the years to come.[33] In early 1930 Meleng's optimism was still understandable. The first three decades of the twentieth century had been a period of expansion and vigorous activity, and the 1920s, in particular, had seen some important changes in the institutes. These included post-war building improvements, new and effective fund-raising methods, the foundation of new institutes which became affiliated with the Institutes Association, the revival of moribund institutes, a new phase of educational work in connection with the WEA, the introduction of new technology such as electricity, telephones, motor cars and radio broadcasting, and the increased participation of women on institute committees. All this activity seemed to point to a secure future for institutes in South Australia. However, Meleng could not have foreseen some of the events that conspired in the 1930s to bring the institute movement to the end of its most successful era.

THE DEPRESSION

The first heavy blow for South Australia's institute movement came in mid-1930 as the effects of the Depression were beginning to be felt, but it was not directly connected with the Depression: Frederick Meleng, secretary of the Institutes Association, died aged sixty-four.[34] The president of the Association, Sir William Sowden, eulogised Meleng's enormous contribution to institutes since the 1890s: "The great champion of self-help, Samuel Smiles, ... would have gloried in honouring such a subject in his Gallery of Men Who have Done Things," he said. Meleng's death had resulted in "a serious loss to South Australia, and indeed to the library world throughout the Southern Hemisphere."[35]

Sowden's words reflected the attitude of almost everybody connected with institutes in the state. Tributes to Meleng's three decades of devotion to institute work, and his expertise, innovations, enthusiasm and encouragement, as well as donations for a permanent memorial medallion, poured into the Institutes Association's headquarters from all over South Australia. Many of the people involved would have met Meleng personally on his numerous visits to country and suburban institutes, when he would advise institute committees on card cataloguing, classification of books, library economy, possible ways to attract new members, the club side of institute life, books suitable for institute libraries, the upkeep of public reading rooms, library legislation, and other "various matters of vital importance to institutes." He also appreciated and enthusiastically participated in the festivities which often coincided with his visits.[36]

The second blow came as a direct result of the depression: In 1931, the annual government subsidies to institutes were withdrawn completely, and were only partly restored in 1934. In reports to the *Institutes Journal*, institutes such as Port Pirie and Renmark complained that their book-buying operations in particular were being severely curtailed by the removal of their government subsidies.[37] In an attempt to create the revenue that was desperately needed to buy library books, and to pay off large building mortgages, institutes generally responded in the traditional way. Judging by the frequency of reports in the *Institutes Journal*, fund-raising ventures such as fêtes, garden parties, dances and concerts became an even more prominent feature of institute activities during the 1930s. At some institutes, local unemployed people were recruited for house-to-house canvassing to gain new subscribers. At an unnamed suburban institute, such canvassers were paid on a commission basis. At Strathalbyn in 1931, canvassers managed to increase the Institute's membership by twenty-one.[38]

The widespread unemployment created by the depression was responsible for severely reduced membership in many institutes. In his report on library services in South Australia published in 1937,[39] Archibald Grenfell Price reported that of South Australia's "effective" institutes, 225 had fewer than one hundred members.[40] Some institutes attempted to cater for the unemployed who could not afford subscriptions; the same suburban institute which paid canvassers on a commission basis also allowed unemployed subscribers to borrow books, even though their subscriptions were seriously in arrears. The committee also granted extensions of time for the payment of subscriptions.[41] At Nadda, a railway town thirty-eight kilometres south-east of Loxton, the Institute accepted donations of wheat in lieu of subscription fees as poor crops added to the general depression in the district.[42]

COMPETITION FROM OTHER LIBRARIES

The third, and arguably the most serious, blow to institutes was again as a result of the depression: the rapid growth of "threepenny shop libraries." Before the depression, commercial subscription libraries were mainly confined to Adelaide. By 1932, however, as wholesale booksellers in the city, suburbs and country towns found that they were unable to sell their stock, they turned their businesses into "threepenny" shop libraries, so called because they rented out their novels at threepence a time. These shop libraries quickly gained in popularity. One of the main reasons was that they were open for business every day during shop hours, whereas most institutes - with either voluntary or lowly-paid staff - opened their libraries for only two or three periods a week, perhaps for only two hours at a time. Most importantly, readers much preferred to pay threepence for a new or recent novel form a large selection than to pay one pound a year subscription fees to an institute whose library books were mostly outdated.[43] Consequently, by 1937, Grenfell Price reported that almost every town and suburb in South Australia had at least one shop library in direct competition with the local Institute, causing it to lose subscribers and suffering, he believed, "a permanent decline."[44]

As an example of this, by 1939 the Glenelg Institute was competing with no fewer than eleven shop libraries. They catered for an estimated thirty percent of Glenelg's population and ninety percent of its book borrowers, whereas the Institute catered for only three percent of the population and ten percent of the borrowers.[45] Shop libraries, declared Grenfell Price, were "here to stay."[46]

A survey of conditions in Australian libraries and suggestions for their improvement, known as the Munn-Pitt Report,[47] was conducted in 1934 and published in 1935 when the institute movement was at the lowest point in its history so far. "It is pathetic to observe the pride and complacency with which local committees exhibit wretched little institutes which have long since become cemeteries of old and forgotten books,"[48] the report claimed. There is no question that this observation was correct as far as the majority of institute libraries in South Australia were concerned. In fact, the President of the Institutes Association, Sir William Sowden, suggested that the most ineffective institutes should be "weeded out,"[49] while S H Skipper, a member of the board of the Public Library and of the Council of the Institutes Association, considered that the surveyors' allegation that "almost every [Australian] city and large town now contains a decadent institute or school of arts" was "justified absolutely."[50]

CONTINUING RELEVANCE OF THE INSTITUTES

One great advantage of institute libraries was that they could be established in even the most remote, sparsely-populated regions with very little financial backing and few books, thanks to the Institutes Association's travelling book boxes and the numerous volunteers who willingly devoted their free time to running local institutes. It was not even necessary for an institute to own or rent a building. This is demonstrated in the case of Callington Institute, which was situated in a room in a private residence. Certainly few, if any, small country towns would have been able to support free municipal libraries. This fact is at least acknowledged in the Munn-Pitt report.[51] Surely the existence of a local institute library in a community, however inadequate, was preferable to having no library at all.

The early 1930s may have marked the end of an era for the cultural side of institute life, but as social centres local institutes were still far from being merely "wretched little institutes."[52] After all, where else could one go to church, visit the dentist, peruse the wares of travelling hawkers, attend lodge meetings, go to dances, concerts and the cinema, visit a local museum, art gallery and library, take classes in various subjects, attend bazaars, fêtes and sports days and perhaps even go skating or play billiards - all in the same place? Institutes had always done much to reduce the isolation of life in the country and in suburbs by cultivating a sense of community. They continued to do so throughout the 1930s and beyond even though, as Bridge commented in his history of the State Library and its forerunners, the Depression had "knocked the stuffing out of them."[53]

The institutes cited in this chapter as case studies have been found to be typical of South Australian institutes in general and, in many senses, of institutes throughout Australia. Institute officials and committee members were always prominent members of communities; their attitudes towards the social and cultural responsibilities of their institutes were similar, as were the kinds of activities they provided. The examples cited also reflect the overall willingness of institutes to assume added responsibilities towards their local communities in times of adversity. They are also an accurate reflection of the ability of most institutes to continually generate revenue by employing a wide range of effective, and sometimes innovative, fund-raising methods.

As an all-purpose social and cultural institution, the local institute has never been wholly replaced. Many of its functions have been taken over by specialist institutions such as community centres, church halls, RSL clubs, public libraries and colleges of TAFE, to name only a few. But as this chapter shows, the institutes of South Australia, aided by many public-spirited volunteers and relatively few paid staff, provided outlets for local creativity and energy and enhanced the social and cultural lives of people in hundreds of urban and rural communities before the general decline of the movement which began after 1930.

NOTES AND REFERENCES

1.*South Australian Institutes Journal (SAIJ)*, February 1920, p.89.

2.*SAIJ*, May 1920, p.111.

3.*SAIJ*, August 1920, pp.158-9.

4.*SAIJ*, March 1921, pp.257-63.

5.*SAIJ*, November 1920, p.203.

6.*SAIJ*, June 1921, p.279.

7.*SAIJ*, November 1921, p.355.

8.*SAIJ*, November 1926, p.275 & 31 August 1930, p.21; and Bridge, C. (1986). *A trunk full of books: History of the State Library of South Australia and its forerunners.* Adelaide: Wakefield Press in association with the State Library of South Australia, p.249.

9.*SAIJ*, August, 1920, p.159.

10.*SAIJ*, October 1924, pp.390-1.

11.Stocks, M. (1953). *The Workers' Educational Association: The first fifty years.* London: Allen & Unwin, pp.9, 20 & 45.

12.*SAIJ*, June 1918, p.286.

13.*SAIJ*, *op. cit.*, p.285.

14.Minutes of Committee Meetings on 12 June 1919 and 15 March 1927, *Thebarton Institute Minute Books, 1918-80*, vol. 1, (State Records, GRG 58, series 212/1).

15.Minutes of Committee Meeting on 14 June and 11 September 1919, *Thebarton Institute Minute Books 1918-80*, vol. 1.

16.*SAIJ*, June 1918, p.285.

17.*SAIJ*, February 1920, p.98; July 1924, p.360.

18.*SAIJ*, April 1927, p.299.

19.*SAIJ*, March 1923, p.116.

20.*SAIJ*, April 1927, p.299.

21.*SAIJ*, March 1924, p.290.

22.*SAIJ*, October 1924, p.414.

23.*SAIJ*, May-June 1929, p.191.

24.*SAIJ*, February 1920, p.70.

25.*SAIJ*, October 1924, p.414.

26.Minutes of Committee Meetings on 27 February 1924, 1 October 1925, 12 November 1927, 31 October 1928, 2 October 1929 & 5 March 1930, *Macclesfield Institute Minute Books, 1891-1972.*

27.Department of Mines and Energy, "Moonta Mines" (pamphlet), March 1988.

28.*Moonta Mines Institute Annual Reports*, 1920-30, *Moonta Mines Institute Minute Book, 1910-44.*

29.*SAIJ*, April 1927, p.299.

30.Minutes of a Committee Meeting on 21 December 1927, *Brighton Institute Minute Book 1927-31.*

31.*Register*, 29 September 1927, cited in *SAIJ*, September - November 1927, p.398.

32.*SAIJ*, December 1923, pp.256-7.

33.*SAIJ*, January - February 1930, p.376.

34.Besides being secretary of the Institutes Association of South Australia, librarian of the Port Adelaide Institute and editor of the *South Australian Institutes Journal* from 1908 until his death in 1930, Frederick Meleng was also, from 1928, secretary of the Australian Library Association and honorary secretary and publicity officer of the Library Association of Australia. (Source: *SAIJ*, 31 August 1930, p.9.)

35.*SAIJ*, 31 August 1930, p.6.

36.*SAIJ*, May-June 1928, p.15.

37.*SAIJ*, 28 February 1931, p.40; 30 June 1931, p.51.

38.*SAIJ*, 28 February 1931, pp.7 & 40.

39.In 1936 Dr Archibald Grenfell Price, geographer, historian and first master of St Mark's College at the University of Adelaide, was appointed by the government to report on South Australia's library system. This was in response to the findings of the Munn-Pitt report of 1935 and changing practices in other states and abroad. (Source: Bridge, *op. cit.*, p.139.)

40.Grenfell Price, A. (1937). *Libraries in South Australia: Report of an inquiry commissioned by the South Australian Government into the system of management of libraries maintained or assisted by the State.* Adelaide: South Australian Government Printer, p.25.

Opening Ceremony of the Waikerie Institute Soldiers' Memorial Hall, SA
(reproduced from the South Australian Institutes' Journal by the Mortlock Library)

Opening Ceremony of the Whyalla Institute, SA
(reproduced from the South Australian Institutes' Journal by the Mortlock Library)

South Australian Institute, ca 1875
(reproduced by permission of the State Library of South Australia - SSL:M:B10931)

41. *SAIJ*, 28 February 1931, p.7.

42. *SAIJ*, 30 June 1931, p.50.

43. Grenfell Price, *op. cit.*, p.27; Bridge, *op. cit.*, p.127.

44. Grenfell Price, *loc. cit.*

45. Bridge, *loc. cit.*

46. Grenfell Price, *loc. cit.*

47. Ralph Munn, Director of the Carnegie Library, Pittsburgh, USA and Ernest Pitt, Chief Librarian of the Public Library of Victoria, conducted and published a survey of Australian libraries in 1934-5. It was prepared under the auspices of the Carnegie Corporation of New York. A request to the Corporation for such a survey was first made by the Library Association of Victoria in 1929. (Sources: Grenfell Price, *op. cit.*, p.7; and Munn, R., & Pitt, E.R. (1935). *Australian libraries: A survey of conditions and suggestions for their improvement*. Melbourne: Australian Council for Educational Research, inside page).

48. Munn & Pitt, *op. cit.*, p.24.

49. Sir William Sowden's suggestion was taken up in the mid-1930s. In 1930 there were 306 institutes in South Australia, whereas by 1940 this number had been reduced to 258, partly as a result of the "weeding out" of institutes with no libraries or with less than ten subscribers.

50. Munn & Pitt, *op. cit.*, p.23.

51. Grenfell Price, *op. cit.*, p.26.

52. Munn & Pitt, *op. cit.*, p.33.

53. Bridge, *op. cit.*, p.148.

CHAPTER NINETEEN

'THIS MEETING IS NOW CLOSED': THE SOCIAL SIGNIFICANCE OF THE INSTITUTES IN RETROSPECT

John Laurent

INTRODUCTION

In the foregoing pages, readers have been presented with a range of perspectives on the schools of arts and mechanics' institute movement in Australia, which reached its peak in the early twentieth century with perhaps some 2,000 of these institutions prospering to a greater or lesser extent throughout the length and breadth of the country.[1] Just how significant a feature they were in Australia's social and cultural life is suggested by this number: At the height of the mechanics' institute movement in England (which, as Jill Eastwood and Stefan Petrow explain, provided the model for the Australian institutions), in the early 1860s, there were around 1,200 institutes in existence in that country[2] - and Britain's population at that time was more than six times that of Australia at the turn of the century. Moreover, as some of the authors in this volume - particularly Carole Inkster, Peter Rose *et.al.*, and Michael Talbot - have shown, schools of arts and mechanics' institutes (or simply 'institutes,' as they were known in South Australia) have survived in numerous localities until surprisingly recent times - indeed a small number continue to provide cultural services to the community of one sort or another, whether as education centres, libraries, community halls, or whatever.

Before proceeding further, it is perhaps worth saying something about this word 'culture.' The term can, of course, mean many things. I read somewhere recently (I am writing this in July 1992) that a curator at the National Museum of Australia currently being established in Canberra was seeking exhibits of 'backyard culture' - that is, outhouses, backyard toilets (or 'dunnies,' as the person concerned preferred to call them). But while we use the term 'culture' fairly broadly, such apparently conscious anti-intellectualism is not the intention in this volume; our meaning would be closer to that used in a recent discussion paper on *The Role of the Commonwealth in Australia's Cultural Development*, produced by the Department of the Arts, Sport, the Environment and Territories: that is, "intellectual and artistic activity" in so far as this bears on our "whole way of life, in both its material and spiritual dimensions."[3] In this chapter, I will concentrate primarily on some aspects of *intellectual* activity in mechanics' institutes and schools of arts in Australia in the late nineteenth and early twentieth centuries (though this will necessarily include some reference to the arts). The 'arts,' as such, are more especially the focus of the chapters by Jean Riley, Steve Kellermeier and Tessa Raath.

So, given the apparent proliferation of mechanics' institutes and schools of arts in Australia by the end of the nineteenth century, what is one to make of the claim so frequently encountered in connection with these institutions, that is to say, that they were a 'failure?' What did authors using this word mean by it? This subject should be addressed before looking at intellectual life in the institutions in some detail.

Generally speaking, what seems to be being argued in the above contention is the point of view originally put forward as long ago as 1851 by James Hudson, in his *History of Adult Education*[4], namely that the British mechanics' institutes of his time had failed to achieve their stated purposes - to instruct the 'mechanic' in the scientific principles underlying his trade, and to promote (as Jean Riley notes) 'mental and moral improvement' of the working classes. Whether or not there was any substance to Hudson's (and others' subsequent[5]) claims concerning Britain, two things need to be considered with respect to Australia: firstly, whether the original objectives of the institutes can be regarded as not having been achieved; and secondly, whether this could be said to constitute 'failure?' There seems little question that Frederick Engels' 1844 assessment of British mechanics' institutes - that their founders were intent on "making them organs for the dissemination of the sciences useful to the bourgeoisie," with the result that "the mass of working men naturally have nothing to do with these institutes"[6] - contains some substance, and as Stefan Petrow persuasively shows, much the same can probably be said of the earliest Australian institutions. What I will try to show in this chapter, however, is that any attempt to understand the ethos of Australian mechanics' institutes and schools of arts needs to take into account certain factors which differentiate them from their British counterparts, including: (1) the much greater role of government in their establishment and sustenance (to which I alluded in my earlier chapter); (2) the very different economic base of nineteenth-century Australian compared with British society; and (3) the generally later start and greater longevity of the Australian institutions and what this meant for their character in terms of the kind of society that was evolving around them.

As Marc Askew and Jean Riley explain, and as I also tried to bring out in my earlier chapter, a major difference between Australian institutes and those of Britain was that whereas the latter were concentrated mainly in industrial centres (especially in the new northern cities spawned by the Industrial Revolution - Manchester, Leeds, Bradford and others), and were intended to cater for the needs of the 'mechanic' (as perceived by employers), a large proportion of the Australian institutions were established in rural and mining communities, where 'mechanics' as such were relatively few in number. Australia then (as now!) was primarily a commodity-based economy, tending to rely on the 'mother country' for its needs in manufactured goods (even if a surprising amount of agricultural and transport equipment was made here from an early date[7]). This was in fact recognised from the institutions' beginnings. Thus, as Jill Eastwood mentions, one of the first lectures at the Melbourne Mechanics' Institute was on 'Agriculture', and similarly, in one of his first lectures to the Brisbane School of Arts, the School's president, W A Duncan, spoke of the need for State "industrial" schools where "boys" could be "instructed in the theory and practice of agriculture and horticulture."[8] In South Australia, two of the earliest institutes established outside Adelaide were built by a mine owner and squatter for miners and quarry workers respectively[9] (mining being that struggling colony's first major industry), and this tradition continued so that a number of later institutes reflected the connection in their names - the Moonta Mines Institute, Wallaroo Mines Institute, etc. The 1882 lecture programme at the Sydney Mechanics' School of Arts (SMSA) included lectures on 'Agriculture,' 'Botany,' 'Dairy Farming,' and 'Mines and Miners.'[10]

To the extent that some of these earlier, and indeed not a few later, institutions were built by employers, they bore some similarity to their British counterparts. Besides those just mentioned, examples include the Mt Morgan School of Arts in Queensland described by Steve Kellermeier, the Stroud and Clifton institutions mentioned by Tessa Raath, and one could add various 'station' schools of arts such as those at Isis Downs and Katandra in Queensland, where station owners might provide accommodation, bookshelves, etc. - and books for a library - in shearers' quarters. But this was as far as the similarity went.

As I have indicated, another major difference between Australian mechanics' institutes and schools of arts and those of Britain existed in the much greater involvement of government in the Australian institutions from the beginning. In Britain, this amounted to little more than the provision of 'payments by results,' stipends to teachers in Department of Science and Art classes at mechanics' institutes, provision of some scientific apparatus, and possibly some small contribution to the upkeep of buildings (and this was later than 1859, long after many of the institutes concerned had been established). In Australia, to begin with, not only was land readily granted to any group willing to form a school of arts or mechanics' institute committee, which would then set about raising the money to erect a building, land was usually set aside (from the mid-nineteenth century onwards) in town plans specifically for this purpose (see illustration showing town plan of Gooroolba, Queensland[11]). Earlier, land was granted on an *ad hoc* basis, as at Launceston (see chapter by Stefan Petrow) and Sydney - where indeed the SMSA's first president, Sir Thomas Mitchell, was Surveyor General of the colony.

Once established, mechanics' institutes and schools of arts could apply for government subsidies towards their running costs. These varied somewhat over time, and from colony to colony (or after 1901, from state to state), but in 1904, just to take a year for which I have the information before me, they were as follows: In New South Wales, the government granted a pound for pound on money raised locally for the cost of a building, and 10/- in the pound on subscriptions or donations towards running costs (including purchase of books for libraries). In South Australia and Tasmania the grant was 15/- per pound raised locally overall, and in Victoria and Queensland it was 10/- per pound overall, in Queensland's case this being to a maximum of £300 per year.[12] Looking at Queensland in more detail, in 1909 the government in that state, in addition to the latter, was subsidising "reading rooms at shearing sheds, sugar mills, and meat works to the extent of £1 for £1, with a view to assisting to provide reading matter, and such suitable recreation games as draughts, chess, etc. for the workers in those industries."[13]

As already indicated, 'station' schools of arts were sometimes provided by station owners (who no doubt were looking to the government for some recompense). But there seems little question that the special provisions just mentioned would also have prompted to some extent initiatives on the part of the employees. In his chapter, Phil Candy reproduces a letter from a group of shearers, wool classers and other station hands at the Peak Downs Station to the Under Secretary of the Queensland Department of Public Instruction which, among other things, maintained that:

> At whatever stations these Schools of Arts have been established, a marked and gratifying change is making itself manifest in many aspects of woolshed life; the improvement in manners and the tone of social intercourse being rapid and continuous;

and went on to explain that a library of 110 volumes had already been accumulated, and that a "Minute Book, Cash Book, Ledger, Register, etc. have been provided and kept."[14] Similarly, in September 1918, the Hon. Secretary of the 'Katandra Station School of Arts' (near Hughenden, Queensland) wrote to the Under Secretary in connection with subsidies, and also insurance of property (required by the Department), explaining that:

> [W]e have not any building of our own. The rooms used as a School of Arts is [sic] lent to us by the owners of the Station and is part of the Shearers and Shed hands' quarters being two of their bedrooms made into one for that purpose. The only property the School of Arts own [sic] here are the books and two book cases valued at £125 which we are willing to ensure if you would kindly let us know what the premium would be.[15]

THE IDEOLOGICAL ENVIRONMENT OF INSTITUTES IN AUSTRALIA

Whatever substance there was to the claims concerning the "tone of social intercourse" in the 1899 letter above, there would seem to be no obvious reason to question the general proposition that schools of arts of this sort (and indeed mechanics' institutes, schools of arts and various other kindred institutions such as the miners' institutes discussed by Peter Rose *et.al.*) would have contributed considerably to the tone of social, cultural and intellectual life in Australia at this time. Australia was just then entering a period of bold political experiment. In December 1899, Queenslanders elected the first (albeit short-lived - it lasted a week) Labor government in the world, and within six years of that date the first effective state government of that complexion had been returned in South Australia. By 1915 Labor had been comfortably installed in six of the seven Australian national and state governments. Along with this was a phenomenal growth in the trade union movement over the same period, such that by 1919, at 50 percent of the workforce, New South Wales for example had the highest union membership in the world.[16] Whatever one's politics, there is no denying the significance of these achievements for Australian working people, and the profound transformation of Australian society, from a former British gaol into one widely believed to be essentially egalitarian, that these changes signified. At least that was the belief: as Cardinal Moran of Sydney was quoted in the Brisbane *Worker* in June 1905 as saying: "We are proud of the triumphs of Democracy in Australia, and I trust they will continue until perfect Democracy prevails amongst us."[17]

Kylie Tennant and Manning Clark have painted dramatic pictures of shearers reading socialist works like Edward Bellamy's *Looking Backward* and Henry George's *Progress and Poverty*, as well as the *Bulletin* and *Worker*, in shearing sheds and by the light of campfires during the political turmoil of the early 1890s,[18] when the Labor Party was born out of the failure of wide-spread strikes at that time. Henry Lawson, that quintessential voice of Australian egalitarian idealism of the time, later recalled miners and farm workers earnestly reading and debating George's *Progress and Poverty* in the Gulgong district.[19] All of this literature was also readily obtainable in schools of arts and mechanics' institute libraries[20] - and indeed, there were enthusiastically received lectures on subjects like George's 'Single Tax' (on land) scheme in institute halls.[21] So, when one considers the intentions of some of the original promoters of mechanics' institutes and schools of arts in this country, something of a transformation of their character would seem to have occurred along with that of society around them. In his 1854 address to the Hobart Town Mechanics' Institute (see earlier

373

chapter), John Lillie spoke of the virtues of "the race of competition" and society's "natural tendency to arrange itself in a gradation of ranks or classes." Such ideas however were becoming suspect in the 1890s, when capitalism seemed to be collapsing, with the welter of bank failures of the time, and people were looking for new societal models.

Much of this new spirit became combined with a heightened nationalist feeling of the time, which had been largely initiated by five-times NSW Premier, Sir Henry Parkes, notably in his famous Federation Speech at the Tenterfield School of Arts on 24 October 1889.[22] There was talk of republicanism, and a widespread idea that somehow the physical isolation of the Australian continent offered protection from the evils and injustices of the old world. A new, egalitarian society could surely flourish here.[23]

Another means by which this intellectual ferment sought expression was in the distinctively Australian school of painting known as Australian Impressionism - significantly launched at an 'Impression Exhibition' in Melbourne at about the same time as Parkes' speech. Painters like those who described themselves as the 'Heidelberg School' in Victoria (Roberts, McCubbin, Conder, Streeton and others) were for the first time able to free themselves from European conventions and to see the Australian landscape in a fresh, new way: eucalypts now *looked* like eucalypts, and not like European trees transplanted to the antipodes. And as Jean Riley mentions, some important painters of this time were associated with schools of arts - for example the SMSA - and this continued into the early 1900s (by which time British painters were just beginning to accept the new insights of impressionism). One artist of note in this connection, whose works are now much prized, was Alfred Coffey, a teacher at the Sydney Technical College (which grew out of the SMSA) and the Granville School of Arts (which, as I explained in my earlier chapter, ran classes for the Technical College) from 1898. An outstanding example of Coffey's work is his 'Terrigal,' which can be seen in Brennan Hall at St John's College at the University of Sydney.[24]

But while many believed a New Jerusalem might be established in this country, others, disillusioned by the failure of the great strikes of the early 'nineties (especially the Maritime Strike of 1890 and the Shearers' Strike of 1891), looked elsewhere for the fulfilment of their Utopian visions. Most notable among these was William Lane, founder of 'New Australia' on 463,000 acres of land granted by the Paraguayan government in 1893. This venture was to end in bitter and acrimonious failure; but it was symptomatic of the hopes and dreams and general intellectual ebullience of these times.[25] Before leaving with 220 other hopefuls for Paraguay, Lane had founded the *Boomerang* (edited by Henry Lawson for a time) and *Worker* in Brisbane. As mentioned, the *Worker* was in schools of arts libraries as were numerous books by the authors to whom readers of the *Worker*, and also Lane's *The Workingman's Paradise* (published in Brisbane in 1892) were directed. Among these authors were Milton, Bunyan ("the Englishman who has never read *Pilgrim's Progress* does not know his mother tongue"[26]), Sir Walter Scott, Shelley, Wordsworth, Dickens, George Elliot, Tennyson, Kingsley, the Brontës, Zola and Flaubert, and others which, as Wayne Murdoch notes, we would now unhesitatingly describe as 'classics' but which at the time were in popular demand. At the SMSA in 1894, for instance, among the authors most requested were Ruskin, George Elliot, Tennyson, Bulwer Lytton, Scott, F Marion Crawford and Kipling,[27] and at the Sandhurst (Victoria) Mechanics' Institute at an earlier date, circulation figures show that its members were reading forty books each per year on average, of which about a quarter were serious works on history, biography, philosophy, science, etc.

At the Warwick (Queensland) School of Arts at a slightly later date (1908), 191 members read 11,317 books between them in a year - or 59 each on average.[28] As Michael Cannon notes, even if part of this borrowing was on behalf of non-members, there was obviously a fertile field in which the more radical ideas contained in works like Bellamy's *Looking Backward*, George's *Progress and Poverty* and Gronlund's *Cooperative Commonwealth* could take root.[29] As Kylie Tennant eloquently expresses it:

> In the 'nineties people read books. Every little country school of arts was solid with classics. One country newspaper boosted circulation by printing Ruskin's *Unto This Last* in its leader columns; navvies, drovers, and miners attended lectures on French poetry, Darwinism, Henry George, and the land laws of Leviticus. There was a stirring quality, a pride of men who found themselves enlisted in great causes. The sap of the future rushed up the nation's stem. It is to the nineties that the modern Australia looks back, almost wonderingly, surprised that men should have wholeheartedly believed and fought and suffered - for what? For ideas which might not even bring them any particular profit. Just for ideas.[30]

THE PLACE OF EVOLUTION IN THIS IDEOLOGY

Another country newspaper - the *Illawarra Mercury* - serialised *Looking Backward*.[31] It was just pipped in being the first Australian newspaper to do so by Lane's *Worker*, the front page of the first issue of which has the words: "[The *Worker*] is a journal of the workers, in touch with their thoughts, inspired by their needs. It aims, as all thinking workers aim, at the securing of a happier state of society, which, though not, perhaps, on the same lines, is imbued with just the same spirit as that which imbues society in Bellamy's *Looking Backward*."[32] Bellamy's book, besides being serialised in these newspapers (the *Illawarra Mercury* was in all local schools of arts reading rooms), was also in libraries in the original, for example in those of the Sydney, Brisbane and Orange Schools of Arts, and the Moonta Mines and Port Adelaide Institutes,[33] and it perfectly expresses the millennial expectations of the times. As the author explains in a postscript to his story:

> *Looking Backward*, although in the form of a popular romance, is intended, in all seriousness, as a forecast, in accordance with the principles of evolution, of the next stage in the individual and social development of humanity.[34]

In this sense the novel - which was set in the year 2000 AD - was in the tradition of Utopian writing going back to Sir Thomas More's original book of that name (indeed Lane's *Workingman's Paradise* was in the same tradition). Bellamy introduced another element into this tradition, however, with his reference to "the principle of evolution."

As I explained in my earlier chapter, and as noted in the above quote from Kylie Tennant, a fascination with Darwinism and evolution was a salient feature of late nineteenth and early twentieth-century intellectual life. This fascination spilled over into political idealism: specifically, the socialism of Bellamy, George and others saw itself as in line with the processes of natural evolution. Bellamy gives a hint of how he saw this connection in his novel, where one of the central characters in the story, Dr Leete, explains to Julian West (the Bostonian who falls asleep in 1887 and wakes into a different world in the year 2000) that whereas in West's day "the field of industry was a battlefield," in Leete's Utopian world "All men were co-labourers to a common end": the "pseudo self-interest of selfishness" has been replaced by "institutions based on the true self-interest of a rational unselfishness, and appealing to the social and generous instincts of men."[35]

What has this to do with Darwinian evolution? The connection can clearly be seen in Darwin's *Descent of Man* which, as I indicated in my earlier chapter, was to be found in most sizeable mechanics' institutes and schools of arts libraries. In that earlier chapter I referred to a marked passage in the Muswellbrook School of Arts' copy of the book. Another marked passage reads as follows:

> Notwithstanding many sources of doubt, man can generally and readily distinguish between the higher and lower moral rules. The higher are founded on social instincts, and relate to the welfare of others. They are supported by the approbation of our fellow-men and by reason.[36]

Here, then, are the "social instincts" to which Bellamy refers. This passage is in a chapter of *Descent of Man* titled 'The Moral Sense,' in which Darwin outlines his theory explaining the evolutionary development of the same in humans: it is based, Darwin believed, in instincts for gregariousness which can be observed in various species, including other primates, and which presumably evolved for the advantage they conferred in the 'struggle for existence.' In humans, these inherited instincts, coupled with the exercise of reason, form the basis for legal, ethical, and social systems generally, and are what allow societies to function. Socialists like Bellamy, Lane and their followers in Australia believed that their vision of a more just society was simply in accord with these basic biological principles. Co-operation, rather than internecine competition, was the source of a nation's strength.

However this may be, an interest in Darwin and evolution, and indeed in science generally, does seem to have been a feature of intellectual life in the late nineteenth and early twentieth centuries, whether or not in an ideological context (though I would question whether one could easily separate the two), and this was reflected in the life of mechanics' institutes and schools of arts at the time. In the NSW State Library there is a small - presumably fairly random - collection of books gold-blocked 'For Country Libraries' shelved in the Shakespeare Room. These are a remnant of the books circulated to schools of arts and mechanics' institute libraries in book boxes, as described (for Victoria and South Australia) by Brian Hubber, Michael Talbot and Amanda Bettesworth, and which system was not only much appreciated by the institutions themselves (the minutes of the Jamberoo School of Arts for 1898, for instance, record the "splendid reading" in the books, which had been "well used"),[37] but also by the Brisbane *Worker*, which carried an article commending the system in January 1913.[38] Among this small collection of about 30 books in the NSW State Library, then, are Darwin's *Life and Letters* (an 1887 printing) and Capt. Robert Fitzroy's (1839) *Narrative of the Surveying Voyages of His Majesty's Ships 'Adventure' and 'Beagle' between the Years 1826 and 1836* (this of course is Fitzroy's volume from the three-volume account of the voyages which included Darwin's *Journal of Researches into the Natural History and Geology of the Countries Visited During the Voyage Round the World of H.M.S. 'Beagle'*). Not only are these books in poor condition, indicating extensive use, Darwin's *Life and Letters* has several marked passages suggesting careful reading. Other books in this collection include Amundsen's (1908) *The North West Passage - Being the Record of a Voyage of Exploration of the Ship Gjöa, 1903-1907* (it contains numerous descriptions of geological investigations, such as at Beechy Island, where "Lt. Hansen...took the opportunity of exploring the nature of the country, and collecting a great number of fossils"[39]), *Wordsworthia: A Selection from Papers Read to the Wordsworth Society* (1889; including a paper on 'Wordsworth's Relations to Science'), and Ruskin's *Ariadne Florentina - Six Lectures on Wood and Metal Engraving* (1890) - which has a chapter titled 'On the Study of Anatomy' and contains the interesting view that "No man can do better than he sees: if he can reach the nature round him, it is well; he may fall short of it; he cannot rise above it."[40]

The only other volume I have seen from the NSW State Library embossed for circulation to country libraries is an old (1889), very worn copy of *Natural Inheritance* by Darwin's cousin, Francis Galton. It too had passages marked in pencil, such as:

> Though one half of every child may be said to be derived from either parent, yet he may receive a heritage from a distant progenitor that neither of his parents possessed as personal characteristics. Therefore the child does not on the average receive so much as one half of his personal qualities from each parent, but something less than half.[41]

Galton, the founder of eugenics, was no egalitarian, let alone socialist - nor was Darwin - but readers of these persuasions could selectively quote both authors in support of their views, as with the above, which *could* be cited as arguments that one wasn't necessarily condemned by one's heredity. (In *Descent of Man*, Darwin refers to Galton's observations of gregariousness in African cattle, published in *Macmillan's Magazine* as 'Gregariousness in Cattle and in Man.'[42]) Whether this was in the mind of the reader who marked the above passage is, again, impossible to tell; the point is, as I noted in my earlier chapter, these books, in an age before the cinema and television, were evidently being read seriously.

In the 1890s and early 1900s the SMSA regularly published in the Sydney press selected lists of recently purchased books, and since this was presumably with a view to attracting subscribers it is reasonable to suppose that the titles chosen for inclusion were those expected to be of interest to readers. An apparent interest in science and Darwinism is again conspicuous in these titles. Lists published in 1892-6, for instance, contained works like H Drummond's *Ascent of Man* (which was also described by the school's secretary as having "aroused some interest"[43]), W Gee's *Short Studies in Natural Knowledge*, C H Burton's *Outlines of Australian Physiography*, G Henslow's *Origin of Plant Structures*, B Lindsay's *An Introduction to the Study of Zoology*, H H Donaldson's *Growth of the Brain*, B W Richardson's *Biological Experimentation*, W McAdam's *Elementary Anatomy and Surgery for Nurses*, O Browning's *Biological Problems of Today* and G C Robertson's *Elements of Psychology*.[44] In 1897 the School's *20 copies* of Nansen's *Farthest North* (which has much zoological discussion) was described by the School's librarian as "bespoken very far ahead."[45] This kind of interest persisted into later years: in July 1922, among the "more serious literature" for which there had been "outstanding inquiry" was *A Photographer with Shackleton in the Antarctic.*[46]

As one might expect in this era of the rise of labour and socialism in Australia, an interest in books on these subjects is also conspicuous at the SMSA at this time. According to the School's secretary, W M Fairland, speaking in 1895, "books of the Socialistic and up-to-date economic and political character" were in particular demand - "There is a great call for them among the working classes," Fairland went on to explain.[47] Two years later the SMSA's librarian claimed that "political works on the labour question and on industrial questions are the most read"[48] (presumably he meant of political works in general). Amongst books listed as being acquired by the library at this time were J S Nicholson's *Historical Progress and Ideal Socialism*, H Dyer's *Evolution of Industry*, M Kaufmann's *Socialism and Modern Thought*, Guyot's *Labor, Socialism and Strikes*, T Mackay's *Methods of Social Reform*, Robert Blatchford's *Merrie England* and E Belfort Bax and William Morris's *Socialism*.[49]

The quoted passage from Kylie Tennant's *Australia: Her Story*, (see p.375), suggests that people attending lectures on Darwinism and the theories of Henry George and others saw some link between these areas of thought, and indeed this suggestion is supported by a glance at the content of some of these lectures. Thus visiting British trade unionist, Tom Mann, in a lecture on 'Eminent Men I have Met and Worked With in the Labor Movement' at the Charters Towers School of Arts in 1905 (see advertisement for lecture program), referred to the socialist and anarchist writer Kropotkin, who, Mann said, "has taken up the Darwinian theories where Darwin left off."[50]   A lecture by a Rev. William Finlay Brown (a Presbyterian minister and one of the ubiquitous Dissenting clergy with an interest in adult education), published in Parkes in 1898 as a booklet entitled *A Treatise on the Evolution of Historical Organism*, deals at length with the philosopher Herbert Spencer's concept of society as a "social organism," an idea that was taken up with enthusiasm by socialist writers at the time, including Henry George.[51] The idea, basically, was that human society could be compared with a complex biological organism, in which social groups, or "units," performed functions analogous to organs in a living body; and just as in biological evolution, so *societies* are evolving towards some higher state. Brown expressed the idea this way:

> In Biology the first step in the production of any living organism, high or low, is a certain differentiation, whereby a peripheral portion becomes distinguished from a central portion; a differentiation of the original homogeneous mass into a co-ordinating and a co-ordinated part is the indispensible first step...[Likewise], along with social aggregation there goes organisation of some kind. The highest form of the Social organism...is only reached by the perfect adjustment of all relations between social units.[52]

Whatever the merits of such arguments, they seriously exercised the minds of thoughtful listeners and readers around the turn of the century. In Victoria, a few years later, the *Socialist*, which was taken by various mechanics' institutes, for example those of Maldon and Williamstown,[53] frequently published lists of literature which the journal commended to readers and which could be purchased from its office post-free. Many of these works were on subjects related to the supposed connection between socialism and evolution. Lists in the *Socialist* for 20 July and 28 December 1907 and 8 January 1909, for instance, contained titles like J A Hobson's *Evolution of Capitalism* (which, Hobson argued, was but a stage in the "inevitable" transition to socialism), C W Saleeby's *Organic Evolution*, J Connell's *Socialism and Survival of the Fittest*, Labriola's *Essay in the Materialistic Conception of History*,

Engels's *The Origin of the Family, Private Property and the State*, and "Works by Spencer, Mill, H G Wells, Darwin, Haeckel [i.e. Ernst Haeckel, author of *The Evolution of Man*], Huxley, etc, each: 6d." Also listed are stories and essays by popular novelists of the time, including *The Jungle* by Upton Sinclair, and *What Communities Lose by the Competitive System*, by Jack London. *The Jungle*, it is interesting to notice, was a topic of contention in a school of arts elsewhere in Australia around this time - at Molong, N.S.W. - where in August 1906 a Mr Simpson, chairman of the School of Arts Library Committee, declared his intention to resign over, among other things, "the fact that the book entitled *The Jungle* was needed and constantly inquired for; yet the Library Committee could not get it without authority" (which the president of the School had apparently refused to grant).[54]

Further evidence of this interest in socialism and evolution in the context of mechanics' institutes and schools of arts at the time is contained in a letter from another 'Station School of Arts' to the Sydney *Worker* in November 1910. The writer advised that "those Australian publications...issued from THE WORKER office have been continually in circulation amongst our readers"[55] (the institution, it was explained, had been "formed by the shearers and other workers here" - however the locality is not given in the *Worker*). Two works specifically mentioned in the letter were W M (later Prime Minister) Hughes' *The Case for Labor*, and H I Jensen's *The Rising Tide*. Both these books make much of the supposed connection between socialism and evolutionary theory. Hughes attempts to deal with 'survival of the fittest' arguments *against* socialism by employing the 'society as organism' idea:

> Many very superior people brush collectivism impatiently aside because they believe it interferes with the survival of the fittest...Belonging to the terminology of writers on organic evolution, [this phrase] has been usefully borrowed by the individualist school of economists...[However] the environment of man is not fixed, but ever in a flux: it embraces the organic and inorganic, the physical and mental, the spiritual and moral, the industrial and social worlds...Competition will be replaced by co-operation because the environment which made competition desirable or possible is changing - has changed, in fact...The social organism as a whole is affected...Competition will soon be as unfit to survive as those monsters of the Carboniferous period, or the land ancestor of the whale.[56]

Jensen, a geologist and soil scientist with the NSW Department of Agriculture, and an active member of the Glebe Parliamentary Labor League (and before that of the Workers' Political Organisation at Irvinebank, Queensland, where "at every possible opportunity the miners...made use of the School of Arts Library," according to a biographical note in the *Worker*[57]), took up the Darwinian argument:

> When social life was commenced...coherence would be the necessary quality to ensure the success of the growing community...Mutual aid gradually became a habit; morality grew, inasmuch as the more persistent social instincts conquered the less permanent selfish instincts.[58]

Other books available to this station school of arts through the *Worker* and possibly in circulation amongst its readers included Rationalist Press Association reprints of works by

Darwin, Spencer, Haeckel etc. (those also available through the *Socialist*), Marx's *Theory of Value*, Bellamy's *Equality*, Ingersoll's works, Blatchford's *Merrie England* and *Not Guilty*, all Zola's works, Annie Besant's *Fruits of Philosophy* (an early tract on contraception), Paine's *Age of Reason*, Gronlund's *Co-operative Commonwealth*, all *Bulletin* publications, *Elements of Social Science* and various technical works such as *The Australian Miner's Guide, Dynamos and Electric Motors, Electricity Made Simple, Practical Gas and Oil Engines, Poultry Keeping*, etc.[59] Also available through the *Worker* was O S Fowler's *Science of Life*, a book originally published in 1870 and interesting for its early, pre-Darwinian views on the inheritance of behavioural characteristics: "All instinctive habits, modes of life, appetites, etc, are equally transmitted...Whence the universality of all the ever-varying instincts of every...species? Are they not obviously consequent on their *hereditary* descent through each parental pair to their offspring?" (etc).[60]

OTHER READING MATTER IN MECHANICS' INSTITUTE AND SCHOOLS OF ARTS LIBRARIES

Of course, thoughtful members of mechanics' institutes and schools of arts interested in science and politics did not have to subscribe to socialistic ideas. Other arguments could be found in the literature available in the libraries, including in novels. A glance through the titles selected by Wayne Murdoch from the catalogues of the Rockhampton School of Arts suggests the range of opinions available, from staunchly conservative (Hallam, J D Lang, Wentworth, Mrs Henry Wood) through mildly radical (Disraeli, Mill, Macaulay) to radical and socialist (George Eliot, Kingsley, Ruskin, Rousseau - in 1904 this library also contained Morris and Bax's *Scientific Socialism*, George's *Progress and Poverty*, Marx's *Revolution and Counter Revolution* and works by Kropotkin).[61] An example of a contrary interpretation of evolutionary theory would be that contained in H L Wilson's novel, *The Wrong Twin*, the Kiama School of Arts' copy of which I have. At one point in the story, the journeyman printer Dave Cowan declaims as follows:

> We fought our way up to be a fish with lungs, and then we fought on till we got legs, and here we are. And the only way we got there was by competition - some of us always beating others. Holy rollers like Socialists would have us back to one cell and keep us there with equal rewards for all. But she won't work that way. The pot's still a-boiling, and competition is the eternal fire under it.

> Look at all the imaginary Utopias they write about - good stories, too, about a man waking up three thousand years hence and finding everything lovely [A slightly exaggerated reference to *Looking Backward*?]. But every one of 'em, and I've read all, picture a society that's froze [sic] into some certain condition - static. Nothing is! They can spray the fire of competition with speeches all they like, but they can't put it out...Old Evolution is still evoluting, and her only tool is competition.[62]

Mention of this novel, and some of the authors above, introduces another important topic; the vexed question of the quality of reading matter generally in mechanics' institute and schools of arts libraries. Books like *Looking Backward, The Jungle* and various works by Jack London (for example, *The Iron Heel*) are well known propagandist pieces, but they are also regarded by many authorities as significant literature. Anthony Trollope's comment after visiting the library of the Mudgee Mechanics' Institute that "Mudgee shepherds certainly prefer novels," as noted by Jean Riley, may well have been true enough, but this does not necessarily imply that these readers were not thereby receiving some educational benefit. As already noted, a number of the fiction authors in popular demand at the SMSA in the 1890s would now unquestionably be regarded as writers of prose of a very high quality. The same can be said of an earlier era. Elizabeth Webby notes the popularity of novels by Sir Walter Scott and James Fenimore Cooper circulated by the Hobart Town Book Society in the 1820s and '30s, and indeed in its 1835 *Annual Report*, the SMSA made a point of placing Scott's 'Waverley Novels' at the head of its list of selected acquisitions for that year.[63] But there would be no question today of the educational value of these works. One of the greatest scientists of all time, the self-educated bookbinder's apprentice, Michael Faraday, warmly acknowledged a debt to Scott in his mental development, and Faraday's own abilities as a stylist have been commented upon by scholars.[64] It is interesting to see that Scott's *Quentin Durward* was one of the works listed for study for the entrance examination to the Diploma courses in science, architecture, and mechanical, electrical and sanitary engineering at the Sydney Technical College in 1916.[65]

If he had arrived in the town just a few years later, Anthony Trollope might easily have included a particular lanky, awkward youth amongst his "Mudgee shepherds" who preferred novel reading - Henry Lawson. In his biography of Lawson, *The Grey Dreamer*, Denton Prout describes the important place of the Mudgee Mechanics' Institute in the great writer's literary education (it was there that he is said to have "discovered Dickens," for example[66]), and this habit of frequenting such libraries continued following Lawson's move to Sydney in the early 1880s. Lawson's first job was as a painter at Hudson's Bros. railway carriage works at Granville, and for a time he was employed at the firm's branch workshop at Wickham, Newcastle, where he "haunted the School of Arts, still with an idea of learning before it was too late."[67] (For a description of this School, see Tessa Raath's chapter.) By 1890, at the time of the Maritime Strike, according to Lawson's mate Arthur Parker,

> We were all back in Sydney. Henry took me round to join the Australian Socialist League. They had a room upstairs with every Labour [sic] paper in the world in it. There he introduced me to McNamara, Holman, Black, Rae, Ferguson, Rosa, Jim Mooney, and all the eager, ardent spirits who were working to bring the first Labour Party into existence. I often met Henry and his mother there on Sunday evenings. She had a printing office in Jamieson Street, and Henry helped her. I used to go there and meet him and his brother Bert, and she called us 'The Secret Society.' Henry was a great student. He was always going up to the Reference Library or down to the School of Arts.[68]

Lawson's first published poem, *Song of the Republic*, was published in the *Bulletin* in 1887, and his first book, *Short Stories in Prose and Verse*, was published by his mother, Louisa Lawson, the feminist and publisher of radical journals like *The Republican* and *Dawn - A Journal for Australian Women* (see illustrations), in 1894. By that year Louisa was on the SMSA Committee (she received the fifth highest number of votes of 25 nominees in February that year[69]), and Henry's close connection with this institution continued. Similarly, Gavin Casey, whose short-story prose at its best has been compared with Lawson's, acknowledged an important place for the Kalgoorlie Mechanics' Institute in his education as he grew up in that tough mining town in the 1920s.[70]

DEBATING CLUBS AND POLITICS

As Lawson's literary education owed a great deal to mechanics' institute and schools of arts libraries, so no doubt did his political education. The wealth of radical literature in the SMSA's library was noted earlier, and besides the opportunity to peruse this, Lawson must surely have attended some of the debates organised by the School's Debating Society in the 1880s and '90s, when the Society was particularly active. As Michael Whiting points out in his chapter, debating clubs and societies made a significant contribution to the intellectual life of mechanics' institutes and schools of arts towards the end of the nineteenth century, when they tended to overtake the earlier educational role of lectures to some extent. These clubs and societies became a common feature of the institutions, no matter how large or small. At the SMSA in 1886, 1,200 people are said to have attended 41 meetings of the Debating Club,[71] and interest remained strong in the following decade. At the Jamberoo School of Arts in 1896 the School's Debating Club did "much to popularise [the] institution,"[72] and similar clubs and societies existed at the Parramatta, Granville, Bondi - Waverley, Liverpool, Brisbane and Charters Towers Schools of Arts, as well as the Mudgee Mechanics' Institute,[73] and no doubt many other institutions. At an opening ceremony for the Newtown (Sydney) School of Arts in September 1916, NSW Premier W A Holman made the following remarks as reported in the *Sydney Morning Herald*:

> 'One might be pardoned for sighing over the departed glories of the old mechanics' institutes, when they [sic] were all democrats together'... The Premier recalled the fact that he had been a mechanic working at the bench in Newtown...In those days he was a member of the Sydney Mechanics' School of Arts, and of its famous debating club. He was also a member of the library committee. He debated a lot and read a lot. To the exchange of ideas and his reading in the library he owed a great deal...Schools of Arts provided splendid social gathering places.[74]

A glance at the SMSA's *Annual Reports* from the early 1890s shows that Holman (who, as Arthur Parker remembered, was a member with Lawson of the Australian Socialist League) was indeed prominent in the School's Debating Club at the time. Topics moved for debate by Holman in 1890, for example, included 'Labor [sic] and Capital,' 'Interest is Spoliation,' 'Socialism' and 'That the franchise should be granted to women.'[75] (In that year Henry Parkes introduced an Electoral Bill in the NSW Legislative Assembly granting female suffrage, which Louisa Lawson hailed as "the boldest and most liberal measure every submitted to any Parliament."[76]) Over the next few years topics debated by the Debating Club included 'That the proposal of Henry George is the best method of nationalising the land,' 'That a system of co-operation would be to the advantage of the workers at large' and 'That state socialism in practicable.'[77] Topics argued by the Liverpool School of Arts' 'Parliamentary Debating Club' between 1901 and 1907 included 'The adult suffrage question' (in 1901, the year before women finally gained the vote in Australia), 'Is the minimum wage adopted by the government prejudicial to the best interests of the Colony?,' 'That a Labor Party is a menace to good government' and 'Are strikes justifiable?'[78] In Charters Towers in 1905 members of the School of Arts Literary and Debating Society joined issue on 'Individualism versus socialism' and whether abolition of the Legislative Council could be good for Queensland;[79] and at the Brisbane School of Arts in 1909 members debated the topic 'Socialism, the only remedy for the evil of unemployment.'[80]

Another eminent Australian politician whose political and general education owed much to schools of arts was Ben Chifley. Chifley, the blacksmith's son and locomotive driver who became Prime Minister (1945-9), was a voracious reader in his youth and made frequent use of the libraries of the Bathurst School of Arts (his name appears in subscribers' lists for the years 1909, 1910, 1912 and 1914-15) and the Bathurst Railway Institute.[81] Most significant among the authors who led Chifley to his lifelong commitment to socialism, according to his biographer, L F Crisp, were Bellamy, Jack London and G B Shaw[82] - interestingly, all fiction writers, and all interested in evolution (in Shaw's case, albeit in that author's characteristically idiosyncratic way in plays like *Man and Superman* and *Back to Methuselah*).[83] In 1917 Chifley was a leader in the momentous NSW Rail Strike of that year, and it is interesting to see that in the rail unions' newspaper, *The Co-operator* (which was taken into various mechanics' institute and schools of arts reading rooms, for example those of Cootamundra and Bowral[84]) evolutionary language is conspicuous: the issue for 17 May 1917, for instance, under 'The Economic Interpretation of History,' argues that "Human life has thus far not been exempt from the inexorable law of nature, with its struggle for existence through natural selection. This struggle [includes] the struggle of group with group...of the labour class with one or all of the capitalist classes" (etc).[85]

By the outbreak of the First World War the involvement of mechanics' institutes and schools of arts with the Labor movement had become very close for a number of institutions, with local branches of the Labor party (called Parliamentary Labour Leagues in NSW and branches of the Workers' Political Organisation in Queensland) meeting in their rooms: for example, at the Yass and Young Mechanics' Institutes, and the Muswellbrook, West Wallsend, Rockdale, Kensington, St Leonards, Bondi-Waverley, Wagga and Leeton Schools of Arts in NSW, and the West End, Corinda, Windsor, Bulimba, Warwick and Chillagoe Schools of Arts in Queensland.[86] Various individual unions also met in the buildings; for example the Millers' Point Mechanics' Institute in Sydney was described as the "rendezvous" of the Coal Lumpers' Union, and the AWU and Engine Drivers' and Engineers' Association met in the Charters Towers School of Arts.[87] In South Australia, a series of campaign meetings aimed at increasing the United Labor Party's *Weekly Herald* in early 1914 were held in the Terowie, Salisbury, Penola, Mt Gambier, Mt Barker and Edwardstown Institutes, among others.[88] And of course, self-educated politicians who themselves had benefited from attending mechanics' institutes and schools of arts were delighted to open and lay foundation stones for such institutions: such as Holman, Sir Henry Parkes, as Tessa Raath notes, and South Australia's first Labor Premier, the former stone mason Tom Price, who laid the foundation stone for the Mt Gambier Institute, for instance.[89]

THE WORKERS' EDUCATIONAL ASSOCIATION

By around this time, then, the transformation of many Australian mechanics' institutes and schools of arts since the time of John Lillie's address in Hobart was about complete: there was frequently virtual identity between the ethos of the institutions and the ascendant Labor politics of the time. (Parkes of course was not Labor, but he saw himself as a radical, and in his last term of office held power in coalition with Labor.) This identity of purpose was soon to be severely strained, and in some cases completely destroyed, by the effects of the First World War, especially in connection with Labor's traumatic split over the conscription issue, but not before the identity was further cemented by the advent of the WEA in Australia just before the war. The first WEA classes appear to have been those held in connection with the Sydney Trades Hall in late 1913, and by June 1914 classes were being run on 'The Social Problem,' 'Trade Union Development' (taught by W M Hughes), 'Australian Ideals,' 'Syndicalism,' 'Biology' and other subjects at the Trades Hall and various other unspecified centres in Sydney.[90] By 1915 the Bathurst School of Arts was hosting a class on 'The Economics of War' (Chifley was almost certainly a member[91]), and the Glebe Workingmen's Institute ran a class on 'The Present War and Democracy' described as "full of interest."[92] Unnamed classes were held at the Kogarah School of Arts in 1914-15,[93] and in 1917-18 a course on 'Reconstruction After the War' was being taught at the Bondi-Waverley School of Arts by Professor Meredith Atkinson of Sydney University.[94]

A series of WEA lectures sponsored by the Brisbane School of Arts in 1917 were suggestively titled 'Human Nature and Politics' and 'The Evolution of Man's Government and Industry.' In one of the latter lectures, the lecturer concerned, T C Witherby of the University of Queensland, declared that "if the people of the world were fighting only to preserve their present social life, then the best blood of Britain, of Australia, of France and of Germany, was now being poured out in vain." There was "a word on the lips of many today," Witherby went on to say - "reconstruction," and that word implied "that we were out to build a fairer and better state out of the present turmoil."[95]

These were indeed stirring times, which paralleled in some ways the ideological ferment of the 'nineties; as capitalism was then held by some to be responsible for the financial disasters of that decade, so was it now seen as responsible for the war (see *Worker* cartoon). In 1919, in another WEA lecture at the Brisbane School of Arts, on 'Who Shall Control Industry,' Witherby informed a "crowded gathering" that,

> There has of late been a recrudescence of a demand for industrial control by the wage earners. From time to time in the past this demand has arisen, for instance in the days of Robert Owen in England, and in the days of Fourier in France...Today the demand is fairly universal and comes from many different countries...Labor is challenging the whole structure of capitalist society as it now exists. It is no longer willing to acquiesce in a system under which industry is conducted for the benefit of the few.[96]

As Amanda Bettesworth shows, the WEA was also active in South Australian institutes as well by this time, and indeed provided a new lease of life for many which had languished during the war due to government stringencies and so many young men being overseas doing the fighting. No doubt lively debates were prompted by some of these lectures and classes, participants perhaps arming themselves with material from magazines like *The World's Work* - the Quorn Institute's December 1918 issue of which I have, and which argues, in an article on 'Self Government in Industry,' that along with the establishment of wool and cotton control boards in Britain,

> Not less important is the establishment in practice of the right of the trade unions to a voice in the control of industry. It is a revolutionary precedent, but after the experience of the past four years, few indeed would deny their competence to take such participation. The acceptance of the principle that an industry has a common duty and discipline, that the maintenance of the reserve of labour is an obligation on an industry, is an indication of how far we have travelled since 1914.[97]

The WEA was particularly active in South Australia in the 1920s. As Amanda Bettesworth explains, a number of institutes became connected with the work of the association during this decade of great hopes for the future - following the founding of the League of Nations - as encapsulated in the H G Wells novel, *The Secret Places of the Heart* published in 1922 (and in various institute libraries, for example, that of the Perth Literary Institute[98]): "Some new sort of world, planned and scientific, has to be got going. Civilisation renewed. Rebuilding civilisation...It's an immense enterprise, but it is the only thing to be done."[99] This sense of 'rebuilding' of the time was reflected in the new injection of government funding into institutes which Amanda Bettesworth describes, which enabled much needed structural repairs - some institute buildings undergoing the distinctive facelift of the decade which shows in California Bungalow - type concrete porticoes, with the obligatory statue of a digger standing out in front (as at Terowie, Wilmington, Wirrabara and Yacka). And indeed a number of new institutes were built, such as at Colonel Light Gardens, a new suburb of Adelaide created out of the South Australian government's 'Thousand Homes' soldier resettlement scheme.[100]

Among WEA lecturers in South Australia was Dr A C Garnett of Adelaide University, who took classes in philosophy and psychology. In 1925-6 Garnett lectured at Berri, Murray Bridge, Gawler, Port Adelaide and Colonel Light Gardens, probably in institute halls in at least some of these centres.[101] His book, *Instinct and Personality*, was set as a text by the WEA,[102] and it is interesting looking through its content in the light of what I have been saying about the prevalence of biological and evolutionary themes in the intellectual life of mechanics' institutes and schools of arts. This interest clearly continued, as can be seen in the following extract:

> Whence come the motives for that human conduct which is moral in the sense of being social?... A careful consideration of animal habits will show that the gregarious tendency is much more widespread than at first appears. It is certainly present in man...[A]ltruism as a practice is, in a certain limited way, very primitive...Those types of conduct which come to be first singled out and liked, and later admired, are, of course, such as confer benefits on numerous individuals or on the group as a whole...[K]indliness (due to the extension of the Parental instinct) toward the weaker members of the tribe; justice or fairness on the part of tribal leaders; skill in performance of the common duties of the tribe or the family; these are the virtues that thus come to be admired and to arouse moral enthusiasm.[103]

Mechanics' institutes and schools of arts, then, were still very much alive and well in the 1920s: Amanda Bettesworth in fact refers to this decade as the South Australian institutes' "most successful era." In New South Wales, as Jean Riley points out, there were as many as 434 schools of arts and kindred institutions receiving government subsidies in 1928; the optimism of the time was encapsulated in the "boom-style" extension to the Young Town Hall and Mechanics' Institute (1924), incorporating a clock tower and niche for the statue of a digger, described by Tessa Raath. In Queensland similarly, as Steve Kellermeier explains, some communities, such as North Tamborine, did not even have a school of arts until the 1920s - another example would be Chelmer, whose School of Arts hall served not only as the library for the district but was also "the focus of much activity of the semi-rural Chelmer community during the 1920s and '30s."[104] (Banyo, Clayfield and Woody Point on the Redcliffe Peninsula near Brisbane are three more 'Memorial Schools of Arts' of the time that I know of). Extensions and improvement to existing buildings - as at Ma Ma Creek, near Gatton, in 1923[105] - were also carried out in Queensland at this time, and as Carole Inkster notes, a School of Arts Association was not formed in Queensland until 1927. In Victoria, the importance of mechanics' institutes in the development of technical education continued well into this decade: the Prahran Mechanics' Institute, for instance, which had been extended to form an adjoining 'Technical School' in 1915 (which eventually became the Prahran College of TAFE) continued to attract subscribers, such that membership did not in fact peak until 1930.[106] One of the Technical School's more illustrious students was Sidney (later Sir Sidney) Nolan, who attended evening art classes there in 1931.[107] In 1927 the Melbourne Working Men's College (later RMIT) was advertising its courses on the cover of the Williamstown Mechanics' Institute and Library magazine.[108]

LAST DAYS OF THE INSTITUTES

Into the 1930s, however, all this was to change for many institutions. While most mechanics' institutes and schools of arts survived the earlier depression of the 1890s, the much worse economic collapse of the 1930s was the finish for many of them. Actually, as Amanda Bettesworth argues, the decline had already begun to set in for some institutions in the 'twenties. The reasons are not hard to find. The motor car was beginning to have a profound impact on the everyday life of Australians (motor vehicle ownership increased from one for every 55 people in 1920 to one for every 11 people in 1930 - putting Australia fourth in the world in car ownership at the time),[109] removing the 'tyranny of distance' for many people. Whereas once, in South Australia for instance, people in, say, Mt Barker or Two Wells would have been thankful for a 'magic lantern' entertainment at the local institute, with the advent of the car, motoring down to Adelaide to see one of the new 'talkies' (from 1927) at the cinema was no major undertaking. Or, with the coming of radio, people could be entertained in their own living room if they wished (and could afford it). Innovative activities such as 'wireless concerts' organised by some institute committees, like that at the Honiton Institute in 1924, and at the Ma Ma Creek and North Tamborine Schools of Arts in Queensland in the next couple of years,[110] could attract renewed interest for a time, but the tide of change was against the institutions. In Young, the Mechanics' Institute continued operations but "night attractions - moving pictures, sporting, both indoor and outdoor, and the coming of home wireless reception reduced its patronage and caused financial difficulties."[111]

And these financial difficulties for an increasing number of institutions were greatly exacerbated by the 1930s Depression. In all States, governments, strapped by loss of revenue, the closure of access to overseas loan capital and commitments to unprecedented welfare pay-outs, were forced to curtail subsidies. Mechanics' institutes and schools of arts never really recovered from this blow, even where reduced subsidies were eventually reintroduced, as in South Australia. Nevertheless, many struggled on, attempting to adapt to the changing times. This was not usually for the better. The vigorous intellectualism of earlier stays was gone; 'popular' culture was now the thing aimed at. In Parkes, for instance, the People's Institute, built in 1909, engaged in an energetic promotional campaign in the late 1930s: "By joining the library...you will leave this dull workaday world and enter the land of enchantment, mystery and romance;" "Read *Gone With The Wind* at the People's Institute for only 5/- per quarter," its slick advertisements in the local press advised[112] - a far cry from the Rev. Finlay Brown's intellectually demanding lecture of forty years before. Notwithstanding these efforts the library was taken over by the Parkes Shire Council in 1945, ironically under the McKell Labor government's Public Libraries Act of the previous year[113] (as was the Young Mechanics' Institute[114]). Prahran Mechanics' Institute, by contrast, resisted this trend; in fact, the period 1940-5 is described in this institutes' history as one of "resurgence" in its popularity and of its role as a local community organisation.[115] Prahran is today one of the very few institutes which has survived as a library.

The mid to late 1940s also - another period of 'new world order' expectations following the favourable turn of events in the latter part of the Second World War, and the return of Federal and State Labor governments - saw a brief period of revitalisation of the old role of mechanics' institutes and schools of arts as centres for political activity. In Eric Lambert's novel *Watermen*, centred in the imaginary fishing community of 'Whale Heads' somewhere south of Geelong (Queenscliff?) at this time, and based on the author's experience of living in such a community, a convincing picture is painted of a meeting in the local mechanics' institute to form a fishermen's co-operative (then being encouraged by the Chifley government). Perhaps Lambert's evocation is as good a reminder as any of the once central place of the mechanics' institutes and schools of arts in the Australian way of life:

> The Mechanics' Institute was full by a quarter to eight...By eight o'clock every fisherman in Whale Heads was in the hall [which was] filled by a low, expectant hum...

> 'And how are yers tonight?' inquired the ingratiating tones of Horrie Dyble, and the Member limped in, wearing a pair of old trousers and a sports coat.

> 'All right. Now I have with me tonight all the data concerning the proposed Fisherman's Co-operative. Now, I'm a busy man.' (Ironical Cheers.) 'So let's get it over with, then we can all go down to Jack Finnigan's for a well-earned beer.' Genuine cheers followed this.

> 'Yers're under no compulsion to join this co-op; as far as I'm concerned yers can all go and drown yourselves - there's no law that can make you join. But if enough of you aren't interested enough in bettering your lot, then the Government certainly *won't* be. I'm here to give you the facts. The rest is up to you.'

> When questions came, they were diffident and few...

> 'All those in favour of a fishermen's co-op raise their right hands!'

> 'That's good enough,' said Horrie amiably. 'The co-op is on its way. This meeting is now closed.'[116]

NOTES AND REFERENCES

1. See Footnote 5 to my earlier chapter.

2.Ludlow, J.M., & Jones, L. (1867). *Progress of the working classes 1832-1867.* London: Alexander Strahan, p.169.

3.Department of the Arts, Sport, the Environment and Territories (1992) *The role of the Commonwealth in Australia's cultural development: A discussion paper.* Canberra: DASET, p.1.

4. See note 2 to my earlier chapter.

5.See, for example, Hunt, E.H. (1981). *British labour history.* London: Weidenfeld & Nicholson; Shapin, S., & Barnes, B. (1977). Science, nature and control: Interpreting mechanics' institutes. *Social Studies of Science, 7* (1), pp.31-74.

6.Quoted in Royle, E. (1971). Mechanics' Institutes and the Working Class, 1840-1860. *The Historical Journal, 14* (2), p.306.

7.See, Carrol, B. (1987). *Australian made: Success stories in Australian manufacturing.* Melbourne: Institution of Production Engineers; and various back issues of *The Olde Machinery Mart* (Caboolture, Qld).

8.*Moreton Bay Courier,* 6 July 1850.

9.Cannon, M. (1978). *Life in the country.* Melbourne: Thomas Nelson, p.252; Illert, C. (1981). *Commemorative biography of Maximilian Ferdinand Wiedenbach.* Berri, SA: Science Art Research Centre, pp.44-45.

10.Sydney Mechanics' School of Arts (1883). *Annual Report to the 31st December, 1882,* pp.20-21.

11.I am grateful to my brother, Robert Laurent, for supplying me with a copy of this plan.

12.*West Australian Librarians' and Institutes' Journal,* November 1904, pp.11-13.

13.anon. (1909). *Our first half-century: A review of Queensland progress.* Brisbane: Anthony J. Cumming, Government Printer, p.85.

14.G.R. Kirkup, (Hon. Secretary, Peak Downs Station School of Arts) to Under Secretary, Department of Education, Brisbane, 28 March 1899 (Queensland State Archives).

15.E.J. Thompson, (Hon. Secretary, Katandra Station School of Arts) to Under Secretary, Department of Education, Brisbane, 26 September 1918 (Queensland State Archives). The following month the Department received a letter from a certain Reg. S. Taylor from Isis Downs, Blackall (4 October 1918) mentioning "the School of Arts here" and agreeing to insure a quantity of books for £100. The style of the handwriting suggests it was written by the station owner or manager. A recent oral-history work has recorded an interview with a former Mourilyan sugar-millworker ("Henry K.") who read Marx's *Capital* and "general science articles" from a School of Arts library, possibly connected with the mill, in the 1920s. (See Lyons, M., & Taksa, L. [1992]; *Australian readers remember: An oral history of reading 1890-1930.* Melbourne: Oxford University Press, pp. 140-141).

16. Markey, R. (1990). A century of labour [sic] and labor [sic]: New South Wales, 1890-1990. In Easson, M. (Ed), *The Foundation of Labor*. Leichhardt, N.S.W.: Pluto Press in association with the Lloyd Ross Forum of the Labor Council of New South Wales, p.41.

17. *Worker* (Brisbane), 10 June 1905.

18. Tennant, K. (1971). *Australia: Her story*. London: Pan Books Ltd., p.211; Clark, C.M.H. (1981). *A history of Australia. Vol. V - The people make laws 1888-1915*. Melbourne: Melbourne University Press, p.57.

19. Lawson, H. (1899/1987). Pursuing literature in Australia. In Cronin, L. (Ed.), *Henry Lawson: Recollections*. Frenchs Forest, NSW: Reed Books, p.180.

20. The Sydney *Worker* was taken by the Goulburn Mechanics' Institute, the Gilgandra and Taree Schools of Arts and the Meningie (SA) Institute, for instance, and its Brisbane counterpart by the Brisbane and Warwick Schools of Arts, among others. (Sydney *Worker*, 8 May 1913; Goulburn Mechanics' Institute, *What Do You Read*? [leaflet, ca. 1900]; Taree School of Arts, *Catalogue, 1913-14*; Linn, R. [1988] *A diverse land: A history of the Lower Murray, Lakes and Coorong*. Meningie, SA: Meningie Historical Society, Inc., p.154; Brisbane School of Arts, *Supplementary Catalogue, 1900-1918; Warwick Examiner*, 26 January 1909). The Sydney *Worker* changed its name at one stage to *Australian Worker*.

21. see Johnston, A.W. (1890). Free railways, or The abolition of tolls and taxes. *A lecture delivered in the Mechanics' Institute, Singleton, June 26 1890*. Sydney: Turner and Henderson.

22. *Sir Henry Parkes' Tenterfield Speech* (1889/1981). Sydney: Published by the Local Management Committee of the National Trust of Australia (NSW) for the Tenterfield School of Arts.

23. See Clarke, R. (1991). *Literary legends of the 1890s*. Melbourne: Australia Post.

24. Undated (1959) and unnamed newspaper supplement celebrating 75 years of technical education at the Granville Technical College in the library of the Granville College of TAFE; Norm Neill, Head, NSW TAFE History Unit, Personal Communication. I am grateful to Fr. Barry Tunks, Rector of St. John's College, for the information about the Coffey painting.

25. For details of this ill-fated Utopian experiment, see Souter, G. (1981). *A peculiar people: The Australians in Paraguay*. Sydney: Sydney University Press.

26. "Miller, John" (William Lane) (1892). *The workingman's paradise*. Brisbane: *Worker* Board of Trustees, p.64.

27. *Daily Telegraph* (Sydney), 18 August 1894; *Sunday Times* (Sydney), 15 September 1895. (Cuttings in book of same held by Sydney School of Arts Committee).

28. *Warwick Examiner*, 30 January 1909

29. Cannon, M. (1978). *Life in the Cities*. Melbourne: Thomas Nelson, p.259.

30. Tennant, K. *op.cit.*, p.217.

31. Ross, E. (1970). *A history of the Miners' Federation of Australia*. Sydney: Australasian Coal and Shale Employees' Federation.

32. *Worker* (Brisbane), 1 March 1890.

33. SMSA *Catalogue, 1901*; Brisbane School of Arts, *Supplementary Catalogue 1900-1918*; Orange School of Arts, *Catalogue, 1914*; Moonta Mines Institute, *Catalogue* (MS, n.d.); Port Adelaide Institute, *Catalogue and List of Books sent to Semaphore Institute* (MS), 1904.

34. Bellamy, E. (1888/1968). *Looking backward*. New York: Magnum Books, p.348.

35. *ibid*, p.268.

36. Darwin, C. (1871). *The descent of man and selection in relation to sex*. London: John Murray, Vol 1, p.100.

37. *Report of the Jamberoo School of Arts for year ending 31st December 1898* (MS in Minute Books).

38. *Worker* (Brisbane), 16 January, 1913.

39. Amundsen, R. (1908). *The North West Passage - Being the record of a voyage of exploration of the ship Gjöa 1903-1907* (2 Vols.) London: Constable & Co., Vol. 1, p.49.

40. Ruskin, J. (1890). *Ariadne Florentina - Six lectures on wood and metal engraving*. London: George Allen, p.279.

41. Galton, F. (1889). *Natural inheritance*. London: Macmillan, p.2. I am grateful to the proprietors of the Sanctuary Cove Antique Gallery for my copy of this book.

42. Darwin, C. *op.cit.* (2nd edit.), p.159.

43. *Daily Telegraph* (Sydney), 18 August 1894.

44. *ibid.*, 11 October 1892; 16 August, 18 November 1895; 15 August, 14 November, 16 December 1896.

45. *Sydney Mail*, 5 June 1897.

46. *Daily Telegraph* (Sydney), 1 July 1922.

47. *Sunday Times* (Sydney), 15 September 1895.

48. *Sydney Mail*, 5 June 1897.

49.*Daily Telegraph* (Sydney), 18 November, 13 December 1895; 16 May, 16 December 1896.

50.*Northern Miner*, 28 April 1905.

51.In *Progress and Poverty* (London: Kegan Paul, Trench & Co., 1888), George wrote as follows: "[T]o use the language in which Herbert Spencer has defined evolution, the development of society is, in relation to its component individuals, the passing from an indefinite, incoherent homogeneity to a definite, coherent heterogeneity. The lower the stage of social development, the more society resembles one of those lowest of animal organisms, which are without organs or limbs, and from which a part may he cut and yet live. The higher the stage of social development, the more society resembles those higher organisms in which functions and powers are specialised, and each member is vitally dependent on the others." (pp.363-364).

52.Brown, W. Finlay (1898). *A treatise on the evolution of historical organism*. Parkes, N.S.W.: Dugold Cameron, Printer and Publisher, pp.8, 120.

53.*Socialist* (Melbourne), 12 March 1909.

54.*Molong Express*, 11 August 1906.

55.*Worker* (Sydney), 10 November 1910.

56.Hughes, W.M. (1910). *The case for labor*. Sydney and Melbourne: *Worker* Trustees, pp.51-53, 85, 91.

57.*Worker* (Sydney), 18 February 1909.

58.As quoted in *Westralian Worker* (Kalgoorlie), 5 August 1910.

59.*Worker* (Sydney), 2 January 1913.

60.Fowler, O.S. (1875), *Science of life*. Philadelphia: National Publishing Co., p.65.

61.Rockhampton School of Arts (1904). *Catalogue of the books contained in the library*, Vol. 1.

62.Wilson, H.L. (1919?), *The wrong twin*. London: John Lane, The Bodley Head Ltd., p.271. This point of view is also contained in Scrimshaw, Ex. Sgt. H., *Natural law versus socialistic nonsense: The only practical way towards equality*. (Sydney: Deaton & Spencer, n.d. [1919]): "the survival of the fittest self-seekers is the basis of progress" (p.14).

63.SMSA (1835). *Third Annual Report*, p.11.

64.Interview with Faraday published after his death in *St Paul's Magazine, 6* (1870), pp.262-303. (I am grateful to Margaret Murphy, Curator of Special Collections, Baillieu Library, University of Melbourne for sending me a copy of this article, and to Professor Rod Home, Department of History and Philosophy of Science, University of Melbourne, Dr Greg Hope,

School of Science, Griffith University, and Chris Spero, Queensland Electricity Commission, for further information about Faraday.)

65.Sydney Technical College *Handbook*, 1916, p.4.

66.Knowles, A.L. (1988). Technical education in Mudgee: A history. *Unpublished BEd (Tech) thesis*, Institute of Technical and Adult Teacher Education, Sydney College of Advanced Education, p.23.

67.Lawson, H. (c.1916/1987), in Cronin, L., *op.cit.*, p.32.

68.Cited in Prout, D. (1973). *Henry Lawson: The grey dreamer*. Adelaide: Rigby Ltd., pp.83-84.

69.*Daily Telegraph* (Sydney), 13 February 1894.

70.Casey, G., & Mayman, T. (1964). *The mile that Midas touched*. Adelaide: Rigby Ltd., pp.173-174.

71.Warburton, J.W. (1963). Schools of Arts. *Australian Quarterly, 35* (4), p.78.

72.Jamberoo School of Arts, *Minutes*, 18 January 1897.

73.Granville School of Arts, *Minutes* 5 March, 2 April, 4 June 1894; Parramatta School of Arts, *Minutes* 17 May 1913; Bondi-Waverley School of Arts, *Annual Report*, 1914; *Liverpool Herald*, 7 September 1901; *Worker* (Brisbane), 26 June 1909; *Northern Miner*, 8 March, 19 July, 30 August 1905; Knowles, A.L., *op. cit.*, p.22.

74.*Sydney Morning Herald*, 4 September 1916.

75.SMSA, *Annual Report*, 1890.

76.Clark, C.M.H., *op. cit.*, p.55.

77.SMSA, *Annual Reports*, 1891, 1892, 1894, 1897.

78.*Liverpool Herald*, 7 September, 1901, 6 June 1903, 7 December 1907.

79.*Northern Miner*, 8 March, 19 July 1905.

80.*Worker* (Brisbane), 26 June 1909.

81.Bathurst School of Arts, *Reports*, 1909, 1910, 1912, 1914-15; Morris, R. (1990). Trade union education in Australia. In Tennant, M. (Ed.), *Adult and continuing education in Australia: Issues and practices*. London: Routledge, p.139.

82.Crisp, L.F. (1963). *Ben Chifley*. Croydon, Victoria: Longmans, p.6.

83.On Shaw's evolutionism, see also his Preface to *Geneva, Cymbeline refinished, and Good King Charles* (London: Constable and Company, 1946), p.26. (My copy of this book is from

UNDER THE AUSPICES OF THE
A.W.U.

MR. TOM MANN,

The World-renowned
LABOR LEADER AND ORGANISER,
will
L E C T U R E
IN THE SCHOOL OF ARTS,
APRIL 26, 27 AND 28.
SUBJECTS :
WEDNESDAY, APRIL 26, 8 P.M.,
" THE LABOR MOVEMENT IN EU-
ROPE, AMERICA AND AUSTRA-
LIA."
THURSDAY, APRIL 27, 8 P.M.,
" EMINENT MEN I HAVE MET AND
WORKED WITH IN THE LABOR
MOVEMENT."
FRIDAY, APRIL 28, 8 P.M.,
" THE CZAR, THE KAISER AND
KING EDWARD."
SUNDAY, APRIL 30.
Subject : " THE RELIGIOUS BASIS
OF THE LABOR MOVEMENT."
(Place of Meeting announced later).
Collection will be taken up at each
Lecture. The whole of the proceeds,
without deduction, will be divid-
ed between the District Hospital, the
Children's Hospital and the Benevo-
lent Society.
W. J. WELLINGTON,
Secretary.
The Organisation of Industry is the
most vital problem of the world.
—Carlyle.

Advertisement for Public Lecture by Tom Mann at the Charters Towers School of Arts, Qld

New Lambton Mechanics' Institute, NSW

Wickham School of Arts, NSW

THE DOUBLE-HEADED GLUTTON.

THE BALD HEAD: "My! Can't he put it away! I'd never be able to get through it if it wasn't for him. Fortunately it all goes to the same place."

Cartoon from the Sydney *Worker*, 24 June 1915

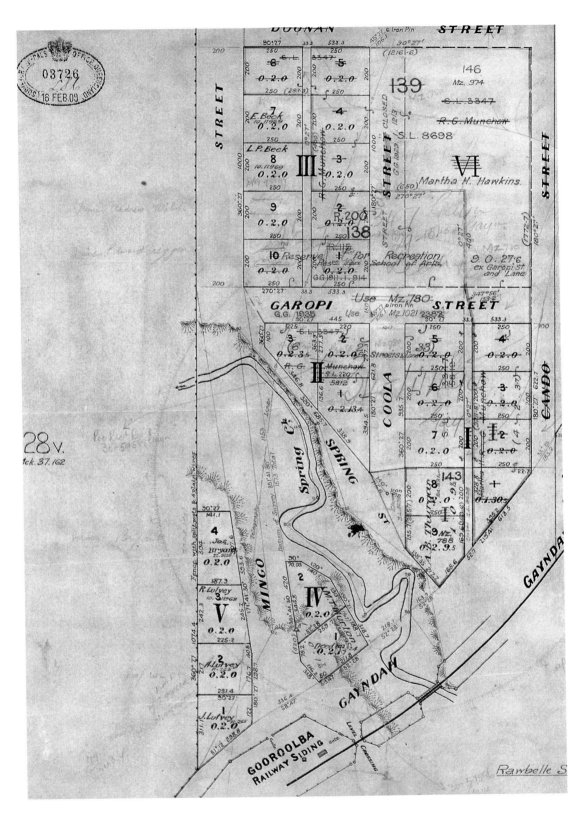

Extract from the Town Plan of Gooroolba, Qld, showing School of Arts Reserve

the Brisbane School of Arts Library).

84. Bowral School of Arts, *31st Annual Report* (1915); Cootamundra Literary Institute, *Annual Report for the Year Ending June 30th 1916*.

85. *The Co-operator*, 17 May 1917.

86. *Worker* (Sydney), 21, 28 January, 25 March, 24 June 1909; 3 March 1910, 14 August 1913; *Worker* (Brisbane), 16, 30 January, 10, 17 April, 22 May 1909; 2 January 1913; *Murrumbidgee Irrigator*, 4 June 1915; Dowd, B.T. (Ed.).(1959). *The history of the Waverley Municipal District*. Sydney: Council of the Municipality of Waverley, p.219.

87. *Socialist*, 15 June 1907; *Evening Telegraph* (Charters Towers), 28 April, 1905.

88. *Daily Herald* (Adelaide), 11, 17, 20, 29 April 1914.

89. *Worker* (Sydney), 10 June 1909. (I am grateful to Margaret Horton of the NSW Parliamentary Library for sending me this item.) See also, Maslen, C.J. (1981). *A history of the Mount Gambier Institute (Incorporated), 1862-1980*. Mt. Gambier: Corporation of the City of Mt. Gambier. p.14.

90. *ibid*, 18 June 1914; Workers Educational Association of New South Wales, *First Annual Report and Statement of Accounts*, 1915, pp.4-5.

91. Bathurst School of Arts, *Report*, 1914-1915, p.4.

92. Glebe Workingmen's Institute, *Report and Balance Sheet*, 1916.

93. Kogarah School of Arts, *30th Annual Report*, 1915.

94. Bondi-Waverley School of Arts, *Annual Report*, 1918.

95. *Daily Mail* (Brisbane), 7 August 1917.

96. Witherby, T. C. (1919). *Who shall control industry?* Brisbane: Workers' Educational Association of Queensland, p.13. W.E.A. classes at the Brisbane School of Arts that year (as advised in the back of this booklet) also included 'Social Science' conducted by Witherby, 'Economics' (E. Stanley), 'Literature' (H.S. Parnell) and 'Biology' (Miss Freda Bage, M.Sc.).

97. Greenwood, G.A. (1918). Self government in industry. *The World's Work*, December 1918, p.32.

98. Perth Literary Institute (1929). *Catalogue of books in the Library*. (3rd Issue). Perth: Imperial Printing Co.

99. Wells, H.G. (1922). *The secret places of the heart*. London: Cassell and Company, Ltd., p.17.

100. See Gibbs, R.M. (1969). *A history of South Australia.* Adelaide: Balara Books, pp.194-5.

101. I am indebted to Dr Dennis Binnion, Co-ordinator of the W.E.A. in South Australia, for this information, which is taken for the *Minutes* of the Association, 1924-6.

102. *ibid.*

103. Garnett, A.C. (1928). *Instinct and personality.* London: George Allen & Unwin Ltd., pp.88-89, 105, 107.

104. *The Satellite* (Sumner Park, Qld), 25 March 1992.

105. Ma Ma Creek School of Arts Committee (1984). *Official opening of the Ma Ma Creek Community Centre*, 25 February 1984 (booklet, n.p.), unpaginated. For an excellent social history of the Gatton-Lockyer area, see Wit, K. (1992). *A history of Left-Hand Branch at Mt. Sylvia.* Gatton: The Author.

106. McCalman, L.B. (1983). *Pioneer and hardy survivor: The Prahran Mechanics' since 1854.* Prahran: Prahran Historical and Arts Society in conjunction with Prahran Mechanics' Institute, pp.25-6.

107. I am grateful to Mr Noel Hutchison, Principal Lecturer in Fine Art at the Prahran College of TAFE, for this information.

108. Working Men's College (Melbourne), *Principal's Monthly Report*, 8 August 1927.

109. See anon. (1986). *Australia's yesterdays: A look at our recent past.* Surry Hills, NSW: Readers Digest Association, pp. 216-219.

110. Ma Ma Creek School of Arts Committee, *op. cit.* See Steve Kellermeier's and Amanda Bettesworth's chapters in this book re the North Tamborine School of Arts and the Honiton Institute respectively.

111. Bayley, W.A. (1977). *Rich earth: History of Young, New South Wales.* Young: Young Municipal Council, p.172.

112. *Parkes News*, 3 November 1939.

113. Tindall, R. (Ed.). (1983). *Parkes: One hundred years of local government.* Parkes: The Council of the Shire of Parkes, p.98.

114. Bayley, W.A., *op. cit.*, p.107.

115. McCalman, L.B., *op. cit.*, p.29.

116. Lambert, E. (1956). *Watermen.* London: Frederick Muller Ltd., pp. 113-5, 118. On Commonwealth Government initiatives in fishing cooperatives, see 'Cooperation in Fishing,' *Adelaide Advertiser*, 7 July 1944.

INDEX

compiled by Helen Stafford

Within headings the term Institute has been used to include Schools of Arts, Literary Institutes and other bodies

INSTITUTIONS

compiled by Helen Stafford

Listed by State and referred to or illustrated in *Pioneering Culture*

NEW SOUTH WALES

Abermain School of Arts
Albury Mechanics' Institute
Alexander Mackie College
Armidale Mechanics' Institute
Australian Circulating Library
Bathurst Mechanics' Institute
Bega School of Arts
Bendigo Institute of Technology
Berry School of Arts
Bibbenluke School of Arts
Binalong Mechanics' Institute
Blackheath School of Arts
Blacktown School of Arts
Blayney School of Arts
Bombala Literary Institute
Bondi-Waverley School of Arts
Bonville School of Arts
Botany School of Arts
Bourke Mechanics' Institute
Bowral School of Arts
Braidwood Literary Institute
Brewarrina Mechanics' Institute
Broken Hill Mechanics' Institute
Bulli and Woonona School of Arts
Bungendore School of Arts
Burraja School of Arts
Burrawang School of Arts
Byron Bay Mechanics' Institute
Casino School of Arts
Clifton School of Arts
Coolamon School of Arts
Coopernook School of Arts
Cootamundra Literary Institute
Corrimal School of Arts
Cowra School of Arts
Crookwell School of Arts
Cundleton School of Arts
Deniliquin Mechanics' Institute
East Maitland Mechanics' Institute
Epping School of Arts
Fairfield School of Arts
Forbes School of Arts
Glebe Workingmen's Institute
Glen Innes School of Arts
Goulburn Mechanics' Institute
Goulburn Technical College

Grafton Mechanics' Institute
Granville School of Arts and Working Men's
 College
Grenfell Literary Institute
Gundaroo Literary Institute
Gunnedah School of Arts
Harden Mechanics' Institute
Harden-Murrumburrah Museum
Harrington School of Arts
Hay Athenaeum
Helensburgh Workmen's Literary and Social
 Club
Hornsby Literary Institute
Inverell School of Arts
Jamboroo School of Arts
Jerilderie Mechanics' Institute
Jerrawa School of Arts
Kangaroo Valley School of Arts
Katoomba School of Arts
Kensington School of Arts
Kiama School of Arts
Killabakh School of Arts
Kincumber School of Arts
Kogarah School of Arts
Krambach School of Arts
Lambton Mechanics' and Miners' Institute
Lansdowne School of Arts
Laurieton School of Arts
Leeton School of Arts
Lismore School of Arts
Liverpool School of Arts
Maclean School of Arts
Maitland Book Society
Maitland Mechanics' Institute
Marlee School of Arts
Menindie Mechanics' Institute
Millers Point Mechanics' Institute
Milton Mechanics' Institute
Minmi Mechanics' Institute
Mitchell's Creek School of Arts
Mitchell's Island School of Arts
Molong School of Arts
Moree School of arts
Morpeth School of Arts
Moruya School of Arts
Moss Vale School of Arts
Mudgee Mechanics' Institute

Mudgee School of Arts
Murrumbidgee Irrigation Trust
Murrumburrah School of Arts
Murrurundi Literary Institute
Murwillumbah School of Arts
Muswellbrook School of Arts
Narrandera Mechanics' Institute
Nelligen Mechanics' Institute
New Lambton Mechanics' Institute
Newcastle Engineering Institute
Newcastle Mechanics' Institute
Newcastle School of Arts
Newton School of Arts
North Ryde Literary Institute
Nowra Mechanics' Institute and School of Arts
Orange School of Arts
Parkes People's Institute
Parramatta Book Society
Parramatta City Library
Parramatta Library
Parramatta Commercial Reading Rooms and
    Library
Parramatta Clerical Book Society
Parramatta Mechanics' Library and Reading
    Room
Parramatta School of Arts
Patrick's Plains Institute
Philosophical Society of Australia
Pilliga Mechanics' Institute
Port Macquarie School of Arts
Pyree Literary Institute
Queanbeyan Mechanics' Institute
Queanbeyan Mutual Improvement Association
Queanbeyan School of Arts
Redfern Railway Institute
Richmond School of Arts
Robertson School of Arts
Rochdale School of Arts
Rockhampton Municipal Library
Rockhampton Natural History Society
Rockhampton School of Art
Rockhampton TAFE College
Rockhampton Technical College
Sackville School of Arts
St Leonards Mechanics' Institute
Scone School of Arts
Singleton Mechanics' Institute
Society for Encouragement of Arts, Science,
    Commerce and Agriculture
Stroud Mechanics' Institute
Sydney Mechanics' School of Arts
Sydney Municipal Library
Sydney Reading Room
Sydney Society for Encouragement of Arts,
    Science, Commerce and Agriculture
Sydney Technical or Working Men's College
Tamworth Mechanics' Institute
Taralga School of Arts

Taree Literary Institute
Taree School of Arts
Tenterfield School of Arts
Tinonee School of Arts
Tomerong School of Arts
Upper Lansdowne School of Arts
Wagga Wagga School of Arts
Useful Book Society
Wallsend Mechanics' Institute
Wallsend School of Arts
Wentworth Falls School of Arts
Wentworth Mechanics' Institute
Wentworthville School of Arts
West Maitland School of Arts
West Wallsend School of Arts
Wetherill Park School of Arts
White Cliffs Mechanics' Institute
Wickham School of Arts
Wilcannia Athenaeum
Windsor School of Arts
Windsor Debating Society
Windsor Mechanics' Institute
Windsor School of Arts
Wingello Mechanics' Institute
Wingham School of Arts
Wollongong School of Arts
Wyalong School of Arts
Yanco School of Arts
Yass Mechanics' Institute
Young Mechanics' Institute
Young School of Arts

QUEENSLAND
Banyo School of Arts
Boonah School of Arts
Bowen School of Arts
Brisbane School of Arts
Buderim School of Arts
Bulimba School of Arts
Bundaberg Historical Society
Bundaberg School of Arts
Charters Towers School of Arts
Chelmer School of Arts
Chillagoe School of Arts
Clayfield School of Arts
Corinda School of Arts
Crows Nest School of Arts
Dalby School of Arts
Dugandan Draught and Chess Club
Gin Gin School of Arts
Goondiwindi School of Arts
Gooroolba School of Arts
Home Hill School of Arts
Howard School of Arts
Ipswich Subscription Library and Reading Room
Ipswich Mechanics' School of Arts
Irvinebank School of Arts

Isis Downs School of Arts
Julatten School of Arts
Kaimkillenbun School of Arts
Katandra School of Arts
Longreach School of Arts
Mackay School of Arts
Maryborough Historical Society
Maryborough School of Arts
Meandarra School of Arts
Morningside School of Arts
Mount Morgan Historical Society
Mount Morgan School of Arts
North Tamborine Progress Association
North Tamborine School of Arts
Nudgee School of Arts
Peak Downs Station
Queensland Country Women's Association
Queensland Public Library
Queensland Library Board
Queensland School of Arts Association
Ravenswood School of Arts
Rockhampton School of Arts
South Brisbane Mechanics' Institute
Tansey School of Arts
Teviot Cinema
Thursday Island School of Arts
Warwick School of Arts
West End School of Arts
Wilston School of Arts
Windsor School of Arts
Woody Point School of Arts
Yangan School of Arts

SOUTH AUSTRALIA
Adelaide Book Club
Adelaide Circulating library
Adelaide Mechanics' Institute
Adelaide Philosophical Society
Balhannah Public Library
Barmera Institute
Beachport Institute
Berri Institute
Brighton Institute
Callington Institute
Clare Institute
Cockburn Institute
Colonel Light Gardens Institute
Crystal Brook Institute
Edwardstown Institute
Freeling Institute
Gawler Institute
Glenelg Institute
Hindmarsh and Bowden Mechanics' Institute
Honiton Institute
Hoyleton Institute
Kalangadoo Institute
Kapunda Institute

Kensington Institute
Kingston Institute
Lyndoch Institute
Macclesfield Institute
Moonta Mines Institute
Mount Barker Institute
Mount Gambier Institute
Murray Bridge Institute
Murraytown Institute
Nadda Institute
Norwood Institute
Penola Institute
Port Adelaide Institute
Port Elliot Institute
Port Lincoln Institute
Port Noarlunga Institute
Port Pirie Institute
Quorn Institute
Renmark Institute
Riverton Institute Robe Institute
Salisbury Institute
South Australian Institute
South Australian Library and Mechanics'
    Institute
South Australian Literary and Scientific
    Association
South Australian Oddfellows library
South Australian Public Library, Museum and
    Art Gallery
South Australian School Society
South Australian Scientific and Literary
    Association
South Australian Subscription Library
Strathalbyn Institute
Tarcowie Institute
Terowie Institute
Thebarton Institute
Truro Institute
Waikerie Institute
Wallaroo Mines Institute
Whyalla Institute
Wilmington Institute
Wirrabara Institute
Wood's Point Institute
Yacka Institute

TASMANIA
Bothwell Literary Society
Campbell Town library
Hobart Book Society
Hobart Public Library
Hobart Reading, Literary and News Room
Hobart Technical College
Hobart Town Book Society
Hobart Town Mechanics' Institute
Hobart Town Mechanics' School of Arts
Hobart Working Men's Club

Launceston Book Society
Launceston Library Society
Launceston Mechanics' Institute
Launceston Public Library
Launceston Working Men's Club
New Norfolk Reading Association
Norfolk Plains Library
Norfolk Plains Book Society
Pontville Literary Society
Richmond Book Society
Richmond Library
Tasmanian Public Library
Tasmanian Society for the Acquisition of Useful
    Knowledge
Union Club, Hobart
Van Diemen's Land Mechanics' School of Arts

VICTORIA

Ballarat East Public Library
Ballaarat Mechanics' Institute
Bathurst Literary Society
Bathurst Mechanics' School of Arts
Bathurst Periodical Book Club
Bathurst Railway Institute
Beechworth Mechanics' Institute
Benalla Mechanics' Institute
Brighton Mechanics' Institute
Castlemaine Institute
Castlemaine Public Library
Collongwood Mechanics' Institute
Collingwood Public Library
Emerald Hill Institute
Geelong Catholic Young Men's Society
Geelong Circulating Library
Geelong Free Library
Geelong Literary and Scientific Association
Geelong Mechanics' Institute
Geelong Presbyterian Young Men's Association
Geelong School of Arts
Geelong Wesleyan Religious and Literary
    Society
Gordon Technical College
Hawthorn Public Library
Healesville Mechanics' Institute
Kew Institute
Kilmore Institute
Maldon Mechanics' Institute
Melbourne Athenaeum
Melbourne Circulating Library
Melbourne Mechanics' Institute
Melbourne Working Man's College
Melbourne Working Man's Technical College
Northcote Public Library
Paddington Mechanics' Institute
Port Phillip Mechanics' Institute
Portland Mechanics' Institute
Portland Scientific and General Literary Society

Prahran College of TAFE
Prahran Free Library
Prahran Mechanics' Institute
Prahran Public Library
Sandhurst Mechanics' Institute
Smythesdale Mechanics' Institute
Union Benefit Society
Warrnambool Mechanics' Institute
Williamstown Mechanics' Institute
Yackandandah Mechanics' Institute

WESTERN AUSTRALIA

Albany Mechanics' Institute
Albany Municipal Library
Albany State School
Armadale Mechanics' Institute
Bardoe Mechanics' Institute
Bonnievale Mechanics' Institute
Boulder Mechanics' Institute
Bridgetown Mechanics' Institute
Broad Arrow Mechanics' Institute
Bulong Mechanics' Institute
Bulong Miners' Institute
Bunbury Mechanics' Institute
Bunbury Working Men's Association
Busselton Mechanics' Institute
Busselton Working Men's Association
Colliefields Miners' Institute
Coolgardie Mechanics' Institute
Day Dawn Mechanics' Institute
Derby Mechanics' Institute
Donnybrook Mechanics' Institute
Eleanor Roberts Youth Library
Field's Find Miners' Institute
Fremantle City Council
Fremantle Literary Institute
Fremantle Mechanics' Institute
Fremantle Workingmen's Association
Geraldton Cultural Trust
Geraldton Mechanics' Institute
Goongarrie Miners' Institute
Greenbushes Agricultural hall
Greenbushes Mechanics' Institute
Greenbushes Miners' Institute
Guildford Mechanics' Institute
Helena Vale Mechanics' Institute
Kalgoorlie Chamber of Mines
Kalgoorlie Mechanics' Institute
Katanning Mechanics' Institute
Kookynie Miners' Institute
Lake Austin Mechanics' Institute
Lennonville Mechanics' Institute
Midland Junction Mechanics' Institute
Midland Junction Railways Institute
Mount Sir Samuel Miners' Institute
Mulline Miners' Institute
Nannine Miners' Institute

North Greenbushes Mechanics' Institute
Northam Mechanics' Institute
Onslow Mechanics' Institute
Paddington Mechanics' Institute
Perth Book Society
Perth Boys' School
Perth City Council
Perth Literary Institute
Perth Technical College
Perth Working Men's Association
South Perth Mechanics' Institute
Southern Cross Mechanics' Institute

Swan River Mechanics' Institute
Swan River Reading Society
Thatched Roof Club, Augusta
Toodyay Mechanics' Institute
Wagin Mechanics' Institute
Weeloona Miners' Institute
Western Australian Book Society
Western Australian Railways and Tramways
    Institute
Yass Subscription Library and Reading Room
York Mechanics' Institute